**The Official
Visitor's Guide
of the National
Park Foundation**

The Complete Guide to

America's
National
Parks

Acknowledgments

This project, encompassing so much detail and new material, would not have been possible without the unstinting cooperation and understanding of the Superintendents of the National Parks and their staffs.

The *Guide,* itself is the result of the painstaking and meticulous sifting and compiling of thousands of items which was ably done by **Patrick J. Quirk** and **Thomas F. Fise**. It is their interest, energy and care which has created this book.

Design Director:
Charles Dorian Walker   810332

While every effort has been made to assure the accuracy of the information included in this *Guide,* the National Park Foundation can assume no responsibility for any inconvenience or damages which may arise from any inaccuracies of information. Visitors should verify the accuracy of important details before beginning a trip.

Library of Congress Catalog Card No. 79-67158
ISBN: 0-9603410-0-5

Introduction

America's National Parks—the concept spans a vast Nation encompassing a multitude of diverse areas and a wealth of experiences. The awesomeness of the Grand Canyon, the quiet splendor of the Great Smokys and the uniqueness of Yellowstone are synonymous with National Parks for most of us. But the Statue of Liberty, Klondike—the Alaskan gold rush city of Skagway, the numerous sites of major Civil War battles, Cumberland Island off the Georgia coast, the Washington Monument—these also are integral segments of our National Park System, pointing out the variety and the expanse of this great resource, held in trust for the enjoyment, recreation and enrichment of all Americans.

Why a Guide?
According to a recent Gallup Poll evaluating park services, 65% of persons visiting National Parks found travel information to be the most useful of all park services—to assist in planning their trips. At a time when the costs of traveling are increasing, it is even more necessary to make as many advance plans as possible, so that you can make the most of your trip, avoiding disappointment and unanticipated diversions which waste valuable vacation time—and money. Many Americans are now planning vacations closer to home. Visits to nearby areas can be less expensive and just as relaxing as extensive trips and can reduce fuel consumption and contribute to our national energy conservation effort.

That is how this book came to be. The National Park Foundation has set out to find as much as possible about all of the 353 National Park areas and affiliated sites (those areas which are not part of the National Park Service, but which draw administrative, technical or financial support from the Park Service) in the United States. This *Guide* is the only travel publication endorsed by the National Park Foundation. We have compiled all of this information in capsulized fashion in hopes that the *Guide* can help you to answer as many questions about your trip as possible, *before* you set out from home.

How the Guide was Compiled
Information was gathered on all National Park areas and affiliated sites. While the *Guide* contains useful visitor information on all of the major, widely recognized park areas, the book also contains information on a number of park areas with which you might be less familiar, but which nonetheless offer opportunities for recreation and for natural, historical and cultural enrichment. Information on all areas was compiled in the standardized format in which it appears here. Then, by letter and by telephone, information was verified for accuracy with appropriate officials of each site. Tremendous time and energy have been expended to assure that this book is the most extensive and reliable reference source on National Parks available to the public today.

Before You Start Your Trip
When you are planning your trip, consult the *Guide* to find out what parks are near your primary destination. You may be close to a fascinating site that you haven't heard about and may be able to plan a side trip for a day or an afternoon.

To orient you with the locations of park sites we have included state maps marking the major roads and relative position of park areas. These maps are meant only to show you what parks are located in the immediate vicinity of your destination. In order to keep the maps simple, we have not made them to the exact scale, and have eliminated some smaller roads which might be necessary to reach the park (more explicit location information is given in the DIRECTIONS section of each park listing). So, the maps in this book cannot substitute for an atlas or detailed road maps which can aid your navigation. If you belong to a travel club, you can probably get a book of detailed maps customized for *your* trip.

Although we have included as much specific information as possible, such as hours, fees, holiday closings, you should verify in advance any details of importance to you. Likewise, every effort has been made to obtain accurate information on hospital and first aid facilities. Persons traveling who are apprehensive about possible health problems, or who have been advised to restrict their activities should investigate the specific nature of the hospital and first aid facilities available in the area of travel. You should carry a first aid kit with you.

Admission Fees

While most parks have no admission charges, some do charge entrance fees, ranging from $1 to $3 for visitors 16 years and older. An annual entrance permit, the Golden Eagle Passport, is issued for $10 at all parks where entrance fees are charged. Persons 62 years of age and older are entitled to a free lifetime entrance permit, the Golden Age Passport. Admission fees are waived to the holder of both the Golden Eagle and Golden Age Passports and those accompanying the holder in a noncommercial vehicle. You can obtain more information on both passports by contacting the **National Park Service** headquarters (202-343-4747) in Washington, D.C. or any of its regional offices: **Mid-Atlantic**, 215-597-7067; **Midwest**, 402-864-3471; **National Capital**, 202-426-6664; **North Atlantic**, 617-223-0058; **Pacific Northwest**, 206-399-0170; **Rocky Mountain**, 303-234-3095; **Southeast**, 404-996-2520; and **Western**, 415-556-4122. Campsite fees are not waived to holders of either passports, although holders of the Golden Age Passport generally receive a reduction in fees.

As an appendix to this *Guide*, we have included information on the period of peak visitation in park areas for which these records are kept. You may wish to use this information in planning your trip.

Camping in National Parks is an excellent way to expand your park experience. Generally, no reservations are accepted for campsites in National Park areas, and therefore, to obtain a campsite you are advised to arrive early in the day (sometimes early in the morning), as the number of prospective campers may surpass the number of available campsites—especially during the peak visitation season. Your destination park can give you more specific information.

An advance reservation system was tested in Yosemite National Park, Grand Canyon National Park and Sequoia/Kings Canyon National Parks during 1979, and such a program may be used at these and other parks during 1980.

When you have laid out your plans for your trip, we suggest that you obtain the brochures available on the parks you will be visiting. These are generally available without charge by writing to: National Park Service, Office of Public Information, Washington, D.C. 20240. The *Guide* includes a mailing address and telephone number for each facility in case you wish to write or call to ask any questions or obtain more extensive information about activities, camping, backcountry travel, overnight accommodations, or any other aspect of your trip.

Enjoy your National Parks—they belong to you!

John L. Bryant, Jr.
President, National Park Foundation

Table of Contents

1 **Alabama**
1 Horseshoe Bend National Military Park
2 Russell Cave National Monument
2 Tuskegee Institute National Historic Site
3 **Alaska**
4 Aniakchak National Monument
4 Bering Land Bridge National Monument
6 Cape Krusenstern National Monument
6 Denali National Monument
7 Gates of the Arctic National Monument
8 Glacier Bay National Monument
9 Katmai National Monument
10 Kenai Fjords National Monument
11 Klondike Gold Rush National Historical Park
12 Kobuk Valley National Monument
13 Lake Clark National Monument
14 Mount McKinley National Park
15 Noatak National Monument
15 Sitka National Historical Park
16 Wrangell-St. Elias National Monument
17 Yukon-Charley National Monument
19 **Arizona**
19 Canyon de Chelly National Monument
20 Casa Grande Ruins National Monument
21 Chiricahua National Monument
22 Coronado National Memorial
22 Fort Bowie National Historic Site
23 Glen Canyon National Recreation Area
24 Grand Canyon National Park
26 Hohokam Pima National Monument
26 Hubbell Trading Post National Historic Site
27 Montezuma Castle National Monument
27 Navajo National Monument
28 Organ Pipe Cactus National Monument
30 Petrified Forest National Park
30 Pipe Spring National Monument
31 Saguaro National Monument
32 Sunset Crater National Monument
33 Tonto National Monument
33 Tumacacori National Monument
34 Tuzigoot National Monument
34 Walnut Canyon National Monument
35 Wupatki National Monument
36 **Arkansas**
36 Arkansas Post National Memorial
37 Buffalo National River
38 Fort Smith National Historic Site
38 Hot Springs National Park
39 Pea Ridge National Military Park
40 **California**
41 Cabrillo National Monument
41 Channel Islands National Monument
42 Death Valley National Monument
43 Devils Postpile National Monument
44 Eugene O'Neill National Historic Site
45 Fort Point National Historic Site
45 Golden Gate National Recreation Area
46 John Muir National Historic Site
47 Joshua Tree National Monument
47 Lassen Volcanic National Park
48 Lava Beds National Monument
49 Muir Woods National Monument
50 Pinnacles National Monument
51 Point Reyes National Seashore
52 Redwood National Park
53 Santa Monica Mountains National Recreation Area
53 Sequoia and Kings Canyon National Parks
54 Whiskeytown-Shasta-Trinity National Recreation Area
55 Yosemite National Park
57 **Colorado**
57 Bent's Old Fort National Historic Site
58 Black Canyon of the Gunnison National Monument
59 Colorado National Monument
59 Curecanti National Recreation Area
60 Dinosaur National Monument
61 Florissant Fossil Beds National Monument
62 Great Sand Dunes National Monument
62 Hovenweep National Monument
63 Mesa Verde National Park
64 Rocky Mountain National Park
66 Yucca House National Monument
67 **District of Columbia**
68 Ford's Theatre National Historic Site
68 Fort Dupont Park and Activity Center
69 Frederick Douglass Memorial Home
69 John F. Kennedy Center for the Performing Arts
70 Lincoln Memorial
70 Lyndon Baines Johnson Memorial Grove on the Potomac
71 National Capital Parks
71 National Mall
72 National Visitor Center
72 Old Stone House
73 Pennsylvania Avenue National Historic Site
73 Rock Creek Park
74 Sewall-Belmont House National Historic Site
74 Theodore Roosevelt Island
75 Thomas Jefferson Memorial
75 Washington Monument
76 The White House
77 **Florida**
77 Big Cypress National Preserve
78 Biscayne National Monument
79 Canaveral National Seashore
80 Castillo de San Marcos National Monument
80 DeSoto National Memorial
81 Everglades National Park

82 Fort Caroline National Memorial
82 Fort Jefferson National Monument
83 Fort Matanzas National Monument
84 Gulf Islands National Seashore
85 Mar-A Lago National Historic Site
86 **Georgia**
86 Andersonville National Historic Site
87 Chattahoochee River National Recreation
    Area
87 Chickamauga & Chattanooga National
    Military Park
88 Cumberland Island National Seashore
89 Fort Frederica National Monument
90 Fort Pulaski National Monument
90 Kennesaw Mountain National Battlefield
    Park
91 Ocmulgee National Monument
92 **Hawaii**
92 Haleakala National Park
93 Hawaii Volcanoes National Park
94 Kaloko-Honokohau National Historical
    Park
95 Pu'uhonua o Honaunau National Histor-
    ical Park
95 Puukohola Heiau National Historic Site
96 U.S.S. Arizona Memorial
97 **Idaho**
97 Craters of the Moon National Monument
98 Nez Perce National Historical Park
99 **Illinois**
99 Chicago Portage National Historic Site
100 Lewis and Clark National Historic Trail
100 Lincoln Home National Historic Site
100 Mormon Pioneer National Historic Trail
101 **Indiana**
101 George Rogers Clark National Historical
    Park
102 Indiana Dunes National Lakeshore
103 Lincoln Boyhood National Memorial
104 **Iowa**
104 Effigy Mounds National Monument
105 Herbert Hoover National Historic Site
106 **Kansas**
106 Cherokee Strip Living Museum
106 Fort Larned National Historic Site
107 Fort Scott National Historic Site
108 **Kentucky**
108 Abraham Lincoln Birthplace National
    Historic Site
109 Cumberland Gap National Historical Park
110 Mammoth Cave National Park
111 **Louisiana**
111 Chalmette National Historical Park
112 Jean LaFitte National Historical Park
113 **Maine**
113 Acadia National Park
114 Appalachian National Scenic Trail
115 Saint Croix Island National Monument
116 **Maryland**
116 Antietam National Battlefield
117 Assateague Island National Seashore
118 Catoctin Mountain Park

119 Chesapeake and Ohio Canal National
    Historical Park
120 Clara Barton National Historic Site
120 Fort McHenry National Monument and
    Historic Shrine
121 Fort Washington Park
121 Glen Echo Park
122 Greenbelt Park
123 Hampton National Historic Site
123 Monocacy Battlefield National Park
124 Oxon Hill Farm
124 Piscataway Park
125 Thomas Stone National Historic Site
125 **Massachusetts**
125 Adams National Historic Site
126 Boston National Historic Park
127 Cape Cod National Seashore
128 Dorchester Heights National Historic Site
129 John F. Kennedy National Historic Site
129 Longfellow National Historic Site
130 Lowell National Historical Park
130 Minute Man National Historical Park
131 Salem Maritime National Historic Site
132 Saugus Iron Works National Historic Site
132 Springfield Armory National Historic Site
133 **Michigan**
134 Father Marquette National Memorial
134 Isle Royale National Park
135 Pictured Rocks National Lakeshore
136 Sleeping Bear Dunes National Lakeshore
137 **Minnesota**
137 Grand Portage National Monument
138 Pipestone National Monument
139 Voyageurs National Park
140 **Mississippi**
140 Brices Cross Roads National Battlefield Site
141 Natchez Trace Parkway
141 Tupelo National Battlefield
142 Vicksburg National Military Park
143 **Missouri**
143 George Washington Carver National
    Monument
144 Jefferson National Expansion Memorial
    National Historic Site
144 Oregon National Historic Trail
145 Ozark National Scenic Riverways
146 Wilson's Creek National Battlefield
146 **Montana**
146 Big Hole National Battlefield
147 Bighorn Canyon National Recreation Area
148 Custer Battlefield National Monument
148 Fort Benton
149 Glacier National Park
150 Grant-Kohrs Ranch National Historic Site
151 **Nebraska**
151 Agate Fossil Beds National Monument
152 Chimney Rock National Historic Site
152 Homestead National Monument of Amer-
    ica
153 Scotts Bluff National Monument
155 **Nevada**
155 Lake Mead National Recreation Area

156 Lehman Caves National Monument
157 **New Hampshire**
158 Saint-Gaudens National Historic Site
159 **New Jersey**
159 Edison National Historic Site
160 Morristown National Historical Park
161 Pinelands National Reserve
162 **New Mexico**
162 Aztec Ruins National Monument
163 Bandalier National Monument
164 Capulin Mountain National Monument
164 Carlsbad Caverns National Park
165 Chaco Canyon National Monument
166 El Morro National Monument
167 Fort Union National Monument
168 Gila Cliff Dwellings National Monument
168 Gran Quivira National Monument
169 Pecos National Monument
170 White Sands National Monument
171 **New York**
171 Castle Clinton National Monument
172 Eleanor Roosevelt National Historic Site
173 Ellis Island
173 Federal Hall National Memorial
174 Fire Island National Seashore
175 Fort Stanwix National Monument
175 Gateway National Recreation Area
176 General Grant National Memorial
177 Hamilton Grange National Memorial
177 Home of Franklin Delano Roosevelt National Historic Site
178 Theodore Roosevelt Birthplace National Historic Site
178 Theodore Roosevelt Inaugural National Historic Site
179 Sagamore Hill National Historic Site
179 Saint Paul's Church National Historic Site
180 Saratoga National Historical Park
180 Statue of Liberty National Monument
181 Upper Delaware National Scenic River
182 Vanderbilt Mansion National Historic Site
183 **North Carolina**
183 Blue Ridge Parkway
185 Cape Hatteras National Seashore
186 Cape Lookout National Seashore
187 Carl Sandburg Home National Historic Site
188 Fort Raleigh National Historic Site
188 Guilford Courthouse National Military Park
189 Moores Creek National Military Park
189 Wright Brothers National Memorial
191 **North Dakota**
191 Fort Union Trading Post National Historic Site
192 International Peace Garden
192 Knife River Indian Villages National Historic Site
193 Theodore Roosevelt National Park
194 **Ohio**
194 Cuyahoga Valley National Recreation Area
195 Mound City Group National Monument
196 Perry's Victory and International Peace Memorial
196 William Howard Taft National Historic Site
197 **Oklahoma**
197 Chickasaw National Recreation Area
198 **Oregon**
198 Crater Lake National Park
199 Fort Clatsop National Memorial
200 John Day Fossil Beds National Monument
201 McLoughlin House National Historic Site
201 Oregon Caves National Monument
203 **Pennsylvania**
203 Allegheny Portage Railroad National Historic Site
204 Benjamin Franklin National Memorial
204 Delaware Water Gap National Recreation Area
205 Edgar Allan Poe National Historic Site
205 Eisenhower National Historic Site
206 Fort Necessity National Battlefield
206 Friendship Hill National Historic Site
206 Gettysburg National Military Park
207 Gloria Dei (Old Swedes') Church National Historic Site
208 Hopewell Village National Historic Site
208 Independence National Historical Park
209 Johnstown Flood National Memorial
210 Middle Delaware National Scenic River
210 Thaddeus Kosciuszko National Memorial
210 Valley Forge National Historical Park
211 **Rhode Island**
212 Roger Williams National Memorial
212 Touro Synagogue National Historic Site
213 **South Carolina**
213 Congaree Swamp National Memorial
213 Cowpens National Battefield
214 Fort Sumter National Monument
215 Kings Mountain National Military Park
215 Ninety Six National Historic Site
216 **South Dakota**
216 Badlands National Park
217 Jewel Cave National Monument
218 Mount Rushmore National Monument
219 Wind Cave National Park
220 **Tennessee**
220 Andrew Johnson National Historic Site
221 Big South Fork National River and Recreation Area
222 Fort Donelson National Military Park
223 Great Smoky Montains National Park
224 Obed Wild and Scenic River
224 Shiloh National Military Park
225 Stones River National Battlefield and Cemetery
226 **Texas**
226 Alibates National Monument
227 Amistad National Recreation Area
228 Big Bend National Park
229 Big Thicket National Preserve
230 Chamizal National Memorial
231 Fort Davis National Historic Site
231 Guadalupe Mountains National Park
232 Lake Meredith National Recreation Area

233 Lyndon B. Johnson National Historic Site
234 Padre Island National Seashore
235 Palo Alto Battlefield National Historic Site
235 Rio Grande Wild and Scenic River
235 San Antonio Missions National Historical Park
236 San Jose Mission National Historic Site
237 **Utah**
237 Arches National Park
238 Bryce Canyon National Park
239 Canyonlands National Park
240 Capitol Reef National Park
241 Cedar Breaks National Monument
241 Dinosaur National Monument
242 Golden Spike National Historic Site
242 National Bridges National Monument
243 Rainbow Bridge National Monument
244 Timpanogos Cave National Monument
245 Zion National Park
246 **Virginia**
247 Appomattox Court House National Historical Park
247 Arlington House, The Robert E. Lee Memorial
248 Booker T. Washington National Monument
248 Colonial National Historical Park
249 Fredericksburg and Spotsylvania County Battlefields Memorial National Military Park
250 George Washington Birthplace National Monument
251 George Washington Memorial Parkway
251 Great Falls Park
252 Jamestown National Historic Site
253 Maggie L. Walker National Historic Site
253 Manassas National Battlefield Park
254 Petersburg National Battlefield
254 Prince William Forest Park
255 Richmond National Battlefield Park
255 Shenandoah National Park
256 Turkey Run Farm
257 U.S. Marine Corps War Memorial and Netherlands Carillon
257 Wolf Trap Farm Park for the Performing Arts
258 Yorktown Battlefield
259 **Washington**
259 Coulee Dam National Recreation Area
260 Ebey's Landing National Historical Reserve
260 Fort Vancouver National Historic Site
261 Lake Chelan National Recreation Area
262 Mount Rainier National Park
263 North Cascades National Park
264 Olympic National Park
265 Ross Lake National Recreation Area
266 San Juan Island National Historical Park
267 Whitman Mission National Historic Site
267 **West Virginia**
268 New River Gorge National River
268 Harpers Ferry National Historical Park
269 **Wisconsin**
269 Apostle Islands National Lakeshore
270 Ice Age National Scientific Reserve
271 Lower St. Croix National Scenic Riverway
272 Saint Croix National Scenic Riverway
273 **Wyoming**
273 Devils Tower National Monument
274 Fort Laramie National Historic Site
274 Fossil Butte National Monument
275 Grand Teton National Park
277 John D. Rockfeller, Jr. Memorial Parkway
278 Yellowstone National Park
280 **Canada**
280 Roosevelt Campobello International Park
280 **Guam**
280 War in the Pacific National Historical Park
281 **Northern Marina Islands**
281 American Memorial Park
281 **Puerto Rico**
281 San Juan National Historic Site
281 **Virgin Islands**
281 Buck Island Reef National Monument
282 Christiansted National Historic Site
283 Virgin Islands National Park

Alabama

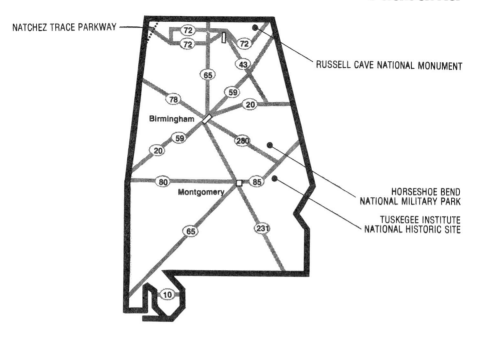

NATCHEZ TRACE PARKWAY

RUSSELL CAVE NATIONAL MONUMENT

Birmingham

Montgomery

HORSESHOE BEND
NATIONAL MILITARY PARK

TUSKEGEE INSTITUTE
NATIONAL HISTORIC SITE

Horseshoe Bend National Military Park
Daviston, Alabama

MAILING ADDRESS: Superintendent, Horseshoe Bend National Military Park, Route 1, Box 103, Daviston, Alabama 36256 **Telephone:** 205-234-7111

DIRECTIONS: The Park, on AL 49, is 19 km (12 miles) north of Dadeville and 29 km (18 miles) northeast of Alexander City via Newsite.

Gen. Andrew Jackson's forces broke the power of the Creek Indian Confederacy and opened Alabama and other parts of the Old Southwest to settlement after fierce fighting here on Mar. 27, 1814, on the "horseshoe bend" of the Tallapoosa River. Authorized for addition to the National Park System on July 25, 1956. Established Aug. 11, 1959.

VISITOR ACTIVITIES: Interpretive and audiovisual exhibits, auto and walking tours, picnicking, boating, hiking, fishing, flintlock rifle demonstrations on Sundays and periodically throughout the week; **Permits:** No; **Fees:** No; **Visitor facilities:** Parking and restrooms at Visitor Center, museum, hiking trails, boat launching ramp, picnic area; **Any limitations on vehicle usage:** Vehicles are restricted to paved roads; **Hiking trails:** Yes, the Park contains both interpretive and nature trails which vary from 4.5 to 11 km (3 to 7 miles) in length. **Backcountry:** battlefield trail; **Camping:** No; **Other overnight accommodations on site:** No; **Meals served in the park:** No; **Food and supplies obtainable in the park:** No; **Food and supplies obtainable nearby:** Yes; **Overnight accommodations:** Dadeville 19 km (12 miles), and Alexander City 29 km (18 miles), both on US 280; **First Aid available in park:** Yes; **Nearest Hospital:** Dadeville, 19 km (12 miles) and Alexander City, 29 km (18 miles), both on US 280; **Days/Hours:** Museum and grounds open daily from 8 a.m. to 4:30 p.m.; **Holiday Closings:** Dec. 25.

GENERAL INFORMATION: Be alert to hazards such as poisonous snakes, poison ivy, and biting fire ants. Exercise caution while boating and walking along the river bank.

Natchez Trace Parkway
For details see listing in Mississippi

Russell Cave National Monument
Bridgeport, Alabama

MAILING ADDRESS: Russell Cave National Monument, Rte. 1, Box 175, Bridgeport, Alabama 35740 **Telephone:** 205-495-2672

DIRECTIONS: The Park is best approached by US 72 leading to Bridgeport, Alabama. Turn north on County Road 91 to the community of Mt. Carmel, then turn right on County Road 75 to the Park entrance. The distance from Bridgeport to the Park is about 12 km (8 miles) over paved road.

An almost continuous archaeological record of human habitation from at least 7000 B.C. to about 1650 A.D. is revealed in this cave, which was "discovered" in 1953. Created by Presidential Proclamation on May 11, 1961.

VISITOR ACTIVITIES: interpretive exhibits and talks, demonstrations of ancient Indian life, guided tours of the cave; **Permits:** No; **Fees:** No; **Visitor facilities:** hiking trails, restrooms; **Any limitations on vehicle usage:** No; **Hiking trails:** Yes, an .8 km (½ mile) nature trail extends to a hiking trail. **Backcountry:** No; **Camping:** No; **Other overnight accommodations on site:** No; **Meals served in the park:** No; **Food and supplies obtainable in the park:** No; **Food and supplies obtainable nearby:** Yes, in Bridgeport, South Pittsburg, Steveson ; **Overnight accommodations:** Kimball, TN, Junction of US 72 and I-24, 29 km (18 miles); **First Aid available in park:** Yes; **Nearest Hospital:** Bridgeport, County 75 to 91 to US 72, 16 km (10 miles); **Days/Hours:** Open daily from 8 a.m. to 5 p.m., until 6 p.m. in summer; **Holiday Closings:** Dec. 25; **Visitor attractions closed for seasons:**None; **Weather:** Summers are hot and humid, winters are relatively mild, with occasional near-zero temperatures and snow.

GENERAL INFORMATION: You are advised not to run on the trails and not to wander from them or to take short cuts. The hiking trail is steep and arduous and you are urged to walk it with care.

Tuskegee Institute National Historic Site
Tuskegee Institute, Alabama

MAILING ADDRESS: Superintendent, Tuskegee Institute National Historic Site, P.O. Box 1246, Tuskegee Institute, Alabama 36088 **Telephone:** 205-727-6390

DIRECTIONS: The Site is located on Old Montgomery Road (126) and is adjacent to the city of Tuskegee, AL. When approaching via Interstate 85, exit onto AL 81 South. Turn right at the intersection of 81 and Old Montgomery Road. The entrance to Grey Columns (Visitor Center and Headquarters) is 2½ blocks from this turn on the left. Just beyond is the Tuskegee Institute campus.

Booker T. Washington founded this college for black Americans in 1881. Preserved here are the student-made brick buildings, Washington's home, and the George Washington Carver Museum. Authorized for addition to the National Park System on Oct. 26, 1974.

VISITOR ACTIVITIES: informal interpretive talks at Grey Columns and Carver Museum, 10-minute audiovisual program on black education, formal tours at The Oaks, self-guiding nature trail, special activities intermittently throughout the year; **Permits:** No; **Fees:** No; **Visitor facilities:** museum, restored home, nature trail; **Any limitations on vehicle usage:** No; **Hiking trails:** Yes, a self-guiding nature trail is behind Grey Columns. **Backcountry:** No; **Camping:** No; **Other overnight accommodations on site:** Yes, for reservations at Dorothy Hall Guest House, contact Tuskegee Institute, Tuskegee Institute, AL 36088, phone 205-727-3400; **Meals served in the park:** No; **Food and supplies obtainable in the park:** No; **Food and supplies obtainable nearby:** Yes, Tuskegee Institute campus or downtown Tuskegee; **Overnight accommodations:** I-85 and Notasulga Highway, 8 km (5 miles); **First Aid available in park:** Yes; **Nearest Hospital:** John Andrew Hospital on Tuskegee Institute campus; **Days/Hours:** Open daily from 9 a.m.-5 p.m.; **Holiday Closings:** Dec. 25 & Jan. 1; **Visitor attractions closed for seasons:** No; **Weather:** Summer is humid, with high temperatures in mid-90's from July-Sept.; Winter is cold, with lows in the 20's from Dec.-Feb.; Spring and Fall have moderate rainfall, with temperatures from 75-85°.

GENERAL INFORMATION: *For Your Safety*—Be especially careful on old walkways and steps. Natural areas have steep slopes, poisonous or spiny vegetation, and animals that sting or bite. Pedestrians have the right-of-way on campus roads.

Alaska

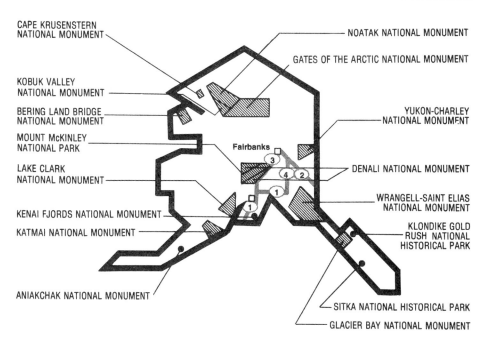

Aniakchak National Monument
Alaska

MAILING ADDRESS: Alaska Office, National Park Service, 540 W. 5th Ave., Anchorage, Alaska 99501 **Telephone:** 907-271-4243

DIRECTIONS: To visit Aniakchak is no simple task. On Monday, Tuesday, and Thursday, Reeve Aleutian Airways, Inc. has a flight between Anchorage and Port Heiden Airfield. The cost of a round trip ticket is around $250. From Port Heiden Airfield a person could walk to the Monument, which is a distance of about 16 km (10 miles), and quite a difficult job. The terrain is tundra meadow, interspersed with scattered thickets of willow, alder, and birch. Very few people have tried to make this walk. A person can also charter an aircraft and fly into the Monument. This cost is about $150 per hour. Wien Air Alaska has a daily flight from Anchorage to King Salmon which costs about $115 round trip. From King Salmon, one can charter an airplane for approximately $150 per hour. As evidenced by the methods available, this is quite an expensive place to visit.

Thirty square-mile Aniakchak Crater, one of the world's largest, contains a lake and a river, and a volcano which erupted in 1931. Aniakchak River flows through the caldera wall to the Pacific. Created by Presidential Proclamation on Dec. 1, 1978.

VISITOR ACTIVITIES: wildlife-watching, float trips, primitive camping, fishing; **Permits:** Alaska fishing license, available in Anchorage, is required; **Fees:** No; **Visitor facilities:** No; **Any limitations on vehicle usage:** No roads; **Hiking trails:** No; **Backcountry trails:** Yes, information can be obtained from Alaska Area Office of the National Park Service. **Camping:** Yes, primitive camping available; **Other overnight accommodations on site:** No; **Meals served in the park:** No; **Food and supplies obtainable in the park:** No; **Food and supplies obtainable nearby:** No, should be obtained in Anchorage; **Overnight accommodations:** King Salmon, about 240 km (150 miles); **First Aid available in park:** No; **Nearest Hospital:** Kodiak, Homer; **Days/Hours:** Monument never closes; **Holiday Closings:** No; **Visitor attractions closed for seasons:** No; **Weather:** The weather will vary a great deal. For Winter, the maximum may be in the low 30°s F to -30° below zero. Summer temperatures range from the mid and upper 40°s to a high of 70°. The caldera is subject to violent wind storms which can make camping inside the caldera very difficult. In June and July, 1973, an individual had his camp destroyed twice during a six-week period and his boat blown away. Local pilots who have flown into the caldera have reported bad experiences with strong turbulent winds.

GENERAL INFORMATION: Visitors in the area should have wool clothing, rubber boots and good rain gear. Bring your own food if camping and be sure that the tent can withstand bad weather conditions. One of the most experienced guide services for this area is Peninsula Airways, Inc., P.O. Box 36, King Salmon, AK 99613, phone 907-246-3372. Other charter aircraft are available in Anchorage, Port Heiden Airfield, and King Salmon.

Bering Land Bridge National Monument
Alaska

MAILING ADDRESS: Alaska Office, National Park Service, 540 W. 5th Ave., Anchorage, Alaska 99501 **Telephone:** 907-271-4243

DIRECTIONS: The Monument is quite isolated. No roads lead to the area, and airports at Nome and Kotzebue that handle jets are rather distant from the Monument's boundaries. Nonetheless, Nome and Kotzebue are for most visitors the intermediate points from which to fly into the Monument or to Native villages in close proximity to the boundaries. Round trip air fare from Anchorage to either Kotzebue or Nome is $182.02, and from Fairbanks to either Kotzebue or Nome is $164.40. Scheduled round trip air flights on alternate days from Nome to Deering cost $68.68 and from Kotzebue to Deering, $55.34. Round trip from Nome to Shishmaref is $111.00. It is possible to charter flights out of Nome and Kotzebue into Serpentine Hot Springs and onto beaches of the Monument. Charter fares run about $125 per hour.

This area on the north side of Seward Peninsula 80 km (50 miles) from Siberia contains remains of land bridge once connecting Asia and North America. The promising archaeological site is also the habitat of polar bear, grizzly bear, wolves, 21 other mammals and 112 bird species. Created by Presidential Proclamation on Dec. 1, 1978..

VISITOR ACTIVITIES: photography, fishing, river floating, boating, canoeing, walking, wildlife- and wildflower-watching. Part of the attraction of the Monument is to see Eskimos from the neighboring villages pursue subsistence lifestyles, manage reindeer herds, and produce pieces of arts and crafts.; **Permits:** Alaska fishing license, available locally, is required; **Fees:** No; **Visitor facilities:** No; **Any limitation on vehicle usage:** No roads; **Hiking trails:** No; **Backcountry:** Yes, information available from Alaska Area Office of the National Park Service; **Camping:** Only primitive camping—no reservations; **Other overnight accommodations on site:** No; **Meals served in the park:** No; **Food and supplies obtainable in the park:** No; **Food and supplies obtainable nearby:** Yes, certain items—food, clothing, beverages, and some gear—may be purchased from merchants in Nome and Kotzebue, but supplies in village stores are generally depleted and are, in fact, intended for local Native consumption; **Overnight accommodations:** Lodging and eating facilities are available at the intermediate points of Nome and Kotzebue. Room reservations are suggested because touring groups book much of the touring space. Rooms average about $50 per day, and meals are proportionately as expensive. Transportation costs for goods and services in "bush" Alaska raise prices considerably in such places as Nome and Kotzebue. Visitors planning to stay in the Monument should plan to arrive self-sufficient. **First Aid available in park:** No; **Nearest Hospital:** Nome and Kotzebue; **Days/Hours:** Monument never closes; **Holiday Closings:** None; **Visitor attractions closed for seasons:** None; **Weather:** Most visitors come into the area between mid-June and mid-September when the temperatures average in the mid-40's F along the coast and mid-60's F inland. During the ice-free periods along the coasts (late May to late October), cloudy skies prevail, fog occurs, daily temperatures remain fairly constant in the long hours of daylight, and the relative humidity is high.

GENERAL INFORMATION: Visitors to the Monument must arrive self-sufficient with their food, clothing, and shelter, and in some cases with fuel. There is some driftwood along the beaches, but inland wood is scarce and should be used chiefly for cooking. You should possess skills, talents, and stamina to survive some difficult conditions. In other words, you should have hiking, backpacking, and camping experience; and be knowledgeable about food, clothing, and gear. Since visitors carry everything on their backs once they've arrived in the Monument, they bring only the *essentials*: good tents with rain flies, sleeping bags and pads, insect repellents and head nets, cooking and eating utensils, first aid items, maps, knife, food, warm clothing and rain gear, calf-high boots with waterproof lowers, fishing tackle, extra socks, and possibly some camera equipment. In parties of two or more—it is advisable to always travel with others in the Monument— many of the above items can be shared, reducing the weight one must carry.

Cape Krusenstern National Monument
Alaska

MAILING ADDRESS: Alaska Office, National Park Service, 540 W. 5th Ave., Anchorage, Alaska 99501

DIRECTIONS: The Monument is in northwestern Alaska. Access is from Kotzebue via charter airplane.

The 114 beach ridges on this Chukchi Sea area, 966 km (600 miles) northwest of Anchorage, tell of successive Eskimo communities living here for 4000 years. Created by Presidential Proclamation on Dec. 1, 1978.

VISITOR ACTIVITIES: wildlife-watching, beach walking, fishing, primitive camping; **Permits:** Alaska fishing license, available locally, is required; **Fees:** No; **Visitor facilities:** No; **Any limitations on vehicle usage:** No roads; **Hiking trails:** No; **Backcountry:** Yes, information can be obtained from Alaska Area Office of the National Park Service; **Camping:** Yes, primitive camping only; **Other overnight accommodations on site:** No; **Meals served in the park:** No; **Food and supplies obtainable in the park:** No; **Food and supplies obtainable nearby:** Yes, at Kotzebue; **Overnight accommodations:** Kotzebue; **First Aid available in park:** No; **Nearest Hospital:** Kotzebue; **Days/Hours:** Monument never closes; **Holiday Closings:** No; **Visitor attractions closed for seasons:** No.

Denali National Monument
Alaska

MAILING ADDRESS: Superintendent, Mt. McKinley National Park, P.O. Box 9, McKinley Park, Alaska 99755 **Telephone:** 907-683-2294

DIRECTIONS: Denali National Monument is generally accessible on the southern side from the Parks Highway; a year-round highway between Anchorage and Fairbanks. A motorist parallels the area beginning near Talkeetna, Alaska, which is about 160 km (100 miles) north of Anchorage, and continues a few miles north of McKinley Station in Mt. McKinley National Park. The total distance is about 200 km (125 miles). General visitor access is presently limited to able bodied hikers, backpackers, cross-country skiers gaining access from service roads that lead from the Parks Highway, and—where allowed—snowmachines, boats, and airplanes. Summer and winter access to the northern portion is possible by charter plane to Lake Minchumina. The Kantishna mining district can be reached by way of the 132 km (82 mile) long road through Mount McKinley National Park but is limited to summer months when the road is open to traffic. Charter air access is available from Talkeetna, Mt. McKinley Station, and from Fairbanks and Anchorage. Depending on the type of aircraft, the cost for a charter can run from $75 to $150 per hour. The Alaska Railroad parallels the southern portion of the National Monument but is not considered satisfactory access to the area except in the Cantwell area. However, it does provide transportation to Talkeetna and McKinley Station where air charters are available. In Summer, public shuttlebus transportation through McKinley Park to Wonder Lake would take you within 10 to 14 km (6 to 8 miles) of Kantishna.

This area, adjacent to Mt. McKinley National Park, assures protection of the entire Mt. McKinley massif, hitherto only about half under National Park Service management. Denali also protects vital wolf, grizzly bear, black bear, caribou and other wildlife habitats. Created by Presidential Proclamation on Dec. 1, 1978.

VISITOR ACTIVITIES: auto tours, charter aircraft tours, backpacking, wilderness camping, cross-country skiing, snowmobiling, fishing; **Permits:** Alaska fishing license required, available at sporting goods stores in Fairbanks or Anchorage; **Fees:** No; **Visitor facilities:** lodging; **Any limitations on vehicle usage:** No formal roads; **Hiking trails:** No; **Backcountry:** Yes, information on backcountry use available at Riley Creek Visitor Center; **Camping:** Yes, no reservations available for primitive campsites; **Other overnight accommodations on site:** Yes, contact Camp Denali, c/o Wally Cole, McKinley Park, AK 99755 or North Face Lodge, Box 66, McKinley Park, AK 99755, Phone 907-683-2265; **Meals served in the park:** No; **Food and supplies obtainable in the park:** No; **Food and supplies obtainable nearby:** Yes, limited food and supplies available along the Parks Highway, but you should stock up in Anchorage or Fairbanks; **Overnight accommodations:** Mount McKinley National Park, McKinley Village, Carlo Creek; **First Aid available in park:** Yes, there is also a clinic in Healy; **Nearest Hospital:** Fairbanks; **Days/Hours:** Park never closes; **Holiday Closings:** None; **Visitor attractions closed for seasons:**None; **Weather:** Alaska Summers are generally cool, wet and windy. A light coat is necessary during Summer particularly in the higher elevations. Winter weather can become very severe with temperatures dropping to 50°F below zero with blowing snow. During moderate weather the winter temperature can be pleasant with sunny skies.

GENERAL INFORMATION: Summer clothing should include rain gear and a light coat in preparation for a sudden storm or cold weather. A sturdy, insect proof tent is necessary and a stove is recommended for backpacking because firewood is scarce. Do not bury or leave trash behind. Insects are troublesome in Alaska from about June until colder weather arrives in the latter part of August. Mosquitoes, no-see-ems and other biting insects abound in wet areas and in the tundra. Bring insect repellent. Keep your distance from bears, moose, and other wild animals. Make noise when you hike to announce your presence. Bears will not be present during the winter months, however, moose are present in their natural habitat year-round. Always keep a clean campsite with your food sealed in containers so odors will not attract animals.

Gates of the Arctic National Monument
Alaska

MAILING ADDRESS: Alaska Office, National Park Service, 540 W. 5th Ave., Anchorage, Alaska 99501 **Telephone:** 907-271-4243

DIRECTIONS: Most visitors to the central Brooks Range fly via scheduled flights from Fairbanks to Bettles (about $52 one-way), and then charter small aircraft in Bettles for flights into the Monument($125-$185 per hour). Charter flights into the Brooks Range can also begin in Fairbanks (air-time is generally paid to and from the destination). Additionally, scheduled flights from Bettles to Anuktuvuk Pass (in the center of the Monument) are available several times a week, at a cost of about $45 per passenger.

This vast tundra wilderness contains seven proposed wild rivers and many lakes and rivers yet unnamed. Broad valleys contrast with razor-like Arrigetch Peaks and turreted Mt. Igipak, high point of the central and western Brooks Range. Here, 324 km (200 miles) northwest of Fairbanks, is habitat vital to the arctic caribou, grizzly bear, sheep, moose, wolf and raptors. Authorized by Presidential Proclamation on Dec. 1, 1978.

VISITOR ACTIVITIES: hiking, backcountry, rock and mountain climbing, fishing, wildlife-watching, canoeing; **Permits:** Alaska fishing license, available in Fairbanks, is required; **Fees:** No; **Visitor facilities:** No; **Any limitations on vehicle usage:** No roads;

Hiking trails: No; **Backcountry:** Yes, information can be obtained from Alaska Area Office of the National Park Service: **Camping:** No; **Other overnight accommodations on site:** Yes, excellent camping sites are available throughout the area. A few private lodges are located within the Monument. **Meals served in the park:** No; **Food and supplies obtainable in the park:** No; **Food and supplies obtainable nearby:** Yes, Bettles, Fairbanks; **Overnight accommodations:** Bettles, 32 km (20 miles) south; **First Aid available in park:** No; **Nearest Hospital:** Fairbanks; **Days/Hours:** Monument never closes; **Holiday Closings:** None; **Visitor attractions closed for seasons:**None; **Weather:** Long, cold Winters and short, mild Summers are the rule. Along the south slopes of the Brooks Range, particularly in the lowlands, mid-summer temperatures may occasionally rise into the 80's and rarely into the 90's. Temperatures in the highlands are generally cooler, and on the northern slopes temperatures range from 30°F to 60°F. In the highlands and on the north slopes freezing temperatures may occur in mid-August and definitely occur in early September. August is often a rainy month.

GENERAL INFORMATION: Because nearly all visitors to the Monument will be backpacking for extended periods, it is essential that clothing, camping gear and food are of good quality and are light in weight. Clothing should include enough "layers", even during the summer months, to provide warmth in sub-freezing temperatures; and rain gear is essential. Tents should be strong, light and have a rainfly. Food will have to consist primarily of dried and freeze-dried items, and should be in greater quantities than what is expected to be consumed during the planned trip. Visitors should be well familiar with their gear before starting a backpacking trip in this area, and should additionally be competent at hiking, camping, and survival skills. Winter travel requires special skills and hardiness, and should only be undertaken after careful planning.

Mosquitoes usually come out in mid-June and begin to disappear in early or mid-August. Gnats and whitesocks hatch in August. Insects are most bothersome in wet lowlands and areas of heavy vegetation, and are not as numerous on dry highlands where breezes are frequent. Carry good mosquito repellent and a headnet as backup.

Glacier Bay National Monument
Gustavus, Alaska

MAILING ADDRESS: Superintendent, Glacier Bay National Monument, P.O. Box 1089, Juneau, Alaska 99801 **Telephone:** 907-586-7127

DIRECTIONS: The Monument is located at the northwest end of the Alexander Archipelago in southeastern Alaska. There are no roads to the Monument, and access is by various types of commercial transport, including regularly scheduled and charter air services, cruise ships and charter boats, private boats, and tours via kayak. By boat, the distance from Juneau is about 160 km (100 miles). Flying time from Juneau is about 30 minutes. An airfield is at Gustavus, just outside the Park.

Great tidewater glaciers, a dramatic range of plant communities, and rare species of wildlife can be found in this unit of the National Park System. Created by Presidential Proclamation on Feb. 26, 1925.

VISITOR ACTIVITIES: glacier-viewing, boating, camping, hiking, fishing, wildlife- and bird-watching, campfire programs; **Permits:** required for fishing; **Fees:** only for concession-operated and commercial transportation to tidewater glaciers; **Visitor facilities:** restrooms, lodge, interpretive programs and hikes, hiking trails, food service, campground. Boaters may obtain gasoline, diesel fuel, water, and limited moorage space at Bartlett Cove. No other public facilities for boats are available at the Park. **Any limitations on vehicle usage:** No; **Hiking trails:** Yes, the Monument's several hundred kilometers of shoreline, numerous islands, and alpine meadows offer nearly unlimited camping and hiking opportunities; **Backcountry:** Yes, a hikers' guide with many suggestions for backcountry users and topographical maps covering the Park can be obtained at Bartlett Cove; **Camping:** Yes, campers should bring food and supplies to Glacier Bay. There are no stores or camping services locally. **Other overnight accommodations on site:** Yes, concessioner-operated Glacier Bay Lodge at Bartlett Cove is open from about mid-May to mid-Sept. Rooms and meals are available. For reservations, write to Glacier Bay Lodge, Glacier Bay National Monument, Gustavus, AK 99826, during the operating season, and Glacier Bay Lodge, Inc., 312 Park Place Bldg., Seattle, WA 98101, phone 206-624-8851 the remainder of the year. A tour boat makes daily cruises from the lodge to the glaciers. For campers and hikers, rain gear, a tent fly, and water-resistant boots are often essential items for a successful trip. **Meals served in the park:** Yes, at Glacier Bay Lodge, in season; **Food and supplies obtainable in the park:** No; **Food and supplies obtainable nearby:** No, at Juneau, AK, 161 km (100 miles) distant; **Overnight accommodations:** Gustavus, 16 km (10 miles) distant. Otherwise Juneau, 161 km (100 miles); **First Aid available in park:** Yes, at Park Headquarters; **Nearest Hospital:** Juneau, 161 km (100 miles) by air; **Days/Hours:** Park always open, concession facilities are open from late May to mid-September; **Holiday Closings:** No; **Visitor attractions closed for seasons:**only concession facilities are closed from mid-Sept. to mid-May; **Weather:** Warm clothing and rain gear are essential when visiting the Park. Summer temperatures seldom exceed 24°C (72°F) and extended periods of wet weather are to be expected. The ground is usually moist and footwear should be selected accordingly.

GENERAL INFORMATION: Publications, maps, and marine charts relating to Glacier Bay may be purchased at Bartlett Cove, or by writing to Alaska Natural History Association, Glacier Bay National Monument, Gustavus, AK 99826. Boaters should be familiar with procedures and regulations. Cooking stoves are recommended because no wood for campfires is available in many portions of upper Glacier Bay.

For Your Safety—Beware of brown and black bears. Keep your food supply separate from campsites and equipment so that no odors linger. Make noise when you hike to announce your presence. Glacial streams may be small in the morning and uncrossable torrents in the afternoon after a warm or rainy day. Tides may fluctuate 7 meters (25 feet) daily and beach meadows that are enticing as campsites may be flooded. Avoid crossing or approaching steep glacial interfaces. Though some stagnant bodies may be crossed safely, extreme caution should be taken when hiking on glacial surfaces.

Katmai National Monument
Alaska

MAILING ADDRESS: Superintendent, Katmai National Monument, P.O. Box 7, King Salmon, Alaska 99613 **Telephone:** 907-246-3305

DIRECTIONS: Katmai is 290 air miles southwest of Anchorage. Daily commercial jet flights connect Anchorage with King Salmon. Travel from King Salmon to Brooks River is by amphibious bush aircraft. Visitor information is available at the Brooks River Ranger Station.

Variety marks this vast land: lakes, forests, mountains, and marshlands all abound in wildlife—including the Alaska brown bear, the world's largest carnivore. Here, in one of the largest areas in the National Park System, Novarupta Volcano erupted violently in 1912, forming the ash-filled "Valley of Ten Thousand Smokes." Today, only a few active vents remain. Created by Presidential Proclamation on Sept. 24, 1918.

VISITOR ACTIVITIES: hiking, walking, wildlife-watching, fishing, camping, backcountry travel, bird-watching, boating, mountain climbing; **Permits:** Fishing licenses can only be obtained at Brooks Lodge; backcountry permits available without charge at Brooks River Ranger Station or at Headquarters in King Salmon; **Fees:** Yes, for Alaska State fishing licenses; **Visitor facilities:** concession boats, bus tours, interpretive talks, charter aircraft, cabins, lodge, dining room, campgrounds, rental tents and stoves, fuel, fishing equipment rental; **Any limitations on vehicle usage:** Katmai is not connected with any road system—access is by aircraft; **Hiking trails:** Yes, detailed information on hiking is provided in a free publication, available by mail or at Brooks River Ranger Station or from Headquarters in King Salmon; **Backcountry:** Yes, permit required; check at Brooks River Ranger Station or at Headquarters in King Salmon; **Camping:** Yes; **Other overnight accommodations on site:** Yes, a lodge is at Brooks River. Wien Air Alaska (4100 International Airport Road, Anchorage, AK 99502, phone 907-243-4100.) provides accommodations and services at Brooks River and Lake Grosvenor. **Meals served in the park:** Yes, at Brooks River and Lake Grosvenor Camp; **Food and supplies obtainable in the park:** Yes, camping supplies and groceries should be obtained before visiting the park. Limited freeze-dried food items and stove fuel available at the park. **Food and supplies obtainable nearby:** Yes, a small general store in King Salmon; **Overnight accommodations:** motel in King Salmon; **First Aid available in park:** Yes, or nearby emergency facilities in King Salmon; **Nearest Hospital:** Anchorage, 290 miles by air; **Days/Hours:** Brooks Camp is accessible only from early June to mid-September. Charter flights over Katmai can be made in Winter. **Visitor attractions closed for seasons:** Lodge and concession facilities closed from Sept. 7 to June 1. **Weather:** Summer high temperatures average 63°F and low temperatures average 44°F. Strong winds and sudden, gusty rainstorms known as williwaws frequently sweep the area. The sky is clear about 20% of the Summer.

GENERAL INFORMATION: Day hikers should have sturdy hiking boots with good support, good gear, and warm clothing. Come prepared for some sunshine and some stormy weather. Clothing that may be useful includes comfortable sport clothes, a warm sweater or windbreaker, walking shoes or boots with thick soles and good support, wool socks, and a rain coat or hat. You will need insect repellent.

Katmai is a wildlife sanctuary. Keep your distance from and do not feed the animals. Keep all food sealed to reduce odors; use food caches. Make lots of noise when you walk.

Kenai Fjords National Monument
Alaska

MAILING ADDRESS: Alaska Office, National Park Service, 540 W. 5th Ave., Anchorage, Alaska 99501 **Telephone:** 907-271-4243

DIRECTIONS: The Monument is completely undeveloped at present. The gateway communities of Homer and Seward, Alaska are within a few hours' drive from Anchorage. Air transportation from Anchorage to the towns is available via commercial and charter flights. In addition, Seward has bus service. Both towns offer the charter boat service to bottomfishing opportunities along the coast. Charters range from $300 to $400 per day and costs may be shared among groups using the same service.

Within a few miles of Seward, this one-half million acre national monument preserves a portion of the southern Kenai Mountains, two interrelated ice fields and a coastal fjord system along which are found abundant marine mammals, seabirds and mountain goats. Created by Presidential Proclamation on Dec. 1, 1978.

VISITOR ACTIVITIES: fishing, sailing, hiking, visiting a glacier, wildlife-watching, charter boats at the Fish House in Seward; **Permits:** Alaska fishing permits required, available in Seward or Anchorage; **Fees:** No; **Visitor facilities:** A State Ferry System links Prince William Sound with Seward, Homer, and Kodiak Island. Flightseeing chartered tours leave from Homer and Seward. Hotels, motels, campgrounds, food and services are available in Seward. **Any limitations on vehicle usage:** No roads; **Hiking trails:** Yes, trails are located around the periphery on adjacent federal and state lands; **Backcountry:** Yes, information can be obtained from the Alaska Area Office; **Camping:** Yes; **Other overnight accommodations on site:** No reservations required for campgrounds in Seward and within adjacent national forest land. Contact the Chamber of Commerce in either Seward, AK, 99664, phone 907-244-3046, or Homer, AK 99603 for information on other facilities; **Meals served in the park:** No; **Food and supplies obtainable in the park:** No; **Food and supplies obtainable nearby:** Yes, at Seward; **Overnight accommodations:** Seward; **First Aid available in park:** No; **Nearest Hospital:** Seward; **Days/ Hours:** Park always open; **Holiday Closings:** No; **Visitor attractions closed for seasons:** Charter boats operate from late May to Labor Day; **Weather:** A coastal maritime climate influences the area. Seward receives more rainfall and cloudy days than does Homer, which is located on the rain-shadow side of the mountain.

GENERAL INFORMATION: Nights are cool along the coast and high humidity can be expected. Comfortable wool clothing and appropriate rain gear are important considerations.

Klondike Gold Rush National Historical Park
Skagway, Alaska and Seattle, Washington

MAILING ADDRESS: Superintendent, Klondike Gold Rush National Historical Park, P. O. Box 517, Skagway, Alaska 99840 *OR* Superintendent, Klondike Gold Rush National Historical Park, 117 S. Main St., Seattle, Washington 98104 **Telephone:** AK:907-983-2400 WA:206-442-7220

DIRECTIONS: Access to Skagway is by auto, plane, bus, cruise ship, rail, or State of Alaska ferry. For further information, contact your travel agent or the City of Skagway, Box 415, Skagway, AK 99840. Visitor Center is on Broadway between 2nd and 3rd Streets. The Seattle Visitor Center is at 117 S. Main Street in the Pioneer Square area.
   The Park is a memorial to the thousands of miners who followed trails from Skagway, AK to the Yukon Territory of Canada during the 1898 gold rush. It preserves historic structures in Skagway, Chilkoot Trail, and White Pass Trail (from Dyea to the Canadian Border), with an interpretive center in Seattle. Authorized for addition to the National Park System on June 30, 1976.

VISITOR ACTIVITIES: Alaska: wildlife-watching, camping, foot, bus, and chartered aircraft tours. Information available at the Skagway Visitor Center. Seattle: interpretive displays, films, special tours and other events; **Permits:** No; **Fees:** No; **Visitor facilities:** Seattle: Visitor Center, restrooms, exhibits; Alaska: Visitor Center, campground, groceries and other limited supplies and restrooms; **Any limitations on vehicle usage:** Vehicles are restricted to designated roadways; **Hiking trails:** In Alaska, the 53 km (33 mile) Chilkoot Trail is accessible only on foot. You must be properly outfitted before embarking on a hike over the Chilkoot Trail. Weather conditions may change rapidly from hour to hour, especially in the summit area. You must be prepared for cold temperatures, snow or rain, fog and travel through swampy areas and snow fields. Proper equipment includes warm clothing (preferably wool), sturdy rain gear (not plastic), a tent with waterproof fly, campstove, and adequate fuel (there is no wood in the summit area and campfires are not allowed at all in the Canadian portion), good hiking boots, adequate food plus emergency rations and first-aid kit. Current trail information available at the Visitor Center in

Skagway or the Parks Canada office in Whitehorse. Hiking the trail north from Dyea is recommended because it is the historic route. Travelling the trail in reverse is not recommended because descending the steep summit scree, the "Golden Stairs" of the gold rush days is dangerous. *For Your Safety*—Be alert for symptoms of hypothermia—a lowering of the body temperature that results in uncontrollable shivering, disorientation, weariness, and possibly dèath. Never feed wild animals. Make noise when you hike, announcing your presence, since animals are most dangerous when startled or cornered. Never approach a potentially dangerous animal. Keep your campsite and equipment clean. Food should be sealed in airtight containers and hung from trees so that animals will not be attracted by food odors. You are advised not to take pets on the Chilkoot Trail. It is a difficult hike. **Backcountry:** Yes; **Camping:** In Alaska, no reservations available for primitive campsites; **Other overnight accommodations on site:** Yes; **Meals served in the park:** Not within either section of the park, but meals are available nearby; **Food and supplies obtainable in the park:** Yes, groceries and limited supplies in Alaska; **Food and supplies obtainable nearby:** Yes, Seattle: 2 blocks north, Alaska: Skagway Historic District; **Overnight accommodations:** Seattle and Skagway; **First Aid available in park:** Yes; **Nearest Hospital:** Seattle: 1.6 km (1 mile) away, Alaska: None; **Days/Hours:** Seattle: 9 a.m. to 7 p.m. in Summer; shorter hours during the off-season, Skagway: Visitor Center open from 9 a.m. to 8 p.m., only in Summer; **Holiday Closings:** Seattle Visitor Center holiday closings have not yet been determined. **Visitor attractions closed for seasons:** Skagway Visitor Center open only in Summer.

GENERAL INFORMATION: International Regulations: Customs and Immigration laws require that anyone travelling to Carcross or beyond must report to Canadian Customs in Whitehorse. Anyone proceeding to Skagway from Canada must report to U.S. Customs and Immigration authorities in Skagway.

Kobuk Valley National Monument
Alaska

MAILING ADDRESS: Alaska Office, National Park Service, 540 W. 5th Ave., Anchorage, Alaska 99501.

DIRECTIONS: Access is via charter aircraft from Kotzebue.
   The Kobuk River, flowing west across this area to the Chukchi Sea, has been a major transportation route for centuries. Archaeological resources are extensive. Other features in this area between the Baird Mountains on the north and Waring Mountains are the Salmon River, caribou migrating routes; habitat of moose,grizzly bear, black bear and wolves; and the Great Kobuk Sand Dunes. Created by Presidential Proclamation on Dec. 1, 1978.

VISITOR ACTIVITIES: float trips, fishing, dune walks, primitive camping; **Permits:** Alaska fishing license, available in Anchorage, is required; **Fees:** No; **Visitor facilities:** No; **Any limitations on vehicle usage:** No roads; **Hiking trails:** No; **Backcountry:** Yes, information can be obtained from Alaska Area Office of the National Park Service; **Camping:** Yes, primitive camping only; **Other overnight accommodations on site:** No; **Meals served in the park:** No; **Food and supplies obtainable in the park:** No; **Food and supplies obtainable nearby:** No, in Kotzebue; **Overnight accommodations:** No; **First Aid available in park:** No; **Nearest Hospital:** Kotzebue; **Days/Hours:** Monument never closes.

Lake Clark National Monument
Alaska

MAILING ADDRESS: Alaska Office, National Park Service, 540 W. 5th Ave., Anchorage, Alaska 99501 **Telephone:** 907-271-4243 ·

DIRECTIONS: Most visitors charter an aircraft from Anchorage to the Lake Clark area at a cost of $120 to $160 an hour depending on the weight load, number of passengers and type of aircraft. Most places in the Monument are within one and a half hours flight time from Anchorage. There is commercial air service available from Anchorage to Iliamna, costing about $85 round trip. Points within the Monument from Iliamna are visited via air charter, at the same cost per hour as Anchorage's air charter services.

Already popular with summer hikers and fishermen, this 2.5 million acre area across Cook Inlet from Anchorage provides major recreational potential. Among the wildlife to be viewed in this rugged country are caribou, grizzly bear, black bear, sheep at the southern limit of its range, wolves, wolverine, mink, marten, lynxes, and other fur bearers. The coastal mountains contain two steaming volcanoes. The Monument preserves the Kivichak River and associated red salmon fishery. Created by Presidential Proclamation on Dec. 1, 1978.

VISITOR ACTIVITIES: hiking, wildlife- and bird-watching, fishing, boating, river trips, primitive camping; **Permits:** for backcountry, available at the Alaska Office, and Alaska fishing licenses are required and are available in Anchorage; **Fees:** No; **Visitor facilities:** boat rental, fishing tackle, guide services on the shores of Lake Clark, Fishtrap Lake, and Lake Iliamna, lodging; **Any limitations on vehicle usage:** No roads; **Hiking trails:** Yes, several primitive and unmarked trails; **Backcountry:** Yes, information can be obtained from Alaska Area Office of the National Park Service; **Camping:** Yes, primitive camping only; **Other overnight accommodations on site:** Yes, Island Lodge is located within the Monument, while 4 other lodges are located outside the boundaries of the Monument and along the shores of Lake Clark. Other lodging is available through commercial and air charter services in Anchorage to points on the periphery of the Monument. Lodging ranges from primitive cabins to a modern lodge with plumbing; **Meals served in the park:** Yes, but only for guests at lodging facilities; **Food and supplies obtainable in the park:** Yes, limited food and supplies at nearby Nondalton and Iliamna; **Overnight accommodations:** No; **First Aid available in park:** Yes; **Nearest Hospital:** Kenai; **Days/Hours:** Monument never closes; **Holiday Closings:** None; **Visitor attractions closed for seasons:**None; **Weather:** Most visitors arrive between mid-June and early September, when high temperatures average between 60° and 75 °, with an occasional 80° day in the interior. Coastline areas are cooler with temperatures between 50° and 65 °. Wind and rainfall are present on the coastal areas, with mostly sunny weather and milder temperatures in the interior.

GENERAL INFORMATION: Insects are numerous and precautions should be made by obtaining adequate tents for camping on open river and lake bars. Having an ample supply of insect repellent is a must. One should plan on wearing clothing that will ward off the extremes of possible freezing temperatures, wet weather, and warm sunny days. Extra socks and tennis shoes are practical for river running travel, plus a rainsuit, wool shirts and pants. Campers should travel light by carrying freeze-dried and high energy foods, dried fruit, powdered milk and packaged soups. Ordinary camping gear such as a warm sleeping bag, tent with rain fly and mosquito-proof webbing, knife, small hatchet, insect repellent, sturdy hat, matches in waterproof container, and maps with protective casing are suggested.

Mount McKinley National Park
McKinley Park, Alaska

MAILING ADDRESS: Superintendent, Mount McKinley National Park, P.O. Box 9, McKinley Park, Alaska 99755 **Telephone:** 907-683-2294

DIRECTIONS: The Park is 386 km (240 miles) north of Anchorage and 193 km (120 miles) south of Fairbanks, on Alaska Highway 3. Buses run regularly from both cities. The Alaska Railroad provides passenger and freight service to the park; 8 hours from Anchorage and 4 hours from Fairbanks. For information write to Alaska Railroad, Traffic Division, P.O. Box 7-2111, Anchorage, AK 99510.

Mount McKinley, at 20,320 feet, is the highest mountain in North America. Large glaciers of the Alaska Range, caribou, sheep, moose, grizzly bears, timber wolves, and other wildlife are highlights of this second largest national park. Established by act of Congress on Feb. 26, 1917.

VISITOR ACTIVITIES: camping, wildlife-watching, interpretive talks and walks, hiking, backcountry use, fishing, dog sledding, cross-country skiing; **Permits:** for backcountry, available in Summer; at Visitor Centers and Ranger Stations, in Winter, at Park Headquarters; **Fees:** for wildlife scenic tours, $20 per person (1979 price). Campground fees vary from free to $4 per night, depending on facilities; **Visitor facilities:** campsites, lodging, food service, groceries, supplies, gas, minor auto repairs. After you leave the entrance area for the park interior, gasoline and food service are not available. **Any limitations on vehicle usage:** Maximum speed limit is 35 mph. During the visitor season, private vehicles are not permitted beyond the Savage River except to proceed to a registered campsite. Trail bikes and motorcycles must not leave the park road. Snowmobiles are prohibited. Since private vehicles are not allowed, there is *free transportation.* Buses regularly run from the Visitor Orientation Center to Eielson Visitor Center and on to Wonder Lake. The buses make regularly scheduled stops at key points along the park road for your convenience, but you should feel free to get on and off *at any point* and to change buses *as many times as you please.* Bring all the food you will need, because there is no food service beyond the entrance area; **Hiking trails:** Yes, most hiking is cross-country. Both long- and short-range trips are available. Take extra caution in crossing streams; they are swifter than they seem; **Backcountry:** Yes, a permit and a stove are required for backcountry use. Obtain information from the Visitor Center upon arrival or by contacting the Park in advance; **Camping:** Yes, if you plan to camp in the Park you must choose a campsite and then register for it at the Visitor Orientation Center in the Headquarters-entrance area. All campsites are available on a first-come, first-served basis. You may drive to Riley Creek or Savage River and select a site, then register, however, for campsites at Sanctuary River, Teklanika River, Igloo Creek and Wonder Lake registration must be made at the Riley Creek Visitor Orientation Center when you arrive. After you have registered, you will be allowed to drive your own vehicle just to the campsite. Once there you must hike or use the free public transportation system to get to other points of interest in the park. There is a privately-owned campground 16 km (10 miles) north of the McKinley Park entrance, and Byer's Lake campground is in the Denali State Park 145 km (90 miles) to the south of the Park entrance. **Other overnight accommodations on site:** Yes, for information and reservations at McKinley Park Station Hotel, contact the hotel at Mount McKinley National Park, P.O. Box 9, McKinley Park, AK 99755, phone 907-683-2215. **Meals served in the park:** Yes, at McKinley Park Station Hotel; **Food and supplies obtainable in the park:** Yes, near McKinley Park Station Hotel. For detailed information on concessioner services, contact Mount McKinley National Park Company, McKinley Park, AK 99755, phone 907-683-2215, from May 18-Oct. 1. From Oct. 2 to May 17, contact the Company at Outdoor World, 307 South B.

Street, San Mateo, CA 94401, phone 414-348-3385; **Food and supplies obtainable nearby:** Yes, 16 km (10 miles) north in Healy, AK. Shopping should be done in Fairbanks or Anchorage, where prices are more reasonable. **Overnight accommodations:** Healy Road House, 16 km (10 miles) north; McKinley Village, 9.7 km (6 miles) south; **First Aid available in park:** Yes, Healy Clinic; **Nearest Hospital:** Fairbanks, 209 km (130 miles) north; **Days/Hours:** Park never closes; **Holiday Closings:** None; **Visitor attractions closed for seasons:** Hotel and related services (gas, food, etc.) closed in Winter. Park road closed to cars beyond Headquarters in Winter, but is open to skiers and dog sledders; **Weather:** Typical summer weather is cool, wet and windy. To be comfortable, you should bring clothing for temperatures that range from 5°C (40°F) to 25°C (80°F). Rain gear, a light coat, sturdy walking shoes or boots, and insect repellent are essential. Winter visitors can expect temperatures between 30°F and -50°F.

GENERAL INFORMATION: Binoculars are valuable for viewing wildlife and mountains. A telephoto lens helps with wildlife photography. *Keep your distance* from animals. Keep your campsite and your equipment clean. All food should be sealed in containers so odors will not attract animals. Make noise when you hike.

Noatak National Monument
Alaska

MAILING ADDRESS: Alaska Office, National Park Service, 540 W. 5th Ave., Anchorage, Alaska 99501 **Telephone:** 907-271-4243

DIRECTIONS: Access is via charter aircraft from Kotzebue.
  The Noatak River has the country's largest mountain-ringed basin unaffected by man's technology, a 105 km (65-mile) Grand Canyon of the Noatak, a transition zone for diverse plant and animal life and a vital caribou migration route. Some of its 200 archaeological sites date back 5000 years. Created by Presidential Proclamation on Dec. 1, 1978.

VISITOR ACTIVITIES: float trips, fishing, primitive camping; **Permits:** Alaska fishing license, available in Anchorage is required; **Fees:** No; **Visitor facilities:** No; **Any limitations on vehicle usage:** No roads; **Hiking trails:** No; **Backcountry:** Yes, information can be obtained from Alaska Area Office of the National Park Service; **Camping:** Yes, primitive camping only; **Other overnight accommodations on site:** No; **Meals served in the park:** No; **Food and supplies obtainable in the park:** No; **Food and supplies obtainable nearby:** No, at Kotzebue; **Overnight accommodations:** None; **First Aid available in park:** No; **Nearest Hospital:** Kotzebue; **Days/Hours:** Monument never closes; **Holiday Closings:** None; **Visitor attractions closed for seasons:**No.

Sitka National Historical Park
Sitka, Alaska

MAILING ADDRESS: Sitka National Historical Park, Box 738, Sitka, AK 99835 **Telephone:** 907-747-6281

DIRECTIONS: Sitka is in Alaska's southeastern panhandle. It can be reached by commercial airline direct from Seattle, Juneau, and Anchorage, and is a port of call for many cruise ships and ferries on the Alaska Marine Highway System.
  The site of the 1804 fort and battle which marked the last major Tlingit Indian resistance to Russian colonization is preserved here. Native artists demonstrate crafts and

discuss their culture. The Park features totem pole exhibits and the restoration of one of the oldest Russian buildings in Alaska. Created by Presidential Proclamation on June 1, 1890.

VISITOR ACTIVITIES: interpretive talks, audiovisual exhibits, and craft demonstrations at the Visitor Center, picnicking, walking tours; **Permits:** No; **Fees:** No; **Visitor facilities:** parking and restrooms, picnic tables, fireplaces, Indian Cultural Center, trails, beach (no swimming permitted); **Any limitations on vehicle usage:** No; **Hiking trails:** Yes, almost 3 km (2 miles) of walkways thread the park; **Backcountry:** No; **Camping:** No; **Other overnight accommodations on site:** No; **Meals served in the park:** No; **Food and supplies obtainable in the park:** No; **Food and supplies obtainable nearby:** Yes, in Sitka, .8 km (1/2 mile); **Overnight accommodations:** Sitka, .8 km (1/2 mile); **First Aid available in park:** Yes; **Nearest Hospital:** Sitka, .8 km (1/2 mile); **Days/Hours:** Open daily from 8 a.m. to 5 p.m. with extended hours in Summer; **Holiday Closings:** Thanksgiving, Dec. 25 and Jan. 1; **Visitor attractions closed for seasons:**None; **Weather:** Summer has frequent rain; temperatures range from the high 50's-mid 60's. Winter is rainy and snowy; temperatures from high teens-high 30's.

GENERAL INFORMATION: Visitors should also see nearby landmarks: St. Michael's Cathedral, Castle Hill, the Russian Memorial, and Old Sitka.

Wrangell-St. Elias National Monument
Alaska

MAILING ADDRESS: Alaska Office, National Park Service, 540 W. 5th Ave., Anchorage, Alaska 99501 **Telephone:** 907-271-4243

DIRECTIONS: Access into the Monument by road is available from the community of Chitina via the Chitina-McCarthy road, a four-wheel drive route, which is generally passable during the summer months, and extends some 104 km (65 miles) up the Chitina River Valley following the historic route of the Cooper River and Northwestern Railroad to the town of McCarthy. Road access into the northern section of the Monument is from Slana (on the Tok cutoff) along a four-wheel drive route which extends some 45 miles into the abandoned mining community of Nabesna. Access to the remaining portions of the Monument is by air. Charter air service is available from the community of Gulkana to a number of interior landing strips. Costs vary but an average round trip cost from Gulkana to McCarthy with pick up at a later point in time would cost about $180 for a Cessna 180 hauling about 3 passengers. The community of Gulkana is some 332 km (200 miles) by paved highway from Anchorage and is reached by regularly scheduled bus and air service. Round trip air fare from Anchorage to Gulkana is about $100. Air access to southern sections including the beaches is available from Yakutat. Costs are about the same as above. At present there are no charter boats available out of Yakutat.

A day's drive east of Anchorage, this Monument contains wilderness not yet visited by non-natives. Here is the country's largest collection of glaciers and of peaks over 16,000 feet, including 18,008-foot Mount St. Elias, the continent's second-highest. Caribou, Dall sheep, and grizzly and black bears, wolves, wolverine, moose and mountain goats are among the wildlife. Created by Presidential Proclamation on Dec. 1, 1978.

VISITOR ACTIVITIES: backpacking, lake fishing, camping, river rafting, cross-country skiing, mountain climbing, hiking, rafting, air tours; **Permits:** Alaska fishing licenses required, available in Anchorage; **Fees:** No; **Visitor facilities:** lodging; **Any**

limitations on vehicle usage: Most roads are for four-wheel drive vehicles; **Hiking trails:** Yes, trails are primitive. Contact the Alaska Area Office for further information; **Back-country:** Yes, contact the Alaska Area Office for information; **Camping:** Yes; **Other overnight accommodations on site:** Yes, rustic overnight accommodations (no electricity, running water, etc.) are available in McCarthy, Kennecott, and at the Ptarmigan Lake Lodge. There are scattered fish camps and guide cabins located throughout the region which will accommodate backcountry parties. The major fish camps are located on Tanada and Copper Lakes in the north, Ptarmigan and Rock Lakes on the northeast, and Tebay and Hanagita Lakes in the southcentral portion of the Monument. More standard accommodations are available in motels and cabins in and around the community of Glennallen, on the Glenn and Richardson highways, and along the Tok cutoff. BLM campgrounds are found at Liberty Creek near Chitina and Sourdough north of Gulkana; **Meals served in the park:** No; **Food and supplies obtainable in the park:** Yes, Glennallen has a good supermarket, and limited supplies available in McCarthy, but all visitors to the backcountry must of necessity be self-sufficient and carry sufficient food to cover unexpected delays in getting picked up; **Overnight accommodations:** Motels are in Glennallen and along the Richardson Hwy.; **First Aid available in park:** No; **Nearest Hospital:** Glennallen; **Days/Hours:** Monument never closes; **Holiday Closings:** None; **Visitor attractions closed for seasons:** Much of the area is inaccessible in winter; **Weather:** Summer weather is cool, often cloudy and rainy. Such conditions will often interfere with scheduled air pickups, resulting in trips longer than scheduled. Clear, hot days are not uncommon, particularly in July which has the best weather. August is cooler and wetter but generally more mosquito-free. The Fall is excellent but of short duration. Winters are cold and dark, but clear weather is common. Average snow cover is about two feet.

GENERAL INFORMATION: Good rain gear and wool clothing are a must.

Yukon-Charley National Monument
Alaska

MAILING ADDRESS: Alaska Office, National Park Service, 540 W. 5th Ave., Anchorage, Alaska 99501 **Telephone:** 907-271-4243

DIRECTIONS: Eagle and Circle are the gateway cities to the Monument. Take either the Taylor Highway to Eagle (the highway connects with the Alcan and with a highway from Anchorage) or the Steese Highway from Fairbanks to Circle. There are scheduled flights from Fairbanks for both Eagle and Circle. Round trip fare to Eagle is $97.74 and to Circle $63.32.

The Monument preserves a 115-mile stretch of the 1800-mile Yukon River and the 88-mile scenic Charley River which drains a million-acre watershed near the Canadian border. Also protected are one of the largest nesting concentrations of the endangered peregrine falcon, and historic resources of the Gold Rush days. Created by Presidential Proclamation on Dec. 1, 1978.

VISITOR ACTIVITIES: Walking and guided tours of historic towns, wildlife- and bird-watching, river floating, hiking, camping, photography, backcountry, picnicking, kayaking, canoeing, gold digging; **Permits:** Alaska fishing license, available at local sporting goods stores, is required; **Fees:** None; **Visitor facilities:** Campgrounds at Eagle; Trading post, bar, liquor store, and picnic area at Circle; **Any limitations on vehicle usage:** No roads; **Hiking trails:** No; **Backcountry:** Information can be obtained from Alaska Area Office of the National Park Service; **Camping:** Yes; no reservations available at Eagle municipal campground;**Other overnight accommodations on site:** No; **Meals served in the park:** No; **Food and supplies obtainable in the park:** No; **Food and supplies obtainable nearby:** Yes, Eagle and Circle; **Overnight accommodations:** Circle Hot Springs or along the Alcan Highway; **First Aid available in park:** No; **Nearest Hospital:** Fairbanks (150 miles); **Days/Hours:** Monument never closes; **Holiday Closings:** None; **Visitor attractions closed for seasons:** Many highways closed in Winter; **Weather:** Most visitors come into the Monument between mid-June and mid-September when the temperatures average between 40° and 70°F and water conditions are most conducive to travel. Thunderstorms with strong winds can arise suddenly. They can become violent, pose dangers, and raise whitecaps on the wider stretches of the Yukon.

GENERAL INFORMATION: If you intend to be out among the elements in Alaska for a few days or longer in Summer, you had best carry clothing for *all* seasons. Within a span of a few hours on the Yukon River you can be very warm and very cold, so you should prepare accordingly. You can always shed garments when temperatures rise, but you can't make a hasty purchase of a jacket when temperatures fall. Tennis shoes are practical for river travel because they dry easily, but you'll need additional footwear. Extra socks and a rain suit or poncho are essential. Your choice of *food* items will depend upon a number of variables: length of planned visit, activities planned, weight you can carry, and kinds of meals planned. If weight is no problem and you want to go "first class" from Eagle to Circle or vice versa, you can carry fresh meat and produce in a cooler packed with *chunk* ice. Local merchants rarely carry these items so make your purchases elsewhere. The weight-conscious traveller such as the backpacker or kayaker, or the person wishing to abandon some of the amenities of civilization for a while will travel lightly and simply: freeze-dried and high-energy foods, packaged soups, dried fruit, powdered milk, etc. Ordinary *camping gear* is sufficient for Summer visitors: a good sleeping bag that will dry, a tent with rain fly, knife, hatchet, insect repellent and head net, matches in waterproof container, cooking and eating utensils, water container, good maps, fishing tackle, and photographic equipment. *Insects* are numerous and irritating from early Summer to early August when they diminish. To avoid some of the irritation from insects, most travellers camp on bars and open shorelines where winds are most likely to prevail.

Arizona

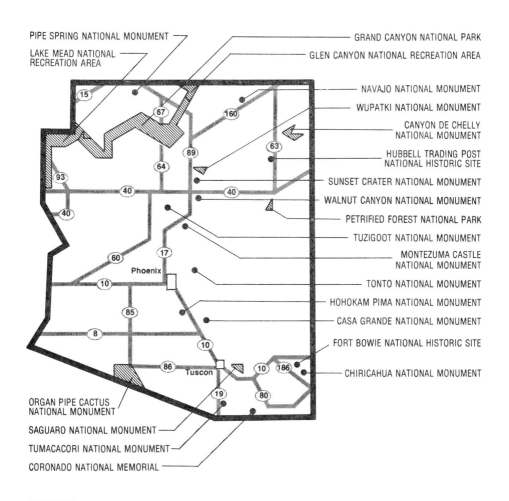

PIPE SPRING NATIONAL MONUMENT

LAKE MEAD NATIONAL RECREATION AREA

GRAND CANYON NATIONAL PARK

GLEN CANYON NATIONAL RECREATION AREA

NAVAJO NATIONAL MONUMENT

WUPATKI NATIONAL MONUMENT

CANYON DE CHELLY NATIONAL MONUMENT

HUBBELL TRADING POST NATIONAL HISTORIC SITE

SUNSET CRATER NATIONAL MONUMENT

WALNUT CANYON NATIONAL MONUMENT

PETRIFIED FOREST NATIONAL PARK

TUZIGOOT NATIONAL MONUMENT

MONTEZUMA CASTLE NATIONAL MONUMENT

TONTO NATIONAL MONUMENT

HOHOKAM PIMA NATIONAL MONUMENT

CASA GRANDE NATIONAL MONUMENT

FORT BOWIE NATIONAL HISTORIC SITE

CHIRICAHUA NATIONAL MONUMENT

Phoenix

Tuscon

ORGAN PIPE CACTUS NATIONAL MONUMENT

SAGUARO NATIONAL MONUMENT

TUMACACORI NATIONAL MONUMENT

CORONADO NATIONAL MEMORIAL

Canyon de Chelly National Monument
Chinle, Arizona

MAILING ADDRESS: Superintendent, Canyon de Chelly National Monument, P.O. Box 588, Chinle, Arizona 86503 **Telephone:** 602-674-5436

DIRECTIONS: The Visitor Center is 4.8 km (3 miles) from Route 63 in Chinle. From Gallup, NM, follow Routes 666, 264 to 63, 159 km (99 miles) to Chinle. From Grand Canyon, AZ, Routes 64, 89, 160, 264 to 63, 370 km (270 miles). From Holbrook-Petrified Forest, I-40, 264 to 63. From Kayenta, Routes 160, 60 to 63, 167.3 km (104 miles). From Mesa Verde, Routes 789, 160 to 63, 254 km (158 miles). From Monument Valley, Routes 163, 160 to 63, 206 km (128 miles). From Page-Lake Powell, Routes 98, 160 to 63, 334.7 km

(208 miles). From Tuba City, Route 160 to 63, 283 km (176 miles).

Ruins of Indian villages built between A.D. 350 and 1300 are at the base of sheer red cliffs and in caves in canyon walls. Modern Navajo Indians live and farm here. Authorized for addition to the National Park System on Feb. 14, 1931.

VISITOR ACTIVITIES: auto tours, hiking, pictograph-viewing, ruin tours, interpretive exhibits and talks, horseback riding (by prior arrangement with the Monument), picnicking, photography; **Permits:** Yes, you must have a tribal permit to fish on the reservation. Write to the park for a list of places where Navajo fishing licenses are available. Concession jeep tours available from Justin's Thunderbird Lodge, P.O. Box 548, Chinle, AZ 86503, Phone 602-674-5443 or -5265. Hiking within the canyon requires a Park Service permit plus an authorized Navajo guide, except along the White House Ruins Trail. A $3 per hour fee for up to 6 people is paid directly to the guide. To drive on the canyon bottom, you must obtain a Park Service permit and be accompanied by an authorized Navajo guide. Fee is $2.75 per hour for 1 vehicle and 50¢ per hour for each additional vehicle, with a 5 vehicle maximum per guide; **Fees:** For concession jeep tours and guided tours. See above; **Visitor facilities:** hiking and auto trails, parking, restrooms, exhibits, concession canyon trips, rental horses (by prior arrangement), campgrounds; **Any limitations on vehicle usage:** Autos should use paved highways only. Jeeps or 4-wheel drive vehicles must be used to travel to the bottom of the canyon; **Hiking trails:** Yes, a 4 km (2-1/2 mile) hiking trail leads to White House Ruin; **Backcountry:** No; **Camping:** Yes, no reservations for individual campsites, which are free of charge and are open year-round. Reservations for group sites, of 14 or more people, can be made by contacting the park; **Other overnight accommodations on site:** Yes, lodging is available at Thunderbird Lodge. Make reservations in advance by writing Thunderbird Lodge, Box 548, Chinle, AZ 86503, phone 602-674-5443 or -5265; **Meals served in the park:** Yes, at Thunderbird Lodge; **Food and supplies obtainable in the park:** No; **Food and supplies obtainable nearby:** Yes, at nearby trading posts; **Overnight accommodations:** Window Rock, AZ 106.2 km (66 miles) away, Monument Valley, Hwy 63 & 160 to 163, 206 km (128 miles); and Gallup, NM, Hwy 63 & 264 to 666, 159 km (99 miles), which has over 50 motels; **First Aid available in park:** No, available at Chinle Clinic, Phone 602-674-5282; **Nearest Hospital:** Ganado Hospital, 56 km (35 miles), phone 602-755-3411. Other hospitals in Gallup, NM, 159 km (99 miles) away; **Days/Hours:** Visitor Center open daily 8 a.m. to 5 p.m.; until 6 p.m. in Summer; **Holiday Closings:** Dec. 25 and Jan. 1; **Visitor attractions closed for seasons:** The canyons become impassable in Winter and at certain other times of the year; **Weather:** Hot Summers and cold Winters, with little precipitation all year.

GENERAL INFORMATION: Quicksand, deep dry sand, cliffs, loose rocks and flash floods make the canyons hazardous.

Casa Grande Ruins National Monument
Coolidge, Arizona

MAILING ADDRESS: Superintendent, Casa Grande Ruins National Monument, P.O. Box 518, Coolidge, Arizona 85228 **Telephone:** 602-723-3172

DIRECTIONS: The Monument is about 1.6 km (1 mile) north of Coolidge on AZ 87, about halfway between Phoenix and Tucson.

Perplexing ruins of a massive four-story building, constructed of high-lime desert soil by Indians who farmed the Gila Valley 600 years ago, raise many unanswered questions for modern man. The Casa Grande Ruin Reservation was authorized by Congress on Mar. 8, 1889 and proclaimed a national monument on Aug. 3, 1918, at which time the

National Park Service assumed administration of the area.

VISITOR ACTIVITIES: interpretive talks and exhibits, walking tours, picnicking; **Permits:** No; **Fees:** entrance fee is $1 per vehicle. Golden Eagle and Golden Age Passports accepted and available; **Visitor facilities:** parking and restrooms at Visitor Center, drinking water, picnic area; **Any limitations on vehicle usage:** No; **Hiking trails:** Yes, a 400-yard round trip self-guiding walking trail leads through the ruins area; **Backcountry:** No; **Camping:** No; **Other overnight accommodations on site:** No; **Meals served in the park:** No; **Food and supplies obtainable in the park:** No; **Food and supplies obtainable nearby:** Yes, in Coolidge; **Overnight accommodations:** Coolidge, AZ 87, 1.6 km (1 mile) south; Florence, AZ 287, 19 km (12 miles) east; Casa Grande, AZ 287, 33 km (22 miles) southwest; **First Aid available in park:** Yes, or nearby in Coolidge, AZ 87, 1.6 km (1 mile); **Nearest Hospital:** Florence, AZ 287, 19 km (12 miles) east; **Days/Hours:** Open from 7 a.m. to 6 p.m., 365 days a year; **Holiday Closings:** None; **Weather:** The most comfortable time for visiting is between early October and early May, because summer temperatures approach 120°F..

GENERAL INFORMATION: *WARNING:* You are in harsh desert area. Beware of the cactus. Intense heat can cause varying degrees of discomfort. Be cautious of poisonous snakes, centipedes, and scorpions.

Chiricahua National Monument
Willcox, Arizona

MAILING ADDRESS: Superintendent, Chiricahua National Monument, Dos Cabezas Star Route, Willcox, Arizona 85643 **Telephone:** 602-824-3560

DIRECTIONS: The Visitor Center is 61 km (38 miles) south of Willcox on AZ 186.

The varied rock formations here were created millions of year ago by volcanic activity, aided by erosion. Created by Presidential Proclamation on April 18, 1924.

VISITOR ACTIVITIES: camping, hiking, auto tours, interpretive exhibits, campfire programs in Summer, picnicking; **Permits:** No; **Fees:** $1 per car entrance fee; $2 per night per site camping fee, with Golden Eagle Passport, free admission, camping $2; Golden Age Passport, free admission, camping $1; **Visitor facilities:** parking and restrooms at Visitor Center, campgrounds, drinking water, fireplaces, tables, shuttle bus, picnic area; **Any limitations on vehicle usage:** No wheeled vehicles are permitted on the trails; **Hiking trails:** Yes, more than 27 km (17 miles) of trails provide views of all the park's features; **Backcountry:** No; **Camping:** Yes, no reservations accepted for campsites; **Other overnight accommodations on site:** No; **Meals served in the park:** No; **Food and supplies obtainable in the park:** No; **Food and supplies obtainable nearby:** Yes, in Willcox; **Overnight accommodations:** Willcox, AZ 186, 61 km (38 miles) north, has motels, restaurants, commercial campgrounds and trailer parks; **First Aid available in park:** Not always; **Nearest Hospital:** Willcox, AZ 186, 61 km (38 miles); **Days/Hours:** Open daily year-round 8 a.m. to 5 p.m.; **Holiday Closings:** None; **Visitor attractions closed for seasons:** Road often closed in Winter; **Weather:** Temperatures are generally moderate. The mean daily temperature in January is 4°C (40°F) and in July, 23°C (74°F). Most of the precipitation occurs in July and August. Except for Winter, the rest of the year is relatively dry.

GENERAL INFORMATION: *For Your Safety*—Be alert for an occasional rattlesnake during warm weather. The scenic drive is winding and mountainous; watch for fallen rocks on the road.

Coronado National Memorial
Hereford, Arizona

MAILING ADDRESS: Superintendent, Coronado National Memorial, Rural Route 1, Box 126, Hereford, Arizona 85615 **Telephone:** 602-366-5515

DIRECTIONS: The Memorial is about 35 km (22 miles) south of Sierra Vista, AZ, and 48 km (30 miles) west of Bisbee, AZ. The Montezuma Canyon Road, which leads to the Memorial, joins AZ 92 about 40 km (25 miles) west of Bisbee. It is 8 km (5 miles) from this junction to Memorial Headquarters.

Our Hispanic heritage and the first European exploration of the southwest, by Francisco Vasquez de Coronado in 1540-42, are commemorated here, near the point where Coronado's expedition entered what is now the United States. Authorized as an international memorial on Aug. 18, 1941. Established by act of Congress on Nov. 5, 1952.

VISITOR ACTIVITIES: interpretive exhibits and talks, picnicking, walking tours, hiking, climbing, horseback riding, Hispanic Indian cultural fiesta and historical pageant on the last Sunday in April each year; **Permits:** No; **Fees:** No; **Visitor facilities:** parking, restrooms, wayside exhibits, picnic area, foot trails, trailside benches; **Any limitations on vehicle usage:** No; **Hiking trails:** Yes, scenic foot trails begin at the parking area and Visitor Center, and at Montezuma Pass area; **Backcountry:** No; **Camping:** No; **Other overnight accommodations on site:** No, a U.S. Forest Service campground is at Parker Lake 29 km (18 miles) west of the Memorial; **Meals served in the park:** No; **Food and supplies obtainable in the park:** No; **Food and supplies obtainable nearby:** Yes, at Sierra Vista, Bisbee; **Overnight accommodations:** Sierra Vista, AZ 92 North, 35 km (22 miles); Bisbee, AZ 92 West, 48 km (30 miles); **First Aid available in park:** Yes; **Nearest Hospital:** Sierra Vista, AZ 92 North, 35 km (22 miles), Bisbee, AZ 92 West, 48 km (30 miles); **Days/Hours:** Park open daily from dawn to dusk, Visitor Center open daily from 8 a.m. to 5 p.m.; **Holiday Closings:** None; **Visitor attractions closed for seasons:**No; **Weather:** Rainy periods are July through Oct. and Dec. through March. Temperatures are generally in the 70's to 90's in Summer and into the 20's in Winter. There are light snowfalls in Winter.

GENERAL INFORMATION: *For Your Safety*—Watch out for unexpected steps, low branches, cactus, poison ivy, black widow spiders and scorpions.

Fort Bowie National Historic Site
Bowie, Arizona

MAILING ADDRESS: Superintendent, Fort Bowie National Historic Site, P.O. Box 158, Bowie, Arizona 85605 **Telephone:** 602-847-2500

DIRECTIONS: There is no road to the ruins proper. They can be reached only by a 2.4 km (1-1/2 mile) foot trail that begins midway in Apache Pass. The trailhead may be reached from two directions: from the town of Willcox, located on Int. 10, drive 35.4 km (22 miles) south on AZ 186 to the graded road leading east into Apache Pass; from the town of Bowie, also on Int. 10, drive southerly 19.3 km (12 miles) on a graded dirt road that then bears westerly into Apache Pass.

Established in 1862, this fort was the focal point of military operations against Geronimo and his band of Apaches. Authorized for addition to the National Park System on Aug. 30, 1964.

VISITOR ACTIVITIES: walking tours, exhibits, wildflower- and wildlife-watching, mountain climbing; **Permits:** No; **Fees:** No; **Visitor facilities:** small museum in the ranger station, parking area, pit toilets; **Any limitations on vehicle usage:** No vehicle access beyond the parking lot at the trail head; **Hiking trails:** Yes, .8 km (1/2 mile) foot trail to ruins; .4 km (1/4 mile) trail to Overlook Ridge; **Backcountry:** Yes, write the Site for information; **Camping:** No; **Other overnight accommodations on site:** No; **Meals served in the park:** No; **Food and supplies obtainable in the park:** No; **Food and supplies obtainable nearby:** Yes, at Willcox and Bowie; **Overnight accommodations:** Willcox and Bowie, Int. 10, 35.4 km (22 miles) and 19.3 km (12 miles); **First Aid available in park:** Yes, at the Contact Station at the ruins; **Nearest Hospital:** Willcox, 19.3 km (14 miles) to Bowie & 40 km (25 miles) more by I-10; **Days/Hours:** A Ranger is on duty at the contact station from 8 a.m. to 5 p.m. daily; **Holiday Closings:** None; **Visitor attractions closed for seasons:** No; **Weather:** Drizzling rain in Winter, heavy rains and muddy roads in July and August, with flash flood warnings.

GENERAL INFORMATION: Water is available at the fort. However, the summer hiker should consider a canteen since temperatures may climb above 100°. Summer storms may suddenly and briefly flood the washes. Simply wait out high water. Be alert for an occasional rattlesnake or Gila monster.

Glen Canyon National Recreation Area
Page, Arizona (also in Utah)

MAILING ADDRESS: Superintendent, Glen Canyon National Recreation Area, P.O. Box 1507, Page, Arizona 86040 **Telephone:** 602-645-2471

DIRECTIONS: Park Headquarters is at 337 North Navajo Drive in Page, Arizona, on US 89. There is a Visitor Center by Glen Canyon Dam, about 1.6 km (1 mile) from Page on US 89.

Lake Powell, formed by the Colorado River, stretches for 299 km (186 miles) behind one of the highest dams in the world. Established by act of Congress on Oct. 27, 1972.

VISITOR ACTIVITIES: camping, swimming, boating, fishing, water skiing, hunting, driving, hiking, dam tours, photography, interpretive exhibits, picnicking; **Permits:** Fishing permits are available at sporting goods stores in Page or at the park's marina. Licenses vary in length of validity and cost; **Fees:** Camping fee is $2 per night per site; **Visitor facilities:** restrooms, marinas, launching ramps, beaches, campgrounds, trailer villages, restaurants, lodging, boat rentals and tours, picnic areas, bathhouse; **Any limitations on vehicle usage:** Drive only on designated roads and trails. Boaters should be familiar with boating regulations; see pamphlet available at the Visitor Center; **Hiking trails:** Yes, Rangers can suggest good routes; **Backcountry:** Yes, write the Superintendent for information on the many miles of backcountry; **Camping:** Yes, no reservations available for campsites; **Other overnight accommodations on site:** Yes, for reservations at other accommodations, contact any of the following concessioners: Canyon Tours, Inc. P.O. Box 1597, Page, AZ 86040, phone 602-645-2433; Bullfrog Resort and Marina, Inc., Bullfrog Basin, Hanksville, UT 84743, phone 801-684-2233; Lake Powell Ferry

Service, Inc., Blanding, UT 84511, phone 801-684-2261; **Meals served in the park:** Yes, at Wahweap, and Bullfrog; **Food and supplies obtainable in the park:** Yes, at Wahweap, Lees Ferry and Bullfrog; **Overnight accommodations:** Page, 1.6 km (1 mile) from the park on US 89; **First Aid available in park:** Yes, at Rainbow Marina and Ranger Stations at Wahweap, Bullfrog, Halls, and Hite; **Nearest Hospital:** Page, 1.6 km (1 mile) from Wahweap; Clinic in Green River, Hospital in Grand Junction, CO; **Days/Hours:** Park never closes; **Holiday Closings:** Visitor Center closes on Dec. 25 and Jan. 1; **Visitor attractions closed for seasons:**None; **Weather:** The intense heat of Summer can limit activities. Winters are rather short. Spring arrives in March, and the weather is mild through the middle of November.

GENERAL INFORMATION: An all-day cruise takes boaters to Rainbow Bridge National Monument (see listing in this book). If you are camping, be sure to pick a campsite on flat or gently sloping terrain, not on talus slopes or underneath ledges where you can see that rock has fallen.

Grand Canyon National Park
Grand Canyon, Arizona

MAILING ADDRESS: Superintendent, Grand Canyon National Park, P.O. Box 129, Grand Canyon, Arizona 86023 **Telephone:** 602-638-2411

DIRECTIONS: There are three separate areas in the park-the South Rim, the North Rim, and the Inner Canyon or Inner Gorge. Each has different facilities, different activities, and even different climates. The South Rim Visitor Center is 6 km (3.5 miles) north of the South Entrance Station, in Grand Canyon Village, 96.6 km (60 miles) north of Williams and 92 km (57 miles) west of Cameron, both on AZ 64. The North Rim Information Station is on State Hwy 67, 70 km (43 miles) south of Jacob Lake (at intersection with Hwy 89). Detailed directions are available in a brochure available at Visitor and Information Centers or from the Superintendent.

The park, focusing on the world-famous Grand Canyon of the Colorado River, encompasses the entire course of the river and adjacent uplands from the southern terminus of Glen Canyon National Recreation Area to the eastern boundary of Lake Mead National Recreation Area. The forces of erosion have exposed an immense variety of formations which illustrate vast periods of geological history. National Park established by act of Congress on Feb. 26, 1919.

VISITOR ACTIVITIES: interpretive exhibits, environmental study area, guided and self-guiding tours, picnicking, camping, backcountry, hiking, horseback riding, boating, fishing, biking, auto tours, mule trips, river tours; **Permits:** required for backcountry and fishing; for fishing, licenses and trout stamps are available at Babbitt's Store in Grand Canyon Village; **Fees:** $2 entrance fee; $2 camping fee at Desert View, $3 at Mather and North Rim Campgrounds. Golden Eagle and Golden Age Passports accepted and available; **Visitor facilities:** picnic areas, campgrounds, hiking trails, bus, limousine and air tours, guided hikes and vehicle tours, river float trips, religious services, post offices, banks, backpacking equipment rentals, food and lodging facilities; **Any limitations on vehicle usage:** Motorcycles, trailbikes, and other off-road vehicles may not be operated outside of established public roads and parking areas; **Hiking trails:** Yes, 38 trails of nearly 644 km (400 miles). Check at Information Centers for details; **Backcountry:** Yes, backcountry reservations and permits are required. Reservations can only be made 3 months in advance of your visit and are recommended for any time of year; beginning

Oct. 1, they are accepted for the calendar year. Contact Backcountry Reservations Office, Grand Canyon National Park, Grand Canyon, AZ 86023, phone 602-638-2474; **Camping:** Reservations are required for Mather Campground sites for the period between Memorial Day and Labor Day: Contact Ticketron Reservation Office, P.O. Box 2715, San Francisco, CA 94126. Any unreserved campsites will be assigned on a first-come, first-served basis. No reservations are available for other campsites at Grand Canyon. Many other sites are available near the Park; contact Grand Canyon for further information; **Other overnight accommodations on site:** Yes; **Meals served in the park:** Yes, on Bright Angel Point at Grand Canyon Lodge, Grand Canyon Village, Desert View, Tusayan; **Food and supplies obtainable in the park:** Yes, Grand Canyon Village, Desert View, and the North Rim; **Food and supplies obtainable nearby:** Yes, Tusayan, AZ, 1.6 km (1 mile) south of the park; **Overnight accommodations:** Tusayan, Cameron, Gray Mountain, Flagstaff, Williams, Kaibab, Jacob Lake, Fredonia, Marble Canyon, & Page, AZ; Kanab, Utah; **First Aid available in park:** Yes, at the Information Desk in North Rim Lodge, or at Grand Canyon Clinic, Center Road between South Entrance Station and Grand Canyon Village. In case of emergency, telephone 602-638-2477; **Nearest Hospital:** Flagstaff, I-40 & AZ 180, 129 km (80 miles); Williams, I-40 & US 64, 97 km (60 miles); **Days/Hours:** South Rim never closes; North Rim open 24 hours a day from mid-May to mid-Oct.; **Holiday Closings:** None; **Visitor attractions closed for seasons:** North Rim closed in Winter, from about mid-Oct. to mid-May; **Weather:** 80°-90°F temperatures in Summer.

GENERAL INFORMATION: For up-to-date recorded information about weather, road conditions, and interpretive activities, phone 602-638-2245, 24 hours a day. *For Your Safety*—Do not climb in the canyon; most of the rock is too crumbly for safety. Avoid overexertion. The air on the rims is extremely thin. Temperatures within the Inner Canyon can reach extremes. Take enough water and food, dress for the weather, and know your own physical limitations. If you are hiking, carry plenty of water.

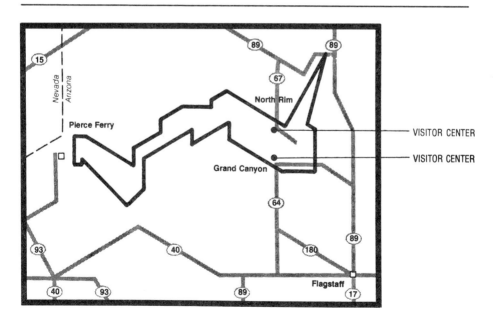

Hohokam Pima National Monument
Coolidge, Arizona

MAILING ADDRESS: Superintendent, Hohokam Pima National Monument, c/o Casa Grande Ruins National Mounument, P.O. Box 518, Coolidge, Arizona 85228 **Telephone:** 602-723-3172

DIRECTIONS: NOT OPEN TO THE PUBLIC.
   The Monument will preserve the Snaketown archaeological site, which contains the remains of a large Hohokam Indian village occupied between 300 B.C. and 1100 A.D. Although the Monument was authorized by Congress for addition to the National Park System on Oct. 21, 1972, it has not yet been established. The area remains closed to the public pending completion of land exchanges necessary to bring the site under National Park Service administration.

Hubbell Trading Post National Historic Site
Ganado, Arizona

MAILING ADDRESS: Superintendent, Hubbell Trading Post National Historic Site, P.O. Box 150, Ganado, Arizona 86505 **Telephone:** 602-755-3475

DIRECTIONS: The Site is on the Navajo Indian Reservation, 1.6 km (1 mile) west of Ganado and 89 km (55 miles) northwest of Gallup, New Mexico. It can be reached by AZ 264 (Navajo Route 3) from the east and west by AZ 63 from the north and south.
   This still-active 100 year-old trading post illustrates the influence of reservation traders on the Indians' way of life. Authorized for addition to the National Park System on August 28, 1965.

VISITOR ACTIVITIES: walking tours, exhibits, weaving demonstrations, picnicking, tours of the Hubbell Home, watching the on-going trading operation and craft demonstrations; **Permits:** tour tickets can be obtained at Information Desk; **Fees:** No; **Visitor facilities:** parking and restrooms at Visitor Center, picnic area; **Any limitations on vehicle usage:** Off-road vehicle travel is prohibited; **Hiking trails:** No; **Backcountry:** No; **Camping:** No; **Other overnight accommodations on site:** No; **Meals served in the park:** No, limited food service in Ganado; **Food and supplies obtainable in the park:** No; **Food and supplies obtainable nearby:** Yes, at Chinle or Window Rock; **Overnight accommodations:** Chinle, 56 km (35 miles) north on AZ 63; Window Rock, 48 km (30 miles) east on AZ 264; Chambers, 61 km (38 miles) south on AZ 63; Second Mesa, 92 km (67 miles) west on AZ 264; **First Aid available in park:** Yes; **Nearest Hospital:** Ganado, 1.6 km (1 mile) east; **Days/Hours:** Open daily from 8 a.m. to 5 p.m., until 6 p.m. in Summer; **Holiday Closings:** Thanksgiving, Dec. 25 and Jan. 1; **Visitor attractions closed for seasons:** None; **Weather:** Elevation is 6300 feet. Climate is mild. Record extremes are -50°F and 100 °F. High winds blow the sand in Spring. Fall and early Spring may bring snow flurries.

GENERAL INFORMATION: You will find Hubbell Trading Post on the way to Grand Canyon National Park, Canyon de Chelly National Monument (see listings in this book) and the Hopi Mesas. *For Your Safety*, be cautious when walking around the grounds as burrs and bits of metal and glass have been left over the years. In many cases the floors are uneven in the buildings, and there is usually a step between rooms. Portable wheel chair ramps are available.

Montezuma Castle National Monument
Camp Verde, Arizona

MAILING ADDRESS: Superintendent, Montezuma Castle National Monument, P.O. Box 219, Camp Verde, Arizona 86322 **Telephone:** 602-567-3322

DIRECTIONS: The Visitor Center is 3.8 km (2-1/2 miles) off Interstate 17, 8 km (5 miles) north of Camp Verde.

One of the best-preserved cliff dwellings in the United States, this 5-story, 20-room pueblo was built by prehistoric farmers over 700 years ago. Montezuma Well, a separate section of the Monument, is 17 km (10-1/2 miles) north of the Castle. This natural sinkhole is continually fed by spring water at the rate of 1-1/2 million gallons a day. Archaeological sites include pueblo ruins, cliff dwellings, and an excavated pithouse. Created by Presidential Proclamation on Dec. 8, 1906.

VISITOR ACTIVITIES: picnicking, photography, self-guiding walking tours, exhibits; **Permits:** No; **Fees:** Yes, entrance fee is $1 per carload. No charge to US residents age 62 and older. Golden Eagle and Golden Age Passports accepted and available; **Visitor facilities:** restrooms, picnic areas, interpretive trails, museum; **Any limitations on vehicle usage:** Visitors should arrive before 10 a.m. or after 3 p.m. during the summer months because of limited parking; **Hiking trails:** Yes, a .6 km (1/3 mile) self-guiding trail leads to the ruins; **Backcountry:** No; **Camping:** No; **Other overnight accommodations on site:** No; **Meals served in the park:** No; **Food and supplies obtainable in the park:** No; **Food and supplies obtainable nearby:** Yes, at Camp Verde; **Overnight accommodations:** Camp Verde, 8 km (5 miles) south; **First Aid available in park:** Yes, or nearby at Camp Verde; **Nearest Hospital:** Cottonwood, Int. 17 to AZ 279 to by pass road to Jerome, 32.2 km (20 miles); **Days/Hours:** Open daily from 8 a.m. to 5 p.m., and from 7 a.m. through 7 p.m. from June to September.

GENERAL INFORMATION: Visitors may wish to explore other nearby monuments, including Tuzigoot, Walnut Canyon, Wupatki & Sunset Crater (see listings in this book). Nearby points of interest include Fort Verde and Jerome State Historical Parks.

Navajo National Monument
Tonalea, Arizona

MAILING ADDRESS: Superintendent, Navajo National Monument, Tonalea, Arizona 86044 **Telephone:** 602-672-2366

DIRECTIONS: The Monument is in north-central Arizona, south to southeast of Lake Powell and the Glen Canyon Recreation Area. It is reached from US 160 which diagonals through the Navajo Reservation 14.5 km (9 miles) north of Black Mesa on AZ 564. At Black Mesa-80.5 km (50 miles) northeast of Tuba City, 35.4 km (22 miles) southwest of Kayenta-you turn north onto Route 564. Route 564 dead-ends at the Monument Head-quarters, 14.5 km (9 miles) from US 160.

Betatakin, Keet Seel, and Inscription House are three of the best-preserved and most elaborate cliff dwellings known. Created by Presidential Proclamation on Mar. 20, 1909.

VISITOR ACTIVITIES: hiking, interpretive exhibits and trails, evening campfire programs in Summer, camping, picnicking, horseback riding; **Permits:** required for tours, apply by mail, phone, or in person; **Fees:** No; **Visitor facilities:** Visitor Center, exhibits, craft shop in summer, hiking trails, picnic area, campgrounds; **Any limitations on vehicle usage:** Vehicles are limited to paved roads; **Hiking trails:** Yes, Sandal Trail is 1.6 km (1 mile) long and leads to the Betatakin Point Overlook. Twice each day tours of not more than 20 people leave from the Visitor Center to Betatakin Ruin across the canyon during the summer season only. It is only about 4 km (2-1/2 miles) but it's not easy. You climb down-and back up-700 *steep* stairs, about the equivalent of a 70-story building! The tour takes about three hours and is Ranger-led. You cannot go into the canyon or the ruin without a Ranger.

Keet Seel, the largest cliff dwelling in Arizona, is about eight miles north of the Visitor Center. It can be reached only on foot or horseback; the trail is rugged and the elevation change is over a thousand feet. You cannot enter Keet Seel without a Park Ranger. All travel is by reservation and there is a limit of 20 people per day. So write or phone ahead if you want to make this trip; **Backcountry:** Yes, for information write or phone Headquarters; **Camping:** Yes, no reservations available for campsites. The Monument maintains a campground at the end of the loop road at the Headquarters area. Trailers up to 25 feet in length can be accommodated. Because of freezing, the water is usually turned off from late September to early May. There is a second "dry campground" about a mile from the Visitor Center, open when weather permits; **Other overnight accommodations on site:** No; **Meals served in the park:** No; **Food and supplies obtainable in the park:** No; **Food and supplies obtainable nearby:** Yes, at the shopping center at Black Mesa, where you turn off US 160 to get to the Monument; **Overnight accommodations:** Kayenta, US 160, 50 km (31 miles) northeast of the Monument; Tuba City, US 160, 95 km (59 miles) southwest; **First Aid available in park:** Yes; **Nearest Hospital:** Flagstaff, AZ, 241.4 km (150 miles); **Days/Hours:** The Visitor Center is open year-round from 8 a.m. to 5 p.m. daily, until 6 p.m. in Summer; **Holiday Closings:** Dec. 25, Jan. 1; **Visitor attractions closed for seasons:** Sandal Trail to the overlook is closed when snow and ice are severe; **Weather:** The Monument is at an elevation of over 7000 feet. Winter comes early and stays late. Snow accumulation is heavy, especially in the small canyons which provide access to the cliff dwellings. All canyon trails are closed after the first snowfall and remain closed until all snow melts in Spring.

GENERAL INFORMATION: When you hike, remember that the altitude is 7200 feet. The air is thin. You may find that walking can tire you out faster than you might expect if you are not used to the elevation. Pace yourself, eat well and don't try to rush. None of the more strenuous trips are recommended for anyone who has heart or respiratory ailments. The formations are sandstone and natural rockfall is a common occurrence. When travelling the Navajo Reservation you should always watch out for livestock wandering on or about the highway.

Organ Pipe Cactus National Monument
Ajo, Arizona

MAILING ADDRESS: Superintendent, Organ Pipe Cactus National Monument, Route 1, Box 100, Ajo, Arizona 85321 **Telephone:** 602-Organ Pipe #1, through Phoenix Operator.

DIRECTIONS: The Monument lies on the border of the United States and Mexico, 225 km (140 miles) south of Phoenix via US 80 and Arizona 85, and 229 km (142 miles) west of Tucson via AZ 86 and AZ 85. Access to the park from Mexico is via Mexico Route 2 from the west and Mexico Routes 2 and 8 from the South. The Visitor Center is 27 km (17 miles) south of the park entrance.

Sonoran Desert plants and animals found nowhere else in the United States are protected here, alongside traces of a historic trail, Camino del Diablo. Created by Presidential Proclamation on Apr. 13, 1937.

VISITOR ACTIVITIES: interpretive talks and walks, scenic drives, hiking, photography, wildlife- and bird-watching, camping, picnicking, backcountry; **Permits:** for backcountry, available at Visitor Center; **Fees:** Camping fee is $2 per night per site; **Visitor facilities:** campgrounds, picnic areas, mail drop, trails, restrooms, general store, snack bar, and gas station in Lukeville; **Any limitations on vehicle usage;** Drive only on established roads and turnouts. Visitors should be prepared for driving on desert roads. Be sure your car is serviced and tuned. Check your tires (including the spare) to make sure the air pressure is high enough. Hot, dry weather can deplete your radiator and battery water, so check them both frequently. Carry a shovel and 4 or 5 liters (a gallon or so) of extra water. In case of emergency during extremely hot weather, stay with your vehicle. If water is flowing across the road, do not try to drive through it. Wait until the water goes down-usually this takes about an hour. During the summer storm season (July and August), check at the Visitor Center for possible park road closures. When driving at night, be alert for wildlife and cattle on the road; **Hiking trails:** Yes, check at Visitor Center for information on the trails; **Backcountry:** Yes, permit is required, check at Visitor Center. Most backpacking is cross-country (no trails); **Camping:** Yes, no reservations for the 208-site campground, except for organized groups using the group campsites; **Other overnight accommodations on site:** No; **Meals served in the park:** No; **Food and supplies obtainable in the park:** No; **Food and supplies obtainable nearby:** Yes, at Lukeville; **Overnight accommodations:** Lukeville, 8 km (5 miles) south, Why, 30 km (20 miles) north, and Ajo, 56 km (35 miles) north; **First Aid available in park:** Yes; **Nearest Hospital:** Ajo, 56 km (35 miles) north on AZ 85; **Days/Hours:** Visitor Center is open 7 days a week from 8 a.m. to 5 p.m., until 4:30 p.m. in Summer; **Holiday Closings:** None; **Visitor attractions closed for seasons:** No interpretive programs from May through October; **Weather:** November-April is mild and usually sunny, May-October is hot, with daytime temperatures over 100°F.

GENERAL INFORMATION: The Monument is a good stopoff while travelling to Mexico via Tucson or Phoenix. *Beware of the cactus!* The spines of these plants and many other trees and shrubs can cause you painful injury. Visitor should be prepared for desert walking. For protection from the sun, rough terrain and the weather, you should have a hat and wear clothing and shoes that are comfortable and sturdy. Carry enough fresh drinking water (4 liters or 1 gallon per day per person). At night, walk carefully and use a flashlight to look for rattlesnakes in your path; six species are found in the park. Snakes play an important role in the ecology of the desert and should not be harmed. Poisonous creatures such as rattlers and gila monsters are rare, but if you see one, observe it quietly and report its location to a ranger.

Travelling in Mexico. There is free access into Sonoyta and westward on Mexico Route 2. However, if you continue into the interior or go to Puerto Penasco, you must have a tourist permit and a car entry permit, both of which may be obtained from Mexican officials at the border. To get a tourist permit, you must have proof of citizenship (birth certificate), and to get a car permit, you will need your automobile registration. To re-enter the United States with pets, you must carry proof of valid pet vaccinations. Transportation of firearms into Mexico is a violation of Mexican law.

Petrified Forest National Park
Petrified Forest National Park, Arizona

MAILING ADDRESS: Superintendent, Petrified Forest National Park, Petrified Forest National Park, Arizona 86028 **Telephone:** 602-524-6228

DIRECTIONS: The Painted Desert Visitor Center is 42 km (26 miles) east of Holbrook on Interstate 40. The Rainbow Forest Entrance Station is 30.6 km (19 miles) east of Holbrook on US 180.

Features of the park include a large section of the colorful Painted Desert, Indian ruins and petroglyphs, and trees that have been petrified, or changed to multicolored stone. Created by Presidential Proclamation on Dec. 8, 1906.

VISITOR ACTIVITIES: paved trail and wilderness hiking, interpretive walks and talks in Summer, film, exhibits in Summer at Painted Desert Inn, picnicking, auto tours; **Permits:** required for backcountry, can be obtained at Rainbow Forest Museum and Painted Desert Visitor Center; **Fees:** $1 entrance fee, which may be raised to $2 pending authorization. Golden Eagle and Golden Age Passports accepted and available.; **Visitor facilities:** picnic areas, restrooms, film about the Park at Painted Desert Visitor Center, interpretive exhibits including specimens of petrified wood. A guide map of the 48 km (29 mile) park road is available at entrance stations; **Any limitations on vehicle usage:** Park only in designated parking areas; **Hiking trails:** Yes,walking trails at Giant Logs (behind Rainbow Forest Museum),Long Logs,Crystal Forest, Blue Mesa, and Kachina Point to Tawa Point. Trails vary in length from .8 km-1.2 km (1/2-3/4 mile). Trailguides available at the Long Logs and Blue Mesa Trails.; **Backcountry:** Yes,approximately 50,000 acres of wilderness area are open for camping and hiking; **Camping:** Yes, camping is limited to the wilderness area, required permits available at either the museum or Vistor Center; **Other overnight accommodations on site:** No; **Meals served in the park:** Yes, at Painted Desert Oasis and Rainbow Lodges; **Food and supplies obtainable in the park:** No; **Food and supplies obtainable nearby:** Yes, at Holbrook, AZ, 42 km (26 miles) west on I-40; Sanders, AZ, 48.3 km (30 miles) east; Gallup, NM, 113 km (70 miles) east; **Overnight accommodations:** Sun Valley, AZ, 29 km (18 miles) west on I-40;Holbrook, 42 km (26 miles) west on I-40; Gallup, NM 113 km (70 miles) east; **First Aid available in park:** Yes; **Nearest Hospital:** Holbrook, AZ, just off I-40,42 km (26 miles) from the Park; **Days/Hours:** The Park is open during daylight hours all year, with occasional closings due to heavy snow and icy roads.; **Holiday Closings:** None; **Weather:** Summer days may be quite warm, and clear weather may be broken by sudden thundershowers. In winter,cold and snowy days are not uncommon. High winds may be expected in any season.

GENERAL INFORMATION: Have sufficient water and notify park personnel if you plan an extended hike. Park elevations range from 5100 to 6235 feet; beware of overexertion in the high altitude. Do not climb on petrified logs; petrified wood can be extremely sharp. Federal law prohibits removal of any petrified wood from this park.

Pipe Spring National Monument
Moccasin, Arizona

MAILING ADDRESS: Superintendent, Pipe Spring National Monument, Moccasin, Arizona 86022 **Telephone:** 602-643-5505

DIRECTIONS: Pipe Spring is 24 km (15 miles) southwest of Fredonia, AZ, and can be reached from US 89 via AZ 389; from US 91, UT 9 and 17 connect with UT 59 at Hurricane, UT, from which a paved road leads to the Monument.

This historic fort and other structures, built here by Mormon pioneers in the 1860's and 1870's, commemorate the struggle for exploration and settlement of the Southwest. Created by Presidential Proclamation on May 31, 1923.

VISITOR ACTIVITIES: walking tours; **Permits:** No; **Fees:** 50¢ per person 16 through 62. Golden Age and Golden Eagle Passports accepted and available; **Visitor facilities:** self-guiding tours around the fort; conducted tours, exhibits, and visual interpretation within; **Any limitations on vehicle usage:** Vehicles must park in the lot at the Visitor Center; **Hiking trails:** Yes, self-guiding .8 km (1/2 mile) loop trail; **Backcountry:** No; **Camping:** No; **Other overnight accommodations on site:** No; **Meals served in the park:** Yes, at snack bar in Summer at the Visitor Center; **Food and supplies obtainable in the park:** No; **Food and supplies obtainable nearby:** Yes, at Kanab or Fredonia; **Overnight accommodations:** Kanab, 33.8 km (21 miles) east on US 89 or Fredonia, 22.5 km (14 miles) east on AZ 389; **First Aid available in park:** Yes, or nearby in Fredonia, 22.5 km (14 miles) east on AZ 389; **Nearest Hospital:** Kanab via AZ 389 & US 89; **Days/Hours:** Monument open daily from 8 a.m. to 5 p.m., until 6 p.m. in Summer; tours closed off at 4:30 p.m., 5:30 p.m. in Summer. Park operates on Mountain Standard Time year-round; **Holiday Closings:** Thanksgiving, Dec. 25 and Jan. 1; **Weather:** Dry and sunny with some summer storms; temperatures range from 85° to 100°F.

GENERAL INFORMATION: Be especially careful of the steep, narrow stairways and low doorways in the buildings. Watch children around the pools.

Saguaro National Monument
Tucson, Arizona

MAILING ADDRESS: Superintendent, Saguaro National Monument, P.O. Box 17210, Tucson, Arizona 85731 **Telephone:** 602-298-2036

DIRECTIONS: The Visitor Center and Park Headquarters in the Rincon Mountain Unit are located on Old Spanish Trail at Freeman Road, 5 km (3 miles) east of Tucson. The Information Center and Visitor Center in the Tucson Mountain section is on Kinney Road, 3.2 km (2 miles) west of the Arizona-Sonora Desert Museum.

Giant Saguaro cactus, unique to the Sonoran Desert of southern Arizona and north-western Mexico, sometimes reach a height of 10 m (40 feet) in this cactus forest. Created by Presidential Proclamation on Mar. 1, 1933.

VISITOR ACTIVITIES: wildlife- and bird-watching, hiking, picnicking, photography, wilderness backcountry, overnight hiking, horseback riding, scenic pleasure driving; **Permits:** required for overnight backcountry, can be obtained at Visitor Center; **Fees:** $1 per car entrance fee. Golden Eagle and Golden Age Passports accepted and available; **Visitor facilities:** audiovisual program and exhibits in the Visitor Center, naturalist walks in winter in the Rincon Mtn. Unit, self-guiding walks and picnic areas in both units; **Any limitations on vehicle usage:** Drive only on established roadways; **Hiking trails:** Yes, nature trails; **Backcountry:** Yes, from Visitor Center in the Rincon Mtn. Unit and Information Center in the Tucson Mtn. Unit; **Camping:** No; **Other overnight accommodations on site:** No; **Meals served in the park:** No, but meals are available at Berkshire Village Shopping Center 9.7 km (6 miles) west near Old Spanish Trail and

Broadway Boulevard; **Food and supplies obtainable in the park:** No; **Food and supplies obtainable nearby:** Yes, at Tucson; **Overnight accommodations:** Tucson, 26 km (16 miles) east of the Rincon Mtn. Unit and 24 km (15 miles) west of the Tucson Mtn. Unit and along Int. 10 and Miracle Mile Strip; **First Aid available in park:** Yes; **Nearest Hospital:** 16 km (10 miles) west of the park via Broadway Blvd, at Wilmot and 5th Streets; **Days/Hours:** Rincon Mtn. Unit is open from 8 a.m. to 8 p.m., Visitor Center 8 a.m.- 5 p.m. Tucson Mtn. Unit open all year, Information Center from 8 a.m. to 5 p.m.; **Holiday Closings:** None; **Visitor attractions closed for seasons:** None; **Weather:** Winter and Summer have rainy periods. Spring and Fall are dry. Annual rainfall is 11″. Temperatures at Tucson Mtn. Unit can be over 110°F in Summer.

GENERAL INFORMATION: On the way to Tucson Mtn. Unit, visit the adjacent Arizona-Sonora Desert Museum to see a presentation of living plants and animals of the desert in simulated natural habitats.

Sunset Crater National Monument
Flagstaff, Arizona

MAILING ADDRESS: Superintendent, Sunset Crater National Monument, Route 3, Box 149, Flagstaff, Arizona 86001 **Telephone:** 602-526-0586

DIRECTIONS: The Visitor Center is 24 km (15 miles) north of Flagstaff on Hwy 89. Go east on the loop road connecting Sunset Crater with Wupatki National Monument.
This colorful volcanic cindercone with summit crater was formed just before 1100 A.D., and looks as if it has barely cooled. Created by Presidential Proclamation on May 26, 1930.

VISITOR ACTIVITIES: audiovisual programs, campfire programs in Summer, exhibits, picnicking; **Permits:** No; **Fees:** No; **Visitor facilities:** information and drinking water at the Visitor Center, picnic areas; **Any limitations on vehicle usage:** You should stay strictly on the road, due to soft shoulders; **Hiking trails:** Yes, two foottrails; **Backcountry:** No; **Camping:** No, no reservations are accepted for U.S. Forest Service campsites which are located across from Sunset Crater Visitor Center. For further information, contact Sunset Crater; **Other overnight accommodations on site:** No; **Meals served in the park:** No; **Food and supplies obtainable in the park:** No; **Food and supplies obtainable nearby:** Yes, in Flagstaff; **Overnight accommodations:** Flagstaff, Hwy 89, 24 km (15 miles); **First Aid available in park:** Yes; **Nearest Hospital:** Flagstaff, 24 km (15 miles) south on Hwy 89; **Days/Hours:** Open daily from 8 a.m. to 5 p.m., 7 a.m. to 7 p.m. in Summer; **Holiday Closings:** Dec. 25 & Jan. 1; **Visitor attractions closed for seasons:** Park is often closed by snow in Winter.

GENERAL INFORMATION: Sunset Crater is an interesting stopoff while driving to the Grand Canyon. Wupatki National Monument (see listing in this book), containing many Indian ruins, is located nearby. The most prominent hazards in the park are deep, narrow earth cracks, razor-sharp lava, unstable backcountry ruins, and wild animals. Watch for sheep and cattle during the winter months, when the area is open range. Do not walk on prehistoric walls or disturb plants, animals, and geological and archaeological features.

Tonto National Monument
Roosevelt, Arizona

MAILING ADDRESS: Superintendent, Tonto National Monument, P.O. Box 707, Roosevelt, Arizona 85545 **Telephone:** 602-467-2241

DIRECTIONS: From Phoenix,take US 60-70 to Apache Junction;turn left on AZ 88 and proceed along the scenic Apache Trail-40.3 km (25 miles) of which is unpaved mountain road-to Roosevelt. The Visitor Center is 4.8 km (3 miles) beyond Roosevelt. Average driving time one way from Phoenix is 2 1/2 hours. From Globe-Miami, take AZ 88 to the park entrance,a distance of 45.1 km (28 miles), driven one way in about 45 minutes.

These well-preserved cliff dwellings were occupied during the early part of the 14th century by Salado Indians, who farmed in the Salt River Valley. Created by Presidential Proclamation on December 19, 1907.

VISITOR ACTIVITIES: interpretive exhibits, guided tours, slide program, hiking, picnicking; **Permits:** required to visit the Upper Ruin, available from the Superintendent; **Fees:** Entrance fee is $1 per vehicle; Golden Eagle and Golden Age Passports accepted and available.; **Visitor facilities:** museum, observation deck, parking, restrooms, picnic area; **Any limitations on vehicle usage:** Vehicles must stay on the paved road; **Hiking trails:** Yes, A self-guiding trail leads to the Lower Ruin. If you wish to visit the Upper Ruin, you must make arrangements with the Superintendent 5 days in advance for the rough, 4.8 km (3 mile), 3-hour round trip hike; **Backcountry:** No; **Camping:** No, Numerous primitive non-reserved campsites can be found in the surrounding Tonto National Forest. For further information contact the forest at 102 S. 28th Street, P.O. Box 13705,Phoenix Arizona, phone 602-467-2236; **Other overnight accommodations on site:** No; **Meals served in the park:** No; **Food and supplies obtainable in the park:** No; **Food and supplies obtainable nearby:** Yes, at Roosevelt Lake Resort and in the Globe-Miami area; **Overnight accommodations:** Roosevelt Lake Resort, 14.5 km (9 miles) and at Globe, 45 km (28 miles); **First Aid available in park:** Yes, aid station located at Roosevelt; **Nearest Hospital:** Globe-Miami area, 45 km (28 miles); **Days/Hours:** Open every day all year, from 8 a.m. to 5 p.m. The trail to the Lower Ruin closes at 4 p.m. each day; **Holiday Closings:** None; **Visitor attractions closed for seasons:**None; **Weather:** The most comfortable weather occurs between late October and early June.

GENERAL INFORMATION: *For Your Safety*—Natural features here could be hazardous. Be on the lookout for steep slopes, falling rocks, spiney vegetation, and poisonous reptiles. Stay on the trails.

Tumacacori National Monument
Tumacacori, Arizona

MAILING ADDRESS: Superintendent, Tumacacori National Monument, P.O. Box 67, Tumacacori, Arizona 85640 **Telephone:** 602-398-2341

DIRECTIONS: Tumacacori is 72.4 km (45 miles) south of Tucson on I-19, 28.97 km (18 miles) north of Nogales and the Mexican border.

This historic Spanish Catholic mission building stands near the site first visited by Jesuit Father Kino in 1691. Created by Presidential Proclamation on Sept. 15, 1908.

VISITOR ACTIVITIES: interpretive exhibits, self-guiding walks, living history demonstrations, picnicking; **Permits:** No; **Fees:** Entrance fee is $1 per carload or 50¢ per person on bus tours. Golden Eagle and Golden Age Passports accepted and available; **Visitor facilities:** parking, picnic area; **Any limitations on vehicle usage:** No; **Hiking trails:** No; **Backcountry:** No; **Camping:** No; **Other overnight accommodations on site:** No; **Meals served in the park:** No; **Food and supplies obtainable in the park:** No; **Food and supplies obtainable nearby:** Yes, in Tucson or Nogales; **Overnight accommodations:** Tucson, 72.42 km (45 miles) north and Nogales, 29 km (18 miles) south; **First Aid available in park:** Yes; **Nearest Hospital:** Nogales, 29 km (18 miles) south; **Days/Hours:** Open year-round from 8 a.m. to 5 p.m., until 6 p.m. in Summer; **Holiday Closings:** Dec. 25; **Weather:** Summers are very hot.

GENERAL INFORMATION: A fiesta is held the first Sunday in December, featuring an outdoor Mariachi Mass, continuous entertainment, and craft and native food sales.

Tuzigoot National Monument
Clarkdale, Arizona

MAILING ADDRESS: Superintendent, Tuzigoot National Monument, P.O. Box 68, Clarkdale, Arizona 86324 **Telephone:** 602-634-5564

DIRECTIONS: The Visitor Center is 3 km (2 miles) east of Clarkdale.

Ruins of a large Indian pueblo which flourished in the Verde Valley between A.D. 1100 and 1450 have been excavated here. Created by Presidential Proclamation on July 25, 1939.

VISITOR ACTIVITIES: interpretive exhibits in the museum, walking tours; **Permits:** No; **Fees:** Entrance fee is $1 per vehicle, Golden Eagle and Golden Age Passports accepted and available; **Visitor facilities:** parking and restrooms at Visitor Center; **Any limitations on vehicle usage:** No; **Hiking trails:** Yes, from the Visitor Center to the ruin and overlook; **Backcountry:** No; **Camping:** No; **Other overnight accommodations on site:** No; **Meals served in the park:** No; **Food and supplies obtainable in the park:** No; **Food and supplies obtainable nearby:** Yes, in Cottonwood, AZ, 4.8 km (3 miles); **Overnight accommodations:** Cottonwood, AZ, 4.8 km (3 miles); **First Aid available in park:** Yes; **Nearest Hospital:** Cottonwood, AZ, 4.8 km (3 miles); **Days/Hours:** Open daily from 8 a.m. to 5 p.m. year-round; **Holiday Closings:** None; **Weather:** Summer is very hot. Spring and Fall are pleasant, Winter is mild.

GENERAL INFORMATION: 40 km (27 miles) from Tuzigoot is Montezuma Castle National Monument, one of the best preserved cliff dwellings in the United States. It can be reached from a good road branching from US 89A. If you plan to continue north on US 89A to Flagstaff, you can easily reach other national monuments: Walnut Canyon, Wupatki, and Sunset Crater (see listings in this book).

Walnut Canyon National Monument
Flagstaff, Arizona

MAILING ADDRESS: Superintendent, Walnut Canyon National Monument, Route 1, Box 25, Flagstaff, Arizona 86001 **Telephone:** 602-526-3367

DIRECTIONS: The entrance road to Walnut Canyon is a 4.5 km (3 mile) highway connecting with Int. 40 at a point 12 km (7.5 miles) east of Flagstaff.

These cliff dwellings were built in shallow caves under ledges of limestone by Pueblo Indians about 800 years ago. Created by Presidential Proclamation on Nov. 30, 1915.

VISITOR ACTIVITIES: interpretive exhibits, hiking, picnicking; **Permits:** No; **Fees:** Entrance fee is $1 per carload in private, noncommercial vehicles, 50¢ per person entering by bus or on foot. Golden Eagle and Golden Age Passports accepted and available; **Visitor facilities:** parking, museum, picnic area, hiking trails; **Any limitations on vehicle usage:** Vehicles are restricted to designated roadways; **Hiking trails:** Yes, a paved foot trail leads to 25 of the cliff dwelling rooms; you can see about 100 others from the trail. There is also a short rim trail; **Backcountry:** No; **Camping:** No; **Other overnight accommodations on site:** No; **Meals served in the park:** No, meals and lodging may be obtained at Flagstaff, Sedona, and Winslow, and along major highways: I-40, I-17, 89N & 89S; **Food and supplies obtainable in the park:** No; **Food and supplies obtainable nearby:** Yes, at Flagstaff, 16 km (10 miles); **Overnight accommodations:** Flagstaff, 16 km (10 miles) west of the Monument; **First Aid available in park:** Yes; **Nearest Hospital:** Flagstaff, 19 km (12 miles); **Days/Hours:** Open all year, from 7 a.m. to 7 p.m. Memorial Day through Labor Day; 8 a.m. to 5 p.m. the rest of the year; **Holiday Closings:** Dec. 25 & Jan. 1; **Visitor attractions closed for seasons:**No.

GENERAL INFORMATION: *For Your Safety*—It is dangerous to walk off designated trails. Those with heart ailments or other infirmities should realize that the ISLAND trail includes a 55-meter (185-foot) climb at an altitude of nearly 2134 meters (7000 feet). These conditions can tax the heart.

Wupatki National Monument
Flagstaff, Arizona

MAILING ADDRESS: Superintendent, Wupatki National Monument, Tuba Star Route, Flagstaff, Arizona 86001 **Telephone:** 602-774-7000

DIRECTIONS: The Visitor Center is on the 30 km (18 mile) loop road which connects Wupatki with Sunset Crater National Monument. Drive 24 km (15 miles) north of Flagstaff on Highway 89, then east on the loop road 35 km (22 miles) to Wupatki Visitor Center.

Ruins of red sandstone pueblos built by farming Indians about A.D. 1065 are preserved here. The modern Hopi Indians are believed to be partly descended from these people. Created by Presidential Proclamation on Dec. 9, 1924.

VISITOR ACTIVITIES: interpretive exhibits, hiking, walking, auto tours; **Permits:** No; **Fees:** No; **Visitor facilities:** parking and restrooms at Visitor Center, hiking trails; **Any limitations on vehicle usage:** Due to soft shoulders, drivers should stay strictly on the road; **Hiking trails:** Yes, self-guiding trails to Nalakiku-Citadel Ruins and to Wupatki Ruin; **Backcountry:** No; **Camping:** No; **Other overnight accommodations on site:** No, no reservations are accepted for U.S. Forest Service campsites, which are located across from Sunset Crater Visitor Center. For further information, contact Sunset Crater at Route 3, Box 149, Flagstaff, AZ 86001, phone 602-526-0586; **Meals served in the park:** No; **Food and supplies obtainable in the park:** No; **Food and supplies obtainable nearby:** Yes, at Flagstaff, 59 km (37 miles) south on Hwy 89; **Overnight accommodations:** Flagstaff, 59 km (37 miles) south on Hwy 89; **First Aid available in park:** Yes; **Nearest Hospital:** Flagstaff, 59 km (37 miles) south on Hwy 89; **Days/Hours:** Visitor

Centers open from 8 a.m. to 5 p.m. daily; 7 a.m. to 7 p.m. in Summer; **Holiday Closings:** Dec. 25 and Jan. 1; **Visitor attractions closed for seasons:**No. The campground at Sunset Crater is open from Apr. 1 until Nov. 15; **Weather:** Summer is moderate to hot; Winter is cold, with snow common at Sunset Crater.

GENERAL INFORMATION: The most common hazards in the park are deep, narrow earth cracks, razor-sharp lava, unstable backcountry ruins, and wild animals. Drinking water is available at Headquarters of Wupatki and Sunset Crater.

Arkansas

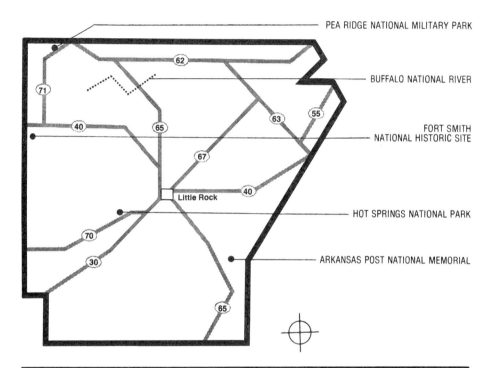

Arkansas Post National Memorial
Gillett, Arkansas

MAILING ADDRESS: Superintendent, Arkansas Post National Memorial, Route 1, Box 16, Gillett, Arkansas 72055 **Telephone:** 501-548-2432

DIRECTIONS: The Memorial is on AR 169, 11 km (7 miles) south of Gillett via AR 1 (The Great River Road) and about 32 km (20 miles) northeast of Dumas via AR 54 and 1.
    The first permanent French settlement in the lower Mississippi Valley was founded on this site in 1686. Authorized for addition to the National Park System on July 6, 1960.

VISITOR ACTIVITIES: exhibits, audiovisual programs, auto and walking tours, picnicking, fishing, biking; **Permits:** an Arkansas fishing license required, available locally; **Fees:** No; **Visitor facilities:** tour road, walking trails, picnic area, restrooms; **Any limitations on vehicle usage:** off-road vehicle use is prohibited; **Hiking trails:** Yes, an .8 km (1/2 mile) nature-history trail; **Backcountry:** No; **Camping:** No; **Other overnight accommodations on site:** No; No reservations are available for campsites at Moore's Bayou, .8 km (1/2 mile) away. This is a developed Corps of Engineers recreation area, with no extra accommodations for trailers. Contact Arkansas Post for further information. **Meals served in the park:** No; **Food and supplies obtainable in the park:** No; **Food and supplies obtainable nearby:** Yes, in Gillett, AR, 11 km (7 miles) north on AR 1; **Overnight accommodations:** Gillett, 11 km (7 miles) north on AR 1; **First Aid available in park:** Yes, or nearby in Gillett, AR 1; **Nearest Hospital:** Dewitt, 32 km (20 miles) north or Dumas, 32 km (20 miles) west; **Days/Hours:** Visitor Center open daily from 8 a.m. to 5 p.m., park open until dark; **Holiday Closings:** Dec. 25; **Visitor attractions closed for seasons:** None.

GENERAL INFORMATION: Be on the lookout for snakes and poison ivy as you walk through the area. Watch your step and stay on the trails. The best time to visit the area is Sept. through May because of the extreme heat, humidity and insects in Summer.

Buffalo National River
Harrison, Arkansas

MAILING ADDRESS: Superintendent, Buffalo National River, P.O. Box 1173, Harrison, Arkansas 72601 **Telephone:** 501-741-5443

DIRECTIONS: Buffalo Point, off AR 14, 27.4 km (17 miles) south of Yellville, is the major center for visitor activities at the river. Information centers are operated at the Buffalo Point, Silver Hill, and Pruitt District Ranger Stations. Information can also be secured at Buffalo National River Headquarters, Federal Building, Walnut and Erie Streets, Harrison 72601.

Offering both swift-running and placid stretches, the Buffalo is one of the few remaining unpolluted, free-flowing rivers in the lower 48 states. It courses through multicolored bluffs and past numerous caves and springs along its 213 km (132 mile) length. Authorized for addition to the National Park System on Mar. 1, 1972.

VISITOR ACTIVITIES: interpretive exhibits, camping, picnicking, canoeing, swimming, hiking, fishing, hunting, campfire programs, guided walks, guided canoe trips; **Permits:** an Arkansas fishing or hunting license is required, available locally for a nominal fee; **Fees:** $3 per site per night camping fee at Buffalo Point Campground; **Visitor facilities:** year-round campground, picnic areas, day-use pavilions, canoe launch areas, hiking trails, guarded swimming beach in Summer, food service, boat and canoe rentals, restrooms, cabin rentals; **Any limitations on vehicle usage:** motor vehicles are restricted to open roadways; **Hiking trails:** Yes, self-guiding hiking trails; **Backcountry:** Yes, information can be obtained by writing Park Headquarters in Harrison; **Camping:** Yes, arrive early in the day in Summer, since all campgrounds are available on a first-come, first-served basis; **Other overnight accommodations on site:** Yes, for cabin information and reservations write to Buffalo Point Concessions, Route A, Yellville, AR 72687; **Meals served in the park:** Yes, at Buffalo Point; **Food and supplies obtainable in the park:** No; **Food and supplies obtainable nearby:** Yes, in Yellville, Harrison, Jasper, Marshall, and Mountain Home; **Overnight accommodations:** Yellville, Harrison, Jasper, Marshall Mountain Home, and Pruitt; **First Aid available in park:** Yes, at Buffalo

Point Ranger Station; **Nearest Hospital:** Harrison, Hwy 62, approx. 80 km (50 miles); Yellville, Hwy 14, 27 km (17 miles) north of Hwy #14; **Days/Hours:** open 24 hours a day, 7 days a week; **Holiday Closings:** None; **Visitor attractions closed for seasons:** No; **Weather:** Summer is hot and humid; Fall and Winter are pleasant.

GENERAL INFORMATION: *For Your Safety*—Stay off the bluffs. Keep alert to river conditions and avoid the river during high water.

Fort Smith National Historic Site
Fort Smith, Arkansas

MAILING ADDRESS: Superintendent, Fort Smith National Historic Site, P.O. Box 1406, Fort Smith, Arkansas 72902 **Telephone:** 501-783-3961

DIRECTIONS: The Site is on Rogers Avenue between Second and Third Streets in downtown Fort Smith. It can be reached from Garrison Ave. (US 64) by turning one block south to Rogers Avenue. A temporary Visitor Center is in the old Barracks Building.
    One of the first U.S. military posts in the Louisiana Territory, the Fort was a center of authority for the untamed region to the West from 1817 to 1896. Authorized for addition to the National Park System on Sept. 13, 1961.

VISITOR ACTIVITIES: interpretive exhibits and walks; **Permits:** No; **Fees:** No; **Visitor facilities:** parking and restrooms at Visitor Center; **Any limitations on vehicle usage:** No; **Hiking trails:** No; **Backcountry:** No; **Camping:** No; **Other overnight accommodations on site:** No; **Meals served in the park:** No; **Food and supplies obtainable in the park:** No; **Food and supplies obtainable nearby:** Yes, in Fort Smith; **Overnight accommodations:** Fort Smith; **First Aid available in park:** Yes; **Nearest Hospital:** Fort Smith, South I Street, 1.6 km (1 mile) from the park; **Days/Hours:** Open daily from 8:30 a.m. to 5 p.m.; **Holiday Closings:** Dec. 25 and Jan. 1; **Visitor attractions closed for seasons:** No; **Weather:** Summer is hot and humid, Winter is generally mild and humid, strong winds occur often in the Spring.

Hot Springs National Park
Hot Springs, Arkansas

MAILING ADDRESS: Superintendent, Hot Springs National Park, P.O. Box 1860, Hot Springs, Arkansas 71901 **Telephone:** 501-624-3383

DIRECTIONS: The Park can be reached by auto via US 70 and 270, and AR 7. The Visitor Center is on the corner of Central and Reserve Avenues.
    Approximately one million gallons of water a day flow from 47 hot springs here, unaffected by climate or seasonal temperatures. Persons suffering from illness or injury often seek relief in the ancient tradition of thermal bathing. Also used by persons who simply want to soak and relax in the soothing, naturally heated water. Set aside as Hot Springs Reservation on Apr. 20, 1832; designated a national park on Mar. 4, 1921.

VISITOR ACTIVITIES: audiovisual and interpretive exhibits at Visitor Center, campfire programs and exhibits at campground Ranger Station, hiking, fishing, auto tours, picnicking, wildflower-watching, biking; **Permits:** No; **Fees:** Fees are charged by bathhouses. Rate schedules available from the Superintendent; **Visitor facilities:** The 12 bathing establishments-7 in the park and 5 in the city-use thermal waters of the park. All are concessions of the Federal Government, subject to regulation and inspection. The baths (full immersion type) may be taken by direct application to the bathhouses, although a physician's advice is recommended. All bathhouses have faciliites for whirlpool baths, showers, massages, and alcohol rubs. The Libbey Physical Medicine Center offers hydro-therapy treatments by registered physical therapists under physician prescriptions; **Any limitations on vehicle usage:** Bicycles, motorcycles, and similar wheeled vehicles are not allowed on the park trails; **Hiking trails:** Yes, many wooded trails; **Backcountry:** No; **Camping;** Yes, the campground is at Gulpha Gorge, 3.2 km (2 miles) northeast of the center of the city. Campers must first register at the campground office. Contact the Park for further information; **Other overnight accommodations on site:** No; **Meals served in the park:** No; **Food and supplies obtainable in the park:** No; **Food and supplies obtainable nearby:** Yes, in city of Hot Springs, adjacent to the Park; **Overnight accommodations:** Yes, the city of Hot Springs, a separate municipality not under National Park Service jurisdiction, nearly surrounds the park. The city has many large hotels offering a choice of American or European plans, smaller hotels, motels, boardinghouses, housekeeping quarters, and furnished or unfurnished cottages. Lists of accommodations and general information are available from the Hot Springs Chamber of Commerce, P.O. Box 1500, Hot Springs, AR 71901, phone 501-372-1700; **First Aid available in park:** Yes; **Nearest Hospital:** Hot Springs, AR, adjacent to the park; **Days/Hours:** Open daily year-round June-Sept: 8 a.m.-7 p.m. Oct.-May 8 a.m.-5 p.m.; **Holiday Closings:** Dec. 25 and Jan. 1; **Visitor attractions closed for seasons:**Novaculite stone exhibit closed Winters; **Weather:** Hot Springs enjoys a favorable climate all year. The Winters are mild and, except for infrequent short intervals, are conducive to outdoor recreation. The mild weather and sunshine are often decided aids to the bath treatments..

GENERAL INFORMATION: *Fires* are one of the park's greatest perils. Campfires are permitted only in designated sites. Cigars and cigarettes should be completely extinguished.

Pea Ridge National Military Park
Pea Ridge, Arkansas

MAILING ADDRESS: Superintendent, Pea Ridge National Military Park, Pea Ridge, Arkansas 72751 **Telephone:** 501-451-8122

DIRECTIONS: The Visitor Center is 16 km (10 miles) north of Rogers off US Hwy 62.
The Union victory here on March 7-8, 1862 led to the Union's total control of Missouri. The battle was one of the major engagements of the Civil War west of the Mississippi. Authorized for addition to the National Park System on July 20, 1956.

VISITOR ACTIVITIES: interpretive exhibits, biking, self-guiding auto tours; **Permits:** No; **Fees:** No; **Visitor facilities:** parking, restrooms, drinking water, picnic area, fireplaces, observation deck, bicycle and nature trails, 11 km (7 mile) self-guiding auto tours; **Any limitations on vehicle usage:** Drive only on paved roads; **Hiking trails:** Yes, .8 km (1/2 mile) nature trail and 16 km (10 mile) Boy Scout trail; **Backcountry:** No; **Camping:** No; **Other overnight accommodations on site:** No, camping is permitted at Beaver Lake, 16 km (10 miles) away, on the north edge of Rogers. **Meals served in the park:** No; **Food and supplies obtainable in the park:** No; **Food and supplies obtainable nearby:**

Yes, in Pea Ridge and Rogers; **Overnight accommodations:** Rogers, US 71S, 16 km (10 miles) from the Park; **First Aid available in park:** Yes, **Nearest Hospital:** Rogers, US 62, 16 km (10 miles); Bentonville, US 62 to AR 102, 24 km (15 miles); **Days/Hours:** Open daily from 8 a.m. to 5 p.m., until 6 p.m. in Summer; **Holiday Closings:** Dec. 25 and Jan. 1; **Weather:** Relatively mild Winters and warm, humid Summers.

California

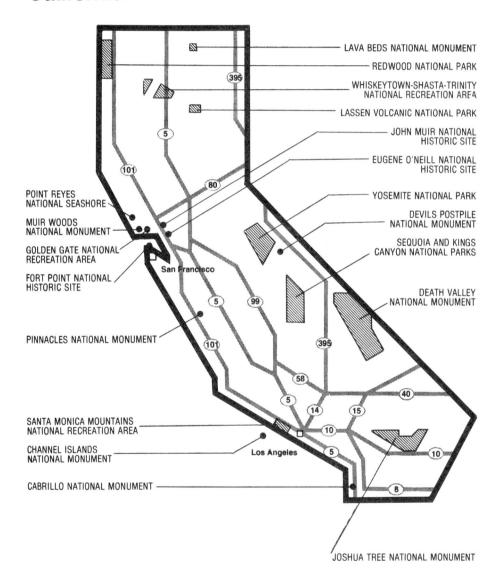

LAVA BEDS NATIONAL MONUMENT

REDWOOD NATIONAL PARK

WHISKEYTOWN-SHASTA-TRINITY NATIONAL RECREATION AREA

LASSEN VOLCANIC NATIONAL PARK

JOHN MUIR NATIONAL HISTORIC SITE

EUGENE O'NEILL NATIONAL HISTORIC SITE

POINT REYES NATIONAL SEASHORE

MUIR WOODS NATIONAL MONUMENT

GOLDEN GATE NATIONAL RECREATION AREA

FORT POINT NATIONAL HISTORIC SITE

San Francisco

YOSEMITE NATIONAL PARK

DEVILS POSTPILE NATIONAL MONUMENT

SEQUOIA AND KINGS CANYON NATIONAL PARKS

DEATH VALLEY NATIONAL MONUMENT

PINNACLES NATIONAL MONUMENT

SANTA MONICA MOUNTAINS NATIONAL RECREATION AREA

CHANNEL ISLANDS NATIONAL MONUMENT

Los Angeles

CABRILLO NATIONAL MONUMENT

JOSHUA TREE NATIONAL MONUMENT

Cabrillo National Monument
San Diego, California

MAILING ADDRESS: Superintendent, Cabrillo National Monument, P.O. Box 6175, San Diego, California 92106 **Telephone:** 714-293-5450

DIRECTIONS: To reach the Monument, follow Rosecrans Street to Canon Street (State Route 209), turn left onto Catalina Boulevard, then go through the gates to the Naval Ocean Systems Center and continue to the tip of Point Loma. Stop first at the Visitor Center.

Juan Rodriquez Cabrillo, Portuguese explorer who claimed the west coast of the United States for Spain in 1542, is memorialized here. Gray whales migrate offshore during the Winter. Created by Presidential Proclamation on Oct. 14, 1913.

VISITOR ACTIVITIES: interpretive exhibits, walking, lighthouse tours, fishing, whale-watching (Dec. through Feb.); **Permits:** No; **Fees:** No; **Visitor facilities:** Visitor Center, parking, restrooms, museum, auditorium, benches, water fountain, walkways, overlooks, lighthouse, wayside exhibits; **Any limitations on vehicle usage:** Vehicles are not allowed in the historic lighthouse complex; **Hiking trails:** Yes, the Monument features a self-guiding ethno-botanical trail through historical coastal defense and chapparal and tide pool walks; **Backcountry:** No; **Camping:** No; **Other overnight accommodations on site:** No; **Meals served in the park:** No; **Food and supplies obtainable in the park:** No; **Food and supplies obtainable nearby:** Yes, ten minutes by auto in the Point Loma-San Diego area; **Overnight accommodations:** San Diego, 8 km (5 miles); **First Aid available in park:** Yes; **Nearest Hospital:** Cabrillo Medical Center, 8 km (5 miles); **Days/Hours:** Open 8:30 a.m. to 7:45 p.m. from June 25 through Labor Day; 9 a.m. to 5:15 p.m. the rest of the year; **Holiday Closings:** None; **Visitor attractions closed for seasons:** No; **Weather:** Mediterranean-type climate: cooler weather in Winter, night and morning fog and clouds in early Summer.

GENERAL INFORMATION: *For Your Safety*—Stay back from the edge of cliffs. Barnacle-encrusted rocks can cut bare feet. Wear rubber-soled shoes if you visit the tide pool areas. Leather soles slip on the wet rocks.

Channel Islands National Monument
Ventura, California

MAILING ADDRESS: Superintendent, Channel Islands National Monument, 1699 Anchors Way Drive, Ventura, California 93003 **Telephone:** 805-644-8157

DIRECTIONS: Southbound on State Route 101-take Seaward offramp in Ventura harbor South to Beechmont, left on Beechmont to headquarters near Port District. Northbound on State Route 101 take Victoria offramp in Ventura, follow Channel Islands signs.

The Monument includes Santa Barbara and Anacapa Islands, and has a large rookery of sea lions, nesting sea birds, and unique plants and animals. Created by Presidential Proclamation on Apr. 26, 1938.

VISITOR ACTIVITIES: hiking, camping, exhibits and audiovisual programs, scuba diving, picnicking, wildlife- and bird-watching, fishing, snorkeling, swimming, boating; **Permits:** for backcountry-call or write Park Superintendent; **Fees:** for concession-operated ferry trips, there is a $16 excursion fee. Inquire with The Island Packers (see below); **Visitor facilities:** Visitor Center, ferry service to and from the islands, campgrounds, comfort facilities, picnic area. For public transportation and tour information write or call: The Island Packers, P.O. Box 933, Ventura, CA 93003, phone 805-642-1393; **Any limitations on vehicle usage:** No vehicles are allowed on the islands; **Hiking trails:** Yes, self-guiding trails; **Backcountry:** Yes, call or write Park Superintendent; **Camping:** Yes, write or call Park Headquarters. You will need to bring water, camping gear, food, cooking equipment, and fuel for campfires. Bring warm clothing, for the nights are cool. You may want a tent as shelter from the ever-present winds. If you are camping on Anacapa, keep in mind that everything must be carried up a steep stairway and then .4 km (1/4 mile) to the camping area; **Other overnight accommodations on site:** No; **Meals served in the park:** No; **Food and supplies obtainable in the park:** No; **Food and supplies obtainable nearby:** Yes, in Ventura, Oxnard; **Overnight accommodations:** Ventura has hotels and motels; **First Aid available in park:** Yes; **Nearest Hospital:** Ventura, 6.4 km (4 miles) from Headquarters; **Days/Hours:** Islands: daylight hours & overnight camping available on Anacapa and Santa Barbara Islands. Visitor Center— 8:30 a.m. - 5 p.m., 7 days a week; **Holiday Closings:** Visitor Center closed Thanksgiving, Dec. 25 and Jan. 1; **Visitor attractions closed for seasons:**No.

GENERAL INFORMATION: *For Your Safety*—hike only on beaches and established trails when on Anacapa.

Death Valley National Monument
Death Valley, California and Nevada

MAILING ADDRESS: Superintendent, Death Valley National Monument, Death Valley, California 92328 **Telephone:** 714-786-2331

DIRECTIONS: US 395 passes west of Death Valley and connects with State Routes 178 and 190 to the park. US 95 passes east of the park and connects with NV 72, 58 and 29 to the park. Interstate 15 passes southeast of the park and connects with State Route 127 to the park.

This large desert, nearly surrounded by high mountains, contains the lowest point in the Western Hemisphere. The area includes Scotty's Castle, the palatial home of a famous prospector, and other remnants of gold and borax mining activity. Created by Presidential Proclamation on Feb. 11, 1933.

VISITOR ACTIVITIES: driving, hiking, jeep riding, camping, photography, biking, interpretive exhibits, guided tours, picnicking, backcountry, horseback riding; **Permits:** backcountry permits are encouraged, available at Ranger Stations; **Fees:** Yes, campground fees at major campgrounds, entrance fee at Scotty's Castle is $1; 50¢ with a Golden Age Passport; **Visitor facilities:** Visitor Center, campgrounds, hiking trails, parking, restrooms, lodging, picnic areas, interpretive programs, post office, bicycle rentals; **Any limitations on vehicle usage:** Drive only on main roads in Summer and always carry water for your car. In case of breakdown, remain with your car until help arrives; **Hiking trails:** Yes, self-guiding walking trails; **Backcountry:** Yes, contact the park for further information; **Camping:** Yes, no reservations for campsites. For further information, write for a copy of the folder *Camping in Death Valley* or pick up a copy at the Visitor Center or any Ranger Station; **Other overnight accommodations on site:** Yes, resorts provide lodging and other commercial services at two locations within the Monument. Facilities at Furnace Creek are operated by Fred Harvey, Inc. P.O. Box 187, Death Valley, CA 92328 phone 714-786-2345; and at Stove Pipe Wells by Stove Pipe Wells Village, Death Valley, CA 92328 phone 714-operator, "Stove Pipe Wells #1". Services at these locations are limited from May through Oct. Call or write for details; **Meals served in the park:** Yes, at Furnace Creek, Stove Pipe Wells, Scotty's Castle; **Food and supplies obtainable in the park:** Yes, at Stove Pipe Wells, Furnace Creek & Scotty's Castle; **Food and supplies obtainable nearby:** Yes, in Beatty, Shoshone; **Overnight accommodations:** Beatty, 19 km (12 miles) from the park; Shoshone, 24 km (15 miles); Trona, 64 km (40 miles); **First Aid available in park:** Yes, or nearby in Beatty, US 95; Trona, State Route 178; Shoshone, State Route 127; **Nearest Hospital:** Lone Pine, 161 km (100 miles) west; Las Vegas, 225 km (140 miles) east; **Days/Hours:** Park never closes. Visitor Center open from 8 a.m. to 9 p.m. from Nov. 1 through Easter; until 5 p.m. the remainder of the year; **Holiday Closings:** None; **Visitor attractions closed for seasons:** No; **Weather:** Summer has extreme heat and low humidity; Winter is cooler with snow at high elevations.

GENERAL INFORMATION: *For Your Safety—the desert can be dangerously hot in summer.* Always carry water for you and your car. *Never enter mines or tunnels;* abandoned shafts are often deep and old timbers rotten. *Forgotten caches of explosives* are occasionally found in mine areas. Do not touch them, but report them to a park ranger as soon as possible. Be alert for *flash floods* when it looks stormy. Do not ford low places when water is running. Flood waters can undercut pavement or sweep a car from the road. *All animals in the park are wild.* They can bite and/or carry diseases. Never feed or touch them. *Never travel alone.* Always tell someone where you are going and when you expect to return. Be extremely cautious in this wild area. If you travel in Death Valley in Summer, pick up a copy of the folder, *Hot Weather Hints,* at distribution boxes at any entrance to the Monument, at the Visitor Center, or any Ranger Station.

Devils Postpile National Monument
Three Rivers, California

MAILING ADDRESS: Superintendent, Sequoia and Kings Canyon National Park, Three Rivers, California 93271 **Telephone:** 209-565-3341

DIRECTIONS: The Monument is reached by a 16 km (10-mile) drive to Minaret Summit on a paved road from US 395, then by 11.2 km (7 miles) of unpaved mountain road.

Hot lava cooled and cracked some 900,000 years ago to form basalt columns 12 to 18 m (40 to 60 feet) high resembling a giant pipe organ. The John Muir Trail between Yosemite and Kings Canyon National Parks crosses the Monument. Created by Presidential Proclamation on July 6, 1911.

VISITOR ACTIVITIES: guided tours, picnicking, fishing, camping; **Permits:** California fishing license, available locally for a nominal fee, is required; **Fees:** $3 camping fee, shuttle bus fee to the Monument from Mammoth Mountain Ski Area parking lot is $1 per person, not to exceed $3 per family unit; **Visitor facilities:** restrooms at Ranger Station, picnic area, campground, shuttle bus; **Any limitations on vehicle usage:** Some park roads may be closed in season, visitors will be required to use a shuttle bus to reach the Monument. Contact the park for further information; **Hiking trails:** Yes, trips may be made north or south along the John Muir Trail and west on the King Creek Trail. Devils Postpile also has several short trails; **Backcountry:** No; **Camping:** Yes, no reservations are available for the campground, which is open from about June 20 to Oct. 1, depending on the weather; **Other overnight accommodations on site:** No; **Meals served in the park:** No; **Food and supplies obtainable in the park:** No; **Food and supplies obtainable nearby:** Yes, at Mammoth Lakes or Reds Meadow; **Overnight accommodations:** Mammoth Lakes, 16 km (10 miles), Reds Meadow, 24 km (15 miles); **First Aid available in park:** Yes; **Nearest Hospital:** Limited facilities at Mammoth Hospital, US 395, 22.5 km (14 miles); more extensive facilities at Bishop, US 395, 87 km (54 miles); **Days/Hours:**

Open 24 hours a day, 7 days a week in season; **Holiday Closings:** None; **Visitor attractions closed for seasons:** The Monument is open from approximately July through Oct.; **Weather:** Summer thundershowers occur frequently in the afternoon.

GENERAL INFORMATION: Warning: Bears inhabit the Monument; proper food storage is required by Federal law. Stay on the regular designated trails since these are the safest places to hike. Use caution when viewing features from near the edge of a cliff or gorge. Footing can be hazardous.

Eugene O'Neill National Historic Site
Danville, California

MAILING ADDRESS: Superintendent, John Muir National Historic Site, 4202 Alhambra Avenue, Martinez, California 94553 **Telephone:** 415-228-8860

DIRECTIONS: There is a significant access problem, i.e., a private road. To arrange for special tours, contact Superintendent, John Muir National Historic Site, 4202 Alhambra Avenue, Martinez, California 94553, phone 415-228-8860, or President, Eugene O'Neill Foundation, P.O. Box 402, Danville, California 94526.

Tao House, near Danville, CA, was built for Eugene O'Neill, who lived here from 1937 to 1944. Several of his best-known plays, including "The Iceman Cometh" and "Long Day's Journey Into Night" were written here-now a memorial to the playwright. Authorized for addition to the National Park System on Oct. 12, 1976.

VISITOR ACTIVITIES: None. The site is affiliated with the National Park System. It is owned by the State of California and at the present time is operated by the Eugene O'Neill Foundation. It is not yet open to the public.

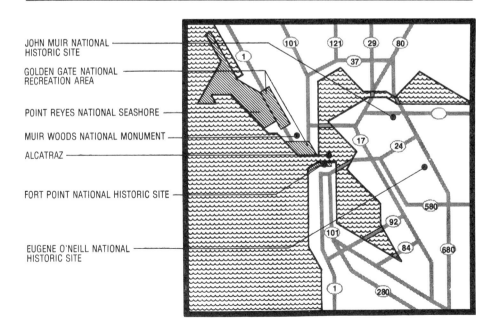

Fort Point National Historic Site
Presidio of San Francisco, California

MAILING ADDRESS: Site Manager, Fort Point National Historic Site, P.O. Box 29333, Presidio of San Francisco, California 94129 **Telephone:** 415-556-1693

DIRECTIONS: Fort Point is located under the south end of the Golden Gate Bridge. Turn off Hwy 101 at the bridge to reach the fort.
  This classic brick and granite mid-19th Century coastal fortification is the largest on the west coast of North America. Established by act of Congress on Oct. 16, 1970.

VISITOR ACTIVITIES: interpretive exhibits and guided tours, fishing; **Permits:** No; **Fees:** No; **Visitor facilities:** parking and restrooms; **Any limitations on vehicle usage:** Vehicles are restricted to passenger cars, which must remain on roads; **Hiking trails:** Yes, short scenic trails through the area; **Backcountry:** No; **Camping:** No; **Other overnight accommodations on site:** No; **Meals served in the park:** No; **Food and supplies obtainable in the park:** No; **Food and supplies obtainable nearby:** Yes, in the immediate area; **Overnight accommodations:** San Francisco—reservations are advisable; **First Aid available in park:** Yes; **Nearest Hospital:** in Letterman, Army Medical Center, Lincoln Blvd., 1.6 km (1 mile); **Days/Hours:** Park open 24 hours a day. Fort open daily from 10 a.m. to 5 p.m.; **Holiday Closings:** Dec. 25 & Jan. 1; **Weather:** Average temperature is 58°F. Wear warm clothes when you visit the area.

GENERAL INFORMATION: Use caution while climbing or descending stairs, which are steep and narrow. Stay on established roadways and off walls, which can be dangerous if climbed.

Golden Gate National Recreation Area
San Francisco, California

MAILING ADDRESS: General Superintendent, Golden Gate National Recreation Area, Fort Mason, San Francisco, California 94123 **Telephone:** 415-556-0560

DIRECTIONS: In San Francisco, Golden Gate National Recreation Area follows the city's northern and western shoreline. These areas are accessible by the Municipal Railway (MUNI) bus system and can easily be reached by car. Ferries provide access to Alcatraz. Across the Golden Gate Bridge in Marin County, the park is reached by various access roads off Hwy 101: Alexander Avenue, Shoreline Highway, and Sir Francis Drake Boulevard. Golden Gate Transit bus system serves Muir Woods, Muir Beach, and Stinson Beach, Visitor information is available at Fort Mason, the Cliff House, Rodeo Beach, and Muir Woods.
  Golden Gate National Recreation Area offers a variety of recreational, scenic, natural, and historic areas on the doorstep of San Francisco. The beauty of the city, the bay, the ocean, and coastal landscape are brought together in one park which contains about 37,000 acres of open space on both sides of the Golden Gate. The park was established in 1972 and represents an effort to bring parks closer to people in urban areas.

VISITOR ACTIVITIES: An endless variety of recreational, cultural, and educational activities are available here, including guided tours of Alcatraz and the National Maritime Museum, picnicking, fishing, camping, swimming, short walks and sightseeing, hiking, and cultural programs at Fort Mason Center; **Permits:** No; **Fees:** No; **Visitor facilities:** picnic sites, fishing piers, beaches, tours of historic areas, campgrounds, snack bars, restrooms, parking, recreational equipment loans; **Any limitations on vehicle usage:** No; **Hiking trails:** Yes, trails vary in length and difficulty. Major trailheads are in the Marin Headlands, near Muir Woods, and Five Brooks in Olema Valley; **Backcountry:** No; **Camping:** Yes, two group campgrounds; An American Youth Hostel offers overnight accommodations in the Marin Headlands Area of the park; **Other overnight accommodations on site:** No; **Meals served in the park:** Yes, food service facilities are available at the Fort Mason Center, The Cliff House, and Muir Woods. In addition, food is easily obtained in the nearby urban community; **Food and supplies obtainable in the park:** No; **Food and supplies obtainable nearby:** Yes, in the nearby urban community; **Overnight accommodations:** The San Francisco Area offers a wide variety of overnight accommodations, many within walking distance of the park; **First Aid available in park:** Yes, at most Visitor Centers and in the surrounding community; **Nearest Hospital:** Letterman, San Francisco General Hospital, and many others in the vicinity; **Days/ Hours:** Most of the park is open all day, all year. Hours for individual facilities vary, but 10 a.m.-5 p.m. are the most common hours of operation; **Holiday Closings:** Alcatraz, Hyde Street Pier, Maritime Museum, and Fort Point are closed on Dec. 25 and Jan. 1; **Visitor attractions closed for seasons:** No; **Weather:** Weather at the park is variable. Wind and fog are common from June to September, especially near the Golden Gate. Fall generally brings the warmest weather. Most rainfall occurs from November to April. Bring a sweater or light jacket that you can carry easily if it warms up.

John Muir National Historic Site
Martinez, California

MAILING ADDRESS: Superintendent, John Muir National Historic Site, 4202 Alhambra Ave., Martinez, California 94553 **Telephone:** 415-228-8860

DIRECTIONS: The Site is located at the foot of the off ramp of the Alhambra Ave. exit of State Route 4, 16 km (10 miles) east of Interstate 80, 8 km (5 miles) west of State Route 680. Access is also available via Bay Area Rapid Transit (BART). Call 415-933-2278 for information on connecting schedules between BART trains and bus service to Martinez.

This 9-acre site preserves the 17 room Victorian home and orchard fragment of the great American writer, naturalist, and defender of the national parks, John Muir. Authorized for addition to the National Park System on Aug. 31, 1964.

VISITOR ACTIVITIES: Guided and self-guiding tours are available. A film about Muir's life and philosophy is shown hourly. Picnicking is available. Guided tours are offered at 10:30 a.m. and 2:30 p.m.; **Permits:** No; **Fees:** 50¢ admission for each person between the ages of 16 and 61. Golden Eagle and Golden Age Passports are accepted and available; **Visitor facilities:** Visitor Center, parking, restrooms, picnic area; **Any limitations on vehicle usage:** No vehicles are allowed in the park, except for those of handicapped visitors; **Hiking trails:** Yes, short trails around the grounds; **Backcountry:** No; **Camping:** No; **Other overnight accommodations on site:** No; **Meals served in the park:** No; **Food and supplies obtainable in the park:** No; **Food and supplies obtainable nearby:** Yes in Martinez; **Overnight accommodations:** Martinez, .8 km (½ mile); **First Aid available in park:** Yes; **Nearest Hospital:** Martinez, 3 km (2 miles) **Days/ Hours:** Open daily from 8:30 a.m. to 4:30 p.m.; **Holiday Closings:** Thanksgiving, Dec. 25 & Jan. 1; **Visitor attractions closed for seasons:** No; **Weather:** Moderate climate; warm Summers.

Joshua Tree National Monument
Twentynine Palms, California

MAILING ADDRESS: Superintendent, Joshua Tree National Monument, 74485 National Monument Drive, Twentynine Palms, California 92277 **Telephone:** 714-367-7511

DIRECTIONS: The Monument is 225 km (140 miles) east of Los Angeles; from the West it is approached via I-10 (US 60) and Twentynine Palms Hwy (Hwy 62) to the North entrances at the town of Joshua Tree and Twentynine Palms. The Cottonwood Springs (South) entrance is 40 km (25 miles) east of Indio, CA, via I-10 (US 60).

The Monument is a desert area of great diversity encompassing the unique ecosystems of both the Joshua Tree-defined Mojave and lower Colorado deserts. Rich in ecological, historical and recreational resources, the Monument was established Aug. 10, 1936.

VISITOR ACTIVITIES: hiking, interpretive walks and talks, picnicking, wildlife-watching, camping; **Permits:** For backcountry, a self-registration system is used throughout the Monument; **Fees:** Not for backcountry use. No general entrance fee—campground use fee at two campgrounds is $2 per night; **Visitor facilities:** campgrounds, tables, fireplaces, toilets, conducted walks, hikes, and campfire talks, drinking water, picnic area; **Any limitations on vehicle usage:** Vehicles must be operated only on established roads; **Hiking trails:** Yes, trails vary in length and difficulty; **Backcountry:** Yes, contact the park or inquire at the Visitor Center; **Camping:** Yes, first-come, first-served. Campers must bring their own water and firewood and be prepared for wide fluctuations in temperature; **Other overnight accommodations on site:** No; **Meals served in the park:** No; **Food and supplies obtainable in the park:** No; **Food and supplies obtainable nearby:** Yes, in Twentynine Palms, Yucca Valley, Joshua Tree; **Overnight accommodations:** Joshua Tree, 13 km (8 miles) from North Park Entrance in Joshua Tree; 8 km (5 miles) from West Park Entrance; Yucca Valley, 17.7 km (11 miles) from West Park Entrance; **First Aid available in park:** Yes; **Nearest Hospital:** Joshua Tree, 13 km (8 miles) from West Park Entrance; **Days/Hours:** Open all year, 24 hours a day. Visitor Center open daily from 8 a.m. to 5 p.m.; **Holiday Closings:** Visitor Center closed Dec. 25; **Visitor attractions closed for seasons:** Guided walks and talks in Spring and Fall only; **Weather:** It is cold from Dec. through mid-Feb. July and Aug. temperatures range from 100°F to 115°F.

GENERAL INFORMATION: When hiking, biking, or driving in Joshua Tree during hot weather, drink four liters (at least one-half gallon) of water per day. Stay clear of mine shafts. Beware of rattlesnakes.

Lassen Volcanic National Park
Mineral, California

MAILING ADDRESS: Superintendent, Lassen Volcanic National Park, Mineral, California 96063 **Telephone:** 916-595-4444

DIRECTIONS: From the north and south, the Park is reached via State Route 89. From the east and west, via State Route 36 and 44. Redding is 77.2 km (48 miles) west of the Park on State Route 44.

The park contains examples of volcanic phenomena, including Lassen Peak, the only recently active volcano in the continental United States, which erupted intermittently from 1914 to 1921. Created by Presidential Proclamation on August 9, 1916.

VISITOR ACTIVITIES: interpretive programs, nature walks, hiking, self-guiding auto tours, camping, cross-country and downhill skiing, picnicking, fishing, boating, back-packing, swimming, winter sports; **Permits:** Wilderness permits are required for over-night stays in the backcountry. Permits are available at Park Headquarters and all Ranger Stations. They may be requested by mail or telephone, but they should be requested at least 2 weeks in advance. California fishing license, available locally, is required. Licenses vary in length of validity and cost; **Fees:** Yes, entrance fee is $1 per car; campground fee is $1 or $2 per campsite, depending on facilities. Golden Eagle and Golden Age Passports are accepted and available; **Visitor facilities:** campgrounds, hiking trails, fast food service, religious services, picnic areas, boat ramp, lodging, supplies, and ski trails, tows, and equipment rental; **Any limitations on vehicle usage:** Motors (electric, etc.,) are not allowed on any park waters; **Hiking trails:** Yes, there are 240 km (150 miles) of foot trails in the park; **Backcountry:** Yes, permit is required for overnight stays; check at Park Headquarters, any Ranger Station, or send for information; **Camping:** Yes, four campgrounds are located along Lassen Park Road. The campgrounds at Manzanita Lake, Crags, Summit Lake, and Butte Lake have sanitary facilities and spaces for trailers (no hookups for electricity, water, or sewage). The Southwest Campground also has modern facilities. The Juniper Lake and Warner Valley Campgrounds have primitive facilities and are not recommended for trailers due to the rough road. Camping is permitted from late-May to October, depending on the weather and the location of the campground. All campgrounds are on a first-come, first-served basis. No reservations can be made. Group campgrounds are also available, and reservations must be made in advance. Complete campground information is provided on request. Call 916-595-4444 for information on lodging facilities; **Other overnight accommodations on site:** Yes, at Drakesbad Guest Ranch, call 916-595-3306; **Meals served in the park:** Yes, fast food services are available at the Manzanita Lake Camper Service Store and Chalet; **Food and supplies obtainable in the park:** Yes, Manzanita Lake Campground; **Food and supplies obtainable nearby:** Yes, in Mineral, 16 km (10 miles) south; Hat Creek, 23 km (16 miles) north; **Overnight accommodations:** Mineral, 16 km (10 miles) south; Hat Creek, 20 km (14 miles) north; **First Aid available in park:** Yes; **Nearest Hospital:** Burney, State Route 44, 77 km (45 miles) west of the north end; Chester, State Route 36, 56 km (35 miles) from the south end; **Days/Hours:** Park is always open; **Holiday Closings:** None; **Visitor attractions closed for seasons:** Transpark Road is closed during Winter; **Weather:** Most of the 48 km (30-mile) Lassen Park Road is closed by snow from the end of October until early June, although the Park is open all year. Winter sports are centered in an area near the southwest entrance.

GENERAL INFORMATION: *For Your Safety*—Stay on established trails at all times in hot springs or steaming areas. Keep small children under strict physical control to avoid burns or accidents. Ground crusts which appear to be safe may be dangerously thin. Hot lunches, ski-rental equipment and accessories are available on weekends and holidays. Ski tows are operated on weekends. Overnight accommodations are available at Mineral, Chester, and Ballard's Childs Meadows Resort.

The terrain and snow conditions are usually excellent for cross-country skiing. For safety reasons, Park Rangers should be notified of all trips. Wilderness permits are required for all overnight stays.

The road is kept open from the northwest entrance to the Manzanita Meadows District Office. Many people visit this section of the park to enjoy the scenery and winter sports.

Lava Beds National Monument
Tulelake, California

MAILING ADDRESS: Superintendent, Lava Beds National Monument, P.O. Box 867,

Tulelake, California 96134 **Telephone:** 916-667-2601

DIRECTIONS: Park Headquarters is 48 km (30 miles) from Tulelake, CA, and 93 km (58 miles) from Klamath Falls, OR, off State Route 139, 8 km (5 miles) south of Tulelake and 42 km (26 miles) north of Canby. Two km (1.3 miles) of the road between Tulelake and the park are not paved.

Volcanic activity spewed forth molten rock and lava here creating an incredibly rugged landscape—a natural fortress used by the Indians in the Modoc Indian War, 1872-73. Created by Presidential Proclamation on Nov. 1, 1925.

VISITOR ACTIVITIES: camping, walking, picnicking, interpretive talks, campfire programs, cave exploration, bird- and animal-watching; **Permits:** No; **Fees:** campground fees are $3 per day per site from mid-June through Labor Day; **Visitor facilities:** picnic areas, campgrounds, drinking water, toilets; **Any limitations on vehicle usage:** Vehicles are restricted to maintained roads; **Hiking trails:** Yes, moderate to rugged both in and outside of the wilderness areas; **Backcountry:** Yes, information available by writing or calling the park, or from Park Headquarters; **Camping:** Yes, no reservations for campsites, which are near Monument Headquarters and are open all year. The 40-unit campground has sites suitable for tents, pickup campers, and small trailers and has water and toilets. From Sept. 15 through May 15 water must be carried from Headquarters. Fleener Chimneys picnic area has no water, and fires may not be built there; **Other overnight accommodations on site:** No; **Meals served in the park:** No; **Food and supplies obtainable in the park:** No; **Food and supplies obtainable nearby:** Yes, at Tulelake and Klamath Falls; **Overnight accommodations:** Tulelake, State Route 139, 48 km (30 miles); Klamath Falls, OR, State Route 139, 93 km (58 miles), and Merrill, OR; **First Aid available in park:** Yes, or nearby in Tulelake, State Route 139, 48 km (30 miles); **Nearest Hospital:** Klamath Falls, OR, State Route 139, 93 km (58 miles); **Days/Hours:** Park never closes, Visitor Center open daily from 8 a.m. to 5 p.m.; until 6 p.m. in Summer; **Holiday Closings:** None; **Visitor attractions closed for seasons:** None; **Weather:** At these altitudes, cold weather is possible anytime; snow has been recorded in nearly all months. Winter daily high temperatures average around 5°C (40'sF); lows are only a few degrees below 0°C (in the 20's F). Fog is frequent. Summers are moderate; with daytime highs averaging from 24° to 27°C (75 to 80°F), lows are about 10°C (40's and 50's F). Precipitation in this area averages 3.18 cm (1.25 inches) or less per month.

GENERAL INFORMATION: Hunting, gathering specimens, and collecting souvenirs is prohibited. Among the potential hazards you may encounter in the lava tubes are low ceilings, steep trails and stairways, and uneven footing. Take more than one light source. Wear protective headgear. Wear adequate clothing—cave temperatures are cool. Notify a Park Ranger before exploring caves other than those listed in the park's brochure, or if you plan to use your own lighting equipment. Be aware that rattlesnakes are found throughout the park; children should be cautioned never to put their hands and feet in places they cannot see.

Muir Woods National Monument
Mill Valley, California

MAILING ADDRESS: Supervising Park Ranger, Muir Woods National Monument, Mill Valley, California 94941 **Telephone:** 415-388-2595

DIRECTIONS: The Monument is 27 km (17 miles) north of San Francisco and is reached by US 101 and State Route 1. Tour bus service is available from downtown San Francisco.

This virgin stand of coastal redwoods was named for John Muir, conservationist and founder of the Sierra Club. Created by Presidential Proclamation on Jan. 9, 1908.

VISITOR ACTIVITIES: interpretive exhibits, walking, hiking; **Permits:** No; **Fees:** No; **Visitor facilities:** Visitor Center, parking, restrooms, souvenir stand, interpretive talks by advance arrangement, trailside markers, signs, and exhibits; **Any limitations on vehicle usage:** No motorized equipment, horses, or bicycles are permitted; **Hiking trails:** Yes, 10 km (6 miles) of trails join those of other public lands. Bridges along Redwood Creek make short loops possible; **Backcountry:** No; **Camping:** No; **Other overnight accommodations on site:** No; **Meals served in the park:** Yes, snacks are available at the concession shop near the Visitor Center; **Food and supplies obtainable in the park:** No; **Food and supplies obtainable nearby:** Yes; **Overnight accommodations:** Mill Valley, 6.4 km (4 miles); **First Aid available in park:** Yes; **Nearest Hospital:** San Rafael, 19.3 km (12 miles); **Days/Hours:** Open daily from 8 a.m. to sunset; **Holiday Closings:** None; **Visitor attractions closed for seasons:** No; **Weather:** 40 inches of rain per year, mostly between November and May.

GENERAL INFORMATION: Weather is often cool and wet, so jackets are advisable. Stay on trails, which can become slippery when wet. Poison oak and nettles are common. Do not pick berries, roots or mushrooms. Several plants found in Muir Woods are poisonous.

Pinnacles National Monument
Paicines, California

MAILING ADDRESS: Superintendent, Pinnacles National Monument, Paicines, California 95043 **Telephone:** 408-389-4578

DIRECTIONS: The Monument is separated into an east and west district with Visitor Service facilities located in both districts. Park Headquarters and the Bear Gulch Visitor Center are on the east side of the Monument and are reached via State Route 25. The Chaparral Ranger Station and Visitor Center are on the west side and can be reached via State Route 146 from Soledad. The road from Soledad to West Pinnacles is narrow. Visitors driving large campers and towing trailers should use extreme caution. There is no road connecting the east and west sides of the monument.

Spirelike rock formations 500 to 1200 feet high, with caves and a variety of organic features, rise above the smooth contours of the surrounding countryside. Created by Presidential Proclamation on Jan. 16, 1908.

VISITOR ACTIVITIES: hiking, climbing, picnicking, camping, evening talks on spring and fall weekends, wildlife-, wildflower-, and bird-watching; **Permits:** none required, but climbers are advised to register with a Park Ranger before and after a climb; **Fees:** $1 per person entrance fee. Golden Eagle and Golden Age Passports accepted and available. $2 per night per site camping fee; **Visitor facilities:** picnic areas, campsites, museum, souvenirs, drinking water, comfort stations, self-guiding trails, hiking trails, amphitheater; **Any limitations on vehicle usage:** Motor vehicles and horses are not allowed on any of the trails; **Hiking trails:** Yes, trails vary in length and difficulty. For further information, inquire at Visitor Center; **Backcountry:** No; **Camping:** Yes, West Side Chaparral campground is reached from Hwy 101, 17.7 km (11 miles) east from the turnoff at Soledad. Reservations are not available for campsites. Picnic tables, fireplaces, water, and modern comfort stations are provided. No gasoline, food or supplies are available. Pinnacles campground is a new, private campground which is adjacent to the park's east boundary on State Route 146. It offers individual and group campsites with tables and grills and modern restrooms. It has showers and laundry facilities, a camper store, recreation vehicle utility hookups and an amphitheatre. Camping fee is $5 per night per site. Reservations may be made by contacting Pinnacles Campground, Inc., 2400 Highway 146, Paicines, CA 95043, phone 408-389-4462; **Other overnight accommodations on site:** No; **Meals served in the park:** No; **Food and supplies obtainable in the park:** No; **Food and supplies obtainable nearby:** Yes, stores at Pinnacles Campground and in Paicines, 37 km (23 miles) to the north; **Overnight accommodations:** Soledad, Hollister, and King City; **First Aid available in park:** Yes; **Nearest Hospital:** Hollister and King City; **Days/Hours:** Park never closes; **Holiday Closings:** None; **Visitor attractions closed for seasons:**None; **Weather:** Winter is the park's busiest season, while Spring is one of the best times to enjoy the park. Summer daytime temperatures can reach 38°C (100°F).

GENERAL INFORMATION: *For Your Safety*—Only experienced climbers and persons under competent leadership should attempt rock climbs in the park. *Stay on regular designated* trails. Rock faces off the trails are unstable and likely to flake off beneath you. *Poison oak* abounds; stay on the trails and in developed areas which are kept reasonably free of this plant. *Rattlesnakes* may be on the trails in the Spring and Fall. *Water* is not always as pure as it seems, so drink only from hydrants and fountains on the park's water supply. Be sure to *wear stout, comfortable shoes*, loose fitting clothing, and in the Summer, a hat. Your summer shoes should have thick soles because thin soles heat quickly and can cause blisters on the bottom of your feet.

Point Reyes National Seashore
Point Reyes Station, California

MAILING ADDRESS: Superintendent, Point Reyes National Seashore, Point Reyes, California 94956 **Telephone:** 415-663-1092

DIRECTIONS: The Seashore is one hour or 65-70 km (40-45 miles) north of San Francisco via US 101 and Sir Francis Drake Blvd., or via US 1 near Mill Valley.
   This peninsula, near San Francisco, is noted for its long beaches backed by tall cliffs, lagoons and esteros, forested ridges and offshore bird and sea lion colonies. Part of the area remains a private pastoral zone. Authorized for addition to the National Park System on Sept. 13, 1962.

VISITOR ACTIVITIES: hiking, biking, picnicking, swimming, surfing, wading, guided tours, surf fishing, horseback riding, bird watching, backcountry; **Permits:** required for camping, obtained by registering at the Park Headquarters Information Center; **Fees:** No; **Visitor facilities:** beaches, campgrounds, hiking trails, horse trails, picnic areas, three Visitor Centers, self-guiding trails, four hike-in campgrounds with 50 sites total; **Any limitations on vehicle usage:** all motor vehicles are restricted to developed, paved roadways and parking areas; **Hiking trails:** Yes, Bear Valley Trailhead is a gateway to more than 273.6 km (170 miles) of trails. The 7 km (4.4 mile) Bear Valley Trail is the most popular route, winding through grassy meadows and forests to the sea. Other trails branch from it and ascend steeply into the high country of the Inverness Ridge and the southern portion of the Seashore. Stay on designated trails; wandering off may result in losing your way or being exposed to poison oak, which abounds here. Carry a canteen-stream water is not potable; **Backcountry:** Yes, informaton can be obtained from the Superintendent; **Camping:** Yes, to obtain a permit, register at Headquarters; **Other overnight accommodations on site:** No; **Meals served in the park:** Yes, at Drakes Beach; **Food and supplies obtainable in the park:** No; **Food and supplies obtainable nearby:** Yes, at Point Reyes Station, Inverness, Olema; **Overnight accommodations:** Point Reyes Station, US 1, 4.8 km (3 miles); Olema, US 1, 1.6 km (1 mile); Inverness, Sir

Francis Drake Hwy, 8 km (5 miles); **First Aid available in park:** Yes or nearby in Point Reyes Station, Inverness, Olema; **Nearest Hospital:** San Rafael and Petaluma, both 32 km (20 miles) away; **Days/Hours:** Park is always open; Visitor Center is generally open from 8 a.m. to 4:30 p.m.; **Holiday Closings:** some facilities close on Dec. 25 and Jan. 1; **Visitor attractions closed for seasons:** None; **Weather:** The ocean strongly influences the weather at Point Reyes. The ocean beaches are frequently foggy and windy enough to make warm clothing welcome. Throughout the Summer these beaches experience more days of fog than sunshine, but Spring and Autumn can be mild and pleasant. The country east of Inverness Ridge, accessible by hiking trails, is free of summer fog, but it has heavy rains in Winter and Spring.

GENERAL INFORMATION: A privately operated tent and trailer campground is 3 km (1/2 mile) from seashore Headquarters. Bicycles and horses can be rented nearby. *Caution!* Pounding surf and rip currents make Point Reyes beaches too dangerous for swimming, surfing and wading.

Redwood National Park
Crescent City, California

MAILING ADDRESS: Superintendent, Redwood National Park, Drawer N, Crescent City, California 95531 **Telephone:** 707-464-6101

DIRECTIONS: The Park can be reached by private auto and scheduled bus lines on US 101 south from the Oregon coast, north from Eureka and Arcata, and from east via US 199 from Grants Pass and Medford, OR. Information stations are in Crescent City and Orick.
　　The Park contains coastal redwood forests with virgin groves of ancient trees, including the world's tallest. It includes 64 km (40 miles) of scenic Pacific coastline. Established by act of Congress on Oct. 2, 1968.

VISITOR ACTIVITIES: driving, hiking, shoreline walks, photography, fishing, picnicking, bird- and wildflower-watching, interpretive services, camping; **Permits:** for fishing and backcountry; backcountry permits issued without charge at trailhead, fishing licenses may be purchased at hardware and tackle shops. Licenses vary in length of validity and cost; **Fees:** $4 per night at campgrounds, $1.50 per vehicle for day-use picnic areas in State parks; **Visitor facilities:** rental cars, hiking trails, exhibits, campgrounds, picnicking facilities are at a number of locations, including Enderts Beach Road, Lagoon Creek, and the State and county parks; **Any limitations on vehicle usage:** Trailers should not be taken off main roads because of weather, general road conditions and steep grades; **Hiking trails:** Yes, on the shore and through redwood forests; **Backcountry:** Yes, inquire at any Park Information Office or write the above address; **Camping:** No, the national park is not as yet operating campgrounds, but camping is available in the state parks and national forests. Each state park has a developed campground suitable for tents, campers, and small trailers up to 8 m (26 feet) long. There are 349 campsites in the 3 state parks. Sites may be reserved through Ticketron outlets or by writing to Reservation Office, Dept. of Parks and Recreation, P.O. Box 2390, Sacramento, CA 95811. Information and forms are available at any California State Park Office. Reservations are helpful from July 1 to after Labor Day. Campsites not filled by reservation are assigned on a first-come, first-served basis. State parks have fees for camping and day-use picnic areas. Interpretive programs are presented daily in the Summer. Four campgrounds are off US 199 in Six Rivers National Forest. They contain 87 campsites, developed for tents, campers, and small trailers, and are about a 30-minute drive from US 101. Campgrounds are also on State

Routes 299 and 96 in Six Rivers, Klamath, and Trinity National Forests. These are 1-to 4-hour drives from US 101; **Other overnight accommodations on site:** No; **Meals served in the park:** No; **Food and supplies obtainable in the park:** No; **Food and supplies obtainable nearby:** Yes, at Crescent City, Eureka, Klamath, Orick; **Overnight accommodations:** A number of motels, private trailer parks, and campgrounds are along US 101 from Eureka, CA to the Oregon line, and on State Routes 299 and 96 and US 199 to the east; **First Aid available in park:** Yes; **Nearest Hospital:** Crescent City, at Front and A Streets, 4 blocks from Headquarters; **Days/Hours:** Open 24 hours a day year-round; **Holiday Closings:** Information Centers closed on Dec. 25 and Jan. 1; **Visitor attractions closed for seasons:** Mill Creek Campground closes in Winter; **Weather:** Summer visits are recommended. Winter is windy and rainy.

GENERAL INFORMATION: For current information on access to new park lands, inquire at an Information Station or ask a Park Ranger.

Santa Monica Mountains National Recreation Area
California

MAILING ADDRESS: Superintendent, Santa Monica Mountains National Recreation Area, 23018 Ventura Blvd., Woodland Hills, California 91364 **Telephone:** 213-888-3440

DIRECTIONS: The National Park Service has not acquired any lands yet.

Beaches, uplands, and highlands north of Los Angeles provide recreational, scientific, archaeological and public health benefits. The area blends public and private lands including state and local parklands. It includes three state parks: Malibu Creek, Point Mugu and Topanga; a state beach, Leo Carrillos; and two large county parks: Topia and Charmlee. All state and local areas are within the boundaries of the 150,000-acre recreation area. Authorized for addition to the National Park System on Nov. 10, 1978.

Sequoia and Kings Canyon National Parks
Three Rivers, California

MAILING ADDRESS: Superintendent, Sequoia and Kings Canyon National Parks, Three Rivers, California 93271 **Telephone:** 209-565-3341

DIRECTIONS: Proceed east on State Route 198 from US 99 to the south entrance of Sequoia Park. To reach Kings Canyon Park, go east on State Route 180 from US 99 to the entrance. Generals Highway connects State Route 198 and 180, and passes through Sequoia Park to the Grant Grove area, Kings Canyon Park, a 2-hour drive.

Two enormous canyons of the Kings River and the summit peaks of the High Sierra dominate Kings Canyon. General Grant Grove, with its giant sequoias, is a detached section of the Park. Attractions at Sequoia include Mount Whitney, the highest mountain in the U.S. outside of Alaska, and giant sequoia groves. Kings Canyon established by act of Congress on Mar. 4, 1940; Sequoia established on Sept. 25, 1890.

VISITOR ACTIVITIES: sightseeing, photography, camping, hiking, fishing, Nordic and downhill skiing, horseback riding, exhibits, campfire programs, guided nature walks; **Permits:** For wilderness use, fishing, entrance, camping: obtain permits at Park Headquarters and Visitor Center; fishing licenses from local stores; **Fees:** $2 per car entrance fee. Camping is $2 per night. Golden Eagle and Golden Age Passports accepted and available; **Visitor facilities:** campgrounds, lodges and cabins, cafeteria, dining rooms, camper supply stores, post offices, rental pack and saddle stock, ski trails; **Any limitations on vehicle usage:** All vehicles are restricted to developed roadways. No vehicles are permitted on trails. Park roads are paved and steep with many turns; drive slowly, keep to the right, and use lower gears to avoid overheating the brakes and transmissions. Trailers are limited to specific campgrounds; **Hiking trails:** Yes, 1190 km (700 miles) of hiking from relatively easy to steep mountain trails. Elevations range from 2,000 to 14, 495 feet; **Backcountry:** Yes, information available by contacting the Superintendent; **Camping:** Yes, campground reservations are required at Lodgepole campground only; other campgrounds are operated on a first come, first-served basis. Reservations can be made in person at over 150 Ticketron outlets in California or by mail from throughout the United States to: Ticketron Reservation Office, P.O. Box 2715, San Francisco, CA 94126. Reservations should be made well in advance; **Other overnight accommodations on site:** Yes, for reservations at cabins, contact: Sequoia and Kings Canyon Hospitality Service, Sequoia National Park, CA 93262, phone 209-565-3373; and Wilsonia Lodge, Kings Canyon National Park, CA 93633, phone 209-335-2310; **Meals served in the park:** Yes, at Giant Forest, Grant Grove, Cedar Grove, Stony Creek, and Wilsonia; **Food and supplies obtainable in the park:** Yes, at Giant Forest, Lodgepole, Grant Grove, Cedar Grove, Stony Creek, Wilsonia; **Food and supplies obtainable nearby:** Yes, in Three Rivers, Visalia, Fresno; **Overnight accommodations:** Kings Canyon: Fresno, State Route 180, 88.5 km (55 miles) from Grant Grove. Sequoia: Three Rivers, State Route 198, 11.3 km (7 miles) from Headquarters: Visalia, State Route 198, 88.5 km (45 miles); **First Aid available in park:** Yes; **Nearest Hospital:** Kings Canyon: Fresno, CA, State Route, CA 180, 88.5 km (55 miles) from Grant Grove. Sequoia: Exeter, CA, State Route 198, 48.3 km (30 miles) from Headquarters; **Days/Hours:** Parks open all year; **Holiday Closings:** None; **Visitor attractions closed for seasons:** Some activities are cancelled and some roads are closed during the winter snow period; **Weather:** Warm mountain climate with cool nights in Summer; snow and relatively severe mountain Winters.

GENERAL INFORMATION: *For Your Safety—Drowning* is the leading cause of fatalities. Extreme caution is advised around rivers, especially in the spring and early Summer when they are swift, deep, and very cold. *Lightning* is dangerous on exposed peaks. *Injuries from falling* are best prevented by staying away from steep places, wearing proper footgear, and hiking in the company of others. *Respiratory or circulatory problems* may be aggravated at higher elevations. *Bears and other wildlife*, though sometimes tame in appearance, are wild and could be dangerous. Regulations that prohibit feeding or aggravating animals are enforced for your safety, as well as for the benefit of the animals.

Whiskeytown-Shasta-Trinity National Recreation Area
Whiskeytown, California

MAILING ADDRESS: Superintendent, Whiskeytown-Shasta-Trinity National Recreation Area, P.O. Box 188, Whiskeytown, California 96095 **Telephone:** 916-241-6584

DIRECTIONS: The main Visitor Center is Overlook Information Station, located at the intersection of CA 299 and Kennedy Memorial Drive.

Whiskeytown Lake, formed by a dam on Clear Creek in a scenic mountain region, is an excellent resource for water-related recreaton. The area's other two units are administered by the U.S. Forest Service. Created by an act of Congress on Nov. 8, 1965.

VISITOR ACTIVITIES: Whiskeytown Lake is excellent for most water-related activities, including swimming, scuba diving, water skiing, boating and fishing. Picnicking, camping, backcountry, hunting, interpretive programs, and horseback riding are also popular; **Permits:** Free backcountry permits available at Overlook Information Station; **Fees:** $3 per day camping fee at Oak Bottom for tent sites or recreational vehicles; **Visitor facilities:** historical museum at Shasta, self-guiding trail, picnic area, campground, bathhouse, boat ramp and rentals, food and supplies, hiking and horse trails; **Any limitations on vehicle usage:** Vehicles are restricted to designated roadways; **Hiking trails:** Yes, 5.9 km (3.7 miles) of hiking trails; **Backcountry:** Yes, information can be obtained from Visitor Stations; **Camping:** Yes, no reservations available for campsites; **Other overnight accommodations on site:** No; **Meals served in the park:** Yes, snack bars at Oak Bottom and Brandy Creek; **Food and supplies obtainable in the park:** Yes, at Oak Bottom Marina and Whiskeytown Store, .4 km (1/4 mile) off CA 299 west; **Food and supplies obtainable nearby:** Yes, at Redding, CA, 12.9 km (8 miles) east of Overlook Information Station; **Overnight accommodations:** Redding, CA 299, 12.9 km (8 miles) east of Overlook Information Station; **First Aid available in park:** Yes; **Nearest Hospital:** Redding, CA 299, 12.9 km (8 miles) east; **Days/Hours:** Open all year, camping and boating hours are unlimited, swimming beaches close at 11 p.m.; **Holiday Closings:** None; **Visitor attractions closed for seasons:** None.

GENERAL INFORMATION: Visitors should inquire at Overlook Information Station for information about the Recreation Area and programs. The most prominent landmark of the region is 1,893 meter (6,029 foot) Shasta Bally, rising in the midst of rolling woodlands and clear-flowing streams. The summit may be reached on foot and by auto.

Yosemite National Park
Yosemite National Park, California

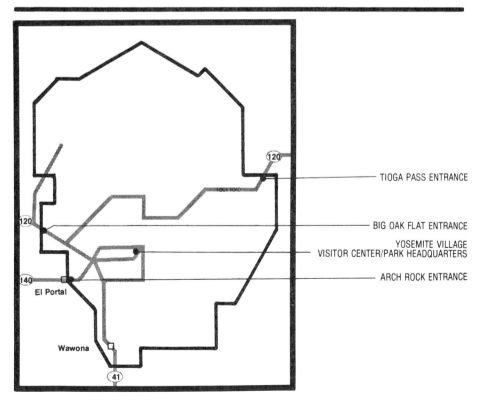

MAILING ADDRESS: Superintendent, Yosemite National Park, P.O. Box 577, Yosemite National Park, California 95389 **Telephone:** 209-372-4605 or -4461

DIRECTIONS: Access to Yosemite is via State Route 140 and 120 eastbound from Merced and Manteca; State Route 41 northbound from Fresno; State Route 120 westbound from Lee Vining (closed in Winter).

Granite peaks and domes rise high above broad meadows in the heart of the Sierra Nevada Mountains; groves of giant sequoias dwarf other trees and wildflowers; and mountains, lakes, and waterfalls, including the Nation's highest, are found here. Established by act of Congress on Oct. 1, 1890.

VISITOR ACTIVITIES: camping, hiking, climbing, horseback riding, fishing, swimming, alpine downhill and cross-country skiing, rock climbing, backpacking, bus tours, walks, talks, cultural demonstrations, self-guiding tours, interpretive exhibits, natural history seminars; **Permits:** Backcountry wilderness permits can be obtained by written application to Park Superintendent between Feb. 1 and May 31, or in person at Wawona, Yosemite Valley, Big Oak Flat Entrance or Tuolumne Meadows; fishing licenses available in person only; **Fees:** Daily vehicle entrance fee is $3; daily campground use fee varies from 50¢ to $2 to $4, depending on facilities; and campground reservation fee is $1.75 (these fees are for the 5 Yosemite Valley campgrounds.) Golden Eagle and Golden Age Passports accepted and available; **Visitor facilities:** individual and group campgrounds, picnic areas, Visitor Centers, showers, laundromat, repair garage, service stations, food service, accommodations, alpine and nordic ski schools, mountaineering school, recreational equipment rental, scheduled transportation and interpretive bus tours; **Any limitations on vehicle usage:** All vehicles are required to stay on surfaced roads. Commercial vehicles are allowed only on Park business; commercial buses require written permission (trip-lease agreement) with the concessioner; **Hiking trails:** Yes, 1207 km (750 miles) of trails; **Backcountry:** Yes, information can be obtained at all Ranger Stations, Visitor Centers, and wilderness permit kiosks. Visitors planning trips during summer holiday weekends and to some destinations should reserve wilderness permits in advance. Contact the Park's Backcountry Office well in advance; **Camping:** Yes, group campsites must be reserved in advance. Individual campsites are assigned on a first-come, first-served basis, except between mid-April and Oct. 31, when the five Yosemite Valley campgrounds are on an advance campsite reservation system. Reservations are required. Otherwise, visitors risk a waiting period of up to six hours or a filled-to-capacity campground. Reservations can be made in person at over 150 Ticketron outlets in California or by mail from throughout the United States to: Ticketron Reservation Office, P.O.Box 2715, San Francisco, CA 94126. *Campsite reservations cannot be made by telephone*; **Other overnight accommodations on site:** Yes, at Yosemite Valley, White Wolf, Wawona, El Portal, Tuolumne Meadows, and the five High Sierra Camps. Reservations are advised at all times for accommodations in hotels, lodges, and cabins. Contact the Yosemite Park and Curry Company, Yosemite National Park, CA 95389, phone 209-373-4171; **Meals served in the park:** Yes, at Yosemite Valley, Wawona, El Portal, White Wolf, Tuolumne Meadows, and the five High Sierra camps; **Food and supplies obtainable in the park:** Yes, Yosemite Valley, Wawona, El Portal, White Wolf, Tuolumne Meadows and the five High Sierra camps; **Food and supplies obtainable nearby:** Yes, in Lee Vining, Groveland, El Portal, Wawona, Oakhurst, Fish Camp, Mariposa; **Overnight accommodations:** Lee Vining, Groveland, El Portal, Wawona, Oakhurst, Fish Camp, Mariposa; **First Aid available in park:** Yes, Yosemite Medical Group provides 24 hour emergency outpatient care; **Nearest Hospital:** Merced, Fresno, Bridgeport; **Days/Hours:** Open 24 hours a day year-round; **Holiday Closings:** None; **Visitor attractions closed for seasons:**Mariposa Grove Road, Glacier Point Road, and Tioga Road closed from mid-November to late May; **Weather:** Cool Summers above 5000 feet, periodic late Summer thunderstorms and snow flurries in high elevations.

GENERAL INFORMATION: Facilities and activities available to and usable by the disabled upon request. Life and death emergency only telephone 209-372-4417 or -4418. For weather, road conditions, etc. telephone 209-372-4605. To report structural and wildland fires, telephone: Yosemite Valley—209-372-4444; Wawona—209-375-6333; El Portal—209-379-2333. Shuttlebus service is available year-round in Yosemite Valley. For illustrated publications describing natural features, write to Yosemite Natural History Association, P.O. Box 545, Yosemite National Park, CA 95389, or stop at a Visitor Center.

Colorado

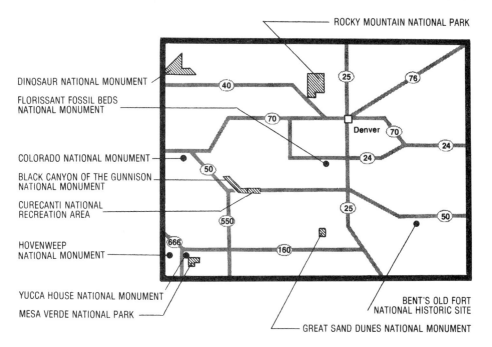

ROCKY MOUNTAIN NATIONAL PARK

DINOSAUR NATIONAL MONUMENT

FLORISSANT FOSSIL BEDS
NATIONAL MONUMENT

COLORADO NATIONAL MONUMENT

BLACK CANYON OF THE GUNNISON
NATIONAL MONUMENT

CURECANTI NATIONAL
RECREATION AREA

HOVENWEEP
NATIONAL MONUMENT

Denver

YUCCA HOUSE NATIONAL MONUMENT

MESA VERDE NATIONAL PARK

BENT'S OLD FORT
NATIONAL HISTORIC SITE

GREAT SAND DUNES NATIONAL MONUMENT

Bent's Old Fort National Historic Site
La Junta, Colorado

MAILING ADDRESS: Superintendent, Bent's Old Fort National Historic Site, P.O. Box 581, La Junta, Colorado 81050 **Telephone:** 303-384-2596

DIRECTIONS: The Site is 13 km (8 miles) east of La Junta and 24 km (15 miles) west of Las Animas on CO 194.

As a principal outpost of civilization on the Southern Plains in the early 1800's and a rendezvous for Indians, the post became the center of a vast fur-trading empire in the West. Authorized for addition to the National Park System on June 3, 1960. Fort reconstructed in 1975-76.

VISITOR ACTIVITIES: interpretive and audiovisual exhibits, guided tours, living history program; **Permits:** No; **Fees:** No; **Visitor Facilities:** Parking area is 600 yards from the fort. Restrooms are available; **Any limitations on vehicle usage:** Visitor vehicles are restricted to the parking terrace; **Hiking trails:** No; **Backcountry:** No; **Camping:** No; **Other overnight accommodations on site:** No; **Meals served in the park:** No; **Food and supplies obtainable in the park:** No; **Food and supplies obtainable nearby:** Yes, in La Junta; **Overnight accommodations:** La Junta, CO 194, 13 km (8 miles) west; **First Aid available in park:** Yes; **Nearest Hospital:** La Junta, CO 194, 13 km (8 miles) west; **Days/Hours:** Open daily 8 a.m. to 5 p.m. from Sept. through May; 8 a.m. to 6 p.m. Memorial Day through Labor Day; **Holiday Closings:** Thanksgiving and Dec. 25; **Visitor attractions closed for seasons:** No.

GENERAL INFORMATION: *For Your Safety*—Remain on the stairs and walks, and watch your step on the steep stairways. Don't let children climb on the walls or run on the upper gallery; there are no handrails.

Black Canyon of the Gunnison National Monument
Montrose, Colorado

MAILING ADDRESS: Superintendent, Black Canyon of the Gunnison National Monument, P.O. Box 1648, Montrose, Colorado 81401 **Telephone:** 303-249-9661

DIRECTIONS: You can drive both rims of the Canyon. The South Rim is open to traffic all year; the North is closed to traffic in Winter. From Montrose, CO, the distance to the South Rim entrance is 18 km (11 miles) - 9.7 km (6 miles) east via US 50 and 8 km (5 miles) north over a hard-surfaced road. You can reach the North Rim from CO 92, just east of Crawford over a 22.5 km (14 mile) graded road. Information is available at Park Headquarters on Hwy 50 East at 2233 East Main, or during the season, at the South Rim Visitor Center.

Shadowed depths of this sheer-walled canyon accentuate the darkness of ancient rocks of obscure origin. Created by Presidential Proclamation on Mar. 2, 1933.

VISITOR ACTIVITIES: camping, fishing, hiking, wildlife- and bird-watching, interpretive exhibits; **Permits:** State fishing license, free backcountry permit are required. Fishing license available from any sporting goods store in Montrose, backcountry permit from a Park Ranger no more than 24 hours in advance of the trip; **Fees:** Yes, camping fee is $1 per site, 7 people per site. Golden Eagle and Golden Age Passports accepted and available. $1 per person entrance fee collected from Memorial Day through Labor Day; **Visitor Facilities:** campgrounds, snack bar, souvenir stand, picnic areas, restrooms and overlooks (both closed in Winter); **Any limitations on vehicle usage:** All vehicles must stay on established roadways; **Hiking trails:** Yes, trails to overlooks and nature trails; **Backcountry:** Yes, you should register at the Ranger Station before starting any inner canyon activity; **Camping:** Yes, no reservations for the two campgrounds/one on each rim; **Other overnight accommodations available on site:** No; **Meals served in the park:** No, but snacks are available on the South Rim; **Food and supplies obtainable in park:** No; **Food and supplies obtainable nearby:** Yes, in Montrose, US 50, 18 km (11 miles); **Overnight accommodations:** Montrose, US 50, 18 km (11 miles); **First aid**

available in park: Yes, but only in season; **Nearest Hospital:** Montrose, US 50 18 km (11 miles); **Days/Hours:** Open 24 hours a day, but occasionally closed in winter due to heavy snow; **Visitor attractions closed for season:**Rim House and Visitor Center are closed in Winter. Rim House open only from mid-May through October; **Weather:** Extremely low temperatures and heavy snows in Winter; travel not advised.

GENERAL INFORMATION: *For Your Safety*— Stay on the trails! View the canyon from behind the railings at the designated overlooks. *Fire* is Black Canyon's greatest peril. Fires are permitted only in the fireplaces in the campground. Be sure your fire is out. All pets must be kept on a leash. No pets are permitted in the inner canyon.

Colorado National Monument
Fruita, Colorado

MAILING ADDRESS: Superintendent, Colorado National Monument, Fruita, Colorado 81521 **Telephone:** 303-858-3617

DIRECTIONS: The Monument is easily accessible by highway: US 6, 50, and I-70 to Grand Junction; and US 6, 50, and I-70 to Fruita. The Monument is 6.4 km (4 miles) west of Grand Junction and 5.6 km (3.5 miles) south of Fruita, CO.
    Sheer-walled canyons, towering monoliths, and strange formations reflect the action of time and weather on colorful sandstone. Created by Presidential Proclamation on May 24, 1911.

VISITOR ACTIVITIES: exhibits, audiovisual programs, auto tours, interpretive talks, nature walks, campfire programs, camping, picnicking, backcountry, hiking, climbing, cross-country skiing; **Permits:** suggested for backcountry, can be obtained at Ranger Stations; **Fees:** $1 entrance fee per single-visit carload, 50¢ per person for commercial tours. Golden Age and Golden Eagle Passports accepted and available. Camping is $2 per night per site, or $1 for Golden Age; **Visitor facilities:** Visitor Center, parking, restrooms, campground, picnic areas, hiking trails; **Any limitations on vehicle usage:** No off-road use. Parking on roads or road shoulders is not allowed; **Hiking trails:** Yes, 34 km (21 miles) of constructed trails, self-guiding nature walks; **Backcountry:** Yes, write or call for more information; **Camping:** Yes, no reservations for campgrounds; **Other overnight accommodations on site:** No; **Meals served in the park:** No; **Food and supplies obtainable in the park:** No; **Food and supplies obtainable nearby:** Yes, Grand Junction, Fruita, and Glade Park Store; **Overnight accommodations:** Grand Junction, 6.4 km (4 miles) east; Fruita, 5.6 km (3 miles) north; **First Aid available in park:** Yes; **Nearest Hospital:** Fruita, 5.6 km (3.5 miles) north; Grand Junction, 6.4 km (4 miles) east; **Days/Hours:** Park is open 24 hours a day. Visitor Center open from 8 a.m. to 4:30 p.m., with extended hours in Summer; **Holiday Closings:** Reduced hours at the Visitor Center on Dec. 25; **Visitor attractions closed for seasons:**No, but snow may hamper access; **Weather:** Summers are hot and dry; Winters are generally cool and snowy.

GENERAL INFORMATION: *For Your Safety*—Do not touch, feed, or harm the animals. Do not hike or climb alone. Register for difficult and technical climbs.

Curecanti National Recreation Area
Gunnison, Colorado

MAILING ADDRESS: Superintendent, Curecanti National Recreation Area, P.O. Box

1040, Gunnison, Colorado **Telephone:** 303-641-2337

DIRECTIONS: The Elk Creek Visitor Center is 25 km (16 miles) west of Gunnison via US 50, on Blue Mesa Lake. An Information Station is at the Cimarron Area.

Forty miles of the scenic Gunnison River and almost 30,000 acres of Colorado high country are included in this unique park area. Established by act of Congress on Feb. 11, 1965.

VISITOR ACTIVITIES: boating, fishing, swimming, water skiing, campfire programs, camping, picnicking, hunting, snowmobiling, naturalist activities, backcountry camping, archaeological walks, ice fishing, interpretive exhibits, boat tours (call 303-641-0403 for information and schedules); **Permits:** Fishing requires a Colorado license, available from the Colorado Division of Wildlife Office and local sporting goods stores. License fees vary in length of validity and cost; **Fees:** camping fee is $2 per night per site; tour boat fees; **Visitor facilities:** parking, campground, launching ramps, scenic overlooks, marina, boat and slip rentals, grocery store, fish observation pond, restrooms, hiking trails, cross-country ski routes, amphitheater, telephones, snowmobile route; **Any limitations on vehicle usage:** Vehicles are restricted to designated roadways; **Hiking trails:** Yes, Pine Creek Trail provides access to Morrow Point Lake; **Backcountry:** No; **Camping:** Yes, no reservations available for campgrounds; **Other overnight accommodations on site:** No; **Meals served in the park:** No; **Food and supplies obtainable in the park:** Yes, some groceries available at the Elk Creek Marina; **Food and supplies obtainable nearby:** Yes, in Gunnison; **Overnight accommodations:** Gunnison, 25.7 km (16 miles) east of the Elk Creek Headquarters area; **First Aid available in park:** Yes; **Nearest Hospital:** Gunnison, US 50, 25.7 km (16 miles) east of the Elk Creek Headquarters Area; **Days/Hours:** Open 24 hours a day, year-round; **Holiday Closings:** None; **Visitor attractions closed for seasons:** Campgrounds with limited facilities are kept open until closed by snow; **Weather:** Winter temperatures drop as low as -37°C (-34°F) at night. Summer daytime highs may reach the mid 20sC (80°F), with around 5°C (upper 30s to 40F) at night.

GENERAL INFORMATION: There are no designated areas for swimming and no lifeguards. Watch out for precipitous shorelines, submerged rocks, and cold water.

Dinosaur National Monument
Dinosaur, Colorado

MAILING ADDRESS: Superintendent, Dinosaur National Monument, P.O. Box 210, Dinosaur, Colorado 81610 **Telephone:** 303-374-2216

DIRECTIONS: The Visitor Center: 21 km (13 miles) east of Vernal, UT, to Jensen, UT on US 40; then 11.3 km (7 miles) north to Quarry on UT 149. Headquarters is 3 km (2 miles) east of Dinosaur, CO on US 40 (60 km [37 miles] east of Vernal, UT on US 40).

The quarry contains fossil remains of dinosaurs and other ancient mammals. Spectacular canyons were cut by the Green and Yampa Rivers through upfolded mountains. Created by Presidential Proclamation on Oct. 4, 1915.

VISITOR ACTIVITIES: Dinosaur fossil displays, auto tours, walking, hiking, picnicking, camping, backcountry driving, fishing, white-water boating, snowmobiling, wildflower-watching; **Permits:** for fishing, white-water boating, and backcountry hiking. For boating apply between Dec. 1 and Jan 15 for the following season; **Fees:** $2 per night camping fee; **Visitor facilities:** Campgrounds, nature walks and trails, rental boat trips, interpretive programs, parking and restrooms at Visitor Center, telephones, boat ramp, snowmobile route; **Any limitations on vehicle usage:** All visitors use a free shuttlebus to the quarry from Memorial Day to Labor Day; **Hiking trails:** Yes, short nature walks at Plug Hat and Harpers Corner and self-guided nature trails at Split Mountain Campground and Lodore; **Backcountry:** Yes, write Park Superintendent in advance, or see any Ranger on arrival. Drinking water in the backcountry is scarce; **Camping:** Yes, no reservations available for campsites; **Other overnight accommodations on site:** No; **Meals served in the park:** No; **Food and supplies obtainable in the park:** No; **Food and supplies obtainable nearby:** Yes, in Dinosaur, Rangely, and Craig, CO; Vernal and Jensen, UT; **Overnight accommodations:** Dinosaur, Rangely, and Craig, CO; Vernal and Jensen, UT; **First Aid available in park:** in Emergency; **Nearest Hospital:** Vernal, US 40, 33.8 km (21 miles); Rangely, CO via CO 64; **Days/Hours:** Visitor Center open 8 a.m.-4:30 p.m. Oct. through May, 8 a.m.-7 p.m. Memorial Day through Labor Day; **Holiday Closings:** Thanksgiving, Dec. 25 and Jan. 1; **Visitor attractions closed for seasons:** Backcountry and canyon roads closed by snow; **Weather:** Summer days 90°, nights 60°; Spring and Fall are mild with cool nights. Winters are cold with 60 days of snow on ground. Low humidity all year.

GENERAL INFORMATION: *For Your Safety*—Most of the accidents at Dinosaur occur while people are boating the rivers or while climbing or hiking in the rugged canyon areas. For your benefit, it is suggested that you check with a Park Ranger about your plans and about local road conditions.

Florissant Fossil Beds National Monument
Florissant, Colorado

MAILING ADDRESS: Superintendent, Florissant Fossil Beds National Monument, P.O. Box 185, Florissant, Colorado 80816 **Telephone:** 303-748-3253

DIRECTIONS: The park can be reached by taking US 24 west from Colorado Springs to the small village of Florissant, 56 km (35 miles) away. At the Village Center, turn south toward Cripple Creek on the unpaved Teller County Road #1. The park is .8 km (1/2 mile) from Florissant.

A wealth of fossil insects, seeds, and leaves of the Oligocene Period is preserved here in remarkable detail. An unusual display of standing petrified sequoia stumps is also here. Authorized for addition to the National Park System on Aug. 20, 1969.

VISITOR ACTIVITIES: interpretive exhibits and walks, hiking, picnicking, horseback riding, cross-country skiing; **Permits:** No; **Fees:** No; **Visitor facilities:** Parking and restrooms at Visitor Center, picnic areas, trails, exhibits; **Any limitations on vehicle usage:** Motor vehicles are restricted to designated roadways; **Hiking trails:** Yes, a nature trail leads to petrified stumps and shale deposits; **Backcountry:** No; **Camping:** No; **Other overnight accommodations on site:** No, there are several well-marked public campgrounds in the surrounding Pike National Forest; **Meals served in the park:** No; **Food and supplies obtainable in the park:** No; **Food and supplies obtainable nearby:** Yes, in Woodland Park, Divide, Florissant, Lake George, and Cripple Creek; **Overnight accommodations:** Woodland Park, Divide, Florissant, Lake George, and Cripple Creek; **First Aid available in park:** Yes; **Nearest Hospital:** Colorado Springs, 56 km (35 miles) east on US 24; **Days/Hours:** Open daily from 8 a.m. to 4:30 p.m., until 7 p.m. in Summer; **Holiday Closings:** Thanksgiving, Dec. 25 and Jan. 1; **Weather:** Heavy snow in Winter may occasionally cause hazardous driving.

GENERAL INFORMATION: *WARNING:* Ticks spreading Colorado tick fever and Rocky Mountain spotted fever are common here in Spring and early Summer. If you are hiking, tuck your pant legs inside your socks and check youself for ticks periodically. If you have any imbedded ticks, contact a ranger or physician.

Great Sand Dunes National Monument
Alamosa, Colorado

MAILING ADDRESS: Superintendent, Great Sand Dunes National Monument, P.O. Box 60, Alamosa, Colorado 81101 **Telephone:** 303-378-2312

DIRECTIONS: The Visitor Center is on Hwy 150, 60 km (37 miles) northeast of Alamosa, Colorado. Write or phone ahead for detailed information on facilities and activities.

Among the largest and highest in the United States, these dunes were deposited over thousands of years by southwesterly winds blowing through the passes of the lofty Sangre de Cristo Mountains. Established by act of Congress on Mar. 17, 1932.

VISITOR ACTIVITIES: hiking, nature walks, dune climbing, camping, picnicking, fishing, 4-wheel drive auto tours, snowshoeing, cross-country skiing, interpretive exhibits, naturalist activities from June through August; **Permits:** Yes, free backcountry permits available at the Visitor Center. Colorado fishing licenses, available locally, are required; **Fees:** $1 per vehicle entrance fee: hikers, bikers, and bus passengers are admitted for 50¢ per day. Golden Age and Golden Eagle Passports are accepted and available. $3 per vehicle per night charge for developed campsites. Entrance and camping fees are not collected from November through March; **Visitor facilities:** Visitor Center, air pump, drinking water, picnic area, campground with restrooms, fire grates & picnic tables, 4-wheel drive road, group campsites; **Any limitations on vehicle usage:** All motor vehicles and their operators must be licensed on all roads within the Monument. The Medano Pass Primitive Road is restricted to 4-wheel drive vehicles and trail bikes. Off road travel or driving on the dunes is prohibited; **Hiking trails:** Yes, trails vary in length and degree of difficulty; **Backcountry:** Yes, contact the park for information. Permits and maps are available at the Visitor Center; **Camping:** Yes, no reservations available for individual campsites. Group camping may be arranged in advance by writing the Superintendent; **Other overnight accommodations on site:** No; **Meals served in the park:** No; **Food and supplies obtainable in the park:** No; **Food and supplies obtainable nearby:** Yes, groceries,snacks, gasoline, showers, campground, gifts, and hookups are located four miles south of the entrance station; **Overnight accommodations:** Alamosa, 60 km (37 miles); Salida, 145 km (90 miles); and Ft. Garland, 46.7 km (29 miles); **First Aid available in park:** Yes; **Nearest Hospital:** Alamosa, Hwy 160, 60 km (37 miles); **Days/Hours:** Open 24 hours a day year-round; **Holiday Closings:** Visitor Center closed Dec. 25.

GENERAL INFORMATION: Hiking on the dunes is most pleasant early and late in the day. Surface temperatures in the Summer can reach 140°F at midday-hot enough to blister your feet or those of your pet. Shoes should be worn or carried. Most visitors begin their walk on the dunes from the picnic area, choosing their own routes because there are no trails on the dunes. A walk to the top and back requires about 3 hours.

Hovenweep National Monument
(near) Cortez, Colorado

MAILING ADDRESS: Superintendent, Hovenweep National Monument, c/o Mesa

Verde National Park, Mesa Verde National Park, Colorado 81330 **Telephone:** 303-529-4469

DIRECTIONS: The Monument is 29 km (18 miles) north of Cortez on Highway 666, and then west at Pleasant View, following a graded dirt road for 40 km (25 miles) to Square Tower Group, Utah.

Pre-Columbian Indians built these 6 groups of towers, pueblos, and cliff dwellings, now preserved as a national monument in Colorado and Utah. Authorized for addition to the National Park System on Mar. 2, 1923.

VISITOR ACTIVITIES: walking tours, camping, picnicking, hiking; **Permits:** No; **Fees:** No; **Visitor facilities:** picnic area, campground, trail, comfort station; **Any limitations on vehicle usage:** The graded dirt roads can become muddy and sometimes impassable during or following storms. Inquire locally during stormy weather regarding road conditions; **Hiking trails:** Yes, a self-guiding trail leads through the prehistoric ruins of Square Tower Group; **Backcountry:** No; **Camping:** Yes, no reservations available for the modern campground near the Ranger Station which is open all year. Camping supplies, firewood and gasoline are not available at the Monument; **Other overnight accommodations on site:** No; **Meals served in the park:** No; **Food and supplies obtainable in the park:** No; **Food and supplies obtainable nearby:** Yes, Hatch Trading Post, 26 km (16 miles) west, and Ismay Trading Post, 22.5 km (14 miles) southeast; **Overnight accommodations:** Cortez, CO, 60 km (37 miles); **First Aid available in park:** Yes; **Nearest Hospital:** Cortez, CO, 60 km (37 miles); **Days/Hours:** The Monument is open from 8 a.m. to 5 p.m. year-round; **Holiday Closings:** None.

GENERAL INFORMATION: Visitors to Hovenweep can also see nearby Mesa Verde National Park (see listing in this book).

Mesa Verde National Park
Mesa Verde National Park, Colorado

MAILING ADDRESS: Superintendent, Mesa Verde National Park, Mesa Verde National Park, Colorado 81330 **Telephone:** 303-529-4465

DIRECTIONS: To get the most out of your visit, you should first go to either the Far View Visitor Center (open only in Summer from 8 a.m. to 5 p.m.) or to the Chapin Mesa Museum (open from 8 a.m. to 6 p.m. in Summer and 8 a.m. to 5 p.m. the rest of the year). The Park entrance is midway between Cortez and Mancos on US 160. It is 34 km (21 miles) from the entrance to the museum and the Chapin Mesa ruins area. The Morfield campground is 6 km (4 miles) from the entrance. The Far View Visitor Center is 25 km (15 miles) away. The narrow, mountainous road has sharp curves and steep grades. Depending on traffic and weather conditions, allow at least 45 minutes to make this drive. Park roads are generally designed as scenic drives with reduced speed limits. The average speed limit in the Park is 55 km (35 miles) per hour.

These pre-Columbian cliff dwellings and other works of early man are among the most notable and best preserved in the United States. Established by act of Congress on June 29, 1906.

VISITOR ACTIVITIES: photography, interpretive exhibits and talks, camping, picnicking, auto tours, guided tours, biking, (limited) hiking, campfire and religious programs in Summer; **Permits:** Yes, for hiking only, available at Chief Ranger's Office; **Fees:** $2 per vehicle entrance fee, 50¢ for bus passengers. Golden Age & Golden Eagle

Passports are accepted and available. Camping fee is $2 per night, $1 with Golden Age. Organized groups are 50¢ per person per day; **Visitor facilities:** bicycle rentals, campgrounds, gas stations, stores, showers, picnic areas, post office, laundry, hiking trails, restaurants, telephones, lodging; **Any limitations on vehicle usage:** Motor vehicles are allowed only on roadways, turnouts, or parking areas; **Hiking trails:** Hiking is restricted to only four trails within the Park. Check at the Ranger Station for their location; **Backcountry:** No; **Camping:** Yes, Morfield campground is open from May 1 through Oct. 31 for tents and trailers. It has restrooms and single and group campsites. Reservations cannot be made. Each campsite has a table, benches, and grills for which fuel can be bought at the store. There are no utility hookups, but the campground has a disposal system for dumping trailer holding tanks. Groceries, souvenirs, carry-out food, a gasoline station, showers, and laundry facilities are also available. All services and facilities are closed from approximately mid-Oct. to mid-May; **Other overnight accommodations on site:** Yes, at Far View, which has a Visitor Center and gas station. Concessioner-operated commercial bus tours of Chapin Mesa and the free tours of Wetherill Mesa leave from this point. *Lodging* is available from mid-May to mid-Oct. From June 1 to Labor Day it is advisable to make reservations with the Mesa Verde Co., P.O. Box 227, Mancos, CO 81328, phone 303-529-4421; **Meals served in the park:** Yes, at Morfield, Far View, and Chapin Mesa; **Food and supplies obtainable in the park:** Yes, at Morfield and Chapin Mesa; **Food and supplies obtainable nearby:** Yes, at Cortez and Mancos, CO; **Overnight accommodations:** Cortez, Hwy 160, 16 km (10 miles) west; Mancos, Hwy 160, 13 km (8 miles) east; **First Aid available in park:** Yes, emergency first aid is provided at the Chief Ranger's Office; first aid at Park Headquarters and the Morfield Ranger Station; **Nearest Hospital:** Cortez, 16 km (10 miles) west of the Park entrance; **Days/Hours:** Accommodations, facilities, and services are available from mid-May to mid-Oct. Maximum interpretive services begin mid-June and last until Labor Day; **Holiday Closings:** Dec. 25 & Jan. 1; **Visitor attractions closed for seasons:** From mid-Oct. to mid-Apr. all concession facilities, including gasoline, food, and lodging are unavailable. The museum and Ruins Road are open year-round. Cliff Palace and Balcony House ruins are closed from mid-November to mid-April by winter snows. Wetherill Mesa ruins (Long House and Step House) open from June 10 through Labor Day only, closed the rest of the winter season. From mid-Oct. to mid-Apr. all concession facilities, including gasoline, food, and lodging are unavailable. Tours of Spruce Tree House are conducted all year when trail and weather conditions permit; **Weather:** In Summer, daytime temperatures are comfortably warm with highs ranging from 29°C (85°F) to 38°C (100°F). Evening temperatures are cool with lows ranging from 13°C (55°F) to 18°C (65°F). Winter highs range from 4°C(40°F) to 10°C(50°F) with lows of -32°C(-25°F) to -10°C(15°F). Snow-covered ground is predominant.

GENERAL INFORMATION: *For Your Safety*—Visits to cliff dwellings, whether on a Ranger-guided tour or a self-guided walk, tend to be quite strenuous. Adequate footwear, such as hiking boots or sturdy shoes, is recommended for these trips. Strenuous activity at the high elevations of the park may adversely affect those persons who experience heart or respiratory ailments. You may wish to reconsider climbing into and out of the cliff dwellings. With the exception of Balcony House, all major cliff dwellings can be viewed from overlooks on the canyon rims. Parents should be especially alert for their childrens' safety when nearing the canyon rim cliff areas. Do not throw rocks or other objects, for other visitors may be below. Be on the lookout for bicycles on the narrow roads. Contact a Ranger if you are involved in an accident or are injured.

Rocky Mountain National Park
Estes Park, Colorado

MAILING ADDRESS: Superintendent, Rocky Mountain National Park, Estes Park,

Colorado 80517 **Telephone:** 303-586-2371

DIRECTIONS: The Park is accessible by Trail Ridge Road, which crosses the Continental Divide. Access from the east is by US 34/36 to Estes Park, from the southwest by US 34 to Grand Lake.

The Park's rich scenery typifies the grandeur of the Rocky Mountains. Peaks towering over 12,000 feet shadow wildlife and wildflowers in 1067 sq. km (412 square miles) of the Rockies' Front Range. Established by act of Congress on Jan 26, 1915.

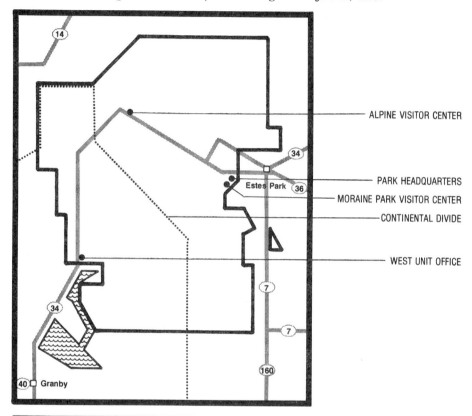

VISITOR ACTIVITIES: interpretive programs, auto touring, camping, hiking, mountain climbing, fishing, horseback riding, downhill and cross-country skiing, snowshoeing, snowmobiling (west side only), bird and animal watching; **Permits:** a Colorado fishing license, available locally, is required. Backcountry use permits for overnight stays available from Park Headquarters or the West Unit Office; **Fees:** Entrance fees, subject to change, are $2 per noncommercial vehicle and 50¢ per person for commercial vehicles or bus passengers. Golden Age and Golden Eagle Passports are accepted and available. Entrance fees are waived for persons under 16 years of age. Campground fees are $4 per night per site. Holders of Golden Age Passports will be given a 50% discount; **Visitor facilities:** Schedules for guided walks, campfire programs, and other activities are available at Information Centers in Summer. Be sure to see the orientation program at Headquarters. Contact the Park for a detailed list of camping facilities; **Any limitations on vehicle usage:** Vehicles must remain on established roads and parking areas; **Hiking trails:** Yes, more than 480 km (300 miles) of trails provide access to remote sections of the Park; **Backcountry:** Day use requires no permit except for technical climbing; a permit for overnight stays is required, and can be obtained without charge on a first-come basis at Park Headquarters or the West Unit Office or by writing no earlier than two weeks ahead of the visit. The number of permits issued is limited. Contact the Park for detailed information on backcountry; **Camping:** Yes, Rocky Mountain has five roadside campgrounds: Moraine Park, Glacier Basin, Aspenglen, Longs Peak, and Timber Creek. Camping is limited to 3 days at Longs Peak and 7 days at the other sites. In Summer, campgrounds have usually been filled to capacity early each day. Organized group sites at Glacier Basin can be reserved. Longs Peak is restricted to tent camping. There are no electrical, water, or sewage connections at any campground. One campground is kept open all year. No reservations available for campsites. Wood fires are permitted in fire grates at campgrounds and picnic areas. A written permit is required for fires outside of those areas. Wood gathering is prohibited parkwide except in the area of certain designated backcountry campsites. Warm clothing and rain gear are advised. Contact the Park for detailed information on camping and campsites. A few privately owned accommodations are available in the vicinity. For information about facilities adjacent to the Park, write to the Chamber of Commerce at either Estes Park, CO 80517 or Grand Lake, CO 80447; **Other overnight accommodations on site:** No; **Meals served in the park:** No, but light lunches at Trail Ridge Store (Fall River Pass) in Summer and at Hidden Valley Winter Use Area in Winter; **Food and supplies obtainable in the park:** No; **Food and supplies obtainable nearby:** Yes, at Estes Park and Grand Lake; **Overnight accommodations:** Estes Park, US 34 or 36, 3.2-6.4 km (2-4 miles) from the Park & Grand Lake, US 34, 1.6 km (1 mile); **First Aid available in park:** Yes, or nearby in Estes Park and Grand Lake; **Nearest Hospital:** Granby, 22.5 km (14 miles) southwest of the Grand Lake Entrance, just beyond the junction of US 40 with US 34; & Estes Park, US 34 or 36, 3.2-6.4 km (2-4 miles) from the Park; **Days/Hours:** Open 24 hours a day year-round; **Holiday Closings:** Visitor Centers closed Dec. 25; **Visitor attractions closed for seasons:**Trail Ridge Road usually closes in October; **Weather:** The high country produces a variable weather pattern primarily due to differences in altitude, slope and exposure. Elevation plays a most important role. Contact the Park for detailed seasonal and monthly weather information.

GENERAL INFORMATION: There are several hazards which you should be aware of. Many serious accidents have occured on *snow and ice fields* in the Summer. Stay away from the edge of steep snow slopes and avoid sliding on snow &/or ice unless you are experienced and properly equipped.

Remember, *mountain climbing* is a technical sport requiring extensive training, skill, conditioning and proper equipment. Registration with a Park Ranger is required for all technical climbs.

Although they appear small, *streams and waterfalls* can be deceptively dangerous, especially in the Spring when they are high and turbulent from melting snow. During *thunderstorms*, stay off ridges and peaks and avoid exposed lone objects such as large rocks, trees, or telephone lines. If you are riding horseback, dismount and get away from your horse.

Trail Ridge Road reaches elevations (max. 12,183') dangerous to persons with heart conditions and other physical impairments. Even healthy persons are normally winded by the slightest exertion at these levels. Plan your activities accordingly.

Yucca House National Monument
Mesa Verde National Park, Colorado

MAILING ADDRESS: Yucca House National Monument, c/o Mesa Verde National Park, Mesa Verde National Park, Colorado 81330 **Telephone:** 303-529-4465

DIRECTIONS: NOT OPEN TO THE PUBLIC

Ruins of these large prehistoric Indian pueblos west of Mesa Verde are not yet excavated or open to the public. Created by Presidential Proclamation on Dec. 19, 1919.

VISITOR ACTIVITIES: No activities.

District of Columbia

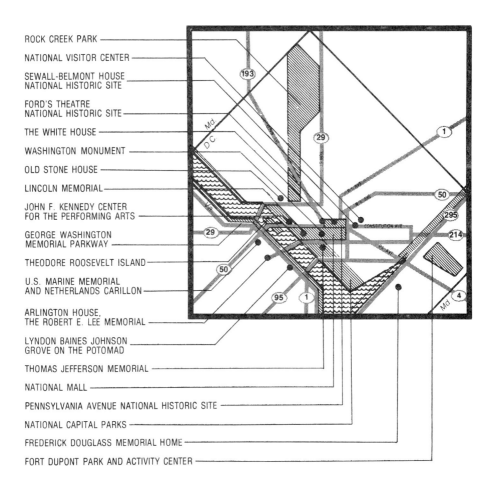

ROCK CREEK PARK

NATIONAL VISITOR CENTER

SEWALL-BELMONT HOUSE NATIONAL HISTORIC SITE

FORD'S THEATRE NATIONAL HISTORIC SITE

THE WHITE HOUSE

WASHINGTON MONUMENT

OLD STONE HOUSE

LINCOLN MEMORIAL

JOHN F. KENNEDY CENTER FOR THE PERFORMING ARTS

GEORGE WASHINGTON MEMORIAL PARKWAY

THEODORE ROOSEVELT ISLAND

U.S. MARINE MEMORIAL AND NETHERLANDS CARILLON

ARLINGTON HOUSE, THE ROBERT E. LEE MEMORIAL

LYNDON BAINES JOHNSON GROVE ON THE POTOMAD

THOMAS JEFFERSON MEMORIAL

NATIONAL MALL

PENNSYLVANIA AVENUE NATIONAL HISTORIC SITE

NATIONAL CAPITAL PARKS

FREDERICK DOUGLASS MEMORIAL HOME

FORT DUPONT PARK AND ACTIVITY CENTER

Ford's Theatre National Historic Site
Washington, D.C.

MAILING ADDRESS: Superintendent, Ford's Theatre National Historic Site, 511 Tenth Street, NW, Washington, DC 20004 **Telephone:** 202-426-6924

DIRECTIONS: The site is at 511 Tenth Street, NW in downtown Washington, DC. The Petersen House is directly across the street from Ford's, at 516 Tenth Street, NW. Both can be reached by subway to Metro Center and by other public transportation.

President Lincoln was shot while attending a play here on Apr. 14, 1865. He was carried across the street to the Petersen House, where he died the next morning. The Lincoln Museum at the theatre contains the Olroyd Collection of Lincolniana, and depicts various phases of Lincoln's life. Live performances and interpretive programs are given in the theatre, and visitors can walk through the Petersen House. Ford's Theatre was purchased by the Federal Government on April 14, 1865; Petersen House authorized for addition to the National Park System on June 11, 1896.

VISITOR ACTIVITIES: live performances, interpretive programs, walking tours; **Permits:** No; **Fees:** Tickets are required for live performances; **Visitor facilities:** restrooms and museum at Ford's, parking adjacent to the theatre; **Food and supplies obtainable nearby:** Yes, in Washington, D.C.; **Overnight accommodations:** Washington, DC; **First Aid available in park:** Yes; **Nearest Hospital:** Washington, DC; **Days/Hours:** Open daily from 9 a.m. to 5 p.m., the auditorium closes for matinees and rehearsals; **Holiday Closings:** Dec. 25.

GENERAL INFORMATION: For information on performances, call 202-347-4833.

Fort Dupont Park and Activity Center
Washington, D.C.

MAILING ADDRESS: Superintendent, Fort Dupont Park and Activity Center, Minnesota Avenue and Randle Circle, S.E. Washington, D.C. 20019 **Telephone:** 202-426-7723

DIRECTIONS: The Park is located just north of Alabama Ave. between Massachusetts Ave. Extension and Ridge Rd. S.W., at Randle Circle. It may be reached by heading east on Pennsylvania Avenue, crossing the Anacostia River and proceeding to the 2nd traffic light, Minnesota Ave. Turn left onto Minnesota; go 10 blocks to Randle Circle and follow signs.

The 375-acre Park is designed for many types of recreational and community activities. Authorized for addition to the National Park System in 1949.

VISITOR ACTIVITIES: basketball, arts and crafts programs, day camp, football, baseball, tennis, walking, ice skating, picnicking, guided talks, nature walks, film programs. summer concerts; **Permits:** Yes, for picnic areas, call 673-7647; **Fees:** None; **Visitor facilities:** basketball courts and football, baseball and soccer fields, year-round ice skating rink, picnic areas, Visitor Center, tennis courts, nature trails; **Any limitations on vehicle usage:** No; **Hiking trails:** Yes; **Backcountry:** No; **Camping:** No; **Other overnight accommodations on site:** No; **Meals served in the park:** No; **Food and supplies obtainable in the park:** No; **Food and supplies obtainable nearby:** Yes, in Washington; **Overnight accommodations:** Washington, D.C. or suburban Maryland; **Nearest Hos-**

pital: Greater Southeast Community Hospital; **Days/Hours:** Park open from dawn to dusk; Activity Center open Mon.-Fri. from 7:45 a.m. to 4:15 p.m.; **Holiday Closings:** Visitor Center closed on all holidays.

Frederick Douglass Memorial Home
Washington, D.C.

MAILING ADDRESS: Superintendent, Frederick Douglass Memorial Home, 1411 W Street, SE, Washington, D.C. 20020 **Telephone:** 202-889-1736

DIRECTIONS: The Home can be best reached by crossing the 11th Street (Anacostia) Bridge to Good Hope Road, turning left on Good Hope Road to 14th Street, and right on 14th Street to W Street. The Home is on top of the hill at 14th and W Streets, SE. Visitors arriving from the north or south on Int. 295 (Anacostia Freeway) should use the "Pennsylvania Avenue East" exit. Proceed east on Pennsylvania Avenue 2 blocks to Minnesota Avenue. Turn right on Minnesota to Good Hope Road. Turn right on Good Hope Road, proceed one-half block, and turn left on 14th Street. Public transportation is available to within a short distance of the site.

This was the home of the Nation's leading 19th-century Black spokesman from 1877 to 1895. He was U.S. minister to Haiti, 1889. Authorized for addition to the National Park System on Sept. 5, 1962.

VISITOR ACTIVITIES: self-guiding house tours, interpretive talks; **Permits:** No; **Fees:** No; **Visitor facilities:** parking area; **Any limitations on vehicle usage:** No; **Hiking trails:** No; **Meals served in the park:** No; **Food and supplies obtainable in the park:** No; **Food and supplies obtainable nearby:** Yes, in Washington, D.C.; **Overnight accommodations:** Washington D.C. or vicinity; **First Aid available in park:** Yes; **Nearest Hospital:** Washington (Southeast Community), Martin Luther King Jr. Ave. to South Capitol Street to Southern Ave., 8 km (5 miles); **Days/Hours:** Open daily from 9 a.m. to 4:15 p.m., until 5 p.m. from Apr. 1 through Aug. 31; **Holiday Closings:** Dec. 25.

GENERAL INFORMATION: *For Your Safety*—Be extra careful when climbing steps and walking on the hilly grounds.

John F. Kennedy Center for the Performing Arts
Washington, D.C.

MAILING ADDRESS: Superintendent, John F. Kennedy Center for the Performing Arts, Washington, DC 20566 **Telephone:** 202-254-3600

DIRECTIONS: The Center is at 2700 F Street, NW, overlooking the Potomac River.

The marble structure, designed by Edward Durell Stone, is the sole official memorial in Washington, DC to the 35th President. It culminates an interest in a National Cultural Center dating back to George Washington. The Center houses five auditoriums-the Opera House, the Concert Hall, the Eisenhower Theatre, and the rooftop Terrace Theatre-and the American Film Institute Theatre. Authorized for addition to the National Park System in 1972.

VISITOR ACTIVITIES: interpretive tours, exhibits, cultural events, rooftop talks;

Permits: No; **Fees:** Tickets are required for many of the cultural events held at the Center; **Visitor facilities:** restrooms, exhibits, restaurants, telephones; **Any limitations on vehicle usage:** Parking is available in a garage underneath the Center; **Meals served in the park:** Yes, restuarants are on the rooftop level; **Food and supplies obtainable in the park:** No; **Food and supplies obtainable nearby:** Yes, in Washington, DC; **Overnight accommodations:** Washington, DC or vicinity; **First Aid available in park:** Yes; **Nearest Hospital:** within .4 km (1/4 mile); **Days/Hours:** The building is open daily from 10 a.m. to midnight. Tours are given every day from 10:00 a.m. to 1:15 p.m.; **Holiday Closings:** No; **Visitor attractions closed for seasons:**No.

GENERAL INFORMATION: The Center is furnished with gifts from 30 foreign governments. Visitors should consult the Center's calendar of events for specific offerings.

Lincoln Memorial
Washington, D.C.

MAILING ADDRESS: Superintendent, Lincoln Memorial, National Capital Parks— Central, 900 Ohio Drive SW, Washington, DC 20242 **Telephone:** 202-426-6841

DIRECTIONS: The Memorial is in downtown Washington at the beginning of 23rd St., NW. From Virginia, follow Rte. 50 east to Washington and turn right on 23rd St. or take George Washington Parkway to Memorial Bridge.
  This classical structure contains Daniel Chester French's monumental sculpture of the 16th President of the United States. Lincoln's Gettysburg Address and Second Inaugural Address are carved on the marble walls. Authorized for addition to the National Park System on Feb. 9, 1911.

VISITOR ACTIVITIES: Interpretive tours are given daily from 8 a.m. to 11:30 p.m.; **Permits:** No; **Fees:** No; **Visitor facilities:** telephones and restrooms, parking on nearby Ohio Drive, handicapped elevator, drinking water, snack bar, bookstore, souvenir stand; **Any limitations on vehicle usage:** No; **Meals served in the park:** Yes, concessioner snack bar is 1 block east of the Memorial; **Food and supplies obtainable in the park:** No; **Food and supplies obtainable nearby:** Yes, in Washington, DC; **Overnight accommodations:** Washington, DC or vicinity; **First Aid available in park:** Yes; **Nearest Hospital:** George Washington University Hospital, 6 blocks from the Memorial; **Days/Hours:** Open daily from 8 a.m. to midnight all year; **Holiday Closings:** No interpretive talks on Dec. 25; **Weather:** Summer is hot and humid, with an average temperature of 88° and occasional thundershowers. Winter is mild, average temperature is 30°.

Lyndon Baines Johnson Memorial Grove on the Potomac
Washington, D.C.

MAILING ADDRESS: Superintendent, George Washington Memorial Parkway, Turkey Run Park, McLean, Virginia 22101 **Telephone:** 703-557-3635

DIRECTIONS: The Grove is in Lady Bird Johnson Park on the George Washington Memorial Parkway, west of I-95 and the 14th Street Bridge. Parking is at nearby Columbia Island Marina.
  A living memorial to the 36th President, the park overlooks the Potomac River,

providing a vista of the Capitol. The design features 500 white pines and engravings on Texas granite. Authorized for addition to the National Park System on Dec. 28, 1973.

VISITOR ACTIVITIES: picnicking, strolling, fishing; **Permits:** No; **Fees:** No; **Visitor facilities:** restrooms, water, picnic tables, parking area; **Any limitations on vehicle usage:** Vehicles are restricted to parking lots; **Hiking trails:** Yes, 1.6 km (1 mile) of woodland walkways; **Meals served in the park:** No, but nearby at Columbia Island Marina; **Food and supplies obtainable in the park:** No; **Food and supplies obtainable nearby:** Yes, in Washington, DC area; **Overnight accommodations:** Washington, DC and vicinity; **First Aid available in park:** No; **Nearest Hospital:** Arlington, VA; **Days/ Hours:** Open during daylight hours year-round; **Visitor attractions closed for seasons:** No; **Weather:** Hot, humid Summers.

National Capital Parks
Washington, D.C. (also in Maryland)

MAILING ADDRESS: National Capital Parks, 1100 Ohio Drive SW, Washington, DC 20242 **Telephone:** 202-426-6700

DIRECTIONS: For information about or directions to any of the more than 300 park units in the Washington metropolitan area, call 202-426-6700. For a recorded message of daily events in metropolitan Washington park areas, call 202-426-6975.

This park system in the Nation's Capital includes parks, parkways and reservations in the Washington metropolitan area, including such properties as the Battleground National Cemetery, the President's Parks (Lafayette Park north of the White House and the Ellipse south of the White House), the parks flanking the Great Falls of the Potomac, and a variety of military fortifications and greenswards. Authorized for addition to the National Park System on Aug. 10, 1933.

National Mall
Washington, D.C.

MAILING ADDRESS: National Mall, c/o National Capital Region, 1100 Ohio Drive SW, Washingon, DC 20242 **Telephone:** 202-426-6842

DIRECTIONS: For general information on the Mall, call the management office at 202-426-6842.

Rows of stately elms mark the sweep of the greensward from the U.S. Capitol to the Washington Monument, a key feature of Pierre Charles L'Enfant's plan for the city of Washington in 1790. The Mall today includes many buildings of the Smithsonian Institution. For further information on the Smithsonian, contact: Information and Reception Center, Smithsonian Institution, Washington, D.C. 20560, phone 202-381-6264. The "Mall area" as distinguished from the "Mall" includes, for management purposes, the major memorials (Washington, Jefferson, and Lincoln), Constitution Gardens and the Sylvan Theater, the President's Parks (the Ellipse, the White House and Lafayette Park), West Potomac Park (including the Reflecting Pool, the polo field and the site of the Folklife Festivals) and the Tidal Basin. (The memorials and the White House are described separately in this book.)

National Visitor Center
Washington, D.C.

MAILING ADDRESS: National Visitor Center, 50 Massachusetts Ave., NE, Washington, D.C. 20002 **Telephone:** 202-523-5300

DIRECTIONS: The Center is located in the restored Union Station, one block off North Capitol Street, across from the Capitol. It is served by bus, subway, and tourmobile service.

The National Visitor Center is the best place to begin your visit to Washington, DC. You can obtain maps and information about the city's many memorials, galleries, museums, government buildings, special events, etc.

VISITOR ACTIVITIES: interpretive exhibits, information services; **Permits:** No; **Fees:** No; **Visitor facilities:** bookstore, souvenir stand, restrooms, information desk, fast-food restaurant, public telephones, restrooms, Traveler's Aid, gift shop; **Any limitations on vehicle usage:** No; **Meals served in the park:** Yes, at a cafeteria in the Gallery section; **Food and supplies obtainable in the park:** No; **Food and supplies obtainable nearby:** Yes, in Washington, DC; **Overnight accommodations:** Washington, DC; **First Aid available in park:** Yes; **Nearest Hospital:** Capitol Hill Hospital, Massachusetts Ave., NE, 7 blocks; **Days/Hours:** Information services are available from 9:30-5:30, 7 days a week. No services are offered on Dec. 25 and Jan. 1.

Old Stone House
Washington, D.C.

MAILING ADDRESS: Old Stone House, 3051 M Street, N.W., Washington, D.C. 20007 **Telephone:** 202-426-6851

DIRECTIONS: The house is located at 3051 M Street, N.W. in Georgetown.

Built in 1765, Old Stone House is a fine example of pre-Revolutionary architecture, and the oldest existing house in the Nation's Capital. Administered by the National Park Service since 1953.

VISITOR ACTIVITIES: guided and self-guiding tours, living history demonstrations, interpretive exhibits, walking through the garden, candlelight evening program with 18th century music on the second Wednesday of each month; **Permits:** No; **Fees:** No; **Visitor facilities:** None; **Any limitations on vehicle usage:** Only commercial or on-street parking is available; **Hiking trails:** No; **Meals served in the park:** No; **Food and supplies obtainable in the park:** No; **Food and supplies obtainable nearby:** Yes, Georgetown or Washington, D.C.; **Overnight accommodations:** within several blocks or anywhere in metropolitan Washington; **First Aid available in park:** Yes; **Nearest Hospital:** Washington, D.C., Pennsylvania Ave., 8 blocks; **Days/Hours:** Open daily from 9:30 a.m. to 5 p.m. Closed on Monday and Tuesday from Jan. through Mar.; **Holiday Closings:** Thanksgiving, Dec. 25 & Jan. 1.

Pennsylvania Avenue National Historic Site
Washington, D.C.

MAILING ADDRESS: Pennsylvania Avenue Development Corporation, Suite 1148, 425 13th Street N.W., Washington, D.C. 20004 **Telephone:** 202-566-1218

DIRECTIONS: The Site includes the architecturally and historically significant area between the Capitol and The White House in Washington, D.C.

The Site includes a portion of Pennsylvania Avenue and the area adjacent to it between the Capitol and the White House encompassing Ford's Theatre National Historic Site, several blocks of the Washington commercial district, and a number of Federal structures. Existing park areas are listed separately in this book. Designated Sept. 30, 1965.

VISITOR ACTIVITIES: walking tours, theatrical performances, shopping, tours of the National Archives, FBI, and National Collection of Fine Arts buildings; **Permits:** No; **Fees:** Only for admission to events at the National Theatre and Ford's Theatre; **Visitor facilities:** museums, theatres, stores, restaurants, lodging; **Any limitations on vehicle usage:** No; **Meals served in the park:** Yes, there are numerous restaurants in the downtown area; **Food and supplies obtainable in the park:** Yes, a grocery store at 12th and F Streets, N.W.; **Food and supplies obtainable nearby:** Yes, Washington and vicinity; **Overnight accommodations:** Washington and vicinity; **First Aid available in park:** Yes, at museums and theatres within the Historic Site; **Nearest Hospital:** George Washington University Hospital, 23rd and Pennsylvania Ave., N.W.; **Days/Hours:** Site always open; **Visitor attractions closed for seasons:** No.

GENERAL INFORMATION: Architour, a non-profit educational organization, is offering regularly scheduled architectural tours of the Pennsylvania Avenue National Historic Site. For information, call 202-223-2472.

Rock Creek Park
Washington, D.C.

MAILING ADDRESS: Superintendent, Rock Creek Park, 5000 Glover Road, N.W. Washington, D.C. 20015 **Telephone:** 202-426-6834

DIRECTIONS: The Nature (Visitor) Center is located south of Military Road and Oregon Avenue at 5200 Glover Road, N.W., Washington, D.C.

One of the largest urban parks in the world, this wooded preserve contains a wide range of natural, historical, cultural, and recreational resources in the midst of metropolitan Washington, D.C. Authorized for addition to the National Park System on Sept. 27, 1890.

VISITOR ACTIVITIES: Nature walks and hikes, horseback riding, picnicking, planetarium, golf, tennis, volleyball, football, baseball, softball, horseshoes, running, and jogging; **Permits:** Required for large picnic areas. To reserve call D.C. Recreation Dept.: 202-673-7647; **Fees:** For rental horses, golf and tennis. Rock Creek Horse Centre, near the Nature Center on Glover Road, offers rental horses and riding instruction. There is a greens fee for golf and a fee for soft tennis courts; **Visitor facilities:** Nature Center and planetarium, hiking trails, horse trails, picnic groves, art barn, tennis courts, amphitheater for summer events, golf course, and facilities for football, baseball, softball, volleyball, horseshoes, jogging, and exercise trail; **Any limitations on vehicle usage:** Vehicles must stay on roads and park in designated areas; **Hiking trails:** Yes, there are about 35 km (20 miles) of trails, with footbridges across Rock Creek. Hikers may also use bridle trails; **Backcountry:** No; **Camping:** No; **Other overnight accommodations on site:** No; **Meals served in the park:** Yes, snacks are available at the golf and tennis courts; **Food and supplies obtainable in the park:** No; **Food and supplies obtainable nearby:** Yes, in Washington, D.C.; **Overnight accommodations:** Washington and vicinity; **First Aid available in park:** Yes, or obtain local assistance by telephoning 911; **Nearest Hospital:** Washington-George Washington Univ. Hosp.; **Days/Hours:** Open dawn to dusk. Parking areas close at dark. No overnight camping or parking allowed. Peirce Mill and Art Barn are closed on Monday and Tuesday; **Holiday Closings:** Nature Center, Peirce Mill, and Art Barn are closed on holidays; **Visitor attractions closed for seasons:**None.

GENERAL INFORMATION: Wading, swimming, and fishing are not recommended in Rock Creek Park or its tributaries because of polluted water. Trails can be slippery.

Sewall-Belmont House National Historic Site
Washington, D.C.

MAILING ADDRESS: Superintendent, Sewall-Belmont House National Historic Site, 144 Constitution Ave., N.E., Washington, D.C. 20002 **Telephone:** 202-546-1210

DIRECTIONS: The house is located near the U.S. Capitol at 144 Constitution Ave., N.E.

Rebuilt after fire damage from the War of 1812, this red brick house is one of the oldest on Capitol Hill. It has been the National Woman's Party headquarters since 1929 and commemorates the party's founder and suffrage leader, Alice Paul, and associates. Authorized for addition to the National Park System on Oct. 26, 1974.

VISITOR ACTIVITIES: guided tours, exhibits; **Permits:** No; **Fees:** No; **Visitor facilities:** memorabilia of suffrage including busts and portraits of suffrage leaders and valuable antique furniture, garden; **Any limitations on vehicle usage:** On-street parking can be scarce; **Meals served in the park:** No; **Food and supplies obtainable in the park:** No; **Food and supplies obtainable nearby:** Yes, in Washington, D.C.; **Overnight accommodations:** Washington, D.C.; **First Aid available in park:** No; **Nearest Hospital:** Capitol Hill Hospital, 7 blocks; **Days/Hours:** Guided tours offered from 10 a.m. to 2 p.m. on weekdays and from noon to 4 p.m. on weekends and holidays; **Holiday Closings:** Thanksgiving, Dec. 25 & Jan. 1; **Visitor attractions closed for seasons:** None.

Theodore Roosevelt Island
Washington, D.C.

MAILING ADDRESS: Superintendent, George Washington Memorial Parkway, Turkey Run Park, McLean, Virginia 22101 **Telephone:** 703-426-6922

DIRECTIONS: The parking area is accessible from the northbound lane of the George Washington Memorial Parkway, Virginia side of the Potomac River. A bridge connects the Island to the Virginia shore.

Wooded trails lead to an imposing statue and memorial to Roosevelt, the 26th President, on this island sanctuary in the Potomac River. Authorized for addition to the National Park System on May 21, 1932.

VISITOR ACTIVITIES: guided tours, hiking, fishing, wayside exhibits; **Permits:** No; **Fees:** No; **Visitor facilities:** restrooms, first aid, drinking water, hiking trails; **Any limitations on vehicle usage:** No vehicles are permitted on the Island; **Hiking trails:** Yes, 4 km (2-1/2 miles) of wooded trails; **Backcountry:** No; **Camping:** No; **Other overnight accommodations on site:** No; **Meals served in the park:** No; **Food and supplies obtainable in the park:** No; **Food and supplies obtainable nearby:** Yes, Arlington, VA or the Washington area; **Overnight accommodations:** Arlington, VA or the Washington metropolitan area; **First Aid available in park:** Yes; **Nearest Hospital:** Arlington, VA or Washington, D.C.; **Days/Hours:** Open year-round during daylight hours; **Holiday Closings:** None; **Visitor attractions closed for seasons:**None; **Weather:** Hot, humid Summers.

Thomas Jefferson Memorial
Washington, D.C.

MAILING ADDRESS: Superintendent, National Capital Parks—Central, 900 Ohio Drive SW, Washington, D.C. 20242 **Telephone:** 202-426-6841

DIRECTIONS: The Memorial is on the south bank of the Tidal Basin, near downtown Washington. From Virginia, take the George Washington Parkway to Memorial Bridge, cross the bridge and follow Ohio Drive to the Memorial.
  The circular, colonnaded Memorial to the 3rd President of the United States contains a bronze statue and is surrounded by Japanese cherry trees. Dedicated May 13, 1943.

VISITOR ACTIVITIES: guided talks by Park Rangers, paddle boating on the Tidal Basin, Cherry Blossom Festival about the first week of April, military band performances in Summer; **Permits:** No; **Fees:** Only for paddle boat rentals; **Visitor facilities:** parking, handicapped parking, paddle boat rentals, telephones, restrooms, drinking water; **Any limitations on vehicle usage:** No; **Meals served in the park:** No; **Food and supplies obtainable in the park:** No; **Food and supplies obtainable nearby:** Yes, in Washington, D.C. and vicinity; **Overnight accommodations:** Washington and vicinity; **First Aid available in park:** Yes; **Nearest Hospital:** 8 blocks from the Memorial; **Days/Hours:** Open 7 days a week from 8 a.m. to Midnight year-round; **Holiday Closings:** No interpretive talks offered on Dec. 25; **Visitor attractions closed for seasons:**No.

Washington Monument
Washington, D.C.

MAILING ADDRESS: Superintendent, Washington Monument, c/o National Park Service, 900 Ohio Drive SW, Washington, DC 20242 **Telephone:** 202-426-6841

DIRECTIONS: The Monument is located on the National Mall between 15th and 17th Streets and Independence and Constitution Avenues. From Virginia follow Rte. 50 east or Int. 395 north to Washington.
  This 555-foot (169 m) obelisk honors the country's first President and is a dominant feature of the Nation's Capital. Construction began in 1848, and the Monument was dedicated on Feb. 12, 1885.

VISITOR ACTIVITIES: Visitors can ascend to the top by elevator and view the city through eight windows; **Permits:** No; **Fees:** Yes, 10¢ elevator fee; **Visitor Facilities:** restrooms, snack bar, parking lot, handicapped parking spaces, information booths; **Any limitations on vehicle usage:** Parking is limited to 1 hour; **Hiking trails:** No, but the

Mall is suitable for short and long walks; **Meals served in the park:** Yes, at concession stand located on 15th St.; **Food and supplies obtainable in the park:** No; **Food and supplies obtainable nearby:** Yes, in downtown Washington or the metropolitan area; **Overnight accommodations:** Washington or the metropolitan area; **First Aid available in park:** Yes, or nearby in Washington; **Nearest Hospital:** 6 blocks from the Monument; **Days/Hours:** Open daily from 9 a.m. to 5 p.m. from Oct.-Apr. and 8 a.m. to Midnight from May through Sept.; **Holiday Closings:** Dec. 25; **Visitor attractions closed for seasons:**No; **Weather:** Summers are hot; average temperature 88°F, with very high humidity and occasional thunderstorms. Winter is mild, with average temperatures of 30° and some snow.

GENERAL INFORMATION: In Summer, entrance to the Monument is by timed reservation tickets, which are distributed at the information booths on the Monument grounds, starting at 8 a.m. Arrive early to arrange for the time you want to ascend. Tickets are not required from 4 p.m. to Midnight but waiting times can reach 2 hours.

The White House
Washington, D.C.

MAILING ADDRESS: Director, Office of Visitor Services, The White House, 1600 Pennsylvania Ave., NW, Washington, D.C. 20500 **Telephone:** 202-456-7041

DIRECTIONS: The White House is at 1600 Pennsylvania Ave., NW in downtown Washington. Visitors should use the East Gate, on East Executive Ave., to enter for tours
     The White House has been the official residence of every American President since November, 1800. The cornerstone was laid on Oct. 13, 1792 on the site selected by George Washington and included in the L'Enfant Plan. The building was renovated between 1949-52. Administration transferred to the National Park Service on Aug. 10, 1943.

VISITOR ACTIVITIES: free public tours, Easter Egg Roll on Easter Monday, Spring and Fall Garden Tours, Candlelight Tours in late December; **Permits:** No; **Fees:** No admission is ever charged. Beware of people selling White House Tours; **Visitor facilities:** "Congressional Tours" are given at 8 a.m. on Tuesdays through Saturdays. Visitors taking these tours do not have to stand in line and can see two rooms that are not included on the regular White House Tours. Tickets are required: obtain them from your Senator's or Representative's office. Tickets are required in Summer for regular White House Tours. A Visitor Waiting Area is set up on the Ellipse, the park area south of the White House grounds. Tickets for the tour will be distributed beginning at 8 a.m. each day. Visitors should proceed directly to the Ellipse when they first arrive rather than going to the East Gate. Each person wishing to tour the White House must pick up his or her own ticket. Tickets are available the day of the tour only. After picking up a ticket, the visitor may leave the park to visit other attractions, or may choose to remain on the Ellipse to view the entertainment that is provided. Covered bleachers are available for seating. At the scheduled time of the tour, visitors will be escorted to the White House by an officer of the National Park Service; **Meals served in the park:** No; **Food and supplies obtainable in the park:** No; **Food and supplies obtainable nearby:** Yes, in Washington, within several blocks; **Overnight accommodations:** Washington, D.C.; **First Aid available in park:** On the Ellipse; **Nearest Hospitals:** George Washington University Hospital, 23rd Streeet, N.W.; **Visitor attractions closed for seasons:**No.

GENERAL INFORMATION: More detailed information about The White House may be found in "The White House, An Historic Guide," "The Living White House," "The Presidents," and "First Ladies of The White House," published by The White House Historical Association, 5026 New Executive Office Building, 726 Jackson Place NW, Washington, DC 20506, phone 202-737-8292.

Florida

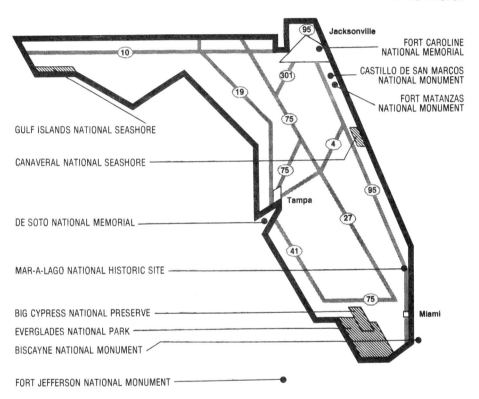

GULF ISLANDS NATIONAL SEASHORE

CANAVERAL NATIONAL SEASHORE

DE SOTO NATIONAL MEMORIAL

MAR-A-LAGO NATIONAL HISTORIC SITE

BIG CYPRESS NATIONAL PRESERVE

EVERGLADES NATIONAL PARK

BISCAYNE NATIONAL MONUMENT

FORT JEFFERSON NATIONAL MONUMENT

Jacksonville

FORT CAROLINE NATIONAL MEMORIAL

CASTILLO DE SAN MARCOS NATIONAL MONUMENT

FORT MATANZAS NATIONAL MONUMENT

Tampa

Miami

Big Cypress National Preserve
Naples, Florida

MAILING ADDRESS: Park Manager, Big Cypress National Preserve, P.O. Box 1247, Naples, Florida 33939 **Telephone:** 813-262-1066

DIRECTIONS: The Park Manager's Office (Preserve Headquarters) is in Central Building, 850 Central Ave., Room 304, Naples, FL. The west boundary of the Preserve is 48 km (30 miles) from Naples, via US 41 and Alligator Alley. The east boundary is 48 km (30 miles) from Miami, FL.

The Preserve comprises 570,000 acres of watershed which provide a natural freshwater supply to the northwest portion of Everglades National Park. It is the ancestral home of the Seminole and Miccosukee Indians, and contains abundant subtropical plant and animal life. Authorized for addition to the National Park System on Oct. 11, 1974.

VISITOR ACTIVITIES: camping, hiking, backpacking, swimming, picnicking, sightseeing, canoeing, boating (small watercraft), fishing, hunting; **Permits:** for hunting and fishing from the Florida Game and Fresh Water Fish Comm.,Tallahassee, FL 32304, phone 904-488-4066; **Fees:** for fresh water fishing; for more information, write: Florida Game and Fish Commission, Tallahasse, FL 32304. Licenses vary in cost and in length of validity; **Visitor facilities:** The only facility is Oasis Ranger Station, the field operational base. Staff is available from 8 a.m.-4:30 p.m. daily; **Any limitations on vehicle usage:** Off-road vehicle use is restricted; **Hiking trails:** Yes, developed hiking trails are located on private lands; **Backcountry:** Yes, information available from Florida Trail Association, P.O. Box 13708, Gainesville, FL 32604; **Camping:** No, camping facilities are at Collier Seminole State Park and Everglades National Park, and at privately owned campgrounds in the vicinity; **Other overnight accommodations on site:** No; **Meals served in the park:** No; **Food and supplies obtainable in the park:** Yes, along US 41; **Food and supplies obtainable nearby:** Yes, in Miami and Naples; **Overnight accommodations:** Ochopee, FL, 32 km (20 miles) from Oasis Ranger Station: Miami and Naples, approx. 80 km (50 miles) from Oasis Ranger Station; All nearby areas are on US 41; **First Aid available in park:** Yes, at Oasis Ranger Station; **Nearest Hospital:** Naples Community Hospital, US 41 west, approx. 93 km (58 miles) from the Oasis Ranger Station; **Days/Hours:** Open year-round; **Holiday Closings:** No; **Visitor attractions closed for seasons:**No.

Biscayne National Monument
Homestead, Florida

MAILING ADDRESS: Superintendent, Biscayne National Monument, P.O. Box 1369, Homestead, Florida 33030 **Telephone:** 305-247-2044

DIRECTIONS: Because no public boat transportation is provided, you must either have your own boat or a hired boat to explore the keys and to swim and dive. You should stop at Park Headquarters on Convoy Point, 14.5 km (9 miles) east of Homestead, or at the Ranger Station on Elliott Key. Park personnel can answer your questions and help you plan your visit.

Most of the park is reef and water, but within its boundaries about 25 keys, or islands, form a north-south chain, with Biscayne Bay on the West and the Atlantic Ocean on the east. The Monument contains a significant example of living coral reef. Most of the shoreline on both mainland and keys is exposed, rough coral rock. Authorized for addition to the National Park System on Oct. 18, 1968.

VISITOR ACTIVITIES: boating, fishing, swimming, snorkeling, scuba diving, camping, picnicking, hiking, interpretive exhibits, bird-watching; **Permits:** fire permits can be obtained from a Park Ranger; **Fees:** No; **Visitor facilities:** At Elliott Key Harbor Ranger Station, primitive campground, picnic area, interpretive trail, restrooms, and saltwater showers. Gasoline is not available at the Monument but it can be obtained near the Headquarters at Homestead Bayfront Park. *Fresh Water is not available.* Meals, lodging, campgrounds, gasoline, and other supplies are available in Homestead. Many well-supplied marinas are located along the mainland coast and in the Florida Keys.

Check your charts or ask a Park Ranger; **Any limitations on vehicle usage:** Be familiar with boating rules. Obtain a copy of them at Headquarters or the Ranger Station; **Hiking trails:** No; **Backcountry:** No; **Camping:** Yes, no reservations for campsites; **Other overnight accommodations on site:** No; **Meals served in the park:** No; **Food and supplies obtainable in the park:** No; **Food and supplies obtainable nearby:** Yes, limited food and supplies at Homestead Bayfront Park; **Overnight accommodations:** Homestead, US 1, 16 km (10 miles); **First Aid available in park:**Yes, at Elliott Key Ranger Station; **Nearest Hospital:** Homestead, US 1, 24 km (15 miles); **Days/Hours:** Open 24 hours a day, 365 days per year; **Holiday Closings:** None; **Visitor attractions closed for seasons:**None; **Weather:** Summers are humid with frequent rain, Winters are cool and clear.

GENERAL INFORMATION: Be sure to read the safety precautions published in the pamphlet on Biscayne available from Headquarters or the Ranger Station. Nearby points of interest include Everglades National Park (see listing in this book) and John Pennekamp Coral Reef State Park.

Canaveral National Seashore
Titusville, Florida

MAILING ADDRESS: Superintendent, Canaveral National Seashore, P.O. Box 2583, Titusville, Florida 32780 **Telephone:** 305-867-4675

DIRECTIONS: Located midway down the Florida east coast between Jacksonville and West Palm Beach, theSeashore is readily accessible via such major arteries as US 1 and Int. I-95, I-4, and I-75. New Smyrna Beach provides access via FL A1A into the Seashore in the vicinity of Turtle Mound, a shell midden made by pre-Hispanic Indians. Titusville, the southern Gateway City, provides access via FL 402. Playalinda Beach on the Seashore's southern end is now the principal visitor use area. It is accessible via FL 402 from Titusville and FL 3, which cuts off to the south from U.S. 1 between Titusville and Oak Hill. In addition, the Intercoastal Waterway linking Florida with the north skirts the western edge of Mosquito Lagoon before entering the Indian River via the Haulover Canal.
    The Seashore offers a great variety of wildlife, including many species of birds, on a segment of largely undeveloped lands. The area includes a portion of the 140,393-acre Merritt Island National Wildlife Refuge, administered by Fish and Wildlife Service, U.S. Dept. of the Interior. Established by act of Congress Jan 3, 1975.

VISITOR ACTIVITIES: bird-watching, boating, swimming, surfing, sun bathing, shell collecting, surf fishing, wildlife observation, photography, wildland hiking, waterfowl hunting, picnicking, walking; **Permits:** No, but hunting in season is subject to U.S. Fish and Wildlife Service state regulations; **Fees:** No; **Visitor facilities:** exhibits, parking, restrooms at Headquarters on FL 402, portable toilets at beaches, picnic tables, walking trail; **Any limitations on vehicle usage:** Vehicles are restricted to established roads and are prohibited on the beach; **Hiking trails:** Yes, Turtle Mound, .4 km (1/4 mile), self-guiding; **Backcountry:** day use only, information can be obtained by contacting the Seashore Headquarters; **Camping:** No; **Other overnight accommodations on site:** No; there are private campgrounds in nearby communities; **Meals served in the park:** No; **Food and supplies obtainable in the park:** Yes; **Food and supplies obtainable nearby:** Yes, at Titusville, 20 km (12 miles); New Smyrna Beach 16 km (10 miles); **Overnight accommodations:** Titusville, 20 km (12 miles); New Smyrna Beach, 16 km (10 miles);

First Aid available in park: limited; **Nearest Hospital:** Titusville, 20 km (12 miles); New Smyrna Beach, 16 km (10 miles); **Days/Hours:** Open 6:30 a.m.-sunset, 7 days a week; **Holiday Closings:** None; **Visitor attractions closed for seasons:**No; **Weather:** The climate is sub-tropical, with short, mild Winters and hot, humid Summers. Ocean temperatures remain relatively warm all year.

GENERAL INFORMATION: Swimming can be dangerous due to strong ocean currents. *For Your Safety,* swim in protected areas. Visitors to inland areas away from the influence of off-shore breezes should carry a repellent to protect themselves from mosquitoes and other biting insects.

Castillo de San Marcos National Monument
St. Augustine, Florida

MAILING ADDRESS: Superintendent, Castillo de San Marcos National Monument, 1 Castillo Drive, St. Augustine, Florida 32084 **Telephone:** 904-829-6506

DIRECTIONS: The Monument is at 1 Castillo Drive in downtown St. Augustine.
   Construction of the oldest masonry fort in the continental United States was started in 1672 by the Spanish to protect St. Augustine, the first permanent settlement by Europeans in the continental United States (1565). Created by Presidential Proclamation on Oct. 15, 1924.

VISITOR ACTIVITIES: interpretive exhibits, guided tours, living history demonstrations, self-guiding tours; **Permits:** No; **Fees:** 50¢ per person entrance fee for those 16 and older. Golden Age and Golden Eagle Passports accepted and available; **Visitor facilities:** parking, restrooms; **Any limitations on vehicle usage:** No; **Hiking trails:** No; **Meals served in the park:** No; **Food and supplies obtainable in the park:** No; **Food and supplies obtainable nearby:** Yes, adjacent to the park in St. Augustine; **Overnight accommodations:** St. Augustine; **First Aid available in park:** Yes; **Nearest Hospital:** 2 major hospitals in St. Augustine; **Days/Hours:** 8:30 a.m.-5:30 p.m. daily; **Holiday Closings:** Dec. 25.

GENERAL INFORMATION: *For Your Safety*-Watch out for rough and uneven floors, fragile walls, and steep drops.

DeSoto National Memorial
Bradenton, Florida

MAILING ADDRESS: Superintendent, DeSoto National Memorial, 75th Street NW, Bradenton, Florida 33505 **Telephone:** 813-792-0458

DIRECTIONS: The Park is on Tampa Bay 8 km (5 miles) west of Bradenton, FL, on 75th Street, NW.
   The landing of Spanish explorer Hernando de Soto in Florida in 1539 and the first extensive organized exploration of what is now the southern United States by Europeans are commemorated here. Authorized for addition to the National Park System on Mar. 11, 1948.

VISITOR ACTIVITIES: interpretive film, exhibit, and trail; fishing; living history demonstration in season; **Permits:** No; **Fees:** No; **Visitor facilities:** parking and restrooms at Visitor Center; **Any limitations on vehicle usage:** No vehicles allowed on the trails or outside the parking area; **Hiking trails:** Yes, an .8 km (1/2 mile) nature trail; **Backcountry:** No; **Camping:** No; **Other overnight accommodations on site:** No; **Meals served in the park:** No; **Food and supplies obtainable in the park:** No; **Food and supplies obtainable nearby:** Yes; in Bradenton; **Overnight accommodations:** Bradenton; Palmetto 16 km (10 miles); **First Aid available in park:** Yes; **Nearest Hospital:** Bradenton, 59th Street, 8 km (5 miles); **Days/Hours:** Open daily from 8 a.m. to 5 p.m.; **Holiday Closings:** Dec. 25; **Visitor attractions closed for seasons:**Living history program closed from Apr.—May and Sept.—Nov.; **Weather:** Temperatures are in the high 90°s F in Summer, with high humidity. Winters are characterized by strong, cold winds and high humidity.

Everglades National Park
Homestead, Florida

MAILING ADDRESS: Superintendent, Everglades National Park, P.O. Box 279, Homestead, Florida 33030 **Telephone:** 305-247-6211

DIRECTIONS: The main Visitor Center is near the park entrance, 20 km (12 miles) southwest of Homestead on FL 27. Other Visitor Centers are at Royal Palm, Flamingo, and Everglades City.
  This largest remaining subtropical wilderness in the conterminous United States has extensive fresh- and salt-water areas, open prairies, and mangrove forests. Abundant wildlife includes rare birds. Park dedicated on Dec. 6, 1947.

VISITOR ACTIVITIES: boating, camping, picnicking, wildlife- and bird-watching, photography, hiking, interpretive talks and exhibits, fishing, backcountry, canoeing, open-air tram and sightseeing boat rides; **Permits:** Florida fishing license, available at local bait and tackle shops, is required. Licenses vary in length of validity and cost. Free backcountry permits available at Key Largo, Everglades City and Flamingo Ranger Stations; **Fees:** $2 per vehicle entrance fee; 50¢ per person on commercial vehicles, hikers and bikers. Overnight camping in developed sites is $3 per night from Nov. 1-Apr. 30; free the remainder of the year. Shark Valley Tram fee is $2 per person; $1 for children 15 and under and persons 62 and over. Golden Age and Golden Eagle Passports accepted and available; **Visitor facilities:** bookstore, parking, restrooms, and telephones at Visitor Center, boat rentals and ramp, marina, nature trails, cafeteria, campgrounds, picnic areas, environmental study area, restaurant, house boat rentals; **Any limitations on vehicle usage:** Airboats and glades buggies are not permitted in the Park. No private vehicles permitted on Shark Valley Road; all vehicles restricted to designated roadways; **Hiking trails:** Yes, many short trails lead from the road to Flamingo; **Backcountry:** Yes, required permit available from Ranger Stations or Park Headquarters. Insect repellent is needed on all backcountry trails throughout the year; **Camping:** Yes, individual campsites cannot be reserved. Group campsites can be reserved by contacting Park Headquarters; **Other overnight accommodations on site:** Yes, there is a motor lodge at Flamingo. Reservations should be made well in advance to The Everglades Park Catering, Flamingo Lodge, Flamingo, FL 33030; 24-hour phone 813-695-3101. Additional camping near Everglades City can be found at Copeland, 11 km (7 miles) north on FL 29, and at Collier-Seminole State Park, 30.5 km (19 miles) west on US 41; **Meals served in the park:** Yes, at Flamingo; **Food and supplies obtainable in the park:** Yes, at Flamingo marina;

Food and supplies obtainable nearby: Yes, at Homestead, Key Largo, Everglades City; **Overnight accommodations:** Homestead/Florida City, 19.3 km (12 miles); Florida Keys, 64.4 km (40 miles); Everglades City, 144.8 km (90 miles); **First Aid available in park:** Yes, at Ranger Stations; **Nearest Hospital:** Homestead, 77 km (48 miles) from Flamingo; **Days/Hours:** Open 24 hours a day year-round; **Holiday Closings:** None; **Visitor attractions closed for seasons:** Shark Valley tram service is not available in Sept. and Oct., although high water in the area may force longer closing; **Weather:** Winters are dry and clear; Summers are rainy with torrential local downpours and lightning storms. Temperatures range in the 80's and 90's during the Summer and on rare occasions drop to the 30's in Winter.

GENERAL INFORMATION: Rates for overnight accommodations are considerably higher throughout South Florida during the winter season (Dec. 15-Apr. 15.) Mosquitoes and other biting insects make camping and backcountry use during the rainy season virtually unbearable by all but the most dedicated outdoorsperson.

Fort Caroline National Memorial
Jacksonville, Florida

MAILING ADDRESS: Superintendent, Fort Caroline National Memorial, 12713 Fort Caroline Road, Jacksonville, Florida 32225 **Telephone:** 904-641-7155

DIRECTIONS: The Memorial is about 16 km (10 miles) east of Jacksonville, and 8 km (5 miles) west of Mayport. It can be reached by FL 10: turn off on the St. Johns Bluff Road or Monument Road, then proceed east on Fort Caroline Road.

The fort overlooks the site of a French Huguenot colony of 1564-65, the second French attempt at settlement within the present United States. The French and Spanish began two centuries of European colonial rivalry in North America here. Authorized for addition to the National Park System on Sept. 21, 1950.

VISITOR ACTIVITIES: interpretive exhibits, walking tours, picnicking; **Permits:** No; **Fees:** No; **Visitor facilities:** Visitor Center, restrooms, picnic area, walking trails; **Any limitations on vehicle usage:** No; **Hiking trails:** Yes, three trails; the longest is 1.6 km (1 mile); **Backcountry:** No; **Camping:** No; **Other overnight accommodations on site:** No; **Meals served in the park:** No; **Food and supplies obtainable in the park:** No; **Food and supplies obtainable nearby:** Yes, in Jacksonville and Mayport; **Overnight accommodations:** Jacksonville, FL 10, 16 km (10 miles) and Mayport FL10, 8 km (5 miles); **First Aid available in park:** Yes; **Nearest Hospital:** Jacksonville, 19 km (12 miles); **Days/Hours:** 8:30 a.m. to 5 p.m. daily; 8:30 a.m. to 6 p.m. in Summer; **Holiday Closings:** Dec. 25 and Jan. 1.

GENERAL INFORMATION: The proximity of the river to the Fort requires additional caution. Summer visitors are advised to bring mosquito repellent.

Fort Jefferson National Monument
112 km (70 miles) west of Key West, Florida

MAILING ADDRESS: Superintendent, Everglades National Park, P.O. Box 279, Homestead, Florida 33030 **Telephone:** 305-247-6211

DIRECTIONS: The Monument can only be reached by boat or seaplane. Several operators of charter boat and air taxi services offer trips to the Dry Tortugas from Key West, Sugar Loaf Key, Marathon, and Naples. Specific information regarding these services may be obtained from the Chambers of Commerce located at: 3330 Overseas Highway, Marathon, FL 33052, phone 305-743-5417; Old Mallory Square, Key West, FL 33040, phone 305-294-2587; and 1700 N. Tamiami Trail, Naples, FL 33940, 813-262-6141.

Built in 1856 to help control the Florida Straits, this is the largest all-masonry fortification in the Western world. It is the central feature of the seven Dry Tortugas Islands and the surrounding shoals and waters of the Gulf of Mexico, some 75 square miles that make up the National Monument. It is famous for its birds and marine life. Created by Presidential Proclamation on Jan 4, 1935.

VISITOR ACTIVITIES: interpretive exhibits, self-guiding tours, bird and wildlife-watching, picnicking, salt-water sport fishing, snorkeling, swimming, and scuba diving; **Permits:** No; **Fees:** No; **Visitor facilities:** exhibit area, picnic area, restrooms; **Any limitations on vehicle usage:** the island is roadless; **Hiking trails:** No; **Backcountry:** No; **Camping:** Yes, no reservations are available for the 5 group sites, which are at Garden Key at Fort Jefferson; **Other overnight accommodations on site:** No; **Meals served in the park:** No; **Food and supplies obtainable in the park:** No; **Food and supplies obtainable nearby:** obtain supplies at Key West, 112 km (70 miles) by water; **Overnight accommodations:** Key West, 112 km (70 miles) by water; **First Aid available in park:** Yes; **Nearest Hospital:** Key West, 112 km (70 miles) by water; **Days/Hours:** Open daily from sunrise to sunset year-round; **Holiday Closings:** None; **Visitor attractions closed for seasons:**Bush Key is closed to visitors from April to the last part of September; **Weather:** Weather is generally sunny and warm. Occasional squalls are common, however, so visitors should be prepared for inclement weather, particularly during the winter months. Hurricane season is from May 1 to Nov. 30.

GENERAL INFORMATION: Since the site is isolated, visitors must provide for their own independent existence. All food, water, and supplies must be brought from the mainland. Visitors must remove all refuse brought into or generated within the Monument. *For Your Safety*—Do not stand near wall edges. Mortar in historic structures may be loose or softened. Watch for uneven walking surfaces, spiral stairways, sudden drop-offs, and darkened areas. Never swim alone. Be cautious in areas with strong currents. Cuts from coral and punctures from the spiny sea urchin may be painful and slow to heal.

Fort Matanzas National Monument
Saint Augustine, Florida

MAILING ADDRESS: Superintendent, Castillo de San Marcos National Monument, 1 Castillo Drive, St. Augustine, Florida 32084 **Telephone:** 904-471-0116

DIRECTIONS: The park is 22 km (14 miles) south of St. Augustine and can be reached by FL A1A on Anastasia Island. The park consists of 298 acres on Rattlesnake Island, where the Fort is located, and on Anastasia Island, where the Visitor Center is. The Fort is accessible only by boat. A ferry crosses to Rattlesnake Island daily between 9:15 a.m. and 4:45 p.m.

This Spanish fort was built between 1740-42 to protect St. Augustine from the British. Created by Presidential Proclamation on Oct. 15, 1924.

VISITOR ACTIVITIES: interpretive walks and talks, ferry boat rides, fishing; **Permits:**

No; **Fees:** No; **Visitor facilities:** restrooms and parking at Visitor Center; **Any limitations on vehicle usage:** Vehicles are restricted to designated roadways; **Hiking trails:** No; **Backcountry:** No; **Camping:** No; **Other overnight accommodations on site:** No; **Meals served in the park:** No; **Food and supplies obtainable in the park:** No; **Food and supplies obtainable nearby:** Yes, in St. Augustine Beach, 16 km (10 miles); **Overnight accommodations:** St. Augustine Beach, 16 km (10 miles), St. Augustine, 24 km (15 miles); **First Aid available in park:** Yes; **Nearest Hospital:** St. Augustine, 24 km (15 miles); **Days/Hours:** Open daily from 8:30 a.m. to 5:30 p.m.; **Holiday Closings:** Dec. 25; **Visitor attractions closed for seasons:** No; **Weather:** a wide variety of weather conditions.

GENERAL INFORMATION: *For Your Safety*—Do not swim in the treacherous waters near the inlet or climb on the fort walls. Be wary of sharp oyster shells.

Gulf Islands National Seashore
Florida and Mississippi

MAILING ADDRESS: Superintendent, Gulf Islands National Seashore, P.O. Box 100, Gulf Breeze, Florida 32561, or Park Manager, 4000 Hanley Road, Ocean Springs, Mississippi 39564 **Telephone:** FL: 904-932-5302, MS: 601-875-9057

DIRECTIONS: Access to Ship Island in the Mississippi section is provided by concession boats from Gulfport and Biloxi, MS, twice daily from Memorial Day through Labor Day, once a day April to Memorial Day and Labor Day to mid-Oct. (twice a day on weekends). Private boats may dock at Fort Massachusetts in the daytime. Horn and Petit Bois Islands are reached by chartered or private boats. Recommended routes for reaching the major visitor areas within the Florida section are: Johnson Beach-take FL 292 southwest from Pensacola; historic mainland forts and Naval Aviation Museum-use the main entrance of Pensacola Naval Air Station off Barrancas Ave. (FL 295); Naval Live Oaks and the Fort Pickens and Santa Rosa beach areas-take US 98 from downtown Pensacola across the Pensacola Bay Bridge.

This series of offshore islands and mainland areas has both historic forts and sparkling white sand beaches near Pensacola, FL, and Pascagoula and Biloxi, MS, with mainland facilities in Mississippi. Authorized for addition to the National Park System on Jan. 8, 1971.

VISITOR ACTIVITIES: interpretive exhibits, tourist programs, picnicking, camping, hiking, sunbathing, swimming, boating, fishing, auto tours, scuba diving, guided fort tours; **Permits:** No; **Fees:** $3 fee for campgrounds without electricity, $4 with; **Visitor facilities:** picnic areas, campgrounds, bathhouse, boat dock and ramp, laundry, boat charters, campground store, restrooms, snack shop, Visitor Contact Stations, guarded beaches, souvenir and bookstore, fishing pier, hiking and bicycle trails, playground, ball field, ball court, wilderness area; **Any limitations on vehicle usage:** Motor vehicles are not allowed on sand dunes and beaches; **Hiking trails:** Yes, interpretive trails are in each state; **Backcountry:** Yes, Horn & Petit Bois Islands are wilderness areas, and can be reached by private or charter boat. Contact MS Gulf Islands for further information; **Camping:** Yes, no reservations available for campsites. Long tent stakes for use in the sand and mosquito netting are a must; **Other overnight accommodations on site:** No; **Meals served in the park:** Yes, snacks at Santa Rosa Area, Ship Island; **Food and supplies obtainable in the park:** Yes, at Ft. Pickens area-campground store; **Food and supplies obtainable nearby:** Yes, in major urban centers along the entire 241 km (150 mile) route from Ship Island, MS to Santa Rose Island, FL; **Overnight accommoda-**

tions: In urban centers: Gulfport, Biloxi, Ocean Springs, & Pascagoula, MS; Pensacola & Ft. Walton Beach, FL; **First Aid available in park:** Yes; **Nearest Hospital:** Ocean Springs, MS, Hwy 90, 8 km (5 miles); Pensacola, FL, Baptist Hosp., 20 km (12 miles); **Days/Hours:** Open 24 hours a day, except Santa Rosa, Ship Island, and Okaloosa Areas; **Holiday Closings:** Dec. 25; **Visitor attractions closed for seasons:**Guarded beaches closed from Sept.-Mar., Redoubt closed from Nov.-Feb.; **Weather:** Hot, humid Summer; cold, moderate Winter; comfortable Spring and Fall.

GENERAL INFORMATION: *For Your Safety*—Be extremely careful of strong currents in heavy surf, and avoid stinging jellyfish and Portuguese man-of-war. Do not swim alone in unguarded waters. Watch your step while exploring the forts and batteries. You should carry a flashlight since the passageways are dimly lighted.

Mar-A-Lago National Historic Site
Palm Beach, Florida

MAILING ADDRESS: Superintendent, Mar-A-Lago National Historic Site, P.O. Box 2527, Palm Beach, Florida 33480

DIRECTIONS: NOT OPEN TO THE PUBLIC.
  This private mansion is representative of the affluent society's way of life in the 1920's. Designated Jan 16, 1969.

Georgia

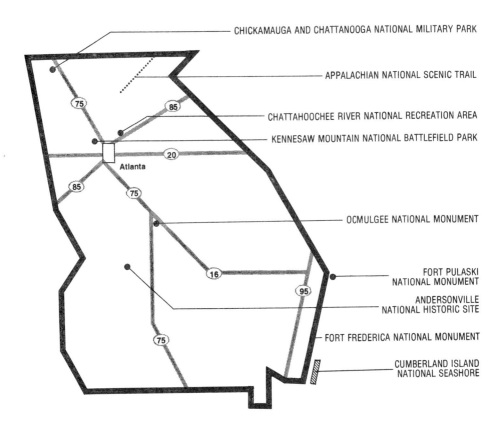

CHICKAMAUGA AND CHATTANOOGA NATIONAL MILITARY PARK

APPALACHIAN NATIONAL SCENIC TRAIL

CHATTAHOOCHEE RIVER NATIONAL RECREATION AREA

KENNESAW MOUNTAIN NATIONAL BATTLEFIELD PARK

Atlanta

OCMULGEE NATIONAL MONUMENT

FORT PULASKI NATIONAL MONUMENT

ANDERSONVILLE NATIONAL HISTORIC SITE

FORT FREDERICA NATIONAL MONUMENT

CUMBERLAND ISLAND NATIONAL SEASHORE

Andersonville National Historic Site
Andersonville, Georgia

MAILING ADDRESS: Superintendent, Andersonville National Historic Site, Andersonville, Georgia 31711 **Telephone:** 912-924-0343

DIRECTIONS: The Site is southwest of Macon and southeast of Columbus on Route 49, 16 km (10 miles) northeast of Americus. Interstate 75 south of Macon intersects Route 49, and further south Routes 224 and 27 connect I-75 with Route 49.

Established by act of Congress on July 1, 1971, this 470-acre site consists of a national cemetery and preserves the Civil War prison camp where more than 12,000 men died and were interred nearby.

VISITOR ACTIVITIES: picnicking, auto tours, walking, commemorative monuments, interpretive exhibits; **Permits:** No; **Fees:** No; **Visitor facilities:** parking and restrooms at Visitor Center, picnic area; **Any limitations on vehicle usage:** Vehicles are confined to parking area and auto tour roads; **Hiking trails:** No; **Backcountry:** No; **Camping:** No;

Other overnight accommodations on site: No; **Meals served in the park:** No; **Food and supplies obtainable in the park:** No; **Food and supplies obtainable nearby:** Yes, Andersonville, .8 km (1/2 mile), Americus, 16 km (10 miles); **Overnight accommodations:** Americus, Hwy 49, 16 km (10 miles), KOA Camp is located approx. 8 km (5 miles) from the Site; **First Aid available in park:** Yes; **Nearest Hospital:** Americus, Hwy 49, 16 km (10 miles); **Days/Hours:** Open 7 days a week; 8 a.m. to 5 p.m., until 7 p.m. from June-Aug.; **Holiday Closings:** Dec. 25; **Visitor attractions closed for seasons:** No.

GENERAL INFORMATION: *For Your Safety*—Wear shoes to protect yourself from sandspurs which grow wild in the grass. Also be wary of snakes, poison ivy, and fire ants (characterized by red sandy mounds) which have a painful sting. Do not climb on monuments, fences, or earthworks.

Appalachian National Scenic Trail
For details see listing in Maine

Chattahoochee River National Recreation Area
Atlanta, Georgia

MAILING ADDRESS: Chattahoochee River National Recreation Area, P.O. Box 1396, Smyrna, Georgia 30081 **Telephone:** 404-952-6009

DIRECTIONS: Hwy 41 is easily reached from the north side of Atlanta via I-285. The Visitor Station is at Hwy 41 and the River.

A 77 km (48-mile) stretch of the Chattahoochee River, extending into Atlanta, is preserved "for public enjoyment" of scenic, recreational, and historical features. Authorized for addition to the National Park System on Aug. 15, 1978.

VISITOR ACTIVITIES: river floating, hiking on primitive trails; **Permits:** No; **Fees:** No; **Visitor facilities:** raft rentals on site and in the area; **Any limitations on vehicle usage:** Vehicle use is restricted in certain areas; **Hiking trails:** Yes, primitive trails; **Backcountry:** No; **Camping:** No; **Other overnight accommodations on site:** No; **Meals served in the park:** No; **Food and supplies obtainable in the park:** No; **Food and supplies obtainable nearby:** Yes, within the Chattahoochee corridor; **Overnight accommodations:** Atlanta and vicinity; **First Aid available in park:** Yes; **Nearest Hospital:** Hwy 41, several miles; **Days/Hours:** Park always open; **Holiday Closings:** None; **Visitor attractions closed for seasons:** No.

GENERAL INFORMATION: *For Your Safety*—No open fires are permitted in the area. Please respect private property rights.

Chickamauga & Chattanooga National Military Park
Fort Oglethorpe, Georgia

MAILING ADDRESS: Superintendent, Chickamauga and Chattanooga National Military Park, P.O. Box 2126, Fort Oglethorpe, Georgia 30742 **Telephone:** 404-866-9241

DIRECTIONS: The Visitor Center is on US 27, off I-75, 16 km (10 miles) south of

Chattanooga, TN.

The Park includes the Civil War battlefields of Chickamauga, Orchard Knob, Lookout Mountain, and Missionary Ridge. Established by act of Congress on Aug. 19, 1890.

VISITOR ACTIVITIES: interpretive exhibits, auto tours, living history demonstrations, hiking, horseback riding; **Permits:** No; **Fees:** Yes, admission fee for Cravens House in the Lookout Mountain Unit is 50¢. Golden Age and Golden Eagle Passports accepted and available; **Visitor facilities:** Parking and restrooms at Visitor Center, museum, hiking trails; **Any limitations on vehicle usage:** No overnight parking is allowed; **Hiking trails:** Yes, self-guiding trails; **Backcountry:** No; **Camping:** No; **Other overnight accommodations on site:** No; **Meals served in the park:** No; **Food and supplies obtainable in the park:** No; **Food and supplies obtainable nearby:** Yes, Fort Oglethorpe and Chattanooga; **Overnight Accommodations:** Fort Oglethorpe, Ga, US 27, continues to Chickamauga Battlefield; Chattanoona, TN (surrounds park areas); **First Aid available in park:** No; **Nearest Hospital:** Fort Oglethorpe, GA, US 27, several blocks from the Visitor Center; **Days/Hours:** Park open 24 hours a day, except Lookout Mountain Unit, which is closed at night; **Holiday Closings:** Dec. 25; **Visitor attractions closed for seasons:** None; **Weather:** Summer is hot and humid; Winter is cold, with a few days below freezing; early Spring is rainy.

Cumberland Island National Seashore
Saint Marys, Georgia 31558

MAILING ADDRESS: Superintendent, Cumberland Island National Seashore, P.O. Box 806, Saint Marys, Georgia 31558 **Telephone:** 912-882-4336

DIRECTIONS: The temporary Park Headquarters and Visitor Center are on US 40, which ends at the St. Marys River. To reach St. Marys, take GA 40 east from I-95 near Kingsland. A National Park Service passenger ferry provides access to the Seashore from St. Marys, GA daily except Tuesday and Wednesday, 7 days a week in June, July and August. Mainland departure times are 9:15 a.m. and 1:45 p.m. Island departure times are 12:15 and 4:45 p.m. The trip takes 45 minutes. Ferry reservations are advisable and can be made by calling 912-882-4335 or by writing to the Superintendent. *Don't miss the ferry from the island.* It leaves as scheduled. If you miss the boat, you must camp or charter a boat to take you to the mainland. The ferry does not transport cars, bicylces, or pets.

Magnificent beaches and dunes, marshes, and freshwater lakes make up this largest of Georgia's Golden Isles, one of the finest remaining natural areas on the East Coast. Established by act of Congress on Oct. 23, 1972.

VISITOR ACTIVITIES: naturalist programs, walking tours, bird- and wildlife-watching, swimming, fishing, photography, hiking, camping, backcountry; **Permits:** required for backcountry, available at Island debarkation point; **Fees:** $2 fee for round-trip ferry tickets, persons 15 and under & 62 and over are charged $1; **Visitor facilities:** restrooms, campgrounds, bath house, beaches, hiking trails; **Any limitations on vehicle usage:** No transportation on the island; **Hiking trails:** Yes, a 3 km (2 mile) nature trail leads to the Dungeness Ruins complex. Maps for other trails are available; **Backcountry:** Yes, information available from Headquarters or Sea Camp Visitor Center; **Camping:** Yes, campers should make reservations with Headquarters and be sure to carry adequate equipment and supplies. Campfires are prohibited so a portable stove is necessary; **Other overnight accommodations on site:** No; **Meals served in the park:** No; **Food and supplies obtainable in the park:** No; **Food and supplies obtainable nearby:** Yes, at St.

Marys; **Overnight accommodations:** Motel accommodations are available in nearby communities. Camping facilities may be found at private commercial campgrounds and 16 km (10 miles) away at Crooked River State Park, Route 1, Box 207, Kingsland, GA 31548, phone 912-882-5256; **First Aid available in park:** Yes; **Nearest Hospital:** St. Marys, GA via emergency boat from the Island; **Days/Hours:** Seashore never closes. Sea Camp Visitor Center is open from 8 a.m. to 5 p.m. daily; **Holiday Closings:** Dec. 25; **Visitor attractions closed for seasons:** No; **Weather:** Cumberland's climate is moderate with short, mild Winters. Summer temperatures range from about 27°C to 35°C (80s to low 90sF) with some humidity.

GENERAL INFORMATION: Before leaving St. Marys, day and overnight visitors should carefully consider what supplies-food, drinks, suntan lotion, film, sunglasses, and insect repellent-they will need, for there are no stores on the Island. Casual dress, comfortable walking shoes, and rain gear are also recommended.

For Your Safety—Dungeness ruins and most of its outbuildings are unstable. For your protection, these structures are closed. The Island is home to several species of poisonous snakes. Visitors are advised to take normal precautions when venturing into areas where vegetation is thick. Lifeguards are not provided; be careful while swimming. Be alert for possible hunting activity on adjacent private lands.

Fort Frederica National Monument
St. Simons Island, Georgia

MAILING ADDRESS: Superintendent, Fort Frederica National Monument, Route 4, Box 286-C, St. Simons Island, Georgia 31522 **Telephone:** 912-638-3639

DIRECTIONS: The Monument is 19.3 km (12 miles) from Brunswick, GA on St. Simons Island. It can be reached by taking the Brunswick-St. Simons toll causeway which connects with US 17 at Brunswick.

Gen. James E. Oglethorpe built this British fort in 1736-48, during the Anglo-Spanish struggle for control of what is now the southeastern United States. Authorized for addition to the National Park System on May 26, 1936.

VISITOR ACTIVITIES: interpretive exhibits and film, walking tours, living history demonstrations in Summer; **Permits:** No; **Fees:** No; **Visitor facilities:** parking and restrooms at Visitor Center, interpretive publications and sales items. Picnicking is available at several points on St. Simons Island; **Any limitations on vehicle usage:** Vehicles are restricted to the entrance road and parking lot; **Hiking trails:** No; **Backcountry:** No; **Camping:** No; **Other overnight accommodations on site:** No; **Meals served in the park:** No; **Food and supplies obtainable in the park:** No; **Food and supplies obtainable nearby:** Yes, St. Simons Island has restaurants, grocery stores, and convenience stores; **Overnight accommodations:** A few motels are on St. Simons Island; majority located in Brunswick, GA and on Jekyll Island, 16 km (10 miles) south of Brunswick; **First Aid available in park:** Yes, there is an emergency squad on St. Simons Island; **Nearest Hospital:** Brunswick, GA, 20 km (12.5 miles); **Days/Hours:** Open daily from 8 a.m. to 5 p.m. Hours may be extended in Summer. Contact the Superintendent for further information; **Holiday Closings:** Dec. 25; **Visitor attractions closed for seasons:** None; **Weather:** Spring and Fall are mild; Winter has occasional cold temperatures. Summers are hot & humid with numerous afternoon thundershowers.

GENERAL INFORMATION: Do not touch the ruins, which are old and fragile and can easily be destroyed. The water is deep and the banks are slippery at the fort. Do not take shelter under the trees during high winds and thunderstorms. Bring an insect repellent in Summer.

Fort Pulaski National Monument
Tybee Island, Georgia

MAILING ADDRESS: Superintendent, Fort Pulaski National Monument, P.O. Box 98, Tybee Island, Georgia 31328 **Telephone:** 912-786-5787

DIRECTIONS: The Visitor Center is in the delta area of the Savannah River, 24 km (15 miles) east of Savannah on US 80.

Bombardment of this early 19th-century fort by Federal rifled cannon in 1862 first demonstrated the ineffectiveness of old-style masonry fortifications. Created by Presidential Proclamation on Oct. 15, 1924.

VISITOR ACTIVITIES: interpretive talks and exhibits, wildlife- and bird-watching, picnicking, fishing; **Permits:** No; **Fees:** Entrance fee is $1 per car. Golden Age and Golden Eagle Passports accepted and available; **Visitor facilities:** parking and restrooms at Visitor Center, picnic area; **Any limitations on vehicle usage:** vehicles are confined to designated roadways; **Hiking trails:** Yes, hiking and nature trails lead around the fort; **Backcountry:** No; **Camping:** No; **Other overnight accommodations on site:** No; **Meals served in the park:** No; **Food and supplies obtainable in the park:** No; **Food and supplies obtainable nearby:** Yes, Tybee Island 6 km (4 miles); Savannah 24 km (15 miles); **Overnight accommodations:** Savannah, 24 km (15 miles) west of the Monument on US 80; **First Aid available in park:** Yes; **Nearest Hospital:** Savannah, Abercorn and Gaston Streets, about 32 km (20 miles); **Days/Hours:** Open daily from 8:30 a.m. to 5:30 p.m.; **Holiday Closings:** Dec. 25; **Weather:** Temperatures range from 7°C (20°F) in Winter to 37°C (100°) in Summer.

GENERAL INFORMATION: *For Your Safety*—Stay off mounds and top-most walls of the fort. Don't run on the terreplein (upper level) of the fort. Come down when there is lightning. Mosquitoes and horseflies are present in Spring and Summer; use a repellent and wear protective clothing. Watch your step in the Fort, and stay on the trails when walking or hiking. Beware of poisonous snakes.

Kennesaw Mountain National Battlefield Park
Marietta, Georgia

MAILING ADDRESS: Superintendent, Kennesaw Mountain National Battlefield Park, P.O. Box 1167, Marietta, Georgia 30061 **Telephone:** 404-427-4686

DIRECTIONS: The Park is 3.2 km (2 miles) north of Marietta, Georgia, a short distance off US 41, and 24 km (15 miles) northwest of Atlanta, off I-75.

Two engagements took place here between Union and Confederate forces during the Atlanta Campaign, June 20-July 2, 1864. Authorized for addition to the National Park System on Feb. 8, 1917.

VISITOR ACTIVITIES: exhibits and audiovisual programs at Visitor Center, walking and auto tours of the park, hiking, horseback riding; **Permits:** No; **Fees:** No; **Visitor facilities:** picnic areas, restrooms, hiking and horseback riding trails; **Any limitations on vehicle usage:** All vehicles are restricted to designated roadways; **Hiking trails:** Yes, the park trails, which start at the Visitor Center, can be used for short walks or long hikes. Hikers should register at the Visitor Center for long hikes; **Backcountry:** No; **Camping:** No; **Other overnight accommodations on site:** No; **Meals served in the park:** No; **Food and supplies obtainable in the park:** No; **Food and supplies obtainable nearby:** Yes, in Marietta or Atlanta; **Overnight accommodations:** Marietta, 3.2 km (2 miles) south; or Atlanta, 24 km (15 miles) southeast; **First Aid available in park:** Yes; **Nearest Hospital:** Marietta, 3.2 km (2 miles); **Days/Hours:** Open daily from 8:30 a.m. to 5 p.m. year-round; **Holiday Closings:** Dec. 25 and Jan 1; **Weather:** Moderate temperatures year round. Daytime temperatures are usually in the 40°+ range in Winter and 80° range in Summer.

Ocmulgee National Monument
Macon, Georgia

MAILING ADDRESS: Superintendent, Ocmulgee National Monument, 1207 Emery Highway, Macon, Georgia 31201 **Telephone:** 912-742-0447

DIRECTIONS: The Monument is on the east edge of Macon, Georgia on US 80 east. Main access is from Int. 75 to Int. 16 east, at the north end of Macon. Take either the first or second exit from Int. 16 and follow the signs 1.6 km (1 mile) to the park entrance.
  The cultural evolution of the Indian civilizations in the southern United States are represented in the remains of mounds and villages here. Authorized for addition to the National Park System on June 14, 1934.

VISITOR ACTIVITIES: auto tours, interpretive exhibits, picnicking, nature walks, hiking, fishing; **Permits:** None; **Fees:** No; **Visitor facilities:** parking and restrooms at Visitor Center, picnic area, craft demonstrations in Summer, nature trail; **Any limitations on vehicle usage:** Vehicles must be parked only in designated parking areas; **Hiking trails:** Yes, 5.5 km (3-1/2 miles) of nature and historical trails; **Backcountry:** No; **Camping:** No; **Other overnight accommodations on site:** No, the closest camping area is Lake Tobasofkee Recreation Area, 13 km (8 miles) west of Macon. No reservations available for campsites. For further information, contact the lake at 6600 Mosley-Dixon Road, Macon, GA 31210, phone 912-474-8770; **Meals served in the park:** No; **Food and supplies obtainable in the park:** No; **Food and supplies obtainable nearby:** Yes, at Macon; **Overnight accommodations:** Macon; **First Aid available in park:** Yes; **Nearest Hospital:** Macon, Hwy 80, .8 km (1/2 mile); **Days/Hours:** Open daily from 9 a.m. to 5 p.m.; **Holiday Closings:** Dec. 25 and Jan. 1; **Visitor attractions closed for seasons:** No earthlodge tours during rain; **Weather:** Summers are hot & humid, Winters are mostly mild.

GENERAL INFORMATION: *For Your Safety*—Mound slopes and steep banks are dangerous. Please use the marked trails. Drivers of camping vehicles should be aware of the 9'9" clearance of the tunnel leading to Greater Temple Mound.

Hawaii

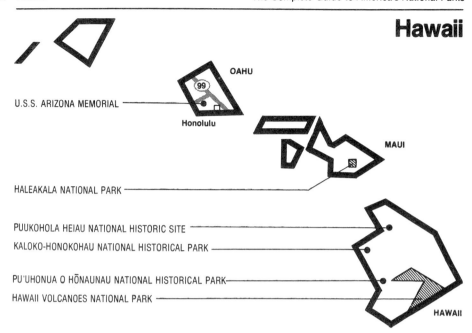

U.S.S. ARIZONA MEMORIAL

OAHU

Honolulu

MAUI

HALEAKALA NATIONAL PARK

PUUKOHOLA HEIAU NATIONAL HISTORIC SITE

KALOKO-HONOKOHAU NATIONAL HISTORICAL PARK

PU'UHONUA O HŌNAUNAU NATIONAL HISTORICAL PARK

HAWAII VOLCANOES NATIONAL PARK

HAWAII

Haleakala National Park
Makawao, Maui, Hawaii

MAILING ADDRESS: Superintendent, Haleakala National Park, P.O. Box 537, Makawao, Maui, Hawaii **Telephone:** 808-572-9177

DIRECTIONS: The Park extends from the 3055 meter (10,023-foot) summit of Mt. Haleakala down the southeast flank to the Kipahulu coast near Hana. These two sections of the Park are not directly connected by road, but can be reached by auto from Kahului, as follows: Haleakala Crater is a 3 hour round trip drive from Kahului via HI 36, 37, 377, and 378. The Kipahulu District of the Park is a 6-to-8 hour round trip drive from Kahului via HI 36 to Hana, then via HI 31 towards Kipahulu. The road around East Maui, which is narrow, winding and slow, is for the adventurous only; it offers roadside state parks, frequent overlooks, and views of rain forests, black lava shores, and rugged coastal cliffs. West of Kipahulu, HI 31 becomes an unpaved road.

The Park preserves the outstanding features of Haleakala Crater on the island of Maui and protects the unique and fragile ecosystems of Kipahulu Valley, the scenic pools along Oheo Gulch, and many rare and endangered species. Authorized for addition to the National Park System on Aug. 1, 1916.

VISITOR ACTIVITIES: Kipahulu: hiking, camping, walking, picnicking, swimming. Haleakala Crater: interpretive exhibits and talks, walking, hiking, camping, picnicking. Park Headquarters, where information, permits, and publications are furnished, is 1.5 km (1 mile) from the entrance to the Park. The Visitor Center, which contains exhibits and is where interpretive talks are held, is about 17.5 km (11 miles) from the park entrance. For detailed information on both areas, contact the Superintendent; **Permits:** for backcountry camping at Haleakala Crater available from Headquarters or from a Park Ranger; **Fees:** Yes, for backcountry cabin rental; **Visitor facilities:** picnic areas, campgrounds, scenic overlooks, interpretive observatory programs, backcountry cabins; **Any limitations on vehicle usage:** Watch out for traffic on narrow roads; **Hiking trails:** Yes, trails vary in difficulty and length; there are several short nature trails; **Backcountry:** Yes, contact the Superintendent for a free brochure; **Camping:** Yes, reservations for campsites available at Park Headquarters. These are primitive campsites with only pit toilets and drinking water. Campers should have equipment appropriate for possible cold, wet weather, and must bring a sleeping bag, tent, and cooking stove with fuel (because of the prohibition against open fires). Three crater cabins are maintained by the National Park Service for visitor use on an advance reservation basis only. Each cabin is allocated to one party at a time, with a capacity of 12 people per night; at least one member of the group must be 18 years of age or older. Each cabin has bunks, blankets, limited water and firewood, cookstove, and eating and cooking utensils. To reserve cabins, write to the Superintendent at least 60 days in advance of your trip. Include your first and alternate choices of dates and cabins preferred. The less restrictive your choices, the better your chance of confirmation. Reservations are limited to 3 nights per month, with no more than 2 consecutive nights at any one cabin. A fee is charged ; **Other overnight accommodations on site:** Yes; **Meals served in the park:** No; **Food and supplies obtainable in the park:** No; **Food and supplies obtainable nearby:** Yes, at Pukalaui, Maui, HI; **Overnight accommodations:** From Kipahulu, 16 km (10 miles) on Rt. 31 to Hana. From Haleakala Crater, 19 km (12 miles) on Rt. 377; **First Aid available in park:** Yes; **Nearest Hospitals:** Kahului, 48 km (30 miles); **Days/Hours:** Open 24 hours a day, 365 days a year, Visitor Center open daily from 8:30 a.m. to 3 p.m.; **Holiday Closings:** None; **Visitor attractions closed for seasons:**No; **Weather:** Weather near the summit varies considerably; Summers are generally dry and moderately warm, but you should come prepared for occasionally cold, windy, damp weather. Winters tend to be cold, wet, foggy, and windy. Generally in the Spring and Fall there is a mixture of all kinds of weather. Call the Park at 808-572-7749 for current weather conditions before beginning your trip.

GENERAL INFORMATION: *For Your Safety*—Hikers should bring comfortable, durable hiking shoes, canteen, light raincoat, sun hat, and suntan lotion. Do not travel alone. Swimmers should never swim during high water. If you notice the water rising, GET OUT FAST! 'Ohe'o stream can become a raging torrent in minutes. Be careful on wet rocks; they are slippery. Check before diving or jumping. In some places there are submerged ledges near the pool's edge.

Hawaii Volcanoes National Park
Hawaii Volcanoes National Park, Hawaii

MAILING ADDRESS: Superintendent, Hawaii Volcanoes National Park, Hawaii Volcanoes National Park, Hawaii 96718 **Telephone:** 808-967-7311

DIRECTIONS: Visitor Centers are at Kilauea and Wahaula. The coastal section of the Park is accessible via HI 13 from Keaau.
 Active volcanism continues here on the island of Hawaii. Rare and luxuriant vegetation provides food and shelter for a variety of animals in lower elevations. Established by act of Congress on Aug. 1, 1916.

VISITOR ACTIVITIES: auto tours, walking, hiking, camping, backcountry, picnicking, fishing, interpretive programs. Schedule of events available from either Visitor Center or by contacting the Park; **Permits:** for backcountry use can be obtained at Headquarters; **Fees:** No entrance fee or camping fee; **Visitor facilities:** parking, restrooms and museums at Visitor Centers, lodging, cabins, picnic areas; **Any limitations on vehicle usage:** All vehicles are restricted to designated roadways; **Hiking trails:** Yes, check at Visitor Center or write for information on the 241 km (150 miles) of trails; **Backcountry:** Yes, hiker shelters and cabins are available, but you must register at Park Headquarters for overnight stays. Detailed maps are sold at Park Headquarters and are highly recommended. Check on trail conditions and water supplies before you start; **Camping:** Yes, no reservations available for individual campsites; **Other overnight accommodations on site:** Yes, Volcano House on the rim of Kilauea Crater is open all year. Reservations are advised, especially during July and August. Cabins with the use of showers are operated at Namakani Paio by the Volcano House. For reservations, contact: The Volcano House, Hawaii Volcanoes National Park, HI 96718, phone 808-967-7321. Kilauea Military Camp, a rest and recreation camp for active and retired military personnel, is 1.6 km (1 mile) west of Park Headquarters; **Meals served in the park:** Yes, at Volcano House Restaurant; **Food and supplies obtainable in the park:** No; **Food and supplies obtainable nearby:** Yes, groceries, gasoline, and camping supplies are available in the community of Volcano, 1.6 km (1 mile) north of the park on HI 11. Stores there are open all year. Groceries and meals are also available in the village of Kalapana, 6 km (4 miles) east of the coastal section of the Park; **Overnight accommodations:** Hilo, Hwy 11, 47 km (29 miles) from the Park; **First Aid available in park:** Yes; **Nearest Hospital:** Hilo, Hwy 11, 47 km (29 miles); **Days/Hours:** Park open 24 hours a day year-round; **Holiday Closings:** None; **Visitor attractions closed for seasons:**None; **Weather:** The northern side of Kilauea's summit is 1200 meters (4000 feet) above sea level, so the climate can be cool and rain can fall at any time of year. At the same time, Kilauea's leeward side is usually dry and warm. There is no record of freezing at Kilauea, but in winter the snow can extend down to 3000 meters (10,000 feet) on Mauna Loa.

GENERAL INFORMATION: *For Your Safety*—Stay on trails. The surface of Kilauea is laced with deep cracks, and many of these are hidden by vegetation. Recent lava flows are shelly and collapse easily. Fumes from volcanoes can compound respiratory problems. If in doubt, heed the warning signs. A number of trails lie along the edges of cliff tops, so be sure of your footing.

Eruption Bulletins: You can get up-to-date information about on-going eruptions or potential activity by calling 808-967-7977 anytime. The automatic answering service is updated whenever Kilauea or Mauna Loa shows signs of change. Because eruptions are the most exciting events at Hawaii Volcanoes, temporary road signs will direct you to access or vantage points where you can confront the power of these events when conditons are safe.

Special publications on the geology, human history, and natural history of Hawaii Volcanoes are published by the Hawaii Natural History Association to help you enjoy the Park. For a price list write to the Association, Hawaii Volcanoes National Park, HI 96718.

Kaloko-Honokohau National Historical Park
On the Kona coast of the Island of Hawaii

MAILING ADDRESS: Hawaii State Director's Office, National Park Service, 300 Ala Moana Blvd., Box 50165, Honolulu, Hawaii 96850 **Telephone:** 808-546-7584

DIRECTIONS: *NOT YET OPEN TO THE PUBLIC.*

The Park contains 234 historic and archaeological features, including the burial site of the first Hawaiian king, Kamehameha I. Native Hawaiians make the Park a center for the perpetuation of Hawaiian culture. Authorized for addition to the National Park System on Nov. 10, 1978.

Pu'uhonua o Honaunau National Historical Park
Honaunau, Kona, Hawaii

MAILING ADDRESS: Superintendent, Pu'uhonua o Honaunau National Historical Park, P.O. Box 128, Honaunau, Kona, Hawaii **Telephone:** 808-328-2326

DIRECTIONS: The Park is located 48 km (30 miles) south of Keahole Airport on HI 160. Take HI 19 to Kailua, thence HI 11 to Honaunau, thence HI 160 to the park.

Until 1819, vanquished Hawaiian warriors, noncombatants and taboo breakers could escape death by reaching this sacred ground. Prehistoric house sites, royal fishponds, coconut groves and spectacular shore scenery comprise the Park. Authorized for addition to the National Park System on July 26, 1955.

VISITOR ACTIVITIES: picnicking, snorkeling, swimming, walking tours, craft demonstrations, interpretive exhibits, hiking, fishing; **Permits:** No; **Fees:** No; **Visitor facilities:** Parking and restrooms at Visitor Center, picnic area; **Any limitations on vehicle usage:** Vehicles are restricted to designated roadways; **Hiking trails:** Yes, self-guiding walking trail through the Park; **Backcountry:** No; **Camping:** No; **Other overnight accommodations on site:** No; **Meals served in the park:** No, the nearest restaurant is 16 km (10 miles) away; **Food and supplies obtainable in the park:** No; **Food and supplies obtainable nearby:** No, limited supplies on HI 11, grocery stores at Captain Cook; **Overnight accommodations:** Captain Cook, HI 11, 16 km (10 miles) away; **First Aid available in park:** Yes; **Nearest Hospital:** Kona, 19 km (12 miles); **Days/Hours:** Open daily from 6 a.m. to midnight; **Holiday Closings:** None; **Visitor attractions closed for seasons:** No; **Weather:** The Park is sunny 95% of the time. Summer is the rainy season; average rainfall is 25 inches per year.

GENERAL INFORMATION: *For Your Safety*—Be alert for unexpected high waves when you are on the shore; don't turn your back on the ocean. Do not climb on the Great Wall or on the framework of the house models. If you leave the trail, watch for falling coconuts and coconut fronds. Do not climb the coconut trees. Visitors to the area can also see Puukohola Heiau National Historic Site (see listing in this book), at Kawaihae Bay, on the island's northwestern shore.

Puukohola Heiau National Historic Site
Kawaihae, Hawaii

MAILING ADDRESS: Superintendent, Pu'uhonua o Honaunau National Historical Park, P.O. Box 128, Honaunau, Hawaii **Telephone:** 808-882-7218

DIRECTIONS: Puukohola Heiau is on the northwestern shore of the island of Hawaii. Airlines make scheduled flights several times daily from Honolulu to airports at Hilo, Keahole, and Waimea-Kohala, which is about 19 km (12 miles) from the park. Taxis and car rentals are available at all airports.

Ruins of Puukohola Heiau ("Temple on the Hill of the Whale"), built by King Kamehameha the Great (1753-1819) during his rise to power are preserved here.

Authorized for addition to the National Park System on Aug. 17, 1972.

VISITOR ACTIVITIES: hiking, guided and self-guiding tours. Swimming and picnicking are permitted at nearby Spencer Beach Park; **Permits:** No; **Fees:** No; **Visitor facilities:** Informal interpretive talks are given at the Visitor Center; **Any limitations on vehicle usage:** If you park in front of Puukohola Heiau on the Spencer Beach Road, use caution while entering and leaving the road, due to heavy traffic; **Hiking trails:** Yes, all points of interest in the Park can be visited on foot; **Backcountry:** No, the Hawaii Visitors Bureau, a non-profit organization with offices in Honolulu, Hilo, Kona, Waikiki, Lihue, and 209 Post Street, San Francisco, CA 94108, phone 415-392-8273, will supply information on trips to and through the Hawaiian Islands; **Camping:** No, information on camping at nearby Spencer Beach Park may be obtained from Hawaii Visitors Bureau, 209 Post Street, San Francisco, CA 94108, phone 415-392-8173; **Other overnight accommodations on site:** No; **Meals served in the park:** No; **Food and supplies obtainable in the park:** No; **Food and supplies obtainable nearby:** Yes, at Kawaihae, 1.5 km (1 mile) away; **Overnight accommodations:** Waimea, 19.3 km (12 miles) southeast; **First Aid available in park:** Yes; **Nearest Hospital:** Honokaa, 46.5 km (29 miles); **Days/Hours:** Open daily from 6 a.m. to midnight; Visitor Center open from 7:30 a.m. to 6 p.m.; **Holiday Closings:** No; **Visitor attractions closed for seasons:**No; **Weather:** Nine inches of rainfall per year; occasional 90°F temperatures.

GENERAL INFORMATION: *For Your Safety*—Stay on the designated trails, and do not climb on the walls of the temple. The trail from the Visitor Center is long, hot, & rugged. If you are not physically fit and attired in proper clothing or footwear, do not attempt the hike. You may view the area from the Spencer Beach Park road. To prevent grass fires, do not smoke. The beach fronting Puukohola is unsuitable for swimming, due to silt and coral collections.

U.S.S. Arizona Memorial
Honolulu, Hawaii

MAILING ADDRESS: Hawaii State Director's Office, National Park Service, 300 Ala Moana Blvd., Box 50165, Honolulu, Hawaii 96850 **Telephone:** 808-546-7584

DIRECTIONS: The Memorial is a 1/2 hour drive from Waikiki. Follow Ala Moana Blvd. from Waikiki to Nimitz Hwy in the direction of Honolulu International Airport. At Puuloa Road, take the elevated freeway above Kamehameha Hwy (Hwy 90) and follow the sign to Arizona Memorial. Go through the traffic light at the intersection of Halawa Gate on Kamehameha Hwy and take the very next left, which is marked "To Ford Island Ferry Landing." Public transportation is available from Waikiki and downtown Honolulu to Ford Island Ferry Landing. For information, call 808-531-1611.
   A floating memorial is suspended over the battleship U.S.S. Arizona, sunk in Pearl Harbor on Dec. 7, 1941. Owned and administered by the U.S. Navy. When shoreside facilities are completed in 1980, the Memorial will be administered by the National Park Service under a cooperative agreement with the U.S. Navy. This affiliated area was authorized for addition to the National Park System on Nov. 10, 1978.

VISITOR ACTIVITIES: walking, free boat tours around Pearl Harbor and to the Memorial. Interpretive exhibits and audiovisual programs are scheduled to be offered starting in Fall, 1980; **Permits:** No; **Fees:** No; **Visitor facilities:** parking, restrooms and souvenirs available at the landing. Museum and audiovisual programs expected starting in Fall, 1980; **Meals served in the park:** Yes, snacks are available on the shore; **Food and supplies obtainable in the park:** No; **Food and supplies obtainable nearby:** Yes, at Pearl Ridge Shopping Center; **Overnight accommodations:** at the Airport or Waikiki; **First Aid available in park:** Yes; **Nearest Hospital:** Queens Hospital, Honolulu; **Days/Hours:** 9 a.m. to 3 p.m. daily except Monday. Hours may be extended when management is assumed by the National Park Service; **Holiday Closings:** Closed all holidays except Memorial Day, Veterans Day, and July 4; **Visitor attractions closed for seasons:**None.

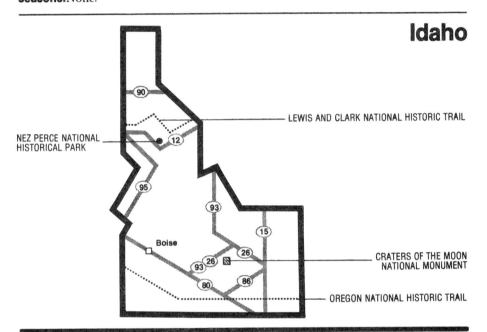

Idaho

LEWIS AND CLARK NATIONAL HISTORIC TRAIL

NEZ PERCE NATIONAL HISTORICAL PARK

CRATERS OF THE MOON NATIONAL MONUMENT

OREGON NATIONAL HISTORIC TRAIL

Craters of the Moon National Monument
Arco, Idaho

MAILING ADDRESS: Superintendent, Craters of the Moon National Monument, P.O. Box 29, Arco, Idaho 83213 **Telephone:** 208-527-3257

DIRECTIONS: The Monument is 29 km (18 miles) west of Arco on US 20, 26, and 93A. Volcanic cones, craters, lava flows, and caves make this an astonishing landscape. Established by act of Congress on May 2, 1924.

VISITOR ACTIVITIES: interpretive exhibits, audiovisual programs, naturalist trips, camping, cross-country skiing; **Permits:** required for backcountry, available at Visitor Center; **Fees:** $1 entrance fee; $2 camping fee; **Visitor facilities:** restrooms, campground, drinking water, nature trails, picnic area, amphitheater, scenic overlooks; **Any limitations on vehicle usage:** Vehicles must remain on paved roads; **Hiking trails:** Yes, self-guiding trails lead to points of interest; **Backcountry:** Yes, write to Superintendent for information; **Camping:** Yes, no reservations for campsites, which have charcoal grills, tables, drinking water, and flush toilets; **Other overnight accommodations on site:** No; **Meals served in the park:** No; **Food and supplies obtainble in the park:**

No; **Food and supplies obtainable nearby:** Yes, in Arco, Idaho; **Overnight accommodations:** Arco, US 20, 26, and 93A, 29 km (18 miles) northeast; **First Aid available in park:** Yes; **Nearest Hospital:** Arco, US 93A, 26 & 20, 29 km (18 miles) northeast; **Days/Hours:** Open Sept. 15-June from 8 a.m. to 5 p.m., until 8 p.m. from June-Sept. 15. Visitor Center open year-round; **Holiday Closings:** Dec. 25, Jan. 1, Washington's Birthday; **Visitor attractions closed for seasons:**The road through the Monument is closed by snow from late November to mid-April; **Weather:** Dry, warm, windy Summers; cold, snowy Winters.

Lewis and Clark Trail
For details see listing in Illinois

Nez Perce National Historical Park
Spalding, Idaho

MAILING ADDRESS: Superintendent, Nez Perce National Historical Park, P.O. Box 93, Spalding, Idaho 83351 **Telephone:** 208-843-2685

DIRECTIONS: The Visitor Center is in Spalding, 17 km (11 miles) south of Lewiston off US 95.

The history and culture of the Nez Perce Indian country are preserved, commemorated, and interpreted here. Four federally-owned sites are administered by the National Park Service, and twenty sites through cooperative agreements. Authorized for addition to the National Park System on May 15, 1965.

VISITOR ACTIVITIES: interpretive exhibits, cultural demonstrations, self-guiding walks, fishing, picnicking; **Permits:** Idaho fishing license, available locally; **Fees:** No; **Visitor facilities:** parking at Visitor Center, restrooms, overlooks, and pullouts throughout the park, picnic area; **Any limitations on vehicle usage:** Vehicles are restricted to paved roads; **Hiking trails:** No; **Backcountry:** No; **Camping:** No; **Other overnight accommodations on site:** No, camping is available in nearby Clearwater and Nez Perce National Forests. Contact the Park for further information; **Meals served in the park:** No; **Food and supplies obtainable in the park:** No; **Food and supplies obtainable nearby:** Yes, Lewiston, Lapwai, Orofino, Kamiah, and Grangeville; **Overnight accommodations:** Lewiston, Lapwai, Orofino, Kamiah, and Grangeville; **First Aid available in park:** Yes; **Nearest Hospital:** Lewiston, US 95, 19.3 km (12 miles); **Days/Hours:** Spalding Unit and Visitor Center is open 8 a.m.-4:30 p.m. Sept. 1-May 31; until 9 p.m. June 1-Aug. 31; **Holiday Closings:** Thanksgiving, Dec. 25, Jan 1; **Visitor attractions closed for seasons:**Watson's Store exhibit and cultural demonstration offered only in Summer.

Oregon National Scenic Trail
For details see listing in Missouri

Illinois

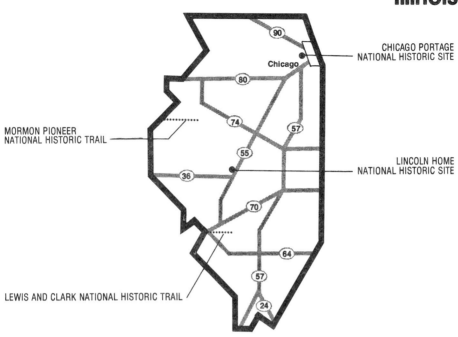

CHICAGO PORTAGE
NATIONAL HISTORIC SITE

Chicago

MORMON PIONEER
NATIONAL HISTORIC TRAIL

LINCOLN HOME
NATIONAL HISTORIC SITE

LEWIS AND CLARK NATIONAL HISTORIC TRAIL

Chicago Portage National Historic Site
River Forest, Illinois

MAILING ADDRESS: Superintendent, Chicago Portage National Historic Site, c/o Cook County Forest Preserve, Cummings Square, River Forest, Illinois 60305 **Telephone:** 312-366-9420

DIRECTIONS: Site is located on the west side of Harlem Ave. (IL 42A), approx. .8 km (1/2 mile) North of Stevenson Expressway (I-55).

A portion of the portage discovered by French explorers Jacques Marquette and Louis Joliet is preserved here. Used by pioneers as a link between the Great Lakes and the Mississippi, the portage was one of the economic foundations of Chicago. Designated Jan. 3, 1952. Owned and administered by Cook County.

VISITOR ACTIVITIES: interpretive story board, picnicking; **Permits:** No; **Fees:** No; **Visitor facilities:** parking, water, picnic area. Formal development has been delayed; **Any limitations on vehicle usage:** Vehicles are restricted to the parking area; **Hiking trails:** No; **Backcountry:** No; **Camping:** No; **Other overnight accommodations on site:** No; **Meals served in the park:** No; **Food and supplies obtainable in the park:** No; **Food and supplies obtainable nearby:** Yes, Lyons, IL; **Overnight accommodations:** Lyons, Hwy 34 (Ogden Ave.), 3 km (2 miles); **First Aid available in park:** No; **Nearest Hospital:**

LaGrange, Willow Springs Road, approx. 9.7 km (4 miles); **Days/Hours:** 9 a.m. to sunset; **Visitor attractions closed for seasons:** Site closed in Winter.

Lewis and Clark National Historic Trail
Illinois (also in Missouri, Kansas, Nebraska, Iowa, South Dakota, North Dakota, Montana, Idaho, Oregon, Washington)

MAILING ADDRESS: Midwest Regional Office, National Park Service, 1709 Jackson Street, Omaha, Nebraska 68102 **Telephone:** 402-221-3472

DIRECTIONS: TRAIL HAS NOT YET BEEN DEVELOPED.
The trail designated the 3,700-mile route of the 1804-06 expedition exploring the Louisiana Purchase from Wood River, IL to Fort Clatsop, OR. The modern trail is 2,200 miles on water and 136 miles on land—about 60% of the original trail. Authorized for addition to the National Park System on Nov. 10, 1978.

Lincoln Home National Historic Site
Springfield, Illinois

MAILING ADDRESS: Superintendent, Lincoln Home National Historic Site, 526 7th Street, Springfield, Illinois 62703 **Telephone:** 217-525-4241

DIRECTIONS: The Site is in downtown Springfield. The Visitor Center is at 526 7th Street, one block west of the Lincoln Home.
While living in this home-now the focal point of this historic area-Abraham Lincoln rose from the practice of a small-town lawyer to become the 16th President of the United States, 1861-65. The two-story structure, built in 1839, was the only home he ever owned and his residence for 17 years. Authorized for addition to the National Park System on Aug. 18, 1971.

VISITOR ACTIVITIES: interpretive exhibits and film, house tours; **Permits:** No; **Fees:** Parking fee is 50¢ per hour; **Visitor facilities:** Visitor Center, restrooms; **Any limitations on vehicle usage:** No vehicle traffic is allowed within the park; **Hiking trails:** No; **Backcountry:** No; **Camping:** No; **Other overnight accommodations on site:** No; **Meals served in the park:** No; **Food and supplies obtainable in the park:** No; **Food and supplies obtainable nearby:** Yes, in Springfield; **Overnight accommodations:** Springfield, surrounding the Site; **First Aid available in park:** Yes; **Nearest Hospitals:** 7 blocks north of the Home; **Days/Hours:** Open daily from 8 a.m. to 5 p.m.; **Holiday Closings:** Dec. 25 and Jan. 1; **Weather:** Winters are cold and snowy; Summers are hot and humid.

GENERAL INFORMATION: Watch out for uneven, slippery boardwalks and steep, narrow staircases.

Mormon Pioneer National Historic Trail
Illinois (also in Iowa, Nebraska, Wyoming, and Utah)

MAILING ADDRESS: Rocky Mountain Regional Ofice, Natinal Park Service, 655 Parfet Street, P.O. Box 25287, Denver, Colorado 80225 **Telephone:** 303-234-3095

DIRECTIONS: TRAIL HAS NOT YET BEEN DEVELOPED.

This 1,300-mile trail follows the route which Mormon leader Brigham Young and his followers took from Nauvoo, IL to the present site of Salt Lake City, UT in 1847. Authorized for addition to the National Park System on Nov. 10, 1978.

Indiana

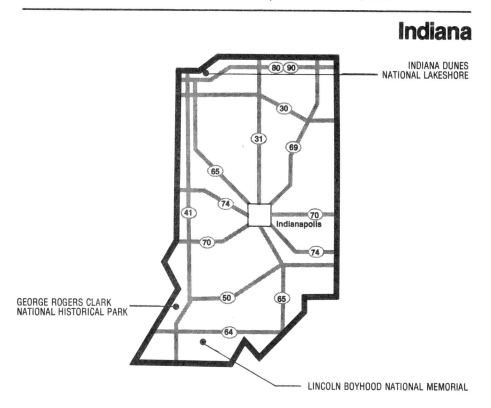

INDIANA DUNES NATIONAL LAKESHORE

GEORGE ROGERS CLARK NATIONAL HISTORICAL PARK

LINCOLN BOYHOOD NATIONAL MEMORIAL

George Rogers Clark National Historical Park
Vincennes, Indiana

MAILING ADDRESS: Superintendent, George Rogers Clark National Historical Park, 401 South Second Street, Vincennes, Indiana 47591 **Telephone:** 812-882-1776

DIRECTIONS: Follow US 50 (east and west) which intersects with US 41 (north and south) at Vincennes. US 50, Business, is on Vigo Street in proximity to the Park. The entrance to the Park is on Second Street, south of US 50.

Near the site of old Fort Sackville, this classic memorial commemorates the seizure of the fort from the British by Lt. Col. George Rogers Clark on Feb. 25, 1779. Authorized for addition to the National Park System on July 23, 1966.

VISITOR ACTIVITIES: interpretive exhibits and film, fishing, biking, living history weapon demonstrations and talks on Sunday afternoons in Summer; **Permits:** No; **Fees:** No; **Visitor facilities:** Visitor Center, bicycle trail, parking. In Summer, a "Trailblazer" train operated by Vincennes University tours points of interest in Vincennes; **Any limitations on vehicle usage:** Motorcycles are not permitted on sidewalks and the river trail; **Hiking trails:** Yes, an unpaved footpath along Wabash River bank, 1/4 mile section of a 2 mile long riverside trail; **Backcountry:** No; **Camping:** No; **Other overnight accommodations on site:** No; **Meals served in the park:** No; **Food and supplies obtainable in the park:** No; **Food and supplies obtainable nearby:** Yes, close to the Park in downtown Vincennes; **Overnight accommodations:** Vincennes; **First Aid available in park:** Yes; **Nearest Hospital:** Vincennes, 7th Street, 6 blocks; **Days/Hours:** Open daily from 8:30 a.m. to 5 p.m.; **Holiday Closings:** Thanksgiving, Dec. 25 & Jan. 1; **Visitor attractions closed for seasons:** The Park may be closed for a day or two in severe winter weather; **Weather:** Expect snow from January through March; the annual temperature range is from -10 to 100°F.

Indiana Dunes National Lakeshore
Chesterton, Indiana

MAILING ADDRESS: Superintendent, Indiana Dunes National Lakeshore, 1100 N. Mineral Springs Road, Porter, Indiana 46304 **Telephone:** 219-926-7561

DIRECTIONS: The lakeshore runs between Gary and Michigan City along the southern shore of Lake Michigan, about 100 km (60 miles) east of Chicago US 12 and 20. Interstate 94, IN 49, and Indiana Toll Road (I-80 and I-90) pass through the area and connect with roads which lead directly to the lakeshore. The Visitor Center is 5 km (3 miles) east of Indiana 49 on US 12 at the Intersection of US 12 and Kemil Road.

Along the southern shore of Lake Michigan between Gary and Michigan City are several sections of clean, sandy beaches backed by huge sand dunes. Many dunes are covered with dense forests, others are continually reshaped by the wind. The parkland, totaling about 12,000 acres, preserves some of these remaining dunes and their associated bogs and marshes and provides recreational opportunities along the beaches and interior lands. Authorized for addition to the National Park System on Nov. 5, 1966.

VISITOR ACTIVITIES: biking, hiking, horseback riding, auto tours, swimming, fishing, photography, interpretive talks, films and programs including a cultural arts festival in mid-July; **Permits:** an Indiana fishing license available locally; **Fees:** Yes, Indiana Dunes State Park, at N. Lakeshore, a $1 per vehicle (50¢ with Golden Age Passport) parking fee at West Beach area; **Visitor facilities:** first aid, horse trail, handicapped facilities, parking lots, restrooms, drinking water, food service, bathhouse, interpretive hikes, trails, talks, and films; **Any limitations on vehicle usage:** Dune buggies, motor bikes, and other motorized vehicles must remain on public roadways; **Hiking trails:** Yes, check at Visitor Center for information on hiking trails in each area; **Backcountry:** No; **Camping:** Yes, camping available at Indiana Dunes State Park, Chesterton, IN 46304, phone 219-926-1215. Reservations are accepted for campsites; contact the park for details. Private campgrounds are in neighboring communities; **Other overnight accommodations on site:** No; **Meals served in the park:** Yes, West Beach area; **Food and supplies obtainable in the park:** Yes, food at West Beach area; **Food and supplies obtainable nearby:** Yes, Michigan City, Gary, Portage; **Overnight accommodations:** Two motels are in the area and many more are in neighboring communities: Michigan City, 9.7 km (6 miles); Portage, 13 km (8 miles), Gary, 4.8 km (3 miles) from the park; **First Aid available in park:** Yes; **Nearest Hospital:** Michigan City, 9.7 km (6 miles), Gary, 4.8 km (3 miles); **Days/Hours:** Visitor Center is open from 8 a.m.-4:30 p.m. daily, and until 8 p.m. in Summer; **Holiday Closings:** Dec. 25 & Jan. 1; **Weather:** 90° Temperatures with high humidity in Summer, 0° and snowy in Winter.

GENERAL INFORMATION: Hunting and open fires are prohibited. Grills and portable stoves using charcoal, gas or liquid fuels are permitted. Private property rights must be respected.

Lewis and Clark Trail
For details see listing in Illinois

Lincoln Boyhood National Memorial
Lincoln City, Indiana

MAILING ADDRESS: Superintendent, Lincoln Boyhood National Memorial, Lincoln City, Indiana 47552 **Telephone:** 812-937-4757

DIRECTIONS: The park is on IN 162, 3.2 km (2 miles) east of Gentryville, 6.5 km (4 miles) south of Dale, IN, and 8 km (5 miles) south of Santa Claus, IN.

On this southern Indiana farm Abraham Lincoln grew from youth to manhood. His mother is buried here. Authorized for addition to the National Park System on Feb. 19, 1962.

VISITOR ACTIVITIES: interpretive tours, exhibits, and film; living history farm, self-guiding walking tours; **Permits:** No; **Fees:** No; **Visitor facilities:** restrooms, parking, telephones, and museum at Visitor Center, walking trails, souvenir sales; **Any limitations on vehicle usage:** Parking is only allowed at the Visitor Center and the exhibit shelter. Drivers should be alert for hikers and the handicapped; **Hiking trails:** Yes, 1.6 km (1 mile) self-guiding loop trail, historical trail; **Backcountry:** No, there are 18 km (12 miles) of connecting hiking trails from Gentryville through the Memorial and Lincoln State Park; **Camping:** No; **Other overnight accommodations on site:** No, a lake with picnic area, campgrounds, and restrooms are at nearby Lincoln State Park. Hiking, swimming, boating, and fishing facilities are also available there. An entrance fee is charged in Summer; **Meals served in the park:** No; **Food and supplies obtainable in the park:** No; **Food and supplies obtainable nearby:** Yes, in Dale and Santa Claus, IN; **Overnight accommodations:** Dale, 6.4 km (4 miles) north on US 231, Huntingburg, 24 km (15 miles) north and Jasper, 30 km (20 miles) north on US 231; **First Aid available in park:** Yes; **Nearest Hospital:** Huntingburg, 24 km (15 miles) north on US 231; **Days/Hours:** Open daily from 9 a.m. to 6 p.m. Jun 1 through Sept. 30, and 8 a.m. to 5 p.m. October 1 through May 30; **Holiday Closings:** Dec. 25 and Jan. 1; **Visitor attractions closed for seasons:**Farm cabin is open on a limited basis in Winter; **Weather:** Summer is humid with temperatures to 95°; Winter is moderate, but snowstorms occur in Jan. & Feb., and roads can be slippery.

GENERAL INFORMATION: The Memorial is on the "Lincoln Heritage Trail," an auto tour route which connects sites relating to Lincoln's life in Kentucky, Indiana and Illinois. *For Your Safety*—Stay on established trails. Beware of insects, poison ivy, and snakes.

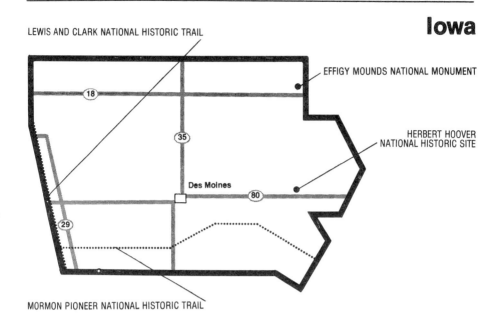

Iowa

LEWIS AND CLARK NATIONAL HISTORIC TRAIL

EFFIGY MOUNDS NATIONAL MONUMENT

HERBERT HOOVER
NATIONAL HISTORIC SITE

Des Moines

MORMON PIONEER NATIONAL HISTORIC TRAIL

Effigy Mounds National Monument
McGregor, Iowa

MAILING ADDRESS: Superintendent, Effigy Mounds National Monument, P.O. Box K, McGregor, Iowa 52157 **Telephone:** 319-873-2356

DIRECTIONS: The Monument is 5 km (3 miles) north of Marquette on IA 76.
   The Monument contains outstanding examples of prehistoric burial mounds, some in the shapes of birds and bears. Created by Presidential Proclamation on Oct. 25, 1949.

VISITOR ACTIVITIES: interpretive exhibits, self-guiding and guided walks; **Permits:** No; **Fees:** No; **Visitor facilities:** parking and restrooms at Visitor Center, walking trail, exhibits and markers, guided walks 4 times daily from Memorial Day through Labor Day; **Any limitations on vehicle usage:** There are no roads; **Hiking trails:** Yes, 1-3 hour self-guiding trail; **Backcountry:** No; **Camping:** No; **Other overnight accommodations on site:** No; **Meals served in the park:** No; **Food and supplies obtainable in the park:** No; **Food and supplies obtainable nearby:** Yes, in Waukon and McGregor; **Overnight accommodations:** Waukon, 30 km (20 miles), McGregor, 7 km (4 miles), and Prairie du Chien, WI, 7 km (4 miles); **First Aid available in park:** Yes; **Nearest Hospital:** Prairie du Chien, WI, 7 km (4 miles); **Days/Hours:** Visitor Center open daily from 8 a.m. until 5 p.m. and remains open until 7 p.m. in Summer; **Holiday Closings:** Dec. 25; **Weather:** Summers are warm to hot with moderate-to-high humidity, Winters are cold and snowy with temperatures in the 15°-30° range.

GENERAL INFORMATION: When hiking, stay on trails and do not venture too close to cliff edges. Hikers should remain on the trail and be alert for poison ivy and stinging nettles.

Herbert Hoover National Historic Site
West Branch, Iowa

MAILING ADDRESS: Superintendent, Herbert Hoover National Historic Site, P.O. Box 607, West Branch, Iowa 52358 **Telephone:** 319-643-2541

DIRECTIONS: West Branch is 11 km (7 miles) east of Iowa City on I-80 and 65 km (40 miles) west of Davenport on I-80. The Visitor Center is on Parkside Drive at the intersection with Main Street.

The birthplace, home, and boyhood neighborhood of the 31st President, 1929-33, the gravesites of President and Mrs. Hoover, and the Hoover Presidential Library-Museum are within the park. Authorized for addition to the National Park System on Aug. 12, 1965.

VISITOR ACTIVITIES: interpretive talks and exhibits, picnicking, walking tours, cross-country skiing; **Permits:** No; **Fees:** No National Park Service fees. The Hoover Presidential Library-Museum is administered by the National Archives and Records Service, and a 75¢ entrance fee is charged; **Visitor facilities:** parking and restrooms at Visitor Center, picnic areas, walking trails, interpretive exhibits, operating blacksmith shop in Summer; **Any limitations on vehicle usage:** Vehicles are restricted to designated roadways; **Hiking trails:** Yes, self-guiding trails; **Backcountry:** No; **Camping:** No; **Other overnight accommodations on site:** No; **Meals served in the park:** No; **Food and supplies obtainable in the park:** No; **Food and supplies obtainable nearby:** Yes, at West Branch; **Overnight accommodations:** West Branch, .8 km (1/2 mile); **First Aid available in park:** Yes; **Nearest Hospital:** Iowa City, IA, 16 km (10 miles) via I-80; **Days/Hours:** Open daily from 8 a.m. to 5 p.m., until 6 p.m. in Summer. Library and Museum open 8 a.m. to 6 p.m. weekdays, and 10 a.m. to 6 p.m. on Sundays from Memorial Day through Labor Day; 9 a.m. to 5 p.m. weekdays and 12 to 5 p.m. on Sundays from Sept. through May; **Holiday Closings:** Thanksgiving, Dec. 25 & Jan. 1.

GENERAL INFORMATION: Please note the historic walkway surfaces. Boardwalks are especially slippery in frost or wet weather.

Lewis and Clark Trail
For details see listing in Illinois

Kansas

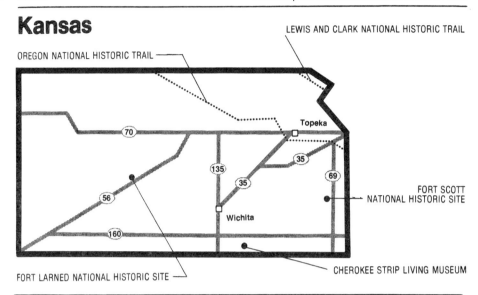

LEWIS AND CLARK NATIONAL HISTORIC TRAIL

OREGON NATIONAL HISTORIC TRAIL

Topeka

70

135

35

35

69

56

160

Wichita

FORT SCOTT
NATIONAL HISTORIC SITE

FORT LARNED NATIONAL HISTORIC SITE

CHEROKEE STRIP LIVING MUSEUM

Cherokee Strip Living Museum
Arkansas City, Kansas

MAILING ADDRESS: Director, Cherokee Strip Living Museum, Arkansas City, Kansas 67005 **Telephone:** 316-442-6750

DIRECTIONS: The Museum is on US 77 south of Arkansas City, Kansas, just across the Cherokee Strip Bridge. It is 25 km (16 miles) east of I-35, 32 km (20 miles) east of US 81, 21 km (13 miles) north of Newkirk, Oklahoma, and 42 km (26 miles) north of Ponca City, OK.

This privately administered museum near the Oklahoma border commemorates the opening of the "Indian territory" to settlement. Authorized for addition to the National Park System on Oct. 12, 1976.

VISITOR ACTIVITIES: interpretive exhibits; **Permits:** No; **Fees:** Entrance fee is $1.50 for adults, $1 for Junior High and High School students. Golden Age and Golden Eagle Passports accepted and available; **Visitor facilities:** museum; **Any limitations on vehicle usage:** No; **Meals served in the park:** No; **Food and supplies obtainable in the park:** No; **Food and supplies obtainable nearby:** Yes, in Arkansas City, KS; **Overnight accommodations:** Within 2.4 km (1-1/2 miles) on Hwy 77; **First Aid available in park:** No, nearby in Arkansas City, KS; **Nearest Hospital:** Arkansas City, KS, Hwy 77, 3 km (2 miles); **Days/Hours:** Open daily from 10 a.m. to 5 p.m.; **Holiday Closings:** Thanksgiving, Dec. 25 and Jan. 1; **Visitor attractions closed for seasons:**No; **Weather:** Moderate weather year-round except for Dec. 15-Feb. 15.

Fort Larned National Historic Site
Larned, Kansas

MAILING ADDRESS: Superintendent, Fort Larned National Historic Site, Route 3,

Larned, Kansas 67550 **Telephone:** 316-285-3571

DIRECTIONS: The Site is 9.5 km (6 miles) west of the city of Larned, KS, on US 156.
A military fort from 1859 to 1878, Fort Larned was used for protection of mail and travellers on the eastern leg of the Santa Fe Trail. It served as an Indian Agency from 1861 to 1868 and a base for military operations against the Southern Plains Indians. Authorized for addition to the National Park System on Aug. 31, 1964; established in 1966.

VISITOR ACTIVITIES: guided tours upon request and daily during Summer, films on Sunday afternoons in Spring, Fall and Winter, Living history programs on weekends during Summer; **Permits:** No; **Fees:** No; **Visitor facilities:** parking, restrooms, exhibits, sales area, and audiovisual facilities at Visitor Center; historic military buildings; interpretive signs; **Any limitations on vehicle usage:** Vehicles are only allowed in the parking area; **Hiking trails:** No; **Backcountry:** No; **Camping:** No; **Other overnight accommodations on site:** No, overnight camping is permitted at a State-operated roadside rest area .4 km (1/4 mile) north of the Site on US 156. Commercial campgrounds are available in Larned. Contact Fort Larned for further information; **Meals served in the park:** No; **Food and supplies obtainable in the park:** No; **Food and supplies obtainable nearby:** Yes, at Larned; **Overnight accommodations:** Larned, 9.6 km (6 miles) on US 156; **First Aid available in park:** No; **Nearest Hospital:** Larned, 9.6 km (6 miles) East on US 156; **Days/Hours:** Open year-round. From early June through Labor Day from 8 a.m. to 7 p.m.; the rest of the year from 8 a.m. to 5 p.m.; **Holiday Closings:** Dec. 25; **Visitor attractions closed for seasons:**Living history programs are offered in Summer only; **Weather:** Summer is warm to hot and often windy. Winter is cold, with snow between late Dec. and early March.

Fort Scott National Historic Site
Fort Scott, Kansas

MAILING ADDRESS: Superintendent, Fort Scott National Historic Site, Old Fort Boulevard, Fort Scott, Kansas 66701 **Telephone:** 316-223-0310

DIRECTIONS: The fort is near the intersection of US 69 and US 54 in Fort Scott, which is 144 km (90 miles) south of Kansas City and 97 km (60 miles) north of Joplin, MO.
The fort commemorates historic events in Kansas prior to and during the Civil War. This affiliated area was authorized for addition to the National Park System on Aug. 31, 1965.

VISITOR ACTIVITIES: tours of reconstructed and restored historic buildings, interpretive exhibits; **Permits:** No; **Fees:** No; **Visitor facilities:** restrooms, book store, museum; **Any limitations on vehicle usage:** No vehicles are allowed within the park; **Hiking trails:** No; **Backcountry:** No; **Camping:** No; **Other overnight accommodations on site:** No, KOA campground is 3 km (2 miles) from the Site; **Meals served in the park:** No; **Food and supplies obtainable in the park:** No; **Food and supplies obtainable nearby:** Yes, at Fort Scott; **Overnight accommodations:** Fort Scott, 2 blocks to 1.6 km (1 mile) from the Site; **First Aid available in park:** Yes; **Nearest Hospital:** Fort Scott, 1.6 km (1 mile); **Days/Hours:** Open daily from 8 a.m. to 5 p.m.; **Holiday Closings:** Thanksgiving and Dec. 25; **Visitor attractions closed for seasons:**None; **Weather:** Summers are hot and humid with an average temperature of 80°. Winters are cold; average temperature is 25°.

GENERAL INFORMATION: The park is still being developed, and will be completed in 1980-81.

Oregon National Scenic Trail
For details see listing in Missouri

Kentucky

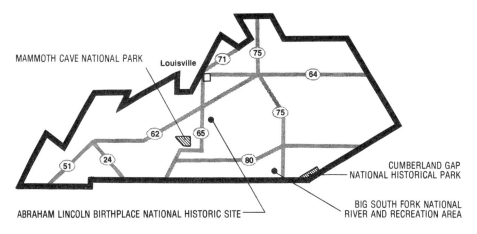

MAMMOTH CAVE NATIONAL PARK   Louisville

CUMBERLAND GAP NATIONAL HISTORICAL PARK

BIG SOUTH FORK NATIONAL RIVER AND RECREATION AREA

ABRAHAM LINCOLN BIRTHPLACE NATIONAL HISTORIC SITE

Abraham Lincoln Birthplace National Historic Site
Hodgenville, Kentucky

MAILING ADDRESS: Superintendent, Abraham Lincoln Birthplace National Historic Site, Route 1, Hodgenville, Kentucky 42748 **Telephone:** 502-358-3874

DIRECTIONS: The Site is 4.8 km (3 miles) south of Hodgenville on US 31E and KY 61, 96 km (60 miles) south of Louisville.

Established by act of Congress on July 17, 1916, this 116.50-acre historic site preserves in its memorial building an early 19th-century Kentucky cabin, symbolic of the one in which Lincoln was born.

VISITOR ACTIVITIES: interpretive talks, exhibits and film, hiking, picnicking; **Permits:** No; **Fees:** No; **Visitor facilities:** parking at Visitor Center, parking and restrooms at picnic area, environmental study area; **Any limitations on vehicle usage:** No; **Hiking trails:** Yes, through forest land; **Backcountry:** No; **Camping:** No; **Other overnight accommodations on site:** No; **Meals served in the park:** No, but available in Hodgenville; **Food and supplies obtainable in the park:** No; **Food and supplies obtainable nearby:** Yes, in Hodgenville; **Overnight accommodations:** Motels are adjacent to the park and in Hodgenville; **First Aid available in park:** Yes, and nearby in Hodgenville, US 31E; **Nearest Hospital:** Elizabethtown, KY 61, 24 km (17 miles); **Days/Hours:** Open daily from 8 a.m. to 7 p.m. from June 1 through Sept. 1; 8 a.m. to 4:45 p.m. the rest of the year; **Holiday Closings:** Dec. 25; **Visitor attractions closed for**

seasons: None; **Weather:** Warm Summers with frequent rain; moderate Winters with light snow.

GENERAL INFORMATION: *For Your Safety*—Watch for exposed roots and uneven ground along trails. Poison ivy and briars are abundant in woodland.

Big South Fork National River and Recreation Area
For details see listing in Tennessee

Cumberland Gap National Historical Park
Middlesboro, Kentucky (also in Tennessee and Virginia)

MAILING ADDRESS: Superintendent, Cumberland Gap National Historical Park, P.O. Box 840, Middlesboro, Kentucky 40965 **Telephone:** 606-248-2817

DIRECTIONS: The Park can be reached by taking US 25E from Kentucky and Tennessee or US 58 from Virginia. The Visitor Center is .8 km (1/2 mile) south of Middlesboro on US 25E.

The mountain pass on the wilderness, explored by Daniel Boone, developed into a main artery of the great trans-Allegheny migration for settlement of "the Old West" and an important military objective in the Civil War. Authorized for addition to the National Park System on June 11, 1940.

VISITOR ACTIVITIES: interpretive and audiovisual exhibits, hiking, camping, picnicking, campfire programs, walking, music and craft demonstrations, bird counts, living history programs, fishing; **Permits:** for backcountry, available from the Superintendent; **Fees:** $2 fee for camping in the Wilderness Road Campground; **Visitor facilities:** primitive and developed campgrounds, hiking trails, restrooms, picnic areas, drinking water, museum; **Any limitations on vehicle usage:** Off-road vehicle use is not permitted; 20' maximum vehicle length on Pinnacle Road; **Hiking trails:** Yes, there are about 80 km (50 miles) of hiking trails in the Park. Trail guides and information are available at the visitor center; **Backcountry:** Yes, get information from the Superintendent; **Camping:** Yes, organized group camping area and primitive campsites are reserved by contacting the Superintendent. No other reservations are available; **Other overnight accommodations on site:** No; **Meals served in the park:** No; **Food and supplies obtainable in the park:** No; **Food and supplies obtainable nearby:** Yes, in Middlesboro, KY, Cumberland Gap, TN, Gibson Station and Ewing, VA; **Overnight accommodations:** Middlesboro, KY, US 25E, several blocks; Cumberland Gap, TN, US 25E, 4 km (2-1/2 miles); Harrogate, TN, US 25E, 6.4 km (4 miles); **First Aid available in park:** Yes; **Nearest Hospital:** Middlesboro, KY, US 25E to Hwy 74, 1.6 km (1 mile); **Days/Hours:** Park gates are open from 8 a.m. to dusk year-round. The Visitor Center is open from 8 a.m. to 5 p.m.; **Holiday Closings:** Dec. 25; **Visitor attractions closed for seasons:**Pinnacle can be closed temporarily due to snow; **Weather:** Summer is hot and humid; Winter is cold to moderate.

GENERAL INFORMATION: *For Your Safety*—Never hike alone. Beware of snakes, poison ivy and poison oak. Nearby points of interest include Cudjo's Cave; the June Tolliver House at Big Stone Gap, VA; Lincoln Memorial University in Harrogate, TN; Pine Mountain State Park, KY; and Dr. Thomas Walker State Park, near Barbourville,

KY. Directions and further information on these sites are available at the Middlesboro Visitor Center.

Mammoth Cave National Park
Mammoth Cave, Kentucky

MAILING ADDRESS: Superintendent, Mammoth Cave National Park, Mammoth Cave, Kentucky 42259 **Telephone:** 502-758-2251

DIRECTIONS: Visitor Center (which includes cave tour information and ticket sales) is 14.5 km (9 miles) northwest of Park City off Interstate 65 via KY 255 or 70.

Mammoth Cave is a series of underground passageways containing travertine, onyx, and gypsum formations, deep pits and high domes and an underground river. Over 305 km (190 miles) of interconnected passageways have been surveyed and mapped, making it the longest recorded cave system in the world. Authorized for addition to the National Park System on May 25, 1926.

VISITOR ACTIVITIES: guided cave tours, guided nature walks and evening programs in Summer, self-guiding walking trails, camping, picnicking, boating, fishing, horseback riding, backcountry hiking, and Green River boat trip; **Permits:** for backcountry camping, available at Park Headquarters or campground station; **Fees:** for cave tours, Green River boat trip, and camping in the main campground. Cave tours vary in length (1 to 6 hours), season offered and time of departure. Green River boat trip available April through Oct. For a description of tours available, current tour schedule and prices, contact the Superintendent; **Visitor facilities:** Visitor Center, hiking trails, picnic area, boat ramps, post office, service station, campgrounds, groceries and camping supplies, coin-operated laundry, showers, lodging, dining room and coffee shop, souvenirs and Green River boat trip; **Any limitations on vehicle usage:** No; **Hiking trails:** Yes, Variety of hiking trails available ranging from short self-guiding nature trails to several miles of hiking trails. Trail information at Visitor Center; **Backcountry:** Yes, information available at Visitor Center or by contacting the Superintendent. Backcountry camping permit required and may be obtained at the Park Headquarters or campground station; **Camping:** Yes, no reservations accepted for the 80 individual campsites. Camping fee is $3 per night per site. A free primitive campground with 12 sites is at Houchins Ferry; **Other overnight accommodations on site:** Yes, Mammoth Cave Hotel is open all year. For reservations, contact National Park Concessions, Inc., Mammoth Cave, KY 42259, phone 502-758-2225; **Meals served in the park:** Yes, at Mammoth Cave Hotel; **Food and supplies obtainable in the park:** Yes, at the service center located next to the main campground. The store is closed from Thanksgiving to Easter Week and is only open on weekends, including Fridays in the Spring and Fall; **Food and supplies obtainable nearby:** Yes, at Bowling Green, Glasgow, Horse Cave, Park City, and Cave City; **Overnight accommodations:** Numerous overnight accommodations are available within a 45 minute drive of the Park which includes the communities of Bowling Green, Glasgow, Horse Cave, Park City and Cave City. For information on areas outside the park write the Department of Public Information, Capitol Annex Building, Frankfort, KY 40601; **First Aid available in park:** Yes; **Nearest Hospital:** Caverna Hospital at Horse Cave, US 31W, 24 km (15 miles); **Days/Hours:** Open year-round: Visitor Center open 7:30 a.m.-7 p.m. in Summer; 8 a.m.-5 p.m. the rest of the year; **Holiday Closings:** Cave tours not available Dec. 25; **Visitor attractions closed for seasons:**Main campground closed Dec. through Feb.

GENERAL INFORMATION: In the caves the temperature remains at 12°C (54°F) and the humidity is a high 87%. Bring along a sweater or light jacket. All cave tours are strenuous, requiring stooping and walking over unlevel terrain. Be sure to select the tour that best meets your physical ability. Portions of cave and surface trails are uneven and wet and slippery, so wear sturdy walking shoes—not sandals. Children under 16 years of age must be accompanied by an adult. While driving, be on the alert for deer crossing the roadway, particularly at night. Poisonous snakes and poison ivy are common, even around the most heavily visited areas.

Louisiana

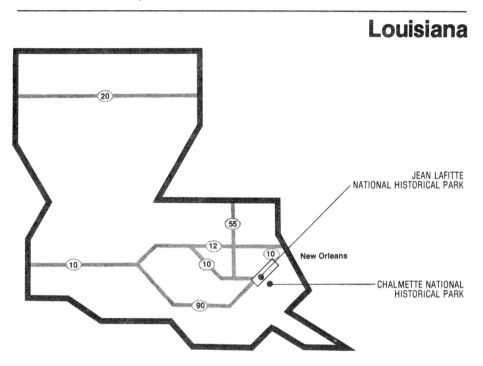

Chalmette National Historical Park
Arabi, Louisiana

MAILING ADDRESS: Unit Manager, Chalmette National Historical Park, P.O. Box 429, Arabi, Louisiana 70032 **Telephone:** 504-271-2412

DIRECTIONS: The Park is in St. Bernard Parish on the east bank of the Mississippi River, 9.7 km (6 miles) from the heart of New Orleans. From Canal Street follow the main thoroughfare that begins at Rampart Street and merges into St. Claude Avenue, then into St. Bernard Hwy., which passes directly in front of the Park. The Visitor Center is located in the Beauregard Home.

America won a brilliant victory here in the Battle of New Orleans in the War of 1812. The Park includes Chalmette National Cemetery. Established by act of Congress on Mar. 4, 1907.

VISITOR ACTIVITIES: audiovisual and interpretive exhibits, auto tours, walking and self-guiding tours, fishing; **Permits:** No; **Fees:** No; **Visitor facilities:** exhibits, parking, restrooms; **Any limitations on vehicle usage:** Vehicles are restricted to designated roadways; **Hiking trails:** No; **Backcountry:** No; **Camping:** No; **Other overnight accommodations on site:** No; **Meals served in the park:** No; **Food and supplies obtainable in the park:** No; **Food and supplies obtainable nearby:** Yes, at Arabi, within 1/2 mile; **Overnight accommodations:** New Orleans and vicinity, approx. 8 km (5 miles); **First Aid available in park:** Yes; **Nearest Hospital:** Arabi, LA 46, 4.8 km (3 miles); **Days/Hours:** Open daily from 8 a.m. to 5 p.m.; **Holiday Closings:** Dec. 25, Jan. 1, and Mardi Gras; **Visitor attractions closed for seasons:** None; **Weather:** Hot, humid Summers, mild Winters.

Jean LaFitte National Historical Park
New Orleans, Louisiana

MAILING ADDRESS: Jean LaFitte National Historical Park, Room 200, 400 Royal Street, New Orleans, Louisiana 70130 **Telephone:** 504-589-3882

DIRECTIONS: *NOT OPEN TO THE PUBLIC AT THIS TIME.* A Visitor Center is expected to open in New Orleans' French Quarter on Jackson Square in early 1980. Contact the Park for further information. See listing in this book for Chalmette National Historical Park, a unit of Jean LaFitte which is currently in operation.

The Park preserves cultural resources of the Delta region including the French Quarter in New Orleans. Chalmette NHP, site of the 1814 Battle of New Orleans, is now a unit of the Park. Authorized for addition to the National Park System on Nov. 10, 1978.

Maine

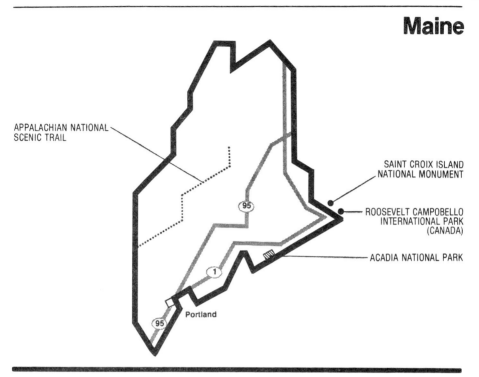

Acadia National Park
Bar Harbor, Maine

MAILING ADDRESS: Superintendent, Acadia National Park, RFD 1, Box 1, Bar Harbor, Maine 04069 **Telephone:** 207-288-3338

DIRECTIONS: The Park is located on ME 3, 75.6 km (47 miles) southeast of Bangor, ME. Schoodic Peninsula, the only part of the Park on the mainland, is accessible via ME 186.

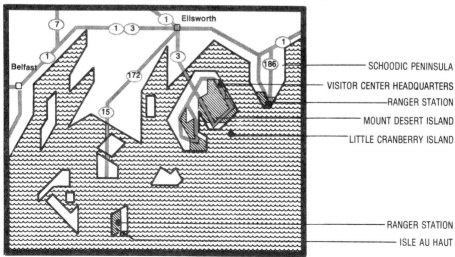

Set aside in 1916 and declared a national park in 1919 and 1929, it combines unusual ocean and mountain scenery over 40 square miles of Mount Desert Island, the mainland Schoodic Peninsula and several small islands.

VISITOR ACTIVITIES: 20-mile scenic drive connects lakes, mountains, and seashore; carriage paths open to hikers, bicycles and horses; foot trails; museums on mainland and Little Cranberry Island; frequent showing of a film at the Visitor Center; naturalist program; boat cruises; **Permits:** No; **Fees:** for boat cruises, the fee ranges from $3.75-$5.00 for adults and $2.25-$2.50 for children under 12. Prices are subject to change; **Visitor facilities:** beaches, campgrounds, museums, nature walks, campfire programs, audiovisual and interpretive programs, cassette tape tours, rental horses, picnic areas, bathhouse; **Any limitations on vehicle usage:** Vehicles are confined to established roadways; **Hiking trails:** Yes, there are more than 192 km (120 miles) of hiking trails; **Backcountry:** No; **Camping:** Yes, two campgrounds are available in the Park, and there are numerous private campgrounds in the area. Camping at designated campgrounds only is limited to 14 days; **Other overnight accommodations on site:** No; **Meals served in the park:** No; **Food and supplies obtainable in the park:** No; **Food and supplies obtainable nearby:** Yes, Bar Harbor, Northeast Harbor, Southwest Harbor, Ellsworth; **Overnight accommodations:** Bar Harbor, ME 3, 4.8 km (3 miles); Northeast Harbor, ME 3, 22.5 km (14 miles); Ellsworth, ME 3, 32 km (20 miles); Southwest Harbor, ME 3, 29 km (18 miles); **First Aid available in park:** No, nearby in Bar Harbor; **Nearest Hospital:** Bar Harbor, ME 3, 4.8 km (3 miles); **Days/Hours:** Open year-round. Visitor Center is open from May 1-Oct. 30, 7 days; 8 a.m. to 4:30 p.m. and 9 a.m. to 5 p.m. in Spring/Fall; 8 a.m. to 8 p.m. in Summer; **Holiday Closings:** None; **Visitor attractions closed for seasons:**Visitor Center, Nature Center, Museum; **Weather:** Cool Summers and fog are common, low temperature 55°-60°, high temperature 68°-75°.

GENERAL INFORMATION: *For Your Safety*—Be particularly careful on the rugged shores of Acadia. Ledges and rocks below high tide are slippery with algae, so walk carefully. Watch out for storm waves, particularly in Spring and Autumn. Occassionally an unusually large one reaches far up on the ledge or beach—it could knock you down and sweep you into the sea. Watch the trail when hiking, to avoid poison ivy or falling loose stones. If you find one trail too steep or precarious, choose another.

Appalachian National Scenic Trail
Maine, New Hampshire, Vermont, Massachusetts, Connecticut, New York, New Jersey, Pennsylvania, Maryland, West Virginia, Virginia, Tennessee, North Carolina, and Georgia

---

MAILING ADDRESS: Appalachian Trail Conference, P.O. Box 236, Harpers Ferry, West Virginia 25425 **Telephone:** 304-535-6331

DIRECTIONS: Contact the Appalachian Trail Conference for detailed information on directions to the Trail.

Approximately 3220 km (2000 miles) of this scenic trail follow the Appalachian Mountains from Mount Katahdin, ME through to Springer Mountain, GA. The Trail is one of the two initial units of the National Trail System. Established by act of Congress on Oct. 2, 1968.

VISITOR ACTIVITIES: short- and long-term hiking, camping, bird- and wildlife-watching, backcountry; **Permits:** A permit is not required to hike the Trail, but camping permits are necessary in the Shenandoah National Park and Great Smoky Mountains National Park. These permits are available at Ranger Stations upon arrival. See listings on these parks in this book for information on facilities and reservations. Camping facilities are also available at Green Mountain National Forest, VT; White Mountain National Forest, NH; and Baxter State Park, ME; **Fees:** at certain Northeast campsites, a $2 fee per site for 158 km (98 miles) through Long Trail Area, VT; **Visitor facilities:** lean-to shelters, fire pits, picnic tables; **Any limitations on vehicle usage:** Motor vehicles are prohibited on hiking trails; **Hiking trails:** Yes, some circuit hikes (blue blazed); **Backcountry:** Yes, Contact the Appalachian Trail Conference, P.O. Box 236, Harpers Ferry, WV 25425, phone 304-535-6331; **Camping:** Yes, no reservations available for campsites; **Other overnight accommodations on site:** No; **Meals served in the park:** Only in some national parks along the trail. Hikers have regular food drop points at post offices near the trail; **Food and supplies obtainable in the park:** No; **Food and supplies obtainable nearby:** Yes, stores are often located near major road crossings. Hut system operates in White Mountains, providing shelter and food at higher fee; **Overnight accommodations:** Accommodations are generally available at nearby towns; **First Aid available in park:** No; **Nearest Hospital:** in most of the larger nearby towns; **Days/Hours:** Park never closes.

GENERAL INFORMATION: Most hikers start in March or April and take 3 to 4 months to hike the entire trail, mostly from south to north.

Saint Croix Island National Monument
Red Beach, Maine

MAILING ADDRESS: Superintendent, Saint Croix Island National Monument, c/o Acadia National Park, Route 1 Box 1, Bar Harbor, Maine 04609 **Telephone:** 207-288-3338

DIRECTIONS: The Monument is at Red Beach Maine, 193 km (120 miles) north of Bar Harbor. It is 19 km (12 miles) south of Calais, Maine along US 1. There is currently no ferry service to the island.
  The attempted French settlement of 1604, which led to the founding of New France, is commemorated on Saint Croix Island, located on the Saint Croix River at the Canadian border. Authorized for addition to the National Park System on June 8, 1949.

VISITOR ACTIVITIES: walking, picnicking; **Permits:** No; **Fees:** No; **Visitor facilities:** There are no facilities on the island at this time. The mainland has a picnic area and pit toilets. No water is available. A mainland visitor interpretive facility is scheduled for the near future; **Any limitations on vehicle usage:** There are no vehicles allowed on the island.It is reached only by boat; **Hiking trails:** No; **Backcountry:** No; **Camping:** No; **Other overnight accommodations on site:** No; **Meals served in the park:** No; **Food and supplies obtainable in the park:** No; **Food and supplies obtainable nearby:** No; **Overnight accommodations:** Calais, US 1, 19 km (12 miles); **First Aid available in park:** No; **Nearest Hospital:** Calais, US 1, 19 km (12 miles); **Days/Hours:** Persons having a boat can visit the island anytime, weather permitting; **Weather:** Summers have cool maritime air, Winters are cold and wet with frequent snowfall.

Maryland

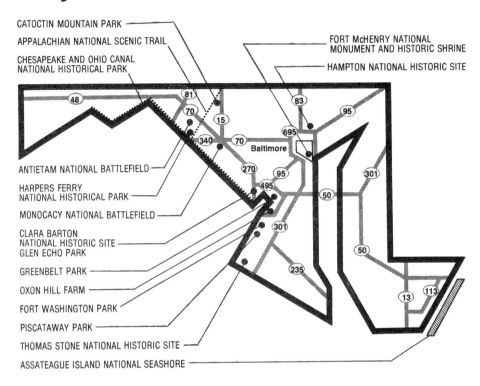

CATOCTIN MOUNTAIN PARK

APPALACHIAN NATIONAL SCENIC TRAIL

CHESAPEAKE AND OHIO CANAL
NATIONAL HISTORICAL PARK

FORT McHENRY NATIONAL
MONUMENT AND HISTORIC SHRINE

HAMPTON NATIONAL HISTORIC SITE

Baltimore

ANTIETAM NATIONAL BATTLEFIELD

HARPERS FERRY
NATIONAL HISTORICAL PARK

MONOCACY NATIONAL BATTLEFIELD

CLARA BARTON
NATIONAL HISTORIC SITE
GLEN ECHO PARK

GREENBELT PARK

OXON HILL FARM

FORT WASHINGTON PARK

PISCATAWAY PARK

THOMAS STONE NATIONAL HISTORIC SITE

ASSATEAGUE ISLAND NATIONAL SEASHORE

Antietam National Battlefield
Sharpsburg, Maryland

MAILING ADDRESS: Superintendent, Antietam National Battlefield, P.O. Box 158, Sharpsburg, Maryland 21782 **Telephone:** 301-432-5124

DIRECTIONS: The site is south of Hagerstown and west of Frederick. Routes I-70 and US 40 or 40-A connect with MD 34 and 65 along which the site lies north of Sharpsburg. The Visitor Center is on MD 65.

Established by act of Congress on Aug. 30, 1890, this site marks the end of General Robert E. Lee's first invasion of the North in 1862, a battle which claimed over 23,000 lives.

VISITOR ACTIVITIES: interpretive and slide programs, exhibits, automobile, bicycle and walking tours, fishing, picnicking; **Permits:** No; **Fees:** No; **Visitor facilities:** Visitor Center with observation deck, exhibit and display room, audiovisual orientation slide program, taped tour for the 13 km (8 mile) self-guiding auto tour; picnic area, nature trail; **Any limitations on vehicle usage:** Vehicles are confined to parking area and park roads; **Hiking trails:** Yes, nature trail, historic trail; **Backcountry:** No; **Camping:** Yes, but only for organized groups. Groups may call 301-432-5124 and ask about camping in the Rohrback area; **Other overnight accommodations on site:** No; **Meals served in the**

park: No; **Food and supplies obtainable in the park:** No; **Food and supplies obtainable nearby:** Yes, in Sharpsburg, 1.6 km (1 mile); **Overnight accommodations:** Along US 40 east of Hagerstown, 16 km (10 miles) from the park; **First Aid available in park:** Yes, or nearby in Sharpsburg, 1.6 km (1 mile); **Nearest Hospital:** Hagerstown, MD 65, 19 km (12 miles); **Days/Hours:** Open daily 8:30 a.m. to 5 p.m.; Summer hours are 8 a.m. to 6 p.m.; **Holiday Closings:** Thanksgiving, Dec. 25, Jan.1; **Visitor attractions closed for seasons:**Historic church closed and audio exhibits not offered in Winter.

GENERAL INFORMATION: *For Your Safety*—Motorists should be aware of one-way roads, pedestrians, and bicyclists. Stop your vehicle while reading interpretive signs.

Appalachian National Scenic Trail
For details see listing in Maine

Assateague Island National Seashore
Maryland and Virginia

MAILING ADDRESS: Superintendent, Assateague Island National Seashore, Route 2, Box 294, Berlin, Maryland 21811 **Telephone:** 301-641-1441 (MD) or 804-336-6577 (VA District Office).

DIRECTIONS: Via US 50, the Seashore is about 241 km (150 miles) from Baltimore or Washington. Via US 13 and 113, it is about 224 km (140 miles) from Philadelphia and 145 km (90 miles) from Norfolk. Visitor facilities are located at the extreme ends of Assateague Island—on the north end near Ocean City, MD and on the south opposite Chincoteague, VA. More than 35 km (22 miles) of roadless barrier island beach and marsh lie between these developed areas. To get from one end of the island to the other, visitors must drive back onto the mainland.

This 60 km (37 mile) barrier island has a sandy beach, pine forests, salt marsh, many kinds of waterfowl and other birds, and a variety of mammals including wild ponies. Most of the Virginia portion consists of the Chincoteague Island National Wildlife Refuge which was established in 1943. Most of the Maryland section was authorized for addition to the National Park System on Sept. 21, 1965.

VISITOR ACTIVITIES: surf fishing, clamming, crabbing, canoeing, hiking, bird-watching, camping, swimming, interpretive programs in Summer, shell collecting, hunting, pony round-up and auction on the last Wednesday and Thursday of July; **Permits:** Oversand vehicle permits required for oversand use. Backcountry permits required; permits for night surf fishing required in Virginia; **Fees:** For camping, day-use and oversand vehicle permits. Camping is $2.50 per night, mid-June through Labor Day. Day-use fee is $1 per car, mid-June through Labor Day. Oversand vehicle permits are $5 each year. Assateague State Park camping and day-use fees are approximately twice as high, but the facilities are more modern; **Visitor facilities:** campgrounds, picnic areas, bathhouses, lifeguarded beaches in Summer, wildlife refuge, self-guided nature trails, crabbing and small-boat launch facilities, Visitor Centers with exhibits; **Any limitations on vehicle usage:** Vehicles must be registered and licensed; all vehicles must stay on marked routes; motorcycles are restricted to hard surfaced roads. Oversand vehicles must have a permit before using the oversand routes. Potential users of oversand routes should contact the park for information on required equipment; **Hiking trails:** Yes, short self-guiding nature trails in both state sections; **Backcountry:** Yes, both hike-in and canoe-in are available. Contact the park or the Visitor Center; **Camping:** Yes, primitive campsites only in Maryland. No reservations for most campsites. Some state park campsites may be reserved in Summer for a full week only. Backcountry sites may be reserved in advance; **Other overnight accommodations on site:** No; **Meals served in the park:** No, but at Assateague State Park, only in Summer; **Food and supplies obtainable in the park:** No; **Food and supplies obtainable nearby:** Yes, Berlin, MD and Chincoteague, VA; **Overnight accommodations:** Chincoteague, VA, 8 km (5 miles); Ocean City, MD, Rte 611, 11.3 km (7 miles); **First Aid available in park:** Yes, or nearby in Chincoteague, VA, Berlin & Ocean City, MD; **Nearest Hospital:** Salisbury, MD, Rte 50 or US 13, approximately 72 km (35 miles) from each end of the island; **Days/Hours:** Virginia section open from 4 a.m.-10 p.m. year-round. Maryland section open from 6 a.m. through 10 p.m. from April through Sept. Contact the seashore for details on Winter hours of operation; **Holiday Closings:** Visitor Center closed Dec. 25 & Jan. 1; **Visitor attractions closed for seasons:**Maryland National Park Service family campgrounds closed from Nov. to mid-Apr.; **Weather:** Summers can be hot & humid with many biting insects. Spring and Autumn offer brisk nights and placid days, allowing a chance to avoid the crowds.

GENERAL INFORMATION: *For Your Safety*—Swim where there are lifeguards; avoid swimming in heavy surf and do not use air mattresses or flotation devices. Seek shelter during lightning. Beware of sunburn and wear shoes in the campgrounds; do not approach ponies; guard against mosquitoes, ticks, and poison ivy. Backcountry canoeing and hiking has its own set of hazards; review the backcountry folders.

Visitors are discouraged from bringing pets, which are prohibited in most areas of the Seashore. The hot, blowing sand and saltwater are hard on dogs' feet and eyes.

Catoctin Mountain Park
Thurmont, Maryland

MAILING ADDRESS: Superintendent, Catoctin Mountain Park, Thurmont, Maryland 21788 **Telephone:** 301-824-2574

DIRECTIONS: Catoctin is located in the foothills of the Appalachian Mountains. From Rte 15 take Rte 77 west for approximately 4.8 km (3 miles). The Visitor Center is on the right.

In 1936 more than 10,000 acres were acquired by the Federal Government and developed to demonstrate the possibilities of creating parks from wornout land. In 1954 the area was divided into two parts, separated by Rte 77. The Federal Government retained the area to the north (Catoctin Mountain Park) and the remaining acreage was deeded to the State of Maryland to be managed for recreational use (Cunningham Falls State Park).

VISITOR ACTIVITIES: hiking, auto tours, camping, picnicking, exhibits, Spring wildflower walks, campfire programs, family walks, children walks, fishing, horseback riding, rock climbing, cross-country skiing, demonstrations of the following: whiskey-making, blacksmithing, leathercraft, pottery, carpentry and shingle riving, kitchen crafts, spinning, and weaving; **Permits:** for the use of Adirondack (hike-in) shelters and for rock-climbing. Both permits available free of charge at the Visitor Center; **Fees:** $2 per night camping fee at Owens Creek campground; **Visitor facilities:** self-guiding trails, picnic areas, bridle trail, craft center, hike-in camp shelters; **Any limitations on vehicle usage:** Motorized vehicles and bicylces are restricted to roads; **Hiking trails:** Yes, hiking is permitted on 19 km (12 miles) of trails and 19 km (12 miles) of bridle trails; **Backcountry:**

Yes, information can be obtained from the Visitor Center; **Camping:** Yes, no reservations accepted for individual campsites; **Other overnight accommodations on site:** Yes, two large Environmental Education Cabin Camps are rented to groups of 60 or more people. They are reserved through applications taken between Dec. 1 and Dec. 15 for Long Term Groups, between Jan. 1 and Jan 30 for Spring Weekend Groups, and between May 1 and May 30 for Fall Weekend Groups; **Meals served in the park:** No; **Food and supplies obtainable in the park:** No; **Food and supplies obtainable nearby:** Yes, Cunningham Falls State Park has a concession at the William Houck Lake Area which is open Memorial Day through Labor Day and also in nearby Thurmont; **Overnight accommodations:** Motels in Thurmont. Camping is also available in Cunningham Falls State Park and in four privately-owned campgrounds within a 24 km (15 mile) radius of the Visitor Center; **First Aid available in park:** Yes, or nearby in Thurmont; **Nearest Hospital:** Frederick and Hagerstown Hospitals are within 32 km (20 miles); **Days/Hours:** The park is open from dawn to dusk. No overnight parking is permitted; **Holiday Closings:** Visitor Center closed Dec. 25 and Jan. 1; **Visitor attractions closed for seasons:** Owens Creek Campground is open Apr. 15 through the third Sunday in Nov. Round Meadow Craft Center is open Memorial Day through Oct. on Saturdays and Sundays only from Noon to 5 p.m.

GENERAL INFORMATION: Activities at Cunningham Falls State Park include camping, picnicking, hiking, swimming, boating, and fishing.

Chesapeake and Ohio Canal National Historical Park
Maryland, Virginia, District of Columbia

MAILING ADDRESS: Superintendent, C&O Canal National Historical Park, P.O. Box 4, Sharpsburg, Maryland 21782 **Telephone:** 301-432-2231

DIRECTIONS: Park Headquarters is 6.4 km (4 miles) west of Sharpsburg, MD on MD 34. Other Visitor Centers and information offices are at Hancock, MD, 108 West Main Street, 301-678-5463; North Branch (intermittent) Visitor Center, 12.8 km (8 miles) south of Cumberland, off MD 51, 301-777-8667; and Great Falls Tavern, MD 301-299-3613.

The Park follows the route of the 296 km (184 mile) canal along the Potomac River between Washington, DC and Cumberland, MD. The canal was built between 1828 and 1850. Set aside Sept. 23, 1938.

VISITOR ACTIVITIES: hiking, biking, camping, horseback riding, canoeing, boating, fishing, picnicking, conducted walks, evening programs, museum at Great Falls, MD, mountain climbing. For information on barge rides, phone 301-299-2026; **Permits:** for camping at one campsite can be obtained from the Park Ranger at Great Falls Tavern, 11710 MacArthur Boulevard, Potomac, MD 20854; **Fees:** No; **Visitor facilities:** picnic areas, campgrounds, museum, boat ramp and rentals, bicycle trail; **Any limitations on vehicle usage:** All motor vehicles, including motorcycles and snowmobiles, and horse-drawn vehicles are prohibited on the towpath; **Hiking trails:** Yes, the towpath follows the canal's entire length; **Backcountry:** No; **Camping:** Yes, no reservations for "Hiker-Biker" campsites. One campsite, with pit toilets only, is midway between Seneca and Georgetown and is available by permit to hiker-bikers; **Other overnight accommodations on site:** No; **Meals served in the park:** No; **Food and supplies obtainable in the park:** No; **Food and supplies obtainable nearby:** Yes, in stores along the various adjacent access routes; **Overnight accommodations:** In major urban areas, near I-70; **First Aid available in park:** Yes, at all Visitor Centers and Park Headquarters; **Nearest Hospital:** Along the route of the canal, in or near Potomac, Seneca, Poolesville,

Brunswick, Sharpsburg, Williamsport, Hancock, Little Orleans, Oldtown, and Cumberland; **Days/Hours:** Park open year-round; **Holiday Closings:** None; **Visitor attractions closed for seasons:**Barge ride operation closed from mid-Oct.—Apr.

GENERAL INFORMATION: *For Your Safety*—Help prevent drownings by keeping your family or group together. Stay on the trail and out of the water. Be prepared to deal with such annoyances as insects, polluted river water, and adverse weather conditions.

Clara Barton National Historic Site
Glen Echo, Maryland

MAILING ADDRESS: Superintendent, George Washington Memorial Parkway, Turkey Run Park, McLean, Virginia 22101 **Telephone:** 301-492-6246

DIRECTIONS: The park is just north of Washington, DC. Take MacArthur Boulevard from Washington or Exit 15 from the Capital Beltway (I-495) to Glen Echo, MD. Turn left at Oxford Road just past Glen Echo Park.

This 38-room home of the founder of the American Red Cross was for 7 years the headquarters of that organization. Authorized for addition to the National Park System on Oct. 26, 1974.

VISITOR ACTIVITIES: guided tours and exhibits; **Permits:** No; **Fees:** No; **Visitor facilities:** restrooms, parking; **Any limitations on vehicle usage:** Vehicles are restricted to the parking lot; **Hiking trails:** No, but hiking is available on the nearby C&O Canal towpath; **Backcountry:** No; **Camping:** No; **Other overnight accommodations on site:** No; **Meals served in the park:** No; **Food and supplies obtainable in the park:** No; **Food and supplies obtainable nearby:** Yes, limited food and supplies in Glen Echo, MD; wider range in Bethesda, MD and Washington, D.C.; **Overnight accommodations:** Washington, D.C. or vicinity; **First Aid available in park:** Yes, or nearby at Glen Echo Fire Dept., Massachusetts Ave.; **Nearest Hospital:** Sibley Hospital, Washington, D.C., 6.4 km (4 miles); **Days/Hours:** Thursday and Friday 10-5 with reservation; Saturday 10-5, Sunday 1-5 from Feb.-Nov.; **Holiday Closings:** Thanksgiving, Dec. 25; **Visitor attractions closed for seasons:**December and January; **Weather:** Hot, humid Summer.

GENERAL INFORMATION: Visitors can see the adjacent Glen Echo Park (see listing in this book).

Fort McHenry National Monument and Historic Shrine
Baltimore, Maryland

MAILING ADDRESS: Superintendent, Fort McHenry National Historic Shrine, Baltimore, Maryland 21230 **Telephone:** 301-962-4290

DIRECTIONS: The Monument is 4.8 km (3 miles) from the center of Baltimore, and is readily accessible over East Fort Avenue, which intersects MD 2.

Successful defense of this fort in the War of 1812, Sept. 13-14, 1814, inspired Francis Scott Key to write "The Star Spangled Banner" Authorized for addition to the National Park System on Mar. 3, 1925.

VISITOR ACTIVITIES: interpretive exhibits and film, walking tours, picnicking, guided tours during summer months and upon request to groups; **Permits:** No; **Fees:** No; **Visitor facilities:** parking and restrooms at Visitor Center, picnic area, seawall walking-jogging path; **Any limitations on vehicle usage:** Vehicles must stay on designated roadways; **Hiking trails:** Yes, a 1.6 km (1 mile) paved foot trail leads around the seawall; **Backcountry:** No; **Camping:** No; **Other overnight accommodations on site:** No; **Meals served in the park:** No; **Food and supplies obtainable in the park:** No; **Food and supplies obtainable nearby:** Yes, in Baltimore; **Overnight accommodations:** Baltimore; **First Aid available in park:** Yes, paramedic ambulance service on call; **Nearest Hospital:** South Baltimore General Hosp., Hanover St., 3 km (2 miles); **Days/ Hours:** Open 7 days a week, 9 a.m. to 5 p.m. and until 8 p.m. from Memorial Day through Labor Day; **Holiday Closings:** Dec. 25 and Jan. 1; **Weather:** Summer is hot and humid; air quality is often poor. Winter is cold, damp and windy; Spring and Autumn are mild.

GENERAL INFORMATION: *For Your Safety*—do not climb on monuments, trees, cannons, or the seawall. Stay away from the edge of the fort walls.

Fort Washington Park
Fort Washington, Maryland

MAILING ADDRESS: Superintendent, National Capital Parks East, 5210 Indian Head Hwy., Oxon Hill, Maryland 20021 **Telephone:** 301-292-2112

DIRECTIONS: The Park is on the Maryland side of the Potomac River. You can reach the Park by crossing the South Capitol Street Bridge and driving south on Int. 295 and east on Int. 495 (Capitol Beltway). Turn right on Indian Head Hwy (MD 210) and again right onto Fort Washington Road. The fort is 3.2 km (2 miles) inside the Park from Fort Washington Road.
This fort, situated across the Potomac from Mount Vernon and built to protect Washington, D.C., was begun in 1814 to replace an 1809 fort destroyed by the British. Recreational facilities are included in the Park. Authorized for addition to the National Park System on May 29, 1930.

VISITOR ACTIVITIES: interpretive tours and living history demonstrations, auto tours, picnicking, hiking; **Permits:** Yes, reserved picnic areas available for groups of 50 or more; **Fees:** No; **Visitor facilities:** picnic areas, parking, restrooms, museum; **Any limitations on vehicle usage:** No trucks are allowed in the Park; **Hiking trails:** Yes, a short trail along the Potomac River and Piscataway Bay; **Backcountry:** No; **Camping:** No; **Other overnight accommodations on site:** No; **Meals served in the park:** No; **Food and supplies obtainable in the park:** No; **Food and supplies obtainable nearby:** Yes, 5.6 km (3.5 miles) from the Park on Fort Washington Road; **Overnight accommodations:** in the Washington metropolitan area; **First Aid available in park:** Yes, or nearby in Oxon Hill, 19.3 km (12 miles), on Oxon Hill Road; **Nearest Hospital:** Washington, D.C., Southern Avenue, 32 km (20 miles); **Days/Hours:** Fort open from 7:30 a.m. to 5:30 p.m. daily; Park open from 7:30 a.m. to dark every day; **Holiday Closings:** Fort closed on Dec. 25 & Jan. 1; **Weather:** Winters are cool & wet, with light snow; Summers are hot and humid.

George Washington Memorial Parkway
For details see listing in Virginia

Glen Echo Park
Glen Echo, Maryland

MAILING ADDRESS: Site Manager, Glen Echo Park, MacArthur Blvd. at Oxford Road, Glen Echo, Maryland 20768 **Telephone:** 301-492-6282

DIRECTIONS: The Park is just north of Washington, DC at MacArthur Boulevard and Oxford Road. Take MacArthur Boulevard from Washington, Capital Beltway Exit 15, or George Washington Memorial Parkway from Maryland. Information on facilities and activities may be obtained at Glen Echo Gallery.

Located on Maryland's Potomac Palisades, the Park was formerly a 19th century Chautauqua assembly center and then an amusement park. It is now a cultural and arts center. Authorized for addition to the National Park System in 1976.

VISITOR ACTIVITIES: walking tours, carrousel rides on summer weekends, arts and crafts courses, special programs, free concerts and festivals, picnicking; **Permits:** No; **Fees:** Carrousel rides are 25¢, tuition fees are charged for courses and admission fees for some performances; **Visitor facilities:** restrooms, parking, gallerys, picnic areas; **Any limitations on vehicle usage:** Vehicles are restricted to the parking lot; **Hiking trails:** No; **Backcountry:** No; **Camping:** No; **Other overnight accommodations on site:** No; **Meals served in the park:** Yes, food service on Sundays only, from May-Oct; **Food and supplies obtainable in the park:** No; **Food and supplies obtainable nearby:** Yes, in town of Glen Echo; **Overnight accommodations:** suburban Maryland or Washington, DC; **First Aid available in park:** Yes; **Nearest Hospital:** Sibley Hospital, MacArthur Blvd. and Loughboro Rd., Washington, DC; **Days/Hours:** Open 24 hours a day, 7 days a week; **Holiday Closings:** None; **Visitor attractions closed for seasons:**Most festivals are held between May and Oct.; **Weather:** Hot, humid Summers; cold, snowy Winters.

GENERAL INFORMATION: Visitors can also see the adjacent Clara Barton National Historic Site (see listing in this book).

Greenbelt Park
Greenbelt, Maryland

MAILING ADDRESS: Superintendent, Greenbelt Park, 6501 Greenbelt Road, Greenbelt, Maryland 20770 **Telephone:** 301-344-3948

DIRECTIONS: From the Capital Beltway (Int. 495), take Exit 28 at Kenilworth Avenue (MD 201) proceed south toward Bladensburg and follow the signs into the Park. From the Baltimore-Washington Parkway, exit at Greenbelt Road (MD 193) and follow signs.

Just 19 km (12 miles) from Washington, D.C., this woodland park offers urban dwellers access to many forms of outdoor recreation. Established by act of Congress in 1933.

VISITOR ACTIVITIES: picnicking, camping, nature walks, horseback riding, biking, hiking; **Permits:** No; **Fees:** Camping fee is $2 per night, $1 if camper has a Golden Age Passport; **Visitor facilities:** picnic areas, campgrounds, nature trails, interpretive walks, talks, and evening programs, fireplaces (only charcoal is permitted), restrooms, bicycle trail on Sundays; **Any limitations on vehicle usage:** Park only in designated areas. All vehicles, including bicycles, are restricted to paved roads. Their use on any trail is strictly prohibited; **Hiking trails:** Yes, nearly 19 km (12 miles) of well-marked trails lead through the Park. A 9.6 km (6 mile) loop, also designated a bridle trail, circles the Park's western half; **Backcountry:** No; **Camping:** Yes, no reservations for the 178-site family campground, which is open all year. In Summer, the campground is usually filled by nightfall. Visitors should plan to arrive by mid-afternoon to be assured of a site. There are no showers or hookups; **Other overnight accommodations on site:** No; **Meals served in the park:** No; **Food and supplies obtainable in the park:** No; **Food and supplies obtainable nearby:** Yes, Greenbelt or vicinity; **Overnight accommodations:** Greenbelt;

First Aid available in park: Yes, but only for emergencies or nearby in Lanham, MD; **Nearest Hospital:** New Carrollton, Good Luck Road, 6.4 km (4 miles); **Days/Hours:** Open 10 a.m. until dark. Campers have access at all times; **Holiday Closings:** No; **Visitor attractions closed for seasons:** Bike trail is closed for winter; **Weather:** High heat and humidity in Summer, cold in Winter with some snow.

Hampton National Historic Site
Towson, Maryland

MAILING ADDRESS: Superintendent, Hampton National Historic Site, 535 Hampton Lane, Towson, Maryland 21204 **Telephone:** 301-823-7054

DIRECTIONS: To reach Hampton from Baltimore, follow the Jones Falls Expressway, the York Road (MD 45), or Charles Street north to Towson. In Towson, take Dulaney Valley Road (MD 146) across the Beltway (I-695) and immediately thereafter turn right into Hampton Lane which leads to the Site. This is a dangerous intersection; make sure that you do not enter the Beltway exit ramp. The Site can also be reached from Beltway exits 27 and 28 North.

This is a fine example of one of the lavish Georgian mansions built in America during the latter part of the 18th century. Designated June 22, 1948.

VISITOR ACTIVITIES: continuous guided tours, self-guiding grounds tours, stable and garden exhibits; **Permits:** No; **Fees:** None; **Visitor facilities:** parking, restrooms, tea room; **Any limitations on vehicle usage:** No; **Hiking trails:** Yes, a 1.6 km (1 mile) walking tour of the grounds; **Meals served in the park:** Yes, lunch is available at the tea room in the east wing; **Food and supplies obtainable in the park:** No; **Food and supplies obtainable nearby:** Yes, at Towson; **Overnight accommodations:** In Towson, MD, approx. 1.6 km (1 mile) south; **First Aid available in park:** Yes; **Nearest Hospital:** Towson, MD, approx. 3 km (2 miles); **Days/Hours:** Open Tuesday through Saturday from 11 a.m. to 5 p.m. and on Sunday from 1 p.m. to 5 p.m. Closed on Mondays; **Holiday Closings:** Jan. 1, Memorial Day, July 4 & Dec. 25; **Visitor attractions closed for seasons:** No.

GENERAL INFORMATION: Be especially careful on the earthen ramps leading into the gardens; they are steeper than they appear. The cobblestone walks are slippery when wet.

Harpers Ferry National Historical Park
For details see listing in West Virginia

Monocacy Battlefield National Park
Frederick, Maryland

MAILING ADDRESS: Superintendent, Antietam National Battlefield Site, P.O. Box 158, Sharpsburg, Maryland 21782 **Telephone:** 301-432-5124

DIRECTIONS: NOT YET OPEN TO THE PUBLIC.
On July 9, 1864, Confederate Gen. Jubal T. Early and his troops met the Union Forces of Brigade General Lew Wallace south of Frederick along the banks of the Monocacy River. Early's forces defeated the Union but Wallace was able to delay Confederate forces long enough for reinforcements to arrive in Washington to defend the Capital against

Southern troops. Battlefield was established on June 21, 1934. All land is currently under private ownership.

Oxon Hill Farm
Oxon Hill, Maryland

MAILING ADDRESS: Superintendent, National Capital Parks East, 5210 Indian Head Highway, Oxon Hill, Maryland 20021 **Telephone:** 301-839-1177

DIRECTIONS: From southbound Indian Head Highway, (MD 210) at the Capital Beltway (Interstate Rt. 95) exit 37S bear right onto Oxon Hill Road. Turn right approx. 200 yards down Oxon Hill Road to the farm parking lot.

The Farm is like many of those found in the Maryland and Virginia countryside around Washington at the end of the 19th Century. It includes pasture lands, woodland, typical farm buildings, animals, and equipment. In operation as a park since 1967, the Farm is especially attractive for children.

VISITOR ACTIVITIES: picnicking, machinery and equipment displays, live animal exhibits, daily demonstrations of 1900 era farm chores, educational programs for children, seasonal farming and craft demonstrations, recreational activities; **Permits:** No, but large groups should make advance arrangements; **Fees:** No; **Visitor facilities:** picnic area, nature trail, restrooms, Visitor Center, exhibits, farm buildings; **Any limitations on vehicle usage:** All vehicles must use the designated parking area; **Hiking trails:** Yes, .8 km (1/2 mile) self-guiding woodlot nature trail; **Backcountry:** No; **Camping:** No; **Other overnight accommodations on site:** No; **Meals served in the park:** No, many fast-food facilities are .8 km (1/2 mile) east on Oxon Hill Road; **Food and supplies obtainable in the park:** No; **Food and supplies obtainable nearby:** Yes, .8 km (1/2 mile) east on Oxon Hill Road; **Overnight accommodations:** in the Washington metropolitan area; **First Aid available in park:** Yes; **Nearest Hospital:** Washington, D.C.-Greater Southeast Community Hosp.—take Indian Head Hwy (MD 201) North 1.6 km (1 mile) to Southern Ave., turn right on Southern Ave. 3 km (2 miles) to hospital on left; **Days/Hours:** Open daily all year from 8:30 a.m.-5 p.m.; **Holiday Closings:** Thanksgiving, Dec. 25 & Jan. 1; **Visitor attractions closed for seasons:** Activities, programs and demonstrations are curtailed from Dec. to Mar. due to weather; **Weather:** Spring and Fall are temperate, pleasant (60°F) and usually sunny. Summer is warm to hot (70-95°F) and humid. Winter is moderately cold and windy.

GENERAL INFORMATION: *For Your Safety*—Do not smoke in any of the buildings. Be cautious around animals and all machines, which are dangerous and have heavy moving parts and sharp edges. Be alert for moving equipment such as wagons and tractors.

Piscataway Park
Oxon Hill, Maryland

MAILING ADDRESS: Piscataway Park, 5210 Indian Head Hwy., Oxon Hill, Maryland 20021 **Telephone:** 301-292-2112

DIRECTIONS: Take Exit 37S from the Capital Beltway (Int. 495) to Route 210S (Indian Head Hwy) 16 km (10 miles) to the intersection in Accokeek. Turn right onto Bryan's Point Road and go 6.7 km (4 miles) to the Potomac River.

The tranquil view of the Maryland shore of the Potomac from Mount Vernon is preserved as a pilot project in the use of easements to protect parklands from obtrusive urban expansion. Authorized for addition to the National Park System on Oct. 4, 1961.

VISITOR ACTIVITIES: picnicking, fishing, bird-watching, farm tours; **Permits:** No; **Fees:** As of 6/79, a fee is charged for tours of the National Colonial Farm, which is located at Piscataway; **Visitor facilities:** picnic area, boat dock, National Colonial Farm; **Any limitations on vehicle usage:** No; **Hiking trails:** No; **Backcountry:** No; **Camping:** No; **Other overnight accommodations on site:** No; **Meals served in the park:** No; **Food and supplies obtainable in the park:** No; **Food and supplies obtainable nearby:** Yes, Shopping Centers are along Route 210; **Overnight accommodations:** Suburban Maryland or metropolitan Washington, D.C.; **First Aid available in park:** No; **Nearest Hospital:** Washington, D.C., Route 210 to Southern Ave., 32 km (20 miles); **Days/Hours:** Open daily during daylight hours; **Holiday Closings:** None; **Weather:** Hot, humid Summers, and cold, wet Winters.

Thomas Stone National Historic Site
Port Tobacco, Maryland

MAILING ADDRESS: Superintendent, George Washington Birthplace National Monument, Washington's Birthplace, Virginia 22575 **Telephone:** 804-224-0196

DIRECTIONS: *NOT YET OPEN TO THE PUBLIC.*
 The Georgian home of Thomas Stone, a signer of the Declaration of Independence, was built by him in 1771. Authorized for addition to the National Park System on Nov. 10, 1978.

Massachusetts

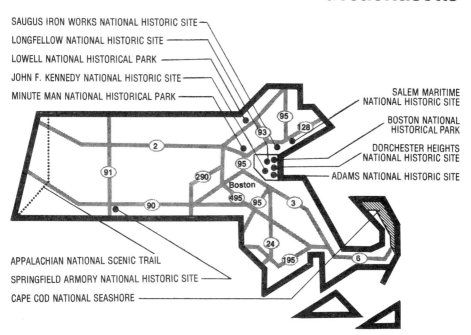

Adams National Historic Site
Quincy, Massachusetts

MAILING ADDRESS: Superintendent, Adams National Historic Site, P.O. Box 531, Quincy, Massachusetts 02269 **Telephone:** 617-773-1177

DIRECTIONS: 12.9 km (8 miles) south of Boston, take Exit 24 (Furnace Brook Parkway interchange) of the Southeast Expressway (Route 3); or Hancock Street to Newport Avenue. Site is located at Furnace Brook Parkway, Newport Avenue and Adams Street.
Established by act of Congress on Dec. 9, 1946, the Site contains 8.45 acres and includes the house, library, garden and stables of Presidents John Adams and John Quincy Adams, and statesman Ambassador Charles Francis Adams and his four illustrious sons.

VISITOR ACTIVITIES: Historic Site tours; **Permits:** No; **Fees:** 50¢ admission fee for adults, children under 16 admitted free when accompanied by an adult. Golden Eagle and Golden Age Passports accepted and available; **Visitor facilities:** None; **Any limitations on vehicle usage:** Parking for visitors is available on the public street in front of the house; **Other overnight accommodations on site:** No; **Meals served in the park:** No; **Food and supplies obtainable in the park:** No; **Food and supplies obtainable nearby:** Yes, Quincy, about .4 km (1/4 mile) south of the Site; **Overnight accommodations:** Boston area along Route 3; **First Aid available in park:** No; **Nearest Hospital:** Quincy City Hospital, less than .4 km (1/4 mile) from the Site; **Days/Hours:** Open 9 a.m.-5 p.m. daily April 19 through Nov. 10; **Holiday Closings:** None; **Visitor attractions closed for seasons:** Closed Nov. 11 through April 18.

Appalachian National Scenic Trail
For details see listing in Maine

Boston National Historical Park
Boston, Massachusetts

MAILING ADDRESS: Superintendent, Charlestown Navy Yard, Boston, Massachusetts 02129 **Telephone:** 617-242-5611

DIRECTIONS: We recommend that you don't drive in downtown Boston; mass transit provides a good option. If you do drive, from Routes 1 north, 93 south and west, take the Charlestown exit, where you will find signs to the Charlestown Navy Yard (berth of USS Constitution). Further directions into downtown Boston can be obtained here.
The Park is comprised of 7 historic sites & a Visitor Center along Boston's Freedom Trail, & Dorchester Heights, a newly-acquired area under development. The Park was founded in 1975.

VISITOR ACTIVITIES: During the peak season (Summer), the sites provide historic information in a variety of ways: tours, lectures, living history. Park Service Rangers are only at Faneuil Hall, Charlestown Navy Yard, Bunker Hill Monument, and the Visitor Center. The programs are relaxed somewhat in Winter; **Permits:** only for special use; **Fees:** Yes, entrance fees are collected at the privately owned and operated sites, by self-supporting associations working cooperatively with the Park; **Visitor facilities:** restrooms at the Visitor Center, Navy Yard & Faneuil Hall; **Any limitations on vehicle usage:** parking is not available in the Navy Yard; **Hiking trails:** Yes, the Freedom Trail follows an urban route; **Camping:** No; **Other overnight accommodations on site:** No; **Meals served in the park:** No; **Food and supplies obtainable in the park:** No; **Food and supplies obtainable nearby:** Yes, in Quincy Market and Northend. There are many restaurants in the vicinity; **Overnight accommodations:** Hotels and motels are throughout the city. Route 1 north has motels, and is a short distance from downtown; **First Aid available in park:** Yes; **Nearest Hospital:** Hospitals near sites include Mass. General, Bunker Hill Community Clinic, Tufts Univ., and Univ. Hospital; **Days/Hours:** Summer: 7 days per week, 9 a.m.-6 p.m. Winter: 7 days per week, 9 a.m.-5 p.m. or 10 a.m.-5 p.m., depending on site; **Holiday Closings:** Thanksgiving, Dec. 25 & Jan. 1; **Visitor attractions closed for seasons:**No; **Weather:** Summer is usually hot and humid with a sea breeze; Winter is windy and usually cold.

Cape Cod National Seashore
South Wellfleet, Massachusetts

MAILING ADDRESS: Superintendent, Cape Cod National Seashore, South Wellfleet, Massachusetts 02663 **Telephone:** 617-349-3785

DIRECTIONS: Visitor Centers are at Salt Pond (in Eastham on Route 6) and Province Lands (in Provincetown on Race Point Road). Headquarters is at the Marconi Station Area.
 Ocean beaches, dunes, woodlands, freshwater ponds, and marshes make up this park on outer Cape Cod. The area preserves notable examples of Cape Cod homes, an architectural style founded in America. Authorized for addition to the National Park System on Aug. 7, 1961.

VISITOR ACTIVITIES: interpretive exhibits and talks, swimming, surfing, driving, horseback riding, camping, picnicking, hiking, shellfishing, biking; **Permits:** for beach vehicles and shellfishing, obtained from the Visitor Centers, and from local towns; **Fees:** $1 per carload entrance fee for July and August only. Golden Eagle and Golden Age Passports accepted and available. Annual beach vehicle fees are $15 for regular ORV's and $25 for self-contained; **Visitor facilities:** bicycle rentals and trails, nature trails, bridle paths and horse rentals, beaches, lifeguard services and other swimming facilities, picnic areas, restaurants, lodging, gift stores; **Any limitations on vehicle usage:** Summer traffic is very heavy—roads are narrow. Motorized vehicles including mopeds are not allowed on paved bicycle trails; **Hiking trails:** Yes, nature trails in each of the four developed areas, day use only; seashore is also good for day hiking; **Camping:** No, camping is available in private campgrounds. Reservations are essential for the summer season. A large state-owned campground is in Nickerson State Park in nearby Brewster. Reservations cannot be made for this campground. Sleeping and campground accommodations, restaurants, gift shops, grocery and other stores, and gas stations are in towns adjoining the seashore. For information and reservations, write to: Cape Cod Chamber of Commerce, Hyannis, MA 02601; **Other overnight accommodations on site:** No; **Meals served in the park:** No; **Food and supplies obtainable in the park:** No; **Food and supplies obtainable nearby:** Yes, along Route 6 and in local towns; **Overnight accommodations:** Available in areas serving the seashore. Contact Chamber of Commerce as noted above; **First Aid available in park:** Yes, emergency only; all towns have rescue squads; **Nearest Hospital:** Hyannis, 48-80 km (30-50 miles) away; **Days/Hours:** Open from 6 a.m. to midnight year-round; **Holiday Closings:** Visitor Center closed Dec. 25 & Jan. 1; **Visitor attractions closed for seasons:**Interpretive services, walks, talks etc. are offered from April-Oct.;

Weather: Summer and Fall are the best times to visit; Spring is often damp; Winter is mild and potentially stormy.

GENERAL INFORMATION: *Caution*—Swim only where lifeguards are on duty. Sand collapses easily. Climbing slopes or digging deep holes is hazardous. The ocean can be dangerous. Be alert for riptides and underwater obstacles. For your safety, do not take glass containers, rafts, rubber tubes, snorkels, or masks to any beach. Watch out for painful sunburn. Place your valuables in the trunk and lock the car.

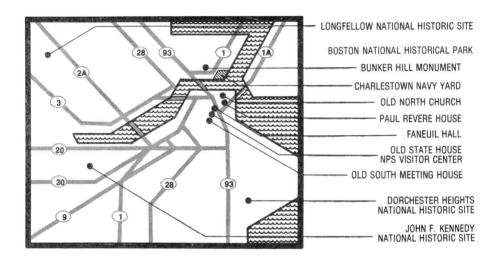

Dorchester Heights National Historic Site
Boston, Massachusetts

MAILING ADDRESS: Site Manager, Dorchester Heights National Historic Site, c/o Boston National Historical Park, 15 State Street, Boston, Massachusetts 02109 **Telephone:** 617-242-5625 or 617-242-5649

DIRECTIONS: The Massachusetts Turnpike and Rte. 128 lead to Fitzgerald Expressway. Take the South Boston exit from the Fitzgerald Expressway. Dorchester Heights can be seen in the distance. On-street parking in the area is limited. To reach the Site by public transportation, take the Red Line subway to Broadway station. Take City Point Bus to G Street. The Site is a short walk on G Street.
 A memorial tower and a green mark the site of the colonial battles that threatened the British in Boston and helped to force them to evacuate the city on March 17, 1776. Designated Apr. 27, 1951. Owned and administered by the city of Boston. The area is to be rehabilitated soon and will be transferred to National Park Service management.

VISITOR ACTIVITIES: touring the Site; **Permits:** No; **Fees:** No; **Visitor facilities:** None; **Any limitations on vehicle usage:** No; **Meals served in the park:** No; **Food and supplies obtainable in the park:** No; **Food and supplies obtainable nearby:** Yes, in South Boston, within a 5-minute walk; **Overnight accommodations:** The nearest accommodations are in Boston, 3 km (2 miles) away; **First Aid available in park:** No; **Nearest Hospital:** Tufts-New England Medical Center; Boston City Hosp.; **Days/ Hours:** Open daily from 8 a.m. to 4:30 p.m.; **Holiday Closings:** None; **Visitor attractions closed for seasons:**No.

John F. Kennedy National Historic Site
Brookline, Massachusetts

MAILING ADDRESS: Superintendent, John F. Kennedy National Historic Site, 83 Beals Street, Brookline, Massachusetts 02146 **Telephone:** 617-566-7937

DIRECTIONS: Take exit #18 from Mass. Turnpike Extension. Proceed towards Allston along Cambridge Street, turn left onto Harvard Street. Turn left from Harvard Street onto Beals Street. Directional signs are posted at nearby intersections. The Site is easily reached by public transportation.

This nine-room, two-story structure is the birthplace and early childhood home (1917-20) of the 35th President of the United States. Authorized for addition to the National Park System on May 26, 1969.

VISITOR ACTIVITIES: self-guiding, tape-recorded tour narrated by the President's mother; **Permits:** No; **Fees:** 50¢ entrance fee per adult. Those under 16 years and over 62 years are admitted free. Golden Eagle and Golden Age Passports accepted and available; **Visitor facilities:** None; **Any limitations on vehicle usage:** Parking is available only on the street, which may be congested. Buses must not idle motors for more than five minutes; **Meals served in the park:** No; **Food and supplies obtainable in the park:** No; **Food and supplies obtainable nearby:** Yes, about four blocks away; **Overnight accommodations:** Brookline, .8 km (1/2 mile). Boston is 4.5 km (3 miles) distant; **First Aid available in park:** Yes; **Nearest Hospital:** Brookline, 1.6 km (1 mile); **Days/Hours:** Open daily from 9 a.m. to 4:30 p.m.; **Holiday Closings:** Thanksgiving, Dec. 25 and Jan. 1.

Longfellow National Historic Site
Cambridge, Massachusetts

MAILING ADDRESS: Superintendent, Longfellow National Historic Site, 105 Brattle Street, Cambridge, Massachusetts 02138 **Telephone:** 617-876-4491

DIRECTIONS: Cambridge is an historic city with both old and new buildings of interest. For visitors unfamiliar with the area the easiest way to see some of Cambridge's sights including the Longfellow House is to park in Boston under the Common, and take the Red Line subway to Harvard Square, the end of the line. From the square walk down Brattle St. about 1 km (.6 mile) to Longfellow House. On your way you will pass two colonial mansions, the William Brattle House and the John Vassal, Sr. House. On your return to Harvard Square, you may wish to go via Mason Street and Cambridge Common. On the Common a bronze plaque marks the site of the "Washington Elm" under whose branches George Washington took command of the Continental Army.

Poet Henry Wadsworth Longfellow lived here from 1837 to 1882. The house had been George Washington's headquarters during the siege of Boston, 1775-76. Authorized for addition to the National Park System on Oct. 9, 1972.

VISITOR ACTIVITIES: guided tours, garden concerts on alternate Sundays during the

Summer beginning on the first Sunday in June; **Permits:** No; **Fees:** Entrance fee is 50¢ for adults. No charge for persons under 16 or 62 and over. Golden Eagle and Golden Age Passports accepted and available; **Visitor facilities:** None on site. A walking tour of historic Cambridge and Harvard Square is suggested. A free brochure is available on request; **Any limitations on vehicle usage:** No parking is available at the Site. Limited parking is 1 km (.6 mile) distant; **Hiking trails:** No; **Meals served in the park:** No; **Food and supplies obtainable in the park:** No; **Food and supplies obtainable nearby:** Yes, in Cambridge (Harvard Square); **Overnight accommodations:** Cambridge, within walking distance, or Boston, 11 km (7 miles); **First Aid available in park:** Yes; **Nearest Hospital:** Cambridge, 2 km (1.3 miles); **Days/Hours:** Open daily from 9 a.m. to 4:30 p.m.; **Holiday Closings:** Thanksgiving, Dec. 25 and Jan. 1; **Weather:** Moderately warm and humid Summer, occasional inconvenience from snow and ice in Winter.

GENERAL INFORMATION: On-site parking for bus groups or handicapped people may be arranged by making advance reservations. Telephone 617-876-4491.

Lowell National Historical Park
Lowell, Massachusetts

MAILING ADDRESS: Superintendent, Lowell National Historical Park, P.O. Box 1098, Lowell, Massachusetts 01853 **Telephone:** 617-459-4136

DIRECTIONS: Take the Lowell Connector from either Int. 495 or US 3. Exit on Thorndike Street North, and proceed approx. 1.6 km (1 mile) to Dutton Street. Take a right turn on Dutton Street. Follow Dutton to the marked parking lot. There is train access to Lowell from the Boston North Station. A free shuttle bus runs from the station to the park every hour. The Visitor Center is at 171 Merrimack Street.

The Park preserves seven original mill complexes, a power canal system and other early 19th Century structures of this planned city of the Industrial Revolution. Authorized for addition to the National Park System on June 5, 1978.

VISITOR ACTIVITIES: Free 3-hour guided tours of the mill and canal are given 9 times a day from 9 a.m. to 5 p.m. on Wednesdays through Sundays in June, July and August. For reservations, call 617-459-4136. Downtown walking tours are also offered; **Permits:** No, but tour reservations are recommended; **Fees:** No admission fees for National Park Service facilities; but the entrance fee at Lowell Museum is $1 for adults and 50¢ for children; **Visitor facilities:** Visitor Center, parking, restrooms; **Any limitations on vehicle usage:** Use of public transportation is recommended; **Hiking trails:** No; **Backcountry:** No; **Camping:** No; **Other overnight accommodations on site:** No; **Meals served in the park:** No; **Food and supplies obtainable in the park:** No; **Food and supplies obtainable nearby:** Yes, in Lowell; **Overnight accommodations:** On the periphery of Lowell, 3 km (2 miles); **First Aid available in park:** Yes; **Nearest Hospital:** St. John's, .4 km (1/4 mile); **Days/Hours:** Visitor Center open from 8 a.m. to 5 p.m. year-round; **Holiday Closings:** None; **Visitor attractions closed for seasons:** Mill and canal tour offered only in Summer; walking tours at other times of the year.

Minute Man National Historical Park
Concord, Massachusetts

MAILING ADDRESS: Superintendent, Minute Man National Historical Park, P.O. Box 160, Concord, Massachusetts 01742 **Telephone:** 617-369-6993

DIRECTIONS: The North Bridge Visitor Center is located off Liberty Street in Concord. The Battle Road Visitor Center is located off Route 2A in Lexington. Information is available at both places.

This is the scene of the fighting on the opening day of the Revolutionary War, April 19, 1775. It includes the Old North Bridge, the Minute Man Statue, 6.4 km (4 miles) of Battle Road between Lexington and Concord, and "The Wayside," Nathaniel Hawthorne's Home. Officially established by act of Congress on May 8, 1976.

VISITOR ACTIVITIES: interpretive exhibits and film, walking tours, interpretive talks. Sales and informational material are available; **Permits:** No; **Fees:** $.75 admission fee at "The Wayside" for persons over 16. Golden Eagle and Golden Age Passports accepted and available; **Visitor facilities:** The North Bridge Unit (includes the famous Minute Man statute by Daniel Chester French), The Battle Road Visitor Center, the Wayside, Fiske Hill, parking, restrooms, and picnic areas available; **Any limitations on vehicle usage:** Use the parking facilities provided. State Route 2A is a heavily travelled road and slowing down for sightseeing could be a hazard; **Hiking trails:** Yes, a 1.6 km (1 mile) self-guiding trail is available at Fiske Hill on Route 2A in Lexington. The restored battle road from the North Bridge leads to the North Bridge Visitor Center; **Backcountry:** No; **Camping:** No; **Other overnight accommodations on site:** No; **Meals served in the park:** No; **Food and supplies obtainable in the park:** No; **Food and supplies obtainable nearby:** Yes, in nearby towns: Concord, Lexington, Acton, & Bedford; **Overnight accommodations:** Concord, Lexington, Acton & Bedford; **First Aid available in park:** Yes; **Nearest Hospital:** Emerson Hospital, Concord, 9 km (6 miles) from the Park; **Days/Hours:** North Bridge Visitor Center is open the year-round except Dec. 25 & Jan. 1. Call 617-369-6993 for hours and days of other facilities; **Weather:** New England climate: cold Winters, dry, warm Summers.

GENERAL INFORMATION: Please respect the rights of private families living within the park boundary. Visitors to the area can also see historic sites relating to the life of Henry David Thoreau.

Salem Maritime National Historic Site
Salem, Massachusetts

MAILING ADDRESS: Superintendent, Salem Maritime National Historic Site, Custom House, Derby Street, Salem, Massachusetts 01970 **Telephone:** 617-744-4323

DIRECTIONS: Site headquarters is at Custom House, 174 Derby Street, Salem, 32 km (20 miles) northeast of Boston.

This seaport town is the only major port never occupied by the British during the Revolution. Later the wharf became one of the nation's great mercantile centers. Other structures of maritime, architectural and literary significance include the Derby House, Custom House, Bonded Warehouse and the Hawkes House. This Living History area was authorized for addition to the National Park System on Mar. 17, 1938.

VISITOR ACTIVITIES: Visitors can enter some or all of these structures, depending on the season and schedule. Audiovisual and living history programs are offered. Cargo samples can be seen, smelled, and handled; cargo hoisting and weighing equipment is demonstrated. Group tours available by reservation; **Permits:** No; **Fees:** 50¢ for Derby House tour; remainder of the Site is free. Golden Eagle and Golden Age Passports accepted and available; **Visitor facilities:** parking, restrooms, visitor information, interpretive exhibits, slide show, snack bar; **Any limitations on vehicle usage:** Autos are prohibited on the historic roadway; **Hiking trails:** No; **Backcountry:** No; **Camping:** No;

Other overnight accommodations on site: No; **Meals served in the park:** Yes, snacks available at West India Goods Store; **Food and supplies obtainable in the park:** No; **Food and supplies obtainable nearby:** Yes, in downtown Salem, within .8 km (1/2 mile); **Overnight accommodations:** Downtown Salem, within .8 km (1/2 mile); **First Aid available in park:** Yes; **Nearest Hospital:** Salem, 2.4 km (1-1/2 miles); **Days/Hours:** Custom House open daily, 8:30 a.m.-5 p.m.; until 7 p.m. in July and Aug. Check here for hours of other structures; **Holiday Closings:** Thanksgiving, Dec. 25 & Jan. 1; **Visitor attractions closed for seasons:** Scale House closed in winter; **Weather:** There is a great weather and temperature range. Weather can be windy or snowy in Winter, with temperatures from 0°F; with sunny or rainy summer days and temperatures ranging as high as 90°F.

Saugus Iron Works National Historic Site
Saugus, Massachusetts

MAILING ADDRESS: Superintendent, Saugus Iron Works National Historic Site, 244 Central Street, Saugus, Massachusetts 09106 **Telephone:** 617-233-0050

DIRECTIONS: Take the "Main Street Saugus" exit from Route 1, which brings you into Saugus Center. Park 2 blocks from Saugus Center—244 Central Street.

This reconstruction of the first integrated iron works in North America, begun in 1646, includes the ironmaster's house, furnace, forge and rolling and slitting mill. Authorized for addition to the National Park System on April 5, 1968.

VISITOR ACTIVITIES: photography, walking tours, exhibits; **Permits:** No; **Fees:** No; **Visitor facilities:** Visitors can tour the Site and museum and watch demonstrations of iron working; **Any limitations on vehicle usage:** No; **Meals served in the park:** No; **Food and supplies obtainable in the park:** No; **Food and supplies obtainable nearby:** Yes, at Saugus Center—2 blocks; **Overnight accommodations:** On Route 1, 1.6 km (1 mile) from the Site; **First Aid available in park:** Yes; **Nearest Hospital:** Wakefield, Lynn; **Days/Hours:** Open daily from 9 a.m. to 4 p.m. from Nov. 1 through March 31 and from 9 a.m. to 5 p.m. from Apr. 1 to Oct. 31; **Holiday Closings:** Dec. 25 and Jan. 1; **Visitor attractions closed for seasons:** Ironmaster's house closed Nov. 1 through March 31; **Weather:** Humid in Summer, cold in Winter. This is an outdoor facility so visitors should dress for inclement weather.

GENERAL INFORMATION: *For Your Safety*—Be careful around the waterwheel pits and do not climb on the waterwheels or other historic structures. The slag can cause severe cuts.

Springfield Armory National Historic Site
Springfield, Massachusetts

MAILING ADDRESS: Superintendent, Springfield Armory National Historic Site, One Armory Square, Springfield, Massachusetts 01105 **Telephone:** 413-734-6477

DIRECTIONS: The Site is in downtown Springfield, MA just off State Street. To reach the Site from the Massachusetts Turnpike take Exit 6 South to Route 291, then Exit 3 to Armory Street and thence to Federal Street. From Interstate 91 exit on State Street, thence to Federal Street. The Site is entered through the gate on Federal Street.

Over a span of 200 years this small-arms manufacturing center produced such weapons as the 1795 flintlock and the 1903 M-1 and M-14 rifles. A large collection of foreign small arms is maintained here. Authorized for addition to the National Park System on Oct. 26, 1974.

VISITOR ACTIVITIES: self-guiding museum tours, guided tours by advance arrangement; **Permits:** No; **Fees:** No; **Visitor facilities:** museum, restrooms; **Any limitations on vehicle usage:** No; **Hiking trails:** No; **Backcountry:** No; **Camping:** No; **Other overnight accommodations on site:** No; **Meals served in the park:** No; **Food and supplies obtainable in the park:** No; **Food and supplies obtainable nearby:** Yes, in Springfield; **Overnight accommodations:** Springfield, within walking distance; **First Aid available in park:** Yes; **Nearest Hospital:** Springfield, directly across from the museum; **Days/Hours:** Open daily from 8 a.m. to 4:30 p.m. year-round; **Holiday Closings:** Thanksgiving, Dec. 25 & Jan. 1; **Weather:** Typical New England conditions prevail.

GENERAL INFORMATION: Visitors should not handle items on open exhibit since fingerprints on bare metal can cause rust.

Michigan

ISLE ROYALE NATIONAL PARK

PICTURED ROCKS NATIONAL LAKESHORE

FATHER MARQUETTE NATIONAL MEMORIAL

SLEEPING BEAR DUNES NATIONAL LAKESHORE

Detroit

Father Marquette National Memorial
St. Ignace, Michigan

MAILING ADDRESS: Straits State Park, 90 Church Street, St. Ignace, Michigan 49781
Telephone: 906-643-8620

DIRECTIONS: The Memorial to Father Jacques Marquette, French priest and explorer, is in Straits State Park near St. Ignace, Mich., where he founded a Jesuit mission in 1617 and was buried in 1678. A memorial structure, restrooms, picnic area, parking lots, foottrails, overlook, and kiosks have been completed. The museum-theatre building and an amphitheatre are now under construction. This affiliated area was authorized for addition to the National Park System on Dec. 20, 1975.

Isle Royale National Park
Houghton, Michigan

MAILING ADDRESS: Superintendent, Isle Royale National Park, 87 North Ripley St., Houghton, Michigan 49931 **Telephone:** 906-482-3310

DIRECTIONS: Transportation from the mainland to Isle Royale is by boat or float-plane. Reservations are recommended. Boats go from Houghton to Rock Harbor from May to Oct. For schedules, rates and reservations for the National Park Service boat, Ranger III, contact the Superintendent, Isle Royale National Park, Houghton MI 49931, phone 906-482-3310. From Copper Harbor to Rock Harbor (late June to Labor Day) and for pre- and post-season charter trips, contact Isle Royale Queen II, Copper Harbor, MI 49918, phone 906-289-4437 (mid-June to Aug.) and 906-482-4950 (Sept. to mid-June). From Grand Portage to Windigo (late June to Labor Day) and Grand Portage to Rock Harbor via Windigo (May to Oct.), contact Sivertson Brothers, 366 Lake Avenue South, Duluth, MN 55802, phone 218-722-0945 year-round. One boat circumnavigates Isle Royale and will discharge and pick up passengers at various points. From Houghton to Windigo via Rock Harbor (late June to Labor Day) contact Isle Royale Seaplane Service, Box 371, Houghton, MI 49931, phone 906-482-8850 (June to Aug.) and 715-526-2465 (Sept. to May).
The largest in Lake Superior, this forested island is also distinguished for its wilderness character, timber wolves and moose herd, and pre-Columbian copper mines. Authorized for addition to the National Park System on Mar. 3, 1931.

VISITOR ACTIVITIES: boating (rentals at Windigo and Rock Harbor Lodge), boat tours, hiking, diving, camping, fishing, wildlife-watching, canoeing, interpretive programs; **Permits:** for camping; and boating and fishing in Lake Superior waters. Permits available at Rock Harbor Lodge and Windigo; **Fees:** No; **Visitor facilities:** boat tours, rental boats and motors, water taxi service, hiking trails, campgrounds, guided fishing trips, self-guiding trails, interpretive programs; **Any limitations on vehicle usage:** No vehicles of any type are allowed on the island and there are no roads; **Hiking trails:** Yes, more than 257.5 km (160 miles) of foot trails; **Backcountry:** Yes, more information available from the Park. A number of combination trips—boat one way and hike the other—can be arranged with commercial boat operators (note phone numbers above); **Camping:** Yes, campsites cannot be reserved. All campers must obtain a camping permit, available at Rock Harbor or Windigo; **Other overnight accommodations on site:** Yes, lodge and housekeeping facilities are available from late June through Labor Day. For reservations and rates during the season, contact Rock Harbor Lodge, Houghton, MI 49931, phone 906-482-2890; out of season, contact National Park Concessions, Inc. Mammoth Cave, KY 42259, phone 502-773-2191; **Meals served in the park:** Yes, food service is available on boats to and from the island and at Rock Harbor and Windigo;

Food and supplies obtainable in the park: Yes, (limited) at Rock Harbor and Windigo; **Food and supplies obtainable nearby:** Yes, in Houghton, MI and Grand Portage, MN; **Overnight accommodations:** Houghton, MI, 96.6 km (60 miles) & Grand Portage, MN, 32.2 km (20 miles); **First Aid available in park:** Yes, at Ranger Stations; **Nearest Hospital:** Houghton, MI. Note: evacuation from the island is done at the cost of the visitor; **Days/Hours:** The Park is open to visitors from about May 15 to Oct. 20. Park seasons and schedules vary from year to year. Call for current information prior to your visit; **Holiday Closings:** None in season; **Visitor attractions closed for seasons:** Park is closed from about Oct. 21 through May 14; **Weather:** Mid-summer temperatures rarely exceed 80°; evenings are usually cool. Rain is frequent throughout the season.

GENERAL INFORMATION: Because the waters of Lake Superior are often rough, it is not safe to use boats of 20 feet or less to go to the island. However, such boats can be transported to Isle Royale on the Ranger III. The private boat operators mentioned in the directions above will transport small runabouts and canoes. Gasoline for your boat cannot be carried on commercial boats or planes but may be purchased at Rock Harbor and Windigo. Firearms and pets are prohibited in the park.

Lake Survey Chart 14976, "Isle Royale" is recommended for anyone navigating the Park's waters. This chart can be purchased from the Park or the U.S. Lake Survey, 630 Federal Bldg., 231 Lafayette Blvd., Detroit, MI 48226. A topographic map of Isle Royale can be purchased at the Park or from the Geological Survey, U.S. Dept. of the Interior, Washington, D.C. 20240.

Pictured Rocks National Lakeshore
Munising, Michigan

MAILING ADDRESS: Superintendent, Pictured Rocks National Lakeshore, P.O. Box 40, Munising, Michigan 49862 **Telephone:** 906-387-2607

DIRECTIONS: The only section of the Pictured Rocks Cliffs accessible by car is Miners Castle, 11.3 km (7 miles) east of Munising off County Road 58. The Visitor Center is at Munising Falls, 4 km (2.5 miles) east of Munising. The headquarters building which contains some exhibits, is at Sand Point, 3 km (2 miles) further east off County Road 58, and is open all year.

Multicolored sandstone cliffs, broad beaches, sand bars, dunes, waterfalls, inland lakes, ponds, marshes, hardwood and coniferous forests, and numerous birds and animals comprise this scenic area on Lake Superior. This is the first national lakeshore, authorized for addition to the National Park System on Oct. 15, 1966.

VISITOR ACTIVITIES: Most formations are visible only from a boat. Privately operated scenic cruises are conducted daily in the Summer from the city dock in Munising. Visitor activities at 12-Mile Beach include sunbathing, hiking, and photography. The water temperature of Lake Superior is normally too cold for all but the most hardy swimmers. Common throughout the area are inland lakes, ponds, streams, waterfalls and bogs, providing educational and recreational potential in the form of boating, fishing, hunting, and swimming. Winter activities include snowmobiling, crosscountry skiing, and snowshoeing; **Permits:** backcountry permits required, available from Park Headquarters or any Ranger; **Fees:** Yes, there is a fee for privately operated scenic boat cruises on Lake Superior; **Visitor facilities:** nature walks and campfire programs in summer; see schedule at camping areas and Ranger Stations; **Any limitations on vehicle usage:** Vehicles are restricted to designated roadways; **Hiking trails:** Yes, a 63 km (39 mile) lakeshore trail plus day use trails; **Backcountry:** Yes, a camping permit is required and is available from Park Headquarters or any Park Ranger; **Camping:** Yes, primitive camping areas accessible by auto are at Hurricane River, Little Beaver Lake and 12-Mile Beach. Developed campgrounds are in nearby Grand Sable State Forest and Hiawatha National Forest; **Other**

overnight accommodations on site: No; **Meals served in the park:** No; **Food and supplies obtainable in the park:** No; **Food and supplies obtainable nearby:** Yes, Munising and Grand Marais, MI; **Overnight accommodations:** Munising, County Road 58; Grand Marais, State Highway 77; **First Aid available in park:** Yes; **Nearest Hospital:** Munising, at west end of the park; **Days/Hours:** Open 24 hours a day, year-round; **Holiday Closings:** None; **Visitor attractions closed for seasons:**Visitor Centers at Grand Marais are only staffed during the Summer; **Weather:** Over 100 inches of snow falls in Winter. Summer is usually pleasant and warm.

GENERAL INFORMATION: *For Your Safety*—Hikers should be especially cautious when near the steep cliffs of the Pictured Rocks. Boaters should note that Lake Superior is always cold, and frequently rough; therefore, only competent boaters with proper equipment should venture on this lake. Summer visitors should be prepared for occasional cold, rainy weather and troublesome insects.

Sleeping Bear Dunes National Lakeshore
Frankfort, Michigan

MAILING ADDRESS: Superintendent, Sleeping Bear Dunes National Lakeshore, 400 Main St., Frankfort, Michigan 49635 **Telephone:** 616-352-9611

DIRECTIONS: The Visitor Center is on Hwy M-109, 4.8 km (3 miles) north of the village of Empire and 3 km (2 miles) south of the main dune climb area. This facility is open daily during Summer and on weekends from Dec. 15 through about Mar. 1. Headquarters is 37 km (27 miles) south, in Frankfort, MI.

Beaches, massive sand dunes, forests and inland lakes are outstanding characteristics of the major mainland portion and the 2 offshore Manitou Islands. Authorized for addition to the National Park System on Oct. 21, 1970.

VISITOR ACTIVITIES: bird- and wildlife-watching, fishing, camping, primitive camping, hiking, interpretive programs, canoeing, swimming, horseback riding, cross-country skiing; **Permits:** Michigan fishing license required; available at local outlets. Free backcountry camping permits required; available from local rangers; **Fees:** $2 per night campground fee at Platte River and D.H. Day Campgrounds; **Visitor facilities:** campgrounds, interpretive programs, canoe rentals, bathhouse, beaches, trails, boat ramp and rentals; **Any limitations on vehicle usage:** All vehicles must remain on designated roads. Snowmobiles are restricted to county roads; **Hiking trails:** Yes, trails lead through forests and dune areas; **Backcountry:** Yes; **Camping:** Yes, no reservations are available for campsites; **Other overnight accommodations on site:** No; **Meals served in the park:** Yes, snacks at Dune Climb and on South Manitou Island in season; **Food and supplies obtainable in the park:** Yes; **Food and supplies obtainable nearby:** Yes, just outside the park and in Empire, Glen Arbor and Platte River campground area; **Overnight accommodations:** Glen Arbor, MI 22, 1.6 km (1 mile); Honor, US 31, 9.7 km (6 miles); Frankfort, MI 22, 19.3 km (12 miles); **First Aid available in park:** Yes; **Nearest Hospital:** Traverse City, MI 72, 48 km (30 miles); **Days/Hours:** Lakeshore open all year. Visitor Center open from 9 a.m. to 5:30 p.m. in season and open 9 a.m. to 5 p.m. on weekends from Dec. 15 through March; **Holiday Closings:** None; **Visitor attractions closed for seasons:**Campgrounds open only in Summer. Visitor Center open weekends only from Dec. 15 through March; **Weather:** Lakeshore is always cool.

GENERAL INFORMATION: *A Safety Note:* High Lake Michigan water levels have created unstable shoreline conditions. Steep lakeshore bluffs are hazardous to climb and descend due to landslides and slumpage. On Lake Michigan, weather conditions can change drastically in a short time. If you are boating, be aware of the weather forecast and carry appropriate safety equipment.

Minnesota

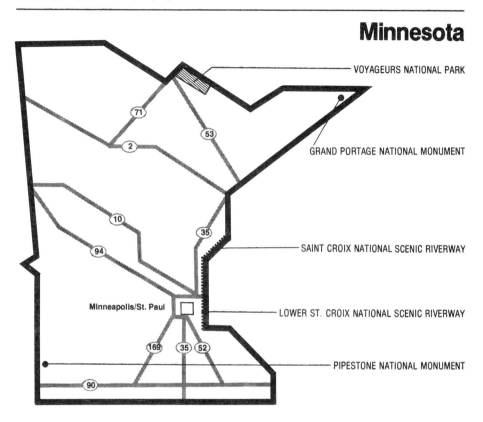

VOYAGEURS NATIONAL PARK

GRAND PORTAGE NATIONAL MONUMENT

SAINT CROIX NATIONAL SCENIC RIVERWAY

LOWER ST. CROIX NATIONAL SCENIC RIVERWAY

Minneapolis/St. Paul

PIPESTONE NATIONAL MONUMENT

Grand Portage National Monument
Grand Marais, Minnesota

MAILING ADDRESS: Superintendent, Grand Portage National Monument, P.O. Box 666, Grand Marais, Minnesota 55604 **Telephone:** 218-387-2788

DIRECTIONS: The Monument is located off US Hwy 61, 58 km (36 miles) northeast of Grand Marais, MN, 232 km (145 miles) from Duluth, MN, and 72 km (45 miles) southwest of the Canadian city of Thunder Bay, Ontario. The portage trail, included as part of the park, bisects the reservation of the Grand Portage Band of the Minnesota Chippewa Tribe.

This 13.6 km (8.5 mile) portage was a rendezvous for traders and trappers on a principal route of Indians, explorers, missionaries, and fur traders into the Northwest. The Grand Portage post of the North West Company has been reconstructed here. Designated Sept. 15, 1951.

VISITOR ACTIVITIES: reconstruction of historic buildings; guided tours, exhibits, demonstrations, audio-visual programs, hiking, cross-country skiing, primitive camping, picnicking; **Permits:** for backcountry, can be obtained at the Monument; **Fees:** No;

Visitor facilities: Information Center, parking, picnic area, hiking/cross-country ski trail; **Any limitations on vehicle usage:** No; **Hiking trails:** Yes, Mount Rose Trail is .8 km (1/2 mile) long. The Grand Portage Trail leads to the site of Fort Charlotte, 13.6 km (8.5 miles) away: **Backcountry:** Yes, information can be obtained at the Monument or at Headquarters; **Camping:** No; **Other overnight accommodations on site:** No; **Meals served in the park:** No; **Food and supplies obtainable in the park:** No; **Food and supplies obtainable nearby:** Yes, Grand Marais, Thunder Bay; **Overnight accommodations:** Grand Marais and town along the shore of Lake Superior. Contact the park for a list of nearby accommodations; **First Aid available in park:** Yes; **Nearest Hospital:** Grand Marais, MN, US 61, 58 km (36 miles); **Days/Hours:** Open daily from 8 a.m. to 5 p.m., mid-May to mid-October; **Holiday Closings:** None; **Visitor attractions closed for seasons:**Closed from mid-Oct. through mid-May; **Weather:** Cool, damp, and windy along the Lake Superior shore.

GENERAL INFORMATION: The portage trail hike requires sturdy hiking shoes and a willingness to endure the discomforts of the trail, which include mud, rocks, mosquitoes and flies. Hikers should remember that emergency assistance is a long way off. A boat leaves daily from the modern dock for Isle Royale National Park, located 35 km (22 miles) offshore (see listing in this book). Beware of uneven ground and irregular steps while visiting Grand Portage. Watch your children near the water; Lake Superior is extremely cold.

Pipestone National Monument
Pipestone, Minnesota

MAILING ADDRESS: Superintendent, Pipestone National Monument, P.O. Box 727, Pipestone, Minnesota 56164 **Telephone:** 507-825-5463

DIRECTIONS: The 283-acre park is adjacent to the north side of the city of Pipestone, in southwest Minnesota, near Sioux Falls, South Dakota. Pipestone can be reached by US 75, and MN 23 and 30. A State Information Center is at Beaver Creek, directly off Interstate 90.

For at least three centuries Indians have obtained materials at this quarry for making ceremonial peace pipes. Established by act of Congress on Aug. 25, 1937.

VISITOR ACTIVITIES: Besides the interesting geology, history, archaeology, and the pipestone crafts, the park offers an opportunity to observe and appreciate the natural environment. Picnicking is available; **Permits:** No; **Fees:** No; **Visitor facilities:** interpretive exhibits, audiovisual program, Indian Cultural Center, souvenir sales; **Any limitations on vehicle usage:** No; **Hiking trails:** Yes, a 1.2 km (3/4 mile) self-guiding trail leads past the quarries and other points of interest; **Backcountry:** No; **Camping:** No; **Other overnight accommodations on site:** No, overnight camping and recreational facilities are available nearby at Split Rock Creek State Park, Route 2, Jasper, MN 56144, phone 507-348-7908, located on MN 23, south of Pipestone; and at Blue Mounds State Park, Route 1, Luverne, MN 56144, phone 507-283-4892, located on US 75, south of Pipestone. No reservations are available for campsites; contact the parks for further information. Check with Park Rangers at Pipestone for locations of private campgrounds and other overnight facilities; **Meals served in the park:** No; **Food and supplies obtainable in the park:** No; **Food and supplies obtainable nearby:** Yes, at Pipestone; **Overnight accommodations:** Pipestone, 1.6 km (1 mile); **First Aid available in park:** Yes; **Nearest Hospital:** Pipestone, 1.6 km (1 mile); **Days/Hours:** Visitor and Cultural Center are open from 8 a.m. to 9 p.m. from Memorial Day to Labor Day and from 8 a.m. to 5 p.m. the rest of the year; **Holiday Closings:** Dec. 25 and Jan. 1; **Weather:** Summer is hot and humid; Spring and Fall are cool and pleasant; Winter brings severe cold, strong winds and possible blizzards.

GENERAL INFORMATION: Visitors should see Winnewisa Falls, one of the stops on the scenic trail.

Lower St. Croix National Scenic Riverway
For details see listing in Wisconsin

Saint Croix National Scenic Riverway
For details see listing in Wisconsin

Voyageurs National Park
International Falls, Minnesota

MAILING ADDRESS: Superintendent, Voyageurs National Park, P.O. Box 50, International Falls, Minnesota 56649 **Telephone:** 218-283-9821

DIRECTIONS: The periphery of the Park is easily approached by surfaced roads from four points along US 53 when travelling from Duluth. County Rte. 23-24 from Orr leads to Crane Lake at the eastern end of the Park; County Rte. 765, or Ash River Trail, provides access to Namakan Lake; County Rte. 122, just south of International Falls, provides access to the south shore of Lake Kabetogama; MN 11, from International Falls, approaches the park area at Black Bay. There are no roads beyond the edge of the Park; access is by canoe, power-boat, float plane, hiking, or a combination of the four.

Once the route of French-Canadian voyageurs, scenic northern lakes are surrounded by forest in this historic and geologically important area. Authorized for addition to the National Park System on January 10, 1972; established on April 8, 1975.

VISITOR ACTIVITIES: fishing, power boating, canoeing, picnicking, camping, hiking, swimming, cross-country skiing; **Permits:** No; **Fees:** No; **Visitor facilities:** guided tours, excursion boat rides, picnic area, campsites, boat ramps and rentals, lodging, food, supplies; **Any limitations on vehicle usage:** Yes, there are only 4.8 km (3 miles) of road in the park. Access is by power boat, float plane, hiking, canoe or a combination of the four; **Hiking trails:** Yes, there are about 40 km (25 miles) of trails; **Backcountry:** Yes, contact Headquarters for details; **Camping:** Yes, primitive sites for boats on major lakes, undeveloped backcountry sites; **Other overnight accommodations on site:** No; **Meals served in the park:** Yes, Whispering Pines Resort, Kettle Falls (reservation only); **Food and supplies obtainable in the park:** Yes, in International Falls, Kabetogama, Crane Lake, Ash River, Orr; **Food and supplies obtainable nearby:** Yes; **Overnight accommodations:** International Falls, Kabetogama, Crane Lake, Ash River, Orr; **First Aid available in park:** Yes; **Nearest Hospital:** International Falls, Cook; **Days/Hours:** Park open year-round. Access is limited during freezing and thawing periods; **Holiday Closings:** No; **Weather:** Summer temperatures range from 40° to 90°F; Winter, -30° to 30°F.

GENERAL INFORMATION: Some of the land is privately owned, and there are many private cottages. Please respect the rights of these property holders. Boaters not familiar with the waters should obtain the services of a guide or use charts, both of which are available locally. The large lakes can suddenly become very rough. Keep informed about weather conditions. Users of small boats and canoes should be particularly cautious and should be prepared to wait out rough water. State boating regulations apply.

Mississippi

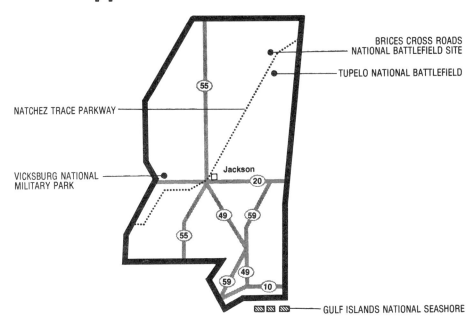

BRICES CROSS ROADS NATIONAL BATTLEFIELD SITE

TUPELO NATIONAL BATTLEFIELD

NATCHEZ TRACE PARKWAY

VICKSBURG NATIONAL MILITARY PARK

Jackson

GULF ISLANDS NATIONAL SEASHORE

Brices Cross Roads National Battlefield Site
Tupelo, Mississippi

MAILING ADDRESS: Superintendent, Natchez Trace Parkway, R.R.1, NT-143, Tupelo, Mississippi 38801 **Telephone:** 601-842-1572

DIRECTIONS: The Site is about 10 km (6 miles) west of Baldwyn on MS 370.
   The Confederate cavalry, under Gen. Nathan Bedford Forrest, was employed with extraordinary skill here during the battle of June 10, 1864. Established by act of Congress on Feb. 21, 1929.

VISITOR ACTIVITIES: The park consists of only a small piece of land, but much of the scene of action is within view. Monuments and markers provide interpretation; **Permits:** No; **Fees:** No; **Visitor facilities:** None; **Any limitations on vehicle usage:** No; **Hiking trails:** No; **Meals served in the park:** No; **Food and supplies obtainable in the park:** No; **Food and supplies obtainable nearby:** Yes, in Tupelo; **Overnight accommodations:** Tupelo, US 45, 40 km (25 miles); Booneville, US 45, 21 km (13 miles); **First Aid available in park:** No, but nearby in Baldwyn, US 45; **Nearest Hospital:** Tupelo, US 45, 40 km (25 miles); **Days/Hours:** Open year-round; **Holiday Closings:** None.

Gulf Islands National Seashore
For details see listing in Florida

Natchez Trace Parkway
Tupelo, Mississippi (Also in Alabama and Tennessee)

MAILING ADDRESS: Superintendent, Natchez Trace Parkway, R.R. 1, NT-143, Tupelo, Mississippi 38801 **Telephone:** 601-842-1572

DIRECTIONS: The Tupelo Visitor Center is 8 km (5 miles) north of Tupelo at the intersection of Natchez Trace Parkway and US 45-North.

This historic route generally follows the old Indian trace, or trail, between Nashville, TN and Natchez, MS. 510 km (317 miles) of the planned 713 km (443 miles) are completed. Established by act of Congress on May 18, 1938.

VISITOR ACTIVITIES: guided tours, hiking, walking, auto tours, camping, swimming, boating, horseback riding, exhibits, biking, interpretive film, fishing, running and jogging, living history program, evening talks, conducted walks, crafts festival in Fall; **Permits:** No; **Fees:** No; **Visitor facilities:** Visitor Center, interpretive film, hiking trails, campgrounds, picnic area, boat ramp; **Any limitations on vehicle usage:** Hauling and commercial trucking are not permitted. Tent and trailer camping are permitted only at authorized campgrounds; **Hiking trails:** Yes, nature and hiking trails up to 4.8 km (3 miles) long; **Backcountry:** No; **Camping:** Yes, campgrounds are at Rocky Springs, Jeff Busby and Meriwether Lewis. Campsites cannot be reserved; stays are limited to 15 days during periods of heavy visitation. You should bring insect netting and repellent. Contact the park for detailed information on locations and facilities at each camping area; **Other overnight accommodations on site:** No; **Meals served in the park:** No; **Food and supplies obtainable in the park:** No; **Food and supplies obtainable nearby:** Yes, at Natchez, Port Gibson, Jackson, Tupelo, Cherokee, and many other towns along the Parkway; **Overnight accommodations:** Same as where food and supplies are available; **First Aid available in park:** Yes; **Nearest Hospital:** Natchez, Jackson, Kosciusko, Tupelo, Columbia, Florence; **Days/Hours:** Park open year-round, 24 hours a day. Tupelo Visitor Center open from 8 a.m. to 5 p.m. 364 days; **Holiday Closings:** Tupelo Visitor Center closed Dec. 25; **Visitor attractions closed for seasons:** None; **Weather:** Summer weather is generally hot and humid. Winter is usually cold and damp with occasional warm periods. Spring and Autumn are mild and warm.

GENERAL INFORMATION: The only service station is at Jeff Busby. You can make the most of your visit by obtaining a brochure on Natchez Trace which is available by mail or at the Visitor Center. It provides detailed information on points of interest and facilities in different areas of the Parkway.

Tupelo National Battlefield
Tupelo, Mississippi

MAILING ADDRESS: Tupelo National Battlefield, c/o Superintendent, Natchez Trace Parkway, R.R. 1, NT-143, Tupelo, Mississippi 38801 **Telephone:** 601-842-1572

DIRECTIONS: The park is within the city limits of Tupelo, MS, on MS 6 about 1.6 km (1 mile) west of its intersection with US 45. It is 1.9 km (1.2 miles) east of the Natchez Trace Parkway.

Here, on July 13-14, 1864, Gen. Nathan Bedford Forrest's cavalry battled a Union force of 14,000 sent to keep Forrest from cutting the railroad supplying Major Gen. William T. Sherman's march on Atlanta. Created by Presidential Proclamation on Feb. 21, 1929.

VISITOR ACTIVITIES: Signs and markers provide interpretation. Information about the area is available at the Tupelo Visitor Center of the Natchez Trace Parkway; **Permits:** No; **Fees:** No; **Visitor facilities: None; Any limitations on vehicle usage:** No; **Hiking trails:** No; **Backcountry:** No; **Camping:** No; **Other overnight accommodations on site:** No; **Meals served in the park:** No; **Food and supplies obtainable in the park:** No; **Food and supplies obtainable nearby:** Yes, at Tupelo; **Overnight accommodations:** Tupelo; **First Aid available in park:** No; **Nearest Hospital:** Tupelo, US 45, 3.2 km (2 miles); **Days/Hours:** Park is always open.

Vicksburg National Military Park
Vicksburg, Mississippi

MAILING ADDRESS: Superintendent, Vicksburg National Military Park, P.O. Box 349, Vicksburg, Mississippi 39180 **Telephone:** 601-636-0583

DIRECTIONS: The Park is just outside of Vickburg on historic US 80.

Fortifications of the 47-day siege of Vicksburg, which ended July 3, 1863, are remarkably well-preserved here. Victory gave the North control of the Mississippi River and cut the Confederacy in two. Vicksburg National Cemetery, containing 18,000 Union graves, adjoins the Park. Confederate dead lie in the city cemetery. Established by act of Congress on Feb. 21, 1899.

VISITOR ACTIVITIES: interpretive audiovisual programs and exhibits, auto tours, guided and auto-tape tours; **Permits:** No; **Fees:** No; **Visitor facilities:** parking and restrooms at Visitor Center; **Any limitations on vehicle usage:** No; **Hiking trails:** No; **Backcountry:** No; **Camping:** No; **Other overnight accommodations on site:** No; **Meals served in the park:** No; **Food and supplies obtainable in the park:** No; **Food and supplies obtainable nearby:** Yes, at Vicksburg; **Overnight accommodations:** Vicksburg, from one block to 8 km (5 miles); **First Aid available in park:** Yes; **Nearest Hospital:** Vicksburg, less than 1.6 km (1 mile) from the Visitor Center; **Days/Hours:** Open daily all year from 8 a.m. to 5 p.m.; **Holiday Closings:** Dec. 25.

GENERAL INFORMATION: The Court House Museum in Vicksburg features an exhibit of relics from the siege.

Missouri

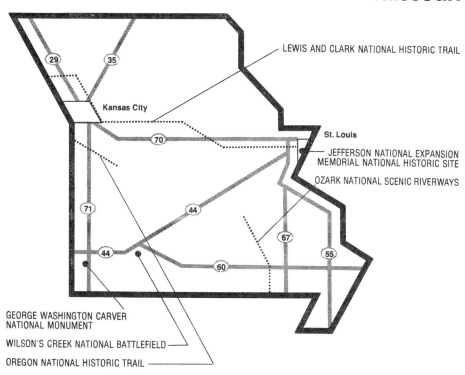

LEWIS AND CLARK NATIONAL HISTORIC TRAIL

Kansas City

St. Louis

JEFFERSON NATIONAL EXPANSION
MEMORIAL NATIONAL HISTORIC SITE

OZARK NATIONAL SCENIC RIVERWAYS

GEORGE WASHINGTON CARVER
NATIONAL MONUMENT

WILSON'S CREEK NATIONAL BATTLEFIELD

OREGON NATIONAL HISTORIC TRAIL

George Washington Carver National Monument
Diamond, Missouri

MAILING ADDRESS: Superintendent, George Washington Carver National Monument P.O. Box 38, Diamond, Missouri 64810 **Telephone:** 417-325-4151

DIRECTIONS: From either Neosho or Carthage take US 71 Alternate to the town of Diamond. Go west 3 km (2 miles) on State Highway V and then south about 1.6 km (1 mile).

The birthplace and childhood home of George Washington Carver, the famous black agronomist, includes the 1881 house, Carver family cemetery and a cultural demonstration area. Authorized for addition to the National Park System on July 14, 1943.

VISITOR ACTIVITIES: interpretive exhibits and film, guided tours, nature walks, picnicking; **Permits:** No; **Fees:** No; **Visitor facilities:** Visitor Center, parking and picnic areas; **Any limitations on vehicle usage:** No; **Hiking trails:** Yes, a 1.2 km (3/4 mile) nature trail; **Backcountry:** No; **Camping:** No; **Other overnight accommodations on site:** No; **Meals served in the park:** No; **Food and supplies obtainable in the park:** No; **Food and supplies obtainable nearby:** Yes, in Diamond; **Overnight accommodations:** Neosho, US 71 A, 16 km (10 miles) & Joplin, 22.5 km (14 miles) northwest on Interstate 44; **First Aid available in park:** Yes; **Nearest Hospital:** Joplin, 22.5 km (14 miles), Interstate

44; Neosho, US 71 A, 16 km (10 miles); **Days/Hours:** Open daily from 8 a.m. to 5 p.m., until 7 p.m. in Summer. Grounds open until dark; **Holiday Closings:** Dec. 25; **Visitor attractions closed for seasons:**None; **Weather:** Rainy Spring, Summer & Fall; snow, sleet, and ice in Winter.

GENERAL INFORMATION: Beware of poison ivy, which abounds in the area.

Jefferson National Expansion Memorial National Historic Site
St. Louis, Missouri

MAILING ADDRESS: Superintendent, Jefferson National Expansion Memorial, 11 North Fourth Street, St. Louis, Missouri 63102 **Telephone:** 314-425-4465

DIRECTIONS: The park is within easy walking distance of downtown St. Louis. The Old Courthouse, with a varied program of exhibits and activities is open daily, as are the Gateway Arch and Museum of Westward Expansion.
  The park, located on the Mississippi riverfront in St. Louis, memorializes Thomas Jefferson and others who directed territorial expansion of the United States. Eero Saarinen's prize-winning, stainless steel Gateway Arch commemorates westward pioneers. Visitors may ascend the 191m (630-foot) high arch by elevator. In the nearby courthouse Dred Scott sued for freedom in the historic slavery case. Designated Dec. 20, 1935.

VISITOR ACTIVITIES: interpretive exhibits, walking, photography, ascending the arch; **Permits:** No; **Fees:** The fee for the elevator ride to the top of the arch is $1 for adults and 50¢ for children under 12; **Visitor facilities:** museum, parking lot, restrooms; **Any limitations on vehicle usage:** No; **Meals served in the park:** No; **Food and supplies obtainable in the park:** No; **Food and supplies obtainable nearby:** Yes, in St. Louis, within 1 block of the site; **Overnight accommodations:** in St. Louis, within walking distance; **First Aid available in park:** Yes; **Nearest Hospital:** St. Louis, within 12 km (8 miles); **Days/Hours:** Open daily from 8:30 a.m. to 5 p.m., 8 a.m. to 10 p.m. from June through Labor Day; **Holiday Closings:** Thanksgiving, Dec. 25 & Jan. 1; **Weather:** Winters are cold and snowy.

GENERAL INFORMATION: Special tours or other programs are available to groups by writing the Superintendent two weeks in advance. Use caution on stone walkways, stairways, and step-down wells. Be extra careful in the Old Courthouse, which has many steps and varying floor levels.

Oregon National Historic Trail
Missouri (also in Kansas, Nebraska, Wyoming, Idaho, Oregon, and Washington)

MAILING ADDRESS: Pacific Northwest Regional Office, National Park Service, 601 Fourth and Pike Building, Seattle, Washington 98101 **Telephone:** 206-442-4830

DIRECTIONS: TRAIL HAS NOT YET BEEN DEVELOPED
  The 2000-mile trail of pioneers from Independence, MO, to Portland, OR vicinity, 1841-48, is commemorated, along with 482 historic places enroute. Included are 115 with high public use potential, including numerous visible segments of the original trail. Authorized for addition to the National Park System on Nov. 10, 1978.

Ozark National Scenic Riverways
Van Buren, Missouri

MAILING ADDRESS: Superintendent, Ozark National Scenic Riverways, P.O. Box 490, Van Buren, Missouri 63965 **Telephone:** 314-323-4236

DIRECTIONS: The park is in Missouri, within an easy day's drive of two large metropolitan centers-282 km (175 miles) south of St. Louis, and 402 km (250 miles) southeast of Kansas City, MO. The Visitor Center at Powder Mill is 56 km (35 miles) north of Van Buren, off MO 106.

The Current and Jacks Fork Rivers flow for about 225 km (140 miles) through a quiet world of nature. Notable features include numerous caves and huge freshwater springs. Authorized for addition to the National Park System on Aug. 27, 1964.

VISITOR ACTIVITIES: canoeing, camping, shore fishing, picnicking, float trips, picnicking, boating, craft demonstrations, interpretive talks, cave tours, hunting, hiking, canoe demonstrations, swimming; **Permits:** No; **Fees:** for campsites, $3 per night per site, collected at Big Spring, Round Spring, Alley Spring, Akers and Pulltite campgrounds from Memorial Day week through Labor Day; **Visitor facilities:** picnic and camping areas, restrooms, stores, canoe and John Boat rentals, bathhouse, boat ramps and rentals, lodging; **Any limitations on vehicle usage:** All vehicles are restricted to designated roadways; **Hiking trails:** Yes, many miles of old logging roads available for hiking but no extended trail system as such. The Ozark Trail is in the planning stage in cooperation with other state and private conservation groups. When completed, this trail will extend the length of the Current River drainage to the Arkansas border; **Backcountry:** Yes, contact Superintendent for more details. No reservations or permits are required; **Camping:** Yes, no reservations for campsites, except for group sites, which are reserved by writing the park; **Other overnight accommodations on site:** Yes, rustic housekeeping cabins available at the Big Spring Unit. Reservations can be made by contacting: Big Spring Concessioner, P.O. Box 73, Van Buren, MO 63965, phone 314-323-4423; **Meals served in the park:** Yes, Big Spring Concessioner; **Food and supplies obtainable in the park:** Yes, at Akers, Round and Alley Springs; **Food and supplies obtainable nearby:** Yes, in adjacent towns: Eminence, Van Buren, Salem, Ellington, Mountain View, Winona, & Birch Tree, MO; **Overnight accommodations:** Eminence, Van Buren, Salem, Ellington, Mountain View, Winona, & Birch Tree; **First Aid available in park:** Yes, small medical clinics also located in Van Buren and Winona, MO; **Nearest Hospital:** Ellington, MO, 34 km (21 miles) from Riverways headquarters in Van Buren via MO State Hwy "D" & 21; **Days/Hours:** Open 24 hours a day; modern camping facilities open Mar. 15-Oct. 30 when freezing is not a threat; **Holiday Closings:** None; **Visitor attractions closed for seasons:** Mild Winters allow almost year round use of the Riverways. The upper stretches of the rivers are often more fun to float during the Winter and Spring because in Summer's low water, portages have to be made around exposed gravel bars and fallen trees.

GENERAL INFORMATION: Visitors should write to obtain an informative pamphlet on the Riverways. Float trips can be hazardous for the unskilled.

For Your Safety: Lifejackets or boat cushions should be carried for each person in the boat or canoe. Non-swimmers and weak swimmers should wear lifejackets at all times. Pick campsites well above river level. Flash flood warnings will be issued when possible. Extinguish campfires before leaving; fire is a great peril here. A lifeline or "trailer" should be attached to all tubes and air mattresses. Know what to expect before launching. Talk to a Park Ranger about river conditions and hazards. Carry first-aid kits, matches, billfolds and other valuables in waterproof containers. Stay out of caves until you check with a Park Ranger. The darkness may conceal mud pools, dropoffs and harmful fungi.

Wilson's Creek National Battlefield
Republic, Missouri

MAILING ADDRESS: Superintendent, Wilson's Creek National Battlefield, 521 N. Hwy 60, Republic, Missouri 65738 **Telephone:** 417-732-2662

DIRECTIONS: The site is 4.8 km (3 miles) east of Republic, MO and 16 km (10 miles) southwest of Springfield, MO. Take Int. 44 Brookline Exit, via Missouri M to Missouri ZZ (south) 8 km (5 miles).

The Civil War battle for control of Missouri took place here on Aug. 10, 1861. Authorized for addition to the National Park System on Apr. 23, 1960.

VISITOR ACTIVITIES: auto tours, interpretive exhibits at Information Station, living history programs on summer weekends; **Permits:** No; **Fees:** No; **Visitor facilities:** picnic areas, restrooms; **Any limitations on vehicle usage:** Vehicles are restricted to designated roadways; **Hiking trails:** Yes; **Backcountry:** No; **Camping:** No; **Other overnight accommodations on site:** No; **Meals served in the park:** No; **Food and supplies obtainable in the park:** No; **Food and supplies obtainable nearby:** Yes, at Republic; **Overnight accommodations:** Springfield, MO, 16 km (10 miles); **First Aid available in park:** Yes; **Nearest Hospital:** Springfield, 16 km (10 miles); **Days/Hours:** Open daily from 8 a.m. to 5 p.m.; **Holiday Closings:** None; **Visitor attractions closed for seasons:**No; **Weather:** Hot, humid Summer, cold with snow and ice in Winter.

GENERAL INFORMATION: New park facilities are under construction.

Montana

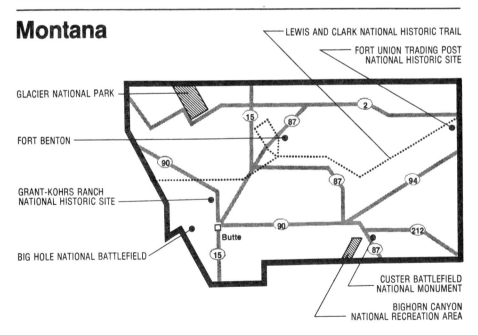

LEWIS AND CLARK NATIONAL HISTORIC TRAIL

FORT UNION TRADING POST NATIONAL HISTORIC SITE

GLACIER NATIONAL PARK

FORT BENTON

GRANT-KOHRS RANCH NATIONAL HISTORIC SITE

BIG HOLE NATIONAL BATTLEFIELD

Butte

CUSTER BATTLEFIELD NATIONAL MONUMENT

BIGHORN CANYON NATIONAL RECREATION AREA

Big Hole National Battlefield
Wisdom, Montana

MAILING ADDRESS: Superintendent, Big Hole National Battlefield, P.O. Box 237,

Wisdom, Montana 59761 **Telephone:** 406-689-2530

DIRECTIONS: The Battlefield is 19.2 km (12 miles) west of Wisdom, MT on MT 43. From Butte, take Interstate 15 southwest to Divide, then to Wisdom on MT 43; from the west, MT 43 intersects US 93 at the State line, between Salmon, Idaho and Hamilton, MT. Stop first at the Visitor Center.

Nez-Perce Indians and U.S. Army troops fought here in 1877—a dramatic episode in the long struggle to confine the Nez Perce, and other Indians, to reservations. Established by Presidential Proclamation on June 23, 1910.

VISITOR ACTIVITIES: audiovisual and interpretive exhibits, self-guiding tours, picnicking, fishing; **Permits:** Montana fishing license can be obtained from local sporting goods dealers; **Fees:** No; **Visitor facilities:** restrooms, parking, and museum at Visitor Center, picnic tables; **Any limitations on vehicle usage:** No; **Hiking trails:** Yes, Big Hole Battlefield Trail follows the route of the Nez Perce War for 36 km (22.5 miles). It is a 2-day hiking and backpacking trail; **Backcountry:** Yes, obtain information from Headquarters; **Camping:** No; **Other overnight accommodations on site:** No, several non-reserved campsites are nearby. Check at Headquarters; **Meals served in the park:** No; **Food and supplies obtainable in the park:** No; **Food and supplies obtainable nearby:** Yes, in Wisdom (limited), Butte & Hamilton, MT, Salmon, ID; **Overnight accommodations:** Wisdom, MT 43, 19.2 km (12 miles) west. Other accommodations are in Butte, MT to the northeast, and Hamilton, MT or Salmon, ID to the West; **First Aid available in park:** Yes; **Nearest Hospital:** Hamilton, ID 93, 108 km (67 miles); **Days/Hours:** Open daily 8 a.m. to 5 p.m., until 8 p.m. from June 1 through Labor Day; **Visitor attractions closed for seasons:**Snow closes hiking trails; **Weather:** Winters are snowy, windy and cold.

GENERAL INFORMATION: *For Your Protection*—animals native to the park are dangerous when startled or approached too closely. Always keep a safe distance. Pets must be under physical control at all times.

Bighorn Canyon National Recreation Area
Fort Smith, Montana and Lovell, Wyoming

MAILING ADDRESS: Superintendent, Bighorn Canyon National Recreation Area, P.O. Box 458, Fort Smith, Montana 59035 **Telephone:** 406-666-2412 (MT) or 307-548-2251 (WY)

DIRECTIONS: North end accessible via MT 313 from Hardin, MT, 69 km (43 miles); south end via WY 14A, Wyoming State Road 37, from Lovell, WY, 21 km (13 miles).

Bighorn Lake, formed by Yellowtail Dam on the Bighorn River, extends 114 km (71 miles), including a large section through scenic Bighorn Canyon. Much of the area borders on the Crow Indian Reservation. Established by act of Congress in 1966.

VISITOR ACTIVITIES: year-round water activities (including winter ice fishing) and recreational activities, sightseeing, weekend visitor programs in Summer; **Permits:** No; **Fees:** Yes, $2 per vehicle per night camping fee at Horseshoe Bend Campground; **Visitor facilities:** campgrounds, boat ramps, Visitor Centers, concessioner services at Horseshoe Bend; **Any limitations on vehicle usage:** All wheeled vehicles must stay on established roads; **Hiking trails:** Yes, short nature trails at both ends of the area; **Backcountry:** Yes, for information in Montana call 406-666-2412, in Wyoming, 307-548-2251; **Camping:** Yes, no reservations available for campsites; **Other overnight accommodations on site:** No; **Meals served in the park:** Yes, fast foods at Horseshoe Bend; **Food and supplies obtainable in the park:** No; **Food and supplies obtainable nearby:** Yes, in Fort Smith, MT & Lovell, WY; **Overnight accommodations:** Hardin, MT, Hwy 313, 69 km (43 miles); Lovell, WY, Hwy 14A, 21 km (13 miles); **First Aid available in park:** Yes; **Nearest Hospital:** Lovell, WY, Hwy 14A, 21 km (13 miles); Hardin, MT 313, 69 km (43 miles); **Days/Hours:** Open year-round; **Holiday Closings:** None; **Visitor attractions closed for seasons:** at North end, Yellowtail Visitor Center closed Oct.-Apr.; **Weather:** Average summer temperature is in the 80'sF; sub-zero temperatures with frequent snow in Winter.

Custer Battlefield National Monument
Crow Agency, Montana

MAILING ADDRESS: Superintendent, Custer Battlefield National Monument, P.O. Box 39, Crow Agency, Montana 59022 **Telephone:** 406-638-2622

DIRECTIONS: The Monument lies within the Crow Indian Reservation in southeastern Montana. US 87 (I-90) passes 1.6 km (1 mile) to the west; US 212 connects the Monument with the Black Hills and Yellowstone National Park. The Crow Agency is 3.2 km (2 miles) north, and Hardin, MT is 29 km (18 miles) north. The nearest cities are Billings, MT, 105 km (65 miles) northwest, and Sheridan, WY, 113 km (70 miles) south.

The famous Battle of the Little Big Horn between 12 companies of the 7th U.S. Cavalry and the Sioux and Northern Cheyenne Indians was fought here on June 25-26, 1876. Lt. Col. George A. Custer and about 268 of his force were killed. Established as a national cemetery on Jan. 29, 1879; changed to Custer Battlefield National Monument by act of Congress on March 22, 1946.

VISITOR ACTIVITIES: interpretive talks and exhibits at Visitor Center, auto tours, hiking; **Permits:** No; **Fees:** No; **Visitor facilities:** parking and restrooms at Visitor Center, interpretive markers; **Any limitations on vehicle usage:** All vehicles are restricted to designated roadways; **Hiking trails:** Yes, self-guiding walking trails; **Backcountry:** No; **Camping:** No; **Other overnight accommodations on site:** No; **Meals served in the park:** No; **Food and supplies obtainable in the park:** No; **Food and supplies obtainable nearby:** Yes, in Hardin, Crow Agency; **Overnight accommodations:** Hardin, MT, 25 km (15 miles) north on I-90; and Crow Agency, 1.6 km (1 mile) north on I-90; **First Aid available in park:** Yes; **Nearest Hospital:** Hardin, MT, 25 km (15 miles) north on I-90; **Days/Hours:** Grounds open from 7 a.m. to sunset year-round. Visitor Center open from 7:30 a.m. to 8:45 p.m. from Memorial Day through Labor Day; from 8 a.m. to 4:30 p.m. from Labor Day through Memorial Day; until 6 p.m. during Daylight Savings Time; **Holiday Closings:** Thanksgiving, Dec. 25 & Jan. 1; **Visitor attractions closed for seasons:** No; **Weather:** Hot Summers, mild Spring and Fall, cold Winter.

GENERAL INFORMATION: *For Your Safety*—Beware of rattlesnakes. Stay on the pathways while walking on the battlefield.

Fort Benton
Fort Benton, Montana

MAILING ADDRESS: Fort Benton Museum, Fort Benton, Montana 59442 **Telephone:** None

DIRECTIONS: Federal facilities are not yet open to the public. In Summer, the community operates a museum, which is located in Old Fort Park.

Founded in 1846, this American Fur Trading Company trading post was an important river port from 1859 through the Montana gold rush of 1862 until rail service surpassed river cargo transport. Authorized for addition to the National Park System on Oct. 16,

1976. The National Park Service will manage the Visitor Center at Fort Benton when construction is completed.

Fort Union Trading Post
For details see listing in North Dakota

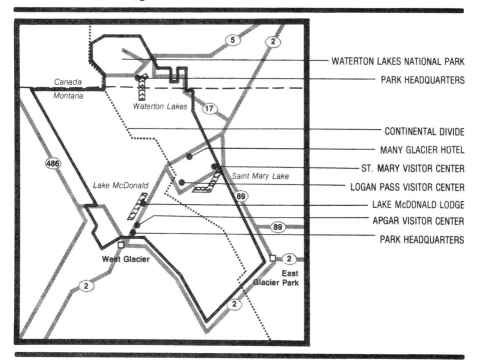

Glacier National Park
West Glacier, Montana

MAILING ADDRESS: Superintendent, Glacier National Park, West Glacier, Montana 59936 **Telephone:** 406-888-5441

DIRECTIONS: The Park is on US 2 and 89 and near US 91 and 93. St. Mary Visitor Center is open mid-May to mid-October; Apgar Information Center from late May through mid-December, and Logan Pass Visitor Center from mid-June to mid-September. For recorded telephone information on the Park, phone 406-888-5551.

This ruggedly beautiful land includes nearly 50 glaciers, many lakes and streams, and a variety of wildflowers and wildlife. Established May 11, 1910.

VISITOR ACTIVITIES: biking, horseback riding and tours, excursion boat cruises, fishing, skiing, snowshoeing, camping, hiking, auto, boat and bus tours, picnicking, interpretive exhibits and programs, backcountry; **Permits:** required for backcountry, can be obtained from Apgar Information Center, St. Mary Visitor Center, and most Ranger Stations; **Fees:** $2 per vehicle entrance fee, 50¢ per person for those entering by means other than private non-commercial vehicles. Persons under 16 years and 62 years or older are not charged. Golden Eagle and Golden Age Passports accepted and available. Campsites are $3 or $2 per night, depending on facilities. Group campsites are 25¢ per night per person, backcountry campsites are free; **Visitor facilities:** Visitor Center, boat rentals, hiking trails, campgrounds, picnic areas, hotels, lodges, cabins, telephones, food service, saddle horse tour concession; **Any limitations on vehicle usage:** Vehicles, including bicycles, are not allowed on trails or off the roads; **Hiking trails:** Yes, there are more than 1120 km (700 miles) of wilderness trails. Check at Visitor Centers for further information· **Backcountry:** Yes, permit required for backcountry, check at any Ranger Station or Information Center; **Camping:** No reservations available for campsites; arrive early for best choice. **Other overnight accommodations on site:** Yes. Accommodations in the Park are available from Glacier Park, Inc.: May 15-Sept. 15 write East Glacier Park, MT. 59434, phone 406-226-9311; Sept. 15-May 15 write 1735 East Fort Lowell Road, Tucson, AZ 85719, phone 602-795-0377; Reservations are advised; deposits are required. Reservations for Granite Park and Sperry Chalets, accessible only by backcountry trails, are available from Belton Chalets, Inc., Box 188, West Glacier, MT 59936, phone 406-888-5511. Privately operated campgrounds are nearby; **Meals served in the park:** Yes, at Apgar, Swift Current, Rising Sun, Many Glacier and Lake McDonald Hotels; **Food and supplies obtainable in the park:** Yes, Apgar, Lake McDonald, Swift Current, Rising Sun & Two Medicine have campers' stores; **Food and supplies obtainable nearby:** Yes, St. Mary, West Glacier, East Glacier; **Overnight accommodations:** St. Mary, West Glacier, East Glacier (adjacent to park entrances); **First Aid available in park:** Yes; **Nearest Hospital:** Cardston, Alberta, Canada, 56 km (35 miles) north of St. Mary on US 89 and in Whitefish, MT, 38 km (24 miles) west of West Glacier on US 93; **Days/Hours:** Park open 24 hours a day, 7 days a week; **Holiday Closings:** None; **Visitor attractions closed for seasons:**Most roads are closed in Winter, except the one between Park Headquarters and Lake McDonald Lodge. Write the park for detailed information on winter activities; **Weather:** Severe storms come quickly, even in Summer, with attendant exposure to low temperatures, rain, snow, sleet and lightning.

GENERAL INFORMATION: *For Your Safety*—Never climb alone. Register before and after the climb. Avoid steep snowfields. Keep your distance from all animals.

Grant-Kohrs Ranch National Historic Site
Deer Lodge, Montana

MAILING ADDRESS: Superintendent, Grant-Kohrs Ranch National Historic Site, P.O Box 790, Deer Lodge, Montana 59722 **Telephone:** 406-846-2070

DIRECTIONS: The ranch is located midway between Yellowstone and Glacier National Parks, .4 km (1/4 mile) from Deer Lodge, off Interstate 90.
　　This was the headquarters area of one of the largest and best known 19th-century range ranches in the country. Today the ranchhouse, bunkhouse, and outbuildings are much as they were in the 1800's. Authorized for addition to the National Park System on Aug. 25, 1972.

VISITOR ACTIVITIES: guided tours of the house, self-guiding walks, exhibits, and fishing (within State requirements); **Permits:** No; **Fees:** No; **Visitor facilities:** Visitor Center, restrooms, self-guiding trail; **Any limitations on vehicle usage:** Vehicles are left at the Visitor Center. The ranch is .4 km (1/4 mile) away by paved trail; **Hiking trails:** No; **Backcountry:** No; **Camping:** No; **Other overnight accommodations on site:** No; **Meals served in the park:** No; **Food and supplies obtainable in the park:** No; **Food and supplies obtainable nearby:** Yes, at Deer Lodge; **Overnight accommodations:** Deer Lodge, Int. 90, .4 km (1/4 mile); **First Aid available in park:** Yes, on emergency basis; **Nearest Hospital:** Deer Lodge, Int. 90, .4 km (1/4 mile); **Days/Hours:** Open daily from 8 a.m. to 4:30 p.m.; until 6 p.m. in Summer; **Holiday Closings:** Thanksgiving, Dec. 25, Jan. 1; **Visitor attractions closed for seasons:**No; **Weather:** Spring is short; Summer, warm; Fall, brisk; Winter, cold.

GENERAL INFORMATION: Smoking is prohibited on the ranch site. Keep your distance from the animals. Pets are not allowed beyond the parking area.

Lewis and Clark Trail
For details see listing in Illinois

Nebraska

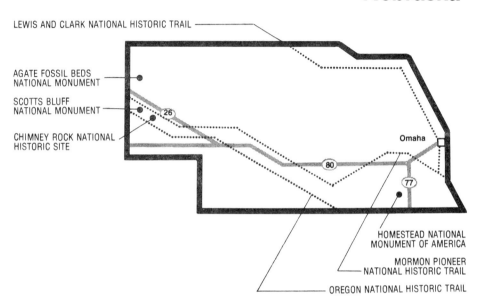

LEWIS AND CLARK NATIONAL HISTORIC TRAIL

AGATE FOSSIL BEDS
NATIONAL MONUMENT

SCOTTS BLUFF
NATIONAL MONUMENT

CHIMNEY ROCK NATIONAL
HISTORIC SITE

Omaha

HOMESTEAD NATIONAL
MONUMENT OF AMERICA

MORMON PIONEER
NATIONAL HISTORIC TRAIL

OREGON NATIONAL HISTORIC TRAIL

Agate Fossil Beds National Monument
Gering, Nebraska

MAILING ADDRESS: Superintendent, Scotts Bluff National Monument, P.O. Box 427, Gering, Nebraska 69341 **Telephone:** 308-436-4340

DIRECTIONS: The site is 54.7 km (34 miles) north of Mitchell on NE 29 and 4.8 km (3 miles) east on County Road; 35 km (22 miles) south of Harrison via NE 29 and 4.8 km (3 miles) east on County Road.
The Monument consists of 1,970 acres, including a 60-acre detached quarry site. The quarries contain numerous concentrated, well-preserved Miocene mammal fossils, representing an important chapter in the evolution of mammals. Established by act of Congress on June 5, 1965.

VISITOR ACTIVITIES: interpretive exhibits, self-guiding hikes; **Permits:** No; **Fees:** No; **Visitor facilities:** Visitor Center exhibits and nearby comfort stations, benches on trails; **Any limitations on vehicle usage:** Vehicles must stay on established roadways; **Hiking trails:** Yes, a 1.6 km (1 mile) dirt trail leads to the fossil beds; **Backcountry:** No; **Camping:** No; **Other overnight accommodations on site:** No; **Meals served in the park:** No; **Food and supplies obtainable in the park:** No; **Food and supplies obtainable nearby:** Yes, in Harrison, NE 40 km (25 miles) north; **Overnight accommodations:** Scottsbluff, Route 26, 72 km (45 miles), Harrison, NE 29, 37 km (23 miles) north,

Mitchell, NE 29, 56 km (35 miles); **First Aid available in park:** Yes; **Nearest Hospital:** Scottsbluff, 72 km (45 miles); **Days/Hours:** Open daily from 8:30 a.m. to 5:30 p.m.; **Holiday Closings:** None; **Visitor attractions closed for seasons:** Closed from Labor Day through Memorial Day.

GENERAL INFORMATION: *For Your Safety*—Watch for rattlesnakes while viewing the fossil areas or walking anywhere in the park.

Chimney Rock National Historic Site
Bayard, Nebraska

MAILING ADDRESS: Superintendent, Chimney Rock National Historic Site, 1500 R, Lincoln, Nebraska 68508 **Telephone:** 402-471-3270 (Lincoln) 308-586-2022 (Trailer at park site)

DIRECTIONS: The Site is 5.6 km (3-1/2 miles) southwest of Bayard, on the south side of the North Platte River. From Bayard, US 26 intersects NE 92 at a point about 2.4 km (1-1/2 miles) from the Site. Gravel roads lead from NE 92 to within .8 km (1/2 mile) of the Site. Travel from there is by foot only, on unimproved path.

Pioneers camped near this famous landmark as they travelled west. It stands 500 feet above the Platte River along the Oregon Trail. Designated a National Historic Site on Aug. 9, 1956.

VISITOR ACTIVITIES: walking tours, picnicking, photography; **Permits:** No; **Fees:** No; **Visitor facilities:** information trailer, picnic area; **Any limitations on vehicle usage:** Vehicles are restricted to designated roadways; **Hiking trails:** Yes; **Backcountry:** No; **Camping:** No; **Other overnight accommodations on site:** No; **Meals served in the park:** No; **Food and supplies obtainable in the park:** No; **Food and supplies obtainable nearby:** Yes, Bayard; **Overnight accommodations:** Bayard, 6.4 km (4 miles); Bridgeport, 19.3 km (12 miles) east; **First Aid available in park:** No; **Nearest hospital:** Scottsbluff, NE 92, approx. 56 km (35 miles); **Days/Hours:** Open during daylight hours, 365 days a year; **Visitor attractions closed for seasons:** Trailer #4 at the rest area on Neb. 92 operates from 8 a.m.-7 p.m. from Memorial Day through Labor Day; **Weather:** Expect violent storms in Summer.

GENERAL INFORMATION: *For Your Safety*—Watch out for rattlesnakes, rough terrain, and yucca plants. Boots and hiking clothes are essential.

Homestead National Monument of America
Beatrice, Nebraska

MAILING ADDRESS: Superintendent, Homestead National Monument of America, R.F.D. 3, Beatrice, Nebraska 68310 **Telephone:** 402-223-3514

DIRECTIONS: The Monument is located in southeastern Nebraska, about 7 km (4.5 miles) northwest of Beatrice and about 65 km (40 miles) south of Lincoln. Take NE 4 from Beatrice to the Monument.

One of the first claims under the Homestead Act of 1862 was filed for this land. Authorized for addition to the National Park System on Mar. 19, 1936.

VISITOR ACTIVITIES: audiovisual and interpretive exhibits, walking tours, living history demonstrations in Summer, hiking, cross-country skiing; **Permits:** No; **Fees:** No; **Visitor facilities:** parking and restrooms at Visitor Center; **Any limitations on vehicle usage:** Motorcycles, bicycles, and snowmobiles are not allowed on the trail or grounds; **Hiking trails:** Yes, a self-guiding trail around the site; **Backcountry:** No; **Camping:** No; **Other overnight accommodations on site:** No, city-operated campsites are available in Beatrice. No reservations are accepted, but there is usually enough space to accommodate all campers. For further information, write Beatrice Park and Recreation Department, City Auditorium, Beatrice, NE 68310, or phone 402-228-3649; **Meals served in the park:** No; **Food and supplies obtainable in the park:** No; **Food and supplies obtainable nearby:** Yes, in Beatrice; **Overnight accommodations:** Beatrice, NE 4, 8 km (5 miles); **First Aid available in park:** Yes; **Nearest Hospital:** Beatrice, NE 4, 8 km (5 miles); **Days/Hours:** Open 7 days a week: Winter, 8 a.m. to 5 p.m. Monday through Friday, 8:30 a.m. to 5 p.m. on Saturday and Sunday. Summer, 8 a.m. to 6 p.m. everyday; **Holiday Closings:** Thanksgiving, Dec. 25, Jan. 1; **Visitor attractions closed for seasons:**Freeman School open regularly only in Summer; **Weather:** Summer is frequently hot with moderate humidity and the possibility of thundershowers. Winter is cold with occasional snow.

GENERAL INFORMATION: *For Your Safety*—Check carefully for ticks, which are most active from May through August. Do not smoke on the trail.

Lewis and Clark Trail
For details see listing in Illinois

Mormon Pioneer Trail
For details see listing in Illinois

Oregon National Scenic Trail
For details see listing in Missouri

Scotts Bluff National Monument
Gering, Nebraska

MAILING ADDRESS: Superintendent, Scotts Bluff National Monument, P.O. Box 427, Gering, Nebraska 69341 **Telephone:** 308-436-4340

DIRECTIONS: The Monument adjoins the south bank of the North Platte River 4.8 km (3 miles) west of Gering via NE 92, which bisects the area from east to west. The Monument is 8 km (5 miles) southwest of the town of Scottsbluff via US 26, which connects with NE 92 north of the river. From I-80 it is 67.6 km (42 miles) to the Monument via NE 71.

Rising 800 feet above the valley floor, this massive promontory was a landmark on the Oregon Trail, associated with the mass migration across the Great Plains between 1843 and 1869. Created by Presidential Proclamation on Dec. 12, 1919.

VISITOR ACTIVITIES: museum, interpretive talks, nature walks, hiking, biking, living history programs; **Permits:** No; **Fees:** $1 per car entrance fee; Golden Eagle and Golden Age Passports accepted and available; **Visitor facilities:** museum, nature, hiking, and bicycle trails; **Any limitations on vehicle usage:** Vehicles must stay on established roads; trailers are not allowed to go to the top of the Monument; **Hiking trails:** Yes, in addition to the Summit Trail, the trough of the old trail, ground down by the passage of a million emigrants, can be seen from the trans-Monument road south of the east entrance, across from the Visitor Center; **Backcountry:** No; **Camping:** No; **Other overnight accommodations on site:** No; **Meals served in the park:** No; **Food and supplies obtainable in the park:** No; **Food and supplies obtainable nearby:** Yes, in Gering, 4.8 km (3 miles) east of Park Headquarters; **Overnight accommodations:** Gering, NE 92, 4.8 km (3 miles); **First Aid available in park:** Yes; **Nearest Hospital:** Scottsbluff, 16 km (10 miles); **Days/Hours:** Open from 8 a.m. to 4:30 p.m. in Winter, extended hours in Summer; **Holiday Closings:** Dec. 25 & Jan. 1; **Visitor attractions closed for seasons:** The road to the top is closed intermittently by snow in Winter.; **Weather:** Winter is snowy and windy.

GENERAL INFORMATION: *For Your Safety*—Remain on the Summit Trail; do not venture toward the cliff's edge.

Nevada

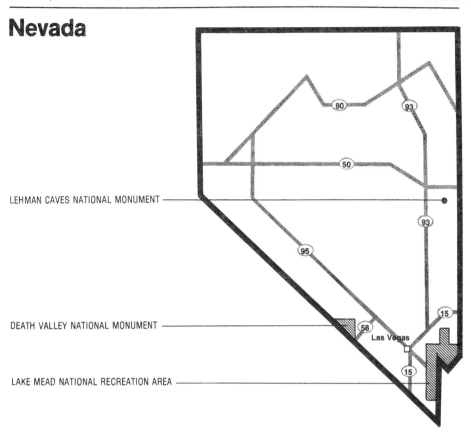

LEHMAN CAVES NATIONAL MONUMENT

DEATH VALLEY NATIONAL MONUMENT

LAKE MEAD NATIONAL RECREATION AREA

Death Valley National Monument
For details see listing in California

Lake Mead National Recreation Area
Boulder City, Nevada

MAILING ADDRESS: Superintendent, Lake Mead National Recreation Area, 601 Nevada Highway, Boulder City, Nevada 89005 **Telephone:** 702-293-4041

DIRECTIONS: The Alan Bible Visitor Center is near the west end of Lake Mead, on US Hwy 93, 6.5 km (4 miles) east of Boulder City.
 Lake Mead in Nevada, formed by Hoover Dam, and Lake Mohave in Arizona, formed by Davis Dam, both on the Colorado River, dominate this first national recreation area. Established by Congress on Oct. 8, 1964.

VISITOR ACTIVITIES: swimming, fishing, boating, water skiing, dam tours, horseback riding, cruising, diving, backcountry, hiking, auto tours, hunting, camping; **Permits:** for fishing, an Arizona or Nevada fishing license, available at most marinas, is required; **Fees:** $2 per night for developed campsites; **Visitor facilities:** Visitor Center, botanical garden, interpretive programs, camping and trailer sites, commercial boat trips, boat, mooring and marine supply rentals; **Any limitations on vehicle usage:** Off-road vehicle travel is prohibited; **Hiking trails:** No, most hiking is cross-country; ask a Ranger about good routes. Carry plenty of water with you. In Summer, the canyons heat up like furnaces. Hikers should have two or more quarts of water per person. There are no creeks or springs that have water suitable for drinking. Never enter abandoned mines or tunnels; shafts are deep and supporting timbers are old and rotten; **Backcountry:** Yes, check at the Visitor Center, see a Park Ranger, or contact the Superintendent in advance; **Camping:** No reservations available for campsites. Nearly all developed areas have campgrounds equipped with individual campsites, fire grates, tables, water, restrooms, any sanitary disposal stations. Only at concessioner trailer courts are there utility hookups. To protect your gear, lock it when you leave camp and notify a Ranger if your campsite is left unattended for more than 24 hours. Be alert for flash floods in stormy weather. Avoid wash bottoms, and never camp on low ground; **Other overnight accommodations on site:** Yes, concession facilities are listed in a pamphlet available by mail from the Superintendent or at the Visitor Center; **Meals served in the park:** Yes, fast food available at each of the seven camping areas; **Food and supplies obtainable in the park:** Yes, at concession facilities; **Food and supplies obtainable nearby:** Yes, in Boulder City, Searchlight, Bullhead City, Overton, Henderson; **Overnight accommodations:** Boulder City, 6.5 km (4 miles); Bullhead City, 9.7 km (6 miles); Henderson, 24 km (15 miles); Las Vegas, 40 km (25 miles); **First Aid available in park:** Yes; **Nearest Hospital:** Boulder City, 6.5 km (4 miles); **Days/Hours:** Park never closes; **Visitor attractions closed for seasons:** No; **Weather:** From late September through late May, the weather is delightful. Even in July and August, when daytime temperatures may rise above 40°C (100°F), many visitors do not find the heat oppressive because of the low humidity. Summer nights are usually comfortable with low temperatures averaging 20°C (70°F). Be prepared for low temperatures on winter mornings and evenings. Bring warm clothing.

GENERAL INFORMATION: *Safety Notes:* For protection against brilliant sunshine, wear a hat and tinted glasses. When swimming, distances to the islands, buoys, and across coves are easily underestimated. Caution-air mattresses and blow-up toys, and inflatables, can blow away even on gentle wind, leaving you stranded far from shore. Never swim alone or from an unanchored boat. Remember, muscles tire quickly in cold water.

Always check the weather forecast and look for storm warning flags before going out boating or water skiing. If bad weather catches you on the water, put on your life jacket, head for the nearest sheltered cove, and wait it out. Call 702-736-3854 for a current forecast from the National Weather Service. Water skiers must wear a lifesaving device, and an observer must accompany the boat operator. Waters below Hoover Dam average in the low 50°s F.; unsafe for swimming in Black Canyon.

Lehman Caves National Monument
Baker, Nevada

MAILING ADDRESS: Superintendent, Lehman Caves National Monument, Baker, Nevada 89311 **Telephone:** 702-234-7331

DIRECTIONS: The Monument is 8 km (5 miles) west of Baker, NV, near the Nevada-Utah boundary. US 6 and 50 are 16 km (10 miles) to the north, and US 93 is 64 km (40 miles) to the west.

Tunnels and galleries decorated with stalactites and stalagmites honeycomb these caverns of gray and white marble. Created by Presidential Proclamation on Jan. 24, 1922.

VISITOR ACTIVITIES: flash photography, cave tours, picnicking, wildlife-watching; **Permits:** Required for cave tours, available at Visitor Center; **Fees:** for tours, guide fees: 50¢ for adults, 25¢ for Golden Age Passport holders and free for children under 16 years; **Visitor facilities:** Trips through the cave are conducted every day over a 1 km (2/3 mile) paved trail with stairways. About 1-1/2 hours are required for the tour. A modern electrical system provides indirect lighting. The temperature averages a chilly 10°C (50°F); warm clothing is suggested. Children under 16 must be accompanied by an adult. Souvenirs are sold at Headquarters. Picnic areas are available; **Any limitations on vehicle usage:** Vehicles are restricted to designated roadways; **Hiking trails:** Yes, a nature trail; **Backcountry:** No, but backcountry is available in Humbolt National Forest, adjacent to the Monument. Contact: US Forest Service, Humboldt National Forest, Baker, NV 89311, phone 702-234-7311; **Camping:** No; **Other overnight accommodations on site:** No, four campgrounds are in the adjacent Humboldt National Forest. Contact: US Forest Service, Humboldt National Forest, Baker, NV 89311, phone 702-234-7311; **Meals served in the park:** Yes, from April through Oct. in a cafe adjacent to the Visitor Center; **Food and supplies obtainable in the park:** No; **Food and supplies obtainable nearby:** Yes, at Baker, NV; **Overnight accommodations:** Baker, NV 74, 8 km (5 miles); **First Aid available in park:** Yes, or nearby in Baker; **Nearest Hospital:** Ely, NV, US 6-50; 112.7 km (70 miles); **Days/Hours:** Open year-round from 8 a.m. to 5 p.m. Tours scheduled at least hourly in Summer; Oct.-May 9, 10:30, 12:30, 2:30 & 4; Evening programs on a varying schedule in Summer; **Holiday Closings:** None; **Visitor attractions closed for seasons:** Cafe closed from Oct. to Easter; **Weather:** Winter: 30°F with lows to 10°F. Snow from Nov. to May. Summer: 80-85°F with highs seldom above 90°F.

GENERAL INFORMATION: *For Your Safety*—while in the cave, watch for low ceilings and slippery conditions. Use the handrails and stay with your group. If you have a heart condition or have difficulty breathing, remember the high elevation and take it easy. Beware of rattlesnakes during the summer months. Avoid going through the brush. Always stay on the pathway when walking the nature trail.

New Hampshire

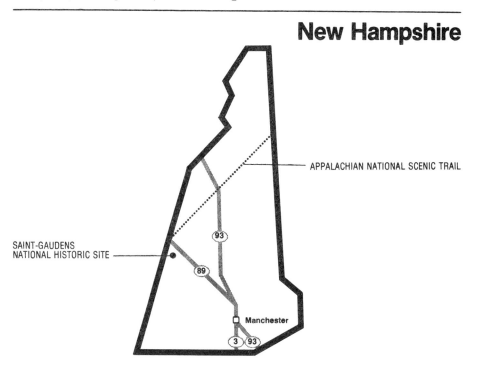

APPALACHIAN NATIONAL SCENIC TRAIL

SAINT-GAUDENS
NATIONAL HISTORIC SITE

93

89

Manchester

3　93

Appalachian National Scenic Trail
For details see listing in Maine

Saint-Gaudens National Historic Site
Cornish, New Hampshire

MAILING ADDRESS: Superintendent, Saint-Gaudens National Historic Site, R.R.2, Windsor, Vermont 05089 **Telephone:** 603-675-2055

· **DIRECTIONS:** The Site is located on NH 12A in Cornish, NH, 12.5 km (9 miles) north of Claremont, NH, and 3 km (2 miles) from Windsor, VT. Visitors travelling via Int. 91 should use the Ascutney or Hartland, VT exits; via 89, they should use the West Lebanon, NH exit.

A memorial to the great American sculptor Augustus Saint-Gaudens (1848-1907) contains his home, "Aspet" and his studios and gardens. Authorized for addition to the National Park System on Aug. 31, 1964. Established in 1977.

VISITOR ACTIVITIES: guided tours, exhibits, picnicking, fishing, concerts and art exhibitions in Summer, snowshoe and cross-country skiing available on the grounds in Winter; **Permits:** No; **Fees:** Entrance fee is 50¢ per person, 16 and under free of charge. Golden Eagle and Golden Age Passports accepted and available; **Visitor facilities:** parking, restrooms, picnic area, museums, garden and grounds; **Any limitations on vehicle usage:** No snowmobiles or other off-road vehicles are allowed; **Hiking trails:** Yes, two 20-minute nature trails; **Backcountry:** No; **Camping:** No; **Other overnight accommodations on site:** No; **Meals served in the park:** No; **Food and supplies obtainable in the park:** No; **Food and supplies obtainable nearby:** Yes, at Claremont, W. Lebanon & Plainfield, NH and Ascutney, Windsor, and Hartford, VT; **Overnight accommodations:** Claremont, W. Lebanon & Plainfield, NH and Ascutney, Windsor, and Hartford, VT; **First Aid available in park:** No; **Nearest Hospital:** Windsor, VT, 3 km (2 miles); **Days/Hours:** Open May 15 through October from 8:30 a.m. to 5 p.m. daily; **Holiday Closings:** None (in season); **Visitor attractions closed for seasons:** House and studios are closed from Nov. through May 15; **Weather:** Temperatures range from 65-80°F in Summer.

New Jersey

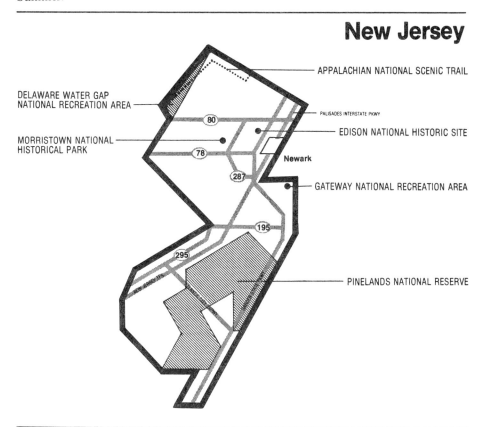

APPALACHIAN NATIONAL SCENIC TRAIL

DELAWARE WATER GAP
NATIONAL RECREATION AREA

PALISADES INTERSTATE PKWY

EDISON NATIONAL HISTORIC SITE

MORRISTOWN NATIONAL
HISTORICAL PARK

Newark

GATEWAY NATIONAL RECREATION AREA

PINELANDS NATIONAL RESERVE

Appalachian National Scenic Trail
For details see listing in Maine

Delaware Water Gap National Recreation Area
For details see listing in Pennsylvania

Edison National Historic Site
West Orange, New Jersey

MAILING ADDRESS: Park Manager, Edison National Historic Site, Main Street at Lakeside Avenue, West Orange, New Jersey 07052 **Telephone:** 201-736-5050

DIRECTIONS: Site headquarters, on Main Street at Lakeside Avenue in West Orange, is 3 km (2 miles) west of Garden State Parkway and .8 km (1/2 mile) north of Interstate 280.
    Buildings and equipment used by Thomas A. Edison for many of his experiments are here, as are his library, papers, and models of some of his inventions. The Site also

includes Glenmont, Edison's 23-room home, with original furnishings. Designated Dec. 6, 1955.

VISITOR ACTIVITIES: walking tours, interpretive exhibits and talks; **Permits:** No; **Fees:** 50¢ per person entrance fee, except for those under 16 or over 62. Golden Age and Golden Eagle Passports accepted and available; **Visitor facilities:** restrooms and parking; **Any limitations on vehicle usage:** No strollers allowed on tour; no buses allowed in Llewellyn Park; **Hiking trails:** No; **Meals served in the park:** No; **Food and supplies obtainable in the park:** No; **Food and supplies obtainable nearby:** Yes, shops within walking distance; **Overnight accommodations:** in the immediate area of West Orange, 2.5-8 km (1-1/2 to 5 miles); **First Aid available in park:** Yes; **Nearest Hospital:** Orange, 3 km (2 miles); **Days/Hours:** Guided tours of the laboratory (1-1/2 hours) are conducted daily, beginning at 9 a.m., with the last tour starting at 3:30 p.m. Tours of Glenmont begin on the hour, 10 a.m. to 4 p.m., Monday through Saturday except holidays by arrangement at headquarters; **Holiday Closings:** Thanksgiving, Dec. 25, & Jan. 1; **Weather:** The site is open year-round, and since tours go between buildings, inclement weather must be tolerated.

Gateway National Recreation Area
For details see listing in New York

Morristown National Historical Park
Morristown, New Jersey

MAILING ADDRESS: Superintendent, Morristown National Historical Park, P.O. Box 1136 R, Morristown, New Jersey 07960 **Telephone:** 201-539-2016

DIRECTIONS: The Park is most easily accessible by Int. 287. Southbound, use exit 32 for Washington's Headquarters and the Ford Mansion. Use exit 26B for the Jockey Hollow Area. Northbound, use exit 32A for the Mansion and Museum, or for the Jockey Hollow Area use the exit for N. Maple Ave./Rte 202. Follow the brown directional signs. Morristown is also easily reached via US 202 or by NJ 24.

For two winters during the Revolution—1777 and 1779-80—the Continental Army established winter quarters here. The Park is divided into two main areas. The Jockey Hollow Area includes the Visitor Center, the Wick House, reconstructed soldier huts, hiking trails, and a tour loop road: Washington's Headquarters includes both the museum and the Ford Mansion. Authorized for addition to the National Park System on Mar. 2, 1933.

VISITOR ACTIVITIES: movies, slide programs, exhibits, soldier life demonstrations, arts and crafts demonstrations, hiking, special events on weekends, wayside exhibits; **Permits:** No; **Fees:** Entrance fee is 50¢ for adults, under 16 and over 62 are free.Golden Eagle and Golden Age Passports accepted and available; **Visitor facilities:** hiking trails, restrooms and sales areas throughout the Park; **Any limitations on vehicle usage:** Park in designated areas only. Park roads are open from 9 a.m. to sunset; **Hiking trails:** Yes, Jockey Hollow has an extensive woodland trail system. Obtain maps at Visitor Center; **Backcountry:** No; **Camping:** No; **Other overnight accommodations on site:** No, within 48-64 km (30-40 miles) there are six State-run parks or forests which have camping facilities. In addition, there are several privately-run campsites closer to Morristown.

Contact the Park for further information; **Meals served in the park:** No, but picnic and eating facilities are available in the Lewis Morris County Park which is adjacent to the Jockey Hollow Area.; **Food and supplies obtainable in the park:** No; **Food and supplies obtainable nearby:** Yes, in Morristown, Bernardsville, Mendham; **Overnight accommodations:** About 8 km (5 miles) north of Morristown, near the intersection of Highways 10 and 202 East and West. Contact the Park for further information on nearby accommodations; **First Aid available in park:** Yes; **Nearest Hospital:** Morristown, South Street, 1.6 km (1 mile); **Days/Hours:** Park buildings open 9 a.m.-5 p.m.; Park roads open 9 a.m.-sunset, 7 days a week year-round; **Holiday Closings:** All park buildings closed Thanksgiving, Dec. 25 & Jan. 1; **Visitor attractions closed for seasons:** Park is occasionally closed by snow or hazardous driving conditions.

GENERAL INFORMATION: Nearby points of interest include Edison National Historic Site (see listing in this book) and Great Swamp Wildlife Refuge.

Pinelands National Reserve
New Jersey

DIRECTIONS: ONLY STATE PARK AREAS HAVE BEEN DEVELOPED AS YET. For further information, contact: State of New Jersey Bureau of Parks, P.O. Box 1420, Trenton, NJ 08625, phone 609-292-2797.

Local, State, and Federal governments and the private sector combine in a new "reserve" policy to protect diversely owned lands from encroachment. This largest undeveloped tract on the Eastern seaboard has the equivalent of a 2000 square-mile lake beneath the dwarfed pines and oaks of its shrubby, porous surface. Authorized for addition to the National Park System on Nov. 10, 1978.

New Mexico

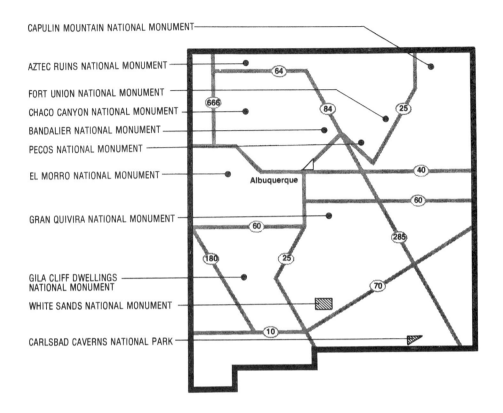

CAPULIN MOUNTAIN NATIONAL MONUMENT

AZTEC RUINS NATIONAL MONUMENT

FORT UNION NATIONAL MONUMENT

CHACO CANYON NATIONAL MONUMENT

BANDALIER NATIONAL MONUMENT

PECOS NATIONAL MONUMENT

EL MORRO NATIONAL MONUMENT

GRAN QUIVIRA NATIONAL MONUMENT

GILA CLIFF DWELLINGS
NATIONAL MONUMENT

WHITE SANDS NATIONAL MONUMENT

CARLSBAD CAVERNS NATIONAL PARK

Albuquerque

Aztec Ruins National Monument
Aztec, New Mexico

MAILING ADDRESS: Superintendent, Aztec Ruins National Monument, P.O. Box U, Aztec, New Mexico 87410 **Telephone:** 505-334-6174

DIRECTIONS: The Monument is northwest of the city of Aztec, near the junction of US 550 and NM 44. You should stop first at the Visitor Center.

Ruins of this large Pueblo Indian community of 12th-century masonry and timber buildings have been largely excavated and stabilized. The ruins, misnamed by early settlers, are unrelated to the Aztecs of Mexico. Created by Presidential Proclamation on Jan. 24, 1923.

VISITOR ACTIVITIES: interpretive exhibits, picnicking, walking tours; **Permits:** No; **Fees:** $1 per car entrance fee. Golden Age and Golden Eagle Passports accepted and available; **Visitor facilities:** parking, restrooms and exhibits at Visitor Center, picnic area; **Any limitations on vehicle usage:** No; **Hiking trails:** Yes, a self-guiding trail leads through the west pueblo, its great Kiva, and the nearby Hubbard Ruin, a tri-walled structure; **Backcountry:** No; **Camping:** No; **Other overnight accommodations on site:** No; **Meals served in the park:** No; **Food and supplies obtainable in the park:** No; **Food and supplies obtainable nearby:** Yes, in Aztec; **Overnight accommodations:** Aztec, a short distance southeast on US 550; **First Aid available in park:** Yes, or nearby in Aztec; **Nearest Hospital:** Farmington, Maple Street, 24 km (15 miles); **Days/Hours:** Open daily from 8 a.m. to 5 p.m., until 6 p.m. from Memorial Day through Labor Day; **Holiday Closings:** Dec. 25 and Jan. 1; **Visitor attractions closed for seasons:**No; **Weather:** Summer: highs in the 90°'s, lows 40°s-50°s, thunderstorms late in the season. Fall & Spring: highs 40°s to 80°s, lows often below 32°, Spring is very windy. Winter: highs 20°s to 40°s, lows well below 32° with some snow.

GENERAL INFORMATION: The 800-year-old walls of these prehistoric Indian ruins are held together with mud: they crumble easily if disturbed.

Bandalier National Monument
Los Alamos, New Mexico

MAILING ADDRESS: Superintendent, Bandalier National Monument, Los Alamos, New Mexico 87544 **Telephone:** 505-672-3861

DIRECTIONS: The Monument is 74 km (46 miles) west of Santa Fe, NM, and is reached from Santa Fe north on US 285 to Pojoaque, then west on NM 4. Approach may also be made through the scenic Jemez country from Albuquerque via NM 44 and NM 4. Inquiry should be made during bad weather before attempting the latter trip. The Visitor Center, 4.8 km (3 miles) inside the Monument, is 16 km (10 miles) southwest of White Rock and 21 km (13 miles) south of Los Alamos, both on NM 4 (loop). The detached Tsankawi section of the Monument is 18 km (11 miles) north of Frijoles Canyon on NM 4.

Ruins of many cliff houses of 15th-century Pueblo Indians lie on the canyon-slashed slopes of the Pajarito Plateau. Created by Presidential Proclamation on Feb. 11, 1916.

VISITOR ACTIVITIES: hiking, camping, interpretive and audiovisual exhibits, self-guiding walking tours, picnicking, horseback riding, campfire programs nightly in Summer; **Permits:** required for backcountry travel, can be obtained from the Visitor Center; **Fees:** $1 per car entrance fee; 50¢ per person for individuals on buses, on foot, or travelling by other means. Golden Age and Golden Eagle Passports accepted and available. $3 per night per site camping fee, 1/2 price for Golden Age Passport holders; **Visitor facilities:** parking, restrooms, and exhibits at Visitor Center, campgrounds, picnic area, snack bar & curio shop in Summer; **Any limitations on vehicle usage:** Vehicles are restricted to paved roads. Trail bikes are not allowed in the Monument; **Hiking trails:** Yes, a 1.6 km (1 mile) round-trip trail from near the Visitor Center to the main ruin, and over 97 km (60 miles) of maintained backcountry trails; **Backcountry:** Yes, get information from a Park Ranger or by telephoning the Visitor Center; **Camping:** Yes, no reservations available for individual campsites. Group sites are reserved through the Superintendent's office; **Other overnight accommodations on site:** No; **Meals served in the park:** Yes, at Frijoles Canyon snack bar; **Food and supplies obtainable in the park:** Yes; **Food and supplies obtainable nearby:** Yes, at White Rock, Los Alamos, Santa Fe; **Overnight accommodations:** White Rock, NM 4, 16 km (10 miles); Los Alamos, NM 4, 21 km (13 miles); Santa Fe, NM 4 to Pojoaque, thence US 285 to Pojoaque, 74 km (46 miles); **First Aid available in park:** Yes; **Nearest Hospital:** Los Alamos, NM 4, 21 km (13 miles); **Days/Hours:** Open daily 8 a.m.-5 p.m.; until 6 p.m. from Memorial Day-Labor Day; **Holiday Closings:** Dec. 25; **Visitor attractions closed for seasons:** Trails are not cleared of snow in Winter; **Weather:** From May-Sept., temperatures range from the low 50°sF at night to the high 80°s F in the daytime. The relative humidity is generally low. Thunderstorms, usually of short duration, are frequent in July and August.

GENERAL INFORMATION: Energy and endurance are required for longer hiking trips. You must be in good physical condition since trails lead into and out of deep, steep-walled canyons of the rough and broken country, and the altitude (about 7000 feet) places an additional burden on the heart and lungs.

Capulin Mountain National Monument
Capulin, New Mexico

MAILING ADDRESS: Superintendent, Capulin Mountain National Monument, Capulin,New Mexico 88414 **Telephone:** 505-278-2201

DIRECTIONS: The Monument is in the northeast corner of New Mexico. The entrance is on NM 325, 4.8 km (3 miles) north of the town of Capulin. From Clayton, Capulin is 87 km (54 miles) west on US 64/87; from Raton, 48 km (30 miles) east. The Visitor Center is on your right, .8 km (1/2 mile) past the entrance.
This symmetrical cinder cone is an interesting example of a geologically recent, extinct volcano. Created by Presidential Proclamation on Aug. 9, 1916.

VISITOR ACTIVITIES: self-guiding trails; interpretive and audiovisual programs; picnicking; photography; flower-, bird-, and wildlife-watching; **Permits:** Yes, obtained at Visitor Center; **Fees:** $1 entrance fee per carload, 50¢ per person on commercial bus. Persons under 16 years of age or over 62 are admitted free. Golden Age and Golden Eagle Passports accepted and available; **Visitor facilities:** parking, restrooms and water in the picnic area at the western base of the mountain; **Any limitations on vehicle usage:** Vehicles are restricted to designated roadways; **Hiking trails:** Yes, trails lead around the rim and into the crater; **Backcountry:** No; **Camping:** No; **Other overnight accommodations on site:** No; **Meals served in the park:** No; **Food and supplies obtainable in the park:** No; **Food and supplies obtainable nearby:** Yes, in Capulin or Raton; **Overnight accommodations:** Raton, 48 km (30 miles) west on US 64-87, to Int. 25; **First Aid available in park:** Yes; **Nearest Hospital:** Raton, 48 km (30 miles) west on US 64-87, to Int. 25; **Days/Hours:** Labor Day to Memorial Day, 8 a.m. to 4:30 p.m.; Memorial Day to Labor Day, 7 a.m. to 8 p.m.; **Holiday Closings:** Dec. 25 & Jan. 1; **Visitor attractions closed for seasons:** The Monument is accessible throughout the year, but the road to the summit may be closed occasionally for a few days by snow.

GENERAL INFORMATION: *For Your Safety*—The trails at Capulin Mountain are well-maintained but loose cinders on them can be hazardous. You should wear rubber-soled shoes on the hiking trails. If you wander away from established trails, be on the lookout for rattlesnakes.

Carlsbad Caverns National Park
Carlsbad, New Mexico

MAILING ADDRESS: Superintendent, Carlsbad Caverns National Park, 3225 National Parks Highway, Carlsbad, New Mexico 88220 **Telephone:** 505-885-8884

DIRECTIONS: The Park is on US 62-180, 32 km (20 miles) southwest of Carlsbad, NM, and 242 km (150 miles) east of El Paso, TX. The Visitor Center is near the cavern entrance, which is 11 km (7 miles) west of Highway 62-180 at the end of NM 7 in Walnut Canyon.

This series of connected caverns, the largest underground chambers yet discovered, has countless magnificent and unusual formations. Created by Presidential Proclamation on Oct. 25, 1923.

VISITOR ACTIVITIES: picnicking, photography, cave tours, nature walks, exhibits, bat flight programs nightly in summer, primitive lantern trips into new cave; **Permits:** No; **Fees:** Entrance fee is $3.00 per carload, or $1.00 per person on commercial carrier. Golden Eagle and Golden Age Passports accepted and available; **Visitor facilities:** picnic areas, nature trails, restaurant, gift shop, nursery, kennel, bicycle trail; **Any limitations on vehicle usage:** No, but be alert for deer and other animals bounding across the roadway; **Hiking trails:** Yes, hiking and backpacking opportunities abound. An adequate supply of water, good boots, and maps are essential; **Backcountry:** Yes, for safety, check with a Park Ranger before going into the backcountry; **Camping:** No; **Other overnight accommodations on site:** No; **Meals served in the park:** Yes, a restaurant is in the Visitor Center. Lunches and refreshments are also available underground; **Food and supplies obtainable in the park:** No; **Food and supplies obtainable nearby:** Yes, in Carlsbad and Whites City; **Overnight accommodations:** Carlsbad, 43 km (27 miles) and Whites City, 11 km (7 miles); **First Aid available in park:** Yes; **Nearest Hospital:** Carlsbad, 43 km (27 miles); **Days/Hours:** The Park and Visitor Center are open 365 days a year; **Holiday Closings:** No; **Visitor attractions closed for seasons:** No; **Weather:** Summers are usually warm and winters mild. However, extreme changes can come at any time of the year. In Spring, winds can be strong. In Summer, thunderstorms accompanied by brief but often heavy downpours may bring flash floods to the canyon bottoms. In Winter the normally mild weather may be broken by a short-lived snowstorm or a bone-chilling "cold front" sweeping through on gale force winds. In the caverns, the temperature remains a constant 13°C (56°F) year round.

GENERAL INFORMATION: *Precautions*: A light sweater or jacket and comfortable walking shoes with rubber soles or heels are recommended. Stay on cavern trails and do not run. If electrical power fails while you are underground, stop and remain quiet until the lights go on again. Watch for rattlesnakes when hiking on the surface. Beware of the cactus and other desert plants; their spines can inflict painful injury.

Chaco Canyon National Monument
Bloomfield, New Mexico

MAILING ADDRESS: Superintendent, Chaco Canyon National Monument, Star Route 4, Box 6500, Bloomfield, New Mexico 87413 **Telephone:** 505-786-5384

DIRECTIONS: The Monument is in northwestern New Mexico. From the north, turn off NM 44 at Blanco Trading Post or Nageezi Trading Post [(11.3 km -7 miles) south of Blanco, 30.6 km (19 miles) to the park entrance] and follow NM 57 for 35 km (22 miles) to the north entrance of the Monument. The Visitor Center is 11.3 km (7 miles) beyond this entrance. From the south, turn north on NM 57 from I-40 at Thoreau and proceed 70.8 km (44 miles) on paved road. A marked turnoff begins a 32 km (20 mile) stretch of unpaved NM Hwy 57, leading to the south entrance. The Visitor Center is just ahead. Because NM 57 is not paved into the Monument, you should inquire locally regarding travel over this route in stormy weather.

The canyon, with hundreds of smaller ruins, contains 13 major Indian ruins unsurpassed in the United States, representing the highest point of Pueblo pre-Columbian civilization. Created by Presidential Proclamation on Mar. 11, 1907.

VISITOR ACTIVITIES: guided tours, campfire talks in season, exhibits, walking tours, picnicking, backcountry, hiking; **Permits:** for backcountry use, no overnight backpacking is permitted. Obtain permits at the Visitor Center; **Fees:** No fees at this time. Depending on the availability of funding, there is a $2 camping fee in summer in some years; **Visitor facilities:** restrooms, campgrounds with fireplaces, picnic area, drinking water, interpretive programs; **Any limitations on vehicle usage:** The Monument's unpaved roads are frequently rough, dusty and narrow; they are very slippery when wet. Do not drive off the graded roadway. Housetrailers longer than 30 feet in length are not recommended in the campground; **Hiking trails:** Yes, self-guiding trails take you through the ruin complex. Walking time for each trail is about 1 hour. There are numerous longer hikes as well. Inquire at Visitor Center; **Backcountry:** Yes, information available by writing the Superintendent; **Camping:** Yes, no reservations accepted for the campsites, which are 1.6 km (1 mile) from the Visitor Center. Write to Chaco for group campsite reservations; **Other overnight accommodations on site:** No; **Meals served in the park:** No; **Food and supplies obtainable in the park:** No; **Food and supplies obtainable nearby:** Only at Blanco and Nageezi Trading Posts; **Overnight accommodations:** Thoreau, 96 km (60 miles); Bloomfield, 96 km (60 miles); Farmington, 129 km (80 miles); **First Aid available in park:** Yes; **Nearest Hospital:** Farmington, 129 km (80 miles); **Days/Hours:** 7 days a week from 8 a.m. to 5 p.m.; **Holiday Closings:** Visitor Center is closed on Dec. 25 and Jan. 1; **Weather:** Although the climate is semiarid, there is snow in Winter, and thunderstorms are possible from June through September. Summers are usually warm and dry.

GENERAL INFORMATION: *For Your Safety*—Do not climb on the walls of the ruins, which are weak and dangerous. Other points of interest in the vicinity are Mesa Verde National Park, 103 km (64 miles) north, and El Morro National Monument, 155 km (96 miles) south (see listings in this book).

El Morro National Monument
Ramah, New Mexico

MAILING ADDRESS: Superintendent, El Morro National Monument, Ramah, New Mexico 87321 **Telephone:** 505-783-5132

DIRECTIONS: The Monument is 90 km (56 miles) southeast of Gallup via NM 32 and NM 53, and 67.6 km (42 miles) west of Grants via NM 53.
    "Inscription Rock" is a soft sandstone monolith on which hundreds of inscriptions are carved, including those of 17th Century Spanish explorers and 19th Century American emigrants and settlers. Pre-Columbian petroglyphs are also here. Created by Presidential Proclamation in 1906.

VISITOR ACTIVITIES: hiking, camping, picnicking, campfire programs in Summer; **Permits:** No; **Fees:** Yes, 50¢ per person, $1 per carload for Trail, no camping or picnicking fees. No charge for educational groups. Golden Age and Golden Eagle Passports accepted and available; **Visitor facilities:** self-guiding walk (tours in summer), campground and picnic area; **Any limitations on vehicle usage:** No off-road vehicles are allowed; vehicles are restricted to park roads; **Hiking trails:** Yes, 3 km (2 miles) of hiking trails (surfaced, with minimum inclines on the lower Inscription Rock Trail, suitable for a guided wheelchair), Mesa Top Trail rises 300 feet via switchbacks, a natural trail over the mesa top; **Backcountry:** No; **Camping:** Yes, no reservations accepted for campsites; **Other overnight accommodations on site:** No; **Meals served in the park:** No; **Food and supplies obtainable in the park:** No; **Food and supplies obtainable nearby:** Yes, limited supplies at Ramah, more extensive supplies at Grants and Gallup; **Overnight accommodations:** Grants, Int. 40, 67.6 km (42 miles); Gallup, Int. 40, 90 km (56 miles); **First Aid available in park:** Yes; **Nearest Hospital:** Grants, NM 53, 67.6 km (42 miles); Gallup, NM 53 & 32 90 km (56 miles); **Days/Hours:** Open daily from 8 a.m. to 5 p.m. year-round; until 8 p.m. in Summer, from approximately Memorial Day to Labor Day; **Holiday Closings:** Dec. 25; **Visitor attractions closed for seasons:** Mesa Top Trail closed during heavy snow accumulation. When the campground is closed for short periods during heavy snow, campers can park at Headquarters parking; **Weather:** Warm sun (daytime) averaging 70's and 80's in Summer; averaging 40's and 50's in Winter; night-time average is 10's and 20's in Winter with some -0 readings, and 30's and 40's in Summer. Usually a nice breeze in Summer, average 10 to 11 inches of rain a year, and 4 to 12 inches of snow per storm.

GENERAL INFORMATION: Be cautious of soft terrain and high cliffs in this natural area. Dogs must be kept on a leash; hiking shoes or shoes with traction are recommended for the trails; children must be accompanied by an adult as the Mesa Top Trail is a natural trail climbing 300 feet. Restrooms have been modified enough to accommodate wheelchair visitors, and the park has a wheelchair for use. The trail has been modified for wheelchair use. Groups are welcome, advance notification is recommended to better accommodate the group.

Fort Union National Monument
Watrous, New Mexico

MAILING ADDRESS: Superintendent, Fort Union National Monument, Watrous, New Mexico 87753 **Telephone:** 505-425-8025

DIRECTIONS: The Monument is 13 km (8 miles) north of I-25, at the end of NM 477. Watrous, NM is 1 km (1/2 mile) south of the intersection of these two highways.
 Three successive U. S. Army forts were build on this site—a key defensive point on the Santa Fe Trail—and were occupied successively from 1851 to 1891. Ruins of the last fort, which was the largest military post in the Southwest, have been stabilized. Established by act of Congress on Apr. 5, 1956.

VISITOR ACTIVITIES: Interpretive exhibits, walking tours, picnicking; **Permits:** No; **Fees:** No; **Visitor facilities:** restrooms and parking at Visitor Center, picnic area, interpretive trail; **Any limitations on vehicle usage:** All vehicles must park at the Visitor Center. No vehicles are allowed on the historic trail; **Hiking trails:** Yes, a 2.5 km (1-1/2 mile) self-guiding trail; **Backcountry:** No; **Camping:** No; **Other overnight accommodations on site:** No; **Meals served in the park:** No; **Food and supplies obtainable in the park:** No; **Food and supplies obtainable nearby:** Yes, in Las Vegas, NM; **Overnight accommodations:** Las Vegas, NM, I-25, 42 km (28 miles) southwest; **First Aid available in park:** Yes; **Nearest Hospital:** Las Vegas, I-25, 42 km (28 miles) southwest; **Days/Hours:** Open daily from 8 a.m. to 5 p.m., until 7 p.m. in Summer; **Holiday Closings:** Dec. 25 and Jan. 1; **Visitor attractions closed for seasons:** No; **Weather:** Summer is warm and windy with afternoon thundershowers. Winter is cold and windy; with infrequent but sometimes heavy snowfalls.

GENERAL INFORMATION: *For Your Safety*—Do not climb on the walls or foundations of the ruins. Stay on the trail, because rattlesnakes can be found in the high grass. The third fort arsenal site is closed to the public.

Gila Cliff Dwellings National Monument
Silver City, New Mexico

MAILING ADDRESS: Gila Cliff Dwellings National Monument, Route 11, Box 100, Silver City, New Mexico 88061 **Telephone:** 505-534-9344

DIRECTIONS: The Monument is 71 km (44 miles) north of Silver City at the end of NM 15, a steep and winding two-lane blacktop highway. The trip to the Dwellings through the mountains takes about 2 hours each way. Silver City is located on US 180, about 193 km (120 air miles) northwest of El Paso, TX. Due to road conditions, trailers over 20 feet are advised to use NM 35 through the scenic Mimbres Valley and by Lake Roberts, instead of NM 15. This is reached from NM 61, north from San Lorenzo which is 30.6 km (19 miles) east of Silver City on Route 90.

These well-preserved cliff dwellings in natural cavities on the face of an overhanging cliff were inhabited from about 1200 to 1350 A.D. Created by Presidential Proclamation on Nov. 16, 1907.

VISITOR ACTIVITIES: camping, picnicking, fishing, exhibits, photography, walking; **Permits:** No; **Fees:** No; **Visitor facilities:** self-guiding interpretive trail to the dwellings. Forest Service picnic and camping area nearby: water, fireplaces, picnic tables; **Any limitations on vehicle usage:** Restricted to pavement at Scorpion camping area; **Hiking trails:** Yes, a steep, 1.6 km (1 mile) trail leads to and through the Dwellings, situated about 180 feet above the canyon bottom. Plan about 1 hour for your visit; **Backcountry:** Yes, the Monument is surrounded by the Gila Wilderness; the trails are well-marked. Information at Gila Visitor Center. Wilderness permits are required, available at Visitor Center without charge; **Camping:** No, but sites are available in Forest Service campgrounds nearby; **Other overnight accommodations on site:** No; **Meals served in the park:** No; **Food and supplies obtainable in the park:** No; **Food and supplies obtainable nearby:** Yes, Gila Hot Springs, about 4.8 km (3 miles) south of the Visitor Center; **Overnight accommodations:** limited accommodations at Gila Hot Springs, NM 15, 4.8 km (3 miles); more extensive facilities at Silver City, NM 15, 71 km (44 miles); **First Aid available in park:** Yes; **Nearest Hospital:** Silver City, NM 15, 71 km (44 miles); **Days/ Hours:** Open daily from 8 a.m. to 6 p.m., June 1 through Labor Day; 9 a.m. to 5 p.m. the rest of the year. Visitor Center open daily from 8 a.m.-5 p.m.; **Holiday Closings:** Dec. 25 & Jan. 1; **Weather:** Daytime temperatures vary between 80 and 100°F; at night, from 45 to 55°F. Temperatures drop lower in the higher elevations. Spring and Fall daytime temperatures range from 70 to 80°F, but nighttime temperatures require a selection of warm clothing. Warm bedding is a necessity, even in Summer.

GENERAL INFORMATION: *For Your Safety*—watch your step on the steep trails.

Gran Quivira National Monument
Mountainair, New Mexico

MAILING ADDRESS: Superintendent, Gran Quivira National Monument, Route 1, Mountainair, New Mexico 87036 **Telephone:** 505-847-2770

DIRECTIONS: From US 60 you can reach the park by turning south at Mountainair and driving 42 km (26 miles) on NM 14. From US 380 you can turn north at Carrizozo and drive 90 km (56 miles) via US 54 and NM 14 which is unpaved for 63 km (39 miles). Or you may turn north on NM 41 at Bingham which is unpaved for 66 km (41 miles). You should use both these roads *only* in good weather.

Ruins of two mission buildings and 21 Pueblo Indian house mounds mark the sites of a 17th century Spanish mission and of an earlier Indian community. Proclaimed Nov. 1, 1909.

VISITOR ACTIVITIES: interpretive exhibits, a 30-minute self-guiding walking tour, picnicking; **Permits:** No; **Fees:** No; **Visitor facilities:** Visitor Center, parking, restrooms, picnic area, guided tours; **Any limitations on vehicle usage:** No; **Hiking trails:** Yes, a .4 km (1/2 mile) self-guiding walking trail; **Backcountry:** No; **Camping:** No; **Other overnight accommodations on site:** No; **Meals served in the park:** No; **Food and supplies obtainable in the park:** No; **Food and supplies obtainable nearby:** Yes, in Mountainair; **Overnight accommodations:** Mountainair, 42 km (26 miles) via NM 14; **First Aid available in park:** Yes, or in Mountainair, NM 14; **Nearest Hospital:** Belen, I-25, 120 km (75 miles); **Days/Hours:** Park never closes. Visitor Center open daily from 8 a.m. to 5 p.m.; until 7 p.m. in Summer; **Holiday Closings:** Dec. 25; **Visitor attractions closed for seasons:** No; **Weather:** Summer is warm and windy, with thundershowers likely. Winter daytime temperatures range from 40°s to 60° F.

Pecos National Monument
Pecos, New Mexico

MAILING ADDRESS: Superintendent, Pecos National Monument, Post Office Drawer 11, Pecos, New Mexico 87552 **Telephone:** 505-757-6414

DIRECTIONS: The park is 40 km (25 miles) southeast of Santa Fe by way of Int. 25, and may be reached from the interchanges at Glorietta, 13 km (8 mile) west of the park via the town of Pecos, and Rowe, 4.8 km (3 miles) south.

Foundations of a 17th-century mission church, ruins of an 18th-century church, ancient pueblo structural remains, and restored kivas comprise the park. The site was once a landmark on the Santa Fe Trail, ruts of which are still in existance. Authorized for addition to the National Park System on June 28, 1965.

VISITOR ACTIVITIES: walking tours, picnicking, Indian craft demonstrations on weekends; **Permits:** No; **Fees:** No; **Visitor facilities:** Visitor Center, picnic area, self-guiding interpretive trails; **Any limitations on vehicle usage:** Vehicles are restricted to designated roadways; **Hiking trails:** Yes, a walking trail leads to the ruins; **Backcountry:** No; **Camping:** No; **Other overnight accommodations on site:** No, camping is available in the Santa Fe National Forest north of the village of Pecos, off State 63, and in other nearby areas. For further information, contact the Forest Supervisor, Santa Fe National Forest, P.O. Box 1689, Santa Fe, NM 87501, phone 505-988-6313; **Meals served in the park:** No, but in Pecos, NM, 3 km (2 miles) north of the Monument; **Food and supplies obtainable in the park:** No; **Food and supplies obtainable nearby:** Yes, in Pecos, 3 km (2 miles) north; **Overnight accommodations:** Pecos, adjacent to the park; Santa Fe, 40 km (25 miles) northwest; Las Vegas, NM, 56 km (35 miles) east; **First Aid available in park:** Yes; **Nearest Hospital:** A small clinic is located in Pecos, NM, 3 km (2 miles) north of the Monument. A hospital is in Santa Fe , via I-25, 45 km (28 miles) distant; **Days/Hours:** Open daily from 8 a.m. to 5 p.m., until 7 p.m. in Summer; **Holiday Closings:** Dec. 25; **Visitor attractions closed for seasons:** Living history demonstrations are offered only in Summer; **Weather:** The elevation is 7000 feet. Summer daytime temperatures average in the 80's and 90's, with cool evenings. July and August are rainy. Winter temperatures are variable, ranging from 0° to the mid 40's, snowfall is heavy at times.

GENERAL INFORMATION: Visitors should use caution due to a few trail irregularities, an occasional prairie rattlesnake, and when using ladders into the restored kivas. Do not climb or stand on the fragile ruins.

White Sands National Monument
Alamogordo, New Mexico

MAILING ADDRESS: Superintendent, White Sands National Monument, Box 458, Alamogordo, New Mexico 88310 **Telephone:** 505-437-1058

DIRECTIONS: The Visitor Center is 24.15 km (15 miles) southwest of Alamogordo on US Hwy 70-82.
   Dunes of sparkling white gypsum sands, 3.05 to 13.71 m (10 to 45 feet) high, are home to small, light-colored animals that have adapted to this harsh environment. Created by Presidential Proclamation on Jan. 18, 1933.

VISITOR ACTIVITIES: guided walks, illustrated evening programs, and star programs in Summer; hiking; picnicking; backcountry; **Permits:** Free backcountry permits available at Headquarters; **Fees:** $1 per car entrance fee. Golden Eagle and Golden Age Passports accepted and available; **Visitor facilities:** museum, gift shop, picnic areas, grills, comfort facilities, drinking water only at the Visitor Center; **Any limitation vehicle usage:** Vehicles are restricted to roads and parking areas. Overnight parking at the Visitor Center parking lot is not allowed; **Hiking trails:** Yes, self-guiding nature trails; **Backcountry:** No; **Camping:** No campgrounds, but primitive backcountry camping is available requiring registration and clearance at Headquarters. The nearest public camping facilities are in Lincoln National Forest, 56 km (35 miles) to the east and at Aguirre Springs, 48 km (30 miles) to the west. Information on National Forest camping can be obtained from the Forest Supervisor, Lincoln National Forest, Alamogordo, N.M. 88310. For information on Aguirre Springs, write the District Manager, Bureau of Land Management, P.O. Box 1420, Las Cruces, N.M. 88001. Several commercial campgrounds are open year-round in Alamogordo and Las Cruces; **Meals served in the park:** No; **Food and supplies obtainable in the park:** No; **Food and supplies obtainable nearby:** Yes, at Alamogordo; **Overnight accommodations:** Alamogordo, Hwy 70-82 24 km (15 miles) northeast; **First Aid available in park:** Yes; **Nearest Hospital:** Alamogordo, Hwy 70-82, 24 km (15 miles) northeast; **Days/Hours:** Visitor Center: Summer 8 a.m. to 7 p.m. Winter 8:30 a.m. to 5 p.m. Dunes Drive 7:30 a.m. to sunset; **Holiday Closings:** Dec. 25; **Weather:** Hot, dry Summers, mild Winters.

New York

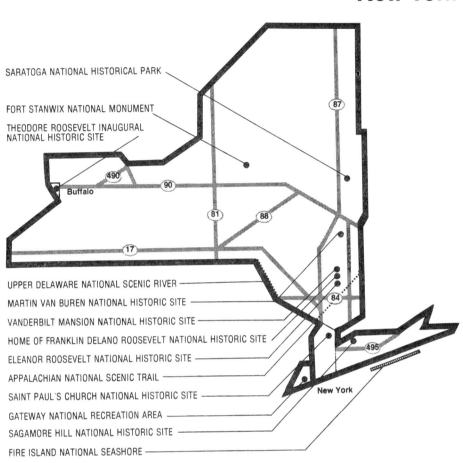

SARATOGA NATIONAL HISTORICAL PARK

FORT STANWIX NATIONAL MONUMENT

THEODORE ROOSEVELT INAUGURAL
NATIONAL HISTORIC SITE

Buffalo

UPPER DELAWARE NATIONAL SCENIC RIVER
MARTIN VAN BUREN NATIONAL HISTORIC SITE
VANDERBILT MANSION NATIONAL HISTORIC SITE
HOME OF FRANKLIN DELANO ROOSEVELT NATIONAL HISTORIC SITE
ELEANOR ROOSEVELT NATIONAL HISTORIC SITE
APPALACHIAN NATIONAL SCENIC TRAIL
SAINT PAUL'S CHURCH NATIONAL HISTORIC SITE
GATEWAY NATIONAL RECREATION AREA
SAGAMORE HILL NATIONAL HISTORIC SITE
FIRE ISLAND NATIONAL SEASHORE

New York

Appalachian National Scenic Trail
For details see listing in Maine

Castle Clinton National Monument
New York, New York

MAILING ADDRESS: Superintendent, Manhattan Sites, National Park Service, 26 Wall Street, New York, New York 10005 **Telephone:** 212-344-7220

DIRECTIONS: The Monument is located in Battery Park at the southern tip of Manhattan.

Built 1807-11, this structure served successively as a defense for New York harbor, a promenade and entertainment center, and an immigration depot through which more than 8 million people entered the United States from 1855 to 1890. Authorized for addition to the National Park System on Aug. 12, 1946.

VISITOR ACTIVITIES: interpretive exhibits, walking tours, living history programs; **Permits:** No; **Fees:** No; **Visitor facilities:** restrooms are available in Battery Park; **Any limitations on vehicle usage:** No vehicles are allowed in the park; **Meals served in the park:** No; **Food and supplies obtainable in the park:** No; **Food and supplies obtainable nearby:** Yes, in lower Manhattan; **Overnight accommodations:** in New York City; **First Aid available in park:** No, but in the firehouse next door; **Nearest Hospital:** Manhattan, Beekman Downtown; **Days/Hours:** 8:30 a.m. to 4:30 p.m. from Monday through Friday; **Holiday Closings:** Thanksgiving, Dec. 25 and Jan 1; **Visitor attractions closed for seasons:** only in very bad weather; **Weather:** Windy and cold in Winter; pleasantly mild in Spring and Fall, Summers are hot and humid.

GENERAL INFORMATION: Nearby points of interest include Federal Hall and the Statue of Liberty (see listings in this book).

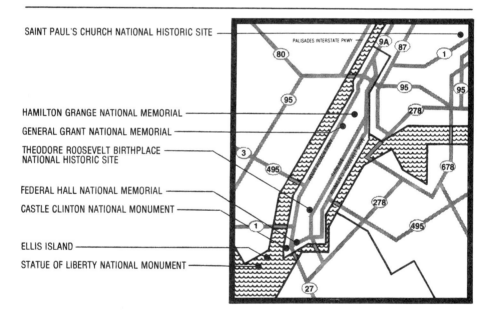

SAINT PAUL'S CHURCH NATIONAL HISTORIC SITE

HAMILTON GRANGE NATIONAL MEMORIAL

GENERAL GRANT NATIONAL MEMORIAL

THEODORE ROOSEVELT BIRTHPLACE
NATIONAL HISTORIC SITE

FEDERAL HALL NATIONAL MEMORIAL

CASTLE CLINTON NATIONAL MONUMENT

ELLIS ISLAND

STATUE OF LIBERTY NATIONAL MONUMENT

Eleanor Roosevelt National Historic Site
Hyde Park, New York

MAILING ADDRESS: Superintendent, Roosevelt-Vanderbilt National Historic Sites, Hyde Park, New York 12538 **Telephone:** 914-229-9115

DIRECTIONS: NOT YET OPEN TO THE PUBLIC.

Mrs. Roosevelt used her "Val-Kill" estate as a retreat and for entertainment of dignitaries and friends. The pastoral setting of the cottage, built for her and two friends in 1925, includes fields, trees, swamps, and ponds. Authorized for addition to the National Park System on May 27, 1977.

Ellis Island
Ellis Island, New York

MAILING ADDRESS: Superintendent, Statue of Liberty National Monument, Liberty Island, New York, New York 10004 **Telephone:** 212-732-1236

DIRECTIONS: Ellis Island is accessible only by ferry. Circle Line Ferries leave Battery Park in lower Manhattan. For schedule and group-rate information, call 212-269-5755.

More than half of the immigrants entering the United States between 1892 and 1924 passed through the gates of Ellis Island. Added by Presidential Proclamation to the Statue of Liberty National Monument on May 11, 1965.

VISITOR ACTIVITIES: guided tours (1 to 1-1/2 hours in length), photographic tours (1 hour, 9:30 a.m. boat only, M-F); **Permits:** No; **Fees:** $1.50 charge for adults and 50¢ for children under 12 for the round-trip ferry boat ride. No fees are charged for the tour; **Visitor facilities:** None. The Island is in primitive condition; **Any limitations on vehicle usage:** No docking is permitted for private boats; **Hiking trails:** No; **Camping:** No; **Other overnight accommodations on site:** No; **Meals served in the park:** No; **Overnight accommodations:** Manhattan; **First Aid available in park:** Yes; **Nearest Hospital:** Manhattan hospitals take about 1 hour to reach; **Days/Hours:** Open daily from Apr. 28 to Oct. 30; **Holiday Closings:** None; **Visitor attractions closed for seasons:** Closed Oct. 31 through Apr. 27.

GENERAL INFORMATION: Buildings are unheated and retain cold and dampness until mid-July. *For Your Safety*—You must remain with your tour group and within protective barricades during your visit. The tour includes a considerable amount of walking and climbing.

School groups should contact the school coordinator for pre-visit materials. Large groups should make reservations with Circle Line Ferries, 212-269-5755.

Federal Hall National Memorial
New York, New York

MAILING ADDRESS: Superintendent, Federal Hall National Memorial, National Park Service, Manhattan Sites, 26 Wall Street, New York, New York 10005 **Telephone:** 212-264-8711

DIRECTIONS: The Memorial is at the corner of Wall and Nassau Streets, just off Broadway. It is within convenient walking distance of South Ferry, the landing place for ferries from Staten Island, Governor's Island, and the Statue of Liberty. By subway, take: the Lexington Ave. IRT Express to Wall St., the EE/RR BMT to Rector Street, the K/J BMT to Broad St., the 7th Ave. IRT Express to Wall St., or the 8th Ave. A/E IND to Fulton St. By bus, take the 2nd Ave. bus to Wall St., or the M15 or 6 South Ferry bus to Broadway and Wall.

This graceful building is on the site of the original Federal Hall where: the trial of John

Peter Zenger, involving freedom of the press, was held in 1735; the Stamp Act Congress convened, 1765; the Second Continental Congress met, 1785; Washington took the oath as first U.S. President, and the Bill of Rights was written, 1789. Present building was a Federal financial center. Designated May 26, 1939.

VISITOR ACTIVITIES: interpretive exhibits and films, guided tours, 18th Century folksong performances and printing press demonstrations; **Permits:** No; **Fees:** No; **Visitor facilities:** restrooms, exhibits; **Any limitations on vehicle usage:** On-street parking in the vicinity is limited, except on Sundays; **Hiking trails:** No; **Meals served in the park:** No, but they are available nearby; **Food and supplies obtainable in the park:** No; **Food and supplies obtainable nearby:** Yes, in New York City; **Overnight accommodations:** New York City; **First Aid available in park:** Yes; **Nearest Hospital:** Beekman Downtown Hospital, New York; **Days/Hours:** Open 9 a.m. to 4:30 p.m. Mon.-Fri. from December through March, 7 days a week in Summer. Call 212-264-8711 to determine weekend hours, which may vary due to budgetary restrictions; **Holiday Closings:** Thanksgiving, Dec. 25 & Jan. 1; **Visitor attractions closed for seasons:** Tour schedule is reduced from December through March; **Weather:** 10°-35°F and rainy in Winter; 70°-90°F and humid in Summer.

GENERAL INFORMATION: Nearby points of interest include Castle Clinton National Monument, Ellis Island, the Statue of Liberty National Monument (see listings in this book), Faunces Tavern, South Street Seaport, on Fulton St., and the U.S. Customs House on Bowling Green.

Fire Island National Seashore
Patchogue, New York

MAILING ADDRESS: Superintendent, Fire Island National Seashore, 120 Laurel Street, Patchogue, New York 11772 **Telephone:** 516-289-4810

DIRECTIONS: By automobile you can reach the island via bridges at the state and county parks. Except for these two points, Fire Island is roadless. Several mainland ferryboat lines, operating from Bayshore, Sayville, and Patchogue, dock on the island. Sailors Haven and the Sunken Forest are served by the ferry terminal in Sayville; Watch Hill by the ferry terminal at Patchogue. All three mainland villages are serviced by the Long Island Railroad. Public ferries run from May 15 to Oct. 15.

This barrier island off the south shore of Long Island possesses opportunities for beach-oriented recreation and ecological observations. Authorized for addition to the National Park System on Sept. 11, 1964.

VISITOR ACTIVITIES: fishing, clamming, swimming, walking, biking, picnicking, guided nature walks and talks in summer, wildlife- and bird-watching, camping, interpretive exhibits, hiking, boating, hunting; **Permits:** for off road vehicle travel, available at Smith Point only; **Fees:** No; **Visitor facilities:** campground, marinas, guarded swimming beaches, snack bars, Visitor Center with exhibits, picnic areas, nature trails, restrooms, bathhouse, telephones, bicycle trails, grocery stores; **Any limitations on vehicle usage:** Vehicle usage is regulated; **Hiking trails:** Yes, nature trails are at Smith Point West, Watch Hill, and Sailors Haven; **Backcountry:** No; **Camping:** Yes, reservations are required for the 32-site primitive campground at Watch Hill. Phone 516-597-6633; **Other overnight accommodations on site:** Yes, contact the park for further information on accommodations on the island; **Meals served in the park:** Yes, snacks are available at Watch Hill and Sailors Haven; **Food and supplies obtainable in the park:**

Yes, Watch Hill and Sailors Haven; **Food and supplies obtainable nearby:** Yes, on mainland at Sayville, Patchogue and Bay Shore; **Overnight accommodations:** Motels are in most major communities on Long Island; **First Aid available in park:** Yes; **Nearest Hospital:** On mainland at Patchogue, Bay Shore; **Days/Hours:** Park open 24 hours a day everyday; **Holiday Closings:** None; **Visitor attractions closed for seasons:** Marinas close in Winter.

GENERAL INFORMATION: *For Your Safety*—Swim at protected beaches. Wear footgear on all boardwalks. Splinters are a common first aid problem. Watch for poison ivy, which abounds on the island. Do not walk on the dunes; their fragile vegetation is easily destroyed by human feet.

Fort Stanwix National Monument
Rome, New York

MAILING ADDRESS: Superintendent, Fort Stanwix National Monument, 112 East Park Street, Rome, New York 13440 **Telephone:** 315-336-2090

DIRECTIONS: The Monument is in downtown Rome, NY, which may be reached by car, bus, train , or plane. State Routes 26, 46, 49, 69, and 365 pass within sight of the Fort. If you are travelling on the NY Thruway, take exits 32 or 33. A city parking garage is on North James Street, within 1/2 block of the Monument's entrance.

The American stand here in August, 1777 was a major factor in repulsing the British invasion from Canada. This was also the site of the Treaty of Fort Stanwix, negotiated with the Iroquois on Nov. 5, 1768. Authorized for addition to the National Park System on Aug. 21, 1935.

VISITOR ACTIVITIES: interpretive film and exhibits, guided tours, living history program from May-Sept. includes drill and occasional weapons-firing demonstrations; **Permits:** No; **Fees:** No; **Visitor facilities:** restrooms inside the Fort; **Any limitations on vehicle usage:** No direct vehicle access to the park; **Hiking trails:** No; **Backcountry:** No; **Camping:** No; **Other overnight accommodations on site:** No; **Meals served in the park:** No; **Food and supplies obtainable in the park:** No; **Food and supplies obtainable nearby:** Yes, in Rome; **Overnight accommodations:** in and around Rome; **First Aid available in park:** Yes; **Nearest Hospital:** Rome Memorial, NY 49, 69, 365, 4.8 km (3 miles); **Days/Hours:** Open daily from 9 a.m. to 5 p.m. from Apr. 1-Dec. 31; until 6 p.m. Memorial Day through Labor Day; **Holiday Closings:** Dec. 25; **Visitor attractions closed for seasons:** Closed during the severest part of Winter; **Weather:** Summers are generally cool.

GENERAL INFORMATION: *For Your Safety*—Follow the staff's instructions during weapon demonstrations. Do not smoke inside wooden buildings.

Gateway National Recreation Area
New York & New Jersey

MAILING ADDRESS: Superintendent, Gateway National Recreation Area, Floyd Bennett Field, Brooklyn, New York 11234 **Telephone:** 212-630-0253

DIRECTIONS: Gateway National Recreation Area consists of four units. Three are in New York: Jamaica Bay Unit, in Brooklyn; Breezy Point Unit, located on the Rockaway

Peninsula in Queens; and the Staten Island Unit, located on the Raritan Bay in Staten Island. The fourth area is the Sandy Hook Unit, situated on a peninsula in the northeast corner of New Jersey. Detailed mass transit and auto directions are available from Headquarters.

The park contains beaches, marshes, islands, and adjacent waters in the New York harbor area, and is one of the first major urban parks in the National Park System. Established by act of Congress on Oct. 27, 1972.

VISITOR ACTIVITIES: swimming, picnicking, sunbathing, sports, interpretive programs, biking, fishing, boating, bird-watching, crabbing, horseback riding; **Permits:** A fishing permit is required at some locations. Permits are also required for baseball, softball, tennis, soccer, archery, football, and basketball facilities at Miller Field in the Staten Island Unit. Information and permits can be obtained by calling 212-351-8700 or by writing the Unit Manager, P.O. Box 437, Staten Island, NY 10306; **Fees:** for boat launching and mooring facilities at Great Kills Park in the Staten Island Unit, mooring facilities at Barren Island Marina, and a parking fee at the Riis Park parking lot, Breezy Point Unit; **Visitor facilities:** marina, boathouse, beaches, sports facilities, restrooms, parking areas, wildlife refuge, bicycle trail, picnic areas; **Any limitations on vehicle usage:** Off-road vehicles are permitted on beaches; **Hiking trails:** Yes, nature trails, ocean and waterfront areas; **Backcountry:** No; **Camping:** Yes, primitive campsites are available for use by organized youth groups on a reservation basis. These reservations must be made through the Unit Manager's office at Sandy Hook Unit, P.O. Box 437, Highlands, NJ 07732 or by calling 201-872-0115; **Other overnight accommodations on site:** No; **Meals served in the park:** Yes, fast food available in Summer at all four units; **Food and supplies obtainable in the park:** No; **Food and supplies obtainable nearby:** Yes, at Sandy Hook, Red Bank, Highlands, Staten Island, Jamaica Bay, Boroughs of Brooklyn and Queens, Breezy Point; **Overnight accommodations:** Sandy Hook, Red Bank, Highlands, Staten Island, Jamaica Bay, Brooklyn and Queens, Breezy Point; **First Aid available in park:** Yes, in all 4 units during the Summer; **Nearest Hospital:** Sandy Hook: Patterson Army Hospital, River View Hospital; Staten Island: Staten Island Hospital; Jamaica Bay: Coney Island Hospital, Brookdale Hospital, Peninsula Hospital; Breezy Point; Peninsula Hospital; **Days/Hours:** Open 7 days a week, 52 weeks a year. Full services are provided from Memorial Day through Sept. 30 from 9 a.m.-8:30 p.m.; **Holiday Closings:** None; **Visitor attractions closed for seasons:** No; **Weather:** Excellent beach weather, with temperatures in the 90'sF in June, July and August.

GENERAL INFORMATION: *For Your Safety*—Swim only where lifeguards are on duty. The ocean can be dangerous. Be alert for riptides. Do not take glass containers, rafts, rubber tubes, snorkels, and masks to any beach. Beware of sunburn. Some of the areas have large patches of poison ivy. Consult park personnel for locations of poison ivy.

General Grant National Memorial
New York, New York

MAILING ADDRESS: Superintendent, General Grant National Memorial, c/o National Park Service, 26 Wall Street, New York, New York 10005 **Telephone:** 212-666-1640

DIRECTIONS: The Memorial is located in Riverside Park near the Intersection of Riverside Drive and West 122nd Street. You can reach it by Fifth Avenue bus, IRT subway to 116th or 125th Street, or 125th Street crosstown bus. Riverside Drive is also accessible from the Henry Hudson Parkway at several points. Parking is permitted near the Memorial.

This Memorial to Ulysses S. Grant, the Union commander who brought the Civil War to an end, includes the sarcophagi of General and Mrs. Grant. As President of the United States (1869-77), Grant signed the act establishing the first national park, Yellowstone, on Mar. 1, 1872. Memorial dedicated on April 27, 1897.

VISITOR ACTIVITIES: interpretive talks and exhibits; **Permits:** No; **Fees:** No; **Visitor facilities:** parking area, exhibit rooms; **Any limitations on vehicle usage:** No; **Meals served in the park:** No; **Food and supplies obtainable in the park:** No; **Food and supplies obtainable nearby:** Yes, several blocks, in Manhattan; **Overnight accommodations:** New York City; **First Aid available in park:** Yes; **Nearest Hospital:** St. Luke's, Amsterdam Ave., about 10 blocks; **Days/Hours:** Open daily from 9 a.m. to 5 p.m.; **Holiday Closings:** Thanksgiving, Dec. 25 & Jan. 1; **Visitor attractions closed for seasons:** No; **Weather:** Cold Winters with occasional snow; hot, humid Summers.

Hamilton Grange National Memorial
New York, New York

MAILING ADDRESS: Superintendent, Hamilton Grange National Memorial, 287 Convent Avenue, New York, New York 10031 **Telephone:** 212-283-5154

DIRECTIONS: The Memorial is at Convent Ave. and West 141st Street. Access by public transportation is recommended. Take the 8th Avenue IND express subway to West 145th Street. You can also catch the Broadway Bus #4 to West 145th St. and Convent Avenue, or Convent Ave. bus #3 to 142nd Street.

"The Grange", named after his grandfather's estate in Scotland, was the home of Alexander Hamilton, American statesman and first Secretary of the U.S. Treasury. Authorized for addition to the National Park System on Apr. 27, 1962.

VISITOR ACTIVITIES: exhibits, guided tours, and an interpretive program planned around themes of drama, music, and colonial crafts; **Permits:** No; **Fees:** No; **Visitor facilities:** None; **Any limitations on vehicle usage:** No vehicle usage in the park; **Hiking trails:** No; **Meals served in the park:** No; **Food and supplies obtainable in the park:** No; **Food and supplies obtainable nearby:** Yes, in New York City; **Overnight accommodations:** New York; **First Aid available in park:** Yes; **Nearest Hospital:** New York City; **Days/Hours:** Open daily from 9 a.m. to 5 p.m.; **Holiday Closings:** Thanksgiving, Dec. 25 & Jan. 1; **Visitor attractions closed for seasons:** No; **Weather:** Cold Winters with snow; hot, humid Summers. Pleasantly mild Spring and Fall.

GENERAL INFORMATION: Be careful walking up and down stairs; they are quite slippery when wet.

Home of Franklin Delano Roosevelt National Historic Site
Hyde Park, New York

MAILING ADDRESS: Superintendent, Home of Franklin Delano Roosevelt National Historic Site, Hyde Park, New York 12538 **Telephone:** 914-229-9115

DIRECTIONS: The Home is on Route 9 in Hyde Park, just north of Poughkeepsie.

This was the birthplace , lifetime residence, and "Summer White House" of the 32nd President, who entertained many distinguished visitors here. The gravesites of President and Mrs. Roosevelt are in the Rose Garden. Designated Jan. 15, 1944.

VISITOR ACTIVITIES: house tours, exhibits in the library; **Permits:** No; **Fees:** $1.50 entrance fee permits access to Roosevelt Home and Library and nearby Vanderbilt Mansion (see listing in this book), just north of the Roosevelt Home. Persons under 16 and over 62 years of age are admitted free. Golden Eagle and Golden Age Passports accepted and available; **Visitor facilities:** parking, restrooms, library; **Any limitations on vehicle usage:** No; **Hiking trails:** Yes; **Meals served in the park:** No; **Food and supplies obtainable in the park:** No; **Food and supplies obtainable nearby:** Yes, Hyde Park; **Overnight accommodations:** Hyde Park and vicinity; **First Aid available in park:** Yes; **Nearest Hospitals:** Poughkeepsie, US 9, 9.7 km (6 miles); **Days/Hours:** Open daily from 9 a.m. to 5 p.m.; until 6 p.m. in Summer; **Holiday Closings:** Dec. 25 and Jan. 1.

GENERAL INFORMATION: *For Your Safety*—Beware of poison ivy and steep slopes.

Theodore Roosevelt Birthplace National Historic Site
New York, New York

MAILING ADDRESS: Superintendent, Theodore Roosevelt Birthplace National Historic Site, 28 East 20th Street, New York, New York 10003 **Telephone:** 212-260-1616

DIRECTIONS: The Site can be reached from the 23rd Street exit of the IRT (Lexington Ave.) or BMT Subway. Parking space in the vicinity is scarce.

The 26th President of the United States was born in this four-story brownstone house on Oct. 27, 1858. Authorized for addition to the National Park System on July 25, 1962.

VISITOR ACTIVITIES: The house is furnished in period style, with two museum rooms; **Permits:** No; **Fees:** Entrance fee is 50¢ ,Golden Eagle and Golden Age Passports accepted and available; **Visitor facilities:** Visitors will receive a guided tour of the house; **Any limitations on vehicle usage:** No; **Meals served in the park:** No; **Food and supplies obtainable in the park:** No; **Food and supplies obtainable nearby:** Yes, in New York City; **Overnight accommodations:** New York City; **First Aid available in park:** Yes; **Nearest Hospital:** 1.6 km (1 mile) east on 20th Street; **Days/Hours:** Open daily from 9 a.m. to 5 p.m.; closed Mon. & Tues. from Labor Day through Memorial Day; **Holiday Closings:** Thanksgiving, Dec. 25, Jan. 1; **Visitor attractions closed for seasons:**No.

Theodore Roosevelt Inaugural National Historic Site
Buffalo, New York

MAILING ADDRESS: Superintendent, Theodore Roosevelt Inaugural National Historic Site, 641 Delaware Ave., Buffalo, New York 14202 **Telephone:** 716-884-0095

DIRECTIONS: The entrance to the house is on Delaware Ave., near North St. Parking at the rear of the house is accessible from Franklin Street, a one-way street leading north from downtown Buffalo. Busses from downtown Buffalo stop in front of the Site.

Here in the Ansley Wilcox House, Theodore Roosevelt took the oath of office as President of the United States on Sept. 14, 1901, shortly after the assassination of President William McKinley. Authorized for addition to the National Park System on Nov. 2, 1966. Site is operated by the Theodore Roosevelt Inaugural Foundation.

VISITOR ACTIVITIES: guided tours, quilt show, Victorian Christmas display, art shows, walking tours; **Permits:** No; **Fees:** 50¢ per person entrance fee; **Visitor facilities:** parking, restrooms, art gallery; **Any limitations on vehicle usage:** No; **Meals served in the park:** No; **Food and supplies obtainable in the park:** No; **Food and supplies obtainable nearby:** Yes, Buffalo, across the street; **Overnight accommodations:** Buffalo; **First Aid available in park:** Yes; **Nearest Hospital:** Buffalo, .8 km (1/2 mile) from the site; **Days/Hours:** Open Mon-Fri: 10 a.m.-5 p.m.; Sat-Sun: Noon-5 p.m.; **Holiday Closings:** Closed on federal holidays; **Visitor attractions closed for seasons:** No.

Sagamore Hill National Historic Site
Oyster Bay, New York

MAILING ADDRESS: Superintendent, Sagamore Hill National Historic Site, Cove Neck Road, Box 304, Oyster Bay, New York 11771 **Telephone:** 516-922-4447

DIRECTIONS: Sagamore Hill is on Cove Neck Road, 3 miles east of Oyster Bay, New York. It can be reached by the Long Island Railroad from New York City's Pennsylvania Station at 7th Avenue and 33rd Street. Taxis meet all trains. If travelling by car, take either Exit 41 from the Long Island Expressway or Exit 35 North from the Northern State Parkway to Route 106 Northbound. Follow Route 106 to the Village of Oyster Bay. Turn right at the third traffic light in Oyster Bay onto East Main Street. Follow the green and white signs marked "Sagamore Hill."

This estate was the home of Theodore Roosevelt, the 26th President of the United States, from 1885 until his death in 1919. Authorized for addition to the National Park System on July 25, 1962.

VISITOR ACTIVITIES: Visitors can tour the Roosevelt home, the pet cemetery, and Old Orchard Museum, containing exhibits relating to Theodore Roosevelt's political career, family life at Sagamore Hill, and the lives of his six children; **Permits:** No; **Fees:** 50¢ entrance fee. Golden Eagle and Golden Age Passports accepted and available; **Visitor facilities:** souvenir and book sales, parking; **Any limitations on vehicle usage:** Vehicles are limited to the entrance road and visitor parking area; **Hiking trails:** No; **Meals served in the park:** Yes, a snack bar operates at Sagamore Shop in Summer; **Food and supplies obtainable in the park:** No; **Food and supplies obtainable nearby:** Yes, in Oyster Bay, 4.8 km (3 miles) west; **Overnight accommodations:** East Norwich, Rt. 25A, 8 km (5 miles); **First Aid available in park:** Yes, in all buildings; **Nearest Hospital:** Glen Cove, St. Andrews Lane, 11.3 km (7 miles); **Days/Hours:** Open daily from 9:30 a.m. to 4:30 p.m.; until 5 p.m. in Spring and Fall; until 6 p.m. in Summer; **Holiday Closings:** Thanksgiving, Dec. 25 & Jan 1; **Visitor attractions closed for seasons:** No; **Weather:** Temperatures range from 65-90° in Summer and 0-40° in Winter.

GENERAL INFORMATION: Poison ivy is common in the area; please keep to the established paths and walkways. Pets must be leashed or carried. Heat exhaustion is common in the Summer, so judge your limits. Park fences are historic and unsafe for climbing.

Saint Paul's Church National Historic Site
Mount Vernon, New York

MAILING ADDRESS: Saint Paul's Church National Historic Site, c/o Corporation of Saint Paul's Church, 897 S. Columbus Ave., Mount Vernon, New York 10550 **Telephone:** 914-667-4116

DIRECTIONS: Take the Conner Street Exit of the New York Thruway-New England Division or US 1-Boston Post Road in Pelham Manor, NY, from the Hutchinson River Parkway.

This 18th-century church is significant because of its connection with the events leading to the John Peter Zenger trial involving freedom of the press, and because of its place in American architectural history, and the Revolution. This affiliated area of the National Park System was designated on July 5, 1943.

VISITOR ACTIVITIES: walking tours of the church, museum, and cemetery; **Permits:** No; **Fees:** No; **Visitor facilities:** parking and restrooms; **Any limitations on vehicle usage:** No; **Meals served in the park:** No; **Food and supplies obtainable in the park:** No; **Food and supplies obtainable nearby:** Yes, at Mount Vernon, in the immediate area; **Overnight accommodations:** Mount Vernon, Bronx, New Rochelle, or anywhere in metropolitan New York City; **First Aid available in park:** No; **Nearest Hospital:** Mount Vernon, N. 7th Ave., 3 km (2 miles); **Days/Hours:** Open by appointment only at this time. Call 914-738-4799 to arrange for a guided tour; **Visitor attractions closed for seasons:**No; **Weather:** Typical New York weather, with seasonal snow or rain.

Saratoga National Historical Park
Stillwater, New York

MAILING ADDRESS: Superintendent, Saratoga National Historical Park, R.D. #1, Box 113-C, Stillwater, New York 12170 **Telephone:** 518-664-9821

DIRECTIONS: The Park entrance lies 48 km (30 miles) north of Albany, NY on US 4 and NY 32. Taxi service is available from Saratoga Springs, Mechanicville, and Schuylerville.

The American victory here over the British in 1777 was the turning point of the Revolution and one of the decisive battles in world history. Major General Philip Schuyler's country home is nearby. Authorized for addition to the National Park System on June 1, 1938. Established by act of Congress on June 22, 1948.

VISITOR ACTIVITIES: Visual programs, lectures, and guided talks are available at the Visitor Center. Craft and weapon demonstrations are given in Summer. The Park is open all year for hiking and skiing; **Permits:** No; **Fees:** No; **Visitor facilities:** An interpretive tour starts at the Visitor Center; **Any limitations on vehicle usage:** snowmobiles are prohibited; **Hiking trails:** Yes, the historic 1777 road system is gradually being turned into hiking trails; **Backcountry:** No; **Camping:** No; **Other overnight accommodations on site:** No; **Meals served in the park:** No; **Food and supplies obtainable in the park:** No; **Food and supplies obtainable nearby:** Yes,in Stillwater and Schuylerville; **Overnight accommodations:** Schuylerville, 13 km (8 miles); **First Aid available in park:** Yes; **Nearest Hospital:** Saratoga Springs, Rte. 32 to 423 to 9P, 27 km (17 miles); **Days/Hours:** Park open from 9 a.m. to 5 p.m. daily. Both the John Neilson House and the Freeman House are usually open in Summer, and park roads are open from about April 1 to Nov. 30 as weather permits; **Holiday Closings:** Visitor Center is closed Thanksgiving, Dec. 25 & Jan. 1.

Statue of Liberty National Monument
New York, New York

MAILING ADDRESS: Superintendent, Statue of Liberty National Monument, Liberty

Island, New York NY 10004 **Telephone:** 212-732-1236

DIRECTIONS: Liberty Island is accessible only by ferry. Circle Line Ferries leave Battery Park in Lower Manhattan every hour and more frequently during Summer. For schedule and group-rate information, call 212-269-5755.

The famous 152-foot copper statue bearing the torch of freedom was a gift of the French people in 1886 to commemorate the alliance of the two nations during the American Revolution. The Monument includes The American Museum of Immigration, in the base of the statue, and Ellis Island, an immigration port from 1892 to 1954. Created by Presidential Proclamation on Oct. 15, 1924.

VISITOR ACTIVITIES: Visitors can reach the top of the pedestal by elevator or stairs. The public is not permitted access to the torch itself. You can climb stairs to the statue's crown.; **Permits:** No; **Fees:** elevator fee-10¢ no charge for children under 16 years of age. Round-trip concession boat fee is $1.50 for adults; children under 12 years - 50¢; **Visitor facilities:** restrooms, public telephones, and books relating to the Statue and to Immigration are available in the Statue lobby. Refreshments and souvenirs are available nearby; **Any limitations on vehicle usage:** No vehicle access available; **Hiking trails:** No; **Backcountry:** No; **Camping:** No; **Other overnight accommodations on site:** No; **Meals served in the park:** Yes, snacks available at refreshment stand; **Food and supplies obtainable in the park:** No; **Food and supplies obtainable nearby:** No; **Overnight accommodations:** New York City; **First Aid available in park:** Yes; **Nearest Hospital:** New York—takes about 1 hour to reach; **Days/Hours:** Open daily year-round from 9 a.m.-5 p.m., with extended hours in season; **Holiday Closings:** Dec. 25.

GENERAL INFORMATION: Ascent to the Statue's crown from the top of the pedestal is by spiral staircase only. The climb is equivalent to 12 stories and those with physical difficulties are urged not to attempt it.

Upper Delaware National Scenic River
New York (also in Pennsylvania)

MAILING ADDRESS: Mid-Atlantic Regional Office, National Park Service, 143 S. Third Street, Philadelphia Pennsylvania 19106 **Telephone:** 215-597-7018

DIRECTIONS: The area is undeveloped at this time.

Nearly 120 km (75 miles) of this free-flowing fishing stream are protected from Hancock, NY to the vicinity of Sparrow Bush, NY. Authorized for addition to the National Park System on Nov. 10, 1978.

VISITOR ACTIVITIES: Canoeing; **Permits:** No; **Fees:** No; **Visitor facilities:** There are no Federal facilities at this time. Boat rentals are available in the vicinity.

Martin Van Buren National Historic Site
Kinderhook, New York

MAILING ADDRESS: Superintendent, Martin Van Buren National Historic Site, P.O. Box 545, Kinderhook, New York 12106 **Telephone:** 518-758-9689

DIRECTIONS: The Site is on Route 9H in Kinderhook, 40 km (25 miles) south of Albany. A tour of the grounds only is offered during restoration.

Lindenwald estate, south of Albany, was the home of the eighth President for 21 years until his death in 1862. Authorized for addition to the National Park System on Oct. 26, 1974.

VISITOR ACTIVITIES: guided tours, cultural activities, off-site programs (slide shows) for community and professional organizations; **Permits:** No; **Fees:** No; **Visitor facilities:** None at present; the Site is undergoing extensive restoration; **Any limitations on vehicle usage:** Parking space is limited; **Hiking trails:** No; **Backcountry:** No; **Camping:** No; **Other overnight accommodations on site:** No; **Meals served in the park:** No; **Food and supplies obtainable in the park:** No; **Food and supplies obtainable nearby:** Yes, in Kinderhook, 2.4 km (1½ miles) north; **Overnight accommodations:** Kinderhook; **First Aid available in park:** Yes; **Nearest Hospital:** Hudson, NY, 19 km (12 miles) south; **Days/Hours:** A tour of the grounds only is offered from 9 a.m. to 5 p.m. daily from May through September; **Holiday Closings:** Thanksgiving, Dec. 25, & Jan. 1; **Visitor attractions closed for seasons:** None; **Weather:** Summer is warm, humid, and breezy. The average temperature is in the high 70's or low 80's.

GENERAL INFORMATION: Restoration is scheduled to be completed in 1982, the bicentennial of the birth of Martin Van Buren.

Vanderbilt Mansion National Historic Site
Hyde Park, New York

MAILING ADDRESS: Superintendent, Vanderbilt Mansion National Historic Site, Hyde Park, New York 12538 **Telephone:** 914-229-9115

DIRECTIONS: The Site is on US 9 about 13 km (8 miles) north of Poughkeepsie, NY. Entrance to the grounds is by the main gate on US 9 north of the village of Hyde Park. The Visitor Center is in the Pavilion near the mansion.

This palatial mansion is a fine example of homes built by 19th century financiers. Designated Dec. 18, 1940.

VISITOR ACTIVITIES: self-guiding tours, interpretive exhibits and audiovisual program, walking tours of the grounds; **Permits:** No; **Fees:** Entrance fee is $1.50, which permits admission to the Vanderbilt Mansion and the nearby Home of Franklin D. Roosevelt National Historic Site (see listing in this book) and the Roosevelt Library. Golden Eagle and Golden Age Passports accepted and available; **Visitor facilities:** parking, restrooms; **Any limitations on vehicle usage:** No; **Hiking trails:** No; **Backcountry:** No; **Camping:** No; **Other overnight accommodations on site:** No; **Meals served in the park:** No; **Food and supplies obtainable in the park:** No; **Food and supplies obtainable nearby:** Yes, at Hyde Park; **Overnight accommodations:** Hyde Park or vicinity; **First Aid available in park:** Yes; **Nearest Hospital:** Poughkeepsie, US 9, 9.7 km (6 miles); **Days/Hours:** Open daily from 9 a.m. to 5 p.m., until 6 p.m. in Summer; **Holiday Closings:** Dec. 25 and Jan.1.

North Carolina

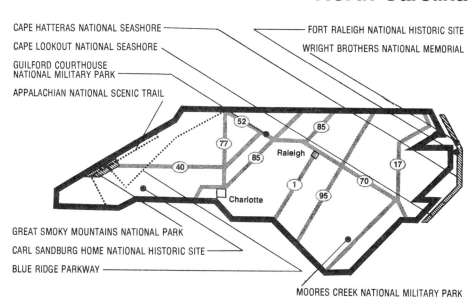

CAPE HATTERAS NATIONAL SEASHORE

CAPE LOOKOUT NATIONAL SEASHORE

GUILFORD COURTHOUSE
NATIONAL MILITARY PARK

APPALACHIAN NATIONAL SCENIC TRAIL

FORT RALEIGH NATIONAL HISTORIC SITE

WRIGHT BROTHERS NATIONAL MEMORIAL

Raleigh

Charlotte

GREAT SMOKY MOUNTAINS NATIONAL PARK

CARL SANDBURG HOME NATIONAL HISTORIC SITE

BLUE RIDGE PARKWAY

MOORES CREEK NATIONAL MILITARY PARK

Appalachian National Scenic Trail
For details see listing in Maine

Blue Ridge Parkway
North Carolina and Virginia

MAILING ADDRESS: Superintendent, Blue Ridge Parkway, 700 Northwestern Bank Building, Asheville, North Carolina 28801 **Telephone:** 704-258-2850, X718

DIRECTIONS: The Parkway intersects many US and State highways, including Interstates 64, 77, 40, & 26, Obtain by mail or in person at any Visitor Center a copy of Blue Ridge Parkway-Accommodations and Services which provides detailed maps and information.

The first national parkway follows the crest of the Blue Ridge and other mountain ranges and includes several large recreation areas. Construction of 755 km (469 miles) of the Parkway is complete. Established by act of Congress on June 30, 1936.

VISITOR ACTIVITIES: auto tours, wildlife- and wildflower-watching, camping, exhibits, picnicking, hiking, fishing, interpretive walks and talks, craft sales and demonstrations; **Permits:** No; **Fees:** $3 campground fee charged at developed areas; **Visitor facilities:** food service, gas, lodging, campgrounds, picnic areas, hiking trails, drinking water, restrooms; **Any limitations on vehicle usage:** Vehicles being used commercially are not allowed on the Parkway; **Hiking trails:** Yes, trails vary in length and difficulty; **Backcountry:** No, the Applachian Trail roughly parallels the Parkway from Mile 0 at

Rockfish Gap to Mile 103 where the trail takes a more westerly route toward the Great Smoky Mountains and Georgia. Shelters, usually 1 day's hike apart, are available on a first-come, first-served basis all along the trail. Information about the trail may be obtained from the Appalachian Trail Conference, P.O. Box 236, Harpers Ferry, WV 25425, phone 304-535-6331; **Camping:** Yes,the nine parkway campgrounds are open from May through Oct. only, but limited camping facilities are available in winter at Otter Creek, Roanoke Mountain, Price Park, and Linville Falls. Sites in each campground are designated for trailer use, but none is equipped for utility connections. Sanitary dumping facilities for trailers are provided at Otter Creek, Peaks of Otter, Roanoke Mountains, Rocky Knob, and Mount Pisgah campgrounds. Camping is limited to 14 days and campsites may not be reserved; **Other overnight accommodations on site:** Yes, Peaks of Otter Lodge, open all year, is operated by Virginia Peaks of Otter Co., Box 489, Bedford, VA 24523, phone 703-586-1081. To reserve at Rocky Knob Cabins, open June through Labor Day, write National Park Concessions, Inc., Meadows of Dan, VA 24120. For Bluffs Lodge (in Doughton Park), open May 1—Oct.31, write National Park Concessions, Inc., Laurel Springs, NC 28644. For Pisgah Inn, open May 1 — Oct. 31, contact Pisgah Inn, Inc., Route 2, Box 441, Canton, NC 28716, phone 704-235-8228; **Meals served in the park:** Yes, at Whetstone Ridge, Otter Creek, Peaks of Otter, Mabry Mill, Doughton Park, Crabtree Meadows, Mount Pisgah; **Food and supplies obtainable in the park:** Yes, limited food and supplies at most Parkway gas stations and at campground stores; **Food and supplies obtainable nearby:** Yes, within a few miles of the Parkway in most of the larger communities; **Overnight accommodations:** at most nearby communities. For further information, obtain a copy of the pamphlet: Blue Ridge Parkway-Accommodations and Services from any Visitor Center or by mail from the Superintendent; **First Aid available in park:** Yes, from Park Rangers; **Nearest Hospital:** Roanoke, Nashville, and many other cities near the Parkway; **Days/Hours:** Open all year. Some sections of the Parkway may be closed in Winter due to snow and ice; **Holiday Closings:** No; **Visitor attractions closed for seasons:**Campgrounds, picnic areas, and other visitor accommodations are open May 1 through Oct. Limited camping facilities are available in Winter; **Weather:** Because of its length and range in elevation, the entire Parkway seldom experiences the same weather at the same time. Most visitors come in Summer but Spring and Fall are pleasant, with fewer crowds. Winter brings snow and ice which may cause temporary closing of the Parkway.

GENERAL INFORMATION: See listings in this book for Great Smoky Mountains National Park, at the southern end of Blue Ridge Parkway, and Shenandoah National Park, to the North.

OTTER CREEK VISITOR CENTER ——

PEAKS OF OTTER VISITOR CENTER

MABRY MILL VISITOR CENTER ——

—— HUMPBACK ROCKS VISITOR CENTER

—— SHENANDOAH NATIONAL PARK

—— SKYLINE DRIVE

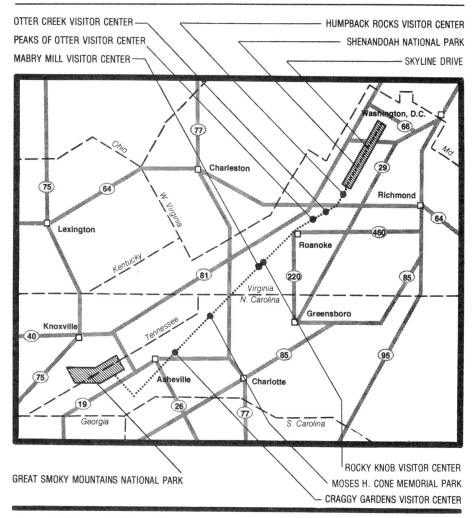

GREAT SMOKY MOUNTAINS NATIONAL PARK

ROCKY KNOB VISITOR CENTER

MOSES H. CONE MEMORIAL PARK

CRAGGY GARDENS VISITOR CENTER

Cape Hatteras National Seashore
Manteo, North Carolina

MAILING ADDRESS: Superintendent, Cape Hatteras National Seashore, Route 1, Box 675, Manteo, North Carolina 27954 **Telephone:** 919-473-2111

DIRECTIONS: The Whalebone Junction Information Center, at the park entrance, is at the intersection of US 158 and NC 12, due south of Nags Head, southeast of Manteo. Information is also available at Visitor Center located at Oregon Inlet Campground, Bodie Island Visitor Center, and Museum of the Sea (Cape Point Campground). Toll ferryboats operate between Ocracoke and Cedar Island (2¼ hours) connecting the park with the mainland. Visitors should check ferry schedules well in advance. Reservations are required. Call Ocracoke 919-928-3841; Cedar Island 919-225-3551.

Beaches, migratory waterfowl, fishing, and points of historical interest, including the Cape Hatteras Lighthouse overlooking the "graveyard of the Atlantic," are special features of the first national seashore. Authorized for addition to the National Park System on Aug. 17, 1937.

VISITOR ACTIVITIES: interpretive exhibits, picnicking, swimming, fishing, guided walks and evening talks in Summer, camping exploring ships wrecks, biking, bird-watching, boating, hunting, surfing; **Permits:** No; **Fees:** only for campsites-$4 per night per site, maximum of 6 people per site; **Visitor facilities:** campgrounds, fishing piers, lifeguarded beaches in Summer, marina, natural trail, showers, restrooms, ferry service, wildlife refuge, picnic area, boat ramps and rentals; **Any limitations on vehicle usage:** Bicyclists should use extreme caution because there are no established bike trails within the park. Park your car only in the designated parking areas to avoid getting stuck in soft sands. Check with Rangers or at Visitor Centers for special regulations governing off-road vehicle travel; **Hiking trails:** Yes, self-guiding nature trail near Cape Hatteras Lighthouse; **Backcountry:** No; **Camping:** Yes, no reservations accepted for individual campsites. Reservations must be made in advance for group camping. Sand and wind conditions require longer than normal tent stakes. Awnings for shade and netting for insect protection will make camping more enjoyable; **Other overnight accommodations on site:** No; **Meals served in the park:** Yes, lunch counter at Oregon Inlet Marina; restaurants in various villages within the Seashore; **Food and supplies obtainable in the park:** No; **Food and supplies obtainable nearby:** Yes, Oregon Inlet Marina and various villages; **Overnight accommodations:** Hotels and motels in nearby communities. For a list, write Dare County Tourist Bureau, Manteo, NC 27954; **First Aid available in park:** Yes, or nearby in Manteo and Nagshead, NC; **Nearest Hospital:** Elizabeth City, NC, 128.7 km (80 miles); **Days/Hours:** Open 24 hours a day. Frisco and Salvo campgrounds close between Labor Day and Memorial Day; **Holiday Closings:** None; **Visitor attractions closed for seasons:** No organized interpretive programs offered during the off season; **Weather:** Summer is hot and humid; Winter is humid and cold. Keep in mind that generally windy conditions make the temperatures feel cooler than they actually are.

GENERAL INFORMATION: *For Your Safety*—Strong littoral currents, rip currents, and shifting sand make swimming particularly dangerous. Tidal currents are hazardous near inlets. Offshore winds can quickly blow air mattresses and other flotation devices out to sea. *Swim* only where lifegurds are on duty. *Sunburn* can ruin your vacation. Short periods of exposure and the use of protective waterproof lotions are recommended. *Hurricanes* are not common but might occur in Aug. or Sept., and winter storms, called Northeasters, should not be taken lightly. Efforts will be made to warn you in time to leave low-lying areas should any of these storms occur. Be sure to walk—never drive—across the *barrier dune* to the sand beaches. *Mosquitoes* and other *insect pests* can make your trip an ordeal if you don't come prepared with repellent and suitable mosquito net-ting for camping. Lightweight *clothing* in Summer should be adequate to protect you from the sun and keep you comfortable in the cool evenings. You should wear shoes when walking to the beach. *Pets must be under physical restraint at all times.*

Nearby points of interest include Wright Brothers National Memorial and Fort Raleigh National Historic Site (see listings in the book).

Cape Lookout National Seashore
Beaufort, North Carolina

MAILING ADDRESS: Superintendent, Cape Lookout National Seashore, P.O. Box 690, Beaufort, North Carolina 28516 **Telephone:** 919-728-2121

DIRECTIONS: Temporary Park Headquarters is located on Front Street in Beaufort, N.C. A permanent administrative site is proposed at Harkers Island, 30 km (20 miles) east of Beaufort. Ferry access to the park is provided from Harkers Island, Davis, Atlantic and Ocracoke. Ferry to Harkers Island transports passengers only. Others transport passengers and vehicles.

The Seashore embraces a series of barrier islands including 93 km (58 miles)of the ocean beach, historic Portsmouth Village, and Cape Lookout lighthouse.Authorized for addition to the National Park System on March 10, 1966.

VISITOR ACTIVITIES: fishing, swimming, boating, shell collecting, photography, primitive camping, bird-watching; **Permits:** Yes, free permit required to drive on islands, obtainable from Park Headquarters; **Fees:** Yes, for Concession Ferry; **Visitor facilities:** Interpretive programs offered in season. This is a developing park and visitor facilities are limited; **Any limitations on vehicle usage:** No roads or bridges, four wheel drive vehicles only; **Hiking trails:** No; **Backcountry:** Yes, information from Park Headquarters; **Camping:** Yes, there are no developed campsites; **Other overnight accommodations on site:** No; **Meals served in the park:** No; **Food and supplies obtainable in the park:** No; **Food and supplies obtainable nearby:** Yes, at Harkers Island and Beaufort; **Overnight accommodations:** Harkers Island and Beaufort; **First Aid available in park:** No; physicians are in Harkers Island and Beaufort; **Nearest Hospital:** Morehead City and Sea Level; **Days/Hours:** Open 24 hours a day; **Holiday Closings:** None; **Visitor attractions closed for seasons:**Interpretive programs offered only in Summer; **Weather:** Hot and humid in Summer.

GENERAL INFORMATION: This is a developing park and visitor facilities are limited. Be prepared to carry with you everything you need, particularly food and water. Don't go out without a shirt and a hat, because there is little shade or shelter on the islands. Make sure your tent is strong and able to withstand wind. It should have a mosquito netting. Be prepared with repellant to combat many biting insects.

Carl Sandburg Home National Historic Site
Flat Rock, North Carolina

MAILING ADDRESS: Superintendent, Carl Sandburg Home National Historic Site, P.O. Box 395, Flat Rock, North Carolina 28731 **Telephone:** 704-693-4178

DIRECTIONS: The Site is 6.4 km (4 miles) south of Hendersonville. Turn off US 25 onto Little River Road at the Flat Rock Playhouse. The park is 42 km (26 miles) south of Asheville via Int. 26.

"Connemara" was the home of the noted poet-author Carl Sandburg for the last 22 years of his life.Authorized for addition to the National Park System on Oct. 17, 1968.

VISITOR ACTIVITIES: Self-guiding tour, guided house tours, exhibits; **Permits:** No; **Fees:** No; **Visitor facilities:** restrooms at Information Center, parking; **Any limitations on vehicle usage:** Visitors must park in the designated area, and walk or take a shuttle bus to the home; **Hiking trails:** Yes, self-guiding paths and trails lead around the Site; **Backcountry:** No; **Camping:** No; **Other overnight accommodations on site:** No; **Meals served in the park:** No; **Food and supplies obtainable in the park:** No; **Food and supplies obtainable nearby:** Yes, Hendersonville; **Overnight accommodations:** Hendersonville, 4.8 km (3 miles) north on US 25; **First Aid available in park:** Yes; **Nearest Hospital:** Hendersonville, 6.4 km (4 miles); **Days/Hours:** Open daily 9 a.m. to 5 p.m. except during Dec., Jan., & Feb., when it is closed on Mondays; **Holiday Closings:** Thanksgiving, Dec. 25, & Jan. 1; **Weather:** Moderate Summers, cool Spring and Fall, cold Winters.

GENERAL INFORMATION: *For Your Safety*— Be cautious around ponds and lakes and while standing on the rock face atop Big Glassy Mountain. Be wary of farm animals that can bite or kick. Stay on established walks and paths, do not climb fences, and be alert for snakes and poison ivy.

Fort Raleigh National Historic Site
Manteo, North Carolina

MAILING ADDRESS: Superintendent, Cape Hatteras National Seashore, Route 1, Box 675, Manteo, North Carolina 27954 **Telephone:** 919-473-2111

DIRECTIONS: The Site is on US 64-264, 4.8 km (3 miles) north of Manteo, NC, 148 km (92 miles) southeast of Norfolk, VA, and 108 km (67 miles) southeast of Elizabeth City, NC.

The first English settlement was attempted here from 1585-87. The fate of Sir Walter Raleigh's "Lost Colony" remains a mystery. Designated Apr. 5, 1941.

VISITOR ACTIVITIES: interpretive exhibits and film, walking tours. In summer, "Lost Colony", a symphonic-drama, is produced in the Waterside Theater; **Permits:** No; **Fees:** only to see "Lost Colony"; **Visitor facilities:** parking, restrooms, picnic area; **Any limitations on vehicle usage:** No; **Hiking trails:** Yes, nature trails around the Site; **Backcountry:** No; **Camping:** No; **Other overnight accommodations on site:** No; **Meals served in the park:** No; **Food and supplies obtainable in the park:** No; **Food and supplies obtainable nearby:** Yes, at Manteo; **Overnight accommodations:** Manteo, 6.4 km (4 miles) or on the Outer Banks, 22.5-29 km (14-18 miles); **First Aid available in park:** Yes, and nearby in Manteo and Nags Head; **Nearest Hospital:** Elizabeth City, NC, US 158, 128.7 km (80 miles); **Days/Hours:** Open daily from 8:30 a.m. to 4:30 p.m. **Holiday Closings:** Dec. 25.

GENERAL INFORMATION: Adjacent to the Historic Site is the Elizabethan Garden, maintained by the Garden Club of North Carolina, Inc. The admission fee is set by that organization.

Great Smoky Mountains National Park
For details see listing in Tennessee

Guilford Courthouse National Military Park
Greensboro, North Carolina

MAILING ADDRESS: Superintendent, Guilford Courthouse National Military Park, P.O. Box 9806, Greensboro, North Carolina 27408 **Telephone:** 919-288-1776

DIRECTIONS: The Visitor Center is near the intersection of Old Battleground Road and New Garden Road, just north of Greensboro.

The battle fought here on March 15, 1781 opened the campaign that led to Yorktown and the end of the Revolution. Established by act of Congress on Mar. 2, 1917.

VISITOR ACTIVITIES: interpretive film and exhibits; auto, bicycle and walking tours, interpretive talks; **Permits:** No; **Fees:** No; **Visitor facilities:** parking and restrooms at Visitor Center, bicycle and foot trails; **Any limitations on vehicle usage:** No; **Hiking trails:** Yes, self-guiding foot trails; **Backcountry:** No; **Camping:** No; **Other overnight accommodations on site:** No; **Meals served in the park:** No; **Food and supplies obtainable in the park:** No; **Food and supplies obtainable nearby:** Yes, in Greensboro; **Overnight accommodations:** Greensboro, 3-16 km (2-10 miles); **First Aid available in park:** Yes; **Nearest Hospital:** Greensboro, 5.8 km (3 miles); **Days/Hours:** Open daily from 8:30 a.m. to 5 p.m., until 7 p.m. in Summer; **Holiday Closings:** Dec. 25 & Jan. 1; **Visitor attractions closed for seasons:** No; **Weather:** Hot, humid Summer; cold moderate Winter.

GENERAL INFORMATION: Watch out for traffic on New Garden Road and Old Battleground Road.

Moores Creek National Military Park
Currie, North Carolina

MAILING ADDRESS: Superintendent, Moores Creek National Military Park, P.O. Box 69, Currie, North Carolina 28435 **Telephone:** 919-283-5591

DIRECTIONS: The Park is about 30 km (20 miles) northwest of Wilmington, NC, and can be reached via US 421 and NC 210.
   The brief, violent battle on Feb. 27, 1776 between North Carolina Patriots and Loyalists is commemorated here.The Patriot victory notably advanced the revolutionary cause in the South, ending Royal authority in the colony. This helped forestall a British invasion of the South and encouraged North Carolina to instruct its delegation to the Continental Congress, on April 12, 1776, to support total independence—the first colony to so act. Established June 2, 1926.

VISITOR ACTIVITIES: exhibits, walking tours, picnicking, wildflower-watching in spring; **Permits:** No; **Fees:** No; **Visitor facilities:** restrooms, exhibits, guide services, picnic areas; **Any limitations on vehicle usage:** No; **Hiking trails:** Yes, a .8 km (½ mile) loop history trail; **Backcountry:** No; **Camping:** No; **Other overnight accommodations on site:** No; **Meals served in the park:** No; **Food and supplies obtainable in the park:** No; **Food and supplies obtainable nearby:** Yes, at Atkinson, Burgaw, or Wilmington; **Overnight accommodations:** Wilmington, 32 km (20 miles) southwest of Moores Creek; or Burgaw, 22 km (14 miles); **First Aid available in park:** Usually or nearby in Burgaw, on Fremont Street; **Nearest Hospital:** Wilmington, 32 km (20 miles); **Days/Hours:** Open daily from 8 a.m. to 5 p.m.; 8 a.m. to 6 p.m. on weekends only during daylight savings time; **Holiday Closings:** Dec. 25 & Jan 1; **Visitor attractions closed for seasons:** No; **Weather:** Spring-sunny and mild; Summer-hot and humid; Fall-sunny and dry; Winter-mild.

GENERAL INFORMATION: When near the creek, be sure to watch your children.

Wright Brothers National Memorial
(near) Manteo, North Carolina

MAILING ADDRESS: Superintendent, Wright Brothers National Memorial, c/o Cape

Hatteras National Seashore, P.O. Box 675, Manteo, North Carolina 27954 **Telephone:** 919-441-7430

DIRECTIONS: The Memorial is located on the Outer Banks of North Carolina about midway between Kitty Hawk and Nags Head. The Visitor Center is 29 km (18 miles) northeast of Manteo on US 158.

The first sustained flight in a heavier-than-air machine was made here by Wilbur and Orville Wright on Dec. 17, 1903. Created by Presidential Proclamation on Mar. 2, 1937.

VISITOR ACTIVITIES: interpretive exhibits, including reproductions of the Wright Brothers' vehicles; picnicking, walking tours, orientation talks year-round; **Permits:** No; **Fees:** No; **Visitor facilities:** picnic area, reconstructions of an airplane hangar and the Wright Brothers' workshop and residence, granite monuments mark the sites of glider experiments and the spot where the first plane left the ground; **Any limitations on vehicle usage:** No; **Hiking trails:** No; **Backcountry:** No; **Camping:** No; **Other overnight accommodations on site:** No; **Meals served in the park:** No; **Food and supplies obtainable in the park:** No; **Food and supplies obtainable nearby:** Yes, at Kitty Hawk, Kill Devil Hills and Nags Head; **Overnight accommodations:** Kitty Hawk, Kill Devil Hills and Nags Head, within a 22.5 km (14 mile) radius; **First Aid available in park:** Yes, or nearby in Nags Head, NC; **Nearest Hospital:** Elizabeth City, NC, 106 km (66 miles); **Days/Hours:** Open daily from 8:30 a.m. to 5 p.m.; **Holiday Closings:** Dec. 25; **Visitor attractions closed for seasons:** No organized interpretive programs during off-season; **Weather:** Weather is generally moderate and windy.

GENERAL INFORMATION: *For Your Safety*—Keep in mind that the generally windy conditions make the temperatures feel cooler than they actually are. Even in relatively warm temperatures high winds can make hypothermia, the loss of body heat, a serious threat. From Spring through early Fall protect against sunburn, especially from 10 a.m. to 3 p.m.

Nearby points of interest include Cape Hatteras National Seashore, which is 16 km (10 miles) south of the Memorial; and Fort Raleigh National Historic Site, located on Roanoke Island about 28 km (17 miles) southwest of the Memorial (see listings in this book). This is the Site of what is known as the Lost Colony, England's unsuccessful first attempt to colonize the North American continent. It can be reached via U.S. 64-264.

North Dakota

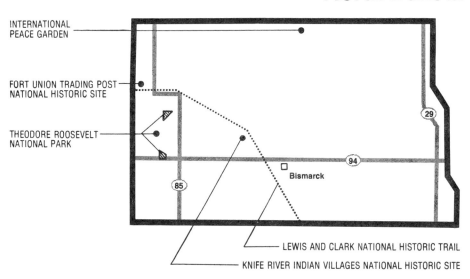

INTERNATIONAL
PEACE GARDEN

FORT UNION TRADING POST
NATIONAL HISTORIC SITE

THEODORE ROOSEVELT
NATIONAL PARK

□ Bismarck

85

94

29

LEWIS AND CLARK NATIONAL HISTORIC TRAIL

KNIFE RIVER INDIAN VILLAGES NATIONAL HISTORIC SITE

Fort Union Trading Post National Historic Site
North Dakota and Montana

MAILING ADDRESS: Superintendent, Fort Union Trading Post National Historic Site, Buford Route, Williston, North Dakota 58801 **Telephone:** 701-572-9083

DIRECTIONS: The Site is on the border of North Dakota and Montana, and can be reached via US 2 and County Road 4 from Williston, ND, which is 40 km (25 miles) to the southeast.

The trading post that stood here was the principal fur-trading depot in the Upper Missouri River region from 1829 to 1867. Only the foundations remain today. Authorized for addition to the National Park System on June 20, 1966.

VISITOR ACTIVITIES: interpretive exhibits, living history programs, walking tours; **Permits:** No; **Fees:** No; **Visitor facilities:** A small Visitor Center is located at the site. Guided tours of the fort site and a teepee display are provided; **Any limitations on vehicle usage:** Vehicles are limited to established roadways; **Hiking trails:** No; **Backcountry:** No; **Camping:** No; **Other overnight accommodations on site:** No; **Meals served in the park:** No; **Food and supplies obtainable in the park:** No; **Food and supplies obtainable nearby:** Yes, at Williston or Sidney, MT; **Overnight accommodations:** Williston, US 2 and County Road 4, 40 km (25 miles); Sidney, MT; **First Aid available in park:** Yes; **Nearest Hospital:** Williston, 40 km (25 miles); **Days/Hours:** Open daily from 9 a.m. to 5:30 p.m.; until 10 p.m. in Summer; **Holiday Closings:** Dec. 25 & Jan. 1; **Visitor attractions closed for seasons:** Living history programs offered only from mid-May through mid-October; **Weather:** Winters are cold with temperatures frequently below zero, Summers are warm and dry. Wet, cool Springs and dry, cool Falls are normal. Windy conditions may be expected during any season.

GENERAL INFORMATION: *For Your Safety*—Exercise caution when touring the fort site. Observe the cellar excavations from a safe vantage point and view the river only from the designated overlooks. Although poisonous snakes are not common to the area, be alert and do not walk in the tall grass.

International Peace Garden
Dunseith, North Dakota

MAILING ADDRESS: Superintendent, International Peace Garden, P.O. Box 116, Dunseith, North Dakota 58329 **Telephone:** 701-263-4390

DIRECTIONS: The Garden is 20 km (13 miles) north of Dunseith on US 281.

Peaceful relations between Canada and the United States are commemorated here. The Garden contains 2,339 acres (888 in North Dakota, 1,451 in Manitoba), which are administered by the International Peace Garden, Inc. The National Park Service has assisted in the master plan. This affiliated area of the National Park System was dedicated on July 14, 1932.

VISITOR ACTIVITIES: hiking, walking, picnicking, camping, guided tours, cross-country skiing, snowshoeing; **Permits:** No; **Fees:** Yes, entrance fee is $1 per vehicle per season; **Visitor facilities:** landscaped gardens, amphitheatre, exhibits, hiking trails, picnic areas, campgrounds, food service, souvenir shops, ski trails, chapel, bell tower, arboretum, International Music Camp, Canadian Legion Sports Camp; **Any limitations on vehicle usage:** Vehicles are restricted to designated roadways; **Hiking trails:** Yes, there are two trails one is about 1.6 km (1 mile) and the other is 5.8 km (3½ miles) in length; **Backcountry:** No; **Camping:** Yes, no reservations available for campsites; fee is $2 per night or $3 per night with electrical hookups. Write or call the Garden for further information on camping facilities; **Other overnight accommodations on site:** No; **Meals served in the park:** Yes, at both American and Canadian concessions; **Food and supplies obtainable in the park:** Yes, at American and Canadian concessions; **Food and supplies obtainable nearby:** Yes, in Dunseith and Boissevain; **Overnight accommodations:** Boissevain, Manitoba, 25 km (16 miles) north on Hwy 10; Dunseith, ND, 21 km (13 miles) south on Hwy 281; **First Aid available in park:** No; **Nearest Hospital:** Boissevain, Manitoba, Hwy 10, 25 km (16 miles); Bottineau, ND, US 281 to ND 5, 48 km (30 miles); **Days/Hours:** Open 24 hours a day year-round; **Holiday Closings:** None; **Visitor attractions closed for seasons:** Activities are curtailed in Winter; **Weather:** Occasional rain and wind with dry, cool evenings. Temperatures range from 60-95°F.

Knife River Indian Villages National Historic Site
Stanton, North Dakota

MAILING ADDRESS: Superintendent, Knife River Indian Villages National Historic Site, P.O. Box 175, Stanton, North Dakota 58571 **Telephone:** 701-745-3636

DIRECTIONS: From I-94 at Bismarck; north on US 83 to ND 200, 64 km (40 miles); west on ND 200 to ND 31, 35 km (22 miles); north on ND 31 to Stanton, 3.2 km (2 miles). The Site adjoins the north city limit of Stanton.

Remnants of five Hidatsa villages, last used in 1845, are an archaeological treasure of the Plains Indians. Visitors to the area include Lewis and Clark, George Catlin and John James Audubon. Authorized for addition to the National Park System on Oct. 16, 1974.

VISITOR ACTIVITIES: No formal visitor facilities at this time. A temporary Visitor Center is expected to be operational sometime in 1980.

Lewis and Clark Trail
For details see listing in Illinois

Theodore Roosevelt National Park
Medora, North Dakota

MAILING ADDRESS: Superintendent, Theodore Roosevelt National Park, Medora, North Dakota 58645 **Telephone:** 701-623-4466

DIRECTIONS: The North Unit is 24 km (15 miles) south of Watford City and 88.5 km (55 miles) north of Belfield, on Highway 85. A stop at the Ranger Station will help you plan and enjoy your visit. The South Unit Visitor Center is at Medora, 27 km (17 miles) west of Belfield and 101 km (63 miles) east of Glendive, off Highway I-94-10. A rough, poorly maintained dirt road of about 32 km (20 miles) leads from the South Unit to the site of Theodore Roosevelt's second ranch, the Elkhorn, Almost nothing of this ranch exists today. Inquiry should be made before attempting this trip.

The Park contains scenic badlands along the Little Missouri River and part of Theodore Roosevelt's Elkhorn Ranch, including bison and some of the original prairie. Established by act of Congress on April 25, 1947.

VISITOR ACTIVITIES: interpretive exhibits, guided walks, campfire programs, auto tours, hiking, camping, snowmobiling, photography, backcountry, horseback riding, picnicking, bird-watching, float trips, cross-country skiing; **Permits:** For backcountry, free permits available at Visitor Center; **Fees:** Yes, entrance fee is $2, camping is $2, group camping is 25¢ per person. Golden Eagle and Golden Age Passports accepted and available; **Visitor facilities:** campgrounds, scenic overlooks, picnic areas, rental horses, hiking trails, restrooms, parking, snowmobiling routes; **Any limitations on vehicle usage:** Off-road and cross-country vehicular travel are prohibited; **Hiking trails:** Yes, information on the many trails is available at the Visitor Center or Headquarters; **Backcountry:** Yes, backcountry use is regulated; for a free backcountry camping permit and further information, check at Visitor Center; **Camping:** Yes, no reservations available for individual campsites, but group camping requires a written reservation from the Park Superintendent. Other Federal and state-maintained campsites are nearby; **Other overnight accommodations on site:** No; **Meals served in the park:** No; **Food and supplies obtainable in the park:** No; **Food and supplies obtainable nearby:** Yes, near the South Unit, Medora. Near the North Unit, Watford City, 24 km (15 miles) north of the park entrance; **Overnight accommodations:** Medora and Watford City; **First Aid available in park:** Yes; **Nearest Hospital:** Watford City and Dickinson Beach; **Days/Hours:** The Park is open all year, but the best time to visit is from May through October; **Holiday Closings:** Thanksgiving, Dec. 25 & Jan. 1; **Visitor attractions closed for seasons:** Portions of the park road may be closed during the winter months, depending on snow conditions; **Weather:** Generally mild, warm to hot days, cool nights. Expect thunderstorms in Summer.

GENERAL INFORMATION: *WARNING: Wildlife is dangerous*—So keep your distance. *Drinking water* should be obtained from approved water sources. Most backcountry water is not fit for human use. The *weather* in the badlands is very harsh with extremes in temperature and sudden violent storms. Prepare yourself for a variety of conditions.

Visitors to the area should also see the Chateau de Mores State Historic Site, a 27-room chateau across the river from Medora. The chateau is open to visitors all year, but may be closed during periods of inclement weather.

Ohio

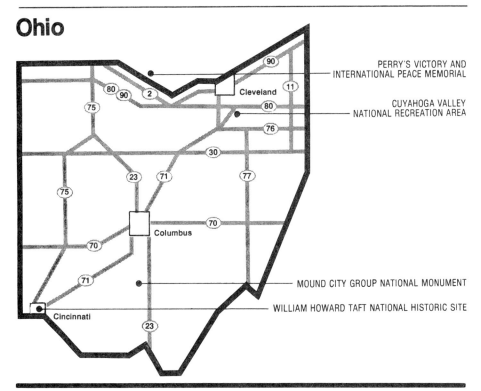

PERRY'S VICTORY AND
INTERNATIONAL PEACE MEMORIAL

CUYAHOGA VALLEY
NATIONAL RECREATION AREA

MOUND CITY GROUP NATIONAL MONUMENT

WILLIAM HOWARD TAFT NATIONAL HISTORIC SITE

Cuyahoga Valley National Recreation Area
Peninsula, Ohio

MAILING ADDRESS: Superintendent, Cuyahoga Valley National Recreation Area, P.O. Box 158, Peninsula, Ohio 44264 **Telephone:** 216-650-4414

DIRECTIONS: Park Headquarters is at 501 W. Streetsboro Road (OH 303), 3 km (2 miles) east of Peninsula and 1.6 km (1 mile) west of OH Route 8.

This recreation area links the urban centers of Cleveland and Akron and preserves the rural character of the Cuyahoga River Valley and the century-old Ohio and Erie Canal system. Authorized for addition to the National Park System on Dec. 27, 1974.

VISITOR ACTIVITIES: hiking, biking, skiing, skating, canoeing, auto tours, sledding, snowmobiling, interpretive exhibits, picnicking, horseback riding, fishing; **Permits:** No; **Fees:** No; **Visitor facilities:** Virginia Kendall Park Unit: trails, picnic areas, fishing, field sports, winter sports, scenic overlooks, Visitor Center, restrooms, nearby-bike trails, horse trails, skiing, historic sites, cultural attractions; **Any limitations on vehicle usage:** No; **Hiking trails:** Yes, there are many foot trails throughout the park; **Backcountry:** No; **Camping:** No; **Other overnight accommodations on site:** No; **Meals served in the**

park: No; **Food and supplies obtainable in the park:** No; **Food and supplies obtainable nearby:** Yes, in any of the numerous communities surrounding the park: **Overnight accommodations:** Motels on OH 8, in Brecksville on OH 21, and in Cleveland and Akron; **First Aid available in park:** Yes; **Nearest Hospital:** Cuyahoga Falls, OH, State Road, approx. 8 km (5 miles). Northern areas of the park have some nearby hospitals in suburbs of Cleveland; **Days/Hours:** 7 days a week 8 a.m.-11 p.m., shorter hours in Winter; **Holiday Closings:** None; **Visitor attractions closed for seasons:** Blossom Music Center open in Summer only: Hale Farm and Village open May-Oct.

Mound City Group National Monument
Chillicothe, Ohio

MAILING ADDRESS: Superintendent, Mound City Group National Monument, 16062 State Route 104, Chillicothe, Ohio 45601 **Telephone:** 614-744-1125

DIRECTIONS: Mound City is on the west bank of the Scioto River, on OH 104, 3.2 km (2 miles) north of the US 35 intersection and 4.8 km (3 miles) north of Chillicothe, OH.

Two thousand years ago (200 B.C. - 500 A.D.), the Ohio River Valley was the focal point of the Hopewell Indian culture. The Hopewell Indians created some of the finest prehistoric art in North America, built vast geometrical earthworks and constructed burial mounds. The largest known concentration of these mounds is preserved at this Monument. The burial mounds yield copper breastplates, tools, obsidian blades, shells, ornaments of grizzly bear teeth and stone pipes carved as birds and animals. Authorized for addition to the National Park System on Mar. 2, 1923.

VISITOR ACTIVITIES: interpretive exhibits, walking, picnicking, organized groups may receive special services, advance arrangements should be made with the Superintendent; **Permits:** No; **Fees:** No; **Visitor facilities:** Visitor Center, restrooms, picnic area, interpretive trails; **Any limitations on vehicle usage:** Vehicles are restricted to designated roadways; **Hiking trails:** Yes, a self-guiding interpretive trail; **Backcountry:** No; **Camping:** No, camping is available in Chillicothe and in nearby state parks. Contact the Monument for further information; **Other overnight accommodations on site:** No; **Meals served in the park:** No; **Food and supplies obtainable in the park:** No; **Food and supplies obtainable nearby:** Yes, in Chillicothe; **Overnight accommodations:** Chillicothe, 4.8 km (3 miles) south on OH 104; **First Aid available in park:** Yes; **Nearest Hospital:** Ross County Medical Center, US 23, 9.7 km (6 miles) north; **Days/Hours:** From Labor Day until June 1 the Visitor Center is open from 8 a.m. to 5 p.m.; from June 1 to Labor Day, from 8 a.m. to 8 p.m. The park is always open during daylight hours; **Holiday Closings:** Dec. 25 & Jan. 1.

GENERAL INFORMATION: *For Your Safety*—Watch for squirrel holes and uneven ground; be extra cautious along the Scioto River trail as it can be very slippery. Keep children under control near the water's edge. Southern Ohio is very rich in prehistoric Indian sites. Among those set aside as State memorials under the custody of the Ohio Historical Society are Fort Ancient, Fort Hill, Miamisburg Mound, Newark Earthworks, Seip Mound and Serpent Mound. You can see historical and archaeological exhibits in the Ross County Historical Society Museum in Chillicothe.

The outdoor drama "Tecumseh" depicts the epic story of the Shawnee leader. It is held at 8:30 p.m. on Tuesday through Sunday from June 17 to Sept. 3 at Sugarloaf Mountain Amphitheatre, which is 8 km (5 miles) from Chillicothe. For further information, write The Scioto Society, Inc., P.O. Box 73, Chillicothe, Ohio 45601. You can call 800-282-2015 from any point in Ohio after June 1; otherwise call 614-775-0700.

Perry's Victory and International Peace Memorial
Put-in-Bay, Ohio

MAILING ADDRESS: Superintendent, Perry's Victory and International Peace Memorial, P.O. Box 78, Put-in-Bay Ohio 43456 **Telephone:** 419-285-2184

DIRECTIONS: The Memorial is on South Bass Island in the village of Put-in-Bay. The island is about 6.44 km (4 miles) from Catawba, Ohio and 22.5 km (14 miles) from Port Clinton, Ohio. Ferry boats from both Catawba and Port Clinton to Put-in-Bay operate from mid-April to mid-Nov. Airplanes provide passenger service year-round.

Commodore Oliver H. Perry won the greatest naval battle of the War of 1812 on Lake Erie. The Memorial(the World's most massive Doric Column)was constructed in 1912-15 "to inculcate the lessons of international peace by arbitration and disarmament." Established by act of Congress on June 2, 1936.

VISITOR ACTIVITIES: A Visitor Center Information Station is near the entrance to the park. An elevator carries visitors to the top of the Memorial. Interpretive programs are presented several times each day during the Summer. Special arrangements may be made for interpretive talks at other times by writing or calling the Superintendent. Fishing is available; **Permits:** No; **Fees:** Entrance fee is 25¢ for persons over 12 years of age. No charge for educational or special groups upon request from administrative office. Golden Eagle and Golden Age Passports are accepted; **Camping:** No, for further information on nearby camping facilities, contact South Bass Island State Park, Put-in-Bay, OH 43456, phone 419-285-2112; **Other overnight accommodations on site:** No; **Meals served in the park:** No; **Food and supplies obtainable in the park:** Yes, grocery store in the village of Put-in-Bay; **Food and supplies obtainable nearby:** Yes,Catawba and Port Clinton; **Overnight accommodations:** within several blocks of the Memorial. Reservations are advised, Contact the park for further information; **First Aid available in the park:** Yes; **Nearest Hospital:** Port Clinton, OH, 22.5 km (14 miles); **Days/Hours:** Mon.-Fri.: 10 a.m. to 5 p.m.; Sat. & Sun. upon request during early Spring and late Fall; 9:30 a.m. to 7:15 p.m., 7 days a week from June through Labor Day; **Holiday Closings:** None during operating season; **Visitor attractions closed for seasons:**The Memorial is closed from the end of Oct. through mid-April.

William Howard Taft National Historic Site
Cincinnati, Ohio

MAILING ADDRESS: Superintendent, William Howard Taft National Historic Site, 2038 Auburn Ave., Cincinnati, Ohio 45219 **Telephone:** 513-684-3262

DIRECTIONS: The Site is at 2038 Auburn Ave. near the intersection of Auburn and Dorchester Avenues.

This house was the birthplace and boyhood home of William Howard Taft, the only man to serve as President (1909-13) and Chief Justice of the United States (1921-30).Authorized for addition to the National Park System on Dec. 2, 1969.

VISITOR ACTIVITIES: walking tours, interpretive exhibits, advance reservations are requested for groups of 25 or more; **Permits:** No; **Fees:** No; **Visitor facilities:** exhibits and walking tours; **Any limitations on vehicle usage:** On-street parking is available; **Meals served in the park:** No; **Food and supplies obtainable in the park:** No; **Food and supplies obtainable nearby:** Yes, within several blocks; **Overnight accommodations:**

Cincinnati and vicinity; **First Aid available in park:** Yes; **Nearest Hospital:** Cincinnati, 2 blocks north of Site; **Days/Hours:** Open from Labor Day through Memorial Day: Mon.-Fri. from 8 a.m. to 4:30 p.m.; from Memorial Day through Labor Day: 8 a.m. to 4:30 p.m. every day; **Holiday Closings:** Thanksgiving, Dec. 25 and Jan. 1; **Visitor attractions closed for seasons:** None; **Weather:** Hot, humid Summers; cold, snowy or icy Winters; moderate Spring and Fall.

GENERAL INFORMATION: Visitors may also want to see the Taft Museum at 316 Pike Street in Cincinnati.

Oklahoma

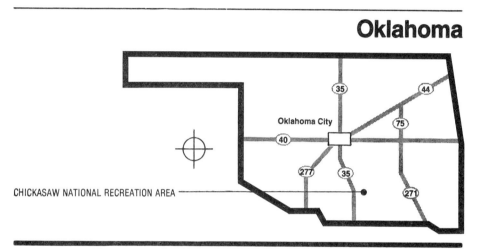

Chickasaw National Recreation Area
Sulphur, Oklahoma

MAILING ADDRESS: Superintendent, Chickasaw National Recreation Area, P.O. Box 201, Sulphur, Oklahoma 73086 **Telephone:** 405-622-3161

DIRECTIONS: Chickasaw lies near Sulphur, Oklahoma on Routes US 177 & OK 7, accessible from Oklahoma City and Dallas-Fort Worth via Int. 35.
The man-made lake of the Arbuckles provides water recreation for an extensive Midwest area, and numerous cold mineral and freshwater springs, including bromide waters, surface here. Established June 26, 1906.

VISITOR ACTIVITIES: interpretive exhibits, camping, picnicking, swimming, water skiing, fishing, boating, skin diving, biking, walking, guided nature walks, hiking, hunting, campfire programs, and nature film; **Permits:** for camping—obtained from the nearest Ranger Station; **Fees:** $3 nightly camping fee; **Visitor facilities:** campgrounds, picnic areas, beach, boat launches, bicycle trails, trailer dump station, nature center; **Any limitations on vehicle usage:** Bicycles are not allowed on trails east of the Nature Center, and are not recommended on Bromide Hill trails; **Hiking trails:** Yes, self-guiding trails; **Backcountry:** No; **Camping:** Yes, reservations for campsites can be made from May to Sept. by calling 405-622-6121 or writing the Superintendent at the above address. Vacant unreserved campsites are available on a first-come, first-served basis; **Other overnight accommodations on site:** No; **Meals served in the park:** No; **Food and supplies obtainable in the park:** No; **Food and supplies obtainable nearby:** Yes, in Sulphur, west on Hwy 177; **Overnight accommodations:** Sulphur, west on Hwy 177; **First Aid**

available in park: Yes; **Nearest Hospital:** Sulphur, 3 km (2 miles) west of the main entrance.; **Days/Hours:** Park never closes; **Holiday Closings:** None; **Weather:** Summers are hot and humid, with severe thunderstorms common in May and June. Temperatures above 37°C (100°F) occur and humidity frequently exceeds 50%. Winters are generally mild and rarely subject to prolonged freezing temperatures.

GENERAL INFORMATION: Be cautious of poisonous snakes and poison ivy.

Oregon

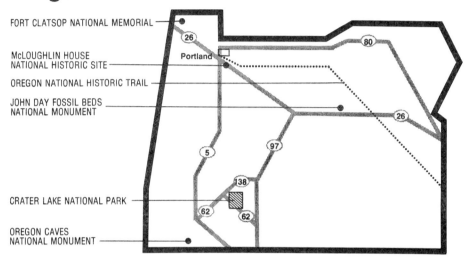

FORT CLATSOP NATIONAL MEMORIAL

McLOUGHLIN HOUSE NATIONAL HISTORIC SITE

OREGON NATIONAL HISTORIC TRAIL

JOHN DAY FOSSIL BEDS NATIONAL MONUMENT

CRATER LAKE NATIONAL PARK

OREGON CAVES NATIONAL MONUMENT

Crater Lake National Park
Crater Lake, Oregon

MAILING ADDRESS: Superintendent, Crater Lake National Park, P.O. Box 7, Crater Lake, Oregon **Telephone:** 503-594-2211

DIRECTIONS: The south and west entrances on US 62 are open all year. The north entrance off Hwy 138 and Rim Drive are open from mid-July to mid-October, weather permitting.

The Park's deep blue lake, formed by accumulated water from rain and snow, reaches 1,932 feet in depth. It lies in the heart of Mount Mazama, an ancient volcanic peak that collapsed centuries ago. Park established by act of Congress on May 22, 1902.

VISITOR ACTIVITIES: summer (mid-June through mid-Sept.) naturalist programs at Mazama Campground and in Rim Village, daily naturalist talks, interpretive walks, concession bus and boat tours around Crater Lake, wildlife-watching, auto tours, fishing, hiking, swimming, picnicking, and camping. Winter slide programs at Headquarters upon request, snowmobiling on the north side of the Park, cross-country skiing, and all types of winter recreational activities; **Permits:** Backcountry permits obtained in Summer from Headquarters, entrance stations, exhibit building, or from a Park Ranger; in Winter, from Headquarters or a Park Ranger; **Fees:** $2 entrance fee; $3 camping fee. Fees are collected from mid-June through mid-Sept., or later if weather permits. Golden

Eagle and Golden Age Passports accepted and available; **Visitor facilities:** picnic areas, restrooms, post office, are available throughout the year. Lodging, food and tour services, curio shop, groceries—all from mid-June through mid-Sept. Light refreshments and souvenirs at the coffee shop in Rim Village during Winter. There are no overnight accommodations at Crater Lake during the winter months. Snowmobile and ski trails are available; **Any limitations on vehicle usage:** All vehicles are restricted to designated roadways; chains or snow tires may be required in Winter; **Hiking trails:** Yes, numerous scenic trails are described in the Park brochure available on request; **Backcountry:** Yes; information can be obtained by writing Park Headquarters or stopping at any Visitor Information point in summer; **Camping:** Yes, campsites are open from mid-June through Sept. No reservations accepted for campsites; **Other overnight accommodations on site:** Yes, reservations for Crater Lake Lodge, open during the Summer, can be made by contacting Crater Lake Lodge, Inc., Crater Lake, OR 97604, phone 503-594-2511; **Meals served in the park:** Yes, at Crater Lake Lodge and Rim Village Coffee shop; **Food and supplies obtainable in the park:** Yes, some groceries available at Rim Village; **Food and supplies obtainable nearby:** Yes, at Fort Klamath, Union Creek; **Overnight accommodations:** Medford, 111 km (69 miles) from the west entrance on OR 62; or Klamath Falls, 87 km (54 miles) from the south entrance on OR 62 and US 97. Union Creek and Fort Klamath on OR 62; **First Aid available in park:** Yes, as well as ambulance service in Chiloquin, OR, OR 62; **Nearest Hospital:** Medford, OR 62, 111 km (69 miles); or Klamath Falls, OR 62 and 97, 87 km (54 miles); **Days/Hours:** 24 hours a day everyday in Summer. In Winter, the south and west road on OR 62 to Park Headquarters is open 24 hours. The road from Park Headquarters to Rim Village is open from 8 a.m. to 5 p.m.; **Holiday Closings:** None; **Visitor attractions closed for seasons:** The north entrance road and Rim Drive are closed from approximately mid-Oct. to early July, depending on snow conditions. The Park averages 50 feet of snowfall annually. In Winter, overnight accommodations are available near the Park. Carry towrope, shovel, and tire chains, which may be necessary at any time.

GENERAL INFORMATION: *For Your Safety-* Stay on trails especially along the caldera rim. Footing can be treacherous on this volcanic rock and soil. Descent to the lake is permitted only on the Cleetwood Trail.

Keep your distance from wildlife. Remember these animals are wild, and can be dangerous. Do *not* feed any wildlife.

Fort Clatsop National Memorial
Astoria, Oregon

MAILING ADDRESS: Superintendent, Fort Clatsop National Memorial, Route 3, Box 604-FC, Astoria, Oregon 97103 **Telephone:** 503-861-2471

DIRECTIONS: The Visitor Center is 10 km (6 miles) southwest of Astoria on US 101.

The Lewis and Clark Expedition camped here in the winter of 1805-6. Authorized for addition to the National Park System on May 29, 1958.

VISITOR ACTIVITIES: interpretive exhibits and slide program, guided tours, living history demonstrations in Summer, walking, picnicking; **Permits:** No; **Fees:** No; **Visitor facilities:** parking and restrooms at Visitor Center, picnic area; **Any limitations on vehicle usage:** No; **Hiking trails:** Yes, walking trails around the fort; **Backcountry:** No; **Camping:** No; **Other overnight accommodations on site:** No, camping facilities are at Fort Stevens State Park, 8 km (5 miles) away. Reserve space by phoning: 503-861-2471; **Meals served in the park:** No; **Food and supplies obtainable in the park:** No; **Food and supplies obtainable nearby:** Yes, at Astoria, Seaside; **Overnight accommodations:**

Astoria, US 101, 10 km (6 miles); Seaside, US 101, 21 km (13 miles); **First Aid available in park:** Yes; **Nearest Hospital:** Astoria, US 101, 10 km (6 miles); **Days/Hours:** Open daily from 8 a.m. to 5 p.m.; until 8 p.m. in Summer; **Holiday Closings:** Dec. 25; **Visitor attractions closed for seasons:**Living history program only operates in Summer; **Weather:** There is frequent rainfall.

GENERAL INFORMATION: Be cautious when visiting the canoe landing, because the banks of the river and slough are often slippery and unstable. Within 40 km (25 miles) of Fort Clatsop are several sites described in the Lewis and Clark journals. These include the salt cairn at Seaside, the trail over Tillamook Head to Cannon Beach, and in the State of Washington, the camp and trail sites at McGowan, Camp Disappointment, and Long Beach.

John Day Fossil Beds National Monument
John Day, Oregon

MAILING ADDRESS: Superintendent, John Day Fossil Beds National Monument, 420 West Main Street, John Day, Oregon 97845 **Telephone:** 503-575-0721

DIRECTIONS: The Monument Headquarters and one Visitor Center are in John Day. The Monument comprises three separate units; Sheep Rock Unit, 16 km (10 miles) north of Dayville; Painted Hills Unit, 16 km (10 miles) northwest of Mitchell; Clarno Unit, 32 km (20 miles) west of Fossil.
  Plant and animal fossils show five epochs, from Eocene to the end of Pleistocene, at this site in north central Oregon. Authorized for addition to the National Park System on Oct. 26, 1974.

VISITOR ACTIVITIES: exhibits, interpretive talks, picnicking, auto tours, wildlife-and wildflower-watching, hiking, fishing; **Permits:** No; **Fees:** No; **Visitor facilities:** Visitor Center, restrooms, picnic areas, hiking trails, loop drives, drinking water available only at Cant Ranch Visitor Center of Sheep Rock Unit; **Any limitations on vehicle usage:** Off road vehicles are prohibited; **Hiking trails:** Yes, one .8 km (½ mile) scenic self-guiding trail at Painted Hills Unit; two more being developed at Turtle Cove in Sheep Rock Unit; **Backcountry:** No; **Camping:** No; **Other overnight accommodations on site:** No, Federal and State-operated campgrounds are in the area. Camping information is posted in each unit; **Meals served in the park:** No; **Food and supplies obtainable in the park:** No; **Food and supplies obtainable nearby:** Yes, at John Day, Fossil, Dayville, & Mitchell; **Overnight accommodations:** John Day, Hwy 26, US 395 intersection; Mount Vernon, also 26-395; Fossil, Hwy 218-19; Mitchell, Hwy 26-207; **First Aid available in park:** Yes, or at clinic in Fossil; **Nearest Hospital:** John Day, Madras, and Prineville; **Days/Hours:** You can visit the formations year-round. Headquarters in John Day are open all year; **Visitor attractions closed for seasons:**Visitor Center at Sheep Rock Unit is open from 8 a.m. to 5 p.m. from Mar. 1 through Nov. 30; **Weather:** Spring, wet and cool; Summer, dry and hot; Fall, warm and sunny.

GENERAL INFORMATION: *For Your Safety*—Do not climb on the geologic formations. Be on the lookout for rattlesnakes. Beware of deer unexpectedly crossing roads at night.

Lewis and Clark Trail
For details see listing in Illinois

McLoughlin House National Historic Site
Oregon City, Oregon

MAILING ADDRESS: Superintendent, McLoughlin House National Historic Site, 713 Center Street, Oregon City, Oregon 97045 **Telephone:** 503-656-5146

DIRECTIONS: The McLoughlin House is in McLoughlin Park between 7th and 8th Streets, less than 4 blocks east of Pacific Hwy (US 99). Bus service is available from Portland, 20 km (13 miles) away.

The house is one of the few remaining pioneer dwellings in the area once known as the "Oregon Country." Dr. John McLoughlin, often called the "Father of Oregon," was prominent in the development of the Pacific Northwest as Superintendent of Fort Vancouver, built the house and lived here from 1846 to 1857. This affiliated area of the National Park System is owned and operated by the McLoughlin Memorial Association and was established by act of Congress in 1941.

VISITOR ACTIVITIES: guided house tours; **Permits:** No; **Fees:** $1 admission fee for adults, 25¢ for those under 18; **Visitor facilities:** house tours; **Any limitations on vehicle usage:** No; **Meals served in the park:** No; **Food and supplies obtainable in the park:** No; **Food and supplies obtainable nearby:** Yes, at Oregon City; **Overnight accommodations:** Portland, I-5 and/or Pacific Hwy (99 E), 20 km (13 miles); Oregon City, McLoughlin Blvd., 1 km (.6 mile); **First Aid available in park:** No; **Nearest Hospital:** Oregon City, Division Street, 2.4 km (1.5 miles);; **Days/Hours:** The house is open four days a week at this time. Inquire locally about days and hours; **Weather:** Winter is the rainy season; incidence of rain is high in late Fall and early Spring, moderating in Summer and Fall.

Oregon Caves National Monument
Cave Junction, Oregon

MAILING ADDRESS: Superintendent, Oregon Caves National Monument, 19000 Caves Highway,Cave Junction, Oregon 97523 **Telephone:** 503-Oregon Caves Toll Station No. 2, through: Medford, OR

DIRECTIONS: The Monument is 32 km (20 miles) southeast of Cave Junction on Oregon 46, and can be reached by travelling either 80 km (50 miles) south of Grants Pass or 122 km (76 miles) north from Crescent City, on US 199. The last 13 km (8 miles) of Oregon 46 are quite narrow and winding. Information is available on OR 46 just as you exit OR 199.

Ground water dissolving marble bedrock formed these cave passages and intricate flowstone formations. Created by Presidential Proclamation on July 12, 1909.

VISITOR ACTIVITIES: cave tours, camping, hiking, wildlife- and bird-watching, campfire programs in Summer; **Permits:** No; **Fees:** All visitors wishing to see the cave must do so on a guided tour provided by the Oregon Caves Company, a private concessioner, for a fee regulated by the U.S. Department of the Interior. Cave tours usually consist of 12-16 visitors and are operated every day except Christmas on the following approximate schedule: June 1 to Sept. 10-8 a.m. to 7 p.m. Sept. 11 to May 31 tour times are 10:30 a.m., 12:30 p.m., 2 p.m., 3:30 p.m. and whenever 12 to 16 visitors are formed. Adults—$3, children 6 through 11—$1.50; **Visitor facilities:** parking, lodge and cabins, campgrounds, hiking trails, restrooms; **Any limitations on vehicle usage:** Towing trailers is not recommended due to narrow roads, infrequent turnarounds, and lack of parking space; **Hiking trails:** Yes, a maintained and marked system of trails provides access to the park for day hikers. Connecting trails lead into the adjacent Siskiyou National Forest. Snowshoes are usually required in Winter and Spring; check trail conditions with Park Rangers before setting out; **Backcountry:** No; **Camping:** No, but the U.S. Forest Service operates two campgrounds in the adjacent Siskiyou National Forest from approximately mid-June through the first week of Sept. Cave Creek campground is 6.5 km (4 miles) from the park on OR 46. No trailers are permitted. Grayback campground is 13 km (8 miles) down OR 46. Trailers are permitted in the campground. Although the campgrounds are rarely filled, campsites are assigned on a first-come, first-served basis. There are no showers and no utility connections. For further information, call 503-592-2166; **Other overnight accommodations on site:** Yes, the Oregon Caves company operates a lodge and cabins from approximately mid-June to the first week in Sept. For reservations and information, write to Oregon Caves Co., Oregon Caves, OR 97523, phone 503-476-2534; **Meals served in the park:** Yes, at the Chateau; **Food and supplies obtainable in the park:** No; **Food and supplies obtainable nearby:** Yes, at Cave Junction, 32 km (20 miles); **Overnight accommodations:** Motel on OR 46, about 19.3 km (12 miles) from the park. Several motels available on OR 199 in and around Cave Junction; **First Aid available in park:** Yes, there is also a doctor and clinic in Cave Junction, OR 46.; **Nearest Hospital:** Grants Pass, 80 km (50 miles); **Days/Hours:** Open daily from 8 a.m. to 6 p.m., until 10 p.m. in Summer; **Holiday Closings:** Dec. 25; **Visitor attractions closed for seasons:**Campfire and interpretive programs during the Summer season only, excluding cave tours.

GENERAL INFORMATION: Because parking is quite limited, you should arrive at the park during the morning hours if you visit the park in Summer. Parking for trailers is extremely limited. If you are hiking, stay on the marked trails. *For Your Safety*—wear proper clothing, including a jacket and walking shoes. The cave temperature varies from 3° to 7°C (38° to 45°F). Cave passageways may be slippery. The cave tour is not recommended for anyone with heart, breathing, or walking difficulty. Stay with your guide. There is an emergency exit one-third of the way through the cave for those who do not wish to continue the tour. Do not touch any of the cave walls or formations. Canes, crutches, tripods, and sticks are not permitted within the cave. Children under 6 are not allowed in the cave. A childcare (babysitting) service is available at the concession for a fee.

Oregon National Scenic Trail
For details see listing in Missouri

Pennsylvania

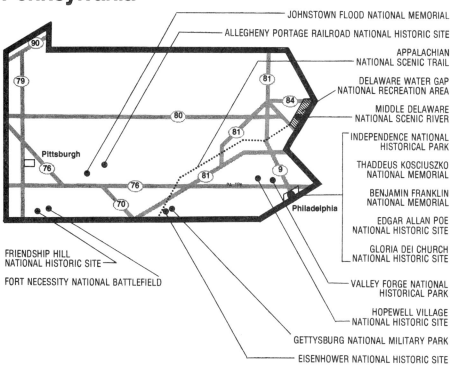

JOHNSTOWN FLOOD NATIONAL MEMORIAL

ALLEGHENY PORTAGE RAILROAD NATIONAL HISTORIC SITE

APPALACHIAN
NATIONAL SCENIC TRAIL

DELAWARE WATER GAP
NATIONAL RECREATION AREA

MIDDLE DELAWARE
NATIONAL SCENIC RIVER

INDEPENDENCE NATIONAL
HISTORICAL PARK

THADDEUS KOSCIUSZKO
NATIONAL MEMORIAL

BENJAMIN FRANKLIN
NATIONAL MEMORIAL

EDGAR ALLAN POE
NATIONAL HISTORIC SITE

GLORIA DEI CHURCH
NATIONAL HISTORIC SITE

FRIENDSHIP HILL
NATIONAL HISTORIC SITE

FORT NECESSITY NATIONAL BATTLEFIELD

VALLEY FORGE NATIONAL
HISTORICAL PARK

HOPEWELL VILLAGE
NATIONAL HISTORIC SITE

GETTYSBURG NATIONAL MILITARY PARK

EISENHOWER NATIONAL HISTORIC SITE

Pittsburgh

Philadelphia

Allegheny Portage Railroad National Historic Site
Cresson, Pennsylvania

MAILING ADDRESS: Superintendent, Allegheny Portage Railroad National Historic Site, P.O. Box 247, Cressson, Pennsylvania 16630 **Telephone:** 814-886-8176

DIRECTIONS: The Site is on US 22 between Duncansville and Cresson, PA. The Visitor Center is at Lemon House, built in 1831 near the summit of Allegheny Mountain as a rest stop and tavern.

The Site preserves structures and traces of the 36-mile incline railroad built between 1831-34 to carry passengers and freight over the Allegheny Mountains between canal basins at Hollidaysburg and Johnstown.Established by act of Congress on June 30, 1969.

VISITOR ACTIVITIES: interpretive talks and costumed demonstrations near Visitor Center, interpretive exhibits and trails, hiking, picnicking; **Permits:** No; **Fees:** No; **Visitor facilities:** Visitor Center with restrooms,walking trails through quiet spots with benches, picnic facilities including water, tables, restrooms and grills; **Any limitations on vehicle usage:** Vehicles are restricted to the parking lot at the Visitor Center; **Hiking trails:** Yes, dirt trails through site; **Backcountry:** No; **Camping:** No; **Other overnight accommodations on site:** No; **Meals served in the park:** No; **Food and supplies obtainable in the park:** No; **Food and supplies obtainable nearby:** Yes, in Cresson and Duncansville; **Overnight accommodations:** Cresson (limited), US 22, 3 km (2 miles);

Duncansville, US 22, 9.7 km (6 miles); Altoona, US 220, 16 km (10 miles); **First Aid available in park:** Yes or nearby in Cresson and Duncansville, US 22; **Nearest Hospital:** Altoona, US 220, 16 km (10 miles); **Days/Hours:** Open 8:30 a.m. to 5 p.m., until 8 p.m. in Summer; **Holiday Closings:** Thanksgiving, Dec. 25 & Jan. 1; **Visitor attractions closed for seasons:** No tours or demonstrations in Winter; **Weather:** Warm days and cool nights in Summer; cold, windy and snowy in Winter.

GENERAL INFORMATION: Visitors to the area can also see the nearby Johnstown Flood National Memorial (see listing in this book), located along US 219 and PA 869 near St. Michael, PA.

Appalachian National Scenic Trail
For details see listing in Maine

Benjamin Franklin National Memorial
Philadelphia, Pennsylvania

MAILING ADDRESS: Director of Audience Development, Benjamin Franklin National Memorial, 20th Street & Benjamin Franklin Parkway, Philadelphia, Pennsylvania 19103 **Telephone:** 215-448-1000

DIRECTIONS: The Memorial is in the Franklin Institute Science Museum at 20th Street and Benjamin Franklin Parkway in Philadelphia.

James Earle Fraser's monumental statue of Franklin honors the inventor-statesman. This affiliated area of the National Park System, owned and administered by The Franklin Institute, was designated on Oct. 25, 1972.

VISITOR ACTIVITIES: exhibits of Franklin artifacts; **Permits:** No; **Fees:** admission to the Memorial is free. There is a separate admission fee for the adjacent Science Museum; **Visitor facilities:** parking, restrooms, snack bar in Science Museum; **Any limitations on vehicle usage:** No; **Hiking trails:** No; **Backcountry:** No; **Camping:** No; **Other overnight accommodations on site:** No; **Meals served in the park:** No, but available at snack bar in the Science Museum; **Food and supplies obtainable in the park:** No; **Food and supplies obtainable nearby:** Yes, in Philadelphia; **Overnight accommodations:** within walking distance in Philadelphia; **First Aid available in park:** No, but through local hospitals and doctors in Philadelphia area; **Nearest Hospital:** Hannemann Hospital, 314 North Broad St., about 3 blocks from the Memorial; **Days/Hours:** Open 10 a.m. to 5 p.m. Mon.-Sat.; 12 noon to 5 p.m. on Sunday; **Holiday Closings:** Dec. 25, Jan. 1, July 4, Thanksgiving; **Visitor attractions closed for seasons:** Science park open Summer only.

Delaware Water Gap National Recreation Area
Bushkill, Pennsylvania (also in New Jersey)

MAILING ADDRESS: Superintendent, Delaware Water Gap National Recreation Area, Bushkill, Pennsylvania 18324 **Telephone:** 717-588-6637

DIRECTIONS: The Area extends from the Delaware Water Gap for 56 km (35 miles) to Milford, PA. Int. 80 crosses the Gap. On the Pennsylvania side follow US 209. The best place to begin your visit is at the Kittatinny Point Information Station, open year-round, located on Int. 80 in NJ. Dingmans Falls Visitor Center, open late Apr. through Oct., is off PA 209.

This scenic area preserves relatively unspoiled land on both the New Jersey and Pennsylvania sides of the Delaware River. Authorized for addition to the National Park System on Sept. 1, 1965.

VISITOR ACTIVITIES: fishing, swimming, canoeing, hiking, hunting, auto tours, ice skating, ice fishing, snowmobiling, picnicking, craft demonstrations, interpretive exhibits, wildlife-watching, rock climbing; **Permits:** State licenses are required for hunting & fishing. Obtain them at nearby sporting goods stores. License fees vary in length of validity & cost; **Fees:** No; **Visitor facilities:** Parking and restrooms at Visitor Center, picnic areas, interpretive and hiking trails, launching ramps, environmental study areas, canoe rentals outside of the park, lifeguarded swimming areas; **Any limitations on vehicle usage:** No; **Hiking trails:** Yes, approx. 32 km (20 miles) of the Appalachian Trail run through the area. Shorter nature trails are available. Check at the Visitor Center or write the Superintendent for further information; **Backcountry:** Yes, information is available from the Visitor Center or the Superintendent; **Camping:** No; **Other overnight accommodations on site:** No; **Meals served in the park:** No; **Food and supplies obtainable in the park:** No; **Food and supplies obtainable nearby:** Yes, Bushkill, Stroudsburg, Milford, Portland, and Delaware Water Gap, PA; Newton, Blairstown, and Branchville, NJ, Port Jervis, NY; **Overnight accommodations:** Bushkill, Stroudsburg, Milford, Portland, and Delaware Water Gap, PA; Newton, Blairstown, and Branchville, NJ, Port Jervis, NY; **First Aid available in park:** Yes; **Nearest Hospital:** East Stroudsburg, PA, Int. 80; Newton, NJ, NJ 206; Port Jervis, NY, US 209; **Days/Hours:** The park is always open. Kittatinny Point Information Station is open daily from 8:30 a.m. to 5 p.m., with extended hours in Summer; **Holiday Closings:** Dec. 25; **Visitor attractions closed for seasons:** Some facilities are closed during Winter, but the park remains open for ice skating, ice fishing, and snowmobiling in designated areas.

GENERAL INFORMATION: Swim only at designated beaches. Climbers must register before climbing and check out after completing the climb.

Edgar Allan Poe National Historic Site
Philadelphia, Pennsylvania

MAILING ADDRESS: Superintendent, Independence National Historical Park, 313 Walnut Street, Philadelphia, Pennsylvania 19106 **Telephone:** 215-627-1364

DIRECTIONS: NOT OPEN TO THE PUBLIC AT THIS TIME
The Poe House in Philadelphia, where this major American literary figure lived, is preserved with North Seventh Street gardens and residences. Authorized for addition to the National Park System on Nov. 10, 1978. Site is expected to be open to the public by Summer 1980.

Eisenhower National Historic Site
Gettysburg, Pennsylvania

MAILING ADDRESS: Superintendent, Gettysburg National Military Park, Gettysburg, Pennsylvania 17325 **Telephone:** 717-334-1124

DIRECTIONS: NOT YET OPEN TO THE PUBLIC
This was the home and farm of President and Mrs. Dwight D. Eisenhower. Designated Nov. 27, 1967.

Fort Necessity National Battlefield
Farmington, Pennsylvania

MAILING ADDRESS: Superintendent, Fort Necessity National Battlefield, The National Pike, Farmington, Pennsylvania 15437 **Telephone:** 412-329-5512

DIRECTIONS: The Battlefield is 17.7 km (11 miles) east of Uniontown on US 40.
Colonial troops commanded by Lt. Col. George Washington, then 22 years old, were defeated here in the opening battle of the French and Indian War on July 3, 1754. The park also includes Jummonville Glenn, site of the first skirmish of the French and Indian War, Braddock's grave, and Mount Washington Tavern, an early 19th-century stage coach inn. Established by act of Congress on Mar. 4, 1931.

VISITOR ACTIVITIES: interpretive exhibits and slide presentation, hiking, picnicking; **Permits:** No; **Fees:** No; **Visitor facilities:** parking, restrooms, picnic area; **Any limitations on vehicle usage:** No; **Hiking trails:** Yes, trails lead around the Battlefield; **Backcountry:** No; **Camping:** No; **Other overnight accommodations on site:** No, private and public campgrounds are located nearby; **Meals served in the park:** No; **Food and supplies obtainable in the park:** No; **Food and supplies obtainable nearby:** Yes, at Uniontown; **Overnight accommodations:** Uniontown, PA 40, 17.7 km (11 miles) west of the park; **First Aid available in park:** Yes; **Nearest Hospital:** Uniontown, PA, US 40, 17.7 km (11 miles) west of the park; **Days/Hours:** Open daily from 8:30 a.m. to 5 p.m., until 6 p.m. in Summer; **Holiday Closings:** Dec. 25 & Jan. 1; **Visitor attractions closed for seasons:** No.

Friendship Hill National Historic Site
Port Marion, Pennsylvania

MAILING ADDRESS: Mid-Atlantic Regional Office, National Park Service, 143 S. Third Street, Philadelphia, Pennsylvania 19106 **Telephone:** 215-597-7018

DIRECTIONS: NOT YET OPEN TO THE PUBLIC
Albert Gallatin (1788-1832), Secretary of the Treasury under Thomas Jefferson, lived in this stone and brick house. Authorized for addition to the National Park System on Nov. 10, 1978.

Gettysburg National Military Park
Gettysburg, Pennsylvania

MAILING ADDRESS: Superintendent, Gettysburg National Military Park, Gettysburg, Pennsylvania 17325 **Telephone:** 717-334-1124

DIRECTIONS: You should start your tour of Gettysburg at the Visitor Center, which is located on PA 134 (Taneytown Road) near its intersection with US 15 (Emmitsburg Road).

The decisive Civil War battle fought here July 1-3, 1863 repulsed the second Confederate invasion of the North. Gettysburg National Cemetery adjoins the Park. President Lincoln delivered his Gettysburg Address here in dedicating the cemetery on Nov. 19, 1863. The Park was established by act of Congress Feb. 11, 1895.

VISITOR ACTIVITIES: auto tours, ranger-conducted walks and talks, living history and campfire programs, hiking, biking, jogging, cross-country skiing, picnicking; **Permits:** No; **Fees:** Yes, for special programs, Electric map is $1 for adults, 50¢ for 11-14 years. Cyclorama is 50¢ for those 16 and older. Battlefield guide, $8 for a 2-hour tour; **Visitor facilities:** Visitor Centers, restrooms, licensed battlefield guides; **Any limitations on vehicle usage:** Park only in designated areas or on the avenues but not on the grass; **Hiking trails:** Yes, trails vary in length and difficulty; **Backcountry:** No, an information brochure on the trails is available by mail or at the Visitor Center; **Camping:** Yes, but only for organized youth groups, Group sites available from mid-Apr. to mid-Oct. (no charge). Groups may wish to make advance reservations for bus tours with a licensed battlefield guide included ($20). Inquiry for both services should be made to the Park at the above address; **Other overnight accommodations on site:** No; **Meals served in the park:** No, in the town of Gettysburg; **Food and supplies obtainable in the park:** No; **Food and supplies obtainable nearby:** Yes, in Gettysburg, 1.6 km (1 mile); **Overnight accommodations:** Numerous motels are adjacent to the Park; **First Aid available in park:** Yes; **Nearest Hospitals:** Gettysburg, .8 km (½ mile) from the Visitor Center; **Days/Hours:** Open daily from 6 a.m. to 10 p.m.; Visitor and Cyclorama Centers open 8 a.m. to 9 p.m. from mid-June to Labor Day; 8 a.m. to 5 p.m. the rest of the year; **Holiday Closings:** Visitor Center and Cyclorama closed Thanksgiving, Dec. 25 & Jan. 1; **Visitor attractions closed for seasons:** Granite (living history) Farm closed in Winter; **Weather:** Summers are hot, 60°-90°F; Winters are cold, 10°-50°F.

GENERAL INFORMATION: *For Your Safety*—Do not climb on cannons and monuments. Running and climbing youngsters frequently fall and injure themselves, so parents are urged to closely supervise their children. Please use extreme caution driving the park roads, especially when they intersect with heavily travelled highways. Bicycle riders are here in ever-increasing numbers; be cautious on blind curves and on one-way roads. Bikers should keep to the right with the flow of auto traffic.

Gloria Dei (Old Swedes') Church National Historic Site
Philadelphia, Pennsylvania

MAILING ADDRESS: Superintendent, Gloria Dei Church National Historic Site, Delaware Ave. and Christian St., Philadelphia, Pennsylvania 19147 **Telephone:** 215-389-1513

DIRECTIONS: Located on the Delaware River, on Delaware Avenue between Christian Street and Washington Avenue; the site is north of the Walt Whitman Bridge and south of the Ben Franklin Bridge, and is next to I-95 on the Delaware River (east) side of I-95.
    This fine example of early Swedish religious architecture was erected about 1700 by a congregation which was founded in 1677. This affiliated area of the National Park System was designated on Nov. 17, 1942. Church site owned and administered by Corporation of Gloria Dei (Old Swedes') Church.

VISITOR ACTIVITIES: The church and grounds are open to the public; arrangements should be made in advance if a guided tour for a group is desired; **Permits:** No; **Fees:** No; **Visitor facilities:** restrooms, church and grounds; **Any limitations on vehicle usage:**

Vehicles not permitted on the church grounds: **Hiking trails:** No; **Backcountry:** No; **Camping:** No; **Other overnight accommodations on site:** No; **Meals served in the park:** No; **Food and supplies obtainable in the park:** No; **Food and supplies obtainable nearby:** Yes, in Philadelphia; **Overnight accommodations:** Philadelphia, 3 km (2 miles); **First Aid available in park:** No; **Nearest Hospital:** Philadelphia, 2.4 km (1½ miles); **Days/Hours:** Open daily from 9 a.m. to 5 p.m.; **Holiday Closings:** No; **Visitor attractions closed for seasons:**No.

Hopewell Village National Historic Site
Elverson, Pennsylvania

MAILING ADDRESS: Superintendent, Hopewell Village National Historic Site, R.D. 1, Box 345, Elverson, Pennsylvania 19520 **Telephone:** 215-582-8873

DIRECTIONS: The Site is 9.7 km (6 miles) south of Birdsboro on PA 345. It is 16 km (10 miles) from the Morgantown interchange on the PA Turnpike, via PA 23 East, and 345 North.

This is one of the finest examples of a rural American 19th-century ironmaking village. The buildings include the blast furnace and its auxiliary structures. Designated Aug. 3, 1938.

VISITOR ACTIVITIES: interpretive programs and exhibits at Visitor Center, living history programs in Summer, hiking, self-guiding walking tours; **Permits:** No; **Fees:** No; **Visitor facilities:** parking and restrooms at Visitor Center, National Environmental Study Area; **Any limitations on vehicle usage:** No; **Hiking trails:** Yes, a nature trail; **Backcountry:** No; **Camping:** No; **Other overnight accommodations on site:** No, swimming, picnicking, and unreserved camping facilities are available in the adjacent French Creek State Park; **Meals served in the park:** No; **Food and supplies obtainable in the park:** No; **Food and supplies obtainable nearby:** Yes, at French Creek State Park; **Overnight accommodations:** Morgantown, PA Turnpike, 11.3 km (7 miles); Pottstown, Rte 100, then 724 or 422, 21 km (13 miles); Reading, Rte 422, 24 km (15 miles); **First Aid available in park:** Yes or at Birdsboro, PA 345 North; **Nearest Hospital:** Reading, 24 km (15 miles); **Days/Hours:** Open daily from 9 a.m. to 5 p.m.; **Holiday Closings:** Dec. 25 and Jan. 1; **Visitor attractions closed for seasons:**No; **Weather:** Hot, humid Summers and cold, icy Winters. Moderate Spring and Fall.

GENERAL INFORMATION: *For Your Safety*—Stay on established tour routes and do not climb on the unstable anthracite furnace ruins, fences, and other historic structures. The sharp slag can cause severe, jagged cuts. Do not enter fenced areas or feed or handle livestock. Those allergic to bee and wasp stings should be especially cautious.

Independence National Historical Park
Philadelphia, Pennsylvania

MAILING ADDRESS: Superintendent, Independence National Historical Park, 313 Walnut Street, Philadelphia, Pennsylvania 19106 **Telephone:** Recorded information—215-627-1776 Visitor Center—215-597-8975

DIRECTIONS: The best place to begin your visit is at the Visitor Center, located at Third and Walnut Streets. The Deshler-Morris House, a unit of Independence National Historical Park, is located at 5442 Germantown Avenue, Philadelphia, PA. It is about 11 km (7 miles) from Independence National Historical Park. The site can be reached either by automobile (metered parking) or by public transportation: Bus No. 23 from the center city or from the park.

The Park includes structures and properties in old Philadelphia associated with the American Revolution and the founding and growth of the United States, including: Independence Hall, the First and Second Banks of the United States, Franklin Court, and Deshler-Morris House in Germantown. Authorized for addition to the National Park System on June 28, 1948.

VISITOR ACTIVITIES: walking tours and photography, summer programs include live drama and children's activities; **Permits:** No; **Fees:** No; **Visitor facilities:** Visitor Center, audiovisual exhibits, films, interpretive displays, post office, various tours. Philadelphia's cultural Loop Bus joins Independence Square with nine other attractions including City Hall, the Zoo and Museum of Art. Schedule varies seasonally; **Any limitations on vehicle usage:** Avoid driving in downtown Philadelphia. Try to walk or use public transportation; **Hiking trails:** No; **Meals served in the park:** Yes, at City Tavern, 2nd and Walnut (concessioner); **Food and supplies obtainable in the park:** No; **Food and supplies obtainable nearby:** Yes, in Philadelphia; **Overnight accommodations:** Philadelphia; **First Aid available in park:** Yes; **Nearest Hospital:** within 4 blocks; **Days/Hours:** Open 7 days a week, 9 a.m. to 5 p.m., with extended hours in Summer. Call the Park for detailed information on hours of various sites; **Holiday Closings:** None; **Visitor attractions closed for seasons:**None; **Weather:** Summers are warm and humid; some snow and sleet in Winter.

GENERAL INFORMATION: The 18th-century brick sidewalks are sometimes rough and uneven. Walk with caution. Try to avoid the midday crowds in Summer by arriving between 9 and 10 a.m. or after 2 p.m.

Johnstown Flood National Memorial
St. Michael, Pennsylvania

MAILING ADDRESS: Superintendent, Johnstown Flood National Memorial, c/o Allegheny Portage National Historic Site, P.O. Box 247, Cresson, Pennsylvania 16630 **Telephone:** 814-886-8176

DIRECTIONS: The area is located along US 219 and PA 869 at the South Fork Dam Site, 16 km (10 miles) northeast of Johnstown near St. Michael, PA.

Remnants of the earthen South Fork Dam on the Little Conemaugh River, which burst on May 31, 1899, causing the devastating flood of Johnstown and nearby communities, are preserved here. Authorized for addition to the National Park System on Aug. 31, 1964.

VISITOR ACTIVITIES: picnicking, hiking, interpretive exhibits at Visitor Center; **Permits:** No; **Fees:** No; **Visitor facilities:** picnic area, interpretive trails, comfort stations, small Visitor Center at the dam site; **Any limitations on vehicle usage:** No; **Hiking trails:** Yes; **Backcountry:** No; **Camping:** No; **Other overnight accommodations on site:** No; **Meals served in the park:** No; **Food and supplies obtainable in the park:** No; **Food and supplies obtainable nearby:** Yes, at St. Michael (limited), Johnstown; **Overnight accommodations:** Johnstown US 219 & PA 869 16 km (10 miles); **First Aid available in park:** Yes, or nearby in St. Michael, Sidman Hospital, PA 869; **Nearest Hospital:** Johnstown, US 219 and PA 869, 16 km (10 miles); **Days/Hours:** Open daily from May 1 to Oct.

1 and on weekends only during the balance of the year; **Holiday Closings:** Thanksgiving, Dec. 25 & Jan 1; **Visitor attractions closed for seasons:** Visitor Center is closed weekdays during the winter season; **Weather:** Warm days and cool nights in Summer; cold, windy Winter with snow.

GENERAL INFORMATION: A short distance from the remains of the South Fork Dam is the Allegheny Portage Railroad National Historic Site (see listing in this book).

Middle Delaware National Scenic River
Pennsylvania (also in New Jersey)

MAILING ADDRESS: c/o Delaware Water Gap National Recreation Area, Bushkill, Pennsylvania **Telephone:** 717-588-6637

DIRECTIONS: See listing for Delaware Water Gap National Recreation Area.
The portion of the river that passes through the Delaware Water Gap National Recreation area is designated the Middle Delaware National Scenic River. Authorized for addition to the National Park System on Nov. 10, 1978.

Thaddeus Kosciuszko National Memorial
Philadelphia, Pennsylvania

MAILING ADDRESS: Superintendent, Thaddeus Kosciuszko National Memorial, c/o Independence National Historical Park, 313 Walnut Street, Philadelphia, Pennsylvania 19106 **Telephone:** 215-597-8974

DIRECTIONS: The Memorial is located at 301 Pine Street, Philadelphia.
This small house, built in 1775, commemorates the life and work of General Thaddeus Kosciuszko, Polish-born patriot and hero of the American Revolution. Created by Presidential Proclamation on Oct. 21, 1972.

VISITOR ACTIVITIES: interpretive exhibits and audiovisual programs; **Permits:** No; **Fees:** No; **Visitor facilities:** restrooms; **Any limitations on vehicle usage:** No; **Meals served in the park:** No; **Food and supplies obtainable in the park:** No; **Food and supplies obtainable nearby:** Yes, in Philadelphia; **Overnight accommodations:** Philadelphia; **First Aid available in park:** Yes; **Nearest Hospital:** Philadelphia, within 6 blocks; **Days/Hours:** Open daily from 9 a.m. to 5 p.m.; **Holiday Closings:** Dec. 25 & Jan 1; **Visitor attractions closed for seasons:**None; **Weather:** Summers are hot and humid; some snow and sleet in Winter.

Valley Forge National Historical Park
Valley Forge, Pennsylvania

MAILING ADDRESS: Superintendent, Valley Forge National Historical Park, Valley Forge, Pennsylvania 19481 **Telephone:** 215-783-7700

DIRECTIONS: The Park is about 32 km (20 miles) west of Philadelphia. Entrances to the Park from the major highways are well-marked. Travelling eastbound or westbound via the Pennsylvania Turnpike, take Exit 24 (Valley Forge). Stay in the right lane for the toll booth and immediately take the next right onto PA 363 North. This will take you to the Visitor Center located at the intersection of PA 363 and 23. Begin your tour here.

Westbound travellers on the Schuykill Expressway (Interstate 76) should take Valley Forge Exit 34 and follow PA 363 North 3.5 km (2.4 miles) to the Park. Travellers on US 202 must take the Valley Forge-Betzwood Bridge exit (truck route US 202 North) and proceed 3 km (2 miles) to the Valley Forge exit (PA 23 West), turn right at the exit and follow PA 23 entrance and Visitor Center.

This is the site of General Washington's Continental Army encampment in the Winter of 1777-78 during the Revolutionary War. A scenic drive through the Park leads to many historical features including Washington's Headquarters and earthen fortifications. Transferred to National Park Service administration on March 31, 1977.

VISITOR ACTIVITIES: interpretive sound/slide program and exhibits, self-guiding auto tour, picnicking, hiking, horseback riding, boating, fishing, biking, auto tape tour Apr.-Oct., historic house tours, living history programs, guided walks; **Permits:** No; **Fees:** No; **Visitor facilities:** parking, hiking and bike trails, bus tours, picnic areas, boat ramp, snack bar; **Any limitations on vehicle usage:** All vehicles must stay on the park roads, which are narrow.; **Hiking trails:** Yes, paved and unpaved trails lead to nearly all of the Park's historical features; **Backcountry:** No; **Camping:** No; **Other overnight accommodations on site:** No; **Meals served in the park:** Yes, sandwiches are available on Route 23 near Washington's Headquarters; **Food and supplies obtainable in the park:** No; **Food and supplies obtainable nearby:** Yes, in King of Prussia; **Overnight accommodations:** Major hotels are within 8 km (5 miles); **First Aid available in park:** Yes; **Nearest Hospital:** Phoenixville, 9.7 km (6 miles); **Days/Hours:** Open daily from 8:30 a.m. to 5 p.m., with extended hours in Summer; **Holiday Closings:** Dec. 25; **Visitor attractions closed for seasons:**None; **Weather:** cold Winters, pleasantly mild Spring, Summer and Fall.

GENERAL INFORMATION: Rail transportation to the Park is available via the Reading Railroad from Philadelphia. For information stop at the Reading Terminal at 12th and Market Streets in Philadelphia or call 215-922-6530.

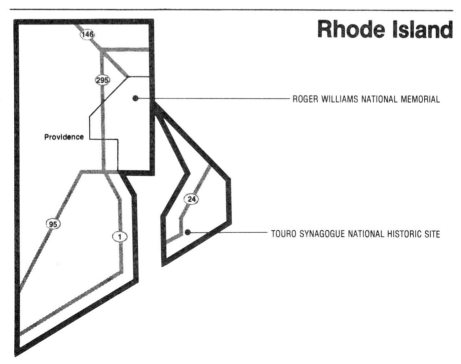

Rhode Island

ROGER WILLIAMS NATIONAL MEMORIAL

Providence

TOURO SYNAGOGUE NATIONAL HISTORIC SITE

Roger Williams National Memorial
Providence, Rhode Island

MAILING ADDRESS: Superintendent, Roger Williams National Memorial, P.O. Box 367, Annex Station, Providence, Rhode Island 02901 **Telephone:** 401-528-4881

DIRECTIONS: The Memorial is between Canal and North Main Streets, at the corner of Smith Street, in Providence.
This Memorial is in honor of the founder of the Rhode Island Colony and a pioneer in religious freedom. Authorized for addition to the National Park System on Oct. 22, 1965.

VISITOR ACTIVITIES: interpretive exhibits; **Permits:** No; **Fees:** No; **Visitor facilities:** The new park includes a small garden and a temporary Visitor Center; **Any limitations on vehicle usage:** No; **Hiking trails:** No; **Backcountry:** No; **Camping:** No; **Other overnight accommodations on site:** No; **Meals served in the park:** No; **Food and supplies obtainable in the park:** No; **Food and supplies obtainable nearby:** Yes, Providence; **Overnight accommodations:** Providence; **First Aid available in park:** Yes; **Nearest Hospital:** within a 3 km (2 mile) radius; **Days/Hours:** Open daily from 8:30 a.m. to 5 p.m. from May 15 through Labor Day. Open by appointment from Sept. through May, unless visitor demand justifies additional openings; **Holiday Closings:** Thanksgiving and Dec. 25; **Weather:** Summers are hot and humid.

GENERAL INFORMATION: Stop at the Visitor Center for a list of nearby points of interest in historic Providence.

Touro Synagogue National Historic Site
Newport, Rhode Island

MAILING ADDRESS: Touro Synagogue National Historic Site, 85 Touro Street, Newport, Rhode Island 02840 **Telephone:** 401-847-4794

DIRECTIONS: Touro Synagogue is on Touro Street in downtown Newport, Rhode Island, about 1½ blocks east of the Old Colony on Washington Square.
Touro Synagogue is one of the most significant buildings in Newport and the oldest existing synagogue in the United States. This affiliated area was authorized for addition to the National Park System on Mar. 5, 1946.

VISITOR ACTIVITIES: guided tours offered from the last week of June until Labor Day; **Permits:** No; **Fees:** No; **Visitor facilities:** souvenir stand; **Any limitations on vehicle usage:** No; **Hiking trails:** No; **Backcountry:** No; **Camping:** No; **Other overnight accommodations on site:** No; **Meals served in the park:** No; **Food and supplies obtainable in the park:** No; **Food and supplies obtainable nearby:** Yes, in Newport; **Overnight accommodations:** In the city of Newport, Rhode Island; **First Aid available in park:** No; **Nearest Hospital:** Newport Hospital is about 1.6 km (1 mile) from the Synagogue; **Days/Hours:** Monday through Friday from 10 a.m. to 5 p.m. and from 10 a.m. until 6 p.m. on Sundays. The rest of the year from 2 p.m. to 4 p.m. on Sundays. Services are held on Fridays during the Summer at 7:30 p.m. and during the rest of the year at sunset. Saturday services are at 9 a.m.

South Carolina

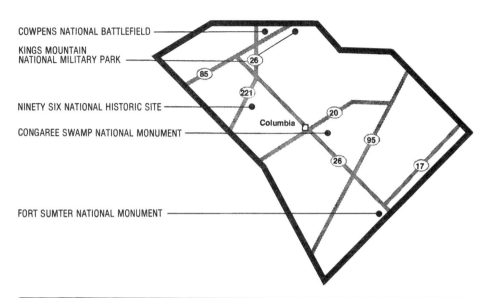

COWPENS NATIONAL BATTLEFIELD

KINGS MOUNTAIN
NATIONAL MILITARY PARK

NINETY SIX NATIONAL HISTORIC SITE

CONGAREE SWAMP NATIONAL MONUMENT

Columbia

FORT SUMTER NATIONAL MONUMENT

Congaree Swamp National Monument
Columbia, South Carolina

MAILING ADDRESS: Superintendent, Congaree Swamp National Monument, P.O. Box 11938, Columbia, South Carolina 29211 **Telephone:** 803-765-5571

DIRECTIONS: Adjacent to State Route 48, S.E. from Columbia, SC (not currently marked by signs).

Located on an alluvial flood plain 32 km (20 miles) southeast of Columbia, the Monument contains the last significant tract of virgin southern bottomland hardwoods in the southeastern United States. This new park area was authorized by an act of Congress on Oct. 18, 1976.

VISITOR ACTIVITIES: access to the park is available only by special permission until establishment, which is projected in the early 1980's; **Permits:** Yes, for entrance to the park. Contact the Superintendent's office; **Fees:** No; **Visitor facilities:** There are presently no Federal facilities; **Any limitations on vehicle usage:** No vehicles are permitted; **Hiking trails:** No; **Backcountry:** No; **Camping:** No; **Other overnight accommodations on site:** No; **Meals served in the park:** No; **Food and supplies obtainable in the park:** No; **Food and supplies obtainable nearby:** Yes, in Columbia, S.C.; **Overnight accommodations:** Columbia, SC 48, 32 km (20 miles); **First Aid available in park:** No; **Nearest Hospitals:** Columbia, Baptist Hospital, SC 48.

Cowpens National Battlefield
Chesnee, South Carolina

MAILING ADDRESS: Cowpens National Battlefield, c/o Superintendent, Kings Moun-

tain National Military Park, P.O. Box 31, Kings Mountain, North Carolina 28086
Telephone: 803-936-7508

DIRECTIONS: The Battlefield is 17.7 km (11 miles) northwest of I-85 and Gaffney, S.C.
and about 3 km (2 miles) southeast of US 221 and Chesnee, S.C.
  Brig. Gen. Daniel Morgan won a decisive Revolutionary War Victory here over British
Lt. Col. Banastre Tarleton on Jan. 17, 1781. Established on Mar. 4, 1929. Additional lands
acquired in 1972.

VISITOR ACTIVITIES: Ranger-conducted walking tours, exhibits and audiovisual
programs at the temporary Visitor Center, auto tours, **Permits:** No; **Fees:** No; **Visitor
facilities:** reconstructed 1830 log cabins, historic monuments, parking, tour road, walking trails, picnic area, information and exhibits; **Any limitations on vehicle usage:**
Recreational vehicles are permitted; commercial vehicles are prohibited; **Hiking trails:**
Yes, 1.6 km (1 mile) walking trail; **Backcountry:** No; **Camping:** No; **Other overnight
accommodations on site:** No; **Meals served in the park:** No; **Food and supplies
obtainable in the park:** No; **Food and supplies obtainable nearby:** Yes, in Chesnee, 3
km (2 miles). Limited food and gas stations within .8 km (½ mile) of the park; **Overnight
accommodations:** Gaffney, SC 11 and I-85, 17.7 km (11 miles) from the park; **First Aid
available in park:** Yes; **Nearest Hospital:** Gaffney, SC 11, 16 km (10 miles); **Days/Hours:**
Open 7 days a week, 364 days a year: Apr. 1-Sept. 1 from 8 a.m. to 6 p.m., 9 a.m. to 5 p.m.
the remainder of the year; **Holiday Closings:** Dec. 25; **Visitor attractions closed for
seasons:** Weather conditions may limit access on roads and trails; **Weather:** Summers are
hot and humid, Winters are mild with occasional snow.

GENERAL INFORMATION: Battlefield is under development, with completion of
Visitor Center expected in mid 1980. Additional trails and picnic areas to be finished in
1981.

Fort Sumter National Monument
Sullivan's Island, South Carolina

MAILING ADDRESS: Superintendent, Fort Sumter National Monument, P.O. Drawer
R, Sullivan's Island, South Carolina 29482 **Telephone:** 803-883-3123

DIRECTIONS: Fort Sumter is in Charleston Harbor and can only be reached by boat.
Tour boats leave from the city boat marina on Lockwood Drive, just south of US 17 in
Charleston. For boat schedules, phone Fort Sumter Tours, 803-772-1691, or write Box 59,
Charleston, SC 29402. Fort Moultrie, administered together with Fort Sumter, is on west
Middle Street on Sullivan's Island. From US 17, take SC 703 to Middle Street. The Visitor
Center is at Fort Moultrie.
  The first engagement of the Civil War took place here on April 12, 1861. The park also
includes Fort Moultrie, scene of the patriot victory of June 28, 1776, one of the early
defeats of the British in the Revolutionary War. Fort Sumter was authorized for addition
to the National Park System on April 28, 1948. Fort Moultrie was added in 1960.

VISITOR ACTIVITIES: interpretive exhibits, film program, walking tours; **Permits:** No; **Fees:** Yes, tour boat to Fort Sumter is $3.50 for adults, $2 for children under
12. There is no admission fee at Fort Moultrie; **Visitor facilities:** restrooms at both forts,
observations deck at Visitor Center; **Any limitations on vehicle usage:** No; **Hiking trails:**
No; **Backcountry:** No; **Camping:** No; **Other overnight accommodations on site:** No;
Meals served in the park: No; **Food and supplies obtainable in the park:** No; **Food and**

supplies obtainable nearby: Yes, in Charleston & vicinity; **Overnight accommodations:** hotels in Charleston and Mount Pleasant; **First Aid available in park:** Yes; **Nearest Hospital:** Charleston, Hwy 17, 19.2 km (12 miles); **Days/Hours:** Open daily from 9 a.m. to 5 p.m.; until 6 p.m. in Summer; **Holiday Closings:** Dec. 25; **Visitor attractions closed for seasons:** No; **Weather:** Summers are hot and humid; Winters are moderately cool with occasional days of extreme cold.

GENERAL INFORMATION: *For Your Safety*—Be especially careful on uneven surfaces, stairways, and near the chain barriers.

Kings Mountain National Military Park
Kings Mountain, South Carolina

MAILING ADDRESS: Superintendent, Kings Mountain National Military Park. P.O. Box 31, Kings Mountain, North Carolina 28086 **Telephone:** 803-936-7508

DIRECTIONS: The Park is easily reached from Charlotte, NC by Int. 85; from Spartanburg, SC by Int. 85; and from York, SC by SC 161. Kings Mountain is on SC Hwy 216, off I-85, about 16 km (10 miles) from Kings Mountain, NC, and about 24 km (15 miles) southwest of Gastonia, NC, and northeast of Gaffney, SC.

American frontiersmen defeated the British here on Oct. 7, 1780, at a critical point during the revolution. Established by act of Congress on Mar. 3, 1931.

VISITOR ACTIVITIES: interpretive exhibits and programs, audiovisual displays, walking tours, photography, living history demonstrations, horseback riding; **Permits:** No; **Fees:** No; **Visitor facilities:** Visitor Center, hiking trail, horseback riding trail; **Any limitations on vehicle usage:** Commercial vehicles are prohibited; drivers should be alert for pedestrians and hikers; **Hiking trails:** Yes, a foot trail leads from the Visitor Center to the chief features of the battlefield: **Backcountry:** Yes, information and brochure available at Visitor Center; **Camping:** No; **Other overnight accommodations on site:** No; camping is permitted only in Kings Mountain State Park, which adjoins the National Military Park on the east. You can also swim (in season) and picnic in the State Park; **Meals served in the park:** No; **Food and supplies obtainable in the park:** No; **Food and supplies obtainable nearby:** Yes, Kings Mountain, NC; Blacksburg, SC; York, SC; **Overnight accommodations:** Gaffney, SC, southwest of the Park; **First Aid available in park:** Yes; **Nearest Hospital:** Kings Mountain, NC, 16 km (10 miles), SC-NC Hwy 216 to US 74 west; **Days/Hours:** Open daily from 9 a.m. to 5 p.m.; until 6 p.m. in Summer; **Holiday Closings:** Dec. 25; **Visitor attractions closed for seasons:** No; **Weather:** Summer is hot and humid. Spring and Fall are pleasantly mild. Winter is cold, but snow and ice are rare.

Ninety Six National Historic Site
Ninety Six, South Carolina

MAILING ADDRESS: Superintendent, Ninety Six National Historic Site, P.O. Box 496, Ninety Six, South Carolina 29666 **Telephone:** 803-543-4068

DIRECTIONS: The Visitor Center is 3 km (2 miles) south of Ninety Six, S.C., off US 248 in Greenwood County.

This colonial trading village dates from the 1730's and became an important government seat after 1768. Held by the British during the Revolutionary War, this Site contains earthwork embankments of 1780 fortifications. Authorized for addition to the National Park System on August 19, 1976.

VISITOR ACTIVITIES: interpretive exhibits, walking, hiking, fishing, horseback riding; **Permits:** No; **Fees:** No; **Visitor facilities:** parking and restrooms at Visitor Center, interpretive trail; **Any limitations on vehicle usage:** No vehicular traffic is allowed in the park; **Hiking trails:** Yes, a 1.4 km (9/10 mile) interpretive trail; **Backcountry:** No; **Camping:** No; **Other overnight accommodations on site:** No; **Meals served in the park:** No; **Food and supplies obtainable in the park:** No; **Food and supplies obtainable nearby:** Yes, Greenwood, 16 km (10 miles) west; **Overnight accommodations:** Greenwood, SC 34, 16 km (10 miles) west; **First Aid available in park:** No; **Nearest Hospital:** Greenwood, SC 34, 14.5 km (9 miles); **Days/Hours:** Open daily from 8 a.m. to 5 p.m.; **Holiday Closings:** Dec. 25; **Visitor attractions closed for seasons:**No; **Weather:** Summer is hot and humid, Winter is mild.

South Dakota

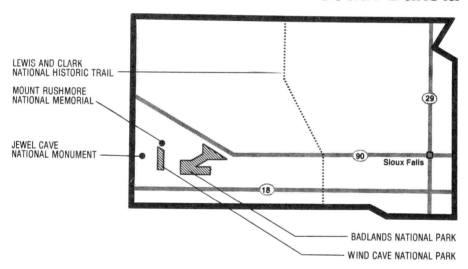

Badlands National Park
Interior, South Dakota

MAILING ADDRESS: Superintendent, Badlands National Park, P.O. Box 6, Interior, South Dakota 57750 **Telephone:** 605-433-5361

DIRECTIONS: The Visitor Center is at Cedar Pass, 4.3 km (2½ miles) northeast of Interior on Route 16A, 45 km (28 miles) southwest of Kadoka and 47 km (29 miles) southeast of Wall— both on I-90.

This Park, carved by erosion, contains animal fossils of 40 million years ago. Prairie grasslands support bison, bighorn sheep, deer, antelope, and prairie dogs. Authorized for admission to the National Park System on Mar. 4, 1929.

VISITOR ACTIVITIES: interpretive and audiovisual exhibits, campfire programs in Summer, camping, hiking, nature walks, wildlife-watching, horseback riding; **Permits:**

No; **Fees:** $1 per vehicle entrance fee, 50¢ per person on commercial buses, $3 per campsite per night. Golden Eagle and Golden Age Passports accepted and available; **Visitor facilities:** campgrounds, foot trails, overlooks, lodge, exhibits, parking, restrooms, church services, picnic areas, restaurant, souvenirs; **Any limitations on vehicle usage:** Do not drive over the grasslands. Be on the lookout for wild animals, especially at night; **Hiking trails:** Yes, self-guiding trails of varying degrees of difficulty lead from the park road; **Backcountry:** Yes, write ahead for complete backcountry and/or trail information. Otherwise, check at Cedar Pass or White River Visitor Centers; **Camping:** Yes, camping available year-round; no campsite reservations except for groups. Commercial campgrounds available at or near Interior, Cactus Flat, Wall, or Kadoka; **Other overnight accommodations on site:** Yes, reservations for lodging should be made with Cedar Pass Lodge (open early May-early Oct.) phone 605-433-5460; **Meals served in the park:** Yes, at Cedar Pass Lodge, from early May-early Oct.; **Food and supplies obtainable in the park:** Yes, at Cedar Pass Lodge; **Food and supplies obtainable nearby:** Yes, in Interior, Wall & Kadoka; **Overnight accommodations:** Wall, I-90, 48 km (30 miles) northwest, Kadoka, 45 km (28 miles) northeast; **First Aid available in park:** Yes at headquarters; doctors in Wall, Kadoka, & Rapid City; **Nearest Hospital:** Kadoka, I-90 45 km (28 miles); **Days/Hours:** Open 24 hours a day, year-round. Cedar Pass Visitor Center open every day except Dec. 25 & Jan. 1; **Holiday Closings:** Dec. 25 & Jan. 1; **Visitor attractions closed for seasons:** The most popular seasons are Spring, Summer, and Autumn. Winter visits can also be rewarding but blizzards may temporarily block roads; **Weather:** Changes in the weather can be sudden and quite drastic in the badlands. Summer is hot, with frequent storms bringing lightning, hail, and high winds. Even on mild days, prolonged exposure to an innocent shower can lead to hypothermia, a potentially fatal reduction in body temperature. Dress adequately and avoid open areas during electrical storms.

GENERAL INFORMATION: *Warning!* Be alert for rattlesnakes, particularly during the warm months. Water should be carried on longer hikes. Drinking water should come from approved sources, such as those at designated campgrounds. Other backcountry water sources are for native wildlife only, and are not fit for human consumption. Do not approach buffalo on foot.

Climbing is discouraged on the steep, barren slopes where moist, slippery clays and soft sediments may suddenly yield under foot.

No open fires or charcoal fires are permitted anywhere in the park. Those wishing to cook must use a stove.

Other points of interest in the Black Hills include Jewel Cave, Wind Cave, and Mount Rushmore (see listings in this book).

Jewel Cave National Monument
Custer, South Dakota

MAILING ADDRESS: Superintendent, Jewel Cave National Monument, c/o Wind Cave National Park, Hot Springs, South Dakota 57747 **Telephone:** 605-673-2288

DIRECTIONS: The area is accessible by US 16, which crosses the northern part of the park between Custer, SD, and Newcastle, WY. The Visitor Center is on US 16, 22.5 km (14 miles) west of Custer.

Limestone formation caverns consist of a series of chambers connected by narrow passages, with many side galleries and fine calcite crystal encrustations. Created by Presidential Proclamation on Feb. 7, 1908.

VISITOR ACTIVITIES: interpretive exhibits, cave tours, picnicking; **Permits:** No;

Fees: There is a guide fee for tours: ages 5 and under, free; 6 to 15, 50¢; 16-61, $1; 62 and over, 50¢. Spelunking tours are $2; **Visitor facilities:** exhibits, information/sales counter, picnic area, drinking water, restrooms; **Any limitations on vehicle usage:** Vehicles must stay on the roads or in the parking area; **Hiking trails:** Yes, a short trail leads from the parking area to the cave entrance; **Backcountry:** No; **Camping:** No; **Other overnight accommodations on site:** No, several campgrounds are near Newcastle, WY and Custer, SD. Contact the Monument for further information; **Meals served in the park:** No; **Food and supplies obtainable in the park:** No; **Food and supplies obtainable nearby:** Yes, in Newcastle, WY or Custer, SD; **Overnight Accommodations:** Yes, in Newcastle, 40 km (25 miles) west of the Monument on US 16, or Custer, 21 km (13 miles) east on US 16; **First Aid available in park:** Yes; **Nearest Hospital:** Custer, 21 km (13 miles) east on US 16; or Newcastle, 40 km (25 miles) west on US 16; **Days/Hours:** the Visitor Center is open daily year-round. Portions of the cave are open to the public, and interpretive tours are offered daily from mid-May through September. Tour schedules, if any, during the rest of the year are irregular and subject to change without notice; **Holiday Closings:** Thanksgiving, Dec. 25 & Jan. 1; **Weather:** Days are warm and sunny, temperatures at night are moderate. There are occasional afternoon thundershowers.

GENERAL INFORMATION: Wear low-heeled walking shoes with non-slip soles while touring the cave. Do not wear sandals or shoes with leather or hard composition soles or with high heels. A light sweater or jacket is desirable - the cave temperature is about 8.3°C (47°F) all year. The tours are not recommended for individuals who have heart trouble or respiratory ailments, or for those who are recovering from a recent operation or hospitalization. Consider each tour description *carefully* before making a choice. *Never* leave a child or pet in a locked car.

Lewis and Clark Trail
For details see listing in Illinois

Mount Rushmore National Memorial
Keystone, South Dakota

MAILING ADDRESS: Superintendent, Mount Rushmore National Memorial, Keystone, South Dakota 57751 **Telephone:** 605-574-2523

DIRECTIONS: The Visitor Center is 4.8 km (3 miles) southwest of Keystone on SD 244 and 40 km (25 miles) south of Rapid City on US 16.
Monumental heads of Presidents George Washington, Thomas Jefferson, Abraham Lincoln, and Theodore Roosevelt were sculpted by Gutzon Borglum on the face of a granite mountain. Authorized for addition to the National Park System on Mar. 3, 1925.

VISITOR ACTIVITIES: evening programs in Summer, interpretive exhibits, audiovisual programs, wildlife- and bird-watching; **Permits:** No; **Fees:** No; **Visitor facilities:** Visitor Center, restrooms, parking lot, feature-length film, floodlighted Memorial in Summer, dining room, gift shop; **Any limitations on vehicle usage:** Leave your vehicle in gear and set your handbrake when parking; **Hiking trails:** Yes, short trails provide varied views of the sculpture; **Backcountry:** No; **Camping:** No; **Other overnight accommodations on site:** No, many commercial, state park, and U.S. Forest Service campgrounds exist in the surrounding Black Hills National Forest, Custer State Park and nearby towns of Rapid City, Rockerville, Keystone, Custer, Hill City, and Hot Springs, South Dakota. Most of these campgrounds can accommodate tents, trailers, and recreational vehicles. Contact: U.S. Forest Service, Black Hills National Forest, 330 Mount Rushmore Road, Custer, SD 57730, phone 605-673-2251; Custer State Park, Hermosa, SD 57744, phone 605-255-4515; South Dakota Division of Tourism, Pierre, SD 57501, phone 605-773-3301; **Meals served in the park:** Yes, complete dining service is available at the concession area during the summer season. Limited food service available during most of the rest of the year; **Food and supplies obtainable in the park:** No; **Food and supplies obtainable nearby:** Yes, at Keystone and Hill City; **Overnight accommodations:** Keystone, 4.8 km (3 miles) northeast; Hill City, 24 km (15 miles) southwest; For further information on accommodations in the vicinity contact the Chamber of Commerce, P.O. Box 747, Rapid City, SD 57701, phone 605-343-1744; **First Aid available in park:** Yes; **Nearest Hospital:** Rapid City, 40 km (25 miles) north on US 16; **Days/Hours:** Visitor Center open from 7 a.m. to 10 p.m. from Memorial Day through Labor Day; from 8 a.m. to 5 p.m. the remainder of the year. Inquire locally to verify hours, which are subject to change; **Holiday Closings:** None; **Visitor attractions closed for seasons:**None; **Weather:** Summer daytime temperatures range from 70-90°F, cool evenings; Winter temperatures range from 40°F to -20°F.

GENERAL INFORMATION: Climbing of Mount Rushmore is prohibited. Stay on trails and stairways. Do not run. Visitors who have heart problems or who have trouble breathing should be aware of the high elevation (5,250 feet). For information on tourist attractions in the Black Hills area, contact the South Dakota Division of Tourism, Pierre, SD 57501, phone 605-773-3301.

Wind Cave National Park
Hot Springs, South Dakota

MAILING ADDRESS: Superintendent, Wind Cave National Park, Hot Springs, South Dakota 57747 **Telephone:** 605-727-2301

DIRECTIONS: The Visitor Center is 17.7 km (11 miles) from the town of Hot Springs on US 385.
This limestone cavern in the scenic Black Hills contains boxwork and calcite crystal formations. Elk, deer, prairie dogs, and bison live in the Park. Established by act of Congress on Jan. 9, 1903.

VISITOR ACTIVITIES: guided cave tour, candlelight and spelunking tours, evening campfire programs, interpretive exhibits, picnicking, camping, fishing, cross-country hiking; **Permits:** No; **Fees:** Yes, for camping and cave tours. Camping is $3 per night per site. Cave tours: Regular (½ mile) tour is $1, Long (1 mile) and Candlelight tours are $1.50 each-½ price for those 6-15 years old; under 6 free. Spelunking tour, $2 (only 14 and over allowed); **Visitor facilities:** parking and restrooms at Visitor Center, picnic area, food service from May-Sept.; **Any limitations on vehicle usage:** Drive only on the roadways. Park on road shoulders or at parking areas only; **Hiking trails:** Yes, 2 self-guiding nature trails; daytime cross-country hikes; **Backcountry:** No; **Camping:** Yes, no reservations accepted for campsites, which are open from about May 15 through Sept. There are many private campgrounds in the Black Hills. For further information, contact the South Dakota Division of Tourism, Pierre, SD 57501, phone 605-773-3301; **Other overnight accommodations on site:** No; **Meals served in the park:** Yes, snacks at Visitor Center in Summer; **Food and supplies obtainable in the park:** No; **Food and supplies obtainable nearby:** Yes, at Hot Springs and Custer; **Overnight accommodations:** Hot Springs, 17.7

km (11 miles) south on Hwy 385; **First Aid available in park:** Only for minor injuries; **Nearest Hospital:** Southern General Hills Hospital, Hot Springs, Hwy 385, 17.7 km (11 miles); **Days/Hours:** Park always open, Cave tours offered daily, with a very limited schedule in Winter; **Holiday Closings:** Cave closed Dec. 25 & Jan. 1; **Visitor attractions closed for seasons:**Many of the Black Hills attractions are open only from Memorial Day through Labor Day. Cave tours are not given as often in Winter; **Weather:** Fall is generally warm and pleasant, Spring can be blustery and is occasionally marred by heavy snowfalls. Winter is mild and moderately severe, but icy roads, lack of accommodations, and closed tourist attractions discourage visitors.

GENERAL INFORMATION: The cave trail is dimly lit, and the surface is paved but uneven. Be sure to wear low-heeled walking shoes with non-slip soles, not sandals or high heels. A light sweater or jacket is desirable, since the cave temperature is about 53°F all year. Beware of bison, which may atttack if disturbed or annoyed. Prairie dogs can bite, and their burrows may harbor rattlesnakes. Poison ivy abounds in the Park and elsewhere in the Black Hills. Learn to recognize and avoid it. If you wish to avoid crowds, plan your visit for Spring or Fall.

Tennessee

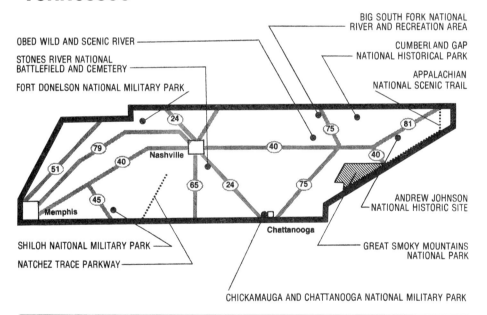

Andrew Johnson National Historic Site
Greeneville, Tennessee

MAILING ADDRESS: Superintendent, Andrew Johnson National Historic Site, Depot Street, Greeneville, Tennessee 37743 **Telephone:** 615-638-3551

DIRECTIONS: The Site is northeast of Knoxville on US 11-E in Greeneville. The Visitor Center is located at the intersection of College and Depot Streets.

This 16-acre Site was established by act of Congress on April 27, 1942 and preserves the two homes, the tailor shop and the cemetery where President Andrew Johnson lived, worked, died, and is buried.

VISITOR ACTIVITIES: interpretive exhibits and historic building tours, auto tours; **Permits:** No; **Fees:** Entrance fee is 50¢ for those 16 years or older, June 1 through Sept. 15. No charge the remainder of the year. Golden Age and Golden Eagle Passports accepted and available; **Visitor facilities:** parking, restrooms; **Any limitations on vehicle usage:** Vehicles are restricted to tour roads and parking area; **Hiking trails:** No; **Backcountry:** No; **Camping:** No; **Other overnight accommodations on site:** No; **Meals served in the park:** No; **Food and supplies obtainable in the park:** No; **Food and supplies obtainable nearby:** Yes, Greeneville; **Overnight accommodations:** Greeneville; **First Aid available in park:** Yes; **Nearest Hospital:** Three hospitals are located in town, 3 blocks from each unit of the site; **Days/Hours:** Open daily from 9 a.m. to 5 p.m.; **Holiday Closings:** Dec. 25; **Visitor attractions closed for seasons:** No.

GENERAL INFORMATION: Visitors to the area can also see Davy Crockett Birthplace State Park, several miles north, and the Samuel Doak house at Tusculum College on the outskirts of North Greeneville.

Appalachian National Scenic Trail
For details see listing in Maine

Big South Fork National River and Recreation Area
Tennessee & Kentucky

MAILING ADDRESS: Project Manager, Big South Fork National River and Recreation Area, P.O. Drawer 630, Oneida, Tennessee 37841 **Telephone:** 615-569-6389

DIRECTIONS: I-75 is the major access route to this area. From I-75 proceed west via KY 80, 90, or 92, or TN 63 to US 27, and thence via US 27 to Whitley City, KY or Oneida, TN which are near the project area.

The free-flowing Big South Fork of the Cumberland River and its tributaries pass through scenic gorges and valleys containing a wide range of natural and historical features. Authorized for addition to the National Park System in 1974.

VISITOR ACTIVITIES: land acquisition began in 1979; **Permits:** No; **Fees:** No; **Visitor facilities:** First recreational facilities will probably be available for visitor use in mid-to-late 1981; **Any limitations on vehicle usage:** No; **Hiking trails:** No; **Backcountry:** No; **Camping:** No; **Other overnight accommodations on site:** No, contact the park for information on campgrounds and facilities in the vicinity; **Meals served in the park:** No; **Food and supplies obtainable in the park:** No; **Food and supplies obtainable nearby:** Yes, at Oneida or Jamestown, TN or Whitley City, KY; **Overnight accommodations:** Oneida or Jamestown, TN and Whitley City, KY; **First Aid available in park:** Yes; **Nearest Hospital:** Oneida, TN.

GENERAL INFORMATION: The U.S. Army Corps of Engineers is responsible for planning, acquisition and development. The National Park Service is responsible for operations.

Chickamauga and Chattanooga National Military Park
For details see listing in Georgia

Cumberland Gap National Historic Park
For details see listing in Kentucky

Fort Donelson National Military Park
Dover, Tennessee

MAILING ADDRESS: Superintendent, Fort Donelson National Military Park, P.O. Box F, Dover, Tennessee 37058 **Telephone:** 615-232-5348

DIRECTIONS: The Park is 1.6 km (1 mile) west of Dover town square and 4.8 km (3 miles) east on Land Between the Lakes National Recreation Area on US 79.

The first major victory for the Union Army in the Civil War occurred here in February 1862 under the leadership of Ulysses S. Grant. The Park was established by act of Congress on March 26, 1928. Fort Donelson National Cemetery (estab. 1867) adjoins the Park.

VISITOR ACTIVITIES: interpretive and audiovisual programs at Visitor Center, museum and wayside exhibits, auto tour, Civil War living history, rifle and cannon demonstrations daily in Summer and on weekends in Spring and Fall, fishing, picnicking, hiking; **Permits:** Tennessee fishing license available from local stores. Licenses vary in length of validity and cost; **Fees:** No; **Visitor facilities:** Visitor Center with exhibits and observation deck, parking, restrooms, picnic area, hiking trails; **Any limitations on vehicle usage:** Park only in pull-offs. Bikers should ride single-file in the direction of traffic; **Hiking trails:** Yes, self-guiding walking tour of natural and historical areas; **Backcountry:** No; **Camping:** primitive camping for Boy and Girl Scout groups only, group leader should contact the Park; **Other overnight accommodations on site:** No; **Meals served in the park:** No; **Food and supplies obtainable in the park:** No; **Food and supplies obtainable nearby:** Yes, Dover; **Overnight accommodations:** Dover, Paris Landing State Park, 25 km (16 miles) southeast on US 79; Clarksville and Paris, TN both on US 79, 48 km (30 miles) in opposite directions; Murry, KY 48 km (30 miles) on KY 121; **First Aid available in park:** Yes, nearby or in Dover; **Nearest Hospital:** Erin, TN 49, 32 km (20 miles); **Days/Hours:** Open daily 8 a.m. to 4 p.m. in Winter, until 5 p.m. all other seasons; **Holiday Closings:** Dec. 25; **Visitor attractions closed for seasons:**Living history program not offered in Winter; **Weather:** Average summer high 95°F; average winter low 20°F; average rainfall 48''; average snowfall 5.6''.

GENERAL INFORMATION: *For Your Safety*—Be cautious near the Cumberland River; it is swift and deep. Watch for poison ivy and poisonous snakes. Hikers should walk facing traffic along park roads.

Great Smoky Mountains National Park
Gatlinburg, Tennessee (also in North Carolina)

MAILING ADDRESS: Superintendent, Great Smoky Mountains National Park, Gatlinburg, Tennessee 37738 **Telephone:** 615-436-5615

DIRECTIONS: The Park Headquarters and a Visitor Center are on US 441, 3.2 km (2 miles) south of Gatlinburg, TN. Obtain a copy of "Smoky Vistas", a newsletter containing up-to-date information on activities, facilities, and medical services.

The loftiest range east of the Black Hills, and one of the oldest uplands on earth, the Smokies have a diversified and luxuriant plantlife, with specimens often of extraordinary size. Authorized for addition to the National Park System on May 22, 1936.

VISITOR ACTIVITIES: hiking, camping (available year-round), interpretive programs, nature walks, fishing, auto tours, horseback riding, wildflower- and bird-

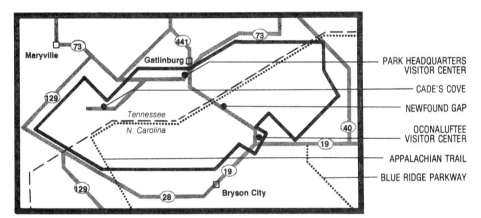

watching, picnicking; **Permits:** Backcountry camping permits available at any Ranger Station or Visitor Center. A TN or NC fishing permit, available locally, is required; **Fees:** $4 per night for developed campsites. No fee for backcountry campsites; **Visitor facilities:** restrooms, developed and primitive campground, picnic areas, trail shelters, horses for hire, lookout tower, nature and foot trails, lodging, supplies; **Any limitations on vehicle usage:** Motorists should be alert for hazards caused by changing natural conditions; **Hiking trails:** Yes, short, self-guiding nature trails, and more than 1286 km (800 miles) of foot and horse trails. Trails are open all Winter; **Backcountry:** Yes, backcountry permit is required; available at Ranger Stations and Visitor Centers. Pick up a free backcountry map and camping guide when you obtain your permit; **Camping:** Yes, camping permits are available after you arrive at the Park. Because of overcrowding, it is necessary to ration overnight use of the 110 km (68 miles) of the Applachian Trail within the Park. Overnight use in five other popular areas, Mt. LeConte, Laurel Gap, Kephart Prong, Scott Gap, and Rich Mountain is also rationed. You must bring your own tent and other camping equipment, since no shelters are provided. There are no showers or hookups for trailers. Primitive campgrounds have no developed water supply; all water must be boiled or chemically treated before it is safe to drink. Pit toilets are provided; **Other overnight accommodations on site:** Yes, LeConte Lodge is accessible only by trail, and offers accommodations within the Park from mid-April to late Oct. Allow ½ day to hike up a mountain trail to this secluded retreat. Reservations are necessary; call or write LeConte Lodge, Gatlinburg, TN 37738, 615-436-4865; **Meals served in the park:** No; **Food and supplies obtainable in the park:** Yes, at Cades Cove Campground; **Food and supplies obtainable nearby:** Yes, at Gatlinburg, Cosby and Townsend, TN and Cherokee, NC; **First Aid available in park:** Yes; **Nearest Hospital:** The Park is served by numerous clinics, medical centers, and hospitals; **Days/Hours:** Open daily year-round; **Holiday Closings:** Visitor Centers closed Dec. 25; **Visitor attractions closed for seasons:**Some picnic areas, clinics, campgrounds, roads and other facilities close in Winter. See "Smoky Vistas" for further information; **Weather:** Wildflowers and migrating birds attract many visitors in late April and early May. If you intend to hike or camp in the Spring, bring warm clothing and be prepared for a variety of weather conditions including frequent rainstorms. Summer days are warm, and nights are usually cool. At higher elevations, temperatures may range from 15-20 degrees lower than those in the valleys. During June and July, the blooming of rhododendron is the outstanding natural event. July and August usually bring the heaviest rainfall, and thunderstorms sometimes come without warning. For greatest comfort on summer hikes, carry a raincoat and insect repellent. Autumn days are cool and clear - ideal for hiking.Winter is the most unpredictable season; yet you shouldn't discount it as a time to visit the Smokies. A quiet peace pervades the Park. Be prepared, however, for sudden snowstorms and icy road conditions.

GENERAL INFORMATION: Hikers must be prepared to meet nature on its own terms. *For Your Safety*—don't travel alone, let someone know your schedule, have proper clothes and equipment, boil all drinking water, and observe park regulations. Stay on the trails, keep off waterfalls and cliff faces, and closely watch and control children. From Nov. through March, winter gear and clothing suitable for survival in deep snow and -20°F temperatures is necessary. This includes a sleeping bag adequate to -20°F, waterproof matches or fire starter, food and other items listed in the *Backcountry Map and Camping Guide* available without charge at Ranger Stations and Visitor Centers. *Bears* may appear tame, but they are dangerous wild animals and should not be approached closely.

Obed Wild and Scenic River
Oneida, Tennessee

MAILING ADDRESS: Superintendent, Obed Wild and Scenic River, P.O. Drawer 670, Oneida, Tennessee 37841 **Telephone:** 615-569-6389

DIRECTIONS: NO FEDERAL LANDS HAVE BEEN ACQUIRED AS YET
The Obed River and its two main tributaries, Clear Cleek and Daddy's Creek, cut into the Cumberland Plateau of East Tennessee, providing some of the most rugged scenery in the Southeast. Authorized for addition to the National Park System on Oct. 12, 1976.

Shiloh National Military Park
Shiloh, Tennessee

MAILING ADDRESS: Superintendent, Shiloh National Military Park, Shiloh, Tennessee 38376 **Telephone:** 901-689-5275

DIRECTIONS: The Park is about 16 km (10 miles) south of Savannah and Adamsville, TN, via 142, and 37 km (23 miles) north of Corinth, MS, via MS 2 and TN 22.
The fierce battle fought here April 6-7, 1862 prepared the way for Major Gen. U.S. Grant's successful siege of Vicksburg. Well-preserved prehistoric Indian mounds overlook the river. Established by act of Congress on Dec. 27, 1894.

VISITOR ACTIVITIES: interpretive film and exhibits at Visitor Center, auto tours, hiking, biking, picnicking; **Permits:** No; **Fees:** No; **Visitor facilities:** The Visitor Center is 19 km (12 miles) south of Savannah, via TN 22 and US 64; **Any limitations on vehicle usage:** Vehicles must stay on designated roadways; **Hiking trails:** Yes, interpretive military trail and environmental trail; **Backcountry:** No; **Camping:** No; **Other overnight accommodations on site:** No; **Meals served in the park:** Yes, snacks and soft drinks at Headquarters area; **Food and supplies obtainable in the park:** No; **Food and supplies obtainable nearby:** Yes, in Shiloh, TN, TN 22; Adamsville and Savannah, TN, US 64; **Overnight accommodations:** Adamsville, TN, 16 km (10 miles) Savannah, TN, 19 km

(12 miles); Selmer, TN, 22 km (15 miles), Pickwick Landing, TN, 22 km (15 miles), Corinth, MS, 32 km (22 miles); **First Aid available in park:** Yes; **Nearest Hospital:** Savannah, TN, US 64, 19 km (12 miles); **Days/Hours:** The Visitor Center is open every day from 8 a.m. to 5 p.m.; **Holiday Closings:** Dec. 25; **Visitor attractions closed for seasons:**None.

GENERAL INFORMATION: You will be sharing the park roads with others. All motorists, hikers, and cyclists should use caution. Be extra careful near the river banks.

Stones River National Battlefield and Cemetery
Murfreesboro, Tennessee

MAILING ADDRESS: Superintendent, Stones River National Battlefield and Cemetery, Route 10, Box 401, Old Nashville Highway, Murfreesboro, Tennessee 37130 **Telephone:** 615-893-9501

DIRECTIONS: The Park is in the northwest corner of Murfreesboro, 43 km (27 miles) southeast of Nashville on US 41/70S. The Visitor Center should be your first stop, since orientation is necessary.

A fierce midwinter Civil War battle which began the Federal offensive to trisect the Confederacy took place here between Dec. 31, 1862 & Jan. 2, 1863. National Cemetery established June 26, 1865 and National Military Park established March 3, 1927.

VISITOR ACTIVITIES: slide program, museum, reference library, publication sales, auto tape tours and Visitor Center, self-guiding auto tours, living history weapon demonstrations from mid-June to Aug., biking; **Permits:** No; **Fees:** No; **Visitor facilities:** parking, restrooms, telephones, small lunch area at Visitor Center, hiking trails, interpretive trails, 13 km (8 mile) bikeway using existing roads; **Any limitations on vehicle usage:** All motorized vehicles must use existing paved roads and parking areas only; **Hiking trails:** Yes, 3 and 8 km (2 and 5 mile) hiking trails, shorter interpretive trails along auto tour; **Backcountry:** No; **Camping:** No; **Other overnight accommodations on site:** No, public campgrounds and motels abound within a 16 km (10 mile) radius of the park; **Meals served in the park:** No, Within 3 km (2 miles) of the park in Murfreesboro; **Food and supplies obtainable in the park:** No; **Food and supplies obtainable nearby:** Yes, in Murfreesboro; **Overnight accommodations:** Murfreesboro, US 41/70S, TN 96, US 231, and 124. Motels are within 8 km (5 miles) of the park; **First Aid available in park:** Yes; **Nearest Hospital:** In the center of Murfreesboro; **Days/Hours:** Park, Cemetery, and Visitor Center open daily 8 a.m. to 5 p.m.; Park and Cemetery open until 8 p.m. from June to August; **Holiday Closings:** Park and Visitor Center closed Dec. 25; cemetery open usual hours; **Visitor attractions closed for seasons:**Living history programs only offered mid-June-August; **Weather:** Temperatures range from 80° - 95°F and dry June-Aug.; 45° - 75°F, occasional rain (mostly pleasant) Sept.-Nov. and Mar.-May; 20° - 40°F, frequent rain, some snow Dec.-Feb.

GENERAL INFORMATION: The oldest Civil War memorial, The Hazen Brigade Monument, is at tour stop 8.

Texas

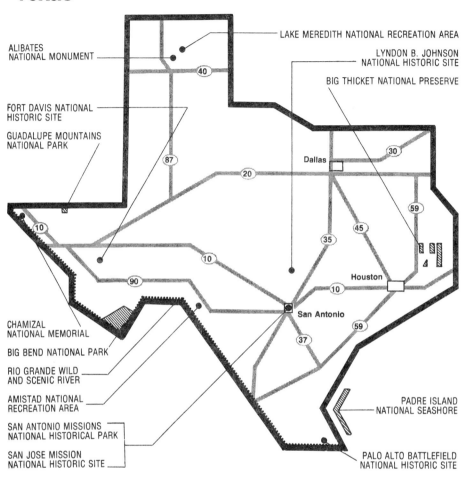

ALIBATES NATIONAL MONUMENT

LAKE MEREDITH NATIONAL RECREATION AREA

LYNDON B. JOHNSON NATIONAL HISTORIC SITE

BIG THICKET NATIONAL PRESERVE

FORT DAVIS NATIONAL HISTORIC SITE

GUADALUPE MOUNTAINS NATIONAL PARK

Dallas

Houston

San Antonio

CHAMIZAL NATIONAL MEMORIAL

BIG BEND NATIONAL PARK

RIO GRANDE WILD AND SCENIC RIVER

AMISTAD NATIONAL RECREATION AREA

SAN ANTONIO MISSIONS NATIONAL HISTORICAL PARK

SAN JOSE MISSION NATIONAL HISTORIC SITE

PADRE ISLAND NATIONAL SEASHORE

PALO ALTO BATTLEFIELD NATIONAL HISTORIC SITE

Alibates National Monument
Fritch, Texas

MAILING ADDRESS: Superintendent, Lake Meredith National Recreation Area, P.O. Box 1438, Fritch, Texas 79036 **Telephone:** 806-857-3151

DIRECTIONS: On Rte. 136, 9.7 km (6 miles) south of Fritch, take Alibates Road 13 km (8 miles) to Bates Canyon Information Station at Lake Meredith. Access to Alibates Flint quarries is available only by ranger-guided tours from Bates Canyon Information Station.

Undeveloped area authorized for addition to the National Park System on Aug. 31, 1965, preserves site where for more than 10,000 years pre-Columbian Indians dug agatized dolomite at these quarries to make projectile points, knives, scrapers and other tools.

VISITOR ACTIVITIES: Ranger-guided tours given twice daily from Bates Canyon Information Station at Lake Meredith National Recreation Area, exhibits; **Permits:** No; **Fees:** No; **Visitor facilities:** None; **Any limitation vehicle usage:** No vehicles permitted; **Hiking trails:** Yes, for Ranger-guided tours only; **Backcountry:** No; **Camping:** No; **Other overnight accommodations on site:** No; **Meals served in the park:** No; **Food and supplies obtainable in the park:** No; **Food and supplies obtainable nearby:** Yes, in Fritch, Borger, Dumas, Amarillo; **Overnight accommodations:** Fritch, Borger, Dumas, Amarillo; **First Aid available in park:** No; **Nearest Hospital:** Borger, TX 136 17.7 km (11 miles); **Days/Hours:** Open 8 a.m. to 5 p.m. from Memorial Day through Labor Day. Tours are generally given at 10 a.m. and 2 p.m.; more frequently if need be. Off-season tours are by appointment only; **Holiday Closings:** None in season; **Visitor attractions closed for seasons:** From Labor Day to Memorial Day, except by appointment; **Weather:** Hot in Summer, cold in Winter, with winds especially high in Spring.

GENERAL INFORMATION: The Panhandle Plains Historical Museum, on the campus of West Texas State University, has several exhibits of archaeological material from this region and a model of what a Panhandle Pueblo structure might look like. The Museum is in Canyon, TX, 26 km (16 miles) south of Amarillo.

Amistad National Recreation Area
Del Rio, Texas

MAILING ADDRESS: Superintendent, Amistad National Recreation Area, P.O. Box 1463, Del Rio, Texas 78840 **Telephone:** 512-775-7491

DIRECTIONS: Park Headquarters and Visitor Center are located in Del Rio on Route 90, west of San Antonio.

Established by act of Congress Nov. 11, 1965, the National Park Service manages the 137 km (85 miles) Lake Amistad under a cooperative international agreement. The lake is formed by the confluence of the Devil's River and the Rio Grande.

VISITOR ACTIVITIES: boating, water skiing, swimming, fishing, hunting and camping on land and from boats, picnicking, hiking; **Permits:** for fishing—If you fish only in United States waters, a Texas State fishing license is all that is required. Texas licenses are sold at any hardware store or at a bait shop in Del Rio, TX. If you cross from the United States portion of the lake to the Mexican portion to fish you must have a Mexican fishing license which costs $10.00 American money. The Mexican licenses may be obtained at a building just across the road from the Mexican Customs checkpoint at the end of the International bridge in the city of Acuna across from Del Rio, Texas; **Fees:** only for fishing permits; **Visitor facilities:** four major boat ramps, designated swim beaches, primitive camping facilities, boat rentals, rental slips, fuel, bait, ice, snacks, and beverages. Gasoline and store facilities are available in nearby towns; **Any limitations on vehicle usage:** Designated areas for driving to the waters' edge and boat launching from vehicles permitted only at those sites; **Hiking trails:** No; **Backcountry:** No; **Camping:** Yes, at the Visitor Center in Del Rio or at Amistad Visitor Center which is operated by the National Park Service near the customs station on the dam during the Summer; **Other overnight accommodations on site:** No; **Meals served in the park:** No; **Food and supplies obtainable in the park:** No; **Food and supplies obtainable nearby:** Yes, some supplies at Diablo East and Rough Canyon marinas; **Overnight accommodations:** Commercial campsites are available near Diablo East, Rough Canyon and Pecos. Motels, travel trailer parks, hotels, restaurant, service stations are in Del Rio and along US 90; **First Aid available in park:** Yes; **Nearest Hospital:** Del Rio, 11.3 km (7 miles); **Days/**

Hours: Open daily from 8 a.m.-5 p.m., until 6 p.m. June-Aug.; **Holiday Closings:** Thanksgiving, Dec. 25 & Jan. 1; **Visitor attractions closed for seasons:** No; **Weather:** Weather is suitable for swimming and water sports for 9 months of the year. December, January, and February will occasionally have low temperatures near 0°C (in the low 30°sF).

GENERAL INFORMATION: *For Your Safety*—Strong winds can make boating extremely hazardous—and in a very short time. Boaters should be familiar with safety precautions listed in a pamphlet available at the Visitor Center. Be sure to use the registration boxes which are provided at each launch ramp.

Big Bend National Park
Big Bend National Park, Texas

MAILING ADDRESS: Superintendent, Big Bend National Park, Big Bend National Park, Texas 79834 **Telephone:** 915-477-2251

DIRECTIONS: From San Antonio, it is 660 km (410 miles) to Park Headquarters at Panther Junction via US 90 to Marathon and south via US 385. From El Paso, it is 520 km (323 miles) to Panther Junction via Int. 10 to Van Horn, US 80 to Alpine, and south via TX 118; and it is 568 km (353 miles) via US 67 to Presidio and Texas Ranch Road 170-the "Camino del Rio". The Headquarters building is 43.5 km (27 miles) off Hwy 385, 113 km (70 miles) south of Marathon.

Mountain scenery contrasts with desert in this great bend of the Rio Grande, where a variety of unusual geological structures are found. Authorized for addition to the National Park System on June 20, 1935.

VISITOR ACTIVITIES: interpretive exhibits, camping, hiking, backcountry, horseback riding, picnicking, fishing, walking and auto tours, boating, biking, wildflower-watching; **Permits:** for backcountry camping and boating on the Rio Grande available from Headquarters; **Fees:** Yes, no entrance fee, but fees are charged for camping at developed campsites and concessioner-operated trailer sites; **Visitor facilities:** camp-grounds, hiking trails, evening talks, lodge, food service, trailer parks, picnic tables, stores, service stations, public telephones, post office, rental saddle horses and pack animals, laundry, restrooms; **Any limitations on vehicle usage:** Do not pass or park on curves; take the numerous road dips slowly; **Hiking trails:** Yes, check at Headquarters for information on the many trails; **Backcountry:** Yes, information can be obtained from Headquarters; **Camping:** Yes, no reservations available for individual campsites; **Other overnight accommodations on site:** Yes, trailer parks and lodge. For reservations at Chisos Mountain Lodge, write to National Park Concessions, Inc., Big Bend National Park, TX 79834, phone 915-477-2291; **Meals served in the park:** Yes, at Chisos Mountain Lodge; **Food and supplies obtainable in the park:** Yes, at the Basin, Rio Grande Village, Castolon, and Panther Junction; **Food and supplies obtainable nearby:** Yes, at Alpine and Marathon; **Overnight accommodations:** Study Butte, TX 118, 37 km (23 miles), Lajitas, TX 118 & TX Ranch Road, 63 km (39 miles) from Headquarters; **First Aid available in park:** Yes; **Nearest Hospital:** Alpine, 183 km (108 miles) from Headquarters; **Days/Hours:** Park is always open. Information desk open from 8 a.m. to 5 p.m.; with extended hours during busy periods; **Holiday Closings:** None; **Visitor attractions closed for seasons:**None; **Weather:** Winter is nippy in the mountains and comfortably warm during the day in the lowlands. Once or twice a year snow falls in the mountains. Spring weather arrives early. Midsummer temperatures in desert and river valley are likely to hover above 100° during the day. This is the best time to go to the mountains. In the Basin (5400-foot elevation), daytime temperatures average a comfortable 85°F, and nights are cool. Autumn is usually warm.

GENERAL INFORMATION: Be sure to obtain a pamphlet describing regulations and precautions, available at Headquarters. Carry your own first-aid supplies, including tweezers to extract cactus spines. Carry drinking water on the trail and in the desert. Check with a Park Ranger before travelling on any of the primitive roads. Wear stout shoes and tough clothing while you are hiking. Stay on the trails.

Big Thicket National Preserve
Beaumont, Texas

MAILING ADDRESS: Superintendent, Big Thicket National Preserve, P.O. Box 7408, Beaumont, Texas 77706 **Telephone:** 713-838-0271

DIRECTIONS: The Preserve is located in southeastern Texas. The twelve separate units are bounded by US 96 on the East, US 90 on the South, US 59 on the West and US 90 on the North. Write or call in advance for a map of the area and information on facilities and activities in each area. The Preserve's temporary headquarters is at 6725 Eastex Freeway, Beaumont, in the Rosedale Shopping Mall near Hwy 105. A small Visitor Station is in the southern end of the Turkey Creek Unit, on FM 420, 4 km (2½ miles) off the Hwy 69.

The Preserve contains 84,550 acres composed of 12 units of various sizes spread over 50 miles square. It is an area of great plant diversity caused by the convergence of several major plant communities from the North, South, and West. The area has potential for a variety of recreational activities. Established by act of Congress on Oct. 11, 1974.

VISITOR ACTIVITIES: Because land acquisition is incomplete, only a few visitor facilities exist within the Preserve. There are two hiking trails in the Turkey Creek Unit. There is also river access for boats and canoes at several points along the Pine Island Bayou and Neches River. A variety of facilities are outside the Preserve. Martin Dies Jr. State Recreation Park located on the B.A. Steinhagen Reservoir includes 3 separate units and provides for boating, camping, fishing, swimming, hiking, and nature study. John K. Kirby State Forest has picnic grounds, a self-guiding nature trail, varied shrubs and many wildflowers. Kirby Nature Trail, in the southern portion of the Turkey Creek Unit contains insect, flower and fungi specimens and takes about 1½ hours to walk. The Roy E. Larson Sandyland Sanctuary protects some of the best examples of Arid Sandy-lands found throughout the Thicket region. It is not yet open to the public, but special tours may be arranged by contacting Caretaker, Roy E. Larson Sandyland Sanctuary, P.O. Box 909, Silsbee, TX 77656. Big Thicket Museum in Saratoga has a slide show and exhibits on the natural and cultural history of the area (closed Mondays). Big Thicket Campground is a private resort campground near Romayor, and has both primitive and developed campsites. The East Texas Indian Reservation has auto tours, a campground, and visitor complex where demonstrations of Indian skills are performed (open seasonally). Woodville has museums and gardens. B.A. Steinhagen Lake area is managed by the Corps of Engineers and has boating, swimming, fishing, and improved campgrounds. The Turkey Creek Trail extends 15 km (9.2 miles) south from road FM 1943 to the unnumbered road that transects the unit. Bring plenty of your own water if you hike this trail; **Permits:** a Texas fishing license, available locally, is required; **Fees:** No; **Visitor facilities:** Facilities are very limited at this time. Hiking trails are available; **Any limitations on vehicle usage:** Vehicles must stay on public roads; **Hiking trails:** Yes, Turkey Creek Unit has a 14.5 (9 mile) trail plus 4 km (2½ miles) loop nature trail; **Backcountry:** Yes, write the Superintendent for information; **Camping:** No; **Other overnight accom-**

modations on site: No; **Meals served in the park:** No; **Food and supplies obtainable in the park:** No; **Food and supplies obtainable nearby:** Yes, at Beaumont, Kountze, Woodville, Silsbee; **Overnight accommodations:** Beaumont, Woodville, Kountze, Silsbee; **First Aid available in park:** No; **Nearest Hospital:** Beaumont, Kountze, Woodville, Silsbee; **Days/Hours:** 24 hours a day, 365 days a year; **Holiday Closings:** No; **Visitor attractions closed for seasons:** No; **Weather:** Summers are hot and humid; Winters are cold and wet.

GENERAL INFORMATION: Additional facilities will be made available as time and money permit. One can expect changes soon. *For Your Safety*—Wear clothing suitable for weather extremes if you hike. To avoid becoming disoriented in the woods, especially on cloudy days, carry a good compass, a map, and stay on the established trails. If you canoe or boat, wear a life jacket, take a partner and a first aid kit, let someone know where you are going and don't overload the boat. Always leave wildlife alone. Beware of snakes. Watch out for poison ivy, bees, wasps, hornets, chiggers, mosquitoes, and fire ants, which are all prevalent. Use plenty of repellent and watch where you sit or stand.

Pets must be on a leash or otherwise restrained at all times. Plants and animals must not be disturbed. All of the lands adjoining the Preserve units are in private ownership. If in doubt, don't trespass.

Chamizal National Memorial
El Paso, Texas

MAILING ADDRESS: Superintendent, Chamizal National Memorial, Room 620, First City National Bank Building, 300 East Main Drive, El Paso, Texas 79901 **Telephone:** 915-543-7780

DIRECTIONS: The Memorial is in south-central metropolitan El Paso immediately adjacent to the international boundary. Entrances to the park are from San Marcial Street and Delta Drive.

The peaceful settlement of a 100-year boundary dispute between the United States and Mexico is commemorated here. The Chamizal Treaty ending the dispute was signed in 1963. An amphitheater and 502-seat auditorium are used by theatrical groups from both nations. Authorized for addition to the National Park System on June 30, 1966.

VISITOR ACTIVITIES: biking, picnicking, interpretive exhibits and film, guided tours, theatrical performances, Border Folk Festival the first weekend in October, Arts festival the week of July 4, Spanish Drama Festival in March; **Permits:** No; **Fees:** No entrance fee is charged, but tickets are sold for some special theatrical performances; **Visitor facilities:** parking and picnic areas, auditorium, restrooms; **Any limitations on vehicle usage:** No; **Hiking trails:** No; **Backcountry:** No; **Camping:** No; **Other overnight accommodations on site:** No; **Meals served in the park:** No; **Food and supplies obtainable in the park:** No; **Food and supplies obtainable nearby:** Yes, downtown El Paso, south of the park; **Overnight accommodations:** El Paso; **First Aid available in park:** Yes; **Nearest Hospital:** El Paso, North Stanton, 4.8 km (3 miles); **Days/Hours:** 8 a.m. to 5 p.m. year-round; **Holiday Closings:** None; **Visitor attractions closed for seasons:** No.

GENERAL INFORMATION: Directly across the Rio Grande, the Republic of the United Mexican States has established a companion park on a portion of Mexico's Chamizal land. You are encouraged to visit the park, which includes formal gardens, outstanding architectural structures, and statuary.

Fort Davis National Historic Site
Fort Davis, Texas

MAILING ADDRESS: Superintendent, Fort Davis National Historic Site, P.O. Box 1456, Fort Davis, Texas 79734 **Telephone:** 915-426-3225

DIRECTIONS: The Site is on the northern edge of the town of Fort Davis, TX. It can be reached from US 290 on the north and 90 on the south by TX 17 and 18. Marfa is 33.8 km (21 miles) to the southeast.

A key post in the West Texas defensive system, the fort guarded emigrants on the San Antonio-El Paso road from 1854 to 1891. Authorized for addition to the National Park System on Sept. 8, 1961.

VISITOR ACTIVITIES: tours of the barracks, warehouses, residences, and the hospital; picnicking, interpretive exhibits, audiovisual programs, hiking; **Permits:** Yes, obtainable at a Visitor Center; **Fees:** Entrance fee is $1 per carload or 50¢ per person. Golden Age and Golden Eagle Passports are accepted and available. No charge for groups from educational institutions; **Visitor facilities:** parking, restrooms at Visitor Center, hiking trails; **Any limitations on vehicle usage:** No driving tours in the park. Electric golf cart is available for handicapped persons only; **Hiking trails:** Yes, 4.8 km (3 miles) of moderately strenuous hiking trails; **Backcountry:** No; **Camping:** No; **Other overnight accommodations on site:** No; **Meals served in the park:** No, but there are several restaurants in the the Fort Davis area; **Food and supplies obtainable in the park:** No; **Food and supplies obtainable nearby:** Yes, in the Fort Davis area and at "Indian Lodge" in the Davis Mountain State Park, 6.4 km (4 miles) west on TX 118; **Overnight accommodations:** In Fort Davis and at nearby Davis Mountain State Park. The telephone number for reservations is 915-426-3254; **First Aid available in park:** Yes. and at firehouse (rescue squad); **Nearest Hospital:** Alpine, TX, 41 km (26 miles); **Days/Hours:** Open daily from 8 a.m. to 5 p.m., until 6 p.m. in Summer; **Holiday Closings:** Dec 25; **Visitor attractions closed for seasons:** Living history programs offered only in Summer; **Weather:** Average annual temperature is 63°, Summer 60° - 90°, Winter, 20° - 60°.

GENERAL INFORMATION: The Fort is a good stopover while traveling to Carlsbad Caverns National Park from Big Bend National Park (see listings in this book).

Guadalupe Mountains National Park
Texas

MAILING ADDRESS: Superintendent, Guadalupe Mountains National Park, 3225 National Parks Hwy, Carlsbad, New Mexico 88220 **Telephone:** 915-828-3385

DIRECTIONS: The Park is in western Texas, on Hwy 62-180 88.5 km (55 miles) southwest of Carlsbad, NM, and 177 km (110 miles) east of El Paso, TX. Van Horn, TX, is 105 km (65 miles) south on Hwy 54. Stop first at Frijole Information Station, on Hwy 62-180.

Rising from the desert, this mountain mass contains portions of the world's most extensive and significant Permian limestone fossil reef. Also featured are a tremendous earth fault, lofty peaks, unusual flora and fauna, and a colorful record of the past. Authorized for addition to the National Park System on Oct. 15, 1966.

VISITOR ACTIVITIES: Mainly hiking and backpacking. Camping available in a drive-in campground. Horseback riding (bring your own horse), guided tours, and evening programs in Summer; **Permits:** for overnight backcountry trips; obtained at Frijole Information Station; **Fees:** No; **Visitor facilities:** Facilities are limited until development is completed. Frijole Information Station provides literature for sale, information, restrooms, and water. Pine Springs Campground, a primitive vehicle campground, offers chemical toilets, picnic tables, and charcoal grills; no fees, no permit required, located 1½ mile west of Frijole Information Station. Very limited road access throughout park. Picnic area at McKittrick Canyon parking lot; **Any limitations on vehicle usage:** Existing roads are limited: approx. 4.8 km (3 miles) of Hwy 62-180 travels through the Park, an 8 km (5 mile) newly paved road provides access from Hwy 62-180 to the mouth of McKittrick Canyon, and a 13 km (7 miles) 4-wheel drive road to Williams Ranch Historic Site requires permission to travel and a key to a locked gate (obtained at Information Station). No off-road vehicle use. no vehicles allowed on foot trails. A gravel road into Dog Canyon (northern side of the Park) is expected to open in the near future; **Hiking trails:** Yes, over 97 km (60 miles) of hiking trails, in rugged mountainous terrain. Trails are primitive and rough; **Backcountry:** Yes, contact Information Station. Hikers must sign in and out at trail registers and obtain permits before starting overnight hikes. Hikers must carry all water. Topographic maps are for sale at Information Station; **Camping:** Yes, primitive vehicle campground at Pine Springs; designated backcountry campsites, all on a first-come, first-served basis. No overnight lodging available in or near the park; **Other overnight accommodations on site:** No; **Meals served in the park:** No; **Food and supplies obtainable in the park:** No; **Food and supplies obtainable nearby:** Yes, Nearest food service: Carlsbad, NM and El Paso, Van Horn, and Dell City, TX; **Overnight accommodations:** Carlsbad, NM, US 62-180 88.5 km (55 miles); Van Horn, TX, 105 km (65 miles) and El Paso, TX, US 62-180, 177 km (110 miles); **First Aid available in park:** limited; **Nearest Hospital:** Carlsbad, NM, US 62-180 88.5 km (55 miles); **Days/Hours:** Frijole Information Station open daily (including holidays and weekends) 8 a.m. to 4:30 p.m. (MST). Campground open daily. McKittrick Canyon hiking area open only during daylight hours, gate closes at night; **Holiday Closings:** No; **Visitor attractions closed for seasons:**Visitor use areas open every day of the year except during occasional emergency situations caused by bad weather conditions or fire danger; **Weather:** Anticipate storms and sudden weather changes. Electrical thunderstorms are common in Summer; freezing rain and occasional snowstorms in Winter. Violent winds in Spring and Winter. Summer temperatures are extreme and winter temperatures usually mild but can suddenly drop to lows below freezing. Potential backpackers can call Frijole Information Station, 915-828-3385, for current weather conditions and forecasts.

GENERAL INFORMATION: *Safety Precautions:* Check with Park Ranger before hiking. Do not climb cliffs; rocks are unstable and considered unsuitable for technical climbing. Beware of cactus and spiny plants. Watch for and respect rattlesnakes during warmer months of the year. If planning a hike or backpack trip, come prepared; sturdy broken-in boots, a tent, tough clothing, cold weather gear in Winter, water repellent clothing for Winter and Summer and capability to carry all your own water (one gallon per person per day is recommended).

Important regulations: Before bringing your pet, remember pets are not allowed on hiking trails and extreme heat in Summer or extreme lows in Winter make leaving your pet in a vehicle uncomfortable and potentially dangerous for the animal. Entry into caves is not permitted without written permission from the Superintendent. The display or use of firearms is prohibited.

Lake Meredith National Recreation Area
Fritch, Texas

MAILING ADDRESS: Superintendent, Lake Meredith National Recreation Area, P.O.

Box 1438, Fritch, Texas 79036 **Telephone:** 806-857-3151

DIRECTIONS: The Park Headquarters building is on Hwy 136 in Fritch. Information about facilities at the various recreation sites is available here.

Man-made Lake Meredith on the Canadian River is a popular water-activity center in the Southwest. On the south side of the lake, Alibates Flint Quarries National Monument can be seen by free guided tours in Summer and by prior appointment at other times of the year. See Alibates listing in this book. Lake Meredith established by act of Congress on Mar. 15, 1965.

VISITOR ACTIVITIES: boating, water skiing, canoeing, fishing, picnicking, swimming, camping, hunting, scuba diving, sailing, motorcycling, interpretive exhibits; **Permits:** Texas hunting and fishing licenses available from Texas Parks and Wildlife Department or at local sporting goods stores; **Fees:** No entrance or camping fees; **Visitor facilities:** marinas, restrooms, drinking water, beaches, launching ramps, picnic and camping areas, snack bar, restaurant; **Any limitations on vehicle usage:** Boats are subject to Federal and State regulations; **Hiking trails:** No; **Backcountry:** Yes, topographic maps and information available from Park Headquarters; **Camping:** Yes, no reservations available for campsites. Campers may stay up to 14 days. No camping is allowed in the launching areas or parking lots. Private campgrounds with hookups are located in nearby towns; **Other overnight accommodations on site:** No; **Meals served in the park:** Yes, snacks available at Sanford-Yake marina; **Food and supplies obtainable in the park:** Yes, limited picnic supplies at Sanford-Yake marina; **Food and supplies obtainable nearby:** Yes, in Fritch, Sanford, Borger, Amarillo, Dumas; **Overnight accommodations:** Fritch, Sanford, Borger, Amarillo, Dumas; **First Aid available in park:** No; **Nearest Hospitals:** Borger, Hwy 136, 24 km (15 miles); Dumas, Hwy 13-19 to 19-13 to 152, 32 km (20 miles); Amarillo, Hwy 136, 40-72 km (25-45 miles); **Days/Hours:** Park never closes; **Holiday Closings:** None; **Visitor attractions closed for seasons:**Activities are curtailed and many areas closed due to inclement weather in Winter; **Weather:** Summers are hot, with temperatures above 100°F on some days. Winters are cold; high winds in Spring.

GENERAL INFORMATION: Boaters should be familiar with Federal and State boating regulations, which can be obtained from Park Rangers or from Lake Meredith Headquarters. Listen for storm warnings! A sudden storm wind can reach 130 km per hour (80 mph) so fast that boats may have trouble geting off the lake. The storm warning signal is a prolonged warbling siren from any National Park Service patrol vessel. Get your boat to shore in a sheltered area and wait out the storm if ramps cannot be reached safely. Sometimes the warning cannot be sounded before sudden storms.

Lyndon B. Johnson National Historic Site
Johnson City, and Stonewall, TX Texas

MAILING ADDRESS: Superintendent, Lyndon B. Johnson National Historic Site, P.O. Box 329, Johnson City, Texas 78636 **Telephone:** 512-868-7128

DIRECTIONS: There are two small park units, one in Johnson City and one in Stonewall. Johnson City and Stonewall are about 80 km (50 miles) west of Austin and 97 km (60 miles) north of San Antonio. Both are located on US 290, an east-west highway connecting Austin and Fredericksburg. North-South US 281 connects San Antonio and Wichita Falls. In Johnson City, stop first at the Visitor Center on the west side of town. In Stonewall, begin your visit at the Visitor Center of the LBJ State Historical Park.

The Site includes the birthplace, boyhood home, and ranch of the 36th President of the United States. Authorized for addition to the National Park System on Dec. 2, 1969.

VISITOR ACTIVITIES: Johnson City: Visitor Center has guided tours of the boyhood home and the ranch of his grandparents, living history programs at the latter. Stonewall: free tour buses to Johnson's school, birthplace, family cemetery, gravesite, and the LBJ Ranch. All bus tours are 90 minutes long; **Permits:** No; **Fees:** No; **Visitor facilities:** restrooms, interpretive activities. A full range of facilities is available in the surrounding area; **Any limitations on vehicle usage:** Access to the LBJ Ranch is by tour bus only. Access to the Johnson Settlement is by wagon or ¼ mile on foot; **Hiking trails:** No; **Backcountry:** No; **Camping:** No, but camping is available in Lady Bird Johnson Municipal Park in Fredericksburg, Pedernales Falls State Park, and Blanco State Park. There are a number of other state and commercial facilities in the immediate area. Contact the Site for further information; **Other overnight accommodations on site:** No; **Meals served in the park:** No; **Food and supplies obtainable in the park:** No; **Food and supplies obtainable nearby:** Yes, in Johnson City and Stonewall, TX; **Overnight accommodations:** Johnson City, Stonewall, Blanco, and Fredericksburg; **First Aid available in park:** Yes; **Nearest Hospital:** Johnson City, 27.4 km (17 miles) from LBJ Ranch; Fredericksburg, 48 km (30 miles) west of Johnson City or 27.4 km (17 miles) west of LBJ Ranch; **Days/Hours:** Johnson City: 9 a.m. to 5 p.m. every day, Visitor Center and wagon operation only offered on weekends in Winter. Stonewall: By tour bus only, 10 a.m. to 4:30 p.m. daily; **Holiday Closings:** Dec. 25; **Visitor attractions closed for seasons:** No; **Weather:** Moderate weather. Summer temperatures are in the mid to upper 90°sF but there is usually a light breeze. Winters average about 40°F with occasional showers. There is very little snow; rain occasionally freezes on the roads.

GENERAL INFORMATION: Advance reservations are required for assured group tours. Groups arriving without reservations may experience long delays prior to being accommodated. Arrangements may be made by calling 512-644-2241.

Padre Island National Seashore
Corpus Christi, Texas

MAILING ADDRESS: Superintendent, Padre Island National Seashore, Corpus Christi, Texas 78418 **Telephone:** 512-937-2621

DIRECTIONS: The only access to the National Seashore is from the North end. There are two approaches: The first leads over a causeway from Corpus Christi to Nueces County Park, the other leads from Port Aransas down Mustang Island via Park Road 53. The Visitor Center is approximately 16 km (10 miles) south of the junction of Park Roads 53 and 22.
   Noted for its wide sand beaches, excellent fishing, and abundant bird and marine life, this barrier island stretches along the Gulf Coast for 129.5 km (80.5 miles). Authorized for addition to the National Park System on Sept. 28, 1962.

VISITOR ACTIVITIES: beach driving, fishing, swimming, surfing, snorkeling, scuba- and skin-diving, bird- and wildlife-watching, hiking, shelling, water-skiing, interpretive exhibits and programs, charter bay fishing trips; **Permits:** Texas State fishing license required for those between 17 and 65 years of age; **Fees:** $2 camping fee ($1 with Golden Age Passports) at Malaquite Beach Campground; **Visitor facilities:** snack bar, gift shop, free showers, locker rooms, rental equipment, nature trails; **Any limitations on vehicle usage:** Vehicles must remain on the roads and the beach. Driving on the beach in front of the campground is prohibited; **Hiking trails:** Yes, self-guiding nature trail. You are free to hike over the entire island except in areas fenced off; **Backcountry:** No; **Camping:** Yes, no reservations available for campsites; **Other overnight accommodations on site:** No, a paved campground with 140 sites, located south of the Ranger Station on the beach, can be used by trailers and recreational vehicles. Hookups are not provided. These facilities are available at the trailer park in Nueces County Park north of the National Seashore boundary and at the trailer park maintained in the Cameron County Park at the south end of the island near Fort Isabel. For information on camping rates and facilities, write: Nueces County Parks, 10901 S. Padre Island Drive, Corpus Christi, TX 78418 or Cameron County Parks, Box 666, Port Isabel, TX 78578; **Meals served in the park:** Yes, at both ends of the island, at Malaquite Beach and in Corpus Christi; **Food and supplies obtainable in the park:** No; **Food and supplies obtainable nearby:** Yes, Port Isabel, Corpus Christi and about 25 km (16 miles) north of the seashore boundary on the Park Road 22; **Overnight accommodations:** Port Isabel, Corpus Christi and South Padre Island; **First Aid available in park:** Yes, year-round at Gulf District Ranger Station; **Nearest Hospital:** Take crosstown freeway to Morgan Exit-Memorial Medical Center has emergency services; **Days/Hours:** Park always open; **Holiday Closings:** Visitor Center closed Dec. 25; **Visitor attractions closed for seasons:**No; **Weather:** Summer is usually quite humid, hot and windy. Late Fall is temperate and mild. Late Winter has many northers; cold and rainy Spring.

GENERAL INFORMATION: *Beware of the following hazards*—overexposure to the sun, swimming alone, rattlesnakes, Portuguese man-of-war, jellyfish, small stingrays, fishing lines, broken glass and boards with nails, getting your car stuck in the sand, vehicle traffic on the beach, and anything that looks like a bomb or gun shell. Always wear shoes when hiking. Phone 512-933-8175 for a recorded informational message on park activities.

Palo Alto Battlefield National Historic Site
Brownsville, Texas

MAILING ADDRESS: Palo Alto Battlefield National Historic Site, P.O. Box 191, Brownsville, Texas 78520 **Telephone:** 512-542-6770

DIRECTIONS: NOT YET OPEN TO THE PUBLIC
This area preserves and commemorates the site of one of two Mexican war battles fought on U.S. soil. Authorized for addition to the National Park Service on Nov. 10, 1978.

Rio Grande Wild and Scenic River
Texas

MAILING ADDRESS: Superintendent, Big Bend National Park, Big Bend National Park, Texas 79834 **Telephone:** 915-477-2251

DIRECTIONS: NO LANDS HAVE BEEN ACQUIRED AS YET.
The area preserves a 307 km (191-mile) segment of Rio Grande from above Mariscal Canyon to Mile 651, averaging not more than 160 acres per mile. Authorized for addition to the National Park System on Nov. 10, 1978.

San Antonio Missions National Historical Park
San Antonio, Texas

MAILING ADDRESS: Southwest Regional Office, National Park System, P.O. Box 728, Santa Fe, New Mexico 87501 **Telephone:** 505-988-6375

DIRECTIONS: You should begin your visit at the Alamo Visitor Center which has information on the missions.

The Park preserves Concepcion, San Jose, San Juan, and Espada Missions which represent, with the Alamo, the country's greatest concentration of Spanish missions. The area also preserves Espada's 18th Century dam, aqueduct and irrigation system, which are still functioning. This affiliated area was authorized for addition to the National Park System on Nov. 10, 1978.

VISITOR ACTIVITIES: walking tours; **Permits:** No; **Fees:** $1 fee charged for admission to all four missions or $.50 for each visit. Ticket for all four missions sold at San Jose Mission; **Visitor facilities:** parking and restrooms; **Any limitations on vehicle usage:** None; **Hiking trails:** No; **Backcountry:** No; **Camping:** No; **Other overnight accommodations on site:** No; **Meals served in the park:** No; **Food and supplies obtainable in the park:** No; **Food and supplies obtainable nearby:** Yes, in San Antonio; **Overnight accommodations:** San Antonio; **First Aid available in park:** No; **Nearest Hospital:** San Antonio; **Days/Hours:** Open daily from 8 a.m. to 5 p.m.; **Holiday Closings:** No; **Visitor attractions closed for seasons:** None.

San Jose Mission National Historic Site
San Antonio, Texas

MAILING ADDRESS: Superintendent, San Jose Mission National Historic Site, 6539 San Jose Drive, San Antonio, Texas 78214 **Telephone:** 512-922-2731

DIRECTIONS: The Site can be reached by travelling south on Int. 37 from downtown San Antonio and exiting at SW Military Dr. Go west to Roosevelt Ave. and turn right. The Mission is on the right, 1 block north. From Int. 35, travel south from downtown to the Southcross Blvd. exit. Travel east on Southcross to Roosevelt Ave. intersection, turn right. Mission is three blocks south, on the left.

This is an outstanding example of the frontier missions that stretched across the Southwest in the 18th century. Designated June 1, 1941.

VISITOR ACTIVITIES: exhibits, group tours on request. Annual events include Los Pastores play in Jan., Harlendale Bilingual/Bicultural Event in May, July 4 celebration, and El Dia De Los Misiones in Aug.; **Permits:** No; **Fees:** Admission fee is 50¢ for adults children 6-12, 25¢; **Visitor facilities:** amphitheater, restrooms, gift shop, snack concession; **Any limitations on vehicle usage:** parking available, no vehicles permitted in the compound; **Hiking trails:** No; **Backcountry:** No; **Camping:** No; **Other overnight accommodations on site:** No; **Meals served in the park:** No; **Food and supplies obtainable in the park:** No; **Food and supplies obtainable nearby:** Yes, at San Antonio; **Overnight accommodations:** motels within 2 blocks, larger hotels and motels within 4.8 km (3 miles); **First Aid available in park:** Yes; **Nearest Hospital:** Robert B. Green Hospital, Int. 35, exit on Houston & Commerce; **Days/Hours:** 9 a.m. to 6 p.m.; until 8 p.m. in Summer; **Holiday Closings:** None; **Visitor attractions closed for seasons:** No; **Weather:** Summer is hot, humid, and sunny. Winter is cool and wet.

Utah

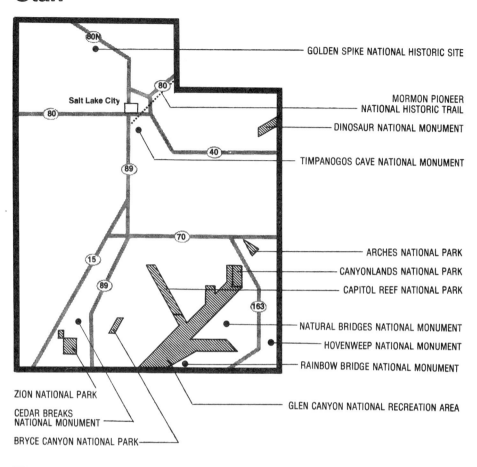

GOLDEN SPIKE NATIONAL HISTORIC SITE

MORMON PIONEER
NATIONAL HISTORIC TRAIL

DINOSAUR NATIONAL MONUMENT

TIMPANOGOS CAVE NATIONAL MONUMENT

ARCHES NATIONAL PARK

CANYONLANDS NATIONAL PARK

CAPITOL REEF NATIONAL PARK

NATURAL BRIDGES NATIONAL MONUMENT

HOVENWEEP NATIONAL MONUMENT

RAINBOW BRIDGE NATIONAL MONUMENT

GLEN CANYON NATIONAL RECREATION AREA

ZION NATIONAL PARK

CEDAR BREAKS
NATIONAL MONUMENT

BRYCE CANYON NATIONAL PARK

Arches National Park
Moab, Utah

MAILING ADDRESS: Superintendent, Canyonlands National Park, 446 S. Main Street, Moab, Utah 84532 **Telephone:** 801-259-7165

DIRECTIONS: The Visitor Center is 8 km (5 miles) northwest of Moab on US 163.
Extraordinary products of erosion in the form of a giant arches, windows, pinnacles, and pedestals change color constantly in the sunlight. Arches National Monument created by Presidential Proclamation on Apr. 12, 1929, designated Arches National Park in 1972.

VISITOR ACTIVITIES: interpretive exhibits, walks and talks, auto tours, wildlife-watching, picnicking, backcountry, camping; **Permits:** requested for backcountry use. They can be obtained from the Visitor Center or the Ranger in the field; **Fees:** $1 entrance fee, $3 camping fee. Golden Age and Golden Eagle Passports accepted and available;

Visitor Facilities: parking and restrooms at Visitor Center, foot trails, campground, picnic area, self-guiding trails; **Any limitations on vehicle usage:** Busses and other large vehicles are discouraged from going past Wolfe Ranch on the dirt road; **Hiking trails:** Yes, obtain brochures describing self-guiding walking tours at the Visitor Center; **Backcountry:** Yes, backcountry hikers should inform Park Rangers at the Visitor Center about trip plans; **Camping:** Yes; individual campsites cannot be reserved, but group sites are on a reservation system. Write the Park for reservations; **Other overnight accommodations on site:** No; **Meals served in the park:** No; **Food and supplies obtainable in the park:** No; **Food and supplies obtainable nearby:** Yes in Moab; **Overnight accommodations:** Moab, US 163, 8 km (5 miles); **First Aid available in park:** Yes; **Nearest Hospital:** Moab, US 163, 8km (5 miles); **Days/Hours:** Open 24 hours a day, 7 days a week year-round; **Holiday Closings:** Visitor Center closes Dec. 25; Park remains open; **Visitor attractions closed for seasons:** Restrooms in the campground closed in Winter; **Weather:** Spring and Fall are the best times to visit Arches. Winters are mild and Summers are very hot, with 110°F temperatures.

GENERAL INFORMATION: *For Your Safety*—You should carry plenty of water, because daytime termperatures here can reach 110°F. Always hike or climb in the company of others. Don't leave your car with children or pets locked inside—the heat of the direct sun can harm them. When hiking, stay on trails and, on sandstone especially, watch your footing. Watch for rattlesnakes and scorpions. Refrain from feeding the wildlife.

Bryce Canyon National Park
Bryce Canyon, Utah

MAILING ADDRESS: Superintendent, Bryce Canyon National Park, Bryce Canyon, Utah 84717 **Telephone:** 801-834-5322

DIRECTIONS: The Park is in southwestern Utah and within a one-day drive of other units of the National Park System. It is most easily reached from US 89 at Bryce Junction, 11.3 km (7 miles) south of Panguitch. Turn east at this junction and continue on UT 12 for 27.4 km (17 miles) to the park entrance. On the East, the Park is not connected by paved roads to state and Federal road systems.

In horseshoe-shaped amphitheaters along the edge of the Paunsagunt Plateau in Southern Utah stand innumerable highly colored and bizarre pinnacles, walls and spires, among the most colorful and unusual erosional forms in the world. Created by Presidential Proclamation on June 8, 1923.

VISITOR ACTIVITIES: Slide programs and exhibits at Visitor Center, guided walks, campfire talks, picnicking, wildlife-watching, hiking, horseback riding. Registration is required for winter activities, which include cross-country skiing, snowshoeing, overnight camping, and snowmobiling; **Permits:** Free permits for backcountry and winter activities available at Visitor Center; **Fees:** $2 per vehicle entrance fee; $2 per campsite per night;Golden Eagle and Golden Age Passports accepted and available;**Visitor Facilities:** parking and restrooms at Visitor Center, church services and interpretive programs, picnic areas, hiking trails, environmental day center for children, campgrounds; **Any limitations on vehicle usage:** Vehicles are restricted to established roads. Use designated pull-offs when stopping. Drive slowly at dusk to avoid colliding with deer crossing roads; **Hiking trails:** Yes, Walking is hardest on return trips—it's all uphill! Wear stout walking shoes. You may wish to carry water; **Backcountry:** Yes, information available by contacting the Visitor Center; **Camping:** Yes, no reservations for campsites, and space is limited. It is best to arrive early in the day to be assured of a campsite; **Other overnight accommodations on site:** Yes, Bryce Lodge, near the rim of Bryce Amphitheater, has food service and sleeping accommodations and is open from May to Oct. For reservations apply to T.W.A. Services, Inc., 4045 S. Spencer St., Suite A-43, Las Vegas, Nevada 89109, Telephone 702-733-2033;**Meals served in the park:** Yes, at Bryce Lodge, from May to Oct.; **Food and supplies obtainable in the park:** Yes, at a store near the Sunrise Point Parking Area; **Food and supplies obtainable nearby:** Yes, at stores and lodges near park entrance; **Overnight accommodations:** Lodging and food are provided outside the Park on a year-round basis at the Pines and Pink Cliffs Motels and from March to Dec. at Ruby's Inn; **First Aid available in park:** Yes, at Headquarters; **Nearest Hospital:** Panguitch, UT 12 to US 89, 42 km (26 miles); **Days/Hours:** Park is always open. Visitor Center open 7 days a week from 8 a.m. to 5 p.m.; until 7 p.m. in Summer; **Holiday Closings:** Visitor Center closed on Dec. 25 & Jan. 1; **Visitor attractions closed for seasons:** Four major viewpoints on the Short Tour from Sunset Point to Paria View are maintained during the Winter; **Weather:** From late Apr. through Oct., days are pleasant and nights are cool. In late July and Aug. thundershowers are fairly common. Winter lasts on the plateau from Nov. through Mar. with days that can be bright and crisp.

GENERAL INFORMATION: *For Your Safety* — Be aware that less oxygen is available to breathe at Bryce because of its altitude (8000 to 9000' above sea level). Therefore, heart patients and visitors with high blood pressure should not subject themselves to strenuous climbs. Keep your distance from park animals. Thunderstorms and lightning are frequent in late Summer. Avoid isolated trees and viewpoints during storms. Lightning frequently strikes objects along the plateau.

Canyonlands National Park
Moab, Utah

MAILING ADDRESS: Superintendent, Canyonlands National Park, 446 South Main Street, Moab, Utah 84532 **Telephone** 801-259-7165

DIRECTIONS: The Park is 56 km (35 miles) southwest of Moab. The Needles area is on UT 211, 56 km (35 miles) west of US 163. Island in the Sky is on UT 313, 48 km (30 miles) southwest of US 163. Maze area is 72 km (45 miles) east of UT 24 via dirt road. The Visitor Center is at Arches National Park (see listing in this book).

The geological area includes rocks, spires, and mesas that rise more than 2377m (7800 feet) & petroglyphs left by Indians about 1000 years ago. Established by act of Congress on Sept. 12, 1964.

VISITOR ACTIVITIES: picnicking, camping, boating, rafting, backcountry, auto and guided tours, interpretive exhibits, hiking, swimming, horseback riding, fishing, bird-watching. Concession-operated jeep tours and jeep rentals available nearby; **Permits:** for backcountry and float trips can be obtained from any Ranger; **Fees:** $1 per auto entrance fee, collected from Easter through Oct. Golden Age and Golden Eagle Passports available and accepted. Campground fee for The Needles Area is $2 per night (collected only in Summer); **Visitor facilities:** restrooms, picnic areas, campgrounds, hiking trails. No services of any kind are available. Be certain you have ample gas, water, tools, emergency supplies, etc; **Any limitations on vehicle usage:** All vehicles must stay on established roads and four-wheel-drive routes. Trail bikes must be licensed, muffled, and operated by a licensed driver; **Hiking trails:** Yes, check with a Ranger for information on the many miles of hiking trails; **Backcountry:** Yes, information can be obtained from a Park Ranger. You must provide your own water for backcountry trips; **Camping:** Yes, no reservations for individual campsites. Campers should bring their own fuel. For group site reservations, telephone 801-259-7167; **Other overnight accommodations on site:** No; **Meals served in the Park:** No, but snacks are available at the Canyonlands Resort; **Food and supplies obtainable in the park:** No; **Food and supplies obtainable nearby:** Yes, in Monticello, Moab, Green River, Hanksfield, Canyonlands Resort; **Overnight accommodations:** Monticello, US 163, 144.8 km (90 miles); Moab, US 163, 56 km (35 miles); Green River, I-70 to 163, 96.6 km (60 miles); **First Aid available in park:** Yes; **Nearest Hospital:** Moab, Hwy 163, 56 km (35 miles); **Days/Hours:** Park Headquarters is open from 8 a.m. to 5 p.m., until 6 p.m. in Summer. The Park is open year-round; **Holiday Closings:** No; **Visitor attractions closed for seasons:** No; **Weather:** This is desert country; Winter is usually short, with little snow. Spring and Autumn are long and pleasant, except for the high winds accompanied by sand or dust storms that are common in Spring.

GENERAL INFORMATION: Piped water is available near Squaw Flat Campground in The Needles area, but nowhere else in the park.

Capitol Reef National Park
Torrey, Utah

MAILING ADDRESS: Superintendent, Capitol Reef National Park, Torrey, Utah 84775; **Telephone:** 801-425-3871

DIRECTIONS: The Visitor Center is 19 km (12 miles) east of Torrey on UT 24.
Narrow high-walled gorges cut through a 1.6 km (1 mile) uplift of sandstone cliffs with highly colored sedimentary formations. Dome-shaped white cap-rock along the Fremont River accounts for the name. Created by Presidential Proclamation on Aug. 2 1937.

VISITOR ACTIVITIES: auto tours, horseback riding, interpretive exhibits, camping, picnicing, naturalist programs, hiking, backcountry; **Permits:** for backcountry available from Park Ranger or Visitor Center; **Fees:** $2 camping fee per vehicle per night, except at Cedar Mesa, where there is no charge for camping; **Visitor facilities:** scenic drive, campgrounds, picnic areas, hiking trails, drinking water; **Any limitations on vehicle usage:** Vehicles are restricted to main roads; **Hiking trails:** Yes, trails vary in length and difficulty; **Backcountry:** Yes, information is available from Visitor Center or by contacting the Superintendent; **Camping:** Yes, no reservations available for individual campsites. Group sites can be reserved in advance by writing the Superintendent. A complete list of accommodations and services is available at the Visitor Center; **Other overnight accommodations on site:** No; **Meals served in the park:** No; **Food and supplies obtainable in the park:** No; **Food and supplies obtainable nearby:** Yes, Torrey, Bichnell, Loa, Hanksville; **Overnight accommodations:** in communities west of the Park and at Hanksville to the east; **First Aid available in park:** Yes; **Nearest Hospital:** Richfield, Utah 24 to 119 to 89, 116 km (72 miles); **Days/Hours:** Park open 24 hours a day year-round; Visitor Center hours vary with the seasons; **Holiday Closings:** closed Thanksgiving, Dec. 25, and Jan 1; **Visitor attractions closed for seasons:**Weather conditions occasionally prohibit access to areas served by dirt and gravel roads; **Weather:** The elevation and desert climate make the area prone to temperature extremes. June and July are the hottest months, with midday temperatures in the upper 30°sC (90°sF) common. Summer evenings cool to the 10°-15°C (50°-60°F) range. Thunderstorms can bring flash floods from July through Sept. Spring and Fall are mild, with warm days and cool nights. Winter daytime temperatures average below 10°C (50°F), dropping below freezing at night. Bitter cold comes occasionally during the Winter, but snowfall is usually light. The average annual precipitation is less than 18 cm (7 inches) with low relative humidity.

GENERAL INFORMATION: *For Your Safety*—Be sure to carry water with you even on short hikes. Most water in Capitol Reef is contaminated with minerals or by animals. Keep pets under physical restraint.

Cedar Breaks National Monument
Cedar City, Utah

MAILING ADDRESS: Superintendent, Cedar Breaks National Monument, P.O. Box 749,Cedar City, Utah 84720: **Telephone:** 801-586-9451

DIRECTIONS: The Monument is reached via UT 14, 43.5 km (27 miles) from US 89 at Long Valley Junction, and 37 km (23 miles) from Int. 15 at Cedar City via UT 14. It can also be reached via UT 143, 22.5 km (14 miles) from Parowan. The Visitor Center is on the rim, 1.6 km (1 mile) from the south entrance.
A huge natural amphitheater has eroded into the variegated Pink Cliffs (Wasatch Formation), which are 607 m (2000 feet) thick at this point. Created by Presidential Proclamation on Aug. 23, 1933.

VISITOR ACTIVITIES: camping, picnicking, interpretive talks, snowmobiling, wild-flower-watching; **Permits:** No; **Fees:** Campground fee is $2 per night; **Visitor facilities:** restrooms at Visitor Center, campground; **Any limitations on vehicle usage:** Drive only on established roads. Do not drive on meadows; **Hiking trails:** Yes, trails vary in length and difficulty. Amphitheater is largely inaccessible; **Backcountry:** No; **Camping:** Yes, no reservations available for campgrounds. One organized group campsite is available for 20-25 persons. Reservation is through the Superintendent's office; **Other overnight accommodations on site:** No; **Meals served in the park:** No; **Food and supplies obtainable in the park:** No; **Food and supplies obtainable nearby:** Yes, in Cedar City, Parowan, Panguitch; **Overnight accommodations:** Cedar City, Parowan, Panguitch or Brian Head; **First Aid available in park:** Yes; **Nearest Hospital:** Cedar City via UT 143-UT 14, 37 km (23 miles); **Days/Hours:** Visitor Center is open 8 a.m. to 6 p.m. from Memorial Day through late Sept.; road open mid-May through Fall depending on the weather; **Holiday Closings:** None in season; **Visitor attractions closed for seasons:**The travel season extends from early June to late October, depending on the weather. At other times, check road conditions before driving to the Monument; **Weather:** usually permits comfortable camping from late June to Labor Day; at other times, freezing temperatures are common at night.

GENERAL INFORMATION: Nearby points of interest include Zion National Park, 127 km (79 miles) away via Cedar City and Int. 15, or 117.5 km (73 miles) via Long Valley Junction and US 89; and Bryce Canyon National Park, 105 km (65 miles) away (see listing in this book).

Dinosaur National Monument
For details see listing in Colorado

Glen Canyon National Recreation Area
For details see listing in Arizona

Golden Spike National Historic Site
Brigham City, Utah

MAILING ADDRESS: Superintendent, Golden Spike National Historic Site, P.O. Box 394 Brigham City, Utah 94302; **Telephone:** 801-471-2209

DIRECTIONS: The Site is about 48 km (30 miles) west of Brigham City. To reach the Site, drive 37 km (23 miles) westward on UT 83 to the Promontory Junction; turn left and go 3.2 km (2 miles) to the next junction; then turn right and go 8 km (5 miles). Roads are well-marked.

Completion of the first transcontinental railroad in the United States was celebrated here when the Central Pacific and Union Pacific Railroads met in 1869. Designated Apr. 2, 1957.

VISITOR ACTIVITIES: interpretive exhibits, audio-visual programs, picnicking, living history program in Summer, steam locomotive displays; **Permits:** No; **Fees:** No; **Visitor facilities:** Visitor Center, parking, restrooms, picnic area; **Any limitations on vehicle usage:** Drive only on established roads; **Hiking trails:** Yes, trails follow the historic roads; **Backcountry:** No; **Camping:** No; **Other overnight accommodations on site:** No; **Meals served in the park:** No, only cold drinks are available; **Food and supplies obtainable in the park:** No; **Food and supplies obtainable nearby:** Yes, Brigham City or Tremonton, UT; **Overnight accommodations:** Brigham City, UT 83, 48 km (30 miles) east on UT 83, or Tremonton, 48 km (30 miles) northeast on UT 83 and 102; **First Aid available in park:** Yes; **Nearest Hospital:** Brigham City, UT 83, 48 km (30 miles east; **Days/Hours:** Open daily from 8 a.m. to 4:30 p.m., until 8 p.m. in Summer; **Holiday Closings:** Dec. 25; **Visitor attractions closed for seasons:** Self-guided auto tours are not available in Winter.

Hovenweep National Monument
For details see listing in Colorado

Mormon Pioneer Trail
For details see listing in Illinois

Natural Bridges National Monument
(near) Blanding, Utah

MAILING ADDRESS: Superintendent, Natural Bridges National Monument c/o Canyonlands National Park, 446 S. Main Street, Moab, Utah 84532 **Telephone:** 801-259-0290

DIRECTIONS: The Visitor Center is 193 km (120 miles) south of Moab on US 163 and State 95 from Blanding, Utah. It is 41 km (26 miles) east of Fry Canyon on Utah 95 and 71 km (44 miles) north of Mexican Hat on Route 261.

Three natural bridges carved out of sandstone are protected here. The highest is 67 m (220 feet) above the streambed, with a span of 268 feet. Created by Presidential Proclamation on April 16, 1908.

VISITOR ACTIVITIES: interpretive exhibits, camping, picnicking, auto tours, hiking; **Permits:** No; **Fees:** $1 per vehicle entrance fee, Golden Eagle and Golden Age Passports accepted and available; **Visitor Facilities:** Visitor Center, campground, picnic area, parking lot, loop road; **Any limitations on vehicle usage:** No; **Hiking trails:** Yes, dirt trails lead to the three bridges. Short trails go to viewpoints at each bridge; **Backcountry:** No; **Camping:** Yes, no reservations available for the 13 campsites; **Other overnight accommodations on site:** No; **Meals served in the park:** No; **Food and supplies obtainable in the park:** No; **Food and supplies obtainable nearby:** Yes, Fry Canyon and Blanding; **Overnight accommodations:** Yes, Blanding, US 163 and State 95, 67.6 km (42 miles); Mexican Hat, Route 261, 71 km (44 miles); **First Aid available in park;** Yes, or nearby in Blanding, US 163; **Nearest Hospital:** Monticello, US 163, 103 km (64 miles) from the park; **Days/Hours:** Visitor Center is open 8 a.m. to 4:30 p.m.; from May 30-Oct. 15 until 6:30 p.m.; **Holiday Closings:** Thanksgiving, Dec. 25 & Jan. 1; **Visitor attractions closed for seasons:** Hiking trails into the canyons are closed in Winter due to snow and ice; **Weather:** best from late April through October.

GENERAL INFORMATION: Visitors can see other points of interest in the area. They include Canyonlands and Arches National Parks (see listings in this book), Lake Powell and Monument Valley. *Warning:* there is hazardous terrain throughout the area; lightning may strike overlooks and viewpoints during storms. Do not enter any ruins you may come across. If these or artifacts are disturbed in any way, a priceless archaeological story could be destroyed forever. The nearest source of gasoline is Fry Canyon, 41 km (26 miles) away.

Rainbow Bridge National Monument
Utah

MAILING ADDRESS: Superintendent, Rainbow Bridge National Monument, c/o Glen Canyon National Recreation Area, P.O. Box 1507, Page, Arizona 86040 **Telephone:** 602-645-2471

DIRECTIONS: You can reach Rainbow Bridge on foot or on horseback on the trail from Navajo Mountain Trading Post (39 km, or 24 miles) or from the abandoned Rainbow Lodge on foot (20 km, or 13 miles). But the most commonly used approach is by boat on Lake Powell. Many visitors now take the water route of 80 km (50 miles) from Wahweap, Bullfrog, or Halls Crossing to the landing at Bridge Canyon and then walk about .5 km (¼ mile) up the Canyon to the bridge.

Greatest of the world's known natural bridges, this symmetrical arch of salmon-pink sandstone rises 290 feet above the floor of Bridge Canyon. Created by Presidential Proclamation on May 30, 1910.

VISITOR ACTIVITIES: hiking, walking trails; **Permits:** No; **Fees:** No; **Visitor facilities:** For people who bring their own boats, there are launching ramps at Wahweap, Halls Crossing, Bullfrog, and Hite. Concessioners at these places sell boating and camping supplies, and they will provide guided boat trips. A floating complex anchored in Forbidden Canyon contains a refueling station, a small store for camping supplies, and a Ranger Station; **Any limitations on vehicle usage:** No road access to Monument; **Hiking trails:** Yes; **Backcountry:** No; **Camping:** No; **Other overnight accommodations on site:** No; **Meals served in the park:** No; **Food and supplies obtainable in the park:** No; **Food and supplies obtainable nearby:** Yes, at Rainbow Marina or in Page, AZ; **Overnight accommodations:** Page, AZ, on US 89, near Glen Canyon Dam, 96 km (60 miles) away by water; **First Aid available in park:** Yes, at Ranger Station in Forbidden Canyon; **Days/Hours:** Park never closes; **Holiday Closings:** No; **Visitor attractions closed for seasons:** No; **Weather:** Extremely hot, sunny Summers.

GENERAL INFORMATION: Before beginning a trail trip, be sure to call Navajo Mountain Trading Post, Tuba City AZ, 602-283-5322, about the following: the condition of the trails, whether or not trading posts are open, and places at which water and supplies are available. Summer visitors should wear cool clothing and thick-soled shoes. Bring a hat, sunglasses, and protective lotion.

Timpanogos Cave National Monument
American Fork, Utah

MAILING ADDRESS: Superintendent, Timpanogos Cave National Monument, Route 3, Box 200, American Fork, Utah 84003 **Telephone:** 801-756-4497

DIRECTIONS: If you are driving south from Salt Lake City on I-15, turn east at UT 80/92, the Alpine exit #285. If you are driving north from Provo, turn east at Pleasant Grove exit #273 or American Fork exit #277. Timpanogos Cave is 11 km (7 miles) from either town via UT 146 or UT 80/92.

This series of three limestone caverns on the side of Mt. Timpanogos is noted for its colorful water-created formations and geological history. The first cave was discovered in 1887 and the Monument was created by Presidential Proclamation on Oct. 14, 1922.

VISITOR ACTIVITIES: Visitors follow a 2.4 km (1.5 mile) trail from the Visitor Center up to the cave entrance rising 1,065 feet in elevation. Picnicking, hiking, fishing, and nature walks are available; **Permits:** No; **Fees:** Purchase tickets for cave tours at the Visitor Center. A user fee of 50¢ is charged for persons 16 and over, under 16 is free. Golden Age Passport holders are admitted for ½ price. Advance reservations are required for groups of 10 or more people; **Visitor Facilities:** picnic area, snacks, and souvenirs in Summer, self-guiding nature trail; **Any limitations on vehicle usage:** Vehicles confined to UT 80/92 and authorized parking areas; **Hiking trails:** Yes, two short trails on site; other hiking trails and backcountry available nearby at Uinta National Forest; **Backcountry:** Information on backcountry available at Visitor Center or by contacting: Supervisor, Uinta National Forest, U.S. Forest Service, 88 West 100 North, Provo, UT 84601, phone 801-377-5780; **Camping:** No; **Other overnight accommodations on site:** No, reserved and non-reserved campsites are available nearby at Uinta National Forest. Contact the forest for reservations and further information; **Meals served in the park:** Yes, snacks at the concession stand from mid-May to mid-Sept.; **Food and supplies obtainable in the park:** No; **Food and supplies obtainable nearby:** Yes, in Highland, American Fork, and Pleasant Grove; **Overnight accommodations:** Minimal accommdations at American Fork, 11 km (7 miles) west of the cave on UT 80/92 and Pleasant Grove, 16 km (10 miles) southeast of the cave on US 89 or I-15; **First Aid available in park:** Yes; **Nearest Hospital:** American Fork, UT 80/92, 11 km (7 miles); **Days/Hours:** The cave is open daily from about May 1 through Oct. 31 depending on weather. Visitor Center is open year-round; **Holiday Closings:** Thanksgiving, Dec. 25, and Jan. 1; **Visitor attractions closed for seasons:** Snow and ice make the trail to the cave impassable from late Oct.-Apr; **Weather:** Cool mornings and warm days in Spring and Fall. July and August day time temperatures in mid-to-high 90°sF. Occasional summer rains close the cave trail temporarily. Winter months are cold with considerable snow accumulation.

GENERAL INFORMATION: About 3 hours are required for the hike and tour of the cave. Because tour sizes are limited, frequently on weekends and holidays it is not possible to accommodate all visitors who wish to tour the cave. Temperature within the caves is a damp, chilly 6°C (43°F). A warm jacket or sweater and comfortable walking shoes with gripping soles are advised.

Zion National Park
Springdale, Utah

MAILING ADDRESS: Superintendent, Zion National Park, Springdale, Utah 84767, **Telephone:** 801-722-3256

DIRECTIONS: I-15 passes west of Zion and connects with UT 9 and 17 to the Park. US 89 passes east and connects with UT 9 to the Park. The Visitor Center is a short distance from the Park's entrance. In Summer, Color Country Tours, Inc. (P.O. Box 1032, Cedar City, Utah 84720, phone 801-586-3777) makes scheduled tours from Cedar City.

Colorful canyon and mesa scenery includes erosion and rockfault patterns and evidence of former volcanic activity. Established by act of Congress on Nov, 19. 1919.

VISITOR ACTIVITIES: interpretive films, exhibits, & programs (schedules posted throughout the Park), driving, walking and hiking, mountain climbing, swimming, camping, biking, horseback trips (make arrangements at Zion Lodge), 1½ hour tram tour of major points of interest leaves from Zion Lodge in Summer, wildlife- and bird-watching; **Permits:** Required for backcountry, available at Visitor Center; **Fees:** $2 per vehicle or 50¢ per person on commercial vehicles is the entrance fee for persons 16 and over. Camping fee is $2 per night per site. Golden Eagle and Golden Age Passports are accepted and available; **Visitor Facilities:** Visitor Center, campgrounds, tap water, fire grates, tables, sanitary disposal station, telephones, picnic sites, religious services, lodging and food service; **Any limitations on vehicle usage:** Do not park on curves. Watch for deer. Your car's lights must be in good working order; they are essential when travelling through the tunnel on East Entrance Road; **Hiking trails:** Yes; a wide variety of trails is available; **Backcountry:** Backcountry permits are required for overnight trips and use of the Narrows; **Camping:** Yes, camping is permitted only in designated campsites and is limited to 14 days. Campgrounds are run on a first-come, first-served basis; **Other overnight accommodations on site:** Zion Lodge is operated by the Utah Parks Division of TWAS (4045 South Spencer St., Suite A43, Las Vegas, Nevada 89109.) Zion Lodge has cabin accommodations within the Park. Reservations are advisable in the Summer. Call toll free, 800-634-6951. Contact Utah Parks Division of TWAS for information on other seasons of the year. Communities in the vicinity offer year-round accommodations; **Meals served in the park:** Yes, Zion Lodge has a dining room and a soda fountain; **Food and supplies obtainable in the park:** No, but available nearby at the campground store; **Food and supplies obtainable nearby:** Yes, at Springdale; **Overnight accommodations:** Springdale and other nearby communities; **First Aid available in park:** Yes, at the Visitor Center year-round and at Zion Lodge in Summer. A physician is in Hurricane, 39 km (24 miles) west of the Park; **Nearest Hospital:** St. George, 72 km (45 miles) west of the Park, Cedar City, 97 km (60 miles) north, and Kanab, 68 km (42 miles) east; **Days/Hours:**

Open 24 hours a day year-round; **Holiday Closings:** None; **Visitor attractions closed for seasons:** Higher hiking trails are closed by snow in Winter; **Weather:** Snow may fall intermittently from Dec. to March; average winter maximum and minimum temperatures are 12°C (53°F) & -1°C (30°F). May to Oct. daytime temps. range from 22°C (72°F) to 39°C (103°F); nighttime, from 7°C (45°F) to 23°C (73°F).

GENERAL INFORMATION: *For Your Safety*—Experienced hikers should take precautions: Obtain detailed information from a Park Ranger before attempting backcountry trails; tell someone where you plan to go and when you plan to return. Do not hike alone. Stay on established trails; taking shortcuts may endanger yourself and others. Stay out of drainage areas during thunderstorms as dry washes can become raging torrents in minutes. Watch your step if taking pictures near cliffs. Be alert for rockfalls and landslides.

The town of Springdale is situated within easy commuting distance of Bryce Canyon, the North Rim of the Grand Canyon and other well-known attractions. Many campers use the campground as a base of operations from which to explore the area. Other nearby attractions include "Ghost Towns" in Washington County and the Shakespeare Festival in Cedar City, which runs from mid-July to mid-August.

Virginia

CHESAPEAKE AND OHIO CANAL NATIONAL HISTORICAL PARK

MANASSAS NATIONAL BATTLEFIELD PARK

PRINCE WILLIAM FOREST PARK

GEORGE WASHINGTON BIRTHPLACE NATIONAL MONUMENT

FREDERICKSBURG AND SPOTSYLVANIA COUNTY BATTLEFIELDS NATIONAL MILITARY PARK

YORKTOWN BATTLEFIELD

SHENANDOAH NATIONAL PARK

APPALACHIAN NATIONAL SCENIC TRAIL

TURKEY RUN FARM

GREAT FALLS PARK

WOLF TRAP FARM PARK FOR THE PERFORMING ARTS

ASSATEAGUE ISLAND NATIONAL SEASHORE

Richmond

Norfolk

CUMBERLAND GAP NATIONAL HISTORICAL PARK

BLUE RIDGE PARKWAY

BOOKER T. WASHINGTON NATIONAL MONUMENT

COLONIAL NATIONAL HISTORICAL PARK

JAMESTOWN NATIONAL HISTORIC SITE

PETERSBURG NATIONAL BATTLEFIELD

RICHMOND NATIONAL BATTLEFIELD PARK

MAGGIE L. WALKER NATIONAL HISTORIC SITE

APPOMATTOX COURT HOUSE NATIONAL HISTORICAL PARK

Appalachian National Scenic Trail
For details see listing in Maine

Appomattox Court House National Historical Park
Appomattox, Virginia

MAILING ADDRESS: Superintendent, Appomattox Court House National Park, P.O. Box 218, Appomattox, Virginia 24522 **Telephone** 804-352-8987

DIRECTIONS: The Visitor Center is in the reconstructed Court House, on VA 24, 4.8 km (3 miles) northeast of the town of Appomattox, VA.

General Robert E. Lee surrendered the Confederacy's largest field army to Lt. Gen. Ulysses S. Grant here on Apr. 9, 1865. The village has been restored. Authorized for addition to the National Park System on June 18, 1930.

VISITOR ACTIVITIES: walking tours (pamphlet available at the Visitor Center), living history talks in Summer, interpretive exhibits; **Permits:** No; **Fees:** $1 per car entrance fee is charged from April 1-October 31; **Visitor Facilities:** parking areas and restrooms, interpretive exhibits, furnished historic buildings; **Any limitations on vehicle usage:** No vehicles are permitted in the village area; **Hiking trails:** Yes, self-guiding trails throughout the Park; **Backcountry:** No; **Camping:** No, but picnic areas and camping facilities are nearby; **Other overnight accommodations on site:** No; **Meals served in the park;** No; **Food and supplies obtainable in the park:** No; **Food and supplies obtainable nearby:** Yes, town of Appomattox; **Overnight accommodations:** Appomattox, VA 24, 4.8 km (3 miles) **First Aid available in park:** Yes, Rescue squad in Appomattox,VA; **Nearest Hospital:** Lynchburg, US 460, 40 km (25 miles); **Days/Hours:** Open daily 8:30 a.m. to 5 p.m.; **Holiday Closings;** Dec. 25; **Visitor attractions closed for seasons:** Living history talks are only offered during the summer months; **Weather:** Warm, humid Summers; cool, humid Winters.

GENERAL INFORMATION: All pets must be kept on a leash while in the Park.

Arlington House, The Robert E. Lee Memorial
Arlington, Virginia

MAILING ADDRESS: Superintendent, Arlington House, c/o George Washington Memorial Parkway, Turkey Run Park, McLean, Virginia 22101 **Telephone:** 703-557-0614

DIRECTIONS: Access from Washington is via the Memorial Bridge. Parking available at the Arlington Cemetery Visitor Center. The Cemetery is both a Tourmobile and a subway stop.

This was the home of Robert E. Lee, which he left to take command of the Southern forces during the Civil War. It is located in Arlington Cemetery, overlooking the Potomac River and the city of Washington. Established by act of Congress on Mar. 4, 1925.

VISITOR ACTIVITIES: interpretive exhibits, guided and self-guiding tours of the house; **Permits:**No; **Fees:**No; **Visitor Facilities:** parking, restrooms at Visitor Center and on site, bookstore; **Any limitations on vehicle usage:** No vehicles are allowed on House grounds; **Hiking trails:** No; **Backcountry:** No; **Camping:** No; **Other overnight accommodations on site:** No; **Meals served in the park:** No; **Food and supplies obtainable in the park:** No; **Food and supplies obtainable nearby:** Yes, Arlington, VA or Washington, D.C.; **Overnight accommodations:** in Washington metropolitan area; **First Aid available in park:** Yes; **Nearest Hospitals;** Arlington, VA and Washington D.C.;

Days/Hours: Open daily from 9:30 a.m. to 4:30 p.m. Oct.-Mar., until 6 p.m. Apr.-Sept.; **Holiday Closings:** None; **Visitor attractions closed for seasons:** No.

Blue Ridge Parkway
For details see listing in North Carolina

Booker T. Washington National Monument
Hardy, Virginia

MAILING ADDRESS: Superintendent, Booker T. Washington National Monument, Route 1, Box 195, Hardy, Virginia 24101 **Telephone:** 703-721-2094

DIRECTIONS: The Monument is 25.7 km (16 miles) northeast of Rocky Mount, VA, via VA 122N, and 32 km (20 miles) southeast of Roanoke, VA, via VA 116S and 122N.

This was the birthplace and early childhood home of the famous black leader and educator. Authorized for addition to the National Park System on Apr. 2, 1956.

VISITOR ACTIVITIES: audiovisual programs, interpretive talks, conducted tours, craft demonstrations daily from mid-June through Labor Day, picnicking, photography; **Permits:** No; **Fees:** No; **Visitor Facilities:** Environmental Education and Cultural Center, picnic area, parking, sales area, restrooms; **Any limitations on vehicle usage:** No; **Hiking trails:** Yes, walking and nature trails; **Backcountry:** No; **Camping:** Primitive organized youth group campground open April 15-Oct. 15; **Other overnight accommodations on site:** No; **Meals served in the park:** No; **Food and supplies obtainable in the park:** No; **Food and supplies obtainable nearby:** Yes, within a 16 km (10 mile) radius; more extensive facilities are at Roanoke, Rocky Mount and Bedford; **Overnight accommodations:** Roanoke, VA, 122S and 46N, 32 km (20 miles); Rocky Mount, VA, 122S, 25.7 km (16 miles); Bedford, VA, VA 122N, 34 km (21 miles); **First Aid available in park:** Yes; **Nearest Hospital:** Roanoke, VA 122S and 116N, 32 km (20 miles); Rocky Mountain, VA 122S, 25.7 km (16 miles); **Days/Hours:** The grounds are open during daylight hours. Visitor Center open Labor Day-Oct. 31:8 a.m.-4:30 p.m. Mon.-Fri.; 9:30 a.m.-6 p.m. Sat. & Sun./Nov. 1-Mar. 31: 8 a.m.-4:30 p.m., 7 days per week. Beginning 1980, Visitor Center open 8:30 a.m. to 5 p.m. daily; **Holiday Closings:** Thanksgiving, Dec. 25 & Jan. 1; **Visitor attractions closed for seasons:** No; **Weather:** Spring is warm and mild; Summer, warm to hot; Fall is mild, cool & pleasant; Winter is generally mild with a few light snowfalls.

GENERAL INFORMATION: *For Your Safety*—Keep your distance from the animals. Do not enter the pastures or pens.

Chesapeake and Ohio Canal National Historical Park
For details see listing in Maryland

Colonial National Historical Park
Yorktown, Virginia

MAILING ADDRESS: Superintendent, Colonial National Historical Park, P.O. Box

210, Yorktown, Virginia 23690 **Telephone:** 804-898-3400

DIRECTIONS: Both Jamestown and Yorktown are located off major highways: Rte. 17 and I-64. Both sites are accessible via the Colonial Parkway which joins Jamestown, Williamsburg and Yorktown. The Park encompasses most of Jamestown Island, site of the first permanent English settlement in America in 1607; Yorktown, scene of the culminating battle of the American Revolution in 1781; the 37 km (23 miles) Colonial Parkway connecting these and other colonial sites including Williamsburg and Cape Henry Memorial, which marks the approximate site of the first landing of Jamestown's colonists in 1607. Authorized for addition to the National Park System on July 3, 1930.

VISITOR ACTIVITIES: self-guided auto and walking tours, guided walking tours, interpretive exhibits, living history and children's programs; **Permits:** Yes, a $3 bus permit is required for Colonial Parkway. Available at Jamestown Entrance Station and Yorktown Visitor Center; **Fees:** Yes, Jamestown Entrance Station fee is $2 per vehicle, or 50¢ per person for those 16 and over who arrive by bus or bicycle. Educational groups and holders of Golden Age and Golden Eagle Passports are admitted free; **Visitor Facilities:** Souvenirs, exhibits, and audiovisual programs are offered at Jamestown and Yorktown (see listings in this book.); **Any limitations on vehicle usage:** Park only in designated areas. There are no service stations, and the road is closed to commercial traffic except buses, for which permits are required; **Hiking trails:** No; **Backcountry;** No; **Camping:** No; **Other overnight accommodations on site:** No, City-and privately-operated campgrounds are nearby. Contact the Park for further information on directions and facilities; **Meals served in the park:** No, there are picnic areas along the Colonial parkway and at Yorktown Beach; **Food and supplies obtainable in the park:** No; **Food and supplies obtainable nearby:** Yes, at Yorktown and Williamsburg; **Overnight accommodations:** Restaurant and motel facilities are available in Yorktown and nearby along Rte. 17, and in Williamsburg; **First Aid available in park:** Yes; **Nearest Hospital:** Riverside Hosp., Newport News, 24 km (15 miles) from Yorktown. Williamsburg Community Hosp. is 15.3 km (9½ miles) from Jamestown; **Days/Hours:** Jamestown Entrance Station open daily from 8:30 a.m. to 4:30 p.m. with extended closing from April through Oct.; **Holiday Closings:** Dec. 25; **Visitor attractions closed for seasons:** Moore House, Nelson House and picnic areas are closed in Winter.

Cumberland Gap National Historical Park
For details see listing in Kentucky

Fredericksburg and Spotsylvania County Battlefields Memorial National Military Park
Fredericksburg, Virginia

MAILING ADDRESS: Superintendent, Fredericksburg and Spotsylvania County Battlefields Memorial National Military Park, P.O. Box 679, Fredericksburg, Virginia 22401 **Telephone:** 703-373-4461

DIRECTIONS: The Visitor Center is in Fredericksburg on US 1 at the foot of Marye's Heights. Another Visitor Center is on the Chancellorsville Battlefield 16 km (10 miles) west of Fredericksburg on VA 3.

Portions of four major Civil War Battlefields-Fredericksburg, Chancellorsville, the Wilderness, Spotsylvania Court House- and several smaller historic sites comprise the

Park. The battles occurred during 1862, 1863, and 1864. Established by act of Congress on Feb. 14, 1927.

VISITOR ACTIVITIES: museums, interpretive exhibits, living history demonstrations in Summer, biking, auto tours, hiking, fishing, picnicking; **Permits:** No; **Fees:** No; **Visitor Facilities:** museums, historic houses, trails, picnic sites; **Any limitations on vehicle usage:** All motorized vehicles must stay on established roadways that are open to the public; **Hiking trails:** Yes, along historic traces and to historic sites; **Backcountry:** No; **Camping:** No; **Other overnight accommodations on site:** No, camping is available at Prince William Forest Park (see listings in this book), 32 km (20 miles) north on Int. 95.; **Meals served in the park:** No; **Food and supplies obtainable in the park:** No; **Food and supplies obtainable nearby:** Yes, in Fredericksburg; **Overnight accommodations:** Fredericksburg; **First Aid available in park:** Yes; **Nearest Hospital:** Fredericksburg, Jefferson Davis Hwy (Rte. 1 bypass); **Days/Hours:** Park roads open from during daylight hours; Visitor Centers open daily, 9 a.m. to 5 p.m., generally until 6 p.m. in Summer; **Holiday Closings:** Dec. 25 and Jan. 1.

GENERAL INFORMATION: *For Your Safety*— Auto tours require turning onto and off of heavily travelled roadways. Beware of poisonous insects, plants and reptiles which may be encountered during your visit. Watch your footing while on the trails.

George Washington Birthplace National Monument
Washington's Birthplace, Virginia

MAILING ADDRESS: Superintendent, George Washington Birthplace National Monument, Washington's Birthplace, Virginia 22575 **Telephone:** 804-224-0196

DIRECTIONS: The Monument is on the Potomac River, 61 km (38 miles) east of Fredericksburg, VA, and is accessible over VA 3 and VA 204.

Birthplace of the first U.S. President, the park includes a Visitor Center, memorial mansion, colonial farm, gardens, and the tombs of his father, grandfather, and great-grandfather. Established by act of Congress on Jan. 23, 1930.

VISITOR ACTIVITIES: picnicking, interpretive exhibits and film, self-guiding tours, nature walks; **Permits:** No; **Fees:** No; **Visitor Facilities:** restrooms and parking area, Visitor Center, historic mansion, colonial farm, burial ground, hiking and nature trails, picnic area; **Any limitations on vehicle usage:** No; **Hiking trails:** Yes, nature trail; **Backcountry:** No; **Camping:** No; **Other overnight accommodations on site:** No; **Meals served in the park:** No; **Food and supplies obtainable in the park:** No; **Food and supplies obtainable nearby:** Yes, in Montross and Colonial Beach; **Overnight accommodations:** Fredericksburg, 61 km (38 miles); Montross, 19 km (12 miles); Colonial Beach, 16 km (10 miles); **First Aid available in park:** Yes; **Nearest hospital:** Fredericksburg, 61 km (38 miles); **Days/Hours:** Open daily from 9 a.m. to 5 p.m.; **Holiday Closings:** Dec. 25 and Jan. 1.

GENERAL INFORMATION: Visitors to the area can also see the birthplace of Robert E. Lee, Stratford Hall, which is several miles south of Washington's Birthplace. *For Your Safety*—Do not feed or tease the animals or enter the pastures or pens. Poisonous plants are common in the area.

George Washington Memorial Parkway
McLean, Virginia

MAILING ADDRESS: Superintendent, George Washington Memorial Parkway, Turkey Run Park, McLean, Virginia 22101 **Telephone:** 703-557-3635

DIRECTIONS: Access to the Parkway is from Exit 14 of the Capital Beltway (Int. 495) from Chain Bridge on Rte. 123; or from Washington, the 14th Street, Memorial or Theodore Roosevelt Bridges.
  The Parkway is a landscape scenic road which parallels the Potomac River for much of its route. There are several places for recreation along the Parkway. Established by act of Congress on May 29, 1930.

VISITOR ACTIVITIES: Areas assigned to the Parkway's administration such as Arlington House, Great Falls Park, Turkey Run Farm, Glen Echo Park and Theodore Roosevelt Island offer opportunities for interpretive walks and talks, exhibits, picnicking, hiking, climbing, biking, & fishing; **Permits:** No; **Fees:** $1 parking fee at Great Falls Park in VA; **Visitor Facilities:** picnic tables, restrooms, parking, boat ramp, bike trail; **Any limitations on vehicle usage:** All vehicles are restricted to paved roads; **Hiking trails:** Yes, trails vary in slope and difficulty; **Backcountry:** No; **Camping;** No; **Other overnight accommodations on site:** No; **Meals served in the park:** Yes, in Great Fall Park, VA; Mount Vernon; Dangerfield Island; Lady Bird Johnson Park; **Food and supplies obtainable in the park:** No; **Food and supplies obtainable nearby:** Yes, in all local towns; **Overnight accommodations:** in the Washington D.C. metropolitan area; **First Aid available in park:** Yes; **Nearest Hospital:** most Washington suburbs in Virginia; **Days/Hours:** Open during daylight hours; the parks close at dark; **Holiday Closings:** None; **Visitor attractions closed for seasons:** None; **Weather:** Hot and humid in Summer, very pleasant and mild Spring and Fall. Moderate Winters.

GENERAL INFORMATION: Visitor use areas managed by the Parkway also include U.S. Navy Marine Memorial, Mount Vernon Bike Trail, Riverside Park, Fort Hunt Park, Fort Marcy and Dyke Marsh.

Great Falls Park
Great Falls, Virginia

MAILING ADDRESS: Superintendent, Great Falls Park, 9200 Old Dominion Drive, Great Falls, Virginia 22066 **Telephone:** 703-759-2915

DIRECTIONS: The Park is about 24 km (15 miles) from Washington, D.C. at the intersection of VA 193 (Georgetown Pike) and VA 738 (Old Dominion Drive) in Great Falls, Virginia.
  The Park provides a fine view of the Great Falls of the Potomac from the Virginia side of the river. Authorized for addition to the National Park System in 1968.

VISITOR ACTIVITIES: tours, hiking, fishing, picnicking, horseback riding, playground activities, rock climbing(registration at Visitor Center is required),cross-country skiing in Winter; **Permits:** a VA or MD fishing license is required; available at local sporting goods stores; **Fees:** $1 per auto parking fee is collected by Fairfax County to pay for land purchase; **Visitor Facilities:** interpretive tours and hikes, picnic tables and grills (charcoal and artificial fuels only), playground, horse trails, snack bar; **Any limitations**

on vehicle usage: Motor vehicles are not allowed on trails or in the picnic area. Park only in designated areas; **Hiking trails:** Yes, novice and expert hikers will find suitably enjoyable trails within the Park; **Backcountry:** No; **Camping:** No; **Other overnight accommodations on site:** No, information on campgrounds in the Washington area is available at the Visitor Center or on request to the Superintendent; **Meals served in the park:** Yes, snacks are available at the Visitor Center; **Food and supplies obtainable in the park:** No; **Food and supplies obtainable nearby:** Yes, in Fairfax County, 8 km (5 miles); **Overnight accommodations:** In Virginia or the Washington, D.C. metropolitan area; **First Aid available in park:** Yes, or nearby in Great Falls & McLean, VA; **Nearest Hospitals:** Fairfax Hospital, 30 km (19 miles); **Days/Hours;** Open from 9 a.m. to dark every day; **Holiday Closings:** Dec. 25; **Visitor attractions closed for season:** None; **Weather;** Summers are hot & humid, temperatures range from 65—95 °; Winters are mild to cold, 25—45 °.

GENERAL INFORMATION: These warnings must be heeded for a safe visit: Strong currents are extremely hazardous at *all* places along the banks of the Potomac River in the park. NO SWIMMING OR WADING OR BOATING; this prohibition is strictly enforced. STAY OFF ROCKS AT WATER'S EDGE.

Jamestown National Historic Site
Jamestown, Virginia

MAILING ADDRESS: Superintendent, Colonial National Historical Park, P.O. Box 210, Yorktown, Virginia 23690 **Telephone:** 804-898-3400

DIRECTIONS: Follow I-64 to Hwy 199 West and take the Colonial Parkway to Jamestown.
    Part of the site of the first permanent English Settlement in North America (1607) is on the upper end of Jamestown Island, scene of the first representative government on this continent, July 30, 1619. Designated Dec. 18, 1940. A portion of the Site is administered by the Association for the Preservation of Virginia Antiquities.

VISITOR ACTIVITIES: auto and foot tours, 15-minute orientation film, exhibits of artifacts, miniature replicas of the three ships and fort, glassmaking demonstrations at the nearby Jamestown Glass House; **Permits:** $3 bus permit is required for Colonial Parkway. Available at Jamestown Entrance Station and Yorktown Visitor Center; **Fees:** Jamestown Entrance Station fee is $2 per vehicle, or 50¢ per person for those 16 and over who arrive by bus or bicycle. Educational groups and holders of Golden Age and Golden Eagle Passports are admitted free; **Visitor facilities:** post office, gift shop, interpretive signs, recorded messages, loop drive, glasshouse, wayside exhibits; **Any limitations on vehicle usage:** Park only in designated areas; **Hiking trails:** No; **Backcountry:** No; **Camping:** No, campgrounds are located nearby in Williamsburg, Newport News, and James City County. Contact the park for further information on directions and facilities; **Other overnight accommodations on site:** No; **Meals served in the park:** No; **Food and supplies obtainable in the park:** No; **Food and supplies obtainable nearby:** Yes, at Yorktown and Williamsburg; **Overnight accommodations:** Williamsburg, Colonial Parkway, 16 km (10 miles); Yorktown, Colonial Parkway; **First Aid available in park:** Yes; **Nearest Hospital:** Williamsburg,15.3 km (9-1/2 miles); **Days/Hours:** Jamestown Entrance Station open daily from 8:30 to 4:30 p.m. with extended closing from April through October; **Holiday Closings:** Dec. 25; **Visitor attractions closed for seasons:** None; **Weather:** Weather is temperate.

GENERAL INFORMATION: *For Your Safety*—Keep on the paths and watch your children. Stay off the ruins and away from the river, which is deep here.

Maggie L. Walker National Historic Site
Richmond, Virginia

MAILING ADDRESS: c/o Richmond National Battlefield Park, 3215 East Broad Street, Richmond, Virginia 23223 **Telephone:** 804-226-1981

DIRECTIONS: NOT YET OPEN TO THE PUBLIC.
Maggie L. Walker, black leader, became the first American woman to establish a bank, the St. Luke Penny Savings Bank, in her native Richmond about 1900. Later she lived here in this 18-room house, located at 110 A E. Leigh Street. Authorized for addition to the National Park System on Nov. 10, 1978.

Manassas National Battlefield Park
Manassas, Virginia

MAILING ADDRESS: Superintendent, Manassas National Battlefield Park, P.O. Box 1830, Manassas, Virginia 22110 **Telephone:** 703-754-7107

DIRECTIONS: The Park is 42 km (26 miles) southwest of Washington, D.C., near the intersection of Int. 66 and VA 234. The Visitor Center is on VA 234, 1.6 km (1 mile) from the intersection of I-66 and VA 234.
The Battles of First and Second Manassas were fought here July 21, 1861 and Aug. 28-30, 1862. The 1861 battle was the first test of Northern and Southern military prowess. Here Confederate Brig. Gen. Thomas J. Jackson acquired his nickname "Stonewall". Designated May 10, 1940.

VISITOR ACTIVITIES: interpretive exhibits, slide programs, conducted tours in season, auto tours, hiking, horseback riding, picnicking, living history programs in Summer;**Permits:** for certain group activities, inquire of superintendent at Visitor Center; **Fees:** No; **Visitor facilities:** parking, hiking and bridle trails, sales, picnic area; **Any limitations on vehicle usage:** Parking is not allowed on the road shoulders. All motorized vehicles must stay on established roadways and may not stop on grassy areas or trails; **Hiking trails:** Yes, there are self-guiding walking tours of Henry Hill and Stone Bridge; **Backcountry:** No; **Camping:** No; **Other overnight accommodations:** No; **Meals served in the park:** No; **Food and supplies obtainable in the park:** No; **Food and supplies obtainable nearby:** Yes, Manassas, south on VA 234; **Overnight accommodations:** Manassas, south on VA 234; **First Aid available in park:** Yes; **Nearest Hospital:** Manassas, VA 234, 3 km (2 miles); **Days/Hours:** Park open daily from sunrise to sunset. Visitor Center open daily from 9 a.m. to 5:30 p.m. and until 6 p.m. in Summer; **Holiday Closings:** Park and Visitor Center closed Dec. 25; **Visitor attractions closed for seasons:** Stone House is closed in Winter; **Weather:** Winters are mild to moderate; Summers are moderate.

GENERAL INFORMATION: *CAUTION:* Two heavily travelled roadways divide the park. Use extreme caution while driving across or turning onto and off of these highways.

Petersburg National Battlefield
Petersburg, Virginia

MAILING ADDRESS: Superintendent, Petersburg National Battlefield, P.O. Box 549, Petersburg, Virginia 23803 **Telephone:** 804-732-3531

DIRECTIONS: The Visitor Center is 4 km (2½ mile) east of the center of Petersburg on Route 36.

The Union Army waged a 10-month campaign here in 1864-65 to seize Petersburg, center of the railroads supplying Richmond and Gen. Robert E. Lee's army. Established by act of Congress on July 3, 1926.

VISITOR ACTIVITIES: A 17-minute map presentation is conducted hourly at the Visitor Center. In Summer, demonstrations of small arms, mortar, and cannon, with actual firings, and soldier life may be seen. Biking, fishing, picnicking, hiking, self-guiding auto tours; **Permits:** No; **Fees:** No; **Visitor facilities:** bike trails, parking, restrooms, picnic area; **Any limitations on vehicle usage:** The Park tour roads are often congested, so drive slowly and carefully; **Hiking trails:** No; **Backcountry:** No; **Camping:** No; **Other overnight accommodations on site:** No, reservations for campsites can be made at Holiday Inn Travel Park which is 11.3 km (7 miles) from the Battlefield. Contact the park at Route 4, Box 500, Petersburg, VA 23803, phone 804-861- 2616; **Meals served in the park:** No; **Food and supplies obtainable in the park:** No; **Food and supplies obtainable nearby:** Yes, 8 km (½ mile) west on Route 36; **Overnight accommodations:** Petersburg, VA, via Route 36, 3.5 km (2½ miles) west; **First Aid available in park:** Yes; **Nearest Hospital:** Petersburg, VA, Rte.36 to Washington St. to Sycamore St., 5.3 km (3½ miles); **Days/Hours:** Battlefield open 8 a.m to dark year-round; Visitor Center open from 8 a.m. to 5 p.m., until 7 p.m. in Summer; **Holiday Closings:** Dec. 25 & Jan. 1; **Visitor attractions closed for seasons:** Living history program operates only from mid-June through Labor Day; **Weather:** Spring and Fall are generally mild. Summers are very hot and humid. Winters are moderately cold and humid.

GENERAL INFORMATION: Visitors to the area can also see the nearby Poplar Grove National Cemetery, which contains the graves of more than 6,000 soldiers. It is on VA 675, 4.5 km (3 miles) south of Petersburg.

Prince William Forest Park
Triangle, Virginia

MAILING ADDRESS: Superintendent, Prince William Forest Park, P.O. Box 208, Triangle, Virginia 22172 **Telephone:** 703-221-7181

DIRECTIONS: The Park is about 52 km (32 miles) south of Washington D.C. The main entrance is on VA 619, just off I-95 near the Quantico Marine Base. The main Information Center is less than 1.5 km (1 mile) from the main entrance. If you are arriving in a travel trailer and desire hookups, take the VA 234 exit from I-95. Follow signs to Travel Trailer Village.

Pines and hardwoods have replaced worn-out farmland in this forested watershed of Quantico Creek. Authorized for addition to the National Park System in 1932.

VISITOR ACTIVITIES: biking, camping, fishing, wildlife-watching, interpretive exhibits, nature walks, picnicking, backcountry, cross-country skiing; **Permits:** Virginia fishing license available from any Ranger. Backcountry permits available at Headquarters; **Fees:** camping fee is $2 per night per site; **Visitor facilities:** parking and exhibits at Visitor Center, restrooms at the campgrounds, nature trails, picnic areas, concessioner trailer camps, backcountry campsites, individual and group campsites, environmental study area, group cabins, cross-country ski trails; **Any limitations on vehicle usage** Vehicles are restricted to designated roadways; **Hiking trails:** Yes, the Park has approx. 56 km (35 miles) of trails and fire roads; **Backcountry:** Yes, backcountry permits are required and are available without charge at Park Headquarters; **Camping:** Yes, no reservations are available for campgrounds, except for group sites. Contact the Park for further information; **Other overnight accommodations on site:** No; **Meals served in the park:** No; **Food and supplies obtainable in the park:** No; **Food and supplies obtainable nearby:** Yes, Triangle or Dumfries; **Overnight accommodations:** Triangle or Dumfries, Rte. 234 and I-95, within a 1.6 to 8 km (1 to 5 mile) radius; **First Aid available in park:** Yes; **Nearest Hospital:** Potomac Hospital, Woodbridge, 14.5 km (9 miles) from the park; **Days/Hours:** Park open during daylight hours; campgrounds always open; **Holiday Closings:** None; **Visitor attractions closed for seasons:** No.

Richmond National Battlefield Park
Richmond, Virginia

MAILING ADDRESS: Superintendent, Richmond National Battlefield Park, 3215 East Broad St., Richmond, Virginia 23223 **Telephone:** 804-226-1981

DIRECTIONS: You should begin your tour at Chimborazo Visitor Center, 3215 East Broad Street, Richmond. Small Visitor Centers with exhibits are available at Cold Harbor and Fort Harrison.

The Park commemorates several battles to capture Richmond, which was the Confederate Capital during the Civil War. Established by act of Congress on Mar. 2, 1936.

VISITOR ACTIVITIES: interpretive exhibits and audiovisual programs, self-guided auto tours, picnicking, living history programs in season; **Permits:** No; **Fees:** No; **Visitor facilities:** parking, restrooms, sales desk, picnic facilities at Fort Harrison and Cold Harbor; **Any limitations on vehicle usage:** Park only in designated areas; **Hiking trails:** No; **Backcountry:** No; **Camping:** No; **Other overnight accommodations on site:** No; **Meals served in the park:** No; **Food and supplies obtainable in the park:** No; **Food and supplies obtainable nearby:** Yes, along the tour route and in Richmond; **Overnight accommodations:** along the tour route and in Richmond; **First Aid available in park:** Yes; **Nearest Hospital:** Medical College of VA, Broad Street, 12 blocks west of Chimborazo Visitor Center; **Days/Hours:** Open only during daylight hours. Chimborozo Visitor Center is open daily year-round; **Holiday Closings:** Jan. 1 and Dec.25; **Visitor attractions closed for seasons:** Fort Harrison Visitor Center is open April-May & Sept.-Oct. weekends; and daily June through August from 9:30 a.m. to 5:30 p.m.; **Weather:** Hot and humid Summers, mild Spring and Fall, moderate Winters.

GENERAL INFORMATION: Whenever possible, spend some time walking in each area; it is the best way to gain a real understanding of its significance.

Shenandoah National Park
Luray, Virginia

MAILING ADDRESS: Superintendent, Shenandoah National Park, Luray, Virginia 22835 **Telephone:** 703-999-2243

DIRECTIONS: The Headquarters of Shenandoah National Park is 6.4 km (4 miles) west of Thornton Gap and 6.4 km (4 miles) east of Luray on US 211. Visitor Centers are at Dickey Ridge and Big Meadows. Skyline Drive winds through hardwood forest along the crest of the Blue Ridge Mountains. Authorized for addition to the National Park System on May 26, 1936.

VISITOR ACTIVITIES: Driving, horseback riding, picnicking, camping, field trips, campfire programs, nature walks. Pick up a *Visitor Activities* folder from any Visitor Center, entrance station, or concession lodge; **Visitor facilities:** Food service, gift shops, service stations, grocery and camping supply stores, showers and laundry buildings, ice and wood sales, 2 lodges, riding stables, self-guiding nature trails; **Any limitations on vehicle usage:** Vehicles must stay on public roads. Commercial trucking is restricted to park business only. Bicycles and other vehicles are prohibited on trails. Chains and snow tires may be required in Winter; **Hiking trails:** Yes, self-guiding nature trails can be enjoyed year-round; **Backcountry:** Yes, information available at Visitor Centers and Park Headquarters, or by mail from the Superintendent; **Camping:** Yes, advance reservations are accepted for organized youth groups at Dundo campground. Other campgrounds are on a first-come, first-served basis.; **Other overnight accommodations on site:** Yes, for lodging information and reservations, contact ARA-Virginia Sky-Line Company, Box 727, Luray, Virginia 22835,Telephone: 703-743-5108; **Meals served in the park:** Yes, at Skyland, Big Meadows, Loft Mountain, Panorama, Elkwallow; **Food and supplies obtainable in the park:** No; **Food and supplies obtainable nearby:** Yes, Big Meadows, Loft Mountain, Panorama, Elkwallow and in towns along Highways 340, 211, 33. Some of these are within 3 km (5 miles) of the Park; **First Aid available in park:** Yes; **Nearest Hospital:** Front Royal, Highway 340, 9.7 km (6 miles); Luray, Highway 211, 16 km (10 miles); Harrisburg, Highway 33; Waynesboro, 250; **Days/Hours:** Park always open. Sections of the drive may be closed due to weather or for resource management; **Holiday Closings:** None; **Visitor attractions closed for seasons:**All facilities are operated in Summer; some are available in Spring and Autumn; **Weather:** Weather is temperate.

GENERAL INFORMATION: *For Your Safety*—wear proper footwear when walking on trails. Most visitor injuries are caused by falls. Do your sightseeing from overlooks and trails, not while driving. Do not feed or approach park animals. Bears roam the Park, so safeguard all food to protect yourself and your property. Know where your children are at all times. Always plan where to meet if you become separated. Stay on trails.

Turkey Run Farm
McLean, Virginia

MAILING ADDRESS: Superintendent, George Washington Memorial Parkway, Turkey Run Farm, McLean, Virginia 22101 **Telephone:** 703-557-1383

DIRECTIONS: From the Capital Beltway (Int. 495), take Exit 13, Route 193 south toward Langley; drive 3.7 (2.3 miles); and turn left at Turkey Run Farm sign to the parking area. From Washington, D.C., take the George Washington Memorial Parkway north to the exit for Route 123 toward McLean (Note: Do not take exit for Turkey Run Picnic Area located nearby); drive almost 1.6 km (1 mile) and bear right on Route 193; make the first right at Turkey Run Farm sign and follow signs to parking lot.

The day-to-day operations of a small-scale, low income colonial farm of the 18th century are re-enacted in this wooded setting. Established by act of Congress in 1973.

VISITOR ACTIVITIES: Living history demonstrations, self-guided walks, picnicking; **Permits:** No; **Fees:** No; **Visitor facilities:** Parking, restrooms, picnic tables; **Any limitations on vehicle usage:** No vehicles; visitors must walk from the parking lot; **Hiking trails:** No; **Backcountry:** No; **Camping:** No; **Other overnight accommodations on site:** No; **Meals served in the park:** No; **Food and supplies obtainable in the park:** No; **Food and supplies obtainable nearby:** Yes, McLean, VA; **Overnight accommodations:** McLean, VA or metropolitan Washington, DC; **First Aid available in park:** Yes; **Nearest Hospital:** Fairfax Hospital, Falls Church, VA; **Days/Hours:** Apr.-Nov.: Wed.-Sun. 10 a.m. 4:30 p.m.;Dec.-Mar.: Fri-Sun. 10 a.m.-4:30 p.m.; **Holiday Closings:** Thanksgiving, Dec. 25 and Jan. 1; **Visitor attractions closed for seasons:**None; **Weather:** The farm is an outdoor experience and can be hot and humid during the summer months and cold through the Winter.

GENERAL INFORMATION: The need to preserve the 18th century atmosphere of the site precludes the use of guided tours by park staff. Visitors are invited to observe the "farm family's" activities and ask questions.

U.S. Marine Corps War Memorial and Netherlands Carillon
Arlington, Virginia

MAILING ADDRESS: Superintendent, George Washington Memorial Parkway, Turkey Run Park, McLean, Virginia 22101 **Telephone:** 703-557-3635

DIRECTIONS: The Memorial and Carillon are located in Arlington, VA, off US 50, and can be reached from Washington, D.C. via Memorial Bridge or Key Bridge.
   Also known as the Iwo Jima Memorial, this monumental sculpture is dedicated to all Marines who have died for their country. Authorized for addition to the National Park System on Nov. 10, 1954. The 49-bell Netherlands Carillon symbolizes the gratitude of the Dutch people for U.S. aid given during and after World War II. Carillon dedicated on May 5, 1960.

VISITOR ACTIVITIES: Sunset parades by the U.S. Marine Drum and Bugle Corps and the Silent Drill Team are held at the Memorial on summer evenings; Carillon concerts Tuesday evenings from June through August; **Permits:** No; **Fees:** No; **Visitor facilities:** Parking area; **Any limimitations on vehicle usage:** Vehicles are restricted to paved roads; **Hiking trails:** No; **Backcountry:** No; **Camping:** No; **Other overnight accommodations on site:** No; **Meals served in the park:** No; **Food and supplies obtainable in the park:** No; **Food and supplies obtainable nearby:** Yes, Arlington, VA or Washington, DC; **Overnight accommodations:** Arlington, VA or metropolitan Washington, DC; **First Aid available in park:** No; **Nearest Hospital:** Arlington, VA; **Days/Hours:** Memorial never closes; **Holiday Closings:** None; **Visitor attractions closed for seasons:**No; **Weather:** Hot, humid Summers; cold, snowy Winters.

Wolf Trap Farm Park for the Performing Arts
Vienna, Virginia

MAILING ADDRESS: Director, Wolf Trap Farm Park, 1551 Trap Road, Vienna, Virginia 22180 **Telephone:** 703-938-3810

DIRECTIONS: From downtown Washington, D.C.: Take the George Washington

Parkway to Capitol Beltway (I-495) heading south into Virginia. Exit I-495 at Exit 11-S (Tysons Corner—VA Rte. 123). Follow Rte 123 briefly to U.S. Route 7 (Leesburg Pike) and turn right. Travel west on Route 7 to Towlston Road. Turn left on Towlston Road at Wolf Trap Farm Park sign. The Park entrance is 1.6 km (1 mile) from this turn and is well-marked. Driving time from downtown Washington, D.C. is 30 minutes in nonrush hour traffic.

At this first national park for the performing arts, the Filene Center can accommodate an audience of 6,500 including 3,000 on the sloping lawn in a setting of rolling hills and woods. The proscenium arch is 70 feet wide and 28 feet high; the stage is 100 feet wide by 64 feet deep. Established by act of Congress on Oct. 15, 1966.

VISITOR ACTIVITIES: attending performances, picnicking, walking, tours of the Filene Center, interpretive programs; **Permits:** No; **Fees:** Yes, tickets are required for most performances. See local newspaper or call the above number for information on events; **Visitor facilities:** refreshment bar, food service, parking, restrooms, picnic areas; **Any limitations on vehicle usage:** Park only in designated areas; **Hiking trails:** No; **Backcountry:** No; **Camping:** No; **Other overnight accommodations on site:** No; **Meals served in the park:** Yes, the dining pavilion adjacent to the Filene Center offers a choice of meal services beginning two hours before each performance. A buffet dinner is available, or a variety of picnic box suppers may be ordered in advance. Reservations are required by 1 p.m. on the day of the performance. Telephone 703-938-4256 or -3810, ext. 276. Snack bars serve sandwiches, soft drinks, and assorted snacks prior to each performance and at intermission; **Food and supplies obtainable in the park:** No; **Food and supplies obtainable nearby:** Yes, Vienna, VA; **Overnight accommodations:** In suburban Virginia or Washington, D.C.; **First Aid available in park:** Yes, physician in attendance at all performances; **Nearest Hospital:** Fairfax Hospital, Access, Reston, Virginia; **Days/Hours:** Park open year-round from 8:30 a.m. to 5 p.m.; until the completion of the performance in Summer. The Filene Center is open for performances from June through August; **Holiday Closings:** None; **Visitor attractions closed for seasons:**The Filene Center is open only in Summer.

GENERAL INFORMATION: Special arrangements for the handicapped can be made in advance by calling 703-938-3810 ext. 234. The Park will also furnish wheelchairs upon request.

Yorktown Battlefield
Yorktown, Virginia

MAILING ADDRESS: Superintendent, Colonial National Historical Park, P.O. Box 210, Yorktown, Virginia 23690 **Telephone:** 804-898-3400

DIRECTIONS: Follow I-64 to Hwy 199 East, then Colonial Parkway to Yorktown.

Yorktown was the scene of the culminating battle of the American Revolution when Washington triumphed over Cornwallis in 1781. Authorized for addition to the National Park System on July 3, 1930.

VISITOR ACTIVITIES: interpretive exhibits, artifact displays, 12-minute film, rooftop overlook, self-guiding auto tour, bookstore, tape and recorder rentals for tours, free 45-minute bus tours in Summer from 10 a.m. to 5 p.m. Free theatrical presentation on Thomas Nelson, Jr., a signer of the Declaration of Independence and the commander of the Virginia militia at the Siege of Yorktown, is offered; **Permits:** $3 bus permit is required for Colonial Parkway available at Jamestown Entrance Station and Yorktown

Visitor Center; **Fees:** No; **Visitor facilities:** interpretive exhibits, Visitor Center, orientation map, film, overlook, bookstore, encampment and battlefield drives, theatrical presentations at Moore House and Nelson House, picnic area at Yorktown Beach; **Any limitations on vehicle usage:** Park only in designated areas; **Hiking trails:** No; **Backcountry:** No; **Camping:** No; **Other overnight accommodations on site:** No, campgrounds are located nearby in Williamsburg, Newport News, and James City County. Contact the park for further information on directions and facilities; **Meals served in the park:** No; **Food and supplies obtainable in the park:** No; **Food and supplies obtainable nearby:** Yes, Yorktown and Williamsburg; **Overnight accommodations:** Along Rte 17 in Yorktown and vicinity and in Williamsburg; **First Aid available in park:** Yes; **Nearest Hospital:** Riverside Hospital, Newport News, 24 km (15 miles) ; **Days/Hours:** Daily from 8:30 a.m. to 5:00 p.m., with later closing from Apr.-Oct.; **Holiday Closings:** Dec. 25; **Visitor attractions closed for seasons:** Moore House, Nelson House and picnic areas closed in Winter.

Washington

Coulee Dam National Recreation Area
Coulee Dam, Washington

MAILING ADDRESS: Superintendent, Coulee Dam National Recreation Area, P.O. Box 37, Coulee Dam, Washington 99116 **Telephone:** 509-633-1360, x441

DIRECTIONS: Information about access to the entire area is available from the National Recreation Area Headquarters in Coulee Dam. There is a Visitor Center at Fort Spokane. Formed by the Grand Coulee Dam (part of the Columbia River Basin project), the 241 km (150 mile) long Franklin D. Roosevelt Lake is the prinicpal recreation feature here. Admitted to the National Park System on Dec. 18, 1946.

VISITOR ACTIVITIES: water skiing, boating, swimming, camping, bird-watching, picnicking, audiovisual programs, interpretive talks and exhibits, fishing, hunting; **Permits:** for fishing and hunting available at local sporting goods stores, Licenses vary in length of validity and cost; **Fees:** $3 camping fee at the following sites: Kettle Falls, Evans (near Kettle), Ft. Spokane, Spring Canyon, & Porcupine Bay; **Visitor facilities:** picnic areas, boat ramps, guarded beaches, individual and group campsites, boat and trailer dump stations, drinking water, bathhouse, ferry service; **Any limitations on vehicle usage:** Off-road vehicle use is prohibited; **Hiking trails:** Yes, two short, 1.6 km (1 mile) nature trails; **Backcountry:** No; **Camping:** Yes, no reservations available for campsites ; **Other overnight accommodations on site:** No, for further information on lodging in the vicinity, contact: Chamber of Commerce, Grand Coulee, WA 99133, phone 509-633-0361; **Meals served in the park:** No; **Food and supplies obtainable in the park:** No; **Food and supplies obtainable nearby:** Yes, in Grand Coulee, Coulee Dam, Colville, Kettle Falls, Northport; **Overnight accommodations:** Grand Coulee, Coulee Dam, Colville, Kettle Falls, Northport; **First Aid available in park:** Yes; **Nearest Hospital:** Grand Coulee, 8 km (5 miles) from Spring Canyon campground; Davenport, 40 km (25 miles) from Fort Spokane campground; and Colville, 16 km (10 miles) from Kettle Falls campground; **Days/Hours:** Park always open. Visitor Centers are open daily from 8 a.m. to 4:30 p.m., with extended hours in season; **Holiday Closings:** None; **Visitor attractions closed for seasons:**The recreation season is May through Oct.; **Weather:** The west arm of the lake is usually quite warm and sunny, while the north arm, influenced by the mountains, tends to be cooler and have more clouds and precipitation. Summer temperatures range from 75°-100°F during the day and between 50 ° and 60 ° at night. It is somewhat cooler in Spring and Autumn. Bring a light jacket for chilly evenings. Occasional foggy and cloudy days occur in Winter and Spring.

GENERAL INFORMATION: *For Your Safety*—Be alert to avoid floating logs and debris. Approach log rafts with caution-cables extend between the rafts and tugboats. Be sure to drown your campfires.

Ebey's Landing National Historical Reserve
Whidbey Island, Washington

MAILING ADDRESS: Pacific Northwest Regional Office, National Park Service, 601 4th and Pike Building, Seattle, Washington 98101 **Telephone:** 206-442-4830

DIRECTIONS: THERE ARE NO DEVELOPED FACILITIES.

The area preserves the 19th century rural community and commemorates Captain George Vancouver's exploration of Puget Sound in 1792 and the settlement of Whidbey Island by Colonel Isaac Ebey, killed by Indians in 1792. Established by act of Congress on Nov. 10, 1978.

Fort Vancouver National Historic Site
Vancouver, Washington

MAILING ADDRESS: Superintendent, Fort Vancouver National Historic Site, Vancouver, Washington 98661 **Telephone:** 206-696-7655

DIRECTIONS: To reach the Site, turn east off I-5 at the Mill Plain Boulevard interchange and then follow signs to the Visitor Center on East Evergreen Boulevard.

As the western headquarters of Hudson's Bay Company from 1825-1860, this was the hub of political and fur-trading activities. A U.S. military reservation—Vancouver Barracks, established in 1849—took over the fort in 1860, remaining active until 1949. Authorized for addition to the National Park System on June 19, 1948.

VISITOR ACTIVITIES: interpretive exhibits and tours of reconstructed buildings at the fort site; **Permits:** No; **Fees:** No; **Visitor facilities:** parking and restrooms at the Visitor Center and at the Fort Site, information and sales desk; **Any limitations on vehicle usage:** No; **Hiking trails:** No; **Backcountry:** No; **Camping:** No; **Other overnight accommodations on site:** No; **Meals served in the park:** No; **Food and supplies obtainable in the park:** No; **Food and supplies obtainable nearby:** Yes, in Vancouver; **Overnight accommodations:** Vancouver; **First Aid available in park:** Yes; **Nearest Hospital:** Vancouver Memorial Hospital, 3 km (2 miles); **Days/Hours:** Open daily from 8:30 a.m. to 4:30 p.m. with extended hours in Summer; **Holiday Closings:** Thanksgiving, Dec. 25, & Jan. 1; **Visitor attractions closed for seasons:** Living history demonstrations are not offered from October through May; **Weather:** Rain is common from October through May; cold weather from November through February. Summers are warm.

GENERAL INFORMATION: *For Your Safety*-Watch your step at the fort because ground is uneven.

Klondike Gold Rush National Historical Park
For details see listing in Alaska

Lewis and Clark Trail
For details see listing in Illinois

Lake Chelan National Recreation Area
Chelan, Washington

MAILING ADDRESS: District Manager, North Cascades National Park, Stehekin, Washington 98852 **Telephone:** 509-682-2459

DIRECTIONS: Access to the North Cascades area from Burlington on the west and Twisp on the east follows WA 20. The main access to Stehekin in LCNRA is by boat or float plane from the town of Chelan on Hwy 97. There is no road access into Stehekin. Service is provided by Lake Chelan Boat Co., Chelan, WA 98852, phone 509-682-2224. Daily boat service from Stehekin to Chelan is maintained from May 15 to Sept. 30. From Oct. 1 to May 14 the boats go on Sunday, Monday, Wednesday, and Friday. There is no Sunday boat from Jan. 1 - Feb. 14. Air service is available for charter year round, weather permitting, from Chelan Airways, Chelan, WA 98816, phone 509-682-5555.

Here the scenic Stehekin Valley, with a portion of fjordlike Lake Chelan, adjoins the southern unit of North Cascades National Park. Established by act of Congress Oct. 2, 1968.

VISITOR ACTIVITIES: interpretive exhibits, guided and self-guiding tours, picnicking, camping, hiking, mountain climbing, horseback riding, boating, fishing, hunting; **Permits:** required for backcountry, are available at Ranger Stations at Stehekin, Chelan, and Marblemount; **Fees:** No; **Visitor facilities:** Picnic area, campground, backcountry, boat and bicycle rentals, restaurant, lodging, supplies, post office, shuttle bus; **Any limitations on vehicle usage:** The Area is inaccessible to vehicles; **Hiking trails:** Yes, a variety from low land day hikes to elevation gains of 6,000 feet; **Backcountry:** No; **Camping:** Yes, no permits are required for boat camps. No reservations are accepted for campsites. Backcountry, crosscountry and trail camps require a permit. Group campgrounds are available by mail reservation. Lodge rooms and housekeeping facilities available year round. Write or call North Cascades Lodge, Stehekin, WA 98852, 509-662-3822.; **Other overnight accommodations on site:** Yes; **Meals served in the park:** Yes, at North Cascades Lodge; **Food and supplies obtainable in the park:** Yes, at North Cascades Lodge; **Food and supplies obtainable nearby:** Yes, Chelan; **Overnight accommodations:** Chelan, 80 km (50 miles); **First Aid available in park:** Yes, at Ranger Station; **Nearest Hospital:** Chelan, 80 km (50 miles); **Days/Hours:** Open 24 hours a day everyday; **Holiday Closings:** None; **Visitor attractions closed for seasons:** guided walks and programs from late June to early Sept. Shuttle bus from mid-May to late Sept.; **Weather:** Outdoor recreation can be enjoyed year-round. The lower levels of the valley are accessible from early Apr. to mid-Nov.

GENERAL INFORMATION: See listing in this book for North Cascades National Park and Ross Lake National Recreation Area, the two other areas of the North Cascades Group. For your safety in the backcountry—hang all food out of the reach of bears. Stream crossings can be hazardous during periods of high water. Check conditions with a Park Ranger before starting out. Snow may linger in higher places. Crossing snowfields may require special equipment. Visitors on horseback should carry adequate feed for their trip, since forage is scarce in most of the Area. A special permit is required for livestock use.

Mount Rainier National Park
Ashford, Washington

MAILING ADDRESS: Superintendent, Mount Rainier National Park, Tahoma Woods, Star Route, Ashford, Washington 98304 **Telephone:** 206-569-2211

DIRECTIONS: The Longmire Visitor Center is 113 km (70 miles) southeast of Tacoma on Route 7 to Elbe, then Route 706 to Longmire. It is 153 km (95 miles) southeast of Seattle, and 166 km (103 miles) west of Yakima.
This greatest single-peak glacial system in the United States radiates from the summit and slopes of an ancient volcano, with dense forests and sub-alpine flowered meadows below. Established by act of Congress on Mar. 2, 1899.

VISITOR ACTIVITIES: hiking, backcountry, climbing, fishing, snowshoeing, camping, crosscountry skiing, picnicking, winter sports, interpretive programs, wildlife-watching, snowmobiling; **Permits:** required for backcountry camping, available at Ranger Stations and Visitor Centers; **Fees:** $2 per auto entrance fee, Golden Age and Golden Eagle Passports are accepted and available; **Visitor facilities:** exhibits at Visitor Centers, restrooms, lodging, hiking trails, picnic areas, mountain climbing equipment rentals, food service, nature trails, snowshoe and crosscountry ski rentals and instruction in Winter; **Any limitations on vehicle usage:** Vehicles must stay on public automobile roads; **Hiking trails:** Yes, self-guiding nature trails in different areas of the Park; **Back-

country: Yes, inquire at Ranger Stations or Visitor Centers; **Camping:** Yes, no reservations available for campsites; **Other overnight accommodations on site:** Yes, accommodations are available at National Park Inn at Longmire (year round) and at Paradise Inn (mid-June to Labor Day). For information on schedule and rates, write or call Mount Rainier National Park Hospitality Service, 4820 S. Washington, Tacoma, WA 98409 phone 206-475-6260; **Meals served in the park:** Yes, Longmire, Paradise, and Sunrise; **Food and supplies obtainable in the park:** Yes, at Longmire and Sunrise; **Food and supplies obtainable nearby:**Yes,at Ashford, Packwood, Enumclaw; **Overnight accommodations:** Ashford, Hwy 706, immediately adjacent to the Park; **First Aid available in park:** Yes; **Nearest Hospital:** Enumclaw, Hwy 410, 64 km (40 miles); Morton, Hwy 12, 74.2 km (40 miles); **Days/Hours:** Open 24 hours a day year-round; **Holiday Closings:** None; **Visitor attractions closed for seasons:**Snow closes roads for short periods. Chains may be required for winter driving. Except for the roads from Nisqually Entrance to Paradise (WA 706), many park roads are usually closed from late Nov. through June or July.

GENERAL INFORMATION: *For Your Safety*—In the backcountry, hike only in the company of others; remember your limitations. Be prepared for sudden and extreme weather changes. Bring your own shelter.

North Cascades National Park
Sedro Woolley, Washington

MAILING ADDRESS: Superintendent, North Cascades National Park, 800 State Street, Sedro Woolley, Washington 98284 **Telephone:** 206-855-1331

DIRECTIONS: Access to the North Cascades area from Burlington on the West and Twisp on the East follows WA 20 with branch routes to Baker River and Cascade River. Hiking access and roadside views of the northwest corner are available from WA 542 east from Bellingham. Access to Stehekin Valley is by boat, float-plane or trail. Vehicle access to Ross Lake is by unimproved road from Canada.

High jagged peaks intercept moisture-laden winds, producing glaciers, icefalls, waterfalls, and other water phenomena in this wild alpine region, with varied plant and animal communities in the valleys. Established by act of Congress on Oct. 2, 1968.

VISITOR ACTIVITIES: camping, backcountry, hiking, mountain climbing, horseback riding, fishing, auto tours, boating, wildlife- and bird-watching; **Permits:** for backcountry, available without charge at Park Offices or Ranger Stations. A Washington State fishing license, available locally, is required; **Fees:** Yes, fees are charged in the developed road access campgrounds; **Visitor facilities:** campgrounds, launching ramps, resorts, hiking trails, horse and mule rentals nearby, professional guide and packtrain services; **Any limitations on vehicle usage:** Vehicles are restricted to maintained roads; **Hiking trails:** Yes, about 556 km (360 miles) of hiking and horse trails throughhout the four North Cascades units; **Backcountry:** Yes, information can be obtained from Park Offices or Ranger Stations.; **Camping:** Yes, no reservations available for campsites; **Other overnight accommodations on site:** Yes, for information on lodging, contact North Cascades Lodge, Stehekin, WA 98852, Diablo Lake Resort; **Meals served in the park:** Yes, Diablo Lake Resort and Stehekin; **Food and supplies obtainable in the park:** Yes, Stehekin and Diablo Lake Resort; **Food and supplies obtainable nearby:** Yes, Marblemount and Newhalem; **Overnight accommodations:** The larger cities and town near the North Cascades group have the usual tourist accommodations, but are 2-to-3 hour drives from park boundaries. Small communities within or adjacent to the areas have limited guest accommodations. The chambers of commerce for each of the counties and towns surrounding the North Cascades group have information on accommodations, packers, guides, and other outdoor services; **First Aid available in park:** Yes, at Ranger Stations; **Nearest Hospital:** Sedro Woolley; **Days/Hours:** Park open all year, but snow conditions prevent access during the Winter; **Holiday Closings:** None; **Visitor attractions closed for seasons:** restricted access to most areas in Winter; **Weather:** Outdoor recreation can be enjoyed year-round. The lower elevations and the big lakes are accessible from early April to mid-October, but at higher elevations the season is from mid-July to mid-Sept. The western side of the North Cascades gets more rain, has more lakes and streams, and more abundant vegetation. Consequently, it has less sunshine and cooler days than the eastern side of the mountains, where more sunshine, warm rock surfaces, and sparse vegetation afford warm days and cool nights typical of a dry climate.

GENERAL INFORMATION: See listings in this book for two other units of the North Cascades Group: Lake Chelan and Ross Lake National Recreation Areas. *For Your Safety in the backcountry*—hang all food out of the reach of bears. Stream crossings can be hazardous during periods of high water. Check conditions with a Park Ranger before starting out. Snow many linger in higher places. Crossing snowfields may require special equipment. Horsemen should carry adequate feed for their trip. Forage is scarce in most of the park. Grazing not permitted in the Park. A special permit is required for livestock use.

Olympic National Park
Port Angeles, Washington

MAILING ADDRESS: Superintendent, Olympic National Park, 600 E. Park Avenue, Port Angeles, Washington 98362 **Telephone:** 206-452-9235

DIRECTIONS: Visitor Centers at Port Angeles and Hoh Rain Forest are open year-round. At Lake Crescent, the Storm King Visitor Center is open only in Summer.
This mountain wilderness contains the finest remnant of Pacific Northwest rain forest (the only temperate zone rain forest in North America), active glaciers, rare Roosevelt elk and 80 km (50 miles) of wild, scenic ocean shore. Proclaimed a national monument on Mar. 2, 1909; established as a national park on June 29, 1938.

VISITOR ACTIVITIES: interpretive and audiovisual programs, camping, auto tours, bird- and wildlife-watching, picnicking, nature walks, hiking, horseback riding, mountain climbing, fishing, backcountry, swimming, skiing, snowshoeing; **Permits:** for backcountry, available at Ranger Stations; **Fees:** for summer camping in developed "class A" campgrounds; **Visitor facilities:** nature trails, parking, restrooms, campgrounds, fireplaces, picnic area, beaches, bathhouse, ski and snowshoe trails, lodging; **Any limitations on vehicle usage:** Vehicles are restricted to designated roadways; **Hiking trails:** Yes, trails vary from those requiring a day or less to wilderness pathways taking up to a week or more. Trail condition reports are available at Visitor Centers and Ranger Stations; **Backcountry:** Yes, information available at Ranger Stations and Visitor Centers; **Camping:** Yes, no reservations accepted for campsites; **Other overnight accommodations on site:** Yes, reserve lodging by the lodging facility: Kalaloch Beach Ocean Village, Route 1, Box 11100, Forks, WA 98331, phone 206-962-2271; Log Cabin Resort, Route 1, Box 6540, Port Angeles, WA 98362, 206-928-3245; Lake Crescent Lodge, Star Route 1, Port Angeles, WA 206-928-3211; Sol Duc Hot Springs, National Park Concessions, Inc., Star Route 1, Port Angeles, WA 98362, 206-928-3211; **Meals served in the park:** Yes, at Hurricane Ridge, Sol Duc, Fairholm, Kalaloch; **Food and supplies obtainable in the park:** Yes, at small grocery stores at some lodges; Shelton and Aberdeen;

Food and supplies obtainable nearby: Yes, at supermarkets at Sequim, Port Angeles, Forks, Shelton, and Aberdeen; **Overnight accommodations:** Port Angeles, Aberdeen, Forks, Sequim and Shelton. For information on facilities near the Park, write the Olympic Peninsula Resort and Hotel Association, Coleman Ferry Terminal, Seattle, WA 98104; **First Aid available in park:** Yes, at most Ranger Stations; **Nearest Hospital:** Port Angeles, Forks, Shelton, Aberdeen-Hoquiam; **Days/Hours:** Park open year-round. Only Visitor Centers and Ranger Stations have closing hours. Most Ranger Stations open 8 a.m.-5 p.m. Hoh Visitor Center: 9 a.m. - 6 p.m. Port Angeles Visitor Center: 8 a.m.-4 p.m.; **Holiday Closings:** Buildings closed Dec. 25 & Jan.1; **Visitor attractions closed for seasons:** Some lodges are open only in Summer. All roads in high elevations are usually open June 1-Oct.1; high elevation trails open July 15-Oct 1.

GENERAL INFORMATION: *For Your Safety*—Stay on trails. Backcountry campers should include a tent and a backpacker's stove in their equipment. Keep your distance from animals. When hiking on the beach, round the headlands only on the outgoing tide to avoid being trapped against the headland cliffs by the incoming tide. The tide and cliffs permit no escape.

Ross Lake National Recreation Area
Sedro Woolley, Washington

MAILING ADDRESS: Superintendent, Ross Lake National Recreation Area, c/o North Cascades National Park, 800 State Street, Sedro Woolley, Washington 98284 **Telephone:** 206-873-4500 or 206-855-1331

DIRECTIONS: Access to the Park is via WA 20 from Burlington on the West and Winthrop on the East.
Ringed by mountains, this reservoir in the Skagit River drainage separates the north and south units of North Cascades National Park. Established by act of Congress on Oct. 2, 1968.

VISITOR ACTIVITIES: hiking, boating, canoeing, rock climbing, camping, wildlife- and bird-watching, auto tours, backcountry, horseback riding; **Permits:** required for backcountry, can be obtained at all Ranger Stations; **Fees:** Camping fee is $3 per night per site at Colonial Creek Campground; $1 per night at Goodell Creek Campground; **Visitor facilities:** boat rentals, campgrounds, lodging, boat launching ramps, wayside exhibits; **Any limitations on vehicle usage:** Only one vehicle is allowed at each campsite; **Hiking trails:** Yes, seven major trails lead outward from Ross Lake into the backcountry; **Backcountry:** Yes, information can be obtained by writing the Superintendent or visiting park offices in Sedro Woolley, Chelan, or Marblemount; **Camping:** Yes, no reservations available for campsites; **Other overnight accommodations on site:** Yes, for information on lodging, contact: Diablo Lake Resort, Rockport, Washington 98283, phone 206 Operator, Newhalem 4735; **Meals served in the park:** Yes, at Diablo Lake Resort; **Food and supplies obtainable in the park:** Yes, at Diablo Lake Resort and Newhalem, WA; **Food and supplies obtainable nearby:** Yes, at Marblemount, WA and Concrete, WA; **Overnight accommodations:** Marblemount, WA, 13 km (8 miles); Concrete, WA, 45 km (28 miles); **First Aid available in park:** Yes, or nearby in Diablo and Newhalem, WA; **Nearest Hospital:** Sedro Woolley, WA 20, 74.2 km (45 miles); **Days/Hours:** Park open year-round; **Holiday Closings:** Office closed Thanksgiving, Dec. 25 and Jan.1; **Visitor attractions closed for seasons:** Hwy 20 and all campgrounds except Goodell Creek are closed in Winter; **Weather:** Summer is warm and sometimes quite hot with temperatures frequently in the high 90°sF. Fall has warm days and cool nights. Strong winds and whitecaps occur frequently and without warning.

GENERAL INFORMATION: See listings in this book for other units of the North Cascades Group: Lake Chelan National Recreation Area and North Cascades National Park. *For Your Safety in the backcountry*—hang all food out of the reach of bears. Stream crossings can be hazardous during periods of high water. Check conditions with the Park Ranger before starting out. Snow may linger in higher places. Crossing snowfields may require special equipment. Horsemen should carry adequate feed for their trip. Forage is scarce in most of the park. Grazing not permitted in the park. A special permit is required for livestock use.

San Juan Island National Historical Park
Friday Harbor, Washington

MAILING ADDRESS: Superintendent, San Juan Island National Historical Park, 300 Cattle Point Road, Friday Harbor, Washington 98250 **Telephone:** 206-378-4180 or 206-378-2240

DIRECTIONS: San Juan Island is reached by Washington State Ferries from Anacortes, WA, 133.6 km (83 miles) north of Seattle; or from Sidney, British Columbia, 24 km (15 miles) north of Victoria. The island is also accessible by private boats. There are good docking facilities at Friday and Roche Harbors. Commercial air flights are scheduled regularly from Bellingham and Seattle, WA, to Friday Harbor. Private one- and two-engine planes can land at airstrips at Friday and Roche Harbors.

The Park commemoriates the peaceful relations maintained by the United States, Great Britain and Canada since the 1872 boundary dispute here. English and American military campsites are included. Authorized for addition to the National Park System on Sept. 9, 1966.

VISITOR ACTIVITIES: picnicking, hiking, interpretive exhibits—no camping is allowed at either American or English Camps; **Permits:** No; **Fees:** No; **Visitor facilities:** A temporary Park Headquarters has been established at American Camp, and visitor facilities and conveniences are minimal. Rangers are on duty during the Summer to answer questions and explain points of interest. Picnic areas are available at both camps. No drinking water is available at English Camp. Water is available at American Camp. Small fires are allowed at South Beach, and at Picnic Ground Beach at American Camp, but they must be 5 feet beyond the driftwood and toward the water's edge; **Any limitations on vehicle usage:** Off-road vehicle travel (by auto, truck, motorcycle, or bicycle) is not allowed within the Park; **Hiking trails:** Yes, American and English Camps have historic trails; **Backcountry:** No; **Camping:** No **Other overnight accommodations on site:** No; **Meals served in the park:** No, but, nearby at Friday and Roche Harbors; **Food and supplies obtainable in the park:** No; **Food and supplies obtainable nearby:** Yes, Friday Harbor (year-round); **Overnight accommodations:** Friday Harbor, 9.7 km (6 miles) from American Camp, and 17.7 km (11 miles) from English Camp; **First Aid available in park:** Yes; **Nearest Hospital:** Friday Harbor, 9.7 km (6 miles) from American Camp, and 17.7 km (11 miles) from English Camp; **Days/Hours:** The roads through the Park are open year-round. The buildings are open from about 9 a.m. to 6 p.m. daily during the Summer and on weekends during Spring and Fall; **Holiday Closings:** Dec. 25 and Jan. 1; **Visitor attractions closed for seasons:** Exhibits shelter at American Camp closed during Winter, inclement weather; **Weather:** Winters can be cold, windy and rainy; Summers are warm, but never hot.

GENERAL INFORMATION: Safety Notes: *Watch your Step*, especially in the vicinity of the American Camp. The San Juan rabbit digs many holes that can cause sprained ankles and broken bones. *Swimming is discouraged* because the water temperature remains below 50 ° all year. Try beachcombing instead. *Tree climbing is dangerous* for you and harmful to the trees. *Look out for insecure footing* on the primitive trails and watch for overhanging branches and downed limbs.

Whitman Mission National Historic Site
Walla Walla, Washington

MAILING ADDRESS: Superintendent, Whitman Mission National Historic Site, Route 2, Walla Walla, Washington 99362 **Telephone:** 509-525-5500, x 465

DIRECTIONS: The Visitor Center is 13 km (8 miles) west of Walla Walla on US 12. It is 6 km (4 miles) west of College Place.

Dr. and Mrs. Marcus Whitman ministered to spiritual and physical needs of the Indians here until slain by a few of them in 1847. The Mission was a landmark on the Oregon Trail. Authorized for addition to the National Park System on June 29, 1936.

VISITOR ACTIVITIES: interpretive exhibits, picnicking, cultural demonstrations; **Permits:** No; **Fees:** No; **Visitor facilities:** self-guiding foot trails, wayside exhibits, museum with audiovisual program, picnic area; **Any limitations on vehicle usage:** No; **Hiking trails:** No, there are 1.4 km (9/10 mile) of foot trails; **Backcountry:** No; **Camping:** No; **Other overnight accommodations on site:** No; **Meals served in the park:** No; **Food and supplies obtainable in the park:** No; **Food and supplies obtainable nearby:** Yes, College Place and Walla Walla; **Overnight accommodations:** Walla Walla and College Place, 9.7-13 km (6-8 miles) east of the park; **First Aid available in park:** Yes, in the Visitor Center; **Nearest Hospital:** Walla Walla, 13 km (8 miles) east of the park; **Days/Hours:** Open daily from 8 a.m. to 4:30 p.m., with extended hours in Summer; **Holiday Closings:** Thanksgiving, Dec. 25 and Jan. 1; **Visitor attractions closed for seasons:** Cultural demonstrations are only offered in Summer; **Weather:** Summer is hot and dry; Winter is cold and dry.

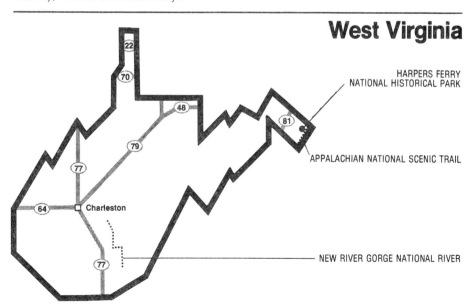

West Virginia

HARPERS FERRY
NATIONAL HISTORICAL PARK

APPALACHIAN NATIONAL SCENIC TRAIL

NEW RIVER GORGE NATIONAL RIVER

Charleston

Appalachian National Scenic Trail
For details see listing in Maine

New River Gorge National River
West Virginia

MAILING ADDRESS: Mid-Atlantic Regional Office, National Park Service, 143 S. Third Street, Philadelphia, Pennsylvania 19106 **Telephone:** 215-597-6379

DIRECTIONS: NO LANDS HAVE BEEN ACQUIRED AS YET.
Contact the Mid-Atlantic Regional Office of the National Park Service for information on outfitters who offer raft trips on the river.
The area preserves 106.2 km (66 miles) of the New River, from Hinton to Gauley as a free-flowing stream abundant in natural, scenic, historic, and recreational values. Authorized for addition to the National Park System on Nov. 10, 1978.

Harpers Ferry National Historical Park
Harpers Ferry, West Virginia

MAILING ADDRESS: Superintendent, Harpers Ferry National Historical Park, P.O. Box 65, Harpers Ferry, West Virginia 25425 **Telephone:** 304-535-6371 x222

DIRECTIONS: The Park is 32 km (20 miles) northwest of Frederick, MD, via US 340. It is 9.7 km (6 miles) south of Charles Town. The Visitor Center is less than 1.6 km (1 mile) off US 340, after a right turn beyond the bridge over the Shenandoah River.
A Federal Armory was established at Harpers Ferry in the late 1700's. Because of its strategic location at the confluence of the Shenandoah and Potomac Rivers, the town changed hands many times during the Civil War. John Brown's raid took place here in 1859. Authorized for addition to the National Park System on June 30, 1944.

VISITOR ACTIVITIES: interpretive audiovisual program, walking tours, mountain climbing, hiking, fishing, living history demonstrations, wildflower-watching, Christmas festival on the first weekend in December; **Permits:** Yes, permit for climbing, can be obtained at Park Ranger's office; **Fees:** No; **Visitor facilities:** Parking, restrooms, restored sites. Picnic areas and campgrounds are in the immediate area, but there are none in the Park itself; **Any limitations on vehicle usage:** Drive carefully; automobile traffic on the narrow streets is often quite heavy; **Hiking trails:** Yes, variety of hiking trails are located nearby; **Backcountry:** No; **Camping:** No; **Other overnight accommodations on site:** No, but several campgrounds are nearby. KOA Campground is within 1.6 km (1 mile) of the Park. For further information and reservations, contact KOA at Harpers Ferry, WV 25425, phone 304-535-6895; **Meals served in the park:** No; **Food and supplies obtainable in the park:** No; **Food and supplies obtainable nearby:** Yes, in the towns of Harpers Ferry, Boliver, Charles Town, and other nearby communities; **Overnight accommodations:** Harpers Ferry, Charles Town, on US 340, 11.3 km (7 miles); **First Aid available in park:** Yes, at the Ranger Office; **Nearest Hospital:** Charles Town, US 340, 11.3 km (7 miles); **Days/Hours:** The Visitor Center and National Park Service sites are open daily all year, from 8 a.m. to 5 p.m., until 6 p.m. in Summer; **Holiday Closings:** Dec. 25, and Jan. 1; **Visitor attractions closed for seasons:** Most of the activities in the Park are centered around the spring and summer months. In the Fall and Spring, park activities are usually restricted to weekends, but the Visitor Center and several of the historic buildings do remain open. Wildflowers abound in late Spring, and fall colors are striking.

GENERAL INFORMATION: Brick and natural stone walkways and steps are sometimes uneven or slippery. Pedestrians, especially children, should be cautious, as automobile traffic is often quite heavy. Mountain climbers should register at the Ranger Station before climbing the cliffs on Maryland Heights. Beware of the rivers. At low water they appear calm and peaceful. This is deceptive, however, as deep holes and swift undercurrents make them treacherous at any time of the year. There are no frequent checks on pollutants. Swimming is not advised. Fishermen and boaters should wear life jackets.

Wisconsin

APOSTLE ISLANDS NATIONAL LAKESHORE

SAINT CROIX NATIONAL
SCENIC RIVERWAY

LOWER ST. CROIX
NATIONAL SCENIC RIVERWAY

ICE AGE NATIONAL SCIENTIFIC RESERVE

53

8

94

51

94

90

43

94
Milwaukee

90

94

Apostle Islands National Lakeshore
Bayfield, Wisconsin

MAILING ADDRESS: Superintendent, Apostle Islands National Lakeshore, P.O. Box 729, Bayfield, Wisconsin 54814 **Telephone:** 715-779-3397

DIRECTIONS: East of Duluth from US 2, WI 13 leads north up the east shore of Bayfield Peninsula to Bayfield, site of the Park Headquarters and Visitor Center.

The Lakeshore comprises twenty picturesque woodled islands and a 17.7 km (11 mile) strip of adjacent Bayfield Peninsula in the southwestern portion of Lake Superior characterized by sand beaches, high clay banks and sandstone cliffs. Established by act of

Congress on Sept. 26, 1970.

VISITOR ACTIVITIES: Island camping, hiking, picnicking, swimming, boating, cross-country skiing, snowshoeing, car ferries, excursion boats, chartered fishing trips, rental power and sail boats and outstanding sport fishing are available; **Permits:** Yes, Wisconsin State fishing license is available locally. Free backcountry permits available at Visitor Center or Ranger Stations; **Fees:** No; **Visitor facilities:** Interpretive exhibits and audiovisual programs at Visitor Center and in Summer, evening programs and nature walks are presented on Stockton Island. Campgrounds in numerous designated areas and concessioners provide shuttle trips between islands, excursion trips, boat rental and charter fishing trips, marina, launch ramps, parking, showers; **Any limitations on vehicle usage:** Restricted by car ferry service; **Hiking trails:** Yes, wide range from maintained trails to old logging and railroad trails overgrown with underbrush or rocky trails which may be slippery or loose; **Backcountry:** Yes, at Bayfield or Little Sand Bay; **Camping:** Yes; **Other overnight accommodations on site:** No; **Meals served in the park:** No; **Food and supplies obtainable in the park:** Yes, at Little Sand Bay in Summer; **Food and supplies obtainable nearby:** Yes, at Bayfield, Cornucopia, Ashland, and Madeline Island; **Overnight accommodations:** Bayfield, Washburn, Cornucopia, and the nearby Chequamegon National Forest; **First Aid available in park:** No; **Nearest Hospital:** Washburn, Hwy 13, 40.2 km (25 miles); Ashland, Hwy 13, 64.4 km (40 miles); **Days/Hours:** Open every day year-round; **Holiday Closings:** None; **Visitor attractions closed for seasons:**None; **Weather:** Winter temperatures of -35°C(-30°F) and wind chill factors of -50°C (-60°F) are not uncommon. Nearly 250 cm (100 inches) of snow falls each year. Winter ice conditions vary with temperature, snowfall, and wind. Extreme caution is required for travelling across ice, as shifting winds may cause cracks and floes.

GENERAL INFORMATION: Biting insects are common from early May to mid-Sept. When hiking or camping, be prepared. Insect repellents are useful, but clothing that covers exposed skin is the best protection. Hiking near cliffs can be dangerous! Wet rocks are slippery and loose rocks may cause falls. Beware of dangerous waters. Even in Summer, Lake Superior's waters are dangerously cold, and sudden storms may break its surface. The temperature of the water a meter or so from shore may be 10°C (50°F) or less-cold enough to cause a strong swimmer to drown in 15 minutes.

About 5 km (3 miles) north of Bayfield is the Red Cliff Indian Reservation, the home of approximately 600 Chippewa Indians. The Red Cliff Cultural Center, open year-round, contains exhibits and artifacts. Hand-crafted items are offered for sale.

Ice Age National Scientific Reserve
Wisconsin

MAILING ADDRESS: Wisconsin Department of Natural Resources, P.O. Box 7921, Madison, Wisconsin 53707 **Telephone:** 608-266-2181

DIRECTIONS: Devils Lake and Mill Bluff are accessible from Int. 90-94. Kettle Moraine is accessible from WI 67, which runs the length of the Unit. Access to Interstate Unit is from US 8 and WI 35.

This first national scientific reserve contains significant features of continental glaciation. There are nine separate units located across the State from Lake Michigan on the East to the St. Croix River on the Minnesota-Wisconsin border. Four of the nine units are operational; The Kettle Moraine State Forest, and Devils Lake, Mill Bluff, and Interstate Parks. Authorized for addition to the National Park System on Oct. 13, 1964.

VISITOR ACTIVITIES: interpretive exhibits, auto tours, camping, hiking, fishing, swimming, picnicking, naturalist services, cross-country skiing; **Permits:** Wisconsin fishing licenses, available from local sporting goods stores or from the Department of Natural Resources, are required; **Fees:** Vehicle use fees are $1.50 per day or $5 annually for residents of Wisconsin; $2.50 per day or $8 annually for non-residents. Camping fees vary from $2.25 to $3.25 per site, depending on facilities. Golden Eagle and Golden Age Passports accepted and available; **Visitor facilities:** scenic drives, hiking trails, beaches, campgrounds, picnic areas, restrooms, ski trails; **Any limitations on vehicle usage:** Motor vehicles should be operated only where permitted; **Hiking trails:** Yes, trails vary from nature walks to a 48 km (30 mile) hiking trail at Kettle Moraine, which offers reserved shelters; **Backcountry:** Yes, by contacting Kettle Moraine, phone 414-626-2116; **Camping:** Yes, information by contacting the following units: Devils Lake, phone 608-356-8301; Northern Kettle Moraine, phone 414-626-2116; Interstate, phone 715-483-3747; **Other overnight accommodations on site:** No; **Meals served in the park:** No; **Food and supplies obtainable in the park:** Yes, at Kettle Moraine and Devils Lake; **Food and supplies obtainable nearby:** Yes, Baraboo, Campbellsport, St. Croix Falls and other nearby towns; **Overnight accommodations:** Baraboo, Campbellsport, St. Croix Falls and other towns near the Ice Age Units. **First Aid available in park:** Yes; **Nearest Hospital:** Fond du Lac, Baraboo, Campbellsport, St. Croix Falls and other nearby communities; **Days/Hours:** Most parks open from 6 a.m. to 11 p.m.; **Holiday Closings:** None; **Visitor attractions closed for seasons:** Naturalist activities are curtailed at most units during the off-season, but are offered year-round at Kettle Moraine and Devils Lake.

GENERAL INFORMATION: *For Your Safety*—When hiking, stay on designated trails. Swim only in authorized areas when lifeguards are on duty.

Lower St. Croix National Scenic Riverway
Wisconsin (also in Minnesota)

MAILING ADDRESS: Superintendent, Lower Saint Croix River, c/o Saint Croix National Scenic River, P.O. Box 708, St. Croix Falls, Wisconsin 54024 **Telephone:** 715-483-3287

DIRECTIONS: Park Headquarters located at the corner of Hamilton and Massachusetts Streets in St. Croix Falls, WI.

Recreational opportunities for much of the upper Midwest are provided here along this 84 km (52 mile) segment of the St. Croix River, a component of the Wild and Scenic River System. Authorized for addition to the National Park System on Oct. 25, 1972. 43.5 km (27 miles) of this segment is administered by the National Park Service with the remaining 40 km (25 miles) administered by the states of Wisconsin and Minnesota.

VISITOR ACTIVITIES: boating, fishing, camping, interpretive exhibits, swimming, hunting, and hiking within state parks located along the Riverway, commercial boat trips; **Permits:** No; **Fees:** No; **Visitor facilities:** campgrounds, boat ramps, canoe rentals, commercial guided boat trip available on the river at Taylor's Falls and Stillwater, MN; **Any limitations on vehicle usage:** Recreational vehicle use discouraged at designated canoe landings with road access; **Hiking trails:** No, but hiking trails are within state parks located along Riverway; **Backcountry:** Yes; **Camping:** No, no reservations for campsites on Federal lands. For information and reservations in state parks write the Departments of Natural Resources in either St. Paul, MN 55155, phone 612-296-6157 or Madison, WI 53702, phone 608-266-2621; **Other overnight accommodations on site:** No; **Meals served in the park:** No; **Food and supplies obtainable in the park:** No; **Food and**

supplies obtainable nearby: Yes, Marine on St. Croix, Osceola, Stillwater; **Overnight accommodations:** Marine on St. Croix, Osceola, Stillwater and other towns along the Riverway; **First Aid available in park:** Yes, at Park Headquarters or State Park Ranger Stations; **Nearest Hospital:** Osceola and St. Croix Falls, WI and Stillwater, MN; **Days/ Hours:** Riverway open year-round but normal season is from Memorial Day through Labor Day with most activities available from about April through Oct.; **Holiday Closings:** Park Headquarters closed Thanksgiving, Dec. 25 & Jan. 1; **Visitor attractions closed for seasons:** Seasonal Visitor Center closed in winter months. Commercial boat trips closed in Winter.

GENERAL INFORMATION: Before setting out for canoeing, make sure you have a life preserver for each person, an extra paddle, insect repellent, a small gasoline stove, and drinking water. Firewood is very scarce in the vicinity of the campsites, and the cutting of trees or brush is prohibited. Drinking water is available at only a few places along the River.

Saint Croix National Scenic Riverway
Wisconsin (also in Minnesota)

MAILING ADDRESS: Superintendent, Saint Croix National Scenic Riverway, P.O. Box 708, Saint Croix Falls, Wisconsin 54024 **Telephone:** 715-483-3287

DIRECTIONS: Park Headquarters is at the corner of Hamilton and Massachusetts Streets in St. Croix Falls. Interpretive pamphlets and maps are available here.
  Over 321 km (200 miles) of the scenic St. Croix River and its Namekagon tributary make up this area, an initial component of the National Wild and Scenic River System. Authorized for addition to the National Park System on Oct. 2, 1968.

VISITOR ACTIVITIES: fishing, canoeing, wildlife- and bird-watching, swimming, boating, interpretive exhibits, camping, hiking in nearby state forests and parks, hunting, commercial launch trips at Hayward Lake near Hayward, WI; **Permits:** No; **Fees:** No; **Visitor facilities:** campsites, boat launching sites, light outfitting services, and canoe rentals. There are limited Federal facilities along the Riverway; **Any limitations on vehicle usage:** Recreational vehicle use is discouraged at designated canoe landings with road access; **Hiking trails:** No, hiking trails available in nearby state forests and parks; **Backcountry:** No; **Camping:** No, but state campgrounds are available nearby. For information, contact: State Departments of Natural Resources, St. Paul, MN 55155, phone 612-296-6157 and Madison, WI 53702, phone 608-266-2621; **Meals served in the park:** No; **Food and supplies obtainable in the park:** No; **Food and supplies obtainable nearby:** Yes, at Hayward, Trego, Saint Croix Falls, Taylor's Falls, Stillwater; **Overnight accommodations:** Hayward, Trego, Saint Croix Falls, Taylor's Falls, Stillwater, and other communities near the Riverway; **First Aid available in park:** Yes, at Ranger Stations on the Riverway; **Nearest Hospital:** Hayward, Spooner, Grantsburg, and St. Croix Falls, WI, all of which are within 16 km (10 miles) of the Riverway; **Days/Hours:** Riverway open year-round but normal season is from Memorial Day to Labor Day with most activities available from about April through Oct. Information Stations closed in Winter; **Holiday Closings:** Park Headquarters closed on Thanksgiving, Dec. 25 and Jan. 1; **Visitor attractions closed for seasons:**Seasonal Visitor Information Stations closed in winter months, as are commercial launch trips on Lake Hayward. The uppermost sections of the St. Croix and Namekagon may become too shallow for canoeing during periods of low water, usually in late Summer and Autumn.

GENERAL INFORMATION: Before setting out for canoeing, make sure you have a life preserver for each person, an extra paddle, insect repellent, a small gasoline stove, and drinking water. Firewood is very scarce in the vicinity of the campsites, and the cutting of trees or brush is prohibited. Drinking water is available at only a few places along the River.

Wyoming

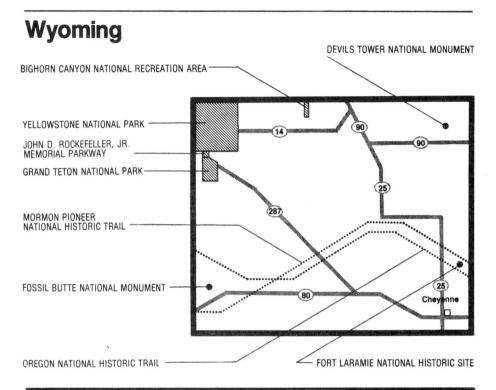

DEVILS TOWER NATIONAL MONUMENT

BIGHORN CANYON NATIONAL RECREATION AREA

YELLOWSTONE NATIONAL PARK

JOHN D. ROCKEFELLER, JR. MEMORIAL PARKWAY

GRAND TETON NATIONAL PARK

MORMON PIONEER NATIONAL HISTORIC TRAIL

FOSSIL BUTTE NATIONAL MONUMENT

Cheyenne

OREGON NATIONAL HISTORIC TRAIL

FORT LARAMIE NATIONAL HISTORIC SITE

Bighorn Canyon National Recreation Area
For details see listing in Montana

Devils Tower National Monument
Devils Tower, Wyoming

MAILING ADDRESS: Superintendent, Devils Tower National Monument, Devils Tower, Wyoming 82714 **Telephone:** 307-467-5370

DIRECTIONS: TheMonument entrance, on WY 24, is 11 km (7 miles) north of US 14; 47 km (28 miles) northwest of Sundance, WY; 53 km (33 miles) northeast of Moorcroft, WY; and 84 km (52 miles) southwest of Belle Fourche, SD. The Visitor Center is about 5 km (3 miles) from the Monument's east entrance and close to the Tower.

This 264 m (865-foot) tower of columnar rock, the remains of a volcanic intrusion, is the Nation's first national monument. Created by Presidential Proclamation on Sept. 24, 1906.

VISITOR ACTIVITIES: interpretive exhibits, photography, walking, camping, hiking, mountain climbing, picnicking, fishing, bird- and wildlife-watching; **Permits:** No; **Fees:** Entrance fee is $1 per vehicle, 50¢ for each bus passenger, 50¢ for individual (biker, hiker, etc.), those under 16 or 62 and over are admitted free. Golden Eagle and Golden Age Passports accepted and available; **Visitor facilities:** parking and restrooms at the Visitor Center, picnic area, campground; **Any limitations on vehicle usage:** Vehicles are restricted to designated roadways; **Hiking trails:** Yes, self-guiding nature trails of varying lengths; **Backcountry:** No; **Camping:** Yes, no reservations accepted for campsites. Fee is $2 per site per night, with a 14 day limit during Summer; **Other overnight accommodations on site:** No; **Meals served in the park:** No; **Food and supplies obtainable in the park:** No; **Food and supplies obtainable nearby:** Yes, within 3 km (2 miles) of the campground; **Overnight accommodations:** Sundance, WY & US 14, 47 km (28 miles); Hulett, 17.7 km (11 miles) east; Moorcroft, WY 24 & US 14, 54.7 km (34 miles); **First Aid available in park:** Yes; **Nearest Hospital:** Sundance, via WY 24 & US 14, 45 km (28 miles); **Days/Hours:** The Monument is open all year. Visitor Center is open from May 1 through Oct.; **Holiday Closings:** No; **Visitor attractions closed for seasons:**Campground is closed by snow in Winter; **Weather:** In Summer, the days are generally sunny, but when the sun sets or during storms you will need a sweater or light jacket.

GENERAL INFORMATION: Be cautious of rattlesnakes, which seldom bite humans unless disturbed or mistreated. Stay clear of prairie dogs, which carry fleas and can bite.

Fort Laramie National Historic Site
Fort Laramie, Wyoming

MAILING ADDRESS: Superintendent, Fort Laramie National Historic Site, Fort Laramie, Wyoming 82212 **Telephone:** 307-837-2221

DIRECTIONS: The Site is about 5 km (3.1 miles) southwest of the town of Fort Laramie, WY, off US 26.
A fur-trade post once stood here, but the surviving buildings are those of a major military post that guarded covered-wagon trails to the West, 1834-90. Created by Presidential Proclamation on July 16, 1938.

VISITOR ACTIVITIES: walking tours, interpretive exhibits, picnicking, living history programs in Summer; **Permits:** No; **Fees:** No; **Visitor facilities:** parking at Visitor Center, self-guided tours, picnic area; **Any limitations on vehicle usage:** No; **Hiking trails:** No; **Backcountry:** No; **Camping:** No; **Other overnight accommodations on site:** No; **Meals served in the park:** No; **Food and supplies obtainable in the park:** No; **Food and supplies obtainable nearby:** Yes, in Guernsey or Torrington; **Overnight accommodations:** Guernsey, 21 km (13 miles) northwest of Fort Laramie or in Torrington, 32 km (20 miles) southeast of Fort Laramie; both on US 26; **First Aid available in park:** Yes, **Nearest Hospital:** Torrington, 32 km (20 miles) southeast of Fort Laramie by US 26; **Days/Hours:** From mid-June through Labor Day, 7 a.m. to 7 p.m.; 8 a.m. to 4:30 p.m. the remainder of the year; **Holiday Closings:** Dec. 25 and Jan. 1; **Visitor attractions closed for seasons:** No living history programs are offered between Labor Day and Memorial Day; **Weather:** Winters can be severe. Summer temperatures can reach 100°F with low humidity. Summer nights are usually cool.

Fossil Butte National Monument
Kemmerer, Wyoming

MAILING ADDRESS: Superintendent, Fossil Butte National Monument, P.O. Box 527,

Kemmerer, Wyoming 83101 **Telephone:** 307-877-3450

DIRECTIONS: The Monument is in southwest Wyoming, about 17.7 km (11 miles) west of Kemmerer. The Butte is located just north of US 30 N and the Union Pacific Railroad, both of which traverse the valley.

An abundance of rare fish fossils, 40-65 million years old, is evidence of former habitation of this now semiarid region. Established by act of Congress on Oct. 23, 1972.

VISITOR ACTIVITIES: picnicking, fossil displays, auto tours, wildlife- and bird-watching, hiking; **Permits:** No; **Fees:** No; **Visitor facilities:** interpretive exhibits, restrooms. The site is largely unimproved; **Any limitations on vehicle usage:** All dirt roads are recommended for four-wheel drive vehicles only. Sufficient rain stops traffic on the dirt roads due to mud; **Hiking trails:** Yes, 2.3 km (1½ mile) interpretive trail; **Backcountry:** No; **Camping:** No; **Other overnight accommodations on site:** No; **Meals served in the park:** No; **Food and supplies obtainable in the park:** No; **Food and supplies obtainable nearby:** Yes, Kemmerer and Cokeville; **Overnight accommodations:** Kemmerer, 17.1 km (11 miles) east on US 30 N, and Cokeville, 53 km (33 miles) west on US 30 N; **First Aid available in park:** Yes, when employees are available. The park is not routinely patrolled; **Nearest Hospital:** Kemmerer; **Days/Hours:** The Visitor Contact Station is staffed from 8 a.m. to 5 p.m. 7 days a week from June 1 through Labor Day, and as weather permits during May and October; **Holiday Closings:** None; **Visitor attractions closed for seasons:** Park is usually closed by snow from Nov.-early May; **Weather:** The climate is semiarid and cool-temperate.

GENERAL INFORMATION: Reservations for accommodations in the area should be made well in advance of the visit. Contact the Monument for further information on local lodging.

Grand Teton National Park
Moose, Wyoming

MAILING ADDRESS: Superintendent, Grand Teton National Park, P.O. Drawer 170, Moose, Wyoming 83012 **Telephone:** 307-733-2880

DIRECTIONS: Park Headquarters and a Visitor Center are at Moose, 21 km (13 miles) north of Jackson on US 26, 89, and 187.

This scenic area of mountain peaks, alpine lakes, and sagebrush flats is filled with moose, elk, trumpeter swans and other wildlife and offers an endless variety of recreational opportunities to the visitor. The Teton Range was established as a National Park on Feb. 26, 1929 and expanded in 1950 to include portions of Jackson Hole.

VISITOR ACTIVITIES: interpretive exhibits, guided tours, picnicking, camping, backcountry, hiking, mountain climbing, horseback riding, swimming, boating, fishing, biking, snowmobiling, skiing, wildlife- and bird-watching; **Permits:** for fishing, backcountry, boating and oversnow travel, available at Visitor Center; **Fees:** $2 entrance fee Golden Eagle and Golden Age Passports accepted and available; **Visitor facilities:** museum, picnic areas, campgrounds, boat ramp and rentals, bicycle trail, snowmobile route, cross-country ski trail, food and lodging, post offices, religious services, restrooms, telephones; **Any limitations on vehicle usage:** Drive only on established roadways. Keep motor vehicles off bikeways; **Hiking trails:** Yes, 320 km (200 miles) of maintained park trails; **Backcountry:** Yes, information can be obtained at Visitor Center or Ranger Station; **Camping:** Yes, no reservations available for individual campsites. Reservations for the trailer village with all hookups at Colter Bay can be made by contacting the Grand

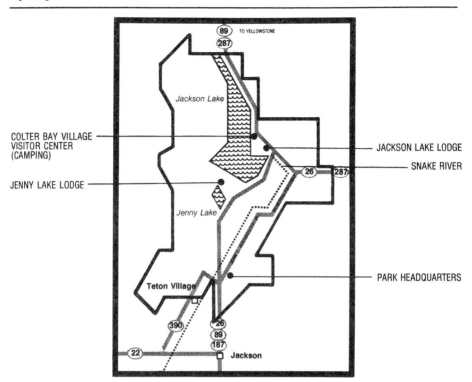

Teton Lodge Company, Moran, WY 83103, phone 307-543-2885. Group campsites are reserved in advance by writing the Superintendent. More than a dozen Forest Service and commercial campgrounds are located near the Park; **Other overnight accommodations on site:** Yes, for information and reservations at other accommodations, contact the Grand Teton Lodge Company, Reservations Dept., P.O. Box 240, Moran, WY 83103, phone 307-543-2855, or Signal Mountain Lodge, Moran, WY 83103, phone 307-543-2831; **Meals served in the park:** Yes, at Colter Bay, and at Jackson Lake, Jenny Lake, and Signal Mountain Lodges; **Food and supplies obtainable in the park:** Yes, at Colter Bay Village, Signal Mountain, Moose, & Kelly; **Food and supplies obtainable nearby:** Yes, at Jackson; **Overnight accommodations:** Jackson, 21 km (13 miles) south; **First Aid available in park:** Yes, emergency first aid at Ranger Stations ; **Nearest Hospital:** St. John's Hospital in Jackson, 6.4 km (4 miles) south of the Park; **Days/Hours:** Open year-round, 24 hours a day; **Holiday Closings:** Moose Visitor Center closed Dec. 25; **Visitor attractions closed for seasons:** Most facilities open from June through Sept.; **Weather:** The seasons at Grand Teton reflect both the mountain heights and the calendar. Spring visitors are attracted by wildflowers, and migrating birds and elk during May and June, despite frequent rains and cold temperatures. If you intend to hike or camp, bring warm clothing and raingear. Be prepared for a variety of weather conditions, since it snows in either month. Temperatures can range from below freezing to over 20°C (about 70°F).

Summer days during July and Aug. are generally warm and occasionally hot. Afternoon thundershowers are possible. Daytime temperatures average near 30°C (80°F), dropping to 4°C (40°F) at night. Park attendance has averaged 1 million people a month, so patience may be necessary if trails are crowded and campsites are taken.

Autumn color is best about the first week of Oct. Days are generally cool & clear during Sept. and Oct.—to many visitors this is the best time to visit. Most park facilities are open in Sept. when it's easy to find space in lodges and campgrounds. During Nov., elk migrate through the Park to their winter range. Expect frosty nights warming to 15-20°C (about 65°F) in early Autumn.

Winter lasts from Nov. through Apr. with an average 5 meters (16 feet) of snowfall. Blizzards may last for several days, making travel hazardous. Daytime temperatures average to near freezing, dropping to well below that at night.

GENERAL INFORMATION: A recorded information service is available on a 24-hour basis all year. Phone 307-733-2220. To talk with park personnel, call 307-733-2880. For State of Wyoming travel information, contact the Wyoming Travel Commission, Cheyenne, WY 82001, 307-777-7777.

For Your Safety—Register at Jenny Lake Ranger Station in Summer and at Park Headquarters during other seasons before starting any off-trail hike or climb. Do not feed or touch any park animal. Lighting-caused fires are allowed to burn in some parts of the Park. If one is in progress, check with a Ranger before planning a trip to the burn area.

John D. Rockefeller, Jr. Memorial Parkway
Moose, Wyoming

MAILING ADDRESS: Superintendent, Grand Teton National Park, P.O. Drawer 170, Moose, Wyoming 83102 **Telephone:** 307-733-2880

DIRECTIONS: The Parkway Ranger Station is located .4 km (¼ mile) north of Flagg Ranch Village on US 89-287. Information on the Parkway is available through Dial-A-Park in Grand Teton: 307-733-2220.

Linking Yellowstone and Grand Teton National Parks, this scenic 132 km (82 mile) parkway commemorates Mr. Rockefeller's role in aiding establishment of many parks, including Grand Teton. Authorized for addition to the National Park System on Aug. 25, 1972.

VISITOR ACTIVITIES: interpretive services, nature walks and evening campfire programs are provided through the Parkway. River float trips, horseback riding, snowmobiling, skiing are available; **Permits:** Required for snowmobiling and boat fishing. Availvable from Ranger Stations on the Parkway and in Grand Teton; **Fees:** No; **Visitor facilities:** At Flagg Ranch Village, gasoline is available throughout the year. From May 15-Sept. 30: lodging, food store, float trips, horseback riding, trailer park with and without full hookups. From Dec. 1-Mar. 15: lodging, food store, snowmobile and cross-country ski rentals and snowcoach rides. At Huckleberry Hot Springs: May 1-Sept. 15: tent camping, swimming pool, general store, laundry, and service station; **Any limitations on vehicle usage:** Drive only on established roadways; **Hiking trails:** Yes, 16 km (10 miles); **Backcountry:** Yes, information available at Ranger Stations on Parkway or Visitor Centers or Ranger Stations in Grand Teton National Park; **Camping:** Yes, Huckleberry Hot Springs, P.O. Box 1934, Jackson, WY 83001 phone 307-543-2402, Flagg Ranch Trailer Village and Snake River Campground; **Other overnight accommodations on site:** Yes, Flagg Ranch Village, Moran, WY 83103 phone 307-543-2861. Both camping and lodge are open in season; inquire about exact dates of operation; **Meals served in the park:** Yes, at Flagg Ranch Village; **Food and supplies obtainable in the park:** Yes, at Flagg Ranch Village year-round and Huckleberry Hot Springs in Summer; **Food and supplies obtainable nearby:** No; **Overnight accommodations:** Jackson, 100 km (62 miles) south; **First Aid available in park:** Yes, emergency first aid at Ranger Station; **Nearest Hospital:** St. John Hospital, Jackson, WY, 100 km (62 miles); **Days/Hours:** Open year-round, 24 hours a day; **Holiday Closings:** None; **Visitor attractions closed for seasons:** No.

GENERAL INFORMATION: Visitors to the area can also see Yellowstone and Grand Teton National Parks (See listings in this book), which are on opposite ends of the Parkway.

Mormon Pioneer Trail
For details see listing in Illinois

Oregon National Scenic Trail
For details see listing in Missouri

Yellowstone National Park
Yellowstone National Park, Wyoming

MAILING ADDRESS: Yellowstone National Park, Yellowstone National Park, Wyoming 82190 **Telephone:** 307-344-7381

DIRECTIONS: The Park can be reached from many directions: from the North US 89; from the Northeast, US 212; from the East through Cody, US 20, 14 and 16, merged; from the South, via the John D. Rockefeller, Jr. Memorial Parkway, US 89 and US 26, and from the West via West Yellowstone, US 191 & 287.

This is the world's greatest geyser area, with Old Faithful and some 10,000 other geysers and hot springs. Here, too are lakes, waterfalls, high mountains, and the Grand Canyon of the Yellowstone-all set apart in 1872 as the world's first national park. It is the largest Park in the National Park System. Established Mar. 1, 1872.

VISITOR ACTIVITIES: fishing, camping, boating, driving, hiking, horseback riding, bird- and wildlife-watching, biking, stagecoach rides, boat and bus tours, snowmobiling, skiing, snowshoeing, interpretive and campfire programs; **Permits:** required for fishing, boating, and backcountry obtained at any Visitor Center or Ranger Station; **Fees:** Yes, fees for campsites vary from free backcountry sites to $3 for well-developed campsites. Fees are also charged for horseback riding, stagecoach rides, boat and bus tours, and trailer park with utilities. There is a combination entrance fee to both Yellowstone and Grand Teton National Parks—$2 per visit for all motor vehicles, including motorcycles. Persons entering on foot, bicycle, or by bus will be charged 50¢ per visit. Golden Eagle and Golden Age passports are accepted and available; **Visitor facilities:** roadside radio interpretation, interpretive display boards, hotels, cabins, amphitheatres, boat rentals, campgrounds, church services, food service, gasoline stations, horse rental, laundries, photo shops, post offices, sewage dump stations, showers, tour bus, fee trailer park with utilities, Visitor Centers, marina, bike trail; **Any limitations on vehicle usage:** Motor vehicles are restricted to designated roads. Bicycles are restricted to roads and designated bicycle trails. Visitors may encounter snow and hazardous driving conditions during Spring and Fall, with temporary road closures. Over-snow vehicles are subject to park rules and regulations; **Hiking trails:** Yes, about 1600 km (1000 miles) of trails lead to remote sections of the Park. Some offer easy part-day trips over gentle terrain, others require strength and endurance because of their elevation. Good topographic maps, which can be purchased at any Visitor Center, are highly recommended. Always check trail conditions with a Ranger before setting out on an overnight or long hike; **Back-**

country: Yes, permits are required and are available at any Ranger Station or Visitor Center on a first-come, first-served basis; **Camping:** Yes, campgrounds are filled on a first-come, first-served basis; **Other overnight accommodations on site:** Yes, reservations for hotels, lodges, cabins, and a trailer park, all open from mid-June through Labor Day, can be made by writing the Yellowstone Park Company, Yellowstone National Park, WY 82190, phone 307-344-7311. Reservations are advised, especially during July and August. Those visitors already in Yellowstone may make advance room reservations at any hotel or lodge anywhere in the Park; **Meals served in the park:** Yes, Yellowstone Lake, Fishing Bridge, Canyon Village, Roosevelt Lodge, Tower Junction, Mammoth Hot Springs, Old Faithful; **Food and supplies obtainable in the park:** Yes, at Yellowstone Lake, Fishing Bridge, Canyon Village, Roosevelt Lodge, Tower Junction, West Thumb, Mammoth Hot Springs, Old Faithful; **Food and supplies obtainable nearby:** Yes, at each community near the 5 park entrances: Livingston, Bozeman, West Yellowstone, Red Lodge, MT; Cody & Jackson, WY; **Overnight accommodations:** Livingston, Bozeman, West Yellowstone, and Red Lodge, MT; Cody and Jackson, WY; **First Aid**

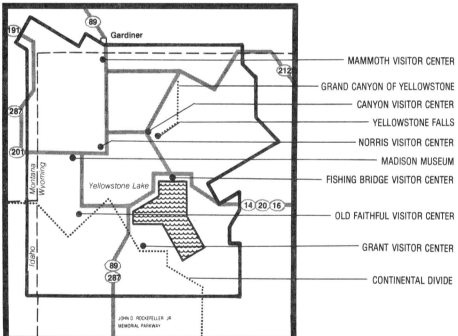

available in park: Yes; **Nearest Hospital:** Lake Hospital, Mammoth Clinic, Old Faithful Clinic; **Days/Hours:** Open 24 hours a day, every day; **Holiday Closings:** None; **Visitor attractions closed for seasons:** Park roads and entrances, except the North Entrance, are ordinarily closed by snow to auto traffic between Oct. 31 and May 1. Most park campgrounds do not open before June, except at Mammoth, where camping is available all year.

Wintertime activities abound. In recent years, thousands of visitors have entered the Park by over-snow vehicle. Heated snow coaches are operated by concessioners from West Yellowstone and South Entrance. Private snowmobiles may also use the unplowed roads, but no cross-country vehicle use is permitted. Ski and snowshoe touring are also on the increase. The Old Faithful Visitor Center is open during the Winter from about mid-Dec. to mid-Mar., providing information, evening programs and winter walks. Meals and overnight lodging are available through the Winter at Old Faithful. The only roads open for auto traffic are Gardiner to Mammoth and from there to the Northeast Entrance and Cooke City. This drive offers an excellent opportunity to see wildlife. Special information on winter activities and services may be obtained by writing to the Park. Reservations for winter facilities may be made by writing to the Yellowstone Park Company, Yellowstone National Park, WY 82190. Reservations are advised, especially during the holidays.

GENERAL INFORMATION: Assistance for any emergency in the Park can be obtained anytime by calling Park Headquarters at 307-344-7381. Write the above address for informative pamphlets and a map. Four national forests providing recreational opportunities border on Yellowstone. To the south lies Grand Teton National Park, with many concessioner and Federal facilities (see listing in this book).

Roosevelt Campobello International Park
New Brunswick, Canada

MAILING ADDRESS: Executive Secretary, Roosevelt Campobello International Park Commission, P.O. Box 97, Lubec, Maine 04652 **Telephone:** 506-752-2922

DIRECTIONS: Follow Maine Route 1 to 189. Cross Roosevelt Memorial Bridge at Lubec, Maine to New Brunswick Route 744. The Park is about 2.4 km (1½ miles) from Canadian Customs.

At the age of 39, President Franklin D. Roosevelt was striken by poliomyelitis here at his summer home. The Park has scenic vistas in a 2600-acre natural area.This is the first international park to be administered by a joint commission. Established by act of Congress in 1964.

VISITOR ACTIVITIES: tours of the Roosevelt Cottage, orientation film, visual aid displays, picnicking, beach activities; **Permits:** No; **Fees:** No; **Visitor facilities:** parking and restrooms at the Reception Center, exhibits; **Any limitations on vehicle usage:** Cars must be parked at the Reception Center in the cottage area; **Hiking trails:** Yes, trails are located in the natural area. Obtain maps at the Reception Center; **Backcountry:** No; **Camping:** No; **Other overnight accommodations on site:** No, tourist facilities are at Welshpool and Wilson's Beach, just north of the Park. The Province of New Brunswick maintains a Park with tent and trailer sites and picnic areas at the northern end of Herring Cove. There are also tourist facilities in and near Lubec. The State of Maine has two parks in the area, with tending and trailer facilities at Cobscook Bay Park in the Moosehorn Game Refuge at Whiting and picnic areas at Quoddy Head State Park; **Meals served in the park:** No; **Food and supplies obtainable in the park:** No; **Food and supplies obtainable nearby:** Yes, Wilson's Beach, NB and Lubec, ME; **Overnight accommodations:** On the Island, within 8 km (5 miles); **First Aid available in park:** No nearby at Welshpool Health Center, 3 km (2 miles); **Nearest Hospital:** Machias, ME, US 95, 48 km (30 miles); **Days/Hours:** Open 7 days per week, 9 a.m. to 5 p.m., from late May through mid-October; **Holiday Closings:** No; **Visitor attractions closed for seasons:** Park is closed from mid-October through May; **Weather:** July and August are warm months. September has warm days and cool nights.

War in the Pacific National Historical Park
Agana, Guam

MAILING ADDRESS: Superintendent, War in the Pacific National Historical Park, P.O. Box 3441, Agana, Guam 96910 **Telephone:** Guam: 477-7561

North Mariana Islands

SAIPAN

Garapan

AMERICAN MEMORIAL PARK

Agana

WAR IN THE PACIFIC
NATIONAL HISTORICAL PARK ——

GUAM

Guam

DIRECTIONS: NOT OPEN TO THE PUBLIC AT THIS TIME. Portions of the Park
are expected to open in 1980.

As a memorial to those participating in the Pacific Theater, this scenic park offers
public enjoyment of natural and World War II historic features. Authorized for
addition to the National Park System on Aug. 18, 1978.

American Memorial Park
Saipan, Northern Mariana Islands

MAILING ADDRESS: Superintendent, War in the Pacific National Historical Park,
P.O. Box 3441, Agana, Guam 96910 **Telephone:** Guam: 477-7561

DIRECTIONS: NOT YET OPEN TO THE PUBLIC.

As a tribute to those who died in the World War II Mariana Islands campaign, this Park
is maintained on Saipan, capital of the Northern Mariana Islands. These South Pacific
islands became a U.S. Commonwealth on Jan. 9, 1979. Park authorized for addition to the
National Park System on Aug. 18, 1978.

San Juan National Historic Site
Old San Juan, Puerto Rico

MAILING ADDRESS: Superintendent, San Juan National Historic Site, P.O. Box 712,
Old San Juan, Puerto Rico 00902 **Telephone:** 809-724-1974

DIRECTIONS: The Site's information desk and other visitor facilities are on the entry
plaza (5th) level of El Morro Castle. The Site includes the Spanish-built forts of El Morro,
San Cristobal, and El Canuelo, and the city walls.

These massive masonry fortifications, the oldest in the territorial limits of the United

Virgin Islands

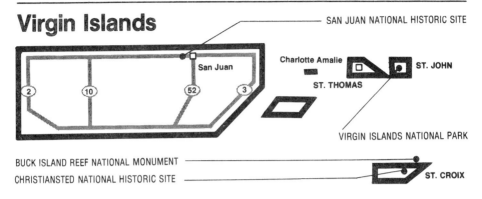

States, were begun by the Spanish in the 16th Century to protect a strategic harbor guarding the sea lanes to the New World. Designated Feb. 14, 1949.

VISITOR ACTIVITIES: guided tours, exhibits; **Permits:** No; **Fees:** No; **Visitor facilities:** audiovisual programs, restrooms, drinking fountains, museums; **Any limitations on vehicle usage:** Limited parking available at Fort San Cristobal; ample parking at El Morro; **Hiking trails:** No; **Backcountry:** No; **Camping:** No; **Other overnight accommodations on site:** No; **Meals served in the park:** No; **Food and supplies obtainable in the park:** No; **Food and supplies obtainable nearby:** Yes, the city of San Juan; **Overnight accommodations:** San Juan, within walking distance; **First Aid available in park:** Yes; **Nearest Hospital:** San Juan, within 8 km (5 miles); **Days/Hours:** Open 7 days a week from 8 a.m. to 5 p.m.; **Holiday Closings:** Dec. 25; **Visitor attractions closed for seasons:** No; **Weather:** Warm to hot all year with no change of seasons.

GENERAL INFORMATION: Walking shoes with rubber soles and low heels are recommended.

Buck Island Reef National Monument
Saint Croix, Virgin Islands

MAILING ADDRESS: Superintendent, Christiansted National Historic Site, P.O. Box 160, Christiansted, Saint Croix, Virgin Islands 00820 **Telephone:** 809-773-1460

DIRECTIONS: Access to the Monument is by charter or private boat. Charters are available at Christiansted Wharf. The Monument is an 8.9 km (5½ mile) sail from Christiansted.
 Coral, grottoes, sea fans, gorgonias, and tropical fishes-along an underwater trail-make this one of the finest marine gardens in the Caribbean. The Island is a rookery for frigate birds and pelicans and the habitat of green turtles. Created by Presidential Proclamation on Dec. 28, 1961.

VISITOR ACTIVITIES: swimming, snorkeling, boat trips, hiking, bird-watching, picnicking, fishing; **Permits:** No; **Fees:** charter boat fees; **Visitor facilities:** picnic tables, charcoal grilles, bathhouse, boat ramp, a sheltered pavilion, restrooms, nature trail; **Any limitations on vehicle usage:** Boats should be maneuvered slowly through park waters. Water skiing, speeding, and reckless boating are prohibited; **Hiking trails:** Yes, nature trail; **Backcountry:** No; **Camping:** No, but you may camp on your boat; **Other over-**

night accommodations on site: No; **Meals served in the park:** No; **Food and supplies obtainable in the park:** No; **Food and supplies obtainable nearby:** No; **Overnight accommodations:** St. Croix; **First Aid available in park:** Yes; **Nearest Hospital:** 3 km (2 miles) from downtown Christiansted; **Days/Hours:** Open daily from 8 a.m. to 5 p.m.; **Holiday Closings:** None; **Visitor attractions closed for seasons:** No; **Weather:** Temperatures range from 72° in Winter to 85° in Summer.

GENERAL INFORMATION: *For Your Safety.* Avoid sunburn. Short periods in the sun and the use of protective waterproof lotions are recommended. Use caution in the water. cuts from coral can inflict painful wounds that may be slow to heal. The common spiny sea urchins are a particularly sharp hazard. Jellyfish, the Portuguese man-of-war, and fire corals can sting and burn, some severely. Treat all underwater creatures with respect. If you haven't snorkelled before, be sure to practice in shallow water before daring the reef. Make sure your face mask fits snugly.

Christiansted National Historic Site
Christiansted, Virgin Islands

MAILING ADDRESS: Superintendent, Christiansted National Historic Site, P.O. Box 160, Christiansted, Virgin Islands 00820 **Telephone:** 809-773-1460

DIRECTIONS: National Park Service Headquarters is in Fort Christiansvearn in downtown Christiansted. Begin your tour at the Fort.
   Colonial development of the Virgin Islands is commemorated by 18th and 19th century structures in the capital of the former Danish West Indies on St. Croix Island. St. Croix was purchased by the United States in 1917. Designated on Mar. 4, 1952.

VISITOR ACTIVITIES: self-guided walking tours, interpretive exhibits; **Permits:** No; **Fees:** No; **Visitor facilities:** restrooms, museum (open 9 a.m. to 4 p.m., Monday through Friday, and 9 a.m. to noon on Saturday); **Any limitations on vehicle usage:** No; **Hiking trails:** No; **Backcountry:** No; **Camping:** No; **Other overnight accommodations on site:** No; **Meals served in the park:** No; **Food and supplies obtainable in the park:** No; **Food and supplies obtainable nearby:** Yes, Christiansted; **Overnight accommodations:** Christiansted; **First Aid available in park:** Yes; **Nearest Hospital:** Christiansted, 3 km (2 miles) from the downtown area; **Days/Hours:** 8 a.m. to 4:30 p.m.; **Holiday Closings:** Dec. 25 & Jan. 1; **Visitor attractions closed for seasons:** No; **Weather:** Average temperatures are 72° in Winter and 85° in Summer.

GENERAL INFORMATION: Beware of uneven walkways and stairs.

Virgin Islands National Park
St. John, Virgin Islands

MAILING ADDRESS: Superintendent, Virgin Islands National Park, P.O. Box 806, Charlotte Amalie, St.Thomas, Virgin Islands 00801 **Telephone:** Cruz Bay Visitor Center: 809-775-2050 or Headquarters: 809-776-6201

DIRECTIONS: Park Headquarters and Visitor Center are in Red Hook at the National Park Service Dock on St. Thomas. A Visitor Center is at Cruz Bay on St. John. You can fly directly to Charlotte Amalie, St. Thomas, or via San Juan, or travel by ship. Taxis and

buses run between Charlotte Amalie and Red Hook. A ferry operates daily across Pills-
bury Sound from Red Hook to Cruz Bay. Water taxi service is available after hours. A
special boat for guests at Caneel Bay Plantation runs between the Red Hook Visitor
Station and Caneel Bay. Very popular with those who can stay only a day are the package
vehicle tours and scenic boat charters that leave from St. Thomas with all transportation
arranged. See a travel agent or make arrangements in advance. Taxi service is provided on
St. John.

The Park covers about three-fourths of St. John and includes quiet coves, blue-green
waters, and white sandy beaches fringed by lush green hills. Early Carib Indian relics and
the remains of Danish colonial sugar plantations are also in the Park. Authorized for
addition to the National Park System on Aug. 2, 1956.

VISITOR ACTIVITIES: interpretive talks and exhibits, hiking, camping, guided snor-
kel trips, hikes, cultural demonstrations, picnicking, swimming, snorkeling, fishing,
auto tours; **Permits:** Persons returning to the US mainland from the Virgin Islands must
go through Customs and Immigration at San Juan, Puerto Rico, St. Thomas or other US
ports of entry. An *import permit* is required for fruits, vegetables, plant cuttings, and
seeds; **Fees:** No; **Visitor facilities:** Self-guiding walking and underwater trails, picnic
areas, beaches, campgrounds, boat rentals and ramps, rental vehicles (make reservations
through the concessioner well in advance); **Any limitations on vehicle usage:** Speed
limit is 32 km (20 miles) per hour. Remember to drive on the left. Sound your horn at
blind curves; **Hiking trails:** Yes, trails range from easy walks to difficult climbs. Bring
hiking shoes and cool clothing. Small knapsacks and belt canteens are also handy. Water
is not available along hiking trails; **Backcountry:** No; **Camping:** Yes; **Other overnight
accommodations on site:** Yes, cottage and tent site reservations must be made well in
advance, but not more than eight months prior to the visit. Primitive campsites can also
be reserved. Contact the Concessioner, Cinnamon Bay Campground, St. John, V.I. 00830,
phone 809-776-6330, or see a travel agent; **Meals served in the park:** Yes, at Cruz Bay,
Trunk Bay, Cinnamon Bay; **Food and supplies obtainable in the park:** Yes, at Cruz Bay;
Food and supplies obtainable nearby: Yes, at St. Thomas; **Overnight accommodations:** St. Thomas, 6.4 km (4 miles) by water; **First Aid available in park:** Yes; **Nearest
Hospital:** The clinic at Cruz Bay is open Monday-Friday from 7 a.m. to 11 p.m.; Saturday
and Sunday, 8 a.m. to 11 p.m., telephone 809-776-6222. A nurse and doctor are on 24-hour
call daily; you can reach them by phoning the Dept of Public Safety, 809-776-6471;
Days/Hours: The Park is open every day. Park Headquarters and Visitor Center in Red
Hook open from 9 a.m. to 6 p.m.; Cruz Bay Visitor Center open from 8 a.m. to 5 p.m.;
Holiday Closings: None; **Visitor attractions closed for seasons:**None; **Weather:** The
yearly temperature averages 26 °C (79°F) and varies little between Winter and Summer.
Temperatures rarely exceed 37°C (98°F) or fall below 18°C (65°F). Rainfall averages
approximately 100 cm (40 inches) per year, coming mostly in brief night showers.

GENERAL INFORMATION: *For Your Safety*—Insect repellent may be useful because
of mosquitos and sand flies. While snorkeling and swimming, use lifeguard-posted
beaches. Protect yourself from sunburn. Avoid heavy surf and never go out alone. While
hiking, avoid long and strenuous hikes in the heat of the day (10 a.m. to 3 p.m.). Bring
drinking water. Avoid eating unidentified plants. Stay on the trails-do not shortcut. Do
not climb around or over ruins. Wear sturdy hiking shoes or boots. Tell someone of your
plans and *do not hike alone.*

Visitors can also see nearby Fort Christian, administered by the Virgin Islands
government.

Peak Visitation

While a visit to one of our National Park areas is almost always enjoyable and enriching, the experience can be all the more relaxing if you can avoid making the visit during the heaviest visitor season. As the crowds disappear, your opportunities to explore more thoroughly, to ask questions, or simply to pause and reflect in an area of spectacular natural beauty or lasting historic significance, all increase. The frustrations of traffic, crowded facilities, and lodging or camping difficulties will be reduced.

To help you in planning to visit National Park areas, we are including a listing of the month when each park area is *most* crowded—the period of peak visitation (according to the National Park Service's 1978 visitation records).

Abraham Lincoln BPL NHS (*July*)
Acadia NP (*August*)
Adams NHS (*August*)
Agate Fossil Beds NM (*July*)
Alibates NM (*July*)
Allegheny Port RR NHS (*August*)
Amistad RA (*June*)
Andersonville NHS (*July*)
Andrew Johnson NHS (*May*)
Antietam NBS (*May*)
Apostle Islands NL (*August*)
Appomattox Crt Hse NHP (*June*)
Arches NP (*August*)
Arkansas Post NMEM (*April, October*)
Arlington Hse RELee NMEM (*April*)
Assateague Island NS (*August*)
Aztec Ruins NM (*July*)
Badlands NM (*July*)
Bandelier NM (*July*)
Bent's Old Fort NHS (*June*)
Big Bend NP (*March*)
Big Hole NB (*July*)
Bighorn Canyon NRA (*August*)
Biscayne NM (*June*)
Black Canyon OTG NM (*August*)
Blue Ridge Parkway (*October*)
Booker T. Washington NM (*May*)
Boston NHP (*August*)
Brices Cross Roads NBS (*August*)
Bryce Canyon NP (*July*)
Buck Island Reef NM (*November*)
Buffalo NR (*July*)
C&O Canal NHP (*May*)
Cabrillo NM (*July*)
Canaveral NS (*March*)

Canyon De Chelly NM (*May*)
Canyonlands NP (*July*)
Cape Cod NS (*August*)
Cape Hatteras NS (*July*)
Cape Lookout NS (*October*)
Capitol Reef NP (*August*)
Capulin Mountain NM (*July*)
Carl Sandburg Home NHS (*July*)
Carlsbad Caverns NP (*July*)
Casa Grande NM (*March*)
Castillo De San Marcos (*July*)
Castle Clinton NM (*July*)
Catoctin Mtn Park (*October*)
Cedar Breaks NM (*July*)
Chaco Canyon NM (*July*)
Chalmette NHP (*May*)
Chamizal NMEM (*July*)
Channel Islands NM (*May*)
Chick Chatt NMP (*July*)
Chickasaw NRA (*July*)
Chiricahua NM (*March*)
Christiansted NHS (*December*)
Clara Barton NHS (*April*)
Colonial NHP (*August*)
Colorado NM (*July*)
Coronado NMEM (*October*)
Coulee Dam RA (*July*)
Cowpens NM (*March*)
Crater Lake NP (*August*)
Craters of the Moon NM (*July*)
Cumberland Gap NHP (*July*)
Cumberland Island NS (*June*)
Curecanti RA (*July*)
Custer Battlefield NM (*July*)
Cuyahoga Valley NRA (*May*)
DeSoto NMEM (*March*)
Death Valley NM (*April*)
Delaware Water Gap NRA (*July*)
Devils Postpile NM (*August*)
Devils Tower NM (*July*)
Dinosaur NM (*July*)
Edison NHS (*August*)
Effigy Mounds NM (*October*)
El Morro NM (*July*)
Everglades NP (*January*)
Federal Hall NMEM (*July*)
Fire Island NS (*July*)
Florissant Fossil Beds NM (*July*)
Ford's Theatre NHS (*April*)
Fort Bowie NHS (*March*)
Fort Caroline NMEM (*November*)
Fort Clatsop NMEM (*July*)
Fort Davis NHS (*July*)
Fort Donelson NMP (*October*)
Fort Frederica NM (*July*)
Fort Jefferson NM (*March*)

Fort Laramie NHS (*July*)
Fort Larned NHS (*July*)
Fort Matanzas NM (*July*)
Fort McHenry NM&HS (*June*)
Fort Necessity NB (*July*)
Fort Point NHS (*July*)
Fort Pulaski NM (*July*)
Fort Raleigh NSH (*July*)
Fort Smith NHS (*July*)
Fort Stanwix NM (*July*)
Fort Sumter NM (*July*)
Fort Union NM (*July*)
Fort Union Trad Post NHS (*July*)
Fort Vancouver NHS (*July*)
Fort Washington Park (*July*)
Fossil Butte NM (*July*)
Fred Spot NMP (*June*)
Fredrk Douglass Home NM (*August*)
Gateway NRA (*July*)
General Grant NMEM (*August*)
Geo Wash Birthplace NM (*July*)
Geo Wash Carver NM (*August*)
Geo Wash Mem Pkwy (*July*)
George Rogers Clark NHP (*July*)
Gettysburg NMP (*July*)
Gila Cliff Dwellings NM (*July*)
Glacier Bay NM (*August*)
Glacier NP (*July*)
Glen Canyon NRA (*July*)
Golden Gate NRA (*July*)
Golden Spike NHS (*August*)
Gran Quivira NM (*July*)
Grand Canyon NP (*July*)
Grand Portage NM (*August*)
Grand Teton NP (*July*)
Great Sand Dunes NM (*July*)
Great Smoky Mtns NP (*July*)
Greenbelt Park (*June*)
Guadalupe Mountains NP (*July*)
Guilford Courthouse NMP (*July*)
Gulf Islands NS (*June*)
Haleakala NP (*August*)
Hamilton Grange NMEM (*May*)
Hampton NHS (*December*)
Harpers Ferry NHP (*July*)
Hawaii Volcanoes NP (*February*)
Herbert Hoover NHS (*July*)
Home of FDR NHS (*August*)
Homestead NM of America (*July*)
Hopewell Village NHS (*July*)
Horseshoe Bend NMP (*July*)
Hot Springs NP (*July*)
Hovenweep NM (*July*)
Hubbell Trad Post NHS (*July*)
Independence NHP (*April*)
Indiana Dunes NL (*July*)
Isle Royale NP (*August*)

Jefferson Memorial (*July*)
Jefferson NEM NHS (*July*)
Jewel Cave NM (*July*)
JFK Ctr Perf Arts (*June*)
John D. Rockefeller Pkwy (*August*)
John Day Fossil Beds NM (*August*)
John F. Kennedy NHS (*August*)
John Muir NHS (*April*)
Johnstown Flood NMEM (*August*)
Joshua Tree NM (*April*)
Katmai NM (*July*)
Kennesaw Mountain NBP (*April*)
Kings Canyon NP (*July*)
Kings Mountain NMP (*October*)
Lake Mead NRA (*June*)
Lake Meredith RA (*June*)
Lassen Volcanic NP (*August*)
Lava Beds NM (*July*)
Lehman Caves NM (*July*)
Lincoln Boyhood NMEM (*July*)
Lincoln Home NHS (*July*)
Lincoln Memorial (*July*)
Longfellow NHS (*June*)
Lyndon B. Johnson NHS (*July*)
Mammoth Cave NP (*July*)
Manassas NBP (*August*)
Mesa Verde NP (*July*)
Minute Man NHP (*June*)
Montezuma Castle NM (*July*)
Moores Creek NMP (*May*)
Morristown NHP (*September*)
Mound City Group NM (*July*)
Mount McKinley NP (*July*)
Mount Rainier NP (*July*)
Mount Rushmore NMEM (*July*)
Muir Woods NM (*July*)
Natchez Trace Parkway (*April*)
National Capital Parks (*July*)
National Visitor Center (*July*)
Natural Bridges NM (*June*)
Navajo NM (*June*)
Nez Perce NHP (*August*)
North Cascades NP (*July*)
Ocmulgee NM (*August*)
Olympic NP (*August*)
Oregon Caves NM (*August*)
Organ Pipe Cactus NM (*March*)
Ozark NSR (*July*)
Padre Island NS (*July*)
Pea Ridge NMP (*October*)
Pecos NM (*July*)
Perry's Victory & IPM (*August*)
Petersburg NB (*April*)
Petrified Forest NP (*July*)
Pictured Rocks NL (*August*)
Pinnacles NM (*April*)
Pipe Spring NM (*July*)

Pipestone NM (*July*)
Piscataway Park (*June*)
Point Reyes NS (*July*)
Prince William For Pk (*September*)
Pu'uhonua O Honaunau NHP (*March*)
Puukohola Heiau NHS (*March*)
Rainbow Bridge NM (*June*)
Redwood NP (*July*)
Richmond NBP (*August*)
Rock Creek Park (*July*)
Rocky Mountain NP (*August*)
Russell Cave NM (*July*)
Sagamore Hill NHS (*July*)
Saguaro NM (*March*)
Saint Croix NSR (*June*)
Saint-Gaudens NHS (*August*)
Salem Maritime NHS (*August*)
San Juan Island NHP (*July*)
San Juan NHS (*July*)
Saratoga NHP (*July*)
Saugus Iron Works NHS (*July*)
Scotts Bluff NM (*July*)
Sequoia NP (*July*)
Shadow Mountain RA (*July*)
Shenandoah NP (*July*)
Shiloh NHP (*July*)
Sitka NHP (*July*)
Sleeping Bear Dunes NL (*August*)
Springfield Armory NHS (*August*)
Statue of Liberty NM (*July*)
Stones River NB (*July*)

Sunset Crater NM (*July*)
Theo Roosevelt Inaug NHS (*April*)
Theo Roosevelt Bpl NHS (*June*)
Theo Roosevelt Is NMEM (*April*)
Timpanogos Cave NM (*July*)
Tonto NM (*April*)
Tumacacori NM (*March*)
Tupelo NM (*August*)
Tuskeegee Institute NHS (*July*)
Tuzigoot NM (July)
Valley Forge NHP (*July*)
Vanderbilt Mansions NHS (*July*)
Vicksburg NMP (*July*)
Virgin Islands NP (*December*)
Voyageurs NP (*August*)
Walnut Canyon NM (*July*)
Washington Monument (*July*)
Whiskeytown NRA (*July*)
White House (*August*)
White Sands NM (*July*)
Whitman Mission NHS (*August*)
William Howard Taft NHS (*May*)
Wilson's Creek NB (*October*)
Wind Cave NP (*July*)
Wolf Trap Farm Park (*July*)
Wright Brothers NMEM (*July*)
Wupatki NM (*July*)
Yellowstone NP (*July*)
Yosemite NP (*August*)
Zion NP (*June*)

Index

Explanation of Abbreviations:

MEM PKWY
Memorial Parkway
NB
National Battlefield
NBS
National Battlefield Site
NHP
National Historical Park
NHS
National Historic Site
NHT
National Historic Trail
NL
National Lakeshore
NM
National Monument
N MEM
National Memorial

NMP
National Military Park
NP
National Park
N PRES
National Preserve
NR
National River or Riverway
NRA
National Recreation Area
NS
National Seashore
NSR
National Scenic River or Riverway
NST
National Scenic Trail
PKWY
Parkway

Abraham Lincoln Birthplace NHS, KY
  108
Abraham Lincoln Memorial, D.C. (See
  Lincoln Memorial)
Acadia NP, ME **113**
Adams NHS, MA **125**
Agate Fossil Beds NM, NE **151**
Alexander Hamilton (See Hamilton
  Grange NM)
Alibates NM, TX **226**
Allegheny Portage Railroad NHS, PA **203**
American Memorial Park, Northern
  Mariana Islands **281**
Amistad NRA, TX **227**
Andersonville NHS, GA **86**
Andrew Johnson NHS, TN **220**
Aniakchak NM, AK **4**
Antietam NB, MD **116**
Apostle Islands NL, WI **269**
Appalachian NST, ME-NH-VT-MA-CT-
  NY-NJ-PA-MD-VA-TN-NC-GA **114**
Appomattox Court House NHP, VA **247**
Arches NP, UT **237**
Arkansas Post N MEM, AR **36**
Arlington House, The Robert E Lee
  Memorial, VA **247**
Assateague Island NS, MD-VA **117**
Aztec Ruins NM, NM **162**
Badlands NP, SD **216**
Bandalier NM, NM **163**
Barton, Clara (See Clara Barton)
Benjamin Franklin N MEM, PA **204**
Bent's Old Fort NHS, CO **57**
Bering Land Bridge NM, AK **4**
Big Bend NP, TX **228**
Big Cypress N PRES, FL **77**
Big Hole NB, MT **146**
Bighorn Canyon NRA, MT-WY **147**
Big South Fork NR and Recreation Area,
  TN-KY **221**
Big Thicket N PRES, TX **229**
Biscayne NM, FL **78**
Black Canyon of the Gunnison NM, CO
  58
Blue Ridge PKWY, NC-VA **183**
Booker T. Washington NM, VA **248**
Boston NHP, MA **126**
Brices Cross Roads NBS, MS **140**
Bryce Canyon NP, UT **238**
Buck Island Reef NM, VI **281**
Buffalo NR, AR **37**
Cabrillo NM, CA **41**
Canaveral NS, FL **79**
Canyon de Chelly NM, AZ **19**
Canyonlands NP, UT **239**
Cape Cod NS, MA **127**
Cape Hatteras NS, NC **185**

Cape Krusenstern NM, AK **6**
Cape Lookout NS, NC 186
Capitol Reef NP, UT **240**
Capulin Mountain NM, NM, **164**
Carl Sandburg Home NHS, NC **187**
Carlsbad Caverns NP, NM **164**
Carver, George Washington (See George
  Washington Carver)
Casa Grande NM, AZ **20**
Castillo de San Marcos NM, FL **80**
Castle Clinton NM, NY **171**
Catoctin Mountain Park, MD **118**
Cedar Breaks NM, UT, **241**
Chaco Canyon NM, NM **165**
Chalmette NHP, LA **111**
Chamizal N MEM, TX **230**
Channel Islands NM, CA **41**
Chattahoochee River NRA, GA **87**
Cherokee Strip Living Museum, KS **106**
Chesapeake and Ohio Canal NHP, MD-
  VA-DC **119**
Chicago Portage NHP, IL **99**
Chickamauga and Chattanooga NMP,
  GA-TN **87**
Chickasaw NRA, OK **197**
Chimney Rock NHS, NE **152**
Chiricahua NM, AZ **21**
Christiansted NHS, VI **282**
City of Refuge NHP (See Pu'uhonua o
  Honaunau NHP)
Clara Barton NHS, MD **120**
Clark, George Rogers (See George Rogers
  Clark)
Colonial NHP, VA **248**
Colorado NM, CO **59**
Congaree Swamp NM, SC **213**
Coronado N MEM, AZ **22**
Coulee Dam NRA, WA **259**
Cowpens NB, SC **213**
Crater Lake NP, OR **198**
Craters of the Moon NM, ID **97**
Cumberland Gap NHP, KY-TN-VA **109**
Cumberland Island NS, GA **88**
Curecanti NRA, CO **59**
Custer Battlefield NM, MT **148**
Cuyahoga Valley NRA, OH **194**
Death Valley NM, CA-NV **42**
Delaware Water Gap NRA, PA-NJ **204**
Denali NM, AK **6**
De Soto N MEM, FL **80**
Devils Postpile NM, CA **43**
Devils Tower NM, WY **273**
Dinosaur NM, CO-UT **60**
Dorchester Heights NHS, MA **128**
Douglass, Frederick (See Frederick
  Douglass)
Ebey's Landing National Historical

Reserve, WA **260**
Edgar Allan Poe NHS, PA **205**
Edison NHS, NJ **159**
Effigy Mounds NM, IA **104**
Eisenhower NHS, PA **205**
Eleanor Roosevelt NHS, NY **172**
Ellis Island, NY **173**
El Morro NM, NM **166**
Eugene O'Neill NHS, CA **44**
Everglades NP, FL **81**
Father Marquette NM, MI **134**
Federal Hall NM, NY **173**
Fire Island NS, NY **174**
Florissant Fossil Beds NM, CO **61**
Ford's Theatre NHS, DC **68**
Fort Benton, MT **148**
Fort Bowie NHS, AZ **22**
Fort Caroline N MEM, FL **82**
Fort Clatsop N MEM, OR **199**
Fort Davis NHS, TX **231**
Fort Donelson NMP, TN **222**
Fort Dupont Park and Activity Center,
    DC **69**
Fort Frederica NM, GA **89**
Fort Jefferson NM, FL **82**
Fort Laramie NHS, WY **274**
Fort Larned NHS, KS **106**
Fort Matanzas NM, FL **83**
Fort McHenry NM and Historic Shrine,
    MD **120**
Fort Moultrie, SC (See Fort Sumter NM)
    214
Fort Necessity NB, PA **206**
Fort Point NHS, CA **45**
Fort Pulaski NM, GA **90**
Fort Raleigh NHS, NC **188**
Fort Scott NHS, KS **107**
Fort Smith NHS, AR **38**
Fort Stanwix NM, NY **175**
Fort Sumter NM, SC **214**
Fort Union NM, NM **167**
Fort Union Trading Post NHS, ND-
    MT **191**
Fort Vancouver NHS, WA **274**
Fort Washington Park, MD **121**
Fossil Butte NM, WY **270**
Franklin, Benjamin (See Benjamin
    Franklin)
Frederick Douglass Memorial Home,
    DC **69**
Fredericksburg and Spotsylvania County
    Battlefields Memorial NMP, VA **249**
Friendship Hill NHS, PA **206**
Gates of the Arctic NM, AK **7**
Gateway Arch, MO (See Jefferson
    National Expansion Memorial NHS)
Gateway NRA, NY-NJ **175**

General Grant N MEM, NY **176**
George Rogers Clark NHP, IN **101**
George Washington Birthplace NM,
    VA **250**
George Washington Carver NM, MO **143**
George Washington MEM PKWY, VA-
    MD **251**
Gettysburg NMP, PA **206**
Gila Cliff Dwellings NM, NM **168**
Glacier Bay NM, AK **8**
Glacier NP, MT **149**
Glen Canyon NRA, UT-AZ **23**
Glen Echo Park, MD **121**
Gloria Dei (Old Swedes') Church NHS,
    PA **207**
Golden Gate NRA, CA **45**
Golden Spike NHS, UT **242**
Grand Canyon NP, AZ **24**
Grand Portage NM, MN **137**
Grand Teton NP, WY **275**
Gran Quivira NM, NM **168**
Grant, U.S. (See General Grant NM)
Grant-Kohrs Ranch NHS, MT **150**
Great Falls Park, VA **251**
Great Sand Dunes NM, CO **62**
Great Smoky Mountains NP, TN-NC **222**
Greenbelt Park, MD **122**
Guadalupe Mountains NP, TX **231**
Guilford Courthouse NMP, NC **188**
Gulf Islands NS, FL-MS **84**
Haleakala NP, HI **92**
Hamilton, Alexander (See Hamilton
    Grange N MEM)
Hamilton Grange N MEM, NY **177**
Hampton NHS, MD **123**
Harpers Ferry NHP, WV-MD **268**
Hawaii Volcanoes NP, HI **93**
Herbert Hoover NHS, IA **105**
Hohokam Pima NM, AZ **26**
Home of Franklin D. Roosevelt NHS,
    NY **177**
Homestead NM of America, NE **152**
Hoover, Herbert (See Herbert Hoover)
Hopewell Village NHS, PA **208**
Horseshoe Bend NMP, AL **1**
Hot Springs NP, AR **38**
Hovenweep NM, CO-UT **62**
Hubbell Trading Post NHS, AZ **26**
Ice Age National Scientific Reserve,
    WI **270**
Independence NHP, PA **208**
Indiana Dunes NL, IN **102**
International Peace Garden, ND **192**
Isle Royale NP, MI **134**
Jamestown NHS, VA **252**
Jean Lafitte NHP, LA **112**
Jefferson Memorial, DC (See Thomas

Jefferson Memorial)
Jefferson National Expansion Memorial NHS, MO **144**
Jewel Cave NM, SD **217**
John D. Rockefeller, Jr. MEM PKWY, WY **277**
John Day Fossil Beds NM, OR **200**
John F. Kennedy Center for the Performing Arts, DC **69**
John Fitzgerald Kennedy NHS, MA **129**
John Muir NHS, CA **46**
Johnson, Andrew (See Andrew Johnson)
Johnson, Lyndon B. (See Lyndon B. Johnson)
Johnstown Flood N MEM, PA **209**
Joshua Tree NM, CA **47**
Kaloko-Honokohau NHP, HI **94**
Katmai NM, AK **9**
Kenai Fjords NM, AK **10**
Kennedy Center, DC (See John F. Kennedy Center)
Kennedy, John F. (See John F. Kennedy)
Kennesaw Mountain NBP, GA **90**
Kings Canyon NP, CA (See Sequoia and Kings Canyon NP)
Kings Mountain NMP, SC **215**
Klondike Gold Rush NHP, AK-WA **11**
Knife River Indian Villages NHS, ND **192**
Kobuk Valley NM, AK **12**
Kosciuszko, Thaddeus (See Thaddeus Kosciuszko)
Lake Chelan NRA, WA **261**
Lake Clark NM, AK **13**
Lake Mead NRA, NV **155**
Lake Meredith NRA, TX **232**
Lassen Volcanic NP, CA **47**
Lava Beds NM, CA **48**
Lee, Robert E. (See Arlington House, The Robert E. Lee Memorial)
Lehman Caves NM, NV **156**
Lewis and Clark NHT, IL-MO-KS-NE-IA-SD-ND-MT-ID-OR-WA **100**
Lincoln Boyhood NM, IN **103**
Lincoln Home NHS, IL **100**
Lincoln Memorial, DC **70**
Longfellow NHS, MA **129**
Lowell NHP, MA **130**
Lower St. Croix NSR, WI-MN **271**
Lyndon B. Johnson NHS, TX **233**
Lyndon Baines Johnson Memorial Grove on the Potomac, DC **70**
McLoughlin House NHS, OR **201**
Maggie L. Walker NHS, VA **253**
Mammoth Cave NP, KY **110**
Manassas NBP, VA **253**
Mar-A-Lago NHS, FL **85**
Martin Van Buren NHS, NY **181**

Mesa Verde NP, CO **63**
Middle Delaware NSR, PA-NJ **210**
Minute Man NHP, MA **130**
Monocacy NB, MD **123**
Montezuma Castle NM, AZ **27**
Moores Creek NMP, NC **189**
Mormon Pioneer NHT, IL-IA-NE-WY-UT **100**
Morristown NHP, NJ **160**
Mound City Group NM, OH **195**
Mount McKinley NP, AK **14**
Mount Rainier NP, WA **262**
Mount Rushmore NM, SD **218**
Muir Woods NM, CA **49**
Natchez Trace PKWY, MS-AL-TN **141**
National Capital Parks, DC-MD-VA **71**
National Mall, DC **71**
National Visitor Center, DC **72**
Natural Bridges NM, UT **242**
Navajo NM, AZ **27**
New River Gorge NR, WV **268**
Nez Perce NHP, ID **98**
Ninety Six NHS, SC **215**
Noatak NM, AK **15**
North Cascades NP, WA **263**
Obed Wild and Scenic River, TN **224**
Ocmulgee NM, GA **91**
Old Stone House, DC **72**
Olympic NP, WA **264**
O'Neill, Eugene (See Eugene O'Neill)
Organ Pipe Cactus NM, AZ **28**
Oregon Caves NM, OR **201**
Oregon NHT, MO-KS-NE-WY-ID-OR-WA **144**
Oxon Hill Farm, MD **124**
Ozark NSR, MO **145**
Padre Island NS, TX **234**
Palo Alto Battlefield NHS, TX **235**
Pea Ridge NMP, AR **39**
Pecos NM, NM **169**
Pennsylvania Avenue NHS, DC **73**
Perry's Victory and International Peace Memorial, OH **196**
Petersburg NB, VA **254**
Petrified Forest NP, AZ **30**
Pictured Rocks NL, MI **135**
Pinelands National Reserve, NJ **161**
Pinnacles NM, CA **50**
Pipe Spring NM, AZ **30**
Pipestone NM, MN **138**
Piscataway Park, MD **124**
Poe, Edgar Allan (See Edgar Allan Poe)
Point Reyes NS, CA **51**
Prince William Forest Park, VA **254**
Pu'uhonua o Honaunau NHP, HI **95**
Puukohola Heiau NHS, HI **95**

Rainbow Bridge NM, UT **243**
Redwood NP, CA **52**
Richmond NBP, VA **255**
Rio Grande Wild and Scenic River,
    TX **235**
Robert E. Lee Memorial (See Arlington
    House)
Rock Creek Park, DC **73**
Rockefeller, John D., Jr. (See John
    D. Rockefeller, Jr.)
Rocky Mountain NP, CO **64**
Roger Williams NM, RI **212**
Roosevelt Campobello International
    Park, Canada **280**
Roosevelt, Eleanor (See Eleanor
    Roosevelt)
Roosevelt, Franklin D. (See Home of
    Franklin D. Roosevelt; Roosevelt
    Campobello)
Roosevelt, Theodore (See Sagamore Hill;
    Theodore Roosevelt)
Ross Lake NRA, WA **265**
Russell Cave NM, AL **2**
Sagamore Hill NHS, NY **179**
Saguaro NM, AZ **31**
Saint Croix Island NM, ME **115**
St. Croix National Scenic Riverway,
    MN-WI **272**
Saint-Gaudens NHS, NH **158**
Saint Paul's Church NHS, NY **179**
Salem Maritime NHS, MA **131**
Sandburg, Carl (See Carl Sandburg)
San Antonio Missions NHP, TX **235**
San Jose Mission NHP, TX **236**
San Juan Island NHP, WA **266**
San Juan NHS, Puerto Rico **281**
Santa Monica Mountains NRA, CA **53**
Saratoga NHP, NY **180**
Saugus Iron Works NHS, MA **132**
Scotts Bluff NM, NE **153**
Sequoia and Kings Canyon National
    Parks, CA **53**
Sewall-Belmont House NHS, DC **74**
Shenandoah NP, VA **255**
Shiloh NMP, TN **224**
Sitka NHP, AK **15**
Skyline Drive, VA (See Shenandoah NP)
Sleeping Bear Dunes NL, MI **136**
Springfield Armory NHS, MA **132**
Statue of Liberty NM, NY **180**
Stones River NB and Cemetery, TN **225**
Sunset Crater NM, AZ **32**
Taft, W. H. (See William Howard Taft)
Thaddeus Koskiuszko NM, PA **210**

Theodore Roosevelt Birthplace NHS,
    NY **178**
Theodore Roosevelt Inaugural NHS,
    NY **178**
Theodore Roosevelt Island, DC **74**
Theodore Roosevelt NP, ND **193**
Thomas Jefferson Memorial, DC **75**
Thomas Stone NHS, MD **125**
Timpanogos Cave NM, UT **244**
Tonto NM, AZ **33**
Touro Synagogue NHS, RI **212**
Tumacacori NM, AZ **33**
Tupelo NB, MS **141**
Turkey Run Farm, VA **256**
Tuskegee Institute NHS, AL **2**
Tuzigoot NM, AZ **34**
Upper Delaware Wild and Scenic River,
    NY **181**
U. S. Marine Corps Memorial &
    Netherlands Carillon **257**
USS Arizona Memorial, HI **96**
USS Constitution, MA (See Boston NHP)
Valley Forge NHP, PA **210**
Van Buren, Martin (See Martin Van Buren)
Vanderbilt Mansion NHS, NY **182**
Vicksburg NMP, MS **142**
Virgin Islands NP, VI **283**
Voyageurs NP, MN **139**
Walker, Maggie L. (See Maggie L. Walker)
Walnut Canyon NM, AZ **34**
War in the Pacific NHP, Guam **280**
Washington, Booker T. (See Booker T.
    Washington; Tuskegee Institute NHS)
Washington Monument, DC **75**
Whiskeytown-Shasta-Trinity NRA, CA **54**
The White House, DC **76**
White Sands NM, NM **170**
Whitman Mission NHS, WA **267**
William Howard Taft NHS, OH **196**
Williams, Roger (See Roger Williams)
Wilson's Creek NB, MO **146**
Wind Cave NP, SD **219**
Wolf Trap Farm Park for the Performing
    Arts, VA **257**
Wrangell-Saint Elias NM, AK **16**
Wright Brothers N MEM, NC **189**
Wupatki NM, AZ **35**
Yellowstone NP, WY-MT-ID **278**
Yorktown Battlefield, VA **258**
Yosemite NP, CA **55**
Yucca House NM, CO **66**
Yukon-Charley NM, AK **17**
Zion NP, UT **245**

Bibliography

■Index of the National Park System and Affiliated Areas as of June 30, 1977.
National Park Service, U.S. Dept. of the Interior, 1977.
■Access National Parks: A Guide for Handicapped Visitors. National Park Service,
U.S. Dept. of the Interior, 1978.
■Washington, D.C. Prepared for the National Visitor Center, National Park Service, U.S.
Dept. of the Interior, 1976.
■Visitor Accommodations, Facilities, and Services—1978 & 1979, furnished by conces-
sioners in the National Park System.
■Camping in the National Park System. National Park Service, U.S. Dept. of the Interior.
■A Group Guide to your National Park Next Door. Golden Gate National Recreation
Area, National Park Service, U.S. Dept. of the Interior.
■1978 Holiday and Vacation Planning Guide to the Federal Parks of the Southwest.
Southwest Public Affairs Office, National Park Service, U.S. Dept. of the Interior.

Summary of Areas and Acreages
Administered by the National Park System

February 27, 1979

Number	Classification	Acreage
39	National Parks	16,038,671.96
92	National Monuments	54,615,323.08
2	National Preserves	654,550.00
4	National Lakeshores	196,456.10
10	National Rivers	522,691.91
	(Includes Wild and Scenic Rivers	
	and Riverways)	
10	National Seashores	597,655.86
59	National Historic Sites	17,970.36
22	National Memorials	7,943.05
11	National Military Parks	34,661.84
3	National Battlefield Parks	6,762.38
9	National Battlefields	10,566.29
1	National Battlefield Site	12.36
22	National Historical Parks	104,852.75
17	National Recreation Areas	3,661,542.70
4	National Parkways	160,825.89
1	National Trail	52,034.25
10	Parks (other)	31,986.18
1	National Capital Parks	6,470.59
1	White House	18.07
1	National Mall	146.35
1	National Visitor Center	0.00
320		76,721,141.97